Communication and Co
in Eastern India

Communication and Colonialism in Eastern India

Bihar, 1760s–1880s

Nitin Sinha

ANTHEM PRESS
LONDON · NEW YORK · DELHI

Anthem Press
An imprint of Wimbledon Publishing Company
www.anthempress.com

This edition first published in UK and USA 2014
by ANTHEM PRESS
75–76 Blackfriars Road, London SE1 8HA, UK
or PO Box 9779, London SW19 7ZG, UK
and
244 Madison Ave. #116, New York, NY 10016, USA

First published in hardback by Anthem Press in 2012

Copyright © Nitin Sinha 2014

The author asserts the moral right to be identified as the author of this work.

All rights reserved. Without limiting the rights under copyright reserved above,
no part of this publication may be reproduced, stored or introduced into
a retrieval system, or transmitted, in any form or by any means
(electronic, mechanical, photocopying, recording or otherwise),
without the prior written permission of both the copyright
owner and the above publisher of this book.

British Library Cataloguing-in-Publication Data
A catalogue record for this book is available from the British Library.

Library of Congress Cataloging-in-Publication Data
The Library of Congress has catalogued the hardcover edition as follows:
Sinha, Nitin.
Communication and colonialism in Eastern India : Bihar, 1760s-1880s / Nitin Sinha.
p. cm.
Revision of the author's thesis (doctoral)–School of Oriental and
African Studies, London, 2007.
Includes bibliographical references and index.
ISBN 978-0-85728-448-8 (hardback : alk. paper)
1. Communication and traffic–India–Bihar–History. 2.
Communication and traffic–Great Britain–Colonies–History. 3. Great
Britain–Colonies–Administration–History–18th century. 4. Great
Britain–Colonies–Administration–History–19th century. I. Title.
HE271.Z7.B55S56 2012
384.0954'12309034–dc23
2012025597

ISBN-13: 978 1 78308 311 4 (Pbk)
ISBN-10: 1 78308 311 5 (Pbk)

This title is also available as an ebook.

CONTENTS

Acknowledgements vii

List of Abbreviations ix

Glossary xi

List of Tables and Illustrations xv

Introduction xvii

Chapter 1 From Affective Forms to Objectification: Spatial Transition from Pre-colonial to Colonial Times 1

Chapter 2 India and its Interiors 23

Chapter 3 Going into the Interiors 57

Chapter 4 Knowing the Ways 91

Chapter 5 Controlling the Routes 117

Chapter 6 Changing Regime of Communication, 1820s–60s 155

Chapter 7 Of Men and Commodities 181

Chapter 8 The Wheels of Change 203

Conclusion 233

Bibliography 241

Index 263

ACKNOWLEDGEMENTS

This book is an outcome of my doctoral thesis completed at the School of Oriental and African Studies, London in 2007. All those who are duly acknowledged in my thesis, therefore, remain acknowledged here also. In particular, I would like to say thanks to B. R. (Tom) Tomlinson, Peter Robb, Daud Ali and David Arnold for their support, guidance and encouragement.

Ian J. Kerr has been generous enough to not only read the different versions of the chapters but the whole manuscript. His comments and criticisms proved the most valuable. Through his suggestions and writings, Ravi Ahuja has unknowingly influenced this work in various ways. I am also thankful to Tirthankar Roy and David Washbrook for their role as 'examiners' to my thesis, and the set of helpful suggestions they offered. The anonymous review organized by Anthem reinforced my belief in the utility of this work for the South Asian historiography.

For specific chapters I often relied on inputs provided in person or over email by a range of scholars, some of which I feel glad in mentioning here (any omissions due to lack of memory is purely unintentional): Muzaffar Alam, Sunil Kumar, Matthew Edney, Kapil Raj, Neeladri Bhattacharya, Chitra Joshi and Radhika Singha.

The thesis was revised into a manuscript at my current work place, the Zentrum Moderner Orient (Centre for Modern Oriental Studies), Berlin. The intellectual milieu of the Zentrum with its engaging group discussions and activities gave me adequate space to put forward some of the new ideas to colleagues and friends working in disciplines other than history and on regions other than South Asia. I am thankful to all of them who offered suggestions and comments. In particular, I would like to say thanks to Heike Liebau, Kai Kresse, Marloes Janson and Katharina Lange for their feedback on certain sections of the book; to Ulrike Freitag, Katrin Bromber, Silke Nagel, Svenja Becherer, Michael Schutz and Thomas Ripper for providing unflinching support, institutional and otherwise; and to Hana Gunkel and Doreen Teumer for filling me in with my last minute requests of books and photocopies from different libraries in Berlin. I am also thankful to Manuela Ciotti for giving her comments on a preliminary version of introduction. A big thanks is reserved for Jolita Zabarskaite without whose help and promptness this book would have taken a much longer time to finish than it did. Christoph Zelke's technical support with maps and plates saved me a lot of time and frustration that I would have otherwise gone through! I am earnestly thankful to Nilanjan Sarkar's friendship and his help in understanding the 'veiled' world of publishing.

Most of the primary sources used in this book have come from the British Library (maps, rare books and Asia and Africa collections), SOAS Library, Bihar State Archives,

Record Room of Water Resource Department, Patna, National Archives of India and Khuda Baksh Library. I am thankful to all the people at these places who helped with my research; in particular to the British Library for giving permission to reproduce sketches and paintings. Chapter 5 is a revised version of an article published in *Indian Economic and Social History Review* in January 2008; I am grateful to the the journal editor for letting me re-use it here.

Some of my friends, not only through their ability to discuss passionately on and beyond history but also through their warmth, help and humour, have made research more pleasurable, and life more enjoyable. Kalyan and Projit's friendship is most cherished in this regard. 'Bihar' in all its seriousness and ironies has remained a favourite topic of discussion with Prabhat and Nitin. Marloes's firm friendship made my life a lot easier in Berlin. Maria's intellectual support, warmth and special friendship has made work and life very exciting.

Support and encouragement from Anthem Press, in particular from Tej Sood and Janka Romero is highly appreciated. Working with Elizabeth Stone, my copy-editor, was fun and an enriching learning experience. I am once again thankful to ZMO for its financial support in letting me undertake the much needed research trips to London and India that substantially helped in revising the thesis into manuscript.

This book is dedicated to my parents, Devendra Mohan Sinha and Neena Sinha. This earnest dedication should make it clear that I lack formal vocabulary (in my second language) to thank them enough for all they have done for me so far. I am equally pleased to say thanks to my *didi*, *bhaiya* and *jijaji* for never stopping the youngest member of the family from getting undue affection.

LIST OF ABBREVIATIONS

AAC	Asia and Africa Collections
AAR	*Asiatic Annual Register*
AARB	*Annual Report on the Administration of the Bengal Presidency*
ABSP	*Hunter's Account of Bhaghalpur and Santhal Pargana*
AGS	*Hunter's Account of Gaya and Shahabad*
AIA	*Annals of Indian Administration*
AJ	*Asiatic Journal*
AMP	*Hunter's Account of Monghyr and Purniah*
APS	*Hunter's Account of Patna and Saran*
AR	*Asiatic Researches*
BC	Bentinck correspondence
Bcl	Board of Control
BCJC	*Bengal Criminal and Judicial Consultations*
BPP	*Bengal Past and Present*
BR	*Bhagalpur Records*, ed. Datta
BRCC	*Bengal Revenue Council Consultations*
BSA	Bihar State Archives
CEHI	*Cambridge Economic History of India*
CR	*Calcutta Review*
CSSH	*Comparative Studies in Society and History*
CTA	Criminal Tribes Act
EIC	East India Company
EIR	East India Railway
EIRC	East Indian Railway Company
FFC	Ferry Fund Committee
GB	General Branch
GISNC	General Inland Steam Navigation Company
GJ	*Geographical Journal*
GOB	Government of Bengal
GOI	Government of India
GOR	*Gaya Old Records*
GSI	Geological Survey of India
GSNC	Ganges Steam Navigation Company
GTR	Grand Trunk Road
GWBRC	Great Western and Bengal Railway Company

HR	*Historical Records*
IESHR	*Indian Economic and Social History Review*
IOR	India Office Records
JASB	*Journal of the Asiatic Society of Bengal*
JBORS	*Journal of Bihar and Orissa Research Society*
JESHO	*Journal of the Economic and Social History of the Orient*
JSSL	*Journal of the Statistical Society of London*
JRGS	*Journal of the Royal Geographical Society of London*
MAS	*Modern Asian Studies*
MHJ	*Medieval History Journal*
NMR	New Military Road
MOR	*Muzaffarpur Old Records*
NAI	National Archives of India
NWP	North-Western Provinces
P&D	Prints and Drawings, British Library
PCRS	*Patna Commissioner Record Series*
PRPWD	*Progress Report of the Public Works Department*
PWD	Public Works Department
QMG	quartermaster general
RCE	*Report by the Chief Engineer*
RBP	Railway Bengal Proceedings
RRWRD	Record Room of the Water Resource Department
SD	*Select Documents*
SE	superintending engineer
SIH	*Studies in History*
SOR	*Singhbhum Old Records*
SS	*Social Scientist*
UP	United Provinces
URG	unpublished record of the government

GLOSSARY

The native and indigenous terms used in the book have been italicized on their first use. The following is the list of important terms used in the book with spellings that were popularly used in British India in the late eighteenth and nineteenth centuries.

aab	water
aalam	world
abkari	excise
akhlaq	set of ethical norms
anna	monetary unit, the sixteenth part of a rupee
arzee	petition
barakat	blessing
batta	extra allowance made to officers, soldiers and other public servants
beegah	unit of land measurement, roughly one-third of an acre
beopari	merchant, trader
bhang	leaves of cannabis plant, cheap and popular intoxicant used in the Indian subcontinent
bhistee	water carrier
bhoges	offerings made during rituals
budgerow	a contemporary anglicized word for one of the most popular types of boat in Bengal called *bajrah*
buggy	two-wheeled horse carriage with a hood
burdasht khana	supply house on trunk lines
burkandazes	police escorts
chaprasie	peon
chattah	umbrella
chaudharies	a loose descriptive term meaning headmen in the local administration, in this book signifying superior revenue officials
chauk	intersection of four streets, usually becoming a vibrant market place
chaukidar (chowkeedar)	a person who mans *choukies*, rural policeman
chillam	upper part of the hookah that contains tobacco and charcoal balls; in common parlance usually associated with ganja smoking
chobdar	mace carrier

choukie	police outpost, halting station for palanquin bearers, toll station where taxes/dues were collected
chuttie	halting place
coss	a locally varying unit of distance measurement popular in pre-colonial and early colonial times
coss minaret	tower built at a fixed distance to measure routes during the pre-colonial times
crore	monetary unit meaning 10 million (10,000,000)
cutchery	court
dafadar	a subordinate native police officer
dak	post(al), palanquin relay system established by post office
dargah	Sufi/holy shrine
darogha	chief native officer in various departments like police, customs or excise, in this book meant as a native police chief
darwesh	mendicant often residing in jungles
dastak	pass allowing free trade, which became a matter of serious contention between the Bengal *nawabs* and EIC in the late eighteenth century
dhonie	country vessel carrying goods
dhoona	product formed from the extracted piece of the sal tree
dhuwangaadi	railway, a popular expression in the Bhojpuri belt of Bihar and UP, *dhuwan* meaning smoke and *gaadi* a car or a wagon
dubhashis	native English interpreters who became an important service group because of their language ability to mediate, *du* meaning two and *bhasi* language
duniya	world
durbar	royal ceremonial space displaying a ruler's authority
feriwalah	peddler
firman	royal order
fouzdari	matters, cases pertaining to the criminal branch of administration
ghariwala	time keeper
ghat (ghaut)	riverbank, hill pass, mountain pass
ghautwal	derived from *ghautwallies*, meaning small *zamindaries* (area of control exercised by a *zamindar*) in which the area was divided
ghee	clarified butter
godown	warehouse
golah	storehouse
gomastha	a native agent, often employed by *zamindars* but also by the EIC who became a powerful class of intermediary administrative structure in the late eighteenth century
gunge	market
gur	jaggery
haat	local market

GLOSSARY

harkara	messenger
havildar	native constable
huqumat	sovereignty/rule
iman	faith
insaan	man
jaghir	land or revenue assignment granted to Mughal officials in lieu of their salary
jamadar	a native officer employed in various branches of civil and military establishment, in this book usually referring to the one employed in a police branch under *darogha*
jarib-kash	road measurer
jholi	bag
kabooleat	deed signed between two individuals or entities
khal	pond, tank
khillat	robes of honour
kutcha	unmetalled road
lakh	monetary unit meaning 100,000
lathial	literally, man with stick; henchman often kept by *zamindars*
lota	a vessel
mir manzil	Mughal equivalent to quartermaster general
mahajan	trader, moneylender
mai-baap	literally, mother and father, a popular expression for a superior individual, authority or a political entity
manjhee	head boatman
mansabdar	a member of Mughal nobility
maund	a unit of weight measurement in the Bengal presidency; one *maund* comprised of 40 *seers*, which was later standardized to roughly 37 kgs
maya	illusion
mela	often a religious gathering on an auspicious day or at a pilgrimage site that also became a vibrant market site
mohurs	coins
muhabbat	love
naukars and *chakars*	a group of domestic helpers, not necessarily servants but those involved in a variety of work
nawab	native rulers, used here for the late Mughal provincial rulers who later became the rulers of 'successor' states
nayaks	leaders, used here for *banjara* leaders
nazar	gift exchange
nullah	stream
paikar	small peddler
palki	palanquin
parwana	deed or title
patella	a type of boat popular in Bihar and Bengal

paubha	wall-hanging
peshkash	gift or tribute
peshkhima	the party that marched ahead of the royal entourage to pitch tents
pucca	metalled road
purab	east, meaning the regions of the present-day eastern Uttar Pradesh and Bihar
puraos	shelter for a cart/carriage
pyke	an armed attendant, usually of the police or revenue establishment, a village watchman
qasbah	a small town with vibrant economic activities
rahdari	road tax
ria'ya	subjects of the imperial rule
rowannah	documents under which goods passed
safarnama	travel accounts
sanad	deed
sardar	leader of a gang of people
sarkar	rule
sayer	group of duties ranging from charges on pastures and fruit trees to tolls on shops, charges on imports and exports, weight of merchandise and transport by land or ferries
sepoy	Indian infantry soldier in the Company army
serai	rest house
shroff	a notable local banker, merchant, trader
siyasat	rule/territory
sowar	police mounted on horses
subah	province
suttranjie	a type of weaved carpet
tanda	*banjara* caravan, camp
tehsildar	a native revenue official
thannadar	chief-of-police outpost or station
thannah	police outpost
topi	hat
wafa	loyalty
watan	homeland
yaari	friendship
zamindar	the actual meaning and range of rights was hugely contested in the period of study, the contemporary dominant English view was to regard a *zamindar* as a legal landholder
zillah	district

LIST OF TABLES AND ILLUSTRATIONS

List of Tables

Table 1	Public works expenditure in Bengal between 1837 and 1850	165
Table 2	Public works expenditure in different presidencies, 1854–55	166
Table 3	Ferry collections in districts of Bihar, 1855–56 to 1858	171
Table 4	Trade in resinous products in Bihar	194
Table 5	Opening of the EIR	217
Table 6	Supply of cotton from Bengal between 1834–35 and 1849–50	225

List of Illustrations

Plate 1	The *Hooghly* steamer near Bhagalpur on the River Ganga, by Thomas Prinsep, 1828	29
Plate 2	Moorcroft and Hearsey, by Hearsey, 1812	36
Plate 3	Ranny Ghaut in the city of Patna from the west	43
Plate 4	View on the River Ganges	43
Plate 5	Patna City	48
Plate 6	Near Bhood Gyah	50
Plate 7	Pen sketch of coalfields of west Burdwan	54
Plate 8	Haider Beg, with the Company's Lucknow resident and Zoffany on a march	61
Plate 9	A touring official	66
Plate 10	Heber's journey	66
Plate 11	Buchanan's visit in Shahabad	67
Plate 12	Major highways in Bihar, south of the Ganga	75
Plate 13	The opium fleet on the Ganga	79
Plate 14	NMR and GTR	82

Plate 15	Principal roads and divisions of Hindustan by James Rennell	109
Plate 16	Roads of Bengal presidency	110
Plate 17	Principal roads	111
Plate 18	Post roads in Bengal presidency	112
Plate 19	Praun Poory	132
Plate 20	Perkasanand	132
Plate 21	An armed watchman	148
Plate 22	Banjara women	152
Plate 23	Government steam tug with accommodation flat	175
Plate 24	GSNC's the *Patna*	175
Plate 25	A dandy	187
Plate 26	Map showing the proposed railway lines in Bengal presidency	215
Plate 27	First railway lines in Bengal presidency	216
Plate 28	Sketch map showing cotton road scheme, 1860s	226

INTRODUCTION

In December 1853, a British officer (whose name we do not know) started his journey from Calcutta towards the Parasnath Hill. He set off in a palanquin, which did not prove very useful because of the poor state of the road. He crossed the ferry at the Hooghly river and proceeded towards the coalfields of Burdwan. All the while he reported on the conditions of roads and bridges, the prospects of railways, topographical details, the beautiful scenery, the Hindu temples and the nature of villages and people. On 26 December he started for the hill from the village of Madhupur where he had hired three native guides (coolies), Kethu aged 18 ('very active and loquacious'), Nilu aged 28 ('very careful and active') and Narain aged 25 ('modest and not conspicuous'). While climbing, these guides started talking about their ascent the previous year, made with four sahibs who lived on the hill for ten days. The sahibs ate fowls and eggs and drank wine. This memory evoked loud laughter among the three guides. Our anonymous traveller suspected that some of those fowls and wine found their way to the guides and that in describing this previous journey they were actually making an indirect appeal to his liberality. For a moment, he paused to think about the caste taboos (which would theoretically regulate dietary practices) but then reasoned: 'What have poor coolies to do with caste?' Tired and lying under the tree, the officer, who was quietly listening to the guides, thought that those were fine times for the poor coolies. After climbing down and reaching the bungalow he did not forget to reward his guides, 'who certainly did know the hill – thoroughly – as they had boasted in the morning'.[1]

This interesting anecdote has many interstices that capture some of the themes this book aims to explore. One, an adventurous exploratory journey undertaken by a European with the help of three native guides, points towards the nature and forms of travel in colonial times, the European travelling gaze and knowledge formation. When the group left the road to go into the jungles the author remarked that he did not see anything but only heard the screams of some large animals. The imagery of impenetrability, however, soon dissipates when he informs that these tracks, which he found steep and slippery, were used by natives to bring fuel wood out from the jungles. The spaces that from a distance seemed inhospitable, inhabitable and impenetrable had strong lived components. Second, in his individual assessment of caste taboos, the officer preferred to privilege the 'class' aspect of his coolies (these were *poor* people) but yet, in the colonial schema, as this book argues, caste provided an easy optic for colonial knowledge

---

1 Anon., Mss Eur. B242, 1853–54, British Library, Asia and Africa Collections (AAC), unpaginated volume.

formation, particularly when it came to identifying criminal propensities of the 'natives'.[2] Third, this anecdote says something about the processes of knowledge formation itself: dependent on the guides he also suspected them of 'appealing to his liberality'. How he understood this, however, remains a moot question: the guides 'uttered in a Hindi Bengali...of which I understand only half'. Dependence on and disdain towards natives were parts of the ways colonial knowledge was formed and formalized. And lastly, the role of communication: if leaving the road to enter into the hill presented an imagery of charting unknown territories, coming close to Madhupur on his return journey gave him the feeling of coming nearer to the road and to civilization. The presence of good roads symbolized the permanence, civility and superiority of civilization. In the rest of this introduction I will elaborate upon some of these issues.

There are four themes 'foregrounded' in this work. The most important is the history of communication between the 1760s and 1880s in colonial India. C. A. Bayly has remarked that 'the study of information, knowledge, and communications is an interesting project which might help close the deplorable gap between studies of economic structures, on the one hand, and of Orientalism and ideology on the other'.[3] The present work, although it does not use communication in the same sense as Bayly does in his work,[4] does share the mid-ground described by him. Here, communication figures both as a site and a link to study the shifting networks of economic structures: trade and travel on the one hand, and ideologies and discourses of colonial rule on the other. This work is therefore about the interrelated histories of various patterns of the circulation of goods, peoples and ideas as and when they interacted with the means and modes of communication. Set against the backdrop of colonial rule in Bihar, the principal objectives of the book are the following: first, to contribute to our historical understanding of the shifting policies and discourses of the colonial state on communication; second, to bring out the changing relationship between trade, transport and mobility through a micro-level historical study of trading and mercantile networks; and third, to add to the existing literature on the forms of colonial knowledge by looking at the practices of travel, tours and surveys.

My entry point into the study of communication is the peculiar spatial category of 'interior' that the colonial state wanted to 'open up'. By showing the different meanings of 'interior' between the 1760s and 1820s, the main argument follows that it was as

---

2 In this book, the word native or natives has been used in two ways: when used within inverted commas, it signifies the colonial homogenizing impetus to classify, quite pejoratively, the colonized group, when used without, it refers to the colonized people of India. There are many other terms that could have been used in the latter sense, such as 'local population', 'indigenous group/people' and so on; but to retain the word native is also an act of political subversion, at least so it appears to the author of this book.

3 C. A. Bayly, 'Knowing the Country: Empire and Information in India', *Modern Asian Studies* 27, no. 1 (1993): 43. [Henceforth *MAS*.]

4 C. A. Bayly, *Empire and Information: Information Gathering and Social Communication in India, 1780–1870* (Cambridge, 1996). See also Michael H. Fisher, 'The Office of Akhbar Nawis: The Transition from Mughal to British Forms', *MAS* 27, no. 1 (1993).

much a constructed category as an encountered one.[5] However, from the 1820s onward, because of the growing nexus of utilitarianism, steam technology, geologically driven idea of natural wealth and resources of the country, and the conviction in 'moral and material' improvement, the economic meaning of 'interior' gained primacy that made 'communication' one of the key features of the colonial discourse on the civilizing mission. The concern for better roads and pathways was not conspicuously absent in the early phase; on the contrary, this book argues that with the acquisition of economic and territorial control in the 1760s the English East India Company (EIC) soon felt the need to know, regulate and improve the means of communication. This reflected in the emergence of road and route surveys, practices of winter tours that contributed to the existing knowledge regarding trade and communication, and in the impulse to maximize revenue by controlling 'illegal' trade through communication surveillance. However, the 1820s did signify a change in the nature of colonial discourse, of which for our purposes, two were most important – first, 'opening up the interiors', and second, public works. These two ideas were tied together and assumed a complementary relationship under the name of communication, which became a dominant theme in the ideology of colonial rule.[6] This was precisely the time when steam, both as a mark of superior technology and a metaphor for the civilizational superiority of the West, was increasingly deployed to legitimize the 'civilizing mission' of colonial rule in India. Henceforth, first the steamships plying the Ganga and then the railway locomotives running on steam power both rhetorically and functionally became the symbol of a new period of growth, advancement and prosperity in India.[7] Such an assertion, however, must be followed by a caveat. Rhetorical vocalism often exuded inherent anxieties, contestations and

---

5 This argument resonates with David Arnold's on the construction of tropics in his *The Tropics and the Traveling Gaze; India, Landscape, and Science 1800–1856* (Delhi, 2005). However, the present work differs not only in terms of the subject matter but also in emphasizing the role of communication in the European travelling gaze, a point discussed below.
6 See for instance, Ravi Ahuja, '"The Bridge Builders": Some Notes on Railways, Pilgrimage and the British "Civilizing Mission" in Colonial India', in Harald Fischer-Tiné and Michael Mann, eds, *Colonialism as Civilizing Mission: Cultural Ideology in British India* (London, 2003), 95–6. For its exclusive application on railways see Ian J. Kerr, 'Representation and Representations of the Railways of Colonial and Post-Colonial South Asia', *MAS* 37, no. 2 (2003).
7 The correspondences, pamphlets and writings of engineers and European officials of this period are full of such expressions; one of the typical writings suggesting the 'remarkable power of steam in awakening the Eastern World' is of G. W. Macgeorge, *Ways and Works in India* (Westminster, 1894), 220–21. On the popular representation of the ideas of the technological superiority of the West and the needs to introduce them in India, see A. Martin Wainwright, 'Representing the Technology of the Raj in Britain's Victorian Periodical Press', in David Finkelstein and Douglas M. Peers, eds, *Negotiating India in the Nineteenth-Century Media* (London and New York, 2000), esp. 185–90. Steamships and their models became prestigious items of gifts in high-profile royal visits. Amongst the most notable gifts that the Prince of Wales carried for the King of Greece was a steam launch; similarly he brought to India some steam fire engines, 'constructed and of course finished in the very highest style of perfection' in London. *Five Months with the Prince in India containing a glance at the Inner life of the Inhabitants, and narrating the chief romantic and picturesque incidents in connection with the visit of the Prince of Wales* (London, 1876), 4–5.

contradictions. So, although the metaphor of steam served to suggest a civilizational chasm between East and West, the same metaphor and technology was also thought to function as a tool to bridge this gap. The civilizational gap was translated into a time-lag, which the 'natives' would overcome with proper supervision and training once the skill they already possessed had been further honed.[8]

Civilizational and technological superiority have been substantially and readily associated with railways, both in contemporary accounts and in the historiography that developed subsequently. The second important 'foreground' issue of this book challenges this easy association by questioning the often misleading rigidity of 'railway studies' in the South Asian case. Representations of technological superiority preceded the railway era; they had become overwhelmingly axiomatic from the 1820s onwards, with increased emphasis on road building on the one hand and the deployment of new technological power – steam – on the other.[9] Most of the studies on transport have focused exclusively on the railways.[10] This selective approach, based on an easy equation of communication with railways, unfortunately reproduces the core of the colonial claims, exemplified best by Juland Danvers, the government director of the Indian Railway Companies in 1877: 'Any history of the material progress of India may well be divided into a pre-railway and a post-railway period.'[11] Although aware of the limitedness and callousness of this rhetoric, scholars who have worked on nineteenth-century transport issues related either with trade or social aspects have barely tried to situate the railway-generated changes amidst the existing patterns and networks of circulation in which the role of roads and ferries

---

8 See for instance, Edward Davidson, *The Railways of India with an Account of their Rise, Progress and Construction* (London, 1868), 1. The inherent dichotomy was the result of the mid-nineteenth-century tension between 'universalism (the idea of one preferred law, ethics, knowledge, functions and methods) and essentialism or relativism (the emphasis on distinct, culturally-appropriate rules and behaviour)'. See Peter Robb, ed., *The Concept of Race in South Asia* (Delhi, 1995), 30, and also 3–10. This divide between rhetoric and practice operated at the level of technology as well; in the construction of bridges in which 'the British engineers in India were to encounter their greatest challenge', European techniques proved inadequate, which forced the engineers to borrow from and blend their technology with traditional Indian bridge-building practices. Ian Derbyshire, 'The Building of India's Railways: The Application of Western technology in the Colonial Periphery 1850–1920' in Roy MacLeod and Deepak Kumar, eds, *Technology and the Raj: Western Technology and Technical transfers to India 1700–1947* (New Delhi, Thousand Oaks and London, 1995), 193.

9 In one of the articles published in 1843, the Roman civilizational legacy of 'good public roads' was invoked to make the point that 'formation of roads must have been amongst the earliest rudiments of civilization', which, of course, allegedly India lacked. 'Letter from Joseph Locke on Advantages of Railways in India', 11 February 1843, in S. Settar (general editor), *Railway Construction in India: Select Documents, Volume I, 1832–1852* (New Delhi, 1999), 18–20. [Henceforth *SD*. Unless otherwise stated, all references are to volume 1.]

10 Notable exceptions are S. K. Munshi, *Geography of Transportation in Eastern India under the British Raj*, Centre for Studies of Social Sciences Monograph 1, (Calcutta, 1980), and Ravi Ahuja *Pathways of Empire: Circulation, 'Public Works' and Social Space in Colonial Orissa, 1780–1914* (New Delhi, 2009).

11 Juland Danvers, *Indian Railways: Their Past History, Present Condition, and Future Prospects* (London, 1877), 7.

was crucial.[12] This is also true for new writings analysing the railway-induced cultural changes. Harriet Bury's attempt to locate the novelty of the travelling experiences of the Hindi elite intelligentsia in the railway era thus unsurprisingly relies on the claim that: 'Prior to the introduction of rail transportation, the modes of circulation and transport used by travellers and traders throughout the subcontinent had barely changed for centuries.'[13] Not explicitly making a similar claim, Prathama Banerjee in her study of the late nineteenth-century Bengali travel suggests that: 'Since the 1860s, the railways had irrevocably changed the Bengali imagination of space and time'.[14] Without challenging the core idea that the ideology of travel in this period led or helped the Bengalis to discover their self vis-à-vis 'the nation's variegated landscape and socialscape' (more immediately vis-à-vis the 'primitives'), her passing comparison between railway and pre-railway mode of travel needs to be qualified. She argues that the latter 'marked the traveller's body with the denials of the road, [while] the new mode of travelling the nation by train eased the path...'[15] The issue at hand here is not to dispute the newness of the technological change that evoked surprise, admiration and criticism from different sections of the society, but of a historiographical value that potentially threatens to flatten the rich and *changing* history of circulation that existed in the pre-railway days. This history is not only related to the *means* of transport in terms of technique and speed that apparently justifies both a certain ahistoricity and unhistoricity of the period previous to the railways. It is in significant ways also related to the ideas, perceptions and practices around the act of travel. 'What did it mean to travel?' should be as important a part of our investigation as our quest to understand the means and modes people took to travel. Our modernist zeal to value

---

12 The works of Ian J. Kerr focus on railways but are in many ways seminally important in rethinking the relationship between transport, communication and space that goes beyond the strict rigidity of the railway-centric approach. For instance see his 'Introduction' in Kerr, ed., *Railways in Modern India* (Delhi, 2001). A new, interesting addition in the railway studies is a collection of essays that professedly aims to 'open up or invigorate research into India's railways' without utilizing or prescribing any 'common methodological and conceptual approach'. Ian J. Kerr, ed., *27 Down: New Departures in Indian Railway Studies* (New Delhi, 2007).
13 Harriet Bury, 'Novel Spaces, Transitional Moments: Negotiating Text and Territory in Nineteenth-Century Hindi Travel Accounts', in Kerr, ed., *27 Down*, 1.
14 Prathama Banerjee, *Politics of Time: Primitives and History-Writing in a Colonial Society* (New Delhi, 2006), 82–3.
15 Ibid., 84. Although Bury's and Banerjee's argumentation seems to sit close to each other, the implications of railway-induced travel in both the accounts are notably different. While Bury concludes that travel by railways homogenized the differentiated understandings of the terrain, Banerjee emphasizes the fact that spatialization reproduced internal frontiers as objectively given, the boundaries of which 'efficient transport could breach but never undo'. In other words, according to Banerjee, the Bengali intelligentsia discovered the 'fragmented and discontinuous' national space while travelling by railway. Bury, 'Novel Spaces, Transitional Moments', 28–9, 34; Banerjee, *Politics of Time*, 91. Another scholar of the mid-Gangetic region has also upheld the view as expressed by the colonial official and chronicler, L. S. S. O'Malley, that the system of transportation had changed so little that 'the mid-nineteenth-century traveler was said to be moving as slowly and as tediously as in the days of [the third-century BCE emperor] Asoka'. Anand Yang, *Bazaar India: Markets, Society, and the Colonial State in Gangetic Bihar* (Berkeley, Los Angeles and London, 1998), 26.

transport in terms of speed does not necessarily mean that the travellers of the eighteenth and nineteenth centuries felt the 'tyranny of distance' in the same way.[16]

The assumed radical change that railways allegedly brought is therefore historically misleading.[17] Favoured by the colonial state, the railways did undercut previous transport routes (and hence the networks of circulation) but they also stimulated the formation of new ones. Further, in many cases the new technology revitalized the old ones: a corollary to the rise of the steam engine was the proliferation of the bullock cart. Locating railways within the broader framework of emerging and changing networks of communication helps us to see 'communication' and its effects in totality, a point of departure that this book uses to move away from the dominant scholarship in South Asian history that focuses narrowly on railways. The book argues that until the 1880s in Bihar the railway-generated changes were part of the larger (and well-entrenched) patterns and networks of circulation with which initially the railways struggled to become a part of; it was only subsequently that railways successfully re-altered those networks, giving rise to a distinct circulatory regime. This approach also stands as a necessary corrective to another glaring historiographical gap: an almost exclusive focus on railways has eclipsed our understanding of colonial policies towards road construction and ferry improvement – an area which has largely remained unexplored either because of the assumption that the EIC had no interest in it or because of the understanding that the pre-railway modes remained unchanging.[18]

Even when a relatively holistic approach is adopted, the history of communication has largely remained appended to an even greater narrative of either the nineteenth-century Indian colonial economy or has appeared at times to explain the social changes of the late nineteenth-century India. Here we can clearly identify the overwhelming presence

---

16 The phrase is from Fernand Braudel, which according to Yang, 'aptly characterizes the system of transportation in South Asia in the late eighteenth and early nineteenth centuries'. Ibid., 26.
17 On two important indexes of social change – caste and gender – an unpublished work convincingly shows that the effect of railways, contrary to what had been thought in terms of its secularizing propensities, was very limited. In fact, so far as caste is concerned, the work argues that improved communication strengthened rather than weakened the fragmentation and conflicts along caste lines. L. L. Appleby, 'Social Change and the Railways in North India, c. 1845–1914' (PhD thesis, University of Sydney, 1990), 27–30. This is also the conclusion of another study on North India; arguably 'far from neutralizing the various social issues dividing Indians, railway travel [in Awadh] had perpetuated them'. Robert Gabriel Varady, 'Rail and Road Transport in Nineteenth Century Awadh: Competition in a North Indian Province' (PhD thesis, University of Arizona, 1981), 147–59, direct quote from 158.
18 Together with Munshi and Ahuja's works mentioned above in fn. 10, Varady's unpublished thesis also closely looks at the role of roads though in Awadh and situates the effects of the Oudh and Rohilkhand Railways in the existing communication web. According to Varady, the concept of 'feeder roads' from the 1860s made roads secondary to the railways, a point which is applicable also in the case of Bihar. A very significant contribution of his research is to show the 'aggressive policy' pursued by the indigenous rulers, the Awadh *nawabs*, in building the network of roads, a point which in subsequent colonial discourse was usually glossed over to score a point of 'uninterested' or 'inefficient' native rulers. Varady, 'Rail and Road Transport'. However, much of this has been presented in terms of 'competition' between rail and road, a notion which this work tries to qualify.

of 'modernist' or modernizing impulses that described the role of communication. This, what I would call a 'functionalist' approach to the history of communication, has not only long informed our line of enquiry but also, as a result, discouraged us from presenting an independent history of communication and the histories related to it. The history of communication (and railways) has been used as a descriptive category which has contributed to our understanding in two ways: first, colonial policies of capital investment and structure of rates; and second, the 'effects' of the means of communication.[19] Little, however, has been done to move beyond the 'effects' paradigm by situating the histories of the means of communication in their immediate socio-political context. In other words, the 'progressive', modernist and technocratic view of transport (the faster and newer the technology the better the effects and integration) has largely remained unexamined. The genesis of this progressive claim lies in the colonial accounts; but some of the best accounts of the late eighteenth- and early nineteenth-century economic histories of India — where communication is functionally used to 'prove' or 'disprove' the changes — have come close to an anachronistic understanding of transport and its effects. This book attempts to present an independent history of communication in which debates on its introduction, improvement and effects are situated in the contemporary contesting discourses and practices of legitimation and rationalization; a history that includes the policies of the colonial state, the discourses that shaped up those policies, and the competitive and complementary role the different means of communication played, together with their varying effects at different spatial scales (for instance macro, micro and nested, see below). While addressing the discursive representations together with the material bases and effects, the book proposes to use communication as an analytic category that exposes the interconnectedness of diverse concerns of colonial rule in India in the late eighteenth and nineteenth centuries, the concerns that otherwise are treated in isolation. Broadening the subject matter of communication by moving beyond the 'railway-centric approach' was one of the key ideas behind writing this book; equally important was to think about the new conceptual framework of communication that ties the seemingly disparate historical developments of the eighteenth and nineteenth centuries. To give an example, studies on crime and criminality have hardly brought out the role of mobility, mobile peripatetic groups and their trading practices in a way that this work does by underscoring the interrelated history of communication and circulation that produced colonial notions on 'native' criminality. Similarly, although the older framework of 'transport' covered the studies on 'effects' it proved inadequate to address the larger issues of colonial knowledge in tandem with practices of mobility and circulation. By looking at communication, which also includes the circulation of ideas, practices and artefacts, a greater synthesis between economic and cultural histories of circulation and transport is possible.

Methodologically, one of the important features of this book is to braid the discursive and materialist aspects related to communication-history to produce an account of both the histories of ideas and practices that characterized colonial rule. This approach

---

19 For references see fn. 41. A recent useful account is by Ian Derbyshire, 'Private and State Enterprise: Financing and Managing the Railways of Colonial North India, 1859–1914', in Kerr, ed., *27 Down*.

is extremely useful and necessary; all the three ingredients – public works, moral and material advancement, and opening up of the interiors – made communication a dominant tool for advertising the civilizational superiority of the West. However, a sole emphasis on discursive strategies or an overreliance on dominant colonial representations of communication potentially runs into danger of presenting a uni-dimensional account in which the internal contradictions and tensions arising within the structure and mechanism of colonial rule (say, in the implementation of the policies) can go amiss. For instance, an unquestioned acceptance of the assertion of the superiority of steam technology might hinder us in appraising the troubled history of steamships on the River Ganga where the peculiarity of the river not only forced technological adaptations but also led to severe loss of capital. The same is very true for the core idea of the book – that opening up the interiors was used to legitimize the introduction of new communication technology and networks. The rhetoric of 'interior' and blank spaces from the 1820s concealed the history of a variety of measures that were undertaken before that period. This work is as much the study of policies and effects as of the discourses that shaped the colonial rule's attitude towards introduction and improvement of the communication network. The analysis of economic policies, practices and choices made by the individuals and groups is interwoven with their competing social institutions, in which of course the state figures prominently; in the power relationships between state and groups and within groups; and in the broad cultural discourses that circulated at the level of empire.

In the present work, the meaning of the term 'communication' partly borrows from and partly adapts the way it was used by colonial officials in India, increasingly so from the second decade of the nineteenth century. Railways, roads, and post and telegraph constituted the newly emerging grid of communication.[20] Clearly, they also constituted a new techno-social network of colonial control not only for securing greater efficacy in maintaining colonial order but also for legitimizing its role in building a modern India. Often, nineteenth-century colonial accounts are overloaded with concepts and representations of a 'stagnant and unchanging India', which means that not only the social space was allegedly static but also the physical space was unchanging.[21] In other words, the physical topography was presented as a *tabula rasa*, and the social composition as static, unchanging and timeless. In the case of communications and physical space, this relationship was reflected in terms such as 'roadless India' and 'unknown interiors', which arguably became one of the reasons for introducing better means of communication to India. This claim and the simultaneous denial extended to the very fact that, as the *Railway Register* noted in 1845: 'there were no travellers in India'.[22]

---

20 For practical reasons, the book covers only railways, roads and water transport, not the post and telegraph.

21 For a detailed discussion of this view along with its critique see Ravi Ahuja, '"Opening up the Country"? Patterns of Circulation and Politics of Communication in Early Colonial Orissa', *Studies in History* 20, no. 1 (2004): 73–5. [Henceforth *SIH*.]

22 Quoted in Hena Mukherjee, *The Early History of the East Indian Railway 1845–1879* (Calcutta, 1994), 20. Contrast it with Emma Roberts' view 'that the "native inhabitants of India appear to be addicted to locomotion"'. This was said just ten years before the *Railway Register*'s views. Quoted in Arnold, *The Tropics*, 12.

The viewpoint of a static and unchanging India has been criticized from numerous angles, caste being one of the most important. The concept of communication could, however, be equally useful – if not more – in addressing both the issues of social and physical space on the one hand and mobility on the other. Recent studies have convincingly shown the diverse itinerant cultures that existed both in the early modern and modern periods.[23] The present work strengthens this line of argument by looking at different levels of mobility and types of mobile groups and the transformations they underwent over the course of a century. The issue of mobility brings us closer to our third 'foreground' issue, which is to look at the diverse aspects of travel and the circulation of people, commodities, artefacts and ideas. In this work, interaction between means of communication and networks of circulation is shown in three ways: first, by arguing how a definite travel circuit either by roads or by river influenced, if not determined, the ways of seeing; second, how the knowledge about routes and roads were circulated in textual and visual mediums both in the colony and between colony and metropolis; and third, the ways in which the changing regimes of communication affected (improved or deprecated) the existing patterns of trade and personnel/group mobility. Different forms of mobility existed along different networks of communication. However, the role of communication (and here I mean it in the fundamental sense of modes of transport) is hardly or very minimally acknowledged in explaining the nature of mobility or the acts/ideas/representations furnished while being mobile. It is in this regard that the present work differs from *Society and Circulation* by stressing to intrinsically integrate the role of means of communication while assessing the historical developments of shifting nature on varying scales of circulatory practices. To further illustrate this point: although in recent years the nature of the imperial travelling gaze has prominently figured as a key area of study in the field of colonial discourse analysis, what has remained unaccounted for or little explained is how far these 'gazes' both depended on and transcended the limits posed by the routinized act of travel, which more often than not followed a few select 'principal' routes. It is argued here that the readily visible standardization in reporting while travelling was not only a function of an emerging standardization of the genre – the travelogue – and thus solely a 'textual' act, but also was a result of the fact that many travellers in the late eighteenth and early nineteenth centuries followed the same tracks. They saw the same things (and they *wanted* to see the same things) albeit *differently*. Their gaze was limited by the high rising *ghats* (riverbanks) and the dense foliage that surrounded the roads. And concomitantly, showing ghats and foliage became *necessary* to truthfully represent what the gaze managed (or did not manage) to penetrate. Ways of seeing, in other words, interacted with the ways of travelling.[24] One would recall the feature of the road in the opening anecdote: roads represented spaces of civilization

---

23 On early modern, see the works of Muzaffar Alam, Sanjay Subrahmanyam and Simon Digby cited in full in Chapter 1; for modern times see Claude Markovits, Sanjay Subrahmanyam and Jacques Pouchepadass, eds, *Society and Circulation: Mobile People and Itinerant Cultures in South Asia* (New Delhi, 2003).
24 In passing, and very generally, Arnold has mentioned about the role of travelling in the ways of seeing. Arnold, *The Tropics*, 20–21.

whereas jungles, interiors, and the seemingly (and rhetorically constituted) unknown terrains and territories represented the spaces of wildness that needed 'improvement'. However, even in this set of representations, rather than being static, the physical space was actively engaged with; it was seen and sketched, represented and constructed, and reported and distorted.

The socioeconomic links existing in and connecting this physical space were also dynamic. The flow of goods and commodities that shaped decisions about the alignment of new communication lines was in turn redirected along those very lines signifying the working of a complex 'nested network'. I use the term 'nested' to distinguish it from 'local' and/or 'other' that comes close to but proves inadequate in defining the nature of the networks we are dealing with. 'Local' does not capture the sheer geographical spread of some of the commodities that circulated in this region; 'other' gives an idea of independently existing rhythms and circuits of transactions, which is misleading. The networks we are talking about are not outside the purview of colonial macro networks either in terms of transport infrastructure or commodity production and exchange. They are enmeshed, and hence nested. The best example comes with the introduction of the railways, which altered some of these networks and led to relative regional decline or ascendancy; but, because of the 'nested network', the book dismisses what is often assumed to be a conflictual relationship between railways and other means of communication. The circuits of railways' mobility were more often than not built *upon* preceding patterns; though of course they adapted and changed them too. In Bihar, when the railways became fully operational from the 1860s, a new communication grid developed around them, but by using the framework of 'nested networks' (of commodity exchange and mercantile ties) this book shows that the overall picture was of interconnectedness of local and supra-local ties, in which the world of peddlers intersected with the world of native merchants and capitalist sahibs (for instance, indigo planters), similar to the way in which the new technology required 'lateral and mutual' growth with the older means of communication rather than being placed directly in competition with them. Emphasis has been given to adopt a commodity-, community-, and region-specific approach to evaluate the overall working of the relationship between modes of communication and patterns of circulation of goods, people and knowledge; this diversity is seen in the way that while the trading networks of peripatetic groups of *banjaras* and *gosains* depreciated due to colonial surveillance (and revenue) policies, the exchange of certain other commodities through annual and bi-annual *melas* adapted to the changing communication networks.

The communication-generated concerns of colonial rule manifested themselves in a variety of ways: in the long overdrawn tussle between the state and the *zamindars* on the issue of improving the conditions of the roads in the early phase and in safeguarding the EIC's trading and revenue rights vis-à-vis the native mobile groups but simultaneously using them for knowing the networks of roads and trade. Colonial rule mobilized its own bureaucracy to collect knowledge about 'interiors'. These concerns visibly contributed to the consolidation of the knowledge pool that the state vitally needed to secure and advance its rule. Accordingly, the last foreground issue of this book concerns the 'politics' of colonial knowledge production, its formations and implications, its contradictions and limitations, and its potential to effect change. Stuart Hall's notion of the 'politics' of representation is useful, with some qualification, in this discussion. He differentiates between the 'politics' and 'poetics' of representation; the latter, he says, is based on the 'semiotics' approach, which 'is concerned with the how of representation, with how language produces meaning'. The other approach, the discursive one, 'is more concerned with the effects and consequences of representation', that is, with its politics. Hall argues that the second approach not only examines 'the how of language and representation, but how the knowledge which a particular discourse produces connects with power, regulates conduct, makes up or constitutes identities and subjectivities, and defines the way certain things are represented, thought about, produced and studied'.[25] The qualification follows at two levels. One, and this stems from the engagement with the colonial context, is to keep open the dialogue between 'colonial' and 'pre-colonial'. This is necessary if we want to chart the ways in which power was conducted, regulated and represented during colonial times. It would be apt here to point out that, methodologically, this approach resonates in agreement with one of the latest influential works on colonial South Asian spatial histories, which argues that social spaces 'do not emerge from self-evident geographies, nor do they exist in mutual isolation. Rather they are co-constituted through the complex "superimposition and interpenetration" of socioeconomic structures, state practices, cultural forms, and collective agency on multiple spatiotemporal scales.'[26] At the temporal scale, investigation of this 'superimposition and interpenetration' thus also requires treading between colonial and pre-colonial practices. The second qualification is about complementing the discursive 'state-centric' formations by looking at the ways such discourses were materialized. It is precisely on this point that I concur with Ravi Ahuja's remark that Manu Goswami's book, the influential work referred above, in its overall treatment, is still entrenched in the colonial (national) discourse analysis framework; in Ahuja's words, Goswami's work 'opens doors for leaving the hermetic world of discourse analysis (though its author appears hesitant to step out fully)'.[27] The sinews of power and its contestation cannot be solely grasped by looking at the dominant colonial discourses alone. They need to be foregrounded in the rather mundane administrative functioning of the Raj, in the ways institutions worked their way out and through competition by and collaboration with the pre-colonial set-up, and in the changing contours of the relationship between the colonial actors and the pre-colonial personnel and ideas. In this way, this work shares a broad thematic and conceptual ground with Ahuja's work,[28] but also makes a new departure by not only accounting for the shifts in the colonial discourse (for instance on public works, which Ahuja has also discussed in depth) and the quotidian circulatory practices but also by looking at the practices and techniques of knowledge generation that informed such discourses and practices. Notwithstanding his pointed identification of Goswami's limitation, one can only wish that Ahuja's own work towards the understanding of social space through 'conflictual material structures' had adopted greater flexibility towards integrating cultural forms of knowledge production. Ahuja's account does not explicitly deal with the production of colonial knowledge or with the role of

---

25 Stuart Hall, ed., *Representation: Cultural Representations and Signifying Practices* (London, Thousand Oaks, CA and New Delhi, 1997), 6.
26 Manu Goswami, *Producing India: From Colonial Economy to National Space* (Chicago and London, 2004), 5–6.
27 Ahuja, *Pathways of Empire*, 21, fn. 7.
28 Ibid.

different techniques and mediums in that production. The absence seems striking if one even passingly reflects on either the role of maps in the history of transport and communication, or in the constitution of boundaries, territories and empires. The result of this approach is that Ahuja, while trying to balance out the present (over/extra) emphasis on discursive analysis mode, has created a new imbalance in privileging only the material aspects of social space without taking into account their necessary cultural accompaniments. In contrast, this book pays closer attention to the ways in which colonial knowledge was produced and circulated; for instance, it discusses a variety of colonial forms of travel, most importantly the administrative winter tours and route surveys that were crucial in knowing the 'interiors'. By doing this, the book shows *how* knowledge about routes, roads, and trade were gathered; how their characteristics changed; and what were the resultant implications of those changes (for example, of steamships partially replacing boats). This is of crucial importance, because in assessing the impact of colonialism either on existing networks or on mobility, the extent to which the rule was able to mobilize and produce knowledge was vital. A focus on this aspect of colonial rule also shows how communication was intrinsically positioned in both the realms: in the acts of travel and representation, in the framing of Orientalist discourses and the picturesque narratives of colonial space; and also in the quotidian colonial administrative concerns and regulations. In doing so, I underpin a fundamental relationship between ideas and practices, both of which had their own contradictory character. Ahuja's *Pathways of Empire* deconstructs the colonial hyperbole and subsequent historiographical complicity, on say the alleged natural barriers and geographical isolation of Orissa that restricted its nature of circulation; it does not directly cover the aspect of colonial production and representation of knowledge on the theme of communication, a subject which the colonial state attached immense importance to.

In this work, four chapters in particular, Chapters 2–5, deal with the nature of processes of knowledge formation, by not only looking at the inter-exchanges between 'Europeans' and 'natives' but also by placing them, as they were, in the asymmetrical power-relations that tied them together. As far as the production of colonial knowledge through travelogues, printed road books, and maps was concerned, the aim is to emphasize the segmented nature of circulation, suggesting that not at every successive level of circulation was knowledge *gained*, but in fact atrophication and omissions were an integral part of the practices.[29] Their segmented nature points towards the varying mediations in which knowledge travelled but which also – and this is a point that this book emphasizes – included not just the extraneous factors that limited circulation but the intrinsic politics of (choice of) those mediations in which knowledge was acquired, produced and disseminated. Reliance on natives rightly suggests the 'limited' nature of the British Raj, yet within that limiting field, the knowledge formed and represented, and the 'regulations' adopted to enforce and justify that knowledge often had an immense potentiality for change, both at the social and spatial levels. The social aspect has been covered by studying a variety of mobile groups, particularly itinerant tradesmen such

---

29 This role of segmentation has been emphasized by Kapil Raj in his book *Relocating Modern Science: Circulation and the Construction of Knowledge in South Asia and Europe, 1650–1900* (Basingstoke, 2007) but has been inadequately demonstrated. See Chapter 4 of this book for further elaboration.

as banjaras and gosains, and by showing how their diverse circulatory practices related to trade, pilgrimage and mercenary militarism, which were perceived as a threat to the colonial state's economic base and political authority. They became marginal and 'criminal' by the end of the first half of the nineteenth century. This requires us to rethink the relationship between knowledge and institutional authority in early colonial India. The limitation in authority, as has been widely argued by scholars in the last two decades, did exist at the institutional level, but that 'limitation' need not imply the 'lack' of knowledge itself. The institutional limitation and continuity did not necessarily define or dictate the pathways and methods of acquiring and representing knowledge. In other words, lack of power and reach of authority during the early colonial rule was not necessarily an impediment created by the condition of lack of knowledge, further implying that knowledge and power did not necessarily follow a synchronic relationship. This has been shown here by juxtaposing (and this relates to the spatial aspect of our above point) the accumulation of knowledge about routes that started right with the inception of the EIC rule in the 1760s to the mechanisms the state devised to control only 'principal' pathways. It was this idea of 'principal' routes that found a place of prominence in the majority of those communication maps that were published from the 1820s onward. Thus, while on the one hand the knowledge base of the state was gradually widening, the physical space as constructed through and around the networks of communication as represented on the maps was becoming blanker over time. This was so because the politics of representation did not necessarily follow the contours of knowledge production. As a result, what becomes necessary to bear in mind is not to overemphasize the homogeneity of colonial control; for instance, although the peripatetic trading features of *sanyasis*, gosains and *fakirs* were controlled, their role in gathering knowledge of the frontier regions continued throughout the nineteenth century. And simultaneously, the need is also not to assume that *institutional continuity* necessarily diluted the changes the colonial rule *intentionally* wanted to introduce.

Often, studies on colonialism and its varied aspects of governance and knowledge formation concentrate solely on the colonial period, thus falling short to provide a necessary linkage with a background to the late pre-colonial conditions. Mapping the nature of 'colonial changes' requires a necessary juxtaposition to the pre-colonial conditions, a task which this book tries to accomplish. At a more general and theoretical level, Chapter 1 lays down the nature of this change taking place, from a pre-colonial affective understanding of space to objectifying colonial interventions. These objectifications in the ways of defining and representing the landscape and its people were, however, not absolute but were internally fractured and contradictory.

Chapter 2 presents the details of different representational tropes and their politics – the tropes that lay at the intersection of travel and communication leading to spatial objectification – suggesting that from the late eighteenth century a spatial descriptive category – interior – was emerging, which by the first two decades of the nineteenth century had coalesced into a larger explanatory schema of 'unchanging and closed India'. Highlighting the role of the ways of travelling and modes of transport through 'roadscapes' and 'Gangascape' in the ways of seeing, the chapter argues that the politico-economic meaning of interior that emerged from the 1820s, in which geological explorations played a crucial role, was informed by the gaze of general travellers and sojourning administrators of the late eighteenth century. However, this gaze and subsequent reporting based on the aesthetic of picturesque did not, as has often been claimed, flatten the topography.[30] I argue that within the forces of spatial objectification that interiorized and inferiorized India, there remained a wider lens through which the people and the landscape were seen and described. What indeed the fixed circuits of travel contributed to was to create a routinized and standardized India.

Chapter 3 focuses on administrative activities that dealt with 'interiors'. While arguing to differentiate between different forms of 'colonial travel' (general sojourns, governor generals' excursions, and district officials' tours), something which at times is overlooked in standard accounts, the chapter's main (although not exclusive) focus is on the district-level touring that was termed as 'going into the interiors'. It shows that the rhetoric of 'unknown interiors' was internally fractured; creation of 'unknown' spaces progressed simultaneously with their 'penetration'.[31] The practice of touring, using a variety of means of transport – horses, palanquins, boats, steamships and not least railways – was central to the colonial administrative efforts in amassing information about roads and ferries, trade and commodities, and taxes and tolls. This knowledge was also useful in improving the communication network. Some of the measures between the 1760s and 1820s included the construction of the New Military Road (NMR), establishment of the Road Fund, and experiments to improve ferries. And still, it is not just the history of investment and policy that concerns us here; the clash of authority between the EIC and the zamindars over the issue of repair and maintenance of roads, for instance, accounts for the social contest that addresses the question of the role of social elites vis-à-vis the state in the backdrop of a continuum of modes of circulation from the late pre-colonial era to those emerging during the colonial rule.

Chapter 4 carries the story of colonial knowledge-gathering and its shifting contexts by looking at route surveys, communication maps, and road and route books that were undertaken and published between the 1760s and 1850s. Identifying the crucial role of 'native' texts and personnel in the formation of colonial knowledge, the chapter suggests that there was a shift in this trend from the beginning of the nineteenth century. Natives, at least in the mainland surveys, became unreliable and the emphasis shifted towards producing 'written' materials – road and route books. The chapter also brings out the implications of varying mediums in which knowledge about the same theme circulated; while the textual corpus provided a thick description of roads and routes, the maps concentrated on 'principal' lines. The role played by print is interesting. Different types of road books and maps suggest the emergence of a varied map-reading audience. The purposes of such publications ranged from maintaining departmental records for posterity to that of helping the travellers in finding their ways in a new country. A growing trend of such publications, which was not specifically 'colonial' in its origin or in its implications,

---

30 Pramod K. Nayar, *English Writing and India, 1600–1920: Colonizing Aesthetics* (Oxford, 2008).
31 In the exploration-cum-travel literature on Africa for the period we are concerned with, the act of knowing which signified the penetration of virgin territories has been brought out by Mary Louise Pratt, *Imperial Eyes: Travel Writing and Transculturation* (London and New York, 1992). Unmistakably, the sexual imagery was not incidental.

however had a colonial flair to it as, for example, it was reflected in the debates on hiring natives for surveys in the mainland.

In most of the communication-maps published after the 1830s, either in India or in London, we see a tendency towards showing only 'principal' routes. I do not contend that it was these publications alone that created a hierarchy of means of communication, thus producing an objectified India of blank spaces. This process was entangled with many other developments, such as the emergence of a diverse nature of map readership, but more importantly with the resources of the state and the choices it made to construct or maintain certain routes depending on their usages (which primarily was military, as the name New Military Road itself suggests), to the practices of travel, and to the politics of investment in related infrastructure such as *dak* bungalows and halting grounds. However, these maps aided in imprinting a hierarchy of routes; the principality of some pushed others into oblivion. This visual trend strengthened the idea of blank spaces and 'roadless' India.

The canvas of empire on which personnel, commands, ideas, artefacts and commodities moved was broad and wide. In the last few years, the idea of circulation and the impulse to understand the history of early modern and modern India through this analytic category has widely been accepted, explored and developed.[32] A recent publication defines the 'great system of circulation' as 'the exchange and interchange of news, ideas and technologies of communication between India and Britain, between Indians and Britons, and between different groups within each of those communities'.[33] Seemingly, this application actually borrows from the increased importance of studies on travel that sought to situate both the text (travelogue) and the textual representation as holding a mid-ground between the metropolis and the colony. Pratt's notion of a 'transcultural zone' and her emphasis that the act of travel is 'complete' only when the traveller returns to his/her home and undertakes to write about it, are necessary cursors to suggest that the circulation of ideas was integral to the making of colonial discourses.[34] Chapter 4 employs the theoretical underpinnings of this category although in a restrained way. The asymmetries of power, the chapter argues, created segmented circuits of flow across different spaces. Identifying the mediations that

---

32 The most recent example is of Raj, *Relocating Modern Science*. In the field of literary studies on the early modern period, seemingly developing from the move towards 'connected histories' and 'global histories', the concept of circulation has been widely put to use in the studies of commodities, texts, personnel, technologies and ideas. Given more to the notion of literary circulation, this strand of investigation has recently been applied to the study of representation of certain spasmodic events. Daniel J. Rycroft, *Representing Rebellion: Visual Aspects of Counter-Insurgency in Colonial India* (New Delhi, 2006). For the circulatory practices in the global context see Tony Ballantyne and Antoinette Burton, *Bodies in Contact: Rethinking Colonial Encounters in World History* (Durham, NC, 2005).
33 Editors, 'A Great System of Circulation: Introducing India into the Nineteenth-Century Media', in David Finkelstein and Douglas M. Peers, eds, *Negotiating India in the Nineteenth-Century Media* (London and New York, 2000), 2.
34 Pratt, *Imperial Eyes*. See also essays in Bart Moore-Gilbert, ed., *Writing India, 1757–1990: The Literature of British India* (Manchester, 1996). Nigel Leask has used Bruno Latour's notion of 'accumulation' to read the late eighteenth-century travel accounts and to explore the theme of colonial encounter, which encompasses the different stages of travel, namely, the appropriation of distant lands, the phenomenology of travel – which for him comprises of 'curiosity' and lastly the temporalization of cultural difference. N. Leask, *Curiosities and the Aesthetics of Travel Writing, 1770–1840: 'From an Antique Land'* (Oxford, 2002), 18–22.

limited the processes of circulation thus becomes important, as does the task of analysing the context and politics of changes in which those mediations worked.

If Chapter 4 looks at the circulatory practices on the broader canvas of empire through the prism of ideas and techniques of print and knowledge production, the social aspects of mobility employs the same analytical concept of circulation in Chapter 5 at a relatively narrower regional and trans-regional level within the area of focus, which is Bihar. The growth in knowledge about routes went hand in hand with their control. Although reluctant to agree with Kerr in presenting groups such as banjaras as 'transport workers',[35] the chapter looks closely at the fate of a few mobile communities vis-à-vis the 'sedentary' policies of the colonial state, thus inviting closer scrutiny and surveillance. That the regime of regulations villainized the 'men-on-the-road' is quite predictable: what is more interesting is the intermeshed role of transport, trade and mobility on the one hand, and colonial surveillance, regulation and control on the other. Seen in this way, many of the arguments about the criminality of wandering tribes that are often made for the second half of the nineteenth century, primarily in and around 1871, would need a better foregrounding on the basis of interlocked histories of communication and circulation as emerging from the late eighteenth century. Arguing against overemphasizing the role of the colonial state in the production of native criminality,[36] two points are emphasized: one, to conceptualize mobility as an integral part of the interrelationship between trade, politics and the colonial state that produced discourses on criminality; and two, to situate the mid-nineteenth-century developments in the socioeconomic and political fabric of the eighteenth century. The emergence of caste as the measuring unit of criminality was already a dominant feature in the late eighteenth century and not a product of changed notions of authority from the mid-nineteenth century.

The elements of colonial discourse that stitched together the notions of communication and modernization, and the regulative practices adopted by the colonial state, started to become conspicuous from the 1820s. At the same time, when the social circulatory practices were getting affected under colonialism, the state's policies were giving rise to new communication regimes from the 1820s. Chapter 6 charts this emergence by arguing that this 'newness' was not located on the site of the railways (as is conventionally done) but in the act of the reassured conviction of the colonial state in the utility of 'public works' that resulted in increased investment on roads and ferries. The period saw the emergence, conceptualization and crystallization of the notion of 'public works' that formed the bedrock of the belief in the 'moral and material Progress' of the colony.[37]

---

35 Ian J. Kerr, 'On the Move: Circulating Labor in Pre-Colonial, Colonial and Post-Colonial India', in Rana P. Behal and Marcel van der Linden, eds, *International Review of Social History: Coolies, Capital and Colonisation: Studies in Indian Labour History*, Supplement 14, 2006.
36 As done by Basudeb Chattopadhyay, *Crime and Control in Early Colonial Bengal* (Calcutta, 2000).
37 See Michael Mann, '"Torchbearers Upon the Path of Progress": Britain's Ideology of a "Moral and Material Progress in India"', in Fischer-Tiné and Mann, eds, *Colonialism as Civilizing Mission*. What emerges from Mann's essay is a clear progression and change in the sites of 'civilizing mission' from the colonial critique of 'Oriental Despotism' in the late eighteenth century to the notion of a civilizing mission in the second decade of the nineteenth century, which emphasized ideas of education, sanitation and communication.

The apparent 'old means' of communication provided the 'new grounds' for the shift in the communication regime. The construction of the Grand Trunk Road (GTR), the streamlining of the Road Fund, the establishment of the Ferry Fund Committees and the introduction of steamships were the chief features of this period. The realignments had already begun; the GTR not only displaced the older thoroughfare (NMR) but also forced re-routing of other connecting roads. The increased expenditure and better connectivity led to realignments of older trading networks and circuits.

However, the period was marked by the existence of diverse patterns of circulation or, as we have called it in Chapter 7, 'nested networks'. The colonial state remained largely successful in curtailing the mobility of certain circulatory groups but the trading networks were not always easily brought under such regulative regimes. It was so because, first, many such patterns of exchange lay outside the purview of the *interest* of the state and, second, the latter had its own institutional limitations in bringing them under control. This is not to say that colonial implications were altogether absent; the shift in the ties of the region of north Bihar with Nepal and northern United Provinces (UP) from the late eighteenth to the nineteenth century, when it increasingly became Calcutta-oriented, had a definitive colonial role.[38] The chapter argues that in imperial commodities such as opium, indigo and English imported cloth, the changes in transport realignments did affect the trading patterns. However, in many other 'local' products that were traded extensively over a vast geographical area, the earlier patterns were sustained.

In this scheme of the study of trade, mobility and communication, attempts have been made to foreground a synthesis between communication and transport. Kerr has argued that 'transport precedes communication', elaborating further that transport symbolizes the infrastructure whereas communication deals primarily with social exchange; that is, the exchange of commodities, of information and of ideas.[39] Ahuja has qualified this understanding; convincingly, he shows that in the period of our study '[t]he word "transport" (or, alternatively, "transit") was not used with regard to infrastructures of mobility but merely to describe the actual movement of goods.'[40] The histories of communication (even by Kerr's definition) and the history of transport operated at too interlocked a level to sustain any distinction. The exchange and volume of goods considerably affected the selection of routes and the opening of a route in turn affected the flow of goods and commodities. What Kerr's distinction does signify is a strong shift in the focus towards the subject-content of studies such as this. The traditional approach

---

38 Kumkum Chatterjee has explained this shift, for instance, by the disappearance of Mughal, Pathan and other merchants who came to Patna from Central Asia, as a result of the weakening of the Mughal control over the parts of North India which consequently led to the insecurity on the roads and some degree of dislocation in the established patterns of life. See her 'Trade and Darbar Politics in the Bengal Subah, 1733–1757', *MAS* 26, no.2 (1992): 240.

39 Kerr, 'British Rule, Technological Change and the Revolution in Transportation and Communication: Punjab in the Later Nineteenth Century' (typescript version personally provided by the author), later published in Tony Ballantyne, ed., *Textures of the Sikh Past: New Historical Perspectives* (New Delhi, 2007).

40 Ahuja, *Pathways of Empire*, 66, especially ch. 3 for a discussion on historical shifts in the meaning of transport and communication.

to transport studies – in both the avatars, the historical narratives and the geographical accounts – dealt more often than not with the 'institutional' history of, say, a railway company, the rate and tariff structures, the volume of trade and so on. In the South Asian case, the element of colonial motive is ever present.[41] The core of the ideological concern of regional geographies written around transport networks was to underline the patterns of rural–urban linkages, primarily owing to the post-independence modernization concern.[42] The broader socio-cultural history of transport, which on the one hand illustrates its effects and on the other contextualizes it in the cultural praxis of the time, is a fairly recent development.[43] This book aims to open the debate in the latter sense.

The last chapter carries forward the story of realignments into the 'railway age' by looking at 'lateral communications'. The age of railways, quite rhetorically, has been defined as one ushering in a period of sea-change in areas of trade, travel and mobility. Against this grain, the chapter argues in favour of taking a more cautious approach by adopting a commodity- and region-specific approach to appraise the nature of the changes, both in terms of spatial shifts (in production zones) and trading linkages. Undeniably, from the 1860s a stable and clear policy was evolving that kept the railways in the centre of the emerging communication grid, followed by four types or categories of roads, devised to connect the 'interiors' with the nodes of railway communication. In this period of lateral realignment, the Grand Trunk Road in Bihar served more for regional than through traffic, but a non-railway-centric nested network still thrived. The earlier networks were galvanized, re-routed and prioritized to cater to the railways but the overall picture that emerges is one that supports the framework of 'alignments and realignments' rather than of competition between the railways and other means of communication.

The railways in their first twenty years of operation did not penetrate deep into existing circulatory patterns so as to diminish or destroy the earlier linkages. The economic and productive zone of wet riparian north Bihar did not see the railway lines before the 1880s, except for a small line built in 1874 during the famine. Rather than opening up the new channels of trade, mobility and circulation, the new technology of communication more often than not relied on earlier existing and prominent modes of commerce and tried to tap their trade. The very choice of the first railways that ran parallel to the Ganga in this region was based on the idea of capturing the *existing* trade rather than opening the

---

41 Some of the works of this nature are Daniel Thorner, *Investment in Empire: British Railway and Steam Shipping Enterprise in India, 1825–1849* (Philadelphia, 1950); W. J. Macpherson, 'Investment in Indian Railways, 1845–1875', *Economic History Review* 8, 2nd series, 1958; Mukherjee, *The Early History of the East Indian Railway*; R. D. Tiwari, *Railways in Modern India* (Bombay, 1941).
42 Jagdish Singh, *Transport Geography of South Bihar* (Varanasi, 1964); Ram Briksh Singh, *Transport Geography of Uttar Pradesh* (Varanasi, 1966).
43 For instance, Ian Carter, *Railways and Culture in Britain: The Epitome of Modernity* (Manchester and New York, 2001).

new one. No wonder the river remained the main channel of communication for bulkier commodities until the end of the century.

Strictly speaking, the chapters in this book are not chronologically arranged but a sense of chronology which also maps out the historical scope of the study comes through. The book starts with the period of acquisition of economic and territorial control by the English East India Company (1760s), who soon felt the need to know, regulate and improve the means of communication. The emergence of road and route surveys, practices of winter tours that led to the accumulation of knowledge regarding trade and communication, and the impulse to maximize the revenue and control the 'illegal' trade through communication surveillance were matters of prime concern for the early colonial rule. The story moves forward into the nineteenth century by charting the changes in the discourses of colonialism, of which, for our study, two were very important – the opening up of the interiors, and public works. The book also looks at the ways in which they materialized, which brings out the inherent limitations and contradictions of colonial rule. From the 1820s onwards, the increased investment – first in road building and then in the railways – symbolized the emergence of a new circulatory regime. The book traces the changes in the nature of investment, the formulation of new policies, and their effects on the circulatory practices until the 1880s, by which time the railways had come to occupy the centre stage of the new communication grid.

This book addresses the issue of the nature of the colonial state–space, explored on the one hand through a close analysis of the colonial travelling gaze, practices of tours and surveys, the politics of representations and mapping, and the formation of colonial knowledge – and, on the other, trading networks, patterns of circulation of commodities and their subsequent realignments. Since, historiographically speaking, communication is regarded as integral to the making of 'dominant colonial space', this work suggests that we perceive colonial space as constituted of a series of layered components of both 'inherited spaces and networks' and also of those which the colonial exigencies altered and relaid over a period of at least one hundred years. To once again return to Goswami, she underlines this character of the colonial state–space by stating that its production was 'made and marked by immanent contradiction'. Yet, there is an insistent tendency in her work to underscore 'profound' and 'spectacular' reconfiguration and restructuration of the social space and time. Goswami traces such changes from immediately after 1857, which serves one major point of departure for this work as it takes into account a much longer period of pre-1857 processes of spatial changes and continuities under colonialism. Although the reader of Goswami gets an idea that the post-1857 colonial state–space had other coordinates of ascendancy, the most important being the global Britain-centred imperial economy, s(he) does not get the concrete historical answers (despite the author's claim that she attempts to 'specify the historicity of colonial state and economy', page 32) to the question of how the post-1857 colonial state related to its own past of a hundred years (1757–1858) in South Asia, during which the state was not just a passive entity but actively participated in territorial control and refashioning of boundaries. Further, Goswami's work does not allow enough help to situate colonial changes within the late pre-colonial developments.[44] Of course the post-1857 changes are explained by Goswami: first through the ideological shifts on the issue of colonization as represented in the writings of Mill and others, and second, through institutional investment, significantly in transport, that for Goswami justifies the formation of 'new colonial state form'.[45] In my understanding, the evaluation of colonial state–space, particularly of its socioeconomic nature through the working of transport and communication, requires a deeper historical investigation – as the last two chapters of this work provide – into the 'sphere of operation': of commodity exchange circuits, regional trends (of ascendancy, decline and disparities) and the lateral development of the transport network. It is thus significantly surprising that roads, even as important feeder lines, figure in Goswami's analysis of colonial state–space as premised on 'new' communication networks.

The work that involves the study of 'macro', 'micro' and 'nested' forms of networks necessarily needs to deal with a range of primary sources. The parts of this book dealing with cultural practices of mobility and issues of representations are based on published and unpublished travelogues, journals, diaries, letters and memoirs of British officers and European sojourners. A range of visual and cartographic materials has been used. The parts dealing with administrative imperatives, trade and communication policy is based on railway company documents and unpublished and published government documents of which the most useful and hitherto scarcely used were found in the local archives of Bihar. These include the Collectors' and Commissioner's Correspondences from the late eighteenth century in the Bihar State Archives and the PWD General Branch and General Branch (Communications) files in the Water Resource Department Record Room in Patna.

One of the key features of this study is its regional focus. The empirical research is focused on the undivided state of Bihar, although while chasing roads, ferries and railroads the story does enter into modern day UP to the west and Bengal to the east.

---

44 One probable reason of this absence could be that although the colonial state–space is an integral part in Goswami's thesis, it primarily serves a staging ground for tracing the processes of how its unevenness opened up the spaces of appropriation by later nationalist formations and formulations. Concerned directly with the problematic of nationalism, she probably is right in claiming for herself the novelty of revising the dominant periodization of nationalism in South Asian scholarship by shifting the zero-ground of study from 1885 to 1857. However, much of this claim appears a muted overstatement if one's core concern is the colonial state itself and its varied technologies and apparatuses of rule, as it is of this work; then this period revision appears rather conventional. The termination of the Company Raj and the beginning of the direct rule has long been treated as a watershed, which needs revision. This work, on the contrary, traces both through colonial discourses and practices, a change taking place in the 1820s. See Goswami, *Producing India*, 5, 7–10, 31–3. My sense of periodization is akin to Arnold's who claims that 'certainly by the 1830s, there emerged a far more complex, expressive and distinctive discourse of Indian landscape, topography and travel.' Arnold, *The Tropics*, 22–3.

45 Goswami, *Producing India*, 42–7; to be fair to the author she does account for the well-known cases of UP's regional shift and differential rate structures of freight; and also the 'emergence of distinct set of regional, urban, and local markets that were more tightly interwoven with imperial markets than with each other' as examples of differentiated homogenization, 59–63, direct quote from 62–3.

Regional anchorage of a work on spatial history dealing with issues of transport and mobility that commonly are thought to link people and regions might appear at odds. And yet delving deep into a region's specificities to bring into sharper relief the patterns of effects or the nature of transactions of objects and ideas that were part of the broader politico-economic systems is too well known to be repeated here. In two of the recent influential works on Bihar's economy of the late eighteenth and nineteenth centuries, the region serves more as a case study than as a site bearing any historical or geographical uniqueness.[46] Both these works use Bihar to illuminate the history of colonial India. In both works Bihar is primarily approached as a 'link' and a 'transitional zone' between north Indian and Bengal plains. So far as the matter of colonial policies and discourses are concerned, this book also uses Bihar as a case study. The debates on 'interiors' and their openings would have remained as true for any other region of colonial India as they were for Bihar. However, so much as it appears to be generally believed, my approach has tried to skirt away from treating Bihar as a transitional sandwiched zone between Hindustan and Bengal. In the approach where Bihar serves merely as a link, the region's geography, very plausibly, could only be imagined as a geographical space squeezed between two imperial clusters. This in turn might give rise to only a limited exploration of other geographical coordinates with which Bihar possibly and historically had remained connected. One such linkage traced in this book is of peripatetic groups travelling through Tibet, Nepal, Northern Bengal, Gangetic Bihar and UP.

Bihar also presented a suitable area of investigation because of the nature of commodities produced there; it was one of the leading production zones in imperial export commodities (opium, indigo and saltpetre) from the late eighteenth century, and in the nineteenth century for grain and seeds. Patna was one of the greatest emporia of trade, with long and extensive trading connections. Besides the old Mughal road that ran alongside the river, the Ganga was the main artery of communication. Substantial sections of the first two imperial lines – NMR and GTR – also ran through Bihar.

However, a socio-spatial account must take into account the topographical variations of the region that are produced as much by its varied ecological settings as by the power-play between state and different influential groups. I hope that this strand illuminates the history of Bihar and the way colonial rule consolidated there in specific ways. This attendance to geographical and ecological diversity is also important to counter the idea that there could be an absolute homogenized space in any historical time. In other words, this work shows that the way the communication network consolidated in a region, together with its effects, were varied and relative. If the region of south Bihar, owing to its hills, plateaus, and difficult passes presented one set of difficulties and created a distinct rhythm of circulation, then north Bihar, where most of the rivers were navigable throughout the year, made ferries extremely important. This is one important point of difference between Bihar and north India where the roads, as Varady has shown, remained extremely important till the late nineteenth century.[47] As in Bengal, at least

---

46 Kumkum Chatterjee, *Merchants, Politics and Society in Early Modern India, Bihar: 1733–1820* (Leiden, New York and Cologne, 1996), 13; Yang, *Bazaar India*, 14–15.
47 Varady, 'Rail and Road Transport'.

in northern and central districts of Bihar, rivers played that role. This diversity created historical richness; north Bihar's trading links with Nepal, the Gangetic valley's extensive linkages with areas both on its east and west, and the southern Bihar's connections with places going as far as Orissa allows for the construction of an interesting history of the complex relationship between networks of trade and modes of communication.

Work on the social history of communication is a fairly new field in South Asian history writing and we must wait for a few more works that assess the region's uniqueness and responses in this respect, and more specifically in relation to colonial policies. This would also help us in appreciating colonialism's varied strategies, discourses and limitations. A brief comparison with Orissa's history, as presented by Ahuja, drives home the point mentioned above. Bihar came under colonial rule quite early on. In fact, politically, administratively and economically the region was as crucial for colonial rule as was the Bengal proper in the late eighteenth century. The grant of Diwani in 1765 led to the emergence of route surveys and within twenty years of territorial and financial control the EIC carried its first biggest investment in road making (the construction of the NMR), to be followed by the creation of a Road Fund within ten years. Orissa, on the other hand, was annexed by the EIC in 1803. Until the 1850s the region witnessed a 'rather low' priority of colonial interest in the development of transport infrastructure.[48] As Ahuja puts it: 'Unlike most of the regions that have so far caught the attention of historians of transport, Orissa was clearly no major target of colonial infrastructure policy and has a rather loosely meshed circulatory network according to subcontinental standards even today.'[49] Not only, therefore, was the priority missing, but also the knowledge mechanism operating in Orissa was very different, and actually weak. To cite Ahuja once again: 'colonial officials had not even a clear perception of the existing patterns of circulation before the 1860s'.[50] In this regard, the difference between Bihar and Orissa is not just of chronology. Bihar, or for that matter UP or Bengal, did not serve as a greenroom for rehearsing the policies that the colonial state wanted to pursue in Orissa. The region's history tells us a very different story of colonial rule – both of its intervention and limitations. The late entry of colonialism in Orissa does not illuminate the early colonial concerns for communication in the same way as it does in the case of Bihar.

---

48 Ahuja, *Pathways of Empire*, 156, 161.
49 Ibid., 8.
50 Ibid., 123. Elsewhere he shows that as late as the 1860s 'the colonial state's ability to "know" circulation in this region was still limited'. Ibid., 147.

Chapter 1

FROM AFFECTIVE FORMS TO OBJECTIFICATION: SPATIAL TRANSITION FROM PRE-COLONIAL TO COLONIAL TIMES

This work primarily deals with the colonial period, that is, from the 1760s onwards, but in order to understand the nature of transition within a much established framework of 'continuity and change', it is important to delineate the trajectories of colonial practices and discourses as they emerged and interacted with the pre-colonial set-up. The changes taking place during the colonial period were both enabled and structured through these interactions. For instance, the colonial perception towards native criminality was not just a product of 'colonial construction' based on caste (and allegedly other enumerative features of colonial rule) but also a phenomenon related to the political decentralization in the early eighteenth century, to the rise of mercenary groups in state-formation and to the changed political conditions in the neighbouring region of Nepal. In the same vein, there existed a dialogue between the early colonial route surveys and map production on the one hand, and the late Mughal and Maratha practices on the other, which makes it clear that mapping, if seen in its essence as a 'tool of empire', was not innately 'colonial' in origin. Nonetheless, there definitely were moments in which colonial practices transcended, reconfigured and even altered the existing practices. Recognizing these moments requires engagement with pre-colonial times. In order to establish the coloniality of colonial spatial interventions, we need to examine some of the geographical and spatial politics and representations that existed before colonialism. What is offered in this chapter is a survey of spatial categories and demarcations as they existed in pre-colonial times and the ways they were used and transformed in the colonial.[1] The importance of this discussion lies in situating and contextualizing the changes taking place in the colonial period, which is the central theme of this book.

Pre-colonial Affective Spatialisms

Let us start with the basic geographical divisions that are readily noticeable in the immediate pre-colonial spatial understanding. Two of the broader units are 'Dakkan' and 'Hindustan', meaning south and north India respectively. Dargah Quli Khan, the traveller in the *Muraqqa-e-Dehli* (a diary written during his stay in Delhi from 1739–41) thus explains

---

1 The discussion is based on English translations of contemporary sources and a variety of secondary works.

his journey from 'Dakkan' to Delhi as going to 'Hindustan'.[2] However, this spatial marking was fluid: for the coastal south, in reference to Portuguese settlements, it was said that 'Farangis are settled on the coast of Hindustan'.[3] This perception was based on the idea of *al-Hind*, which according to al-Biruni, author of the *Kitab-al-Hind* (1305), was 'limited in the south by the above mentioned Indian ocean, and on all three other sides by the lofty mountains, the waters of which flow down to it'.[4] Here we find an encompassing view of 'Hindustan' that was not restricted to north India alone. However, the geographical connotation of this word, the contours of geographical boundaries, spatial demarcations and their socio-political implications kept on shifting over a period of a few centuries, say between the fourteenth and eighteenth. In the thirteenth and fourteenth centuries, the idea of Hindustan radiated out from the capital city of Delhi: as Simon Digby remarks, the 'Dehli usage [of] "Hindostan" was…for the Gangetic lands to the southeast, Awadh and beyond'.[5] Going to Lakhnavti (Bengal) meant going to Hindustan.[6] By the eighteenth century, however, Hindustan and Bengal had become distinct spatial units, as is evident from Dargah Quli Khan's work, where the former specifically meant north India. In the same period, that is, from the fourteenth to eighteenth century, the European understanding of Indian geography, boundaries and frontiers hinged along the axis of a river – the Ganga. The two omnipresent terms – both in texts,[7] but especially in maps – are 'India Intra Gangem' and 'India Extra Gangem'.[8] The former meant the land between the Indus

---

2 Dargah Quli Khan, *Muraqqa-e-Dehli*, trans. Chander Shekhar and Shama Mitra Chenoy (Delhi, 1989); see also Bhimsen's reference to Aurungzeb's march from Deccan towards the north as 'march towards Hindustan'. Bhimsen, *Tarikh-i-Dilkasha*, trans. Jadunath Sarkar, ed. and introd. V. G. Khobreakar (Bombay, 1972), 15.
3 Sanjay Subrahmanyam, *Penumbral Visions: Making Polities in Early Modern South India* (Ann Arbor, 2001), 204.
4 M. Athar Ali, 'The Evolution of the Perception of India: Akbar and Abu'l Fazl', *Social Scientist* 24 (January–March 1996): 81. [Henceforth *SS*.] Isami in his *Futuhus-salatin*, which was written in around 1350 in Daulatabad (which was in Deccan), uses the expression 'Hindustan' in al-Biruni's sense. A few centuries later, Abul Fazl incorporated the peninsular India (Dakkan) in his idea of Hindustan. See Ali, 85 and 87, fn. 8.
5 Simon Digby, 'Before Timur Came: Provincialization of the Delhi Sultanate through the Fourteenth Century', *Journal of the Economic and Social History of the Orient* 47, no. 3 (2004): 319. [Henceforth *JESHO*.] Also the term 'umara-i atraak', which evidently referred to royal slave households in the late fourteenth century, was applied mainly to slaves of eastern Indian provenance who were also known in urban Delhi as 'the Hindostanis'. Simon Digby, 'Iletmish or Iltutmish: A Reconsideration of the Name of the Delhi Sultan', *Iran* 8 (1970): 57, fn. 1.
6 Digby, 'Before Timur Came', 320.
7 For instance, Father Friar Ambrose travelling in the mid-seventeenth century used the expression 'the whole of India extra and intra Gangetic'. Rev. H. Hosten, 'Relation of the Capuchin Missions in Egypt, Syria, Mesopotamia, Persia and East Indies (1644–47)', *Bengal Past and Present* 37, no. 74, pt 2 (1929): 107. [Henceforth *BPP*.] These expressions were in use as late as the late eighteenth century. For instance, see 'Account of the Manners of the INHABITANTS of India within the Ganges', *Weekly Miscellany; or Instructive Entertainer*, 2, 38, June 1774. In this article the Ganga has been used to define the whole of the subcontinent. Some authors also used the 'within the Ganges' phrase for peninsular India. See 'Account of the Peninsula of the INDIES within the Ganges: Being that Part of Asia where the Chief European Settlements are Situated, and the Seat of the War in India', *Royal Magazine*, August

and the Ganga and the latter that beyond the Ganga to the east. These two traditions – Indic and European – were not exclusive. Early European officers of the late eighteenth century were aware of and in fact employed the Indic divisions, often describing north India as Hindustan, in distinction to Bengal. Similarly, the European expression about a river determining the limits of territory finds resonances in various folktales of South Asia wherein a body of water is treated as a boundary, both in territorial and cultural senses.[9]

Beyond the Indic and European paradigms, there existed other axes, *ala* or 'connected histories' between South Asian Islamic polities and notably Persia that generated some other forms of spatial perception. If Persia was viewed as *wilayat* (foreign), the Persian embassy visiting Calicut and the Vijaynagar kingdom (in south India) in 1445 described these places as 'dark regions'.[10] Like Hindustan, the meaning of wilayat also shifted over time. Its current meaning – signifying the West and primarily Britain – evolved in the course of the eighteenth century. Before, it was used for the region of Khurasan, Transoxiana and Iran. Literally, wilayat meant a 'dominion', a 'territory governed' and 'an inhabited country, district'.[11] The geographical situations did not limit the imaginative political and ideological bonding; the 'connected histories' questions the neat division of political boundaries, frontiers and cultural flows. While Dakkan was distinctly seen by the Mughal north Indian power first as its frontier region and subsequently as *mamalika-mahrusa* (well-protected territories), the Deccan rulers, particularly from the Bijapur and Golconda dynasties, saw their territories as part of the Safavid empire. This was explicitly mentioned

---

1761. Similarly, for places such as Arakan in the east, the phrase 'land beyond the Ganges' was used even in the early nineteenth century. 'Singular Customs at Arracan, in India beyond the Ganges', *La Belle Assemblee, or Bell's Court and Fashionable Magazine*, London, 1 August 1814.

8 See Susan Gole, *Indian within the Ganges* (New Delhi, 1983).

9 Not only in folktales but also in political treatises of pre-colonial times a river in indeterminate and contested ways formed the boundary between the kingdoms. Throughout the medieval period the River Kosi was regarded as the indisputable boundary between Tirhut and Bengal. Again, according to Minhaj, the River Begmati (or Karatoya), which he called the river of the first order, was treated as the boundary between the 'Muslim' territory of Bengal and the 'Hindu' country of Kamrup. Jadunath Sarkar, ed., *The History of Bengal, Vol. 2: Muslim Period, 1200–1757*, second impression (Dacca, 1972), 13, fn. 13, and 53. The concept of rivers acting as boundaries of cultural affiliations and practices is also present in current times; people living on the either side of the Ganga in Bihar are reluctant to form marriage alliances. In general on the role of river, see the interesting collection of folktales by Simon Digby, *Wonder-Tales of South Asia*, reprint (New Delhi, 2006).

10 Kamaluddin Abdul-Razzaq Samarqandi in his mission to Calicut and Vijayanagar in 1445 used this phrase. W. M. Thackston, *A Century of Princes, Sources of Timurid History and Art* (Cambridge, MA, 1989), 300.

11 Simon Digby, 'Beyond the Ocean: Perceptions of Overseas in Indo-Persian sources of the Mughal Period', *SIH* 15, no. 2 (1999): 258–9, fn. 31. In the latter sense wilayat is mentioned in *Maasir-i-Alamgiri*, a work completed by Saqi Must'ad Khan in 1710, trans. and annot. Jadunath Sarkar (Calcutta, 1947), 158 and also in J. Sarkar, trans., 'A Description of North Bengal in 1609 A. D.', *BPP* 35 (1928): 146. Babur used this term to distinguish between 'civilized' and 'uncivilized' spaces: wilayat to him meant an agrarian or sedentary region, often in contrast to the steppes. Stephen Dale, 'The Poetry and Autobiography of the Babur-nama', *Journal of Asian Studies* 55, no. 3 (1996): 641.

by the Bijapur ruler in a letter to the Safavid ruler in 1613.[12] Another connected region – Afghanistan – to which north India was inseparably tied, was also seen as 'foreign' and its rulers 'foreigners', at least by contemporary Mughal chroniclers who saw Mirza Hakim, half-brother of Akbar, who ruled from Kabul, in such a way. Interestingly, Father Rudolf Acquaviva, a Jesuit missionary at the court of Akbar shared the same view, pointing at shared spatial prejudices, which might have been consciously developed to win over Akbar to accept Christianity, the objective the Jesuits so badly wanted to achieve.[13]

Along with and within these broad geographical classifications there existed further demarcations. One was the area of Bengal. Ibn Batutta informs us that the 'Muhammadans of Upper India called it *Dojakh-i-Purniyamat*, i.e. a Hell full of good things!' The Mughal chronicler and historian, Abul Fazl, says that the 'country [Bengal] was notorious under the name of *Bulghak-i-Khana*, i.e. the House of Strife from the earliest times'.[14] Equally important was its characterization as a place of wonder and marvels: many of the fables that circulated not only in the court of Mughal rulers in north India but also in the Iberian Peninsula and Europe in general came from the fringes of the Mughal Empire. In fact 'curious objects and animals' were transported as gifts to the Mughal court.[15] What becomes important, as Flores has argued, is that such stereotypes were not plain European constructs; they exhibited 'Eurasian continuum' in which the role of 'ideas and images circulating within India' were also crucial. These ideas and images definitely gained from and contributed to the idea of unknowability of these lands. Distant lands were wondrous, fear-evoking and unhealthy.[16] The contradictions were clear: prospects of good commerce were counterbalanced by the swamps and marshy lands with their insalubrious air that made the entire place unwholesome. Added to this was the turbulent political situation (Bulghak-i-Khana). Dominant tropes on climate, land and politics complemented each other in producing a space. Bengal's image of an unhealthy space lingered long even in the colonial times. Like early colonial expressions of swampy, marshy and unhealthy Bengal, Mirza Abu Taleb Khan of Lucknow, who went to Europe in the late eighteenth century, described the death of his four-year-old son during one of the journeys from Lucknow to Calcutta as 'a sacrifice to the unhealthy climate'. The ignorance of the (native) physician of Calcutta was also mentioned.[17]

---

12 M. Alam and S. Subrahmanyam, 'The Deccan Frontier and Mughal Expansion, ca. 1600: Contemporary Perspectives', *JESHO* 47, no. 3 (2004): 368, 373.

13 Munis D. Faruqui, 'The Forgotten Prince: Mirza Hakim and the Formation of Mughal Empire in India', *JESHO* 48, no. 4 (2005): 490.

14 N. K. Bhattasali, 'Bengal's Chiefs Struggle for Independence in the Reign of Akbar and Jahangir', *BPP* 35, no. 70, pt 2, (1928): 135.

15 Jorge Flores, 'Distant Wonders: The Strange and the Marvelous between Mughal India and Habsburg Iberia in the early Seventeenth Century', *Comparative Studies in Society and History* 49, no. 3 (2007): 560, 562. [Henceforth *CSSH*.] For more such stereotypes on Bengal, see 574–5.

16 It was reported that the poisonous air of Assam caused a pestilence that carried off vast numbers of soldiers during the Khan-i Khanan's conquest of Assam. *Maasir-i-Alamgiri*, 26.

17 Abu Taleb Khan, *The Travels of Mirza Abu Taleb Khan in Asia, Africa and Europe during the Years 1799, 1800, 1801, 1802, and 1803*, trans. Charles Stewart (London, 1810), vol. 1, 16.

Land is often taken as the unit of analysis in spatial studies. This nexus stems from the close link between studies of cartography and space, which understandably but inadequately limits the investigation to only 'land'. We argue, instead, that spatial representation, or, in other words, knowledge produced about a place or space, both in pre-colonial and colonial times included elements other than land; air and water were two such important elements. It is no surprise, then, that in many of the accounts of this period we find an essential mention of not only the resources of water available in a place – a spring, lake, river and rivulet – but also, and sometimes in quite extended discussion – of the taste of the water, its sweetness or disagreeableness. In spatial appraisal, water (*aab*) played a crucial role.[18] Politically too, in the milieu of constant courtly intrigues and conspiracies, it was an element that was under scrutiny. To ward off the possibility of poisoning by water Humanyun had instructed his ewer-bearer thus: 'You are not to allow any other person to offer me water to drink without your seal being affixed, do not permit the water to remain empty during the night; when you give me to drink, pour water into the china cup, and on the march have the bottle on the horse with you.'[19]

The descriptions of sound and smell in the production of space were equally important, which again was true for both Mughal and colonial times. One of the common Mughal examples would be, as Bhimsen notes in his memoirs, the presence of 'scented breeze in gardens', which in this particular garden in Burhanpur, added 'colour and decency to the entire place'.[20] For early colonial 'encounters' as represented in travel writings, one could chiefly look at the description of pagodas (temples), which attracted attention not only because of their riches but also because of their closed interiors: concerning a temple in Tranquenbar, the Revd H. Hoston in the 1640s said: 'such temples have no windows, but are very dark and *evil-smelling*'.[21] Such indexes – sound or smell – were not exclusively

---

18 One typical example could be given here: during his visit to Bengal in 1608–09, Abdul Latif came across a tank – *pukhar* in the Bengali tongue – in a village called Bagha, whose water he mentioned 'might excite the rivalry of the *Kausar* spring in heaven'. Sarkar, 'A Description', 143. In the same *safarnama* he mentioned another river – the Karmanasha – in Bihar, infamous for destroying (*nash*) deeds (*karma*), in these words: 'Its water is extremely distasteful and disagreeable to the sight. A look at it turns a man's bile cold, – not to speak of his merits'. J. Sarkar, 'Travels in Bihar, 1608 A. D.', *Journal of Bihar and Orissa Research Society* 5 (1919): 598. [Henceforth *JBORS*.]
19 Ruby Lal, '"The 'Domestic world" of Peripatetic Kings: Babur and Humanyun, c. 1494–1556', *The Medieval History Journal* 4, no. 1 (2001): 81. [Henceforth *MHJ*.]
20 Bhimsen, *Tarikh-i-Dilkasha*, 6. Gardens provided the most suitable setting for such renderings. One could also see this in Sheik Sajjad Hosain, *The Amir Hamza: An Oriental Novel*, part 1 (Calcutta, 1892) in English; republished as *An Oriental Novel Dastan-e Amir Hamza* (Patna, 1992), 112, 115.
21 Hosten, 'Relation of the Capuchin Missions', 108 (emphasis added). Pagoda, from as early as the sixteenth century, was seen as central to the 'Gentile' (Hindu) culture, which was regarded as 'the repository of immense wealth, where blood was split ceaselessly in sacrifices, hook-swinging rituals, temple-car festivals, and ritual self-dismemberments'. Subrahmanyam, *Penumbral Visions*, 30. Such stereotypes persisted and probably exist even today. In an essay published in 1861, the interior of a Hindu temple was described as the Other of the European idea of a place of public worship; the author commented: 'During the whole performance the air rang with shouts, the gongs boomed out funeral chimes, the people were in a religious frenzy, capable of any wild act of enthusiasm.' 'A Fair on the Ganges', *All the Year Round* 5 (August 1861): 524.

used for 'writing India' in Otherizing terms, either by Indics or Europeans. European perceptions about at least musical sound, as reflected in the seventeenth-century travel writing, were riddled with contradictions. For some the music was 'sweet and tuneable', for others 'loud and barbarous'.[22] In fact the same person 'heard' two or more types of sounds depending on the context. During her travels in the Upper India in the early nineteenth century, A. Deane noted that although the Hindu musical instruments 'do not in general produce agreeable sounds to an English ear', in this particular instance (of a temple function) the sound was rather 'pleasing than otherwise'. However, a 'detestable' ritual such as hook-swinging 'commenced by loud shouting, accompanied with what they miscall music, alias, a combination of barbarous sounds produced from different instruments'.[23] Even if Otherizations happened, Europe itself was under the same type of scrutiny from Indian eyes and ears. One of the most important conclusions that Mirza Abu Taleb drew from his European trip was: 'If I may safely aver, from the day I arrived in Dublin, till I quitted Paris, the *sound of coach wheels* was never out of my ears.'[24] And if Europeans stereotyped Indians, the same happened the other way round. Abu Taleb trenchantly scrutinized English law and English character and concluded that the 'French are greatly superior to the English; they are always courteous, and never betray those symptoms of impatience, so conspicuous and reprehensible in the English character.'[25]

Another cultural–spatial zone, discerned from the *Muraqqa-e-Dehli*, is *Purab* (east), which meant the regions of the present-day eastern Uttar Pradesh and Bihar. So for Sheikh Sultan, a musician in his own day, Dargah Quli Khan says, 'Although he hails from the East, his manner of speech is similar to any person of eloquence of Hindustan',[26] thus clearly signifying that Hindustan now came to mean north India as against the idea that existed in the preceding centuries. Evidently, such terms – Hindustan, Bengal or Purab – were not neutral denotations. Spatial representation was tied not only to the exigencies of rule, authority, commerce and agriculture – the classic example being the 'frontier-izing' of Bengal as shown by Richard Eaton[27] – but was also based on the ideas and hierarchies of religion and cultural refinement (which most notably included *zubaan*, or speech). *Purabiya*, the language (and speech) from the Purab was considered lowly in relation to the eloquence of Persian that placed Hindustan on a higher pedestal. During the same years (1739–41) as Dargah Quli Khan was staying in Delhi, Anand Ram Mukhlis, a Punjabi-Hindu nobleman employed in the Mughal services, had gone to the outskirts of Delhi with some of his friends to visit an *urs* festival (in 1739). After struggling with insomnia, he asked his servant to tell him

---

22 Katherine Brown, 'Reading Indian Music: The Interpretation of Seventeenth-Century European Travel-Writing in the (Re)construction of Indian Music History', *British Journal of Ethnomusicology* 9, no. 2 (2000): 7–8.

23 A. Deane, *Tour through the Upper Provinces of Hindostan; Comprising a Period between the Years 1804 and 1814: with Remarks and Authentic Anecdotes to which is Annexed, a Guide up the River Ganges with a Map from the Source to the Mouth* (London, 1823), 71, 51 respectively.

24 Khan, *The Travels of Abu Taleb Mirza*, trans. Stewart, 119 (emphasis added).

25 http://sitemaker.umich.edu/emes/sourcebook/da.data/82629/FileSource/1810_abu_taleb. pdf 'Impressions of Europe from Mirza Abu Taleb Khan's *The Travels of Taleb in Foreign Lands*, 1810', preface Gail Minault (2004), 6 (accessed 31 March 2009).

26 Khan, *Muraqqa-e-Dehli*, 69.

27 R. Eaton, *The Rise of Islam and the Bengal Frontier, 1204–1760* (Berkeley and Los Angeles, 1993).

a tale, and the latter recited the colourful tale of Padmavat in 'the Broad Eastern Dialect'. Listening to the tale Mukhlis said to himself, 'If this Hindi Beloved were to be displayed in the robes of a Persian writer [Qalamkar-e-Farsi] then it is possible that this work of art might appear *elegant* and *permissible* in the estimation of the *people of taste*.'[28] Speech was seen as an integral aspect of civility: Amir Khusraw, while deploring the presence of Afghans near his living quarters, had said in 1280, 'Well has a wise man said that when speech was sent to men from the sky, the Afghans got the last and least share of it.'[29] As late as the nineteenth century this interplay between region, religion and language was conspicuous. Salar Jang, the ruler of Hyderabad (in Deccan), reacted in the following way when his ministers advised switching the language of governance from Persian to Urdu:

> You Hindustani (Northern Indian) people have little practice in Persian speech and writing Persian language is the symbol of the victory of the Muslims. We have conquered this land with the sword. Having destroyed this symbol in your own country [north India], you people now want darkness here too. Persian shall remain here and flourish so long as I am alive.[30]

Clearly by the eighteenth century, for the people from the south, non-Persianized speech had in many ways become synonymous with north India and within north India with the 'eastern dialect', which represented the eastern regions of the Gangetic plain. It was not the language alone that was contested; the spaces identifiable with different language enclaves were also caught in the dynamics of power struggle. The resurgence of Hindi/Hindavi in Delhi in the late eighteenth century, as opposed to Persian, which had remained the language of that area, was intricately linked to the rise of new elites based not on aristocratic wealth but on trade; this in turn signified, as Alam puts it, 'the region's rise against the Persianized Mughal centre'.[31] Such fine distinctions must have been lost on British ears, but the association of region and language was not; A. Deane described the Doab as a 'Persian territory'.[32]

---

28 Shantanu Phukan, 'The Rustic Beloved: Ecology of Hindi in a Persianate World', *The Annual of Urdu Studies* 15 (2000): 4, 5. The italicized words (which are mine) make two things clear: first, there remained a hierarchy based not only on the limits of artistic ethics and permissibility, but also on the aesthetics of respectability and acceptance to a refined taste. And second, within this hierarchy a strong culture of retelling and translation thrived. See also S. Phukan '"Through throats were many rivers meet": The ecology of Hindi in the world of Persian', *Indian Economic and Social History Review* 38, no. 1 (2001). [Henceforth *IESHR*.] The status of the languages changed with time. Arguably, in Islamicate polities before the Mughal period, Hindavi and not Persian enjoyed a privileged position. Muzaffar Alam, 'The Pursuit of Persian: Language Politics in Mughal India', *MAS* 32, no. 2 (1998): 318–19. Later on, 'Command over good Persian [became] a matter of pride, and deficiency in elegant expression in Persian meant cultural failure.' M. Alam, *The Languages of Political Islam: India 1200–1800* (Chicago, 2004), 133.
29 Sunil Kumar, 'The Ignored Elites: Turks, Mongols and a Persian Secretarial Class in the Early Delhi Sultanate', *MAS* 43, no. 1 (2008): 10.
30 Quoted in Alam, 'The Pursuit of Persian', 331.
31 Alam, *The Languages of Political Islam*, 184.
32 Deane, *A Tour*, 198.

In our brief identification of spatial–cultural terms in pre-colonial times,[33] next (not sequentially) comes the role of faith and religion, which complemented or accompanied the remarks made on climate and land that further rounded off the spatial observations. Saqi Must'ad Khan in his *Maasir-i-Alamgiri* described Arakan as the 'land of infidels'.[34] *Dar-al Harb* was always juxtaposed to *Dar-al Islam*. Despite acknowledging the fact that Calicut had a resident Muslim population with two congregational mosques and a religiously observant Qazi, where people prayed on Fridays 'with peace of mind', it was still described by Samarqandi as a 'city of infidels'.[35] One simple reason behind calling places Dar-al Harb was to legitimize the act of political and military conquest.

However, it would be misleading to see such representations only in functional terms: they were not just the legitimizing apparatus of territorial expansion, they also represented the ideological underpinnings of the Islamicate classification of landforms, topography and climate, from which religion and faith were not inseparable. Of course, there is no simplistic binary involved here. Samarqandi's own expressions prove this. Although the city of Calicut was a Dar-al Harb, Samarqandi intelligently maintained an ambiguous distinction between Muslims and infidels who both resided in the Dar-al Harb: he said he met both Muslims and hordes of infidels; he said both king and beggars (the hordes of infidels) wear the same thing but that Muslims wear fine clothing in the Arab fashion.[36] Although in this schema it was the land that was seen and labelled – Dar-al Harb or Dar-al Islam – central to such distinctions were the characteristics of the people (he said he was used to moon-like faces but not to every ill-proportioned black thing) – ranging from their physical appearance to their dress habits. Almost a century later, for the Turkish admiral Sidi Ali Reis similar characterizations held true: landing at the Gujarat coast was described as coming to an 'infidel coast'. Moving away from the coast, the sight of Zokum trees – which according to the Quran grow only in Hell and whose first fruits serve as food for the condemned – must have further convinced Sidi Ali of his presence in Dar-al Harb.[37] This classification of land based primarily on the religious practices of the inhabitants (together with their social and cultural worldview) did not drastically change with the advent of colonialism. Although the official version of colonial power strived to stay clear of the religious views of the natives, the coming of the European missionaries led to the rise of the trope of 'heathenscape' – a spatial classification based on religion.

---

33 I am aware of other sets of divisions which I do not deal with here. One is the administrative structure of spatial division – *samrajya* (empire), *subah* (province), *pargana, zillah* (district), *mofussil, gaon* (village) and so on. Still others, and part of the administrative apparatus are the types of land – *khalisa, jaghir, maddad-e-maash, iqta* and so on.
34 *Maasir-i-Alamgiri*, 18.
35 Thackston, *A Century of Princes*, 303–4.
36 Ibid., 305.
37 *The Travels and Adventures of the Turkish Admiral Sidi Ali Reis in India, Afghanistan, Central Asia and Persian during the Years 1553–1556*, trans. with notes A. Vambery (London, 1899), 22, 31. He also used the expression – 'land of banians' – which apparently would not sit very uncomfortably with the land of infidels considering Islam's canonical view on usury. But one could definitely argue for greater representational fluidities: amongst the things which he thought were most strange and wonderful that he saw, he mentioned that 'the unbelievers are called in Gujarat "banian" and in India "Hindu"'. Ibid., 59.

This way of defining the landscape and the people was in fact not only restricted to the writings of the eighteenth and nineteenth century missionaries but can be found amongst European travellers in general.[38]

In the war of kingship amongst brothers that ensued after the death of their father, the Mughal ruler Aurungzeb, in 1707, Bahadur Shah sent a message to his brother, Azam Shah, to divide the empire. Azam Shah, due to receive four provinces in the Deccan, objected to the lack of 'fairness', and the rhetoric of kingdom and territoriality is worth mentioning here. He replied to Bahadur Shah (whom he called a *baniya* meaning pejoratively a merchant and a miser): 'a Kingdom was not a thing which could be divided like an inheritance… two kings cannot be contained within one kingdom'.[39] As a result, Azam Shah marched to fight Bahadur Shah and camped at Samugarh, ten miles southeast of Agra. He chose that place because it was the same ground on which his father Aurangzeb had encamped some fifty-two years previously to defeat his brother, Dara Sukoh, in their time of rivalry for the throne.[40]

These two anecdotes sufficiently demonstrate the uncompromising attitude towards land or territory in its political meaning on the one hand and its affective nature on the other. One of the most important sites of representation of space was the body-politic of the empire as reflected in the persona of the ruler. In many cases it was also reflected in the individualized cosmos of the Sufis, particularly when the issue revolved around the conflicting ideas of wilayat either amongst the Sufis or between them and the sultan.[41] Again, this strand of possession was not restricted to land alone; it encompassed rivers and climate, trees and mountains, and smell and sound. When the campaign in which Anand Ram Mukhlis participated was drawing to an end, the emperor, who with his army was camped on the banks of the Sut rivulet, thought it necessary to incorporate that body of water into his success profile. He gave it a title, 'The Loyal Friend and Brave Companion' (*yaar-i-wafaadaar wa hamdil-i tehtmaan*). The irony, however, was that soon a rainstorm broke out and the rivulet was flooded and 'thousands of snakes were found once the camp was cleared up'. Mukhlis was not unperceptive in commenting on this irony: 'This rivulet, so recently dubbed a loyal friend, turns out to be a threat at such a moment.'[42] But it was only for a moment; the river was ascribed with the friendship of the emperor.

There were other ways in which roles of loyalty were rehearsed. For instance, for Sidi Reis, and for travellers in general, the embodiment of landscape in his Padishah became evident

---

38 Arnold shows how a spatial sense of mortality was inscribed on the Indian landscape, both in terms of 'White deaths' and in terms of the death practices of the natives, such as Sati, which of course was seen as related to heathenistic practices. Arnold, *The Tropics*, ch. 2.
39 William Irvine, *The Later Mughals*, ed. Jadunath Sarkar, 2 vols bound in one (New Delhi, 1971), 22.
40 Ibid., 72.
41 Sunil Kumar, 'Assertions of Authority: A Study of the Discursive Statements of Two Sultans of Delhi', in M. Alam, F. N. Delvoye and M. Gaborieau, eds, *The Making of Indo-Persian Culture* (New Delhi, 2000); Simon Digby, 'The Sufi Shaykh and the Sultan: A Conflict to Claims of Authority in Medieval India', *Iran* 28 (1990).
42 M. Alam and S. Subrahmanyam, 'Discovering the Familiar: Notes on the Travel-Account of Anand Ram Mukhlis, 1745', *South Asia Research* 16, no. 2 (1996): 150.

when he reached Turkey: 'Let him [the traveller] never cease to long for the day that he shall see his native shores again, and always, whatever befall, cling loyally to his Padishah.'[43] The act of reaching native shores was both an act of entering into a zone of familiarity and also unambiguously fulfilling the task of loyalty – a reverberation of which could also be found in Amir Khusraw's work *Nuh Siphr* (1318) in which the love for *watan* (homeland) is part of one's *iman* (faith).[44] Space/landscape/place/territory and all their constituents were affective ascriptions of *wafa* (loyalty), iman, *huqumat* (sovereignty/rule) and *siyasat* (rule/territory). This claim in no way purports that the notion of space in pre-colonial times was more inclined towards attributes such as iman (and thus 'non-secular') and in colonial times towards 'commerce' (and therefore 'secular'). Alternatively, what is emphasized here is that in the pre-colonial period, the material conditionalities (such as gift, exchange, *khillat* (robes of honour), tomb, monument and so on), the territorial concerns (such as watan, huqumat and siyasat) and the cultural representations and appropriations (wafa, *yaari* (friendship), truthfulness and sacredness) combined to create a distinct affective nature of space.

Acts such as travel, which made spaces intelligible, had implicit emotive aspects bound to them that unwittingly addressed one or the other of the above factors. We have seen how, in Sidi Reis' case, the act of travel served the function of proving loyalty to the sovereign king and territory. The ideology behind travel in the early modern period, at least in the South Asian case, was riddled with contradictions. It is true that this was a time of great bureaucratic, artistic, military and commercial mobility,[45] but travel was still something that was disliked if not deprecated. The fear of reaching a place safely demanded many ritual performances and divine propitiations (sometimes to animals too) because travel was seen as fraught with danger. Amar, the friend of Amir Hamzah in the *Dastan-e Hamza*, voiced one such fear of not being able to return when he was to be part of Amir's expedition to Ceylon.[46] One could also gather this from the woes of Hafiz who, in spite of decline in the patronage of music and poetry in Shiraz, had said: 'The zephyr-breeze of Musalla and the stream of Ruknabad/Do not permit me to travel or wander afield.'[47] And when people did travel, they did not forget to mention the terrifying 'smell of the ship' and the 'terror of the sea' that made them unconscious; the constant weeping 'in memory of friends and homeland' and for 'the region of the beloved' that gave rise to ceaseless want and appeal to the 'Ever-Vigilant' to 'return me to my comrades'.[48] However, Hafiz and Samarqandi were from the previous centuries.

---

43 Vambery, *Travels and Adventures of Sidi Ali Reis*, 107.
44 Ali, 'The Evolution', 81–2. Long distance journeys served this purpose even better. The wonders that were observed in far-flung areas, Digby argues, strengthened belief in God. Digby, 'Beyond the Ocean', 253.
45 Sanjay Subrahmanyam sees this elite circulation across political boundaries as an essential element in understanding the early modern state-building activity: 'Connected Histories: Notes Towards a Reconfiguration of Early Modern Eurasia', *MAS* 31, no. 3 (1997): 748.
46 *An Oriental Novel*, 132. In fact, later Amar pleaded with Amir to leave him out, which Amir of course did not allow. See 135–7 on Amar's traumatic experience of the sea journey.
47 The *sher* (couplet) expressing his frustration-induced thought to travel is: 'There is no place in Shiraz for poetry and Music/Come Hafiz, let us migrate to a new country.' Sardar Jafri, 'Hafiz Shirazi (1312–1387–89)', *SS* 28 (2000): 8.
48 Samarqandi's expressions, Thackston, *A Century of Princes*, 300–301.

By the seventeenth century, travel was defined as a means of acquiring manliness and also a new cosmopolitan image. But still, it was said that 'a man must be prepared to travel' in order to find services 'only if there is no possibility of ascendancy in one's own homeland'; only in that case should he be prepared to endure the pain of separation from his family and loved ones.[49] Seeking jobs in Mughal India was one of the most important reasons for Iranians to come to India in the sixteenth century. This is best reflected in this contemporary couplet: 'The means of acquiring perfection do not exist in Iran/The henna does not acquire colour till it comes to India.'[50] Such travelling from compulsion gave rise to new ways of seeing. For those leaving Persia, India became *Dar-al Aman* (the abode of peace) where their skills were recognized and appreciated in contrast to alleged tyrannical Safavid rule in Iran, where the atmosphere of religious persecution together with lack of courtly patronage persisted.[51] And unsurprisingly, this perception had changed once again by the early nineteenth century. A Persian, Sheikh Mohammed Ali Hazir residing in Delhi, maintained that if he were to turn the reins of his pen 'to the description of the remaining adventures of my own life, [he would] inevitably be led to depict some of the crimes and shameful things in the circumstances and qualities of this country, traced as it is with foulness, and trained to turpitude and brutality; and [he] should grieve for [his] pen and paper'.[52]

In addition to diverse ways, there existed varied sites on which such affective spaces, comprising both animate and inanimate objects, were conjured up.[53] One important site was monuments – mosques, *dargahs* (Sufi/holy shrines), tanks, domes and gateways. At the most general level, the best example of personal investment in space and thus 'making space' comes from the act of renaming towns and cities after their conquest: for instance, Rajmahal was renamed Akbarabad after its conquest by Akbar.[54] There are numerous

---

49 R. O'Hanlon has sampled some of the perceptions towards travel in her 'Manliness and Imperial Service in Mughal North India', *JESHO* 42, no. 1 (1999): 63–8. Even as late as the eighteenth century, Abu Taleb accepted the offer to travel to Europe only in despair. 'Impressions of Europe', 1.
50 Alam, 'The Pursuit of Persian', 323. All but one of the poet laureates at the Mughal court were Iranians. 'Introduction', Alam et al., *The Making*, 25. For artistic influences, styles and mobility of personnel see also Priscilla P. Soucek, 'Persian Artists in Mughal India: Influences and Transformations', *Muqarnas*, 4, 1987.
51 Alam, 'The Pursuit of Persian', 321; S. Digby, 'Some Asian Wanderers in Seventeenth Century India: An Examination of Sources in Persian', *SIH* 9, no. 2 (1993): 251.
52 'Autobiography of Sheikh Mohammed Ali Hazir (1692–1779)', *The Asiatic Journal* (new series) 4 (1831): 184. [Henceforth *AJ*.]
53 From the point of view of the exercise of power by the Mughal rulers, it has been argued that Jahangir administered justice not only to human subjects but also to animals of his kingdom. Corinne Lefevre, 'Recovering the Missing Voice from Mughal India: The Imperial Discourse of Jahangir (r. 1605–1627) in his Memoirs', *JESHO* 50, no. 4 (2007): 470.
54 But still the spatial identity varied. So even when it became Akbarabad, it was known to many, especially in the military service as Aagmahal, for two reasons. First, it served as an advanced stage (*aag*) for military marches and a camping ground, a place where the advance tents of the Bengal nawabs were sent; and second, it derived its name *aag* (fire) from the event in which most parts of the town were gutted by fire. Again, although the official papers used the name Akbarabad, it was still known as Rajmahal because after the conquest Raja Man Singh had built a fort and mansions there. As recounted by Abdul Latif in his safarnama. Sarkar, 'Travels in Bihar', 601–2.

such examples from this period. After renaming came the construction of new buildings or 're-writing space' with a new flair of conquest and new principles of legitimacy. The conquest of the Rohtas fort in 1576 by Akbar was followed by the construction of a mosque, the inscription of which read that the command of the ruler 'is followed by birds and beasts'.[55] In a separate context on the construction of a dome over a building it was proclaimed, that 'the entire territory now became the centre of the splendour of the kingdom of faith'.[56]

The frontiers of body, polity and space were interlinked and enmeshed. Emotions were spatialized and monuments helped to gain legitimacy. Territorial conquests and reclamations involved bodily dispositions. This has been made clear by the studies done on khillat wherein the ruler invested the subjugated rulers with a robe that signified bodily incorporation.[57] The central issue was 'loyalty'. In the textual production of ideas on kingship, the *akhlaqi* tradition was prominent in this period.[58] Its dominant feature was the presence of humble subjects and a benevolent king. The king, having 'attained perfection through equipoise and a perception of union with the Supreme Being', was then supposed to complete existing things that were incomplete. The main points of reference in such discussions were *insaan* (man), *amr-i ma'ash* (his living) and *aalam* (world). In this set of ethical norms (*akhlaq*) justice was the cornerstone. The king was supposed to deliver and maintain social harmony amongst his subjects (*ria'ya*) lest, it was argued, state, society and the world (often expressed as the prosperity of the country) should suffer and decline. I argue that the akhlaqi norms as practised during the Mughal times are also crucial for our understanding of spatial dimensions not because such norms already explicitly covered physical space – the misguided city, the evil-doing and the ignorant city, the aalam and the *duniya* (world), and the prosperity of the country – but also because they underscored the primacy of justice. It was this concept of justice that informed attitudes towards space and landforms, towards animate and inanimate objects, prevailing in those landforms.[59]

In the textual production, words and actions of the emperor (i.e. commands) were shown as creating a new 'loyal' landscape, a landscape subordinate to its ruler, siyasat and iman. Either through his bodily disposition or royal commands, the emperor was one of the prominent mediations through which affective spaces were created and maintained. Another important site was the embodiment of the leading Sufis characterized by their doctrinal concepts of wilayat and *barakat* (blessings). In this mode, space was perceived in

---

55 Qeyamuddin Ahmed, *Corpus of Arabic and Persian Inscriptions from Bihar (A.H. 640–1200)* (Patna, 1973), 163–4.
56 Ibid., 89, inscription dated 1486–87 in Biharsharif.
57 Stewart Gordon, ed., *Robes of Honour: Khil'at in Pre-Colonial and Colonial India* (Oxford and Delhi, 2003).
58 M. Alam, *The Languages of Political Islam*, and his 'Akhlaqi Norms and Mughal Governance' in Alam et al., *The Making*. The ensuing quote is from the latter, 72.
59 There were competing viewpoints on the nature of justice. For a few, justice required the intervention of the ruler and the state and hence was an artificial way of promoting social harmony. The loftier ideal was through *muhabbat* (love). But, for others, the use of force and the suppression of dissent was permissible.

terms of an individualized idiom, which was transitive in character and dependent upon an individual. An instance of such understanding is in Isami's writing on Nizam al-Din Auliya:

> He was one of the friends of God.
> Through whom the realm of Hindostan was maintained.
> First that man of wise dominion
> Set out from Dehli to another kingdom;
> After this that city and country were ruined;
> Discord persisted in that realm.[60]

Clearly, one can see that the tranquility of the space called Hindustan (of which the city of Delhi was a part) was maintained through the goodwill of a Sufi sheikh; the spatial equilibrium destabilized once the individual decided to move away from the city. Further, the legitimation of that spatial equilibrium rested on the fact that the individual was the friend of God, although the quotidian network of patronage in which Sufi sheikhs operated is well known. Drawing legitimacy by invoking the supreme authority nonetheless discursively ensured that if factors like iman, wafa and huqumat were producing a space then that space, when maintained in its proper equilibrium, would in turn contribute to the flourishing of the very same virtues and ideas, that is, of iman, wafa and huqumat. In other words, the affective nature created a dialogical relationship between actors and their spaces. Landscape was not a static entity; it exhibited an interactive attribute. It was an ever-changing entity that donned new meanings according to new contexts. The presence of dargahs as described by Dargah Quli Khan made their immediate atmosphere akin to 'Rauza-e-Rizwan' (the garden of paradise) where 'the smell of the breeze blowing...is as sweet as the air of paradise'.[61] A monument, tomb, gateway, mosque or other forms of material investment in a space did not mean much on its own; they became part of the spatialism when imputed with meanings: it was said that in the vicinity of the dargah of Hazrat Shah Turkman Biyabani 'when the zephyr surrounds the atmosphere the *smell of truth* comes to mind'.[62]

Similar to the ways that ria'ya were expected to conform and re-enact the codes of loyalty, the deviation from which warranted punishment, the spatial aspects of possessing, ordering and representing territory also included the idea of punishment, the ultimate goal of which was to uphold justice. Landscape was subject to both production and discipline. Along the line of C. Lefevre's argument that the authority of the monarch not only extended over human beings but encompassed the whole of creation,[63] one could see this happening in what Bhimsen mentioned about the Battle of Ujjain: 'The brave [Mughal] soldiers struck their feet so strongly on the ground that the trees around learned the lesson firmness [sic].'[64] Similar to the bodily incorporation of subjugated

---

60 Digby, 'The Sufi Shaykh', 71.
61 Khan, *Muraqqa-e-Dehli*, 10, 11, 33. For the grave of Iltutmish, he said: 'the atmosphere...is akin to rauza-e-rizvan... the softness of the breeze touches the heart', 34.
62 Ibid., 12 (emphasis added).
63 Lefevre, 'Recovering the Missing Voice'.
64 Bhimsen, *Tarikh-i-Dilkasha*, 18.

rulers through khillats, I argue that landscape and its elements were also part of moral suasion and incorporation. They were to be incorporated and disciplined either by muhabbat (love) or by punishment, the two cases exemplified by the Sut rivulet and the trees respectively.

This affective nature, however, did not override or undermine the rather more pragmatic political usages and meanings ascribed to territorial space. Territorial consolidation, domination and possession were integral to both pre-colonial and colonial establishments. Architectural investments, as we have discussed earlier, were one part of this. Other measures included royal hunts (which usually preceded royal campaigns), building roads and caravanserais, geographical mapping through route measurement in *coss* (a unit of measurement) and building *coss minarets* at regular intervals.[65] In many of these branches of knowledge, such as measuring and mapping, texts and maps, skills and memory, touring and inspection and so on – that is, the matters that were crucial for the consolidation of rule – the early colonial phase was in dialogue with its previous regimes. However, within these frameworks of dialogue were also set the modus of change which we aim to describe below.

Colonial Objectifications

We will start the concluding part of this chapter by bringing in the issues of intention and ideology. Using the example of translation of native texts during the Mughal and colonial times to highlight the nature of transition between the two periods and regime, Muzaffar Alam and Seema Alavi argue:

> ...even if the community of indigenous scholars and translators remained the same, the intentions of their English and European patrons were different from those of their pre-colonial patrons. Native texts needed to be collated and translated not merely for social harmony and to bridge the distance between indigenous religious and ethnic communities, but for a variety of reasons concerning both the reinforcement of English political power in India and the European and English rediscovery of their intellectual and cultural past in India.[66]

We take one example from our own discussion to illustrate this point. As we saw, both under the Mughals and the EIC, Bengal was long seen as a swampy place. It represented a space that invited contempt. But based on our discussion in the previous section we can actually attempt to identify the different ideological moorings behind the apparent sameness,

---

65 Differences remained according to individual proclivity and ideological bases. Akbar, following the Iranian tradition, lined his imperial roads with minarets studded with trophies of the hunt, while Sher Shah, the Afghan ruler, followed a more philanthropic direction and implemented strategic measures of building trunk roads and caravanserais. See Ebba Koch, 'Dara-Shikoh Shooting Nilgais: Hunt and Landscape in Mughal Painting', *Freer Gallery of Art Occasional Papers*, vol. 1 (Arthur M. Sackler Gallery, Smithsonian Institute, Washington DC, 1998), 12.

66 M. Alam and S. Alavi, *A European Experience of the Mughal Orient: The I'jaz-I Arsalani (Persian Letters, 1773–1779) of Antoine-Louis Henri Polier* (New Delhi, 2007), 36.

which effectively meant that there existed different strategies of spatial reclamations in pre-colonial and colonial times. In the pre-colonial times, landscape was seen as an affective space, so the way of redeeming that space was through its integration into the body-politic of the empire. This happened either through the three-fold process of 'making', 're-writing' and 'disciplining' (as outlined above) the landscape, or through the personal and institutional investment of the ruler and the ruling apparatus by creating bonds of incorporation and loyalty. This was different from the early colonial attitude towards the damp and swampy climate of Bengal. Then it was not an affective space that needed to be subsumed within the body-politic of the EIC. Rather, it was so full of poisonous effects that instead of incorporation, prevention was suggested in different ways, as in dressing habits, regulating meals, alcohol, sleep and so on. These were the great debatable issues of the time, exemplifying concerns about how to preserve lives in the 'tropics'.[67] Theoretically, this is quite similar to what Bernard Cohn has argued in his study of robes and ceremonies, that is, the transition from the idea of 'incorporation' in pre-colonial to 'subordination' in colonial times that exhibited the process of 'contractualization' of rituals.[68] A minor point of qualification is that in the early phase of colonial rule this transition was protracted and riddled with contradictions. Hence there was a strong practice, albeit not widely admired amongst the Europeans, of 'going native'.

In the early colonial period there are numerous instances of British officers founding a *haat* (market) or a bazaar or a small *qasbah* in their name, a process that was structurally similar to the renaming of towns as happened after victories by Mughal rulers and chiefs. The difference, however, was at two levels: first, the colonial instances were examples of the ascription of individuals over space. It did not necessarily represent investment in the form of corporate identity of British rule/English company or Pax Britannica, unlike the Mughal times where the persona of the ruler and the body-politic of the empire fused together to reproduce/reclaim that space.[69] Second, and as a corollary, the early colonial instances were

---

67 For an interesting account of many of these themes through practices of body, see E. M. Collingham, *Imperial Bodies: The Physical Experience of the Raj* (Cambridge, 2001). Administratively, the condition of Calcutta was described as changing, which is evident from the following remark of Lord Valentia made in the beginning of the nineteenth century: 'The place is certainly less unhealthy than formerly, which advantage is attributed to the filling up of the tanks in the streets, and the clearing more and more jungle; but in my opinion it is much more owing to an improved knowledge of the diseases of the country, and of the precautions to be taken against them; and likewise to greater temperance in the use of spirituous liquors and a superior construction of the houses.' However, the poetical romanticized expressions about Bengal's unhealthy climate lingered for a long time: 'Eyes too, that lighted once, with languor speak/ As pale Bengal is written on the cheek.' For the former, see 'Accepted Travellers', *The Calcutta Review* 24 (December 1856): 295. [Henceforth *CR*]; for the latter, 'Life in India', *AJ* 2 (1816): 483.

68 Cohn, 'From Indian Status to British Contract', 463–82 and 'Representing Authority in Victorian India', in *The Bernard Cohn Omnibus, with a Foreword by Dipesh Chakrabarty* (New Delhi, 2004), 632–82.

69 There would be some dissenting voices, especially from the scholars working in the field of cartography, to show how subsumption took place at the level of and through mapping, how the role of a *company* benefitting from the exploits of a colony was diminished in favour of highlighting the role of the *British* nation itself. While accepting this, two points further need to be stated: one, following the work of Linda Colley, the eighteenth century was still the

therefore not downright *incorporation* into the body-politic. It was adaptation and acquisition, at best an act to become *identified* with the place/space (with obvious economic implications) rather than to *incorporate* them, which arguably was the case in pre-colonial times. As a result, although colonial socio-spatial practices borrowed and built upon pre-existing patterns, even in its early phase colonialism involved a certain degree of objectification of such practices.[70] Interestingly, in the debate that took place in the nineteenth century about whether or not India should be made a *colony*, some of the arguments presented in opposition to the idea compared English rule with the preceding Mughal rule to suggest that since the Mohammedans were successful in colonizing, they degenerated and were thus extinguished. Very emphatically it was stated that India was a conquest and not a colony and it would be enough if England could just *hold* on to that space.[71]

It is this urge to hold and control that gave rise to practices of spatial objectification. Such an objectification is reflected in the repetitiveness of certain tropes, which stabilizes as well as standardizes any particular discourse. It also marked variance from indigenous representations. If for Dargah Quli Khan the atmosphere of Delhi with its shrines and monuments gave the impression of Rauza-e-Rizwan, to the British sojourners only fifty years later the city appeared nothing more than an extended space of ruined monuments. Similarly, while Francis Buchanan during his surveys in eastern India described Patna as one of the dirtiest cities of India,[72] an Iranian traveller, Ahmed Behbahani who lived in India between 1805 and 1809, regarded Patna as one of the most beautiful cities.[73] And yet there were notable similarities in these accounts. While passing through Rajmahal, Behbahani remarked: 'The remains of those magnificent edifices are still extant on the bank of the Ganges. It has a very pleasant climate and being situated in the proximity to a mountain, wild games…are found in abundance in those regions.'[74] This description is

---

period when British national identity was in the process of consolidation, more so because of the contact with the 'Others' and, second, the nature, structures and mediations of spatial (or otherwise) subordination in pre-colonial times differed from the colonial times. One important aspect in this regard was the varying notions of hierarchy and control between the metropolis and colony (both in terms of physical space and knowledge) that characterized subordination in colonial times. Linda Colley, *Britons: Forging the Nation, 1707–1837* (Yale, 1992).

70 Studies of rituals and ceremonies for the later colonial period distinctly bring out the aspect of bureaucratic classification and attempted objectification. See Dick Kooiman, 'Meeting at the Threshold, at the Edge of the Carpet or Somewhere In Between? Questions of Ceremonial in Princely India', *IESHR* 40, no. 3 (2003); and, Douglas Haynes, 'Imperial Ritual in a Local Setting: The Ceremonial Order in Surat, 1890–1939', *MAS* 24, no. 3 (1990).

71 Maxwell, 'Colonization in India', *CR* 31 (1858): 180–88.

72 His exact words were '…as it is difficult to imagine a more disgusting place'. Francis Buchanan, *An Account of the Districts of Behar and Patna in 1811–12*, 2 vols (Patna, 1934). Reference is from vol. 1, 58.

73 His actual words were: 'In the whole of Bangala, nay, in India, a city of such a totality is very few. It is apt to call it the "Paradise of India".' Ahmad Behbahani, *Mir'at Ul-Ahwal-i Jahan Numa*, trans. A. F. Haider, *India in the Early Nineteenth Century: An Iranian Travel Account* (Patna, 1996), 130. It would indeed be erroneous to count Behbahani's impressions as 'indigenous'. The example is used here to point out the differences in 'ways of seeing' which did vary even amongst colonialists of this time.

74 Ibid., 128.

no different from those of the many European travellers who commented upon the wild jungle surrounding the region and sketched the decaying yet still magnificent buildings from Mughal times. But again, the hint as to what discursively distinguished these accounts comes from Behbahani's account itself. Not surprisingly, the dirty, narrow and irregular streets of Patna made it a disgusting place for Buchanan; Behbahani, on the other hand, in spite of admitting that it was a 'beggar-fostering city', called it the paradise of India. The sensibilities of travelling men together with their ideological underpinnings differed. I argue that under colonialism the pragmatics of rule, the routinization of the act of travel, the disciplining of the gaze that looked for 'familiar' and 'different' at the same time, the regulative regimes that were required by the EIC to maintain its profits, all contributed towards growing control and the objectification of both physical space and socio-spatial practices.

The way the term 'objectification' has been used here needs explanation. There are two embedded ideas in the processes of objectification as emerging from the late eighteenth century. Both were part of the growing mercantile network of global capitalism on the one hand and the progressive 'implementation' of geographical Enlightenment ideas on the other. First was the production of national and imperial spaces in terms of territories through techniques of survey, recording, inventories, maps, property (usually land-related) and aesthetics of 'viewing'. The production of 'scientific knowledge' (empirical and natural sciences) in this period was allegedly based on the capacity to observe and classify, which required a necessary distance between the viewer and the viewed.[75] Specifically in the field of cartography, bringing a vast chunk of land as arrayed in a gridded space into hand or within sight, that was premised on the 'fixing' of the places in the space (as imagined on a paper), gave those places an identity, which was based on objectified coordinates of the grid – latitude and longitude. Of course, the contemporary technology, as Edney shows, could not measure longitude with precision.[76] Also, the processes of mapping and recording involved a subjectivist tinge of the observer's position and his cultural locations.

The second aspect of the objectification process – as a few dominant scholarships especially coming from the field of cultural history and studies on the theme of colonial encounter and travel have recently demonstrated – was a wholesale 'unhistoricization' of either the people or the landforms of the colony in colonial accounts. These two processes were not divorced from each other; the spatial ordering of the first level arguably led to the removal of not only the observed, as Edney has argued,[77] but also of the observer as we can see in what Mary Louise Pratt has suggested in the case of European male travellers in Africa:

> The landscape is written as uninhabited, unpossessed, unhistoricised, unoccupied even by the travellers themselves. The activity of describing geography and identifying flora and fauna structures an asocial narrative in which the human presence, European or

---

75 See Matthew H. Edney, *Mapping an Empire: The Geographical Construction of British India, 1765–1843* (Chicago and London, 1997), ch. 2.
76 Ibid., 39.
77 Ibid., 41.

African is absolutely marginal, though it was, of course, a constant and essential aspect of the travelling itself.[78]

In the South Asian case, Nicholas Dirks has argued that the picturesque mode of representation of India tried to put India's history under colonial erasure.[79] According to this formulation, the lived components of the colonial spaces were abstracted out of the space to make the latter appear blank with no temporal progression and spatial competition (amongst inhabitants). My use of the term objectification and its explication in this work does not signify an end result leading to a complete erasure of 'native' people and landscape from the colonizing narratives but denotes a process, often *immanently contradictory*, in which the landscape or the people of the colony were in fact conspicuously present; this presence forced many of the colonial narratives towards 'negativization' rather than unhistoricization. As a matter of fact, almost every geographical description of a place in colonial travel accounts and geographical narratives necessarily carried 'an account of the customs and manners' of the people. It was not the absence of the details of social fabric and practices that characterized colonial accounts, but their often repetitive negativized retelling that produced standardization and objectification of such practices. Pratt's argument of creating asocial narratives while describing the geography of the colony, or more commonly, distant lands, points towards the processes of objectification, which cannot be denied, but her further claim that such narratives were devoid of human presence seems overdrawn. From the 1760s onwards, with the 'Linnaean watershed'[80] from whence she traces this trend, the Indian context is significantly different. Travellers describing the topography and geography of India were actually keen on registering the types of communities living there, their trade, the networks of people and commodities, the association of their past with their places and so on. This makes the argument of the marginality of people difficult to sustain. For instance, William Hodges, while travelling in the Fatehpur region, wrote: 'I was much entertained, during our several marches, by the variety of characters I saw: the people of the bazaar with their wives and children; the cavalry, who were continually manifesting their dexterity, in the oriental manner.'[81] In fact, Hodges claimed that 'pictures achieve their highest value when they are 'connected with the history of the various countries, and...faithfully represent the

---

78 Pratt, *Imperial Eyes*, 51. Arnold's 'diffusion and denial' model to understand the formation of colonial knowledge and the practices of introduction of 'modern' knowledge is close to Pratt's understanding. David Arnold, *Science, Technology and Medicine in Colonial India* (Cambridge, 2000), 15–17.
79 Nicholas Dirks, 'Guiltless Spoliations: Picturesque Beauty, Colonial Knowledge, and Colin Mackenzie's Survey of India', in Catherine B. Asher and Thomas R. Metcalfe, eds, *Perceptions of South Asia's Visual Past* (New Delhi, 1994).
80 On this see also William Beinart, who argues for a more 'fluid' matrix of the male European travelling and scientific explorations than, what he says, has been given to us by the followers of 'ecofeminism'. 'Men, Science, Travel, and Nature in the Eighteenth and Nineteenth Centuries Cape', *Journal of South African Studies* 24, no. 4 (1998).
81 William Hodges, *Travels in India During the Years 1780, 1781, 1782, and 1783*, 2nd edn (London, 1794). I am using the reprint of this edition (Delhi, 1999), 127.

manners of mankind'.[82] This was not only true for a landscape artist such as Hodges, but also for men of other pursuits. Charles Ramus Forrest's avowedly picturesque text starts with the 'History of India' in which he says:

> ...the more closely we pry into, and the more intimate we become with, the wonderful and enchanting country of Hindoostan and India at large, the more we must feel convinced, that in no part of the world have so many and such awful changes occurred, no where have such torrents of human blood been shed, or such great and wonderful revolutions been so frequently experienced. India is a field on which have been accumulated the largest armies, the greatest mass of force the world perhaps has ever witnessed; where the most dreadful and awful struggles have taken place, and the most astonishing results arisen.[83]

One could definitely chafe at the Orientalist depictions of 'bloodshed', 'armies' and 'dreadful and awful struggles' that catered to the image of 'violent and despotic orientals' on the one hand and at the 'wonderful and enchanting country of Hindoostan' that one discovers on a closer look, leading to a certain amount of intimacy as representing some form of idyllic picturesque propensity of the country on the other. Yet the core of the Orientalist depictions were also based on 'great and wonderful revolutions' – which means that the space and its people were historically moving, in fact at a pace that produced 'astonishing results'.

Certainly, a more specified genre of topographical accounts other than travelogues was evolving; but it is important to bear in mind that early colonialism (1760s–1820s) was also a period in which several genres and branches of knowledge and mediums of expression (textual and visual) overlapped, creating a pool of understanding in regard to the history and culture of India.[84] For example, Colin Mackenzie, who figures prominently in the history of Indian topographical surveys, created one of the most extensive 'ethnographic archives' of his time. The interests of like-minded individuals ranged from recording distances, carrying out surveys, collecting manuscripts, either sketching themselves or commissioning natives to prepare albums containing ethnographic knowledge from the types of people, to types of trade, conveyances, dress and so on, all contributing to the understanding of the 'manner and customs'

---

82 As quoted in Harriet Guest, 'The Great Distinction: Figures of the Exotic in the Work of William Hodges', *The Oxford Art Journal* 12, no. 2 (1989): 40.
83 Charles Ramus Forrest, *A picturesque Tour along the river Ganges and Jumna in India, consisting of Twenty-Four highly finished and coloured views, a map, and vignettes, from original drawing made on the spot: with illustrations, historical and descriptive* (London, 1824), 1.
84 I therefore disagree with Edney's classification that the scientific gaze's analogous subjects were 'a wide array of plants, animals, rock outcroppings, whole vistas, and cultural artifacts' whereas the picturesque gaze's analogous individuals were 'landscapes'. He later does concede that both the gazes 'provided basic and complementary tools for the British geographical investigation of the human and physical landscapes of South Asia'. Arnold's proposition that 'science' and 'scenic' were part of the same colonial descriptive and gazing practices, at least in its earlier phase, is more acceptable in this regard. Edney, *Mapping an Empire*, 54, 64; Arnold, *The Tropics*, 24–5.

of Indians.[85] In a nutshell, this was a period of 'administrative ethnography', which overlapped with travel and topographical literature. Indeed, the method of collation and presentation of this knowledge was formulaic: this can be discerned by turning the pages of any of these officers' albums of sketches and paintings (which were usually produced by native artists). Together they created a 'typology' of viewing and representing Indian history, its landscapes and people. There were a few 'set pieces' that characterized this representation. When it came to representing people, the groups that got widely represented belonged to '*naukars* and *chakars*' (groups of domestic help): *khansaamah* (head cook), *aabdar* (water holders), *khidmatgar* (attendants), *hookahbadars* (person preparing hookah), *jhalarwala* (person carrying canopy), *punkah bearer* (fan bearer), *syce* (groom), and so on. And it was not so because of the fact that in the contemporary gaze they appeared as 'picturesque' objects but because these were the people who were conspicuously present in every aspect of European life in India. Similarly, when it came to depicting professional and occupational classes, it was not the big businessmen but rather the ordinary and popular groups such as *bhistee* (water carriers), tailors, boatmen, porters, *harkaras* (messengers) and so on that found a place in the pages of pictorial albums and in a number of travel writings of the period. Clearly, the thrust was to understand Indian society through 'groups' and 'castes' (and not individuals), which is one form of objectification we are describing here. The Europeans who made or commissioned such albums were not interested in 'trading persons' but in 'trade and occupations' as represented through some form of communal solidarity such as caste.[86] Indeed, this formulaic expression was a process of objectification; but it differs from the argument of marginalization or erasure. Rather than being erased, landscape and people were *used* to illuminate history. This history was of decay in which things like 'ruins' and 'banditry' became the facts of illustration. Subsequently, progress in cultivation with curtailment in robberies and banditry, mostly under the British, became the grounds for legitimation of rule.[87] For instance, Hodges, on climbing up the tomb of Akbar, saw a 'prodigious circuit of country', 'the whole of which is flat, and filled with ruins of ancient grandeur'. He continues:

> This fine country exhibits, *in its present state*, a melancholy proof of the consequences of a bad government, of wild ambition, and the horrors attending civil dissensions; for when the governors of this country were in plenitude of power, and exercised their rights of

---

85 And precisely during this time, books such as 'Picturesque Representations of the Dress and Manners of the English' (1814) or T. L. Bushby's 'Costumes of the Lower Orders of London' (1826) were published in England. Mildred Archer, *Company Paintings: Indian Paintings of the British Period* (London, 1992), 16.
86 My views are based on seeing a number of albums from this period stored in the Prints and Drawings section of the British Library. [Henceforth *P&D*.] The set pieces also reflected the changed subject matter: the new stylistic demands thrust upon the native artists by new European patrons. See Mildred Archer, *Company Paintings*, 73–4.
87 Major James Bayley's account is interspersed with such obvious meanings. For the Saharanpur district see 36–7; for Delhi, 42. Bayley, *Journal of a route from Calcutta to the Upper Provinces of Bengal and from there thro' Bundelkhand, and the Territories of the Bhoousbah or Rajah of Nagpour to the Head Quarters of the Hydrabad Subsidiary Force near Ellichpoor in the year 1814*, Mss Eur. D 970.

wisdom, from the excellence of its climate, with some degree of industry, it must have been a perfect garden; but *now all is desolation and silence*.[88]

The contradictions between 'some degree of industry' and 'a perfect garden' on the one hand and 'bad government' and 'wild ambition' on the other are too obvious to be highlighted. These contradictions, which were typical of many of the accounts of this period, and which I argue were part and parcel of the processes of objectification did not, however, jeopardize the colonial agenda of rule. In fact, they became the legitimizing grounds for it. Forrest's comments were also directed towards presenting the history of decline 'from its first origin in the gloomy clouds of superstition, through its gradual rise to a splendour rarely attained by nations, and thence to its sad and disastrous decline and downfall', which justified current colonial rule.[89] Narrating her travels in Upper India, A. Deane's account slipped into describing the pindaris and the British efforts to curtail their infamous raids. Further on, she said about Jats: 'The *Jauts* are brave soldiers and good cultivators; but in order to make good subjects, they must be divested of all power.'[90] Thus British conquest was definitely the subject of representation, but a representation that, at least in the textual medium, took place not by erasing but by strategically invoking the often contradictorily 'negativized' history of the colony that provided a necessary mirror image to justify colonial rule.[91] This is in accordance with Dirks' argument, which also makes a distinction between the visual collections of Mackenzie, telling a story of British military conquest and erasure, and his historiographical and ethnographical data that have a firmer grounding in the local historical context.

Like landscapes, people also became repositories of history. For Thomas and William Daniell, the people of India and their manners still 'with unexampled fidelity have preserved the image of a remote and almost obsolete antiquity'.[92] Balthazar Solvyns' rhetoric was even more forceful. For him, the native retained their 'unchanging behaviour in spite of all the invasions right from Alexander to the Mughals'; they retained their 'primitive purity', which was 'neither undermined by the slow operation of time, nor overthrown by the violence of man'. And yet this textual structuration gave way to immanent contradiction, to a historical change, when he said that only 'perceptive power can distinguish the primitive and pure cast [sic] from the mixed tribes, which are now so frequent in many parts of India'.[93] The indirect observation here is that people in India have not remained unchanged through time immemorial. History was thus perceived to be both static and dynamic in the same text. And the same person who talked about 'guiltless spoliations' in transporting back to Europe the picturesque beauty of the newly

---

88 Hodges, *Travels*, 121 (emphasis added).
89 Forrest, *A Picturesque Tour*, preface.
90 Deane, *A Tour*, 125.
91 The larger implication of this argument, which is something this work does not directly deal with, is that rather than erasing the history of the native people and land, the picturesque movement led to its own genre of 'picturesque history'.
92 Thomas Daniell and William Daniell, *A Picturesque Voyage to India; by the way of China* (London, 1810), ii.
93 François Balthazar Solvyns, *Les Hindoûs*, 4 vols (Paris, 1808–12), vol. 1, 19–21.

subservient place also aimed to familiarize the European public 'with a country to which we are now attached by the ties of consanguinity and affection'.[94]

Conclusions

The aim of this chapter is to allow the colonial changes to stand in dialogue with, and in parallel and contrast to, the pre-colonial practices that set the context of our study of communication and colonialism, of which one axis of the analysis is the spatial forms of objectification under colonialism. The colonialist underpinnings of capitalism had inherited the institutional structures of pre-colonial societies and economies but had reshaped them to produce new categories of spaces for serving the techno-politico-economic necessities and priorities of colonial rule. This has been described here as constituting the processes of objectification. However, colonial rule's interaction with natives, their customs and their landscapes meant that even while inferiorizing and negativizing them, the processes of objectification were not always absolute; they were relative and relational.[95] This would mean that even under colonialism, at one point of time the given impulse to objectify spaces and practices could not only be driven by divergent needs of the rule but that some of those impulses and needs ran contrary to each other. These processes were therefore internally fractured and fragmented. For instance, much like the fluid categories of Hindustan, wilayat, and Purab in pre-colonial times, the colonial category, for instance of interior, was also fluid and changing. It was contextual and liminal. Amidst the asymmetrical relations between the metropolitan and colonial sites of power, historiographically, it means that our effort here is to question the assumed universalization and monochromatic characterization of colonial discourse. The next chapter takes up the issue of interior, which serves as an entry point into the history of colonial communication as framed in this work, in greater detail.

---

94 Thomas Daniell and William Daniell, *A Picturesque Voyage*, introduction.
95 I borrow here the conceptual framework provided by David Harvey, who sees space in three ways: absolute, relative and relational, and argues that at any point of time all of these three exist simultaneously. David Harvey, 'Space as a Key Word', in Noel Castree and Derek Gregory, eds, *David Harvey: A Critical Reader* (Oxford, 2006).

Chapter 2

INDIA AND ITS INTERIORS

Perusing Indian colonial records from the 1820s onwards one cannot but note the frequency of the phrase 'opening up the interiors'. This holds true not only for state records, but also for many other books, tracts and pamphlets written and published around this time. If, in the preceding decades, the spread of Christianity had fuelled the idea of a civilizing mission,[1] from the 1820s it was charged with the power of steam. The oft-repeated phrase 'opening up the interiors' and its means – new improved technology of communication, steamships and railways, together with *good* roads – became an emblem of this civilizational thrust. The general argument ran like this: since India had never enjoyed good means of communication, the country needed to be opened up; the increase in commerce, which would follow the opening up, would at the same time also civilize the indolent natives of the country. From the viewpoint of the state, such an opening up would enable it to control the country better, to speed up the dispersal of troops and information. Hence, communication in general and the opening up in particular was writ large on the colonial agenda of this period.

'Opening up the interiors' is a catchphrase that begs a very basic question: what was meant by 'interior'? Was it a pocket of land or a pattern of untapped commerce through an unknown/uncontrolled area, or a corner of habitation where the *jungli* and the uncivilized resided? In other words, was the term 'interior' framed for its commercial attributes (resources and trade), or for politico-administrative purposes (strengthening the empire) or in a sociological context (bringing the 'unknown' social quarters under the aegis of knowability and control)? The simple and right answer is all three. The issue that became central was the 'moral and material' development of the colonized that actually combined all these three aspects. The remarks of the commissioner of Chota Nagpur illustrate this well: 'There can be no doubt,' he said in 1855, 'that the construction of good roads through the Singhbhum division will eventually do much towards the *moral and material improvement of the wild tribes inhabiting that part of the coun try.*' He further provided proof for his hypothesis by arguing that: 'experience has shown that the *Lurka Coles* who are brought in contact with strangers for commercial purposes became much more tractable and less barbarous than the inhabitants of the more distant Cole villages which are seldom visited by traders or travellers'.[2]

---

1 Mann, 'Torchbearers Upon the Path of Progress', 8.
2 'Extract from a letter from the Commissioner of Chota Nagpur to the Secretary to the Government of Bengal', no. 45, 19 March 1855, in P. C. Roy Chaudhury, *Singhbhum Old Records* (Patna, 1958), 79 (emphasis added). [Henceforth *SOR*.]

The nexus between commerce and civilization, and commerce and interior, was thus self-evident. Similar to the logic of good roads, when the debate on interiors had intensified even the selective view of railways as just an instrument of governance was often criticized. For instance, in strong opposition to the view of C. H. Cameroon who had argued that, 'independently of commercial considerations, railroads might have been invented and used as instruments of government in India',[3] J. C. Ward emphasized the civilizing influence of commerce aided by the railways.[4] For him and many others, 'moral' and 'material' were parts of the same discourse. From the 1820s onwards, notwithstanding the political needs, which undeniably were strong, commerce had increasingly become the fulcrum on which the wheels of communications and ideas of the interior rotated. In fact, in most cases they went side by side, as part of the same discourse that privileged improvement of the means of communication.[5]

The first section of this chapter evaluates the essence of the interior and its opening up. Texts and documents produced from the second decade of the nineteenth century onwards present certain biases and claims that contribute to the *myth* of roadless India and its unknown interiors. Once the space had been whitened off, it became easier and necessary for the colonial state, in association with private investors, to talk about reoccupying that space afresh. A roadless India thus awaited the alleged superior technology and better communications. However, what needs to be emphasized is that such a production was not only materialistically a function of new technologies of rule, that is, communications, police, census and other legal and financial apparatuses, but a product of both colonial rhetoric and of actual administrative realities and institutional growth or decay. The primacy of this spatial view – interior – had its own history. The politico-economic nature of this term became more sharply focused from the mid-nineteenth century, though it was built upon the gaze of general travellers and sojourning administrators of the late eighteenth century. The second section of the chapter looks at some of these sources for both continuity and break that defined the meaning of interior.

'Opening up the interiors': A Polemical Cry?

If one goes through the letters and correspondences of railway companies, of different officials of the colonial state, and not least the Court of Directors in London, it would not take long to appreciate how 'opening up the interiors' had become a commercial slogan between the 1830s and 1850s.[6] The following quote of Dalhousie, the governor

---

3 *SD*, doc. no. 57, 162.

4 James Ward, 'Note on the Policy of Organizing a System of Railways for India, submitted to the President of the Board of Control', 11 March 1847, *SD*, 231–3. This was similar in tone and emphasis to that from the Chota Nagpur commissioner, as noted above.

5 This question of whether to privilege commercial prospects or political benefits was also largely one of the politics of representation, and thus did not represent a difference *per se*. Colonial officers (governor generals for instance) highlighted political benefits; investors dwelt on commercial profits. Far from being rigid, such representations played on overlapping terrains; to secure guarantee on capital the investors also underscored political advantages.

6 I am not unaware of the contradictory views expressed over the subject of the introduction of railways. The most amusing of these was when, in 1841, the Court of Directors dismissed

general of India from 1848 to 1856 (minute dated 28 April 1853) is representative of the commercial underpinning of the opening up exercise:

> Ships from every part of the world crowd our ports in *search of produce, which we have or could obtain in the interior*, but which at present we cannot probably fetch to them, and new markets are opening to us on this side of the globe, under circumstances which defy the foresight of the wisest to estimate their probable value, or calculate their future extent.[7]

The wealth of India, in terms of produce that could 'enrich her population and benefit the whole world', was becoming 'visible' to the colonial eye in this period. An anonymous author argued: 'It is only now that we are beginning to be alive to their [India's productions] importance.'[8] The source of this wealth, according to this author, ranged from soil to rivers, from forests to mines, not excluding the 'abundant population', by which he probably meant manpower. All this, he argued, was unexplored; these resources existed but were unknown.[9] The author further reminded us that what is needed for improvement are good roads, railways and telegraphs.[10] Most of the agency houses and business firms, including Indian establishments — to which R. M. Stephenson, one of the first to think of introducing railways in India, approached to get some 'feedback' to ascertain the commercial viability of his project — spoke in the language of 'unknown and unknowable', 'incalculable', and not least 'opening up the hidden resources'. The resources were unknowable and hidden and the profits, which would follow the opening up, were incalculable. A sense of such notions is evident in the following statement, which is typical of many expressions on the subject:

> The commercial benefits that are likely to arise from the safe and rapid transit of goods and passengers by locomotive power on railways are unquestionable, and we add *incalculable*. That it will benefit the country by developing her *hidden* and partially-opened resources — that it will infuse a spirit of enterprise hitherto unknown to her merchants and that it will increase the consumption of British and other goods that are known, and create a demand for them where they are not — are inferences which even the cautious must admit.[11]

R. M. Stephenson's proposal as a 'wild project'. However, barring a few initial suspicions, the debate did not focus much on whether India needed railways but upon practical subjects and terms of negotiations between railway companies and the state. Issues included the nature and percentage of the guarantee on investment, the lease of lands, the gauge to be adopted and so on. For above reference see 'Note' of the 'Letter from R. M. Stephenson to F. J. Halliday, Secretary to the Government of Bengal, regarding Construction of Railroad in Bengal', 15 July 1844, *SD*, doc. no. 12, 24.

7 Quoted in C. Boulnois, 'East India Railway', *CR* 31 (July–December 1858): 232 (emphasis added).
8 Anon., 'India: Its Products and Improvement', *CR* 30 (January–June 1858): 33.
9 Ibid., 37.
10 Ibid., 42.
11 'Reply form Messrs. Kelsall and Ghose to R. M. Stephenson', 14 September 1844, *SD*, doc. no. 35, 68. For this idea of 'unknown products and resources' see, 'Reply from H. Burkinyoung, Master Trade Association', 7 September 1844; 'incalculable benefits' in 'Letter from Col. George Warren, the Town Major of Fort William', 17 September, 1844; 'incalculable importance' in 'Letter from Messrs White and Borrett, the Solicitors of the Great Indian Peninsula

'Unknown' and 'unknowable' in this schema were used interchangeably, and in fact, seem to have worked as presenting a continuum: the better means of communications would develop the resources which were unknown to an extent that would become unknowable and incalculable. It is intriguing that while India was portrayed as a 'storehouse' of wealth, it was also being represented as static and unchanging. This latter concept looms large in various types of texts of the nineteenth century. A set of studies, both colonial and nationalist, made use of the idea of self-sufficient village economy and stagnant society and civilization to justify their claims. For colonial authors such depictions helped to validate their attempt at 'modernizing' Indian society; for nationalists they provided a comfortable site for criticizing the economic fallouts and the disruptions of the colonial rule.[12] Clive Dewey points out that the utilitarian idea of 'progress' regarded the village community as its Other, one that perpetuates 'stagnation'.[13] The image of *self-sufficiency* and *stagnation* also bred an image of unmoving people under the rubric of 'pre-colonial immobility'.[14] Echoes of such colonial voices have unwittingly surfaced in an otherwise critically engaging work on the history of communication; S. K. Munshi has argued that 'throughout the period of its rule the British government in India never seriously concerned itself with the development of the rural road system, *which had existed in embryo in the preceding period, as a part of a self-sustaining rural economy centring around local, sub-regional and regional marts*'.[15]

This idea of changelessness was central to denying 'natives' their history of communication and circulation. The development of resources might have closely followed improvement in the means of communication,[16] but the ways the measures of development were ideologically rationalized need to be recognized and probed. David Arnold's model of diffusion and denial is partly helpful in understanding this process. The universalist claim to diffuse modern knowledge in the colonies was based on the denial of knowledge(s) existing there previously. Such denials could also extend to the realm of materialist aspects of civilization. So, in our case, the diffusion of new technology required the denial of any form of communication. Not only that, it also extended to the denial of mobility. However, this denial simultaneously also meant a deferral – a time gap (as explained in the introduction). The new universalist scientific knowledge was to be diffused but in a deferred (and not denied) way because the natives, although allegedly unfit 'to receive the benefits of scientific modernity',[17] would, under European supervision,

---

Railway Company, to J. C. Melvill, Secretary of the East India Company', 8 November 1844; 'development of the latent resources of our subjects and profession in the east' in 'Reply from George Arthur, Governor of Bombay, to John Stuart Wortley, M.P. and the Chairman of GIPR', 1 October 1845, *SD*, doc. nos. 30 (59–60), 37 (73), 39 (76), 52 (132) respectively.

12 There were various strands in which both these ideological schools presented their case. See, Peter Robb, 'British Rule and Indian "Improvement"', *Economic History Review*, 34, 4, 1981, particularly section II, and Clive Dewey, 'Images of the Village Community: A Study of Anglo-Indian Ideology', *MAS*, 6, 3, 1972.
13 Dewey, ibid., 297.
14 Ravi Ahuja, '"Opening up the country"?' 74.
15 Munshi, *Geography of Transportation*, 1980, 28–9 (emphasis added).
16 For instance, the introduction of steamships and railways led to a considerable increase in the production of coal, a subject which awaits further historical exploration.
17 Arnold, *Science, Technology and Medicine*, 15–17.

soon overcome this inability. Reverberations of this approach can be clearly seen in the debates over the remunerability of railways in India. The hope to make railways profitable in India was pinned upon capturing goods traffic because it was already concluded that the 'passive', 'resistant', 'apathetic', 'torpid', 'unenterprising' bunch of 'natives', 'invariably wedded to the practice and routine of bygone centuries', would hardly avail themselves of the benefits of speed and travel generated by the technologies of steam.[18]

It was no coincidence that the utilitarian advocates of the notion of the village community were also proponents of laissez-faire in the metropolis and champions of free trade in the colony. By the late 1820s and 1830s, when liberal/utilitarian values became dominant in metropolitan discourse, the demands and petitions from the commercial and professional middle class – the backbone of this ideology – to open up India to British trade and private enterprise considerably increased.[19] The demands for good roads, together with railway promotional literature, should be seen as a part of this larger ideological–economic campaign. What remained in the metropolis the 'opening up of Indian trade' was translated as the 'opening up of the interiors' in the colony. The financial profit of the metropolitan industrialist–capitalist and the moral and material advancement of the colony were seamlessly stitched together.

However, it was not the capital alone that provided the push factor. The idea of empire was strengthening and the need for consolidation was seen to be acute. We have observed how some people had justified the necessity of railways solely on political grounds. For a few it had also become a tool of colonization, to turn India into a 'white colony'. Hyde Clarke, one of the members of the Simla Railway Company, argued for developing hill railways that would help to provide an escape route from the tropical heat to the hill stations, which would in turn facilitate the permanent settlement of Europeans in India. He argued that the telegraph, another instrument of the new communication technology, would keep officials posted with necessary information. The idea was to harness technological advancement to overcome the long-standing issue of the premature death of Europeans in the colony due to the alleged tropical heat, and to create suitable living conditions in the cool and temperate regions of the colony that would not affect administrative efficiency.[20]

---

18 See MacGeorge, *Ways and Works*, 220–21. A few also went on to suggest that it was part of the Indian custom not to have roads: 'Should a Hindu be asked why his countrymen do not have roads, wheel carriages, and furnished hotels, his reply would be, "It is not our custom."' Caleb Wright and J. A. Brainerd, *Historic Incidents and Life in India*, rev. edn (Chicago, 1867), 23. However, some engineers, using surveys done locally, concluded otherwise. For instance, according to John Bourne, an engineer in the East India Railway Company (EIRC), the passenger traffic through which the proposed EIR line crossed was twice greater than that which existed upon the London and Birmingham Railway. Such views nonetheless remained marginal. John Bourne, *Railways in India*, 2nd edn (London, 1848), 5. For a deconstruction of colonial stereotype of 'Indian custom' for not having roads, see the useful discussion in Ahuja, *Pathways of Empire*, 162–75.
19 G. D. Bearce, *British Attitudes Towards India 1784–1858* (Oxford, 1961), 6–9. Summing up the values of liberal tendencies between 1828 and 1838, Bearce says that their proponents believed that 'India needed the colonization of British capitalists…who would develop the resources of the country.' Ibid., 160.
20 Hyde Clarke, *Colonization, Defence, and Railways in Our Indian Empire* (London, 1857).

The nexus between empire and new technology was a prominent feature of the 1840s and 1850s but one can see it evolving from the late 1820s. William Bentinck's various minutes on steam navigation and roads represent this in the best possible way. He vociferously advocated the importance of the 'steam engine', which could 'conquer at once the great inconveniences and the great weakness of vastly extended empire by approximation of distant parts by the quick collection of widely separated force, and by ready control and superintendence'.[21] Of the many expositions, the following best captures the mood:

> Steam power must be included amongst the most powerful means of reducing the difficulties of protection and support to such extensive and distant lines of defence, and of multiplying the military resources that we already possess…an efficient marine steam establishment in India is called for by considerations more powerful even those of commercial advantage, or improved political control. It would multiply in relation, little understood, the defensive means of the empire.[22]

The immediate reason behind this was the first Anglo–Burmese War between 1823 and 1826. In 1825, soon after the conquest of Assam, David Scott, commissioner of the North-East Frontier, called for the necessity of building steamers to navigate the Brahmaputra River in order to convey troops and supplies to Assam.[23] Accordingly, two engines were sent out to India, on receipt of which two steamers, the *Hooghly* and the *Brahmaputra*, were built in Calcutta. They were launched in 1828, but before they could be employed on the Brahmaputra River, Bentinck became the governor general, and he thought it more prudent to employ them on the Ganga.[24] This change of decision was influenced as much by the termination of the war as by the potential of tapping the Gangetic trade. However, the miscalculation that the government displayed in the early period of the steamships' arrival in India shows how differentiated were the colonial concerns regarding utilizing this new technology. First of all, the lead in introducing steamships to India came from private interests. Before the government appreciated their benefits, individuals such as Waghorn and James Henry Johnston were devoted to the idea of using steamships for speedy communication between England and India.[25]

---

21 'Minute on Steam Navigation', 8 June 1833, in C. H. Philips, ed., *The Correspondence of Lord W. C. Bentinck, Governor General of India, 1828–35*, (Oxford, 1977), vol. 2 (1832–35), serial no. 599, 1081. The correspondence was published in two volumes. [Henceforth *BC.*]
22 'Minute on Military Policy', *BC*, II, serial no. 810, 1455.
23 It is interesting to note that Thomas Prinsep, who later did a sketch of the *Hooghly*, was the one who served in the First Burma War. He was also a surveyor with the commissioners of the Sunderbans between 1821 and 1824. In 1826, he was appointed the superintendent of canals. He was associated with the first experimental voyage of the *Hooghly* from Calcutta to Allahabad, which was officially launched on the Ganga on 29 March 1828. Patricia Kattenhorn, *British Drawings in the India Office Library*, vol. 3 (London, 1994), 264.
24 Douglas Dewar, *Bygone Days in India: with Eighteen Illustrations* (London, 1922), 91–2; G. A. Prinsep, *An Account of Steam Vessels and of Connected Proceedings with Steam Navigation in British India* (Calcutta, 1830), 37–43.
25 Dewar, *Bygone Days*, 87–91; also see S. N. Sen, 'Steam Johnston', *BPP* 60, serial no. 121–22 (January–June 1941).

Plate 1. The *Hooghly* steamer near Bhagalpur on the River Ganga, by Thomas Prinsep, 1828

© British Library Board, Online gallery, shelfmark: WD4194, item no. 4194.

Until 1823 the government had refused to purchase the ships; this late appreciation cost it dearly. The case in point is the steamship *Diana*. It was originally planned to use it on the Canton River but the idea was abandoned by the Court of Directors in order to not hurt the 'Chinese sentiments'. It was then reshipped to Calcutta where it arrived in 1823. The Bengal government refused to purchase it, following which it was taken up by the Calcutta agency houses' merchants. Though *Diana* was found to be extremely useful as a passage boat for the port of Calcutta in all seasons, the ship was not able to cover its expenses. In April 1824, soon after the commencement of the Burmese War, the government bought it for Rs. 80,000 when earlier it had refused the price of Rs. 60,000. The purchase was strongly recommended by Captain Marryat, who then commanded the ship *Larne*, and conducted the naval part of the expedition to Rangoon, to which the *Diana* was attached.[26] Another steamship, the *Enterprise*, was sold at £40,000 payable in England. The ship was despatched for Rangoon on 7 January 1826, which according to one estimate 'saved [the] government over 6 lakhs of rupees'.[27] The idea and utility of steam as a necessary connecting agent between metropolis and colony was slowly becoming appreciated. Bentinck and his officials

---

26 Prinsep, *An Account*, 4–10.
27 Dewar, *Bygone Days*, 91.

acknowledged that, as Europeans, they were still 'strangers' in the colony and they had failed 'to acquire a knowledge of the relevant Indian languages and laws' and had 'neglected everything which should have been done to consolidate their power'.[28] Being 'strangers', the only thing they could look forward to was the 'quickest conveyance of public mails and exchange of information and instruction between authorities in India and England'.[29]

The use of steam was not discussed in isolation. The complementary nature of communication is evident in the way Bentinck also complained about the absence of roads in Bengal.[30] Official reports accused native rulers of not directing their minds and money to building roads.[31] But at the personal level, people such as Bentinck described the lack of good roads as a positive scandal and disgrace to the English government in India.[32] Lord Valentia's comments are also noteworthy in this regard:

> During the full power of the house of Timour, they made magnificent causeways from one end of their dominions to the other and planted trees on the sides to shelter travellers from the sun, a most useful plan, in a country where men are the chief instruments of conveyance. Surely we ought to follow so good an example now that we are in tranquil possession of the same empire. But alas! Its sovereigns are too apt to confine their views to a large investment, and an increase of dividend, and have usually opposed every plan for the improvement of the country, which has been brought forward by the different Governor Generals.[33]

The absence of roads signified an absence of mobility. 'With the exception of a very limited number of persons,' said the *Railway Register*, 'almost exclusively men in official positions, who perform tedious and expensive journeys on stated occasions, *there are no*

---

28 See 'Introduction', *BC*, I, xxiii. Also, 'Minute on Steam Navigation', 8 June 1833; 'Minute on Military Policy', 13 March 1835; 'Observations by Major-General Sir S. F. Whittingham', 5 March 1834 in *BC*, II, serial nos. 599 (1080), 810 (1441–5), 681 (1218) respectively.
29 Bentinck's 'Minute on Steam Navigation', 12 June 1832; 'Minute on Steam Navigation', 8 June 1833; 'Minute on Military Policy', 13 March 1835 in *BC*, II, serial nos. 456 (833–4), 599 (1079), 810 (1445) respectively. Also see 'Sir John Malcolm to Bentinck', Private, 28 September 1830 wherein he says, 'Quick communication with England is an important point and the recent establishment of steam vessels affects this part of the question.' *BC*, I, serial no. 250, 517.
30 'Minute on Steam Navigation', 8 June 1833, *BC*, II, serial no. 599, 1081.
31 *The East India Company Memorandum of 1858 on the Progress of Administration in India* unabashedly put forth: 'it was never their [native rulers] practice to lay out money in the construction of permanent roads'. Quoted in John Freeman, *British India or A Reply to the Memorandum of the East India Company: Or An Insight into British India* (London, 1858), 44. This view dominated the official understanding for the better part of the rule; John Strachey said in 1888, 'No Native prince made a road. Before the establishment of our Government there was hardly a road deserving the name in all India.' John Strachey, *India: Its Administration and Progress*, 3rd enlarged and rev. edn, 1903 (Delhi, 1997) with a foreword by M. C. J. Kagzi, 212. First published 1888.
32 'Bentinck to Robert Campbell', 7 May 1831, *BC*, I, serial no. 315, 627.
33 Quoted in 'Accepted Travellers', *CR*, 24, December 1856, 287.

travellers in India.'[34] James Mill's *History* provided ample quotable remarks for the officials of this period to admonish the lack of communications in India. The quintessential character of the Hindus – their 'petty divided sovereignties, injustice, dethronements, bloodshed-marked-polity, conquests and wars' – rendered 'the undertaking of works of public improvement next to impossible'. The 'Muhammadan period' for both Mill and George Tremenheere, a civil engineer in Bengal, was relatively better; but the 'amount of money expended by the emperors in the construction of roads remained questionable'.[35] However, it was not the native rulers alone who became the object of criticism, since EIC rule was also condemned. It was found 'difficult to account for the neglect of the English rulers of Hindostan for objects of public improvement'.[36] The EIC defended itself by saying 'roads in India were not of absolute necessity'.[37] Some members did criticize the Company, however, for this neglect, though they nevertheless tried to excuse the neglect by pointing to the Company's preoccupation with wars and territorial expansion, which did not leave it much time to improve communications.[38] But the Company's defence was weak in the light of mounting criticisms from different quarters.

We can already discern different seams of colonialism in our discussion, seams that both resonate with and qualify our understanding of models such as 'diffusion and denial'. First, the cultural essentialism most often gave way to time lag. The very values and metaphors – such as steam – that explained differences also became the connecting link between cultures. Undeniably, this connection meant better supervision of control and conquest of the colonies. Second, denial (of either the materialist aspect or of knowledge systems existing in the colonies) did not imply complete erasure; rather it was characterized by negotiation and quick revisions. For instance, the colonial view about natives' unwillingness

---

34 This came out in the July issue of 1845, as quoted in Mukherjee, *History of the East Indian Railway*, 20.
35 George Borlase Tremenheere, *On Public Works in the Bengal Presidency, with an Abstract of the Discussion upon the Paper*, ed. Charles Manby (London, 1858), 4. For Mill, Hindus provided an exception for their 'monuments of irrigation', though Tremenheere disagreed on this. For the latter, the 'best monuments of public convenience were carvaserais'.
36 Tremenheere, *On Public Works*, 21.
37 'The plains of India are traversable by carts and even by armies, without made roads, throughout the dry season. Roads, therefore in India, were not, as in some countries, a matter of absolute necessity.' This was the logic given by the EIC, as quoted in Freeman, *British India*, 41.
38 Tremenheere, *On Public Works*, 6–7. The immediate context of this criticism was the difficulties faced during the 1857 Mutiny. Both Tremenheere and Freeman wrote in 1858, just after the event. Economically too, since the period was of increasing trade, the Company came in for severe criticism from the English residents engaged in private trade. Freeman's *British India* represents this view. However, even in works before 1857, we see the same tone of apologia. Albert Robinson, a civil engineer, thus remarked: 'Courtly wars prevented the earlier "enlightened and liberal rulers of India" towards improving communications.' Other reasons according to him were the vast extent of the regions 'under their sway' and the 'peculiar political relations' in which they stood to several states. Robinson, *Account of Some Recent Improvements in the System of Navigating the Ganges by Iron Steam Vessels* (London, 1848), 5–6. For a brief note on 1857 and discussion around communication, see Nitin Sinha, 'Contest and Communication: The Geography of Rebellion in Bihar', *Biblio: A Review of Books: A Special Issue on 1857* 12 (2007).

to travel by railway was riddled with contradictions. While, on the one hand, dominant views such as those of the Court of Directors maintained that the poverty of the natives would force the railways to rely on goods traffic,[39] locally settled officers such as J. B. Higginson, writing from Mirzapur, exuded confidence that 'the natives will readily avail themselves of the saving in time and money which such facilities [railways] may afford them'.[40] Third, colonialism as a state structure had elements of strong self-criticism. As we have seen, not only the natives were blamed but Company administrators were also not spared for making India roadless. The historiographical value of the above discussion lies in our appreciating the fact that although debates about opening up the interiors of India were strongly connected to railways, the period of the 1820s was crucial for the ways in which concerns regarding better communication were formulated by colonial officials, primarily along the lines of extending the commerce and safeguarding the empire. The railway-centric debates signified an extension rather than a break from these concerns.

Are we reading too much into the importance of words like 'incalculable', 'hidden', 'unknown', 'unknowable' and 'unexplored' to capture the essence of 'interiors'?[41] Obviously, the existing volume of trade was known, the routes which the railway lines had to pass through were recognized (although some were contested) and the benefits were also largely estimated.[42] This information was essential to assess the potential return of the line and also to convince the Court of Directors to provide a guarantee on capital. Were not these ways of representing expected effects 'obvious'? Should we not treat 'opening up the interiors' just as a form of presentation, a narrative device, a way of presenting the effects in the most impressive way? Could the 'incalculable benefit' be read simply as one of those stock phrases, meaning that the expected results were so potentially huge and grand that they were incalculable? If we accept such an interpretation, we miss the histories, both constructed on and underlying these phrases. Things that are obvious should not be left unexamined, for they not only create their own history, but also, if influential, try to erase other histories. The politico-economic dimensions of the term 'interior', which gained momentum from the second decade of the nineteenth century, were built upon the dynamics of spatial representation in the preceding period. Interestingly, if in the latter phase communication became one of the crucial ways to open up the interior, in the earlier period it played a vital role in marking the landscape in different spatial hierarchies.

Interiorizing India/Inferiorizing India

As noted in the Introduction and Chapter 1, the travelling gaze was one important medium of creating hierarchies of spatial visions both in pre-colonial and colonial times. It is true

---

39 'First despatch from the Court of Directors of the East India Company to the Government of India', *SD*, 122–3.
40 'Reply from J. B. Higginson', 10 September 1844, *SD*, 69. Captain H. Goodwyn, garrison engineer and civil architect at Fort William, was also sure that 'passengers of all descriptions' will use the railways because there already existed an 'enormous traffic' on steamships, which will increase further. 'Reply from Captain H. Goodwyn', 12 August 1844, *SD*, 30–31.
41 I am grateful to Ian Kerr for his criticism on a preliminary draft of this chapter, which helped me rethink some of the issues.
42 See, for example, Bourne, *Railways*, ch. 2.

that trade- and economy-oriented texts, which strongly advocated the introduction of railways and improvement in other means of communication, conspicuously created the nexus of empire, improvement and interior. But it would be a mistake to take this as the starting point of efforts at 'interiorizing' India. A different kind of literature, travelogues, together with printed visuals, which obviously circulated more widely than official and railway promoters' correspondence had, at least by the end of the eighteenth century, come to use the term 'interior' fairly frequently. This usage was not necessarily economic in its implications; it nevertheless might have carried economic connotations. But primarily it was a way of creating a spatial vision along certain hierarchic binaries such as centre–periphery, mainland–inland, and coast–interior. It is among other reasons that 'interior' became so popular in colonial usage: one of the most prominent and obvious was a complete reversal in the flow and direction of the gaze in the colonial period as compared with that in the Mughal. The perception during Mughal rule was land oriented. The coast did not play a significant role in spatially visualizing the empire; it did so only to the extent of recognizing its frontiers as seen in the thoughts of al-Biruni or Abul Fazl. With the coming of the European East Indian Companies, oceans, ports and coasts became the central sites from which the gaze radiated 'inwards' towards land.[43] It is not a matter of coincidence that while al-Idrisi, a twelfth-century Arab geographer, showed in his map a landlocked Indian Ocean, the European coastal navigational charts from the late seventeenth century 'gave small inset views of the land, as seen from the sea, making it easier for sailors to recognize where they were'.[44] Coming to the coast and then proceeding further 'into' the land thus became an act of 'going into the interiors'. Land was seen *from* sea, whereas in the Mughal times the sea was by and large approached *from* the land. Taking coastal settlements and presidency capitals (in our case Calcutta) as the 'centre', the act of travelling into the mainland became the act of going into the 'interiors'.[45]

Almost all European travellers and administrators who came to take up their jobs in India arrived at coastal port-cities and then went, at least in the northern and eastern part of the country, 'up the Ganges', which was either an act of 'going up the country' or 'going into the interiors'. I argue that this way of routinized journey also disciplined and stabilized descriptions and thus in a course of the fifty to sixty years up to the 1820s–30s when the pronounced interventionist and developmentalist discourses around

---

43 Some recent studies have brought forth the point of politicization of oceanic space as a chief characteristic of the early modern period. For instance, Elizabeth Mancke argues that oceanic rather than terrestrial dominance characterized the modern European empires. Mancke, 'Early Modern Expansion and Politicization of Oceanic Space', *Geographical Review* 89, no. 2 (1999).

44 Gole, *India within the Ganges*, 17, 66–7.

45 Anil Chandra Das Gupta, comp. and ed., *The Days of John Company: Selections from Calcutta Gazette, 1824–1832* (Calcutta, 1959), 117. One could not miss this Calcutta-centric tone in the high-praising phrases of the Daniells: 'Calcutta is now the metropolis of British India, the seat of a powerful and prosperous empire, which has already communicated to those remote regions a portion of its national laws and liberties; and is probably destined to disseminate those arts and sciences which have conferred such honourable distinction on the people of Europe.' *A Picturesque Voyage to India*, text opposite 'Old Fort Gaut, Calcutta'.

communication began to appear, the 'interior' was already an established spatial form of denoting inaccessibility, seclusion and backwardness.[46] Thus, this spatial category allegedly also tried 'inferiorizing' India. In cultural and postcolonial studies, travel literature has been accorded a high place in delineating the pervasiveness of the colonial gaze, something that significantly contributed to the project of 'colonial rule'.[47] Arguably, travel was an act that not only produced 'useful knowledge' but also helped define the colonial Self vis-à-vis the colonized Other. It was an exercise in both going beyond the boundaries of familiarity and yet maintaining or creating a boundary. In that process, as Mary Louise Pratt has argued, a transcultural zone was created.[48] Other studies accept the centrality of travel in the production of colonial knowledge but argue for a greater diversity in its purposes.[49] Still others argue for tensions and anxieties embedded in the act of travel.[50]

The present discussion aims not to contribute to the debate of 'coloniality' involved in the act of travel but to unravel the meanings of 'interior'. The ways of seeing and the creation of spatial boundaries and markers naturally link up with the issue of the power of the colonial gaze to construct the Indian landscape into a representational mode that signified control and authority. My reading of some of the materials from the late eighteenth and early nineteenth centuries suggests it to be otherwise. In the north and east of India at least, the act of 'going up the Ganges' or 'going up the country' meant that the colonial gaze was limited. The linear stretch of land along the river or the road that unfolded to the travelling eye was the only area subject to 'control'; beyond that, the land was closed, the interiors were dense and the jungles inaccessible. Further, if one considers some other types of sources, which also self-professedly gave 'picturesque' accounts, and thus allegedly should have demonstrated 'unchanging India' and a pervasive colonial gaze, the India represented in them was far from static.[51]

---

46 I am not arguing that all forms of colonial travel took place by the Ganga. For a variety, see Chapter 3.
47 See Bernard Cohn, *Colonialism and its Forms of Knowledge: The British in India* (Princeton, 1996).
48 Pratt, *Imperial Eyes*.
49 Sachidananda Mohanty, ed., *Travel Writing and the Empire* (Delhi, 2003), introduction. Although suggesting a close link between travel and empire, a recent volume also highlights the importance of 'failures' which 'sometimes [constitute] the most interesting aspects of the travelogues…because of their potential to uncover the multiplicity of colonizing projects and the diversity of possible responses to them'. See 'Introduction' in Helen Gilbert and Anna Johnston, eds, *In Transit: Travel, Text, Empire* (New York, 2002). Direct quote is from 5.
50 Nigel Leask, *British Romantic Writers and the East: Anxieties of Empire* (Cambridge, 2002).
51 I am referring to private journals and diaries of the travelling officers. This source also, at least amongst the friends and families of the persons employed in India, had a wider circulation and demand. Most of the time, such diaries were published. Highlighting its significance a reviewer commented that no sooner is any information acquired about a district, however remote, 'its peculiar properties are discussed in conversation, information communicated in public journals, and the diary of some tourist is quickly printed and eagerly perused'. 'Review of Tracts, Historical and Statistical, on India by Benjamin Heynes', *AJ* 2 (1816): 365. Mildred Archer records one such demand made by Mrs Lewin to her son, William, in the Company's artillery at Calcutta, in 1826, asking for 'some drawings and sketches of yourself en militaire. I don't mean a formal miniature but a drawing coloured with your horse and uniform'. After William had moved to Arakan, she wrote again, 'as you have a turn for drawing, I hope

The ascribed homogeneity therefore needs to be questioned and qualified. The formulaic representation is not necessarily a representation of colonial conquest, and it also does not necessarily tell a story of the erasure of the colony's history; but is a representation that produced routinized India, that too unevenly. It was a disciplining gaze, not only in terms of disciplining the 'native' landscape, but also disciplining the gaze of subsequent travellers. The Daniells, visiting India some seven years after Hodges' visit, wanted to traverse the latter's footsteps. Tillotson states:

> ...travelling into the country from Calcutta, they [the Daniells] shared his [Hodges'] ambition to visit the major sites. Yet they had seen some of his prints, and their choice of sites was motivated also by a wish not to be outdone by him. From William's [Daniell] journal it is evident that they made a point of 'passing through the caravanserai that Hodges had made an aquatinta of'.[52]

This aspiration to see the same things but *differently* was creating both routinization and spaces of contradictions. The interior was a part of this routinized gaze, which, like these texts, brought both closure and opening. Harriet Guest argues that while consolidating his previous works on the South Pacific, Hodges 'became the first European professional landscape painter to portray the interior of Northern India'.[53] Writing about the late eighteenth century, Bayly says, 'Knowledge of the interior of the country, its manufacture, population and agricultural statistics remained similarly patchy, confined to Bengal and Madras hinterland.'[54] In this kind of understanding the notion of 'interior' is hardly problematized. These views inadvertently echo the colonial complaint about the lack of knowledge of the 'interior'. This point is also missing in an otherwise perceptive recent study on the landscape and topography of India as viewed by British travellers.[55] The notion of the interior, to borrow Edward Said's framework of 'imaginative geography', was a colonial construction. However, such a spatial imagination symbolized both the

---

you will send me sketches of the country and the natives, of yourself, your Bungalow, your horses etc'. Mildred Archer, *British Drawings in the India Office Library*, vol. 1 (London, 1969), 10. Although Archer's understanding of the standard picturesque depiction is different from scholars like Dirks, she concedes that there was 'belittlement of India, an elimination, conscious or unconscious, of all those details in a landscape which made it characteristically Eastern' (in the sense that one couldn't know if by looking at these sketches one was looking at India, Italy or England), 55. This argument, however, appears tricky; so if India is painted like Italy or England, the charges of Eurocentrism are obvious. On the other hand, if, to sooth Archer's lament, the things characteristically Eastern were incorporated, the likely accusation would be of 'essentialisation' of culture.

52 G. H. R. Tillotson, 'A Fair Picture: Hodges and the Daniells at Rajmahal', in Pauline Rahotgi and Pheroza Godrez, eds, *Under the Indian Sun: British Landscape Artists* (Bombay, 1995), 61. The Daniells followed Hodges so closely that many of the drawings that they made were from exactly the same angle. Mildred Archer and Ronald Lightbown, *India Observed: India as Viewed by British Artists, 1760–1860* (London, 1982), 57.
53 Guest, 'The Great Distinction', 36.
54 Bayly, *Empire and Information*, 56.
55 Arnold, *The Tropics*.

Plate 2. Moorcroft and Hearsey, by Hearsey, 1812

© British Library Board, Online gallery, shelfmark: WD350, item no. 350.

lack of colonial power and the need the colonial state felt to attain it in the late eighteenth and early nineteenth centuries. The term interior symbolized a sense of 'distance' – a distant, detached spatial entity – which nonetheless, technically and knowingly, resided *within* the purview of the colonial gaze and control. The interiors were constructed and dissolved simultaneously.

One of the chief functions of the 'interior' was to provide a much needed justification for the claims made by each of the travellers that they alone were representing the truth. Traversing the allegedly hitherto unvisited 'interiors' lent credibility to the account and the gaze. This does not mean that 'interior' was a pre-given space. Rather, as suggested above, it was a constructed entity that was invoked to make the narrative or the picture truthful.[56] In the preface to his book, Hodges expressed surprise that 'of a country [India] so nearly allied to us, so little should be known'. Thus, among other tasks, he set out to fill the gap of information about the 'face of the country'.[57] And that truthful representation and useful information had to come from the interior: 'After residing a year at Madras,

---

56 There exists a good number of literature on the ideology of truthfulness in picturesque depiction, which is not directly the concern of this chapter. Archer's above cited works discuss this. Also see, Giles Tillotson, *The Artificial Empire: The Indian Landscapes of William Hodges* (Richmond, 2000), ch. 1.

57 Hodges, *Travels*, iii, iv. After almost thirty years, Forrest was using the same narrative device to justify his work, that is, to excite the interest of readers who were little acquainted with India. Forrest, *A Picturesque Tour*, preface.

as no prospect presented itself of seeing and making drawings in the interior part of the country, I determined to pursue my voyage to Bengal.'[58] This is presumably the sense in which Harriet suggests that Hodges was the first European artist to portray north Indian interiors; he travelled up the Ganga through Bihar, away from the presidency capital. The Daniells theorized the nature of the gaze more ambitiously: 'the pencil is the narrative to the eye... its representations are not liable to the omissions of memory, or the misconceptions of fancy, whatever it communicates is a transcript from nature'.[59] Solvyns also described his travels as going into the interior.[60] And, like Hodges, he also claimed to represent the truth, which others had not:

> Henceforth the public will not be exposed to admit false or confused ideas upon a subject so interesting to curiosity and so well deserving of attention, nor led astray in the track of authors more disposed to the chimeras of system, than to strictness of observation, and severity of truth.[61]

Travelling was one of the ways to discover this truth. It was both an act of transgressing and a restructuring of spatial boundaries and limitations. But it served other purposes as well. In the postcolonial, post-Saidian Orientalism approach, travel has been so much integrally defined as a colonial project that its other meanings and implications have been glossed over. One of them is very akin to the early modern aspect of acquiring manliness (as discussed in the last chapter). Hawkins Francis James who started his journey from England in February 1827 was initially reluctant to travel to India. But during his sea voyage he discovered a new identity of being 'a Traveller' that opened up possibilities of seeing foreign countries and different nations. He chastised himself for having been so foolish and narrow-minded earlier. However, curiosity was not enough of a reason for his new enthusiasm; it was, in his own words, a feeling that he had 'begun to feel quite like a Man' that he cherished most. Becoming a man for him meant becoming independent (financially) and also contributing to the pleasures and happiness of his family (again pecuniary).[62]

The nature of travel also differed according to the spaces traversed. While travelling in the frontier regions, many Europeans disguised themselves as fakirs and gosains in order to enter into a physical space that was not only hostile to the European presence – hence the need for disguise – but also into a cultural and political space in which the European 'gaze' was unwelcome. George Forster, who journeyed overland from Bengal

---

[58] Hodges, *Travels*, 13.
[59] Thomas Daniell and William Daniell, *A Picturesque Voyage*, ii.
[60] Solvyns, *Les Hindoûs*, vol. 1, 28.
[61] Ibid., 23. It was on the ground of 'truthful' representation that Lady Valentia, during her travels, 'chastised one of the Daniells' prints for relating "incorrectly" a matter of fact, and a Hodges print for bearing "no resemblance" to the subject'. Tillotson, 'A Fair Picture', 64.
[62] *Diaries and Letters of Hawkins Francis James (1806–1860)*, Mss Eur. B365/2 ff. 1–24. (I am following the pagination given at the top of the pages). The above reference is from vol. 2, 32–3. Later, his brother Henry Curry James (1817–66) also joined him in India and they both wrote in the same diary/journal.

to England, partly in disguise, had some pertinent comments to make on the notions of power, travel and appearance:

> If the sahib in India, the grandee 'in the fullness of his power, seated in a palanquin, perhaps on an elephant, surrounded with those bands of stickmen and pikemen, who disperse every man and beast that dares to cross his way', if this personage convinced of his own importance could be suddenly transported to Herat, where a European was an object of contempt, 'how speedily would he be divested of his plumes, and reduced to his simple value'![63]

Similarly, 'When the Daniells wanted to go further north up Delhi, they had to send a letter to the raja of Garhwal for permission to enter his territory, [after which] a new escort was arranged and porters were recruited.'[64] In another instance, William Moorcroft, accompanied by an Anglo Indian, Hyder Young Hearsey (who had already been into the region before with one Captain Webb in 1808), travelled in Indian dress but on their return journey were caught by the Gurkhas who identified them because of their European boots.[65] Somehow, even in the late nineteenth century when the colonial rule had attained supremacy, the detection of disguised Europeans reportedly led to outrages, to an extent that T. G. Montgomerie, the head of the trans-Himalayan survey parties, commented that it has 'put a stop to exploration by Europeans'.[66] In contrast, travel in the heartland of India did not require Europeans to disguise themselves. This travelling was an act to infuse command and generate knowledge, to control the familiar and to know the unfamiliar. This heartland, an undefined space, was seen as a series of interlinked spaces. The zones of familiarity and unfamiliarity that defined frontiers in specific moments of time were closely linked to the political and territorial acquisition; in the South Asian case a definite chronology is discernable. The early sketches of Indian landscapes furnished, say between 1760 and 1810, are usually confined to the presidencies of Bengal and Madras and to Mysore. In this time, the 'heartland' of the region which this book focuses on meant the Gangetic belt. After that, the scenes of upper north India and the northwest frontier became conspicuous, reflecting the British political expansion. To take the case of Delhi for example, until the early nineteenth century, journeys to Delhi were rare and hazardous. The Daniells were one of the first to reach it, albeit with great difficulty. However, from the second decade of the nineteenth century, many travellers visited the city, and often described it as a city of ruins, in

---

63 K. K. Dyson, *A Various Universe: A Study of the Journals and Memoirs of British Men and Women in the Indian Subcontinent, 1765–1856* (Delhi, 1978), 150.
64 Mildred Archer, *Artist Adventurers in Eighteenth Century India; Thomas and William Daniell* (London, 1974), 5.
65 See Plate 2. Moorcroft later became the superintendent of the Pusa stud in Bihar, and the visiting officials did not forget to mention that he had brought shawl wool goats from Tibet, which, in fact, was true. Bayley, *Journal of a Route*, 11. Bayley was also refused by the Gurkhas to go to Dehradun, 36.
66 'Report of a Route-Survey Made by Pundit, from Nepal to Lhasa, and Thence Through its Upper Valley of the Brahmaputra to Its Source', *Journal of the Royal Geographical Society of London* 38 (1868): 129. [Henceforth *JRGS*.]

contrast to 'early travellers such as Bernier, who had given romantic descriptions of the city, its fabulous buildings and beautiful gardens'.[67] It gradually became a place that the European travellers sought to know. Entering into the 'newly conquered provinces', as A. Deane described them, made her feel 'fortunate' to have a 'perfect view of the manners and customs of the natives', seeing areas to which 'Europeans have never been before'.[68] 'Never been before' nonetheless raises an interesting question about the ways in which colonial knowledge, particularly the stereotypical parts of it, was formed. Without any attempt at generalization, the anecdote provided by William Parry Okeden is worth retelling here. During his travels in the Oudh region, Okeden, on hearing some gunshots, inquired of a peasant and was told that the nawab's soldiers were practising. He then asked to confirm if this particular zillah (district) came under the nawab's jurisdiction, to which the peasant replied: 'Look at the ruins and uncultivated lands, how can it be anybodys but the Nawaub's? The Company's Zillahs are not like this.'[69]

As Arnold has put it, the progression of the journey into the heartland was both spatially and culturally seen as a 'journey into Hinduism's "heart of darkness"'.[70] The interiors symbolized this darkness. The binary of centre–interior, a binary of imaginative geography, however, was not a fixed one. It was relational, or at best 'liminal'. A series of such centres existed, with a series of corresponding 'interiors'. For Calcutta a place like Patna became an interior, while in Patna the districts north of Bihar became the interior. The relationality was evident in the way the Indian landscape was simultaneously depicted as familiar and different in these accounts. While for A. Deane the absence of hedgerows in India, in contrast to England, was somewhat surprising, for an anonymous traveller a small village situated at the foot of the hills near Pattergota reminded him of England.[71] Okeden, while driving round the park at Kishnagur during his upcountry travel in 1821, felt that he was in England.[72] James Bayley, while travelling by the Ganga, also expressed similar sentiments when crossing Barrackpur.[73] And yet at points of crises, this relationality broke down. The anonymous traveller referred above, noted: 'no Englishman, with his clean and well-cultivated and well-drained country can have the idea of insects of all shapes, sizes and species that swarm into the windows'.[74] The absolute spatial–cultural differences came to the forefront, thus denying the text and textual representation any one tone that

---

67 For the point of chronological expansion and visual depiction see Mildred Archer, *British Drawings*, 1; for Delhi, Mildred Archer, *Company Paintings: Indian Paintings of the British Period*, 129.
68 Deane, *A Tour*, 139.
69 William Parry Okeden, *Diary and Sporting Journal of William Parry Okeden, India, 1821–41*. Mss Eur. A. 210, 31.
70 Arnold, *The Tropics*, 53.
71 For Deane see *A Tour*, 8, 30–31; for the latter view, Anon., *Journal of a voyage of exploration of the River Ganges upstream to Patna, 28th July–30th August, 1821*, Mss Eur. E 271, 46. He also noted the absence of hedges, 81–2. I am following the pagination given at the bottom of the pages.
72 Okeden, *Diary and Sporting Journal*, 7.
73 Mss. Eur. D 970, 2. This volume is paginated only until page no. 28. Reference to this source beyond that page number follows the pattern of the initial sequence.
74 Anon., *Journal of a voyage*, 8.

can be labelled as homogenizing. Or, in other words, they highlighted their immanent contradictory nature.

The point of progression holds the key for our discussion because it highlights the role of the means of communication that facilitated the travelling gaze and the simultaneous making and dissolving of the interior. The relationship between communication and the gaze resembled the nature of two-way traffic. If the gaze depended on the lines of the communication to present 'views' and 'scenes' while journeying, the lines of communication became the sites for situating everything that was desirable to be *seen* and integral for defining what India was. All scenic properties and cultural practices, like Sati and the rituals of death (leaving sick persons on riverbanks) were woven into the narrative along the lines of communication. Such depictions utilized the then current ideas of 'sublime', 'picturesque' and the 'exotic', to create a romantic Indian landscape with an implicated negative value that required 'reform' and colonial intervention. But this very framing also exhibited the limited gaze of the travelling personnel, adding to the worries of being strangers (as Bentinck and his officials felt), and thus finally merged with the idea of introducing reforms. The difference between this line of argument presented here and other standard arguments is that the urge to reform flowed not always from the belief in the pervasive power of colonial rule, but quite considerably from its anxious status of being limited. We will follow the itinerary of Hodges and others to see some of these anxieties and limitedness.

In his first upland visit, Hodges travelled by road, using the government-established dak (postal) services.[75] The 'objects to attract the attention of the curious traveller from Calcutta' were situated along the road, that is, the town of Plassey (more for its politico-nostalgic importance than for its landscape); the stone bridge built by Sultan Shuja at Oodoonulla, which was 'one of the most elegant specimens in architecture of those times'; and, not least, the ruins of the buildings at Rajmahal.[76] By capturing a few 'highly picturesque' snapshots from nature, as Hodges did with the pass of Sicri Gully, he went on to illuminate 'the general character of this part of the country'.[77] In other words, snippets completed the picture; a particular scene of a pass described the general nature of the landscape. The vastness of the landforms was measured from a point situated along the line of communication:

> After returning to Sicri Gully, I continued my route across the pass of Terriagully, from the top of which a beautiful scene opens itself to the view; namely, the meandering of the river Ganges through the flat country, and glittering through an immense plain, highly cultivated, as far as the extent of the horizon, where the eye is almost at a loss to discriminate the termination of sky and land.[78]

This scenic repertoire changed when he made the downward journey from Monghyr to Calcutta by the Ganga. In his own words, Hodges encountered 'a series of scenery

---

75 Hodges, *Travels*, ibid., 16.
76 Ibid., 17–22. The quotes are from pages 17 and 20 respectively.
77 Ibid., 23.
78 Ibid., 24.

perfectly new'.[79] The vastness of the river caught his attention: 'even the Rhine, appear[s] as rivulets in comparison with this enormous mass of water'.[80] The objects appeared in their miniature forms, and the vast sheet of the water restricted the long, casting gaze: 'The largest boats sailing up or passing down, appear, when in the middle of the stream, as mere points, and the eastern shore only as a dark line marking the horizon.'[81] The downward journey was always quicker and this further made the observation patchier. Hodges admitted, 'My former passage down to the river to Calcutta was too rapid to allow of more observation than what related to the general appearance of the villages and towns on its banks.'[82] However, on close reading of the text, his second trip up the river also presented an account of routine observation. Near Serampur, where 'there is a neat town', 'both sides of the river are decorated with a few houses belonging to English gentlemen'; the town of Chinsura 'is distinguishable from a distance' with a 'handsome appearance'; and until reaching Patna 'Every where on either side of the river there are collections of villages, and the country is high in cultivation.'[83] In terms of noting the sequence of places and their characteristics, there is hardly any divergence in the accounts of these travellers who went up the Ganga: the Danish settlement at Serampur, the French Chandernagar, the Dutch factory at Chinsura, the huts on the banks of the river at Murshidabad, the hills of Rajmahal, the fort at Monghyr, the Fakir Rocks, the ghats of Patna, the granary at Bankipur, the ruins of the palace at Ghazipur, the sprawling ghats and the Aurungzeb's tomb at Benares – almost every traveller observed, wrote and sketched these 'views'. This was the 'Gangascape'[84] that, because of the virtue of the river being an important medium of communication in this region, produced a routinized India in which each traveller wanted to follow his/her predecessor. This Gangascape produced a limited gaze. Most of the time the gaze was restricted to banks, river rocks, ghat monuments, socio-ritual observations, and trading activities performed on the ghats, together with some observation on groups of people (such as women and Brahmins) coming to the ghats. The contemporary general European travelling interest was by and large restricted to these views, which satiated the search for the picturesque; these views were conveniently found or situated along the means of communication. On a closer reading, we observe the nature of the gaze in these accounts. While coming down the Ganga from Kanpur A. Deane remarked that the 'river was bounded on either side by high, and almost perpendicular banks'.[85] For another, the woody banks beyond the

---

79 Ibid., 32.
80 Ibid., 32–3.
81 Ibid.
82 Ibid., 41. Exactly similar was the lament of Robert Smith, 'I often regretted, from the speed of our progress down, my inability to transfer many of these scenes to paper, and my sketchbook presents numerous fragments of drawings begun, truly "pencillings by the way", which I must now trust to memory to fill up.' Robert Smith had prepared a *Pictorial journal of travels in Hindustan from 1828–33*. Quoted from Archer, *British Drawings*.
83 Hodges, *Travels*, direct quotes are from pages 41, 42 and 43 respectively.
84 I have borrowed this term from Dyson, *A Various Universe*, 135.
85 Deane, *A Tour*, 227.

town often 'terminated the view down the river'.[86] At many points there was nothing visible but water.[87] For still another, the 'prospect was hounded mostly by the banks of the river'.[88] Cities and towns were seen from a distance and this was the preferred perspective because the 'approach-view' provided the most picturesque frame. Looking out of his window, our anonymous traveller, on approaching Rajmahal, said:

> Except in one spot, where a few huts were huddled together near the slope of one of the lowest Hills and a little of the Jungle cleared away in that vicinity I could observe no signs of habitation, neither Road nor path were discernable. But notwithstanding all these drawbacks on the Picturesque there was still a general fascination about the scene which was highly pleasing and I spent the greater part of the day in feasting my eyes on the green mass of mountain and trying to catch some of the beauties on paper.[89]

How a space could seem uninhabited, blank and without any sign of civilization (and also without any picturesque traces for the author, which shows how vaguely the picturesque genre was understood) is best illustrated in the above remark. Long before the author had made this journey, the Rajmahal hills and its inhabitants were visited and written about by Europeans.[90] However, if these remarks are read on their own they present a perfect case of erasure, an erasure which was not only an ideological construct of the travelling gaze but also an outcome of the obstructed limited gaze that a moving boat allowed. The obverse side of this limitedness was that the distant view of the towns, the invisibility while travelling on the river and the limited opportunity to go into the towns, was creating an idea of a closed space, a space that was close enough but nevertheless distant. The travellers did disembark from the boats to take a walk on the shore or to sketch, and even sometimes rode into the town but, as A. Deane put it, 'the travel by the river was literally confined to the river'.[91] Sometimes many of the *budgerows* (a contemporary Anglicized word for one of the most popular type of boats in Bengal, *bajrah*) did not allow a direct view of the outside for those seated inside, and even if they did, some of the travellers preferred to gaze out while being seated on a sofa with their 'glass eyes' (in all probably they meant telescope).[92] They seldom came out on the deck because the deck and the roof of the boat were occupied by 'native' boatmen and other servants.[93] In Charles D'Oyly's

---

86 Anon., *Journal*, 21. On pages 25–6, he complains that the 'usual line of wood always contracts one's views in this level country to a narrow Boundary'.
87 Ibid., 29.
88 Bayley, *Journal of a route*, 9.
89 Anon., *Journal*, 40–41.
90 Thomas Shaw, 'On the Inhabitants of the Hills near Rajamahall', *Asiatic Researches*, 4, 1801. [Henceforth *AR*.]
91 Deane, *A Tour*, 226.
92 Anon., *Journal*, 11.
93 In a Benares/Patna style of mica painting of 1830 a British European military officer is shown travelling in a budgerow with a Union flag flying on its mast. While the officer is shown inside the cabin, the open space on the deck and the rooftop is occupied by the dandies and servants, fourteen in number. Three of them are sitting on the deck, one of which, who appears to be the head *manjhee* (boatman), is smoking hookah. Add. Or. 2672, *P&D*. Sometimes, in the evenings, as Hawkins and his friends used to, they did go atop the boat to catch the fresh breeze. *Diaries and Letters*, B 365/4, 3.

INDIA AND ITS INTERIORS 43

Plate 3. Ranny Ghaut in the city of Patna from the west

© British Library Board, D'Oyly, *Behar Amateur Lithographic Scrap Book*, 1828, plate 32.

Plate 4. View on the River Ganges

© British Library Board, D'Oyly, *Behar Amateur*, plate 24.

numerous sketches, the river is the main subject depicted. His long stay at Patna and his travels by river account for this. The ghats occupied an important place. He sketched almost all the ghats of Patna. With the ghats came the depiction of boats, *patellas*, bathing scenes, a decaying fort or temple on the riverside with a huge *peepal* or banyan tree (see Plates 3 and 4).[94]

However, it would be erroneous to impute any homogeneity to this Gangascape. And this also leads, as we will soon note, to the simultaneous and paradoxical processes of resurrecting the interior from a distance and also going into it; in other words, to the double process of erasure and recognition, which together characterized colonial objectification. First, the river itself changed its nature at different stages of travel. Starting from Calcutta, most of the observers experienced 'a new epoch in the voyage' after crossing places such as Sooty, when the 'Ganges burst upon the view' with an 'endless expanse of water ahead'.[95] In fact, even for those who travelled by the road running parallel to the river (the old Gangetic road), this change was perceptible. After passing Murshidabad, Forrest described his journey as 'coming upon the main body of the Ganges' (remember that he was travelling by road), which gave a view of 'an immense and grand expanse of water, rather resembling an inland sea than a river'.[96] Second, the constant shift in the course of the river changed the landscape in every season and perceptive eyes were adept at noticing this. We are here not referring to professional surveyors such as James Rennell, who, during his survey of the Ganga, reached Saatpur (a place that he had visited the previous year in June) in September 1764 and observed: 'There had been so much of the Bank carried away by the Freshes, that we hardly knew the place again; & could not have found the Mark out had it not been for a remarkable Tree which I had formerly took ye [the] bearings of.'[97] The shifts were also evident to the general travellers.[98] Third, the nature of landforms as seen along or from the river was not static either. The change in the course of the Ganga, reflected in corresponding changes in landforms, was described as a subject of 'wonder to the generality of Europeans residing in these provinces'.[99] New islands were regularly formed, cultivation carried out, settlements established which led, among other things, to litigation and disputes over the possession of land.[100] The role of the weather in

---

94 Charles, D'Oyly, *Behar Amateur Lithographic Scrap Book* (1828); *Selection from the Early Experiments of the Bahar Amateur Lithographic Press* (1828?); *Amateur Repository of Indian Sketches*, pt 1 (Calcutta, 1828); *Behar Amateur Lithographic Scrap Book* (1828). All these volumes are in AAC.
95 Anon., *Journal*, 26.
96 Forrest, *A Picturesque Tour*, 132.
97 T. H. D. la Touche, ed., *The Journals of Major James Rennell* (Calcutta, 1910), 26.
98 Anon., *Journal*, 11–12. The encroachment by the river at Plassey was so extensive that the author identified the place only after he was halfway past it. See page 16. For the same place in a review of the travel account it was said that the encroachment has been so extensive that 'every trace is obliterated' and only 'a few miserable huts' now remain. The work under review was *Sketches of India; Or Observations Descriptive of the Scenery, & c. of Bengal. Written in India, in the years 1811, 12, 13, 14; together with Notes on the Cape of Good Hope and St. Helena, written at those Places in February, March, and April, 1815* (London, 1816). The author and the reviewer are anonymous. It appears that the reviewer had spent some time in India (although it is not known in which capacity, that is, as a traveller or as an administrator). The review was published in *AJ* 2, 1816. Direct quotes are from 589–90.
99 R. H. Colebrooke, 'On the Course of the Ganges through Bengal', *AR* 7 (1803): 1.
100 For such instances on the River Gandak see Meena Bhargava, 'Changing River Courses in North India: Calamities, Bounties, Strategies – Sixteenth to Early Nineteenth Centuries',

this diversity was crucial. On his second visit upland with Hastings, which commenced in the rainy month of June in 1781, Hodges observed that every natural object had donned a new face. The dense foliage, rich luxuriance and the green vegetation – standard ways of describing the landscape – were thus not just a fixed representative style, but, at least for Hodges, a function of the cyclical change in weather.[101] Colebrooke accounted for the rain-induced change in the face of the country in the following manner:

> ...large portion of the bank sunk into the channel, nay, even whole fields and plantations have been in sometimes destroyed and trees, which with the growth of the century, had acquired strength to resist the most violent storms, have suddenly undermined and hurled into streams.[102]

Amidst the processes of colonial objectifications, the space retained its flexible character. Of course, the colonial thrust was to have a fixed understanding of it, which can be seen in the travelling practices. Rennell's guides and maps were often part of the itinerary, as they were for our anonymous traveller, but still, the limitation can be seen in his frustration to locate the grove, the hunting house and other details near Plassey, which Rennell had denoted in the corner of his map. Inundation of the plains was possibly the reason.[103] Any attempt to understand the processes and mechanisms of the 'production of space', especially for a region like mid-Gangetic Bihar, thus needs to take into account the complementarity of land and water. Together they formed, changed and diversified the nature of space and the way it was seen. Territorially speaking, there was a uniformity ascribed to the stretch of land whose contours were defined by the Ganga. The political implications were also well defined, that is, to uphold British possession and rule. Thus for Forrest the land from the south of the Ganga valley extending from the Bay of Bengal to the source of the river in the Upper Hindustan formed one territorial unit, which was now in British possession.[104] But within this unified space there existed many localities that even to the generalizing European eyes were radically different from each other in terms of landscape and the manners of the people. The scenery kept on changing every few miles from rich cultivation to wooded country, from high-grass jungle to hills and streams. Such details do not present a critique of the picturesque convention; they do, however, question the implications of that convention, which suggests that the gaze was all flattening. My contention is that within the convention that routinized and interiorized India the gaze was both confirming and diverse. It is true, as Archer has argued, that from a number of picturesque prints one cannot make out the specificities of the place, but the accompanying or associated textual information that falls under the same convention of the picturesque

---

The Medieval History Journal 10, no. 183 (2007): 202–4; for the River Kosi see, Christopher V. Hill, *River of Sorrow: Environment and Social Control in Riparian North Bihar, 1770–1994* (Ann Arbor, 1997).
101 Hodges, *Travels*, 37–8.
102 Colebrooke, 'On the Course', 2.
103 Anon., *Journal*, 16.
104 Forrest, *A Picturesque Tour*, 136.

mode of representation seems to suggest a more complex relationship between travel, landscape and colonial power. For instance, administratively, although Bihar was part of the Bengal presidency, the picturesque travelling gaze made sharp distinctions between these two provinces. Telia Gully and Sicri Gully were the two passes through which travellers described entering Bihar (also mentioned as Bahar in early accounts), the 'country' of which was 'more open' than that of Bengal.[105] In every aspect – language, custom, manner and physical appearance of the people, appearance of landscape and huts, and climate – A. Deane noted sharp differences between Bengal and Hindustan, the extents of the latter, for her, starting after Rajmahal.[106] Dietary differences were also accounted for: rice was the staple diet of the Bengalis whereas the people of Hindustan devoured mainly wheat and barley.[107] However, so forceful was the drive to have a fixed and objectified sense of space that when the perpetually fluctuating topography and geography failed to attain that, the imaginative faculty was invoked through a word-view to stabilize the space:

> If we present to our imagination a wide extended plain, with pens for cattle, and a few humble huts, whose tops are crowned with gourds, and the intervening space highly cultivated; suppose wheat, barley, and pulse of all sorts, to be growing in abundance, the flowers of the latter presenting to the eye the variety of rich tints; let us conceive numerous herds of cattle to be grazing, and a few scattered villages at a distance; suppose the horizon to bound the view, with no other remote objects than a long line of grass jungle, and a few trees, which from their great distance on the main land, are barely describable; and we shall have a tolerable picture of an island in the Ganges.[108]

The fourth factor that qualifies the nature of Gangascape is the very act of travel; almost all the travellers whom we have so far discussed travelled both by water and by road. This was akin to a modern-day hop-out/hop-in travel practice in which the long-distance journeys of going up or down the country were accomplished by a variety of mediums: boats, palanquins, horses, elephants and by foot.[109] Leaving the river and going to see some places off the bank was common. This constituted an act of going 'inland'. Hodges went inland, five coss, to 'view the mosque of Moonheir' (present-day Maner), on the River Soane. Similarly, he went 'two miles inland' from the river in Ghazipur to see the remains of a *serai* (rest house).[110] In going inland, Hodges did not fail to account for the 'unfathomable and perhaps impenetrable darkness of Eastern

---

105 Ibid., 139.
106 Deane, *A Tour*, 10–12. For the traveller getting 'instantly struck with the dissimilitude of the two countries', that is, Bengal and Bihar, also see 'Review of *Sketches of India*', 591. As noticed earlier, I suggest that this early colonial spatial understanding of frontiers of Bengal and Hindustan was in common with the late Mughal notions. What subsequently did change was the terminology; starting the journeys from Calcutta upwards some of the travellers used 'Lower Provinces' for Bengal and 'Upper Provinces' for Hindustan (the latter was also used). These two phrases also had administrative meanings. Interestingly, Purab was a term which did not occur in the European vision.
107 Anon., *Journey*, 80–82. For difference in physical appearance and character see 83.
108 Colebrooke, 'On the Course', 2 fn. 6.
109 The account that follows does not suggest that only Europeans travelled by multiple means. In 1776, Mirza Abu Taleb Khan's first journey (of his life or first to Bengal is not clear) with his mother was by land from Lucknow to Patna, and then by boat to Murshidabad. *The Travels*, 10.
110 Hodges, *Travels*, 45, 47.

antiquities'.[111] Access to ruined forts, like that at Lutteefpoor, was described as 'impenetrable'.[112] Accompanying Augustus Cleveland, the collector of Bhagalpur, on his tour to the Jungle Terry areas, Hodges remarked: 'This interior part of the country consists of much wood, intermixed with cultivated ground, and many villages chiefly inhabited by husbandmen.'[113] The inland journey to Sasseram, twenty coss from Buxar, was not only full of inconveniences but the ruined monument itself was standing in a closed space, covered with shrubs and trees.[114] By reading Hodges it becomes clear that the notion of interior or inland was functionally derived from a position linked to the means of communication. To leave the main routes and travel any distance varying from two to twenty cosses involved going 'inland'. The inland was therefore not a fixed spatial entity but a representational mode marking the boundaries of space, which travel and communication together defined. This is what we would call a 'roadscape', whose nature was different from Gangascape. Unless journeying on the road alongside the river, as Forrest did, the roadscape did not present the vastness and sea-like form of the water body, or the appearance of objects as minimal points wherein the high banks obstructed the view. Approaching the city from the road presented a different view. This distinction is best reflected in William P. Okeden's remark about Benares, a city that 'is only handsome from the river' but whose streets are 'too narrow for four people to go abreast'.[115] Similar was Deane's change of perception: the town of Serampur, which presented a 'magnificent front to the river', on a nearer approach was found 'to abound in narrow streets [which were] ill paved, dirty and offensive'.[116] The most significant difference in Deane's account is the treatment of Benares. While inevitably all the travellers arriving there by the river talked about the ghats and minarets, Deane's long description of the city started with the religious segregation of the city-space between Hindus and Muslims, on their festivals that breached the communal faultlines, and the manufactures of the city.[117] Bayley, who

---

111 Ibid., 63.
112 Ibid., 84.
113 Ibid., 86–7.
114 Ibid., 147–8. This mausoleum of Shershah was of great interest to many travellers. The earliest known sketch is by Peter Mundy (1632). Francis Swain Ward, a cadet posted in Bengal and Bihar in 1759–60, made an oil painting of the mausoleum, which was the only north Indian monument among the ten paintings presented to the directors. Catherine Asher argues that the mausoleum did undergo decay as the Daniells' sketch of the monument showed arches in ruins, a work which Asher regards as having 'a high degree of accuracy'. Hodges also referred to the fact that the monument was 'now greatly ruined'. Asher might be correct in believing that the building truly decayed but she fails to consider that this could also have happened because of the penchant for showing buildings in decay. Strangely, Buchanan, who visited the mausoleum in a few years' time, complained precisely about the lack of vegetational cover that 'might have added to the grandeur of the place'. See, Catherine B. Asher, 'The Mausoleum of Sher Shah Suri', *Arribus Asiae* 39, nos. 3–4 (1977): 277; Pauline Rohatgi, 'Preface to a Lost Collection: The Pioneering Art of Francis Swain Ward', in Pauline Rohatgi and Pheroza Godrez, eds, *Under the Indian Sun: British Landscape Artists* (Bombay, 1995), 35.
115 Okeden, *Diary*, 21.
116 Deane, *A Tour*, 6. Reviewing the work of one Mr James Wathen, who after his long travels in Europe and England, came to India and China in the early nineteenth century, the reviewer commented that the 'appearance of Madras from the roads, is new and surprising to the eyes of an Englishman'. The title of Wathen's book was *Journal of a Voyage in 1811 and 1812 to Madras and China*; it was reviewed in *AJ* 2 (1816): 373.
117 Deane, *A Tour*, 78–80.

travelled to Benares by dak, held a similar view. His experience of being *inside* the city was very different from what he expected when viewed from the *outside*, that is, from the river. The varying aspects of monuments with people on the ghats presented to him an eye-arresting scene.[118] Roadscape provided a different set of objects to be seen, sketched and reported. Conspicuous amongst them were the nature of houses, streets, bazaars and the commodities sold therein, village/town productions, people's dress, different types of monuments close to the road and so on.[119] Thus our first point is that the 'roadscape narratives' provided thicker descriptions of not just views and scenes but social and material aspects of the country – unlike the 'Gangascape narratives', which tended to describe standard 'scenic points' from the 'exterior', by viewers who did not know what the 'interior' looked like.[120] While reading Deane's account one observes a brief description given of every town and village that she passed through. The descriptions deal with things 'inside' the place/city, in the same way that her portrayal of Moradabad constituted an act of seeing the interior.[121]

Plate 5. Patna City

© British Library Board, Online gallery, shelfmark: WD2060, item no. f.50.[122]

---

118 Bayley, *Journal of a Route*, 15.
119 Harriot Mary Woodcock, wife of William Woodcock who served in Bihar and UP in the early 1830s, drew sketches of her travel on the NMR and on the north Bihar roads. Most of the sketches depicted monuments, either temples or mosques or gates situated at the roadside. Archer, *British Drawings*.
120 The anonymous traveller thus remarked that although the exterior of the Murshidabad town was 'extremely prepossessing' the interiors (of the town) were unknown as he had no opportunity to know them. Anon., *Journal*, 21.
121 Deane, *A Tour*, 203–4.
122 Precisely from the same point as D'Oyly did, Sita Ram had earlier sketched 'Another view of the Great Choke' which is radically different from D'Oyly's representation of cramped and desolated Patnascape. The houses in Ram's paintings are plastered. The street is wide and clean. See Add. Or. 4700, *P&D*. Greater difference between his and D'Oyly's perception comes out in another watercolour entitled 'Great Choke at Patna' in which the houses are

However, the roadscapes also varied according to the specific pathways taken for travel. In the late eighteenth century, the newly built New Military Road (NMR) provided many picturesque views to the traveller as it crossed through jungles and ghats (hill passes).[123] Here again, precisely because of the jungles, hills and woods, the gaze was allegedly limited and obstructed. Victor Jacquemont, who travelled on a newly built section of the GTR from Calcutta northwards, described, after seven days of travel, the topographical features between Burdwan and Damodar in these terms: 'I have proceeded a hundred leagues along a road, traversed by no path, *bordered, shut in, walled on either side by the forest or desert plains* through which it has been opened.'[124] Even on the more frequented Gangetic road the view was often said to be obstructed by jungles on one side and by the vast expanse of water on the other.[125] Thus the second point about roadscape is that while it provided a more detailed description of the places visited, the journey through the main thoroughfares of the period also added to the notion of impenetrability. High grasses, jungles, the hazards of travelling in terms of fear and attacks by animals created an image of uncontrolled, untamed, dangerous, wild and savage space. The dense foliage compounded the notion of impenetrability, thus highlighting the limits of and risks involved in accessing the interior. Except for the river and the ghat, one can see the remarkable structural similarity in the idea of 'closed space' as represented in Plate 3 (an instance of Gangascape) and Plate 6 depicting roadscape.

Steam, interior, picturesque

This chapter started by outlining the prescribed role of steam in reaching out to the interior as part of the new transport technology that crucially shaped the discourse on the civilizing mission of colonialism. We have looked closely at the travelling gaze and argued that the role of the mode of travelling was an important factor in shaping spatial descriptions. From the late eighteenth century, travel up and down the Ganga was taken as a 'picturesque' journey. It would now be appropriate to note what the introduction of steam did to the interconnected notions of interior and picturesque.

From the second decade of the nineteenth century onwards, many travellers expressed disappointment at the 'loss of picturesque' in their journey up or down the Ganga. In the whole stretch from Bengal to Simla, Emily Eden 'complained of not seeing anything else but flat plains'. Already, after only a few days had elapsed, when they came out of the Sundarbans into the Ganga, G. (referring to her brother, Governor General

---

neatly built, standing in a row, and are usually of three floors. Their fronts usually have carved wooden pillars (of *mehrab* style). Some houses have open terraces, others are thatched (*khappad* style). In the foreground there is a big open field. Pictorially, these two sketches do not give an impression of dirt and wretchedness, the terms in which almost every traveller described Patna. See Add. Or. 4699, *P&D*.
123 Charles D'Oyly, *Sketches of the New Road in a Journey from Calcutta to Gyah* (Calcutta, 1830). More on the NMR in Chapter 3.
124 Victor Jacquemont, *Letters from India Describing a Journey in the British Dominions of India* (London, 1834; repr. Delhi, 1993), 151 (emphasis added).
125 Forrest, *A Picturesque Tour*, 132.

Plate 6. Near Bhood Gyah

© British Library Board, D'Oyly, *Behar Amateur Lithographic Scrap Book*, plate 10.

Auckland) 'was bored to death with having nothing to do'.[126] The Rajmahal hills that had enthralled many earlier travellers now presented to her the ugliest scenery. The only picturesque beauty of that place was its population.[127] In fact, even Calcutta with its splendid buildings and river views had ceased to be regarded as picturesque beauty. This was due to two reasons. First, the neighbouring landscape was seen as uninteresting – flat and tame. Second, as Forrest wrote, the city 'has been so much talked of, and so often described, that nothing new or interesting concerning it can be offered to the reader'. Thus, Forrest advised all those travellers who wanted to explore Bengal's grander and wilder beauties, not to tarry long at Calcutta.[128] To Oakfield, the autobiographical hero of the novel of the same title, 'northern India afforded only a dull landscape in which the rain-swollen Ganges in the evenings afforded "the one beautiful sight"'.[129] Bishop Heber praised the picturesque quality of D'Oyly's landscape sketches of Bihar and argued that 'India is full of beautiful and picturesque country if people would stir but a little away from the banks of the Ganges.'[130] Heber's comment clearly brings home the point that

---

126 Emily Eden, *Up the Country: Letters Written to her Sister from the Upper Provinces of India* (London, 1866), vol. 1, 12 and 6 respectively. The journey started on 27 October 1837 with a fleet that consisted of two steamers.
127 Dyson, *A Various Universe*, 112.
128 Forrest, *A Picturesque Tour*, 123.
129 Dyson, *A Various Universe*, 112.
130 Quoted in J. P. Losty, 'A Career in Art: Sir Charles D'Oyly', in Rohatgi and Godrez, eds, *Under the Indian Sun*, 100. Gradually, the stage of adventure and search for the picturesque shifted

the production of dull and monotonous north India was because of the routinization of the gaze, which in turn was the result of sticking to just one means of communication. Apart from having some excitement at seeing the Government House at Barrackpur and the Dutch town of Chinsura, the cheerless prospect of seeing flat plains on the one side and sandbanks on the other had little interest for James Bayley and his party. Only when they reached Rajmahal did they show some interest in the topography; the reason being the hills that surrounded the region.[131] The second reason for the alleged monotonous landscape was the steam itself. Greater speed attained in travelling via steamships changed the aesthetic gaze of the traveller. The earlier picturesque beauty ceased to be picturesque not only because of the routinization but also because steam induced new levels of speed that did not provide enough time to gaze in leisurely fashion upon the various objects encountered during the journey.[132] While traversing Patna, Eden accepted that 'there never was anything so provokingly picturesque' but lamented that 'the steamer goes boring on without the slightest regard for our love of sketching'.[133] As shown in Prinsep's sketch of the *Hooghly* or in William Simpson's sketch of a steamer on one of the rivers in the Punjab,[134] one notices that a steamer was incorporated into the framework of picturesque representation; but it would be misleading to assume that such depictions did not work the other way round. In other words, if steam were incorporated into the existing representational mode, the act of 'steaming' also changed the nature of the latter. The loss of the picturesque was anticipated by many, more acutely with the prospects of railway travelling. Reminiscing about her journey, Eden wrote that now, after considerable changes in the modes of transport in India having taken place, her account 'of a journey that was picturesque in its motley processions' would appear amusing.[135] Accepting the fact that now 'travelling is destined to become less picturesque', Henry Lawrence nevertheless consoled himself (and his journal audience) that journeys would, however, become easier and faster. He also was hopeful that, in the long run, railways

---

    to the mountainscape. The hills now presented a new site of relationality – home away from home where the cold climate reminded Europeans of the English landscape. As late as 1877 Lord Lytton had said: 'I affirm it [Ootacamund] to be a paradise… The afternoon was rainy and the road muddy… but such *English* rain and such delicious *English* mud.' Similarly, many of the travel guides described the Nilgiris hills as 'half-English'. Judith T. Kenny, 'Climate, Race, and Imperial Authority: The Symbolic Landscape of the British Hill Station in India', *Annals of the Association of American Geographers* 85, no. 4 (1995): 702, 708. Before starting his tour in 1837, Auckland had purchased a house in Simla in 1836, 'without informing anybody'. Emily Eden described this house as 'a cheerful middle-sized English country-house, and extremely enjoyable'. Jagmohan Mahajan, *The Grand Indian Tour: Travels and Sketches of Emily Eden* (New Delhi, 1996), 78–9. On the idea of 'preventive and recreational values of hill stations' see, J. E. Spencer and W. L. Thomas, 'The Hill Stations and Summer Resorts of the Orient', *Geographical Review* 38, no. 4 (1948): 639–40.
131 Bayley, *Journal of a Route*, 29.
132 A point made in regard to early railway travelling experiences in Wolfgang Schivelbusch, *The Railway Journey: The Industrialisation of Time and Space in the Nineteenth Century* (Berkeley and CA, 1986).
133 Eden, *Up the Country*, 15.
134 Archer, *British Drawings*, 2, plate 78.
135 Eden, *Up the Country*, v–vi.

would 'supply quite as many objects of interest as they [would] take away'.[136] We will follow another anonymous traveller in his downward journey from Benares to Calcutta in the steamer named *Mirzapore* to observe this change.[137]

Presenting many interesting details of life on board relating to food, the recreational activities engaged in by the passengers, the composition (class and gender wise) of the passengers and so on, the author mentions that places such as Chunar, Benares, Monghyr, Rajmahal and the whole stretch from Berhampur to Calcutta turned every passenger 'to whom the scene was not familiar' into a gazer.[138] Some ideas as to the nature of this gaze can be formed from his own words:

> The rich cities of Bengal – Moorshedabad, Bandal, Hoogly, Chinsura, Chandernagore, Serampore – crowd each other so fast that one cannot remember their order. All contain well built houses inhabited by all colours and castes; crowds of boats, crowds of uncovered black heads of Bengalis. Here a tall chimney with black smoke tells of a printing press, another there is a cannon foundry…[139]

Not only, evidently, did speed affect the likelihood of registering the basic order of progression (of places), but the landscape described was different. It was not a landscape marked with ruins and falling buildings but one of new institutions and sites of governance. The latter was not a steam-propelled change but a shift that signified a change in the ideology of colonial rule, of which steam was a part. This shift can be seen even without steam being the travelling agent, although it is one in which the new steam technology was conspicuous; in another journey undertaken by the same writer in November 1853 by a budgerow, he observed and talked about a suspension bridge, a railway bridge and the railway stations at Barrackpur, Chandernagar, Hooghly and Burdwan. He reported on telegraph posts on the road and expected that with the coming of the railways the roads would improve and amenities such as hotels would follow. The existing picture was of a 'dusty plain and apparent confusion' which, however, would soon change.[140]

Conclusions

In attaining this change the alleged superiority of British scientific knowledge and enterprise, of which new means of communication were a part, was crucial. Highlighting the advantages

---

136 Lawrence's note in *Homeward Bound* 23 (September 1856), 168. The loss of aesthetic was not specific to colonialism; on similar debates in the West see Schivelbusch, *The Railway Journey*.
137 Anon., Mss Eur. B 242, 1853–54.
138 The visual representation of travelling does confirm this in some indirect ways. In a watercolour (lithographed) painting from 1863 made by one Becaram Das Pande, three Europeans, two male and a female, are shown on the deck; one of the males is gazing with a telescope while the other is standing beside the lady who is seated on a chair. This representation is symbolic: this is a steam pedal boat with only three Europeans on board, which given the cost and hazards involved in the steam navigation, would practically never have happened. Add. Or. 3803, *P&D*.
139 Anon., Mss Eur. B 242, 1853–54.
140 Ibid.

of railways, it was claimed: 'As a proof that without the intervention of British enterprise and British science the soil might remain a desert forever, glance at the state of communication throughout India at this moment, and save in a few instances where roads have been opened by Government, what is it?'[141] This change in technology and ideology accompanied the change in the meaning of interior. On the one hand, by reducing the duration of the gaze, increased speed reinforced the idea of closed spaces and interiors; on the other, the interior itself, from being earlier seen as a reservoir of picturesque objects, changed into a repository of hidden wealth and resources that needed to be exploited by opening them up – the debate with which we started this chapter. It was not that this change suddenly presented itself in the 1820s and 1830s, to consolidate thereafter. More subtly, the shift was related to the necessities of the variety of knowledge that the colonial state had been acquiring since the late eighteenth century. The picturesque movement ran parallel to many other forms of narration and representation of/about India. One such was the knowledge of minerals and resources. Since this aspect came to closely define 'interior' in the period of the 1820s and 1830s, we will conclude by briefly discussing some of the features of this aspect.

The trend in geological collections (dealing directly with minerals, the 'natural wealth' of the country) started under the aegis of the Asiatic Society of Bengal set up in 1784. By the turn of the century, geology, together with natural science, had become a prime subject in the society's journal. An increasing number of articles were submitted in the field of mineralogy, geology and meteorology between the 1780s and 1820s.[142] Many amateur geologists from within the Company establishment, such as surgeons, botanists, engineers, revenue officials, officials of the Trigonometrical Survey of India, and also missionaries, sent in contributions.[143] A number of professionals also tried making a mark in this field. Notable amongst them was one Mr Andrew Duncan who arrived in Bengal in 1810 to explore the possibilities of founding an ironworks in the province.[144] Duncan was allowed only a limited sum to set up a foundry, because although the Bengal government regarded such works as objects of extreme importance, the financial restriction imposed by the higher authorities in London was severe: 'But as we entertain strong doubts as to the policy of encouraging the prosecution of such works to any extent, we direct that no further expense may be incurred than what may be

---

141 'Letter from Joseph Locke on Advantages of Railways in India', 11 February 1843, *SD*, doc. no. 10, 20.
142 In a survey of articles published in the *Journal of the Asiatic Society*, Deep Kanta L. Choudhuri shows that the number of average articles published on geology increased from 0.6 in 1788 to 11.4 (1825), 8.4 (1834), 9.0 (1839) and 8.6 (1844). The interest in geography was also on rise: from 1.0 in 1788 to 3.6 (1825), 8.2 (1834), 7.4 (1839) and 5.4 in 1844. Choudhuri, 'Communication and Empire: The Telegraph in North India c. 1830–1856' (unpublished MPhil dissertation, Centre for Historical Studies, Jawaharlal Nehru University, 1997), 48.
143 Savithri Preetha Nair, 'Science and the Politics of Colonial Collecting: The Case of Indian Meteorites, 1856–70', *British Journal for History of Science* 39, no. 1 (2006): 98–9.
144 Duncan had served in the iron manufactory at Carron, in Scotland, before proceeding to Russia with Sir Charles Gascoigne, who employed him in establishing the ironworks at Petersavasky. He remained there for fifteen years during which time he reportedly became qualified to manage the business of an iron foundry. He left Russia and returned to England in 1807. See 'Erection of Iron Works under the Superintendence of Mr Duncan', Board of Control, F/4/489 11862. [Henceforth Bcl.]

Plate 7. Pen sketch of coalfields of west Burdwan

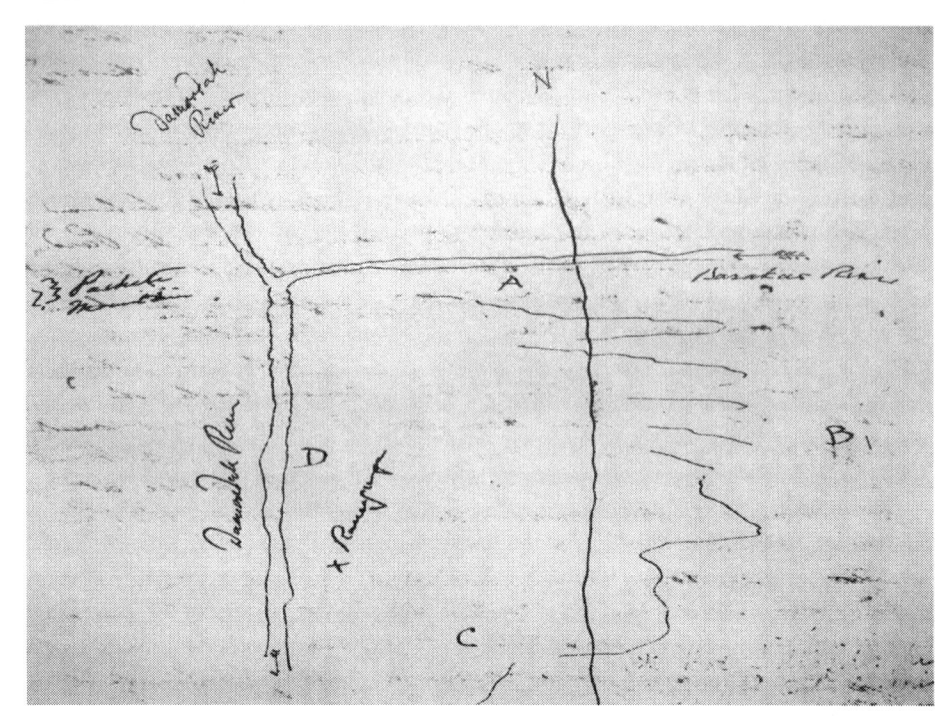

© British Library Board, Mss Eur B 242, 1853–55.

necessary to enable you to report to us the result of Mr Duncan's experiments.'[145] In spite of such stringency, the interior continued to be visited by interested people. In the 1810s, under the direction of Mr Colebrooke, one Mr Jones was sent to examine the Burdwan coalbeds, which were discovered by a Mr Stark in 1804. In the same decade, Mr Stark discovered coal in the Sylhet district. After the introduction of steam navigation, the already known coalbeds in the Palamow region attracted the attention of the principal civil officer, Mr A. Prinsep. Following this, the region was 'visited by scientific and practical men'.[146]

'A more serious dimension to geological collecting and research' came in the 1830s.[147] Though it took another two decades for a professional institution, the Geological Survey

---

[145] 'Extract Public Letter to Bengal', 29 July 1814, ibid.
[146] J. M. McClelland, *Report of a Committee for Investigating the Coal and Mineral Resources of India* (Calcutta, 1838), 47–52, 64. Another region that was explored was the Bhagalpur district by one Mr Tanner of the revenue survey department. His encouraging findings were published in the *Government Gazette* with a conclusion that several other coal deposits as indicated by him could be rendered useful 'by an improvement of roads'; in fact, the article even proposed a railway from the hills to the Ganga in case the demand for the mineral justified the cost. 'Native Coal', *AJ* (new series) 5 (1831): 202–3.
[147] Nair, 'Science and the Politics', 98–9. Also see Daniel J. Rycroft, *Representing Rebellion*, ch. 1. In the light of the above discussion it would, however, be difficult to accept Rycroft's claim that 'The impact of economic geology in India was marked by the arrival of the Committee for Mineral Resources in 1836' (17).

of India (GSI), to be established in 1850, 'every friend of India and practical men, with whose departments the physical character of the country is nearly connected' were enjoined to contribute to the 'full development of the agricultural and mineral resources of the country'.[148] A number of amateurish geologists were surveying the regions where mineral wealth was in concentration, and reporting on subjects such as the process of production, the nature of monopoly and the further ways of improving production and control. The samples collected were sent to the Museum of the Economic Geology.[149] Individuals such as W. S. Sherwill contributed on almost all the important 'themes' of colonial knowledge, ranging from revenue survey, which was his most immediate concern, to geology.[150] Such a mapping of resources led to curious namings, for instance, 'Coal Districts', which numbered twenty-seven between 1804 and 1837.[151] Many of the texts on economic geology written in this period, which were based on extensive tours, can be understood as a corpus revealing the transition from picturesque narrations to those displaying an intense professionalized gaze.[152] The picturesque monument was turned into a utilitarian building; for instance, the ruined marble building of Rajmahal became the reservoir for coal supply to small steamboats navigating the Ganga.[153] However, picturesque sensibilities lingered.[154] These texts were at the cusp of 'statistical reports' in the Buchanian format and latter-day departmentalized knowledge blocks. For instance, people such as Sherwill, although inclined to report on specific issues like revenue or geology, in reality touched upon a wide range of subjects, from rock types to crop production and from social practices to trading circuits and routes and the condition of roads. The pen sketch of the coal tracks of Burdwan in the diary of our anonymous steamship traveller is interesting, as it suggests this shift in what was desirable to be seen in the changed context of the utilization of resources and facilitation of trade through better means of communications.

This opening up of the resources and wealth that became instrumental to secure and promote British metropolitan growth tagged itself on to the debates on communication

---

148 Nair, 'Science and the Politics', 100.
149 Welby Jackson, 'Memorandum on the Iron Works of Beerbhoom', *JASB* 14, pt 2, no. 166 (December 1845): 754–6.
150 See his 'A Sketch of the Behar Mica Mines', *JASB* 20, no. 4 (1851); 'Notes Upon a Tour through the Rajmahal Hills', *JASB* 20, no. 7 (1851).
151 McClelland, *Committee for Investigating the Coal*, 19.
152 A very apt comparison can be made between the D'Oyly's *Sketches of the New Road* and Dr J. Row's 'Geological Remarks'. They both travelled on the same road and saw the same places but their gaze differed. For D'Oyly it was the 'picturesque' that mattered the most; for Row, the nature of rocks and their abundance characterized the landscape. See, J. Row, 'Geological Remarks during the March from Benares (Old Road) via Hazareebaugh, Bankoora and Burdwan to Barrackpoor', *JASB* 13, pt 2, no. 155 (1844): 862–6.
153 *Diaries and Letters*, Mss Eur. B 365/4 ff. 1–28.
154 Thomas Oldham, 'Notes upon the Geology of the Rajmahal Hills: Being the Result of Examinations Made During the Cold Season of 1852–53', *JASB* 23, no. 3 (1854): 264, 267, 270. It should be remembered that Rajmahal was regarded as the most picturesque region since the early days of colonial rule. It was also of peculiar interest to the English reader because of the 'happy triumphs of civilization' that A. Cleveland achieved through his efforts in 'civilizing' the hillmen. 'Review of *Sketches of India*', 590.

circulating in this period, promising not only to deliver tighter administrative control over the colony but also to help achieve the necessities of economy and commerce. The zones of the interior came under the scrutiny of successive tours, each aiming to attain a higher level of understanding and explore the possibility of opening them up. For instance, the Rajmahal hills underwent three successive tours in a period of five years. McClelland gave a description of the 'small portion of the southern end of the range' in 1848–49; Sherwill toured in 1851, and Oldham in 1852–53.[155] The earlier picturesque-generated hierarchies did not dissolve. Rather they were consolidated, but with meanings that were closer to utilitarian logic, 'useful knowledge' and 'moral and material' progress. Sherwill's following remarks best represent this change:

> Although every European proceeding up the Ganges passes immediately under these hills, and although they are only two miles removed from the banks of the river, the hills and their contained valleys are not only unexplored, but not even generally known that the hills are inhabited; the general received opinion being that the Rajmahal Hills are as uninhabited jungle; that such is not the case I hope to show, having penetrated into almost every valley and climbed all the principal hills, during the progress of the survey under my charge.[156]

As argued throughout this chapter, rather than a fixed spatial zone, the 'interior' represented a floating ideational category that was both seen from a distance and traversed through. I chose to end this chapter with examples from geological tours because in the 'opening up' debate it was the resources that became the main characteristic of the interior. But, in addition, the act of 'going into the interiors' had other implications, and to these we now turn.

---

155 Similarly, the Singhbhoom region also attracted conspicuous attraction not only because of its iron and coal deposits but also its gold mines. Mr Robinson toured fifty miles in the region in 1849; J. C. Haughton surveyed the area again in the early 1850s. Haughton, 'Memorandum on the Geological Structure and Mineral Resources of the Singhbhoom Division', *JASB* 23, nos. 1–7 (1854): 108–9.
156 Sherwill, 'Notes upon a Tour through the Rajmahal Hills', 544.

Chapter 3

GOING INTO THE INTERIORS

Aware of the 'limited gaze' and institutional dependence on existing pre-colonial structures, the English East India Company-state's bureaucracy was clear right from the beginning about attaining maximum self-reliance in its administrative functioning. One way of trying to achieve this was to promote administrative mobility, which was based on the idea of seeing things in person. Among the variety of tours, some of which we have discussed in the previous chapter and some we will see in the next, were official tours, which are the main focus of this chapter. They were performed at different bureaucratic levels according to the cultural–bureaucratic functions of the Raj. They had graded meanings; the ones undertaken by higher officials, for instance, were more like public displays, to both constitute and represent authority. They also aimed at 'inspecting' things. In contrast, the local-level tours of district collectors on horses, elephants apart from representing authority, were of the nature of ground exercises in maintaining 'law and order', reviewing the work of the judiciary and police *thannahs* (police outposts), holding on-the-spot courts to settle judicial and revenue cases, collecting information about local trade networks, weather, communication and so on. They were acts of 'knowing the countryside' by 'going into the interiors'.

The purposes of such tours were utilitarian (to generate knowledge) and also, complementarily, to strike a personal chord with the 'natives'. One strand in the argument about the power of local-level officials is that 'the British district officer was a prisoner if not a puppet of the local social forces'.[1] Another argues that administrative tours crucially helped in transforming the identity of 'white sahibs' from strangers to sovereigns.[2] On the timescale of colonial rule the idea of 'itinerant empire' can be clearly traced, following Bayly, from the 1780s onwards.[3] A further qualitative impetus came in the 1820s–30s when the colonial state tried to mould itself into a 'welfare state'. In this period, as a result of the shifting ideological premises of colonial rule, greater emphasis was put on the collectors' tours. But, in turn, this growing emphasis was matched by the increasingly frequent reproach that collectors often neglected this aspect of their duty, that is, touring. It is not surprising, then, that communication become a panacea for covering up this neglect. Thus, on the one hand, 'communication' and networks of trade constituted one of the main subjects of 'enquiry' during the tours while, on the other, the same subject

---

1 Eric Stokes, 'The First Century of British Colonial Rule in India: Social Revolution or Social Stagnation', *Past and Present* 58 (1973): 147.
2 Gayatri C. Spivak, 'The Rani of Sirmur: An Essay in Reading the Archives', *History and Theory* 24, no. 3 (1985).
3 Bayly, 'Knowing the Country', 26–7. The phrase 'itinerant empire' is borrowed from Arnold, *The Tropics*.

was thought to bolster up the touring efficiency of the *mai-baap* of the British *sarkar*. The flip side of such arguments, however, was surprisingly paradoxical. Contrary to the later official belief that better means of communication would consolidate the Raj, the change in techniques of communication made the nodes of power more fluid and thus more debilitating from the Raj's point of view. True, the latter half of the nineteenth century was marked by an enormous increase in and employment of new techniques of knowledge generation, such as the census, and by the growth of specialized areas of knowledge, such as archaeology, geology and so on; but this expansion was akin to departmental routinization that paradoxically came at the expense of the erosion of the image of mai-baap. This chapter will later outline some of the links between the expansion in communication networks and the simultaneous erosion of the paternalist disposition of colonial legitimacy.

There is another link that, although not paradoxical, should be noted. At the same time as the new steam technology and the idea of communication reform emerged in the 1820s, so too did the urge to regulate and regularize officials' touring activities. Furthermore, some serious and at times rhetorical critiques of the EIC's policies in regard to communication came to light. Claims such as one made by Tremenheere that until the 1820s 'nothing was done' and that 'beyond twenty miles from Calcutta the roads communicating with the principal stations in the Upper Provinces, were in no better state than in the time of the Moguls' were frequently made.[4] A closer look at the earlier phase nonetheless tells a different story. Trade being one of the mainstays of the early period, the Company-state was not only aware of the importance of good roads but also tried improving them. This does not contradict the nature of colonial rule as noted above in relation to adoption of steam technology. It is true that the early response was slow but this does not warranty a historiographical recounting that swings between the absolute position of 'no work' or 'great works'. The second half of this chapter delineates some of the efforts made under the early colonial rule, which serve as a corrective to the charges made by officials such as Bentinck and Tremenheere and to the silences in the standard historiography. Interestingly, touring once again had an important administrative contribution to make as it was one of the important mediums through which knowledge about road conditions was obtained, and further actions taken.

At the time when the notion of 'interior' was becoming established, a simultaneous drive to traverse the interior was also developing strongly. Some of the travellers whom we have discussed earlier were also going 'inland'. Most of those journeys were made along thoroughfares (either on the river, or on the Gangetic route and later on the NMR), covering a wide geographical area. The travellers, apart from seeing routinized places of interest, occasionally – and especially from the 1820s onwards when this routinization was making travelling and landscape dull – left the main routes and ventured into the 'interiors'. This was, however, just one kind of going into the interiors. Another, which existed in parallel, was the official tour that had a different and diverse purpose and circuit of mobility. This was not just a journey in the search of the picturesque or a vocational trip propelled by the urge to sketch the Indian landscape. Of course, officers

---

4 Tremenheere, *On Public Works*, 7.

on tour reported and also sketched 'picturesque scenes', but the fundamental difference between this form of mobility and others was that their administrative nature made such tours primarily acts of information gathering. The information acquired was of a wide range, from topography to geography, from climate to crop production, from routes and roads to trade and local markets – the itinerant collector tried to observe everything.[5] This difference added another characteristic to these tours: administrative tours in the localities inevitably required officials to leave the main routes and enter into the byways, into unknown territory and routes. Many a time, this made the touring officials the first Europeans to be seen in the regions they visited, often causing a mixed range of reactions from the natives, from surprise and curiosity to fear and flight. During his tour Rennell remarked on 'countrey [sic] People deserting the Villages on our approach' and informing them that 'that they never saw any Europeans pass this way'.[6] However, as noted in the last chapter, the claim of 'being the first' was also a rhetorical ploy to ascribe credibility and truthfulness to the account, and hence needs to be treated with caution. On entering the city of Patna, Francis Buchanan's *palki* (palanquin) was overrun by women and by children in particular, making him feel that they had not seen a European before. Buchanan might have felt this, but factually it was not so.[7] However, a factor that crucially differentiated the tours of the likes of Buchanan from the tours of higher officials, such as the up-country tours of governor generals, was that the latter were conducted along a fixed itinerary, with great planning done in advance. An example of this can be deduced from Governor General Amherst, who, in January (while already on tour), took the decision that on his return to Calcutta he would leave for 'Eurmutogar Ghant' ghat five months later on 20 June. To plan this trip, the accompanying officers were requested to send in their indents for the boats required.[8]

Vice-Regal Processions

Touring the empire both in colonial and pre-colonial times had always been part of the bureaucratic attempt to know the conditions of and pacify the ruled, and also to demonstrate the authority of the ruler. The British believed that they were following the already established practice of native princely tours. Early nineteenth-century British views confirmed this; on his journey to India Lord Valentia remarked, 'I wish India to be ruled from a palace, not from a counting house, with the ideas of a prince, not with those of a retail dealer in muslin and indigo.'[9] India was seen as a land of opulence, splendour, extravagance and of outward appearances,

---

5 Not only collectors but route surveyors also (on which we will see further in the next chapter) were instructed to enter details in their journals such as 'river crossings, access to portable water, all impediments, descriptions of every town and villages passed, remarks on the wind and the weather, the composition of the soil, the variety and health of crops, and a sketch of the journey'. Ian Barrow, *Making History Drawing Territory: British Mapping in India, c. 1765–1905* (Oxford and New Delhi, 2003), 78.
6 Touche, ed., *The Journals*, 14, 20.
7 Buchanan, *An Account of the Districts of Behar and Patna in 1811–12* (Patna, 1934), vol. 1, 9, 62.
8 Edward Ward Walter Raleigh, '*The Log of a Griffin*', Mss Eur. D 786, 46.
9 'Accepted Travellers', 297.

and hence he further argued that the '[h]ead of a mighty empire ought to conform himself to the prejudices of the country he rules over'.[10] One such prejudice was the act of making extravagant tours, as he himself did, with a long entourage. Pre-colonial royal and imperial journeys, campaigns and hunting expeditions numbered in the thousands. The excursions were well planned; *mir manzil* (equivalent to the quartermaster of the colonial times) looked after the organization of the *peshkhima*, the party that marched ahead of the royal entourage to pitch the tents. A strict hierarchy was followed in the allocation of space in the camps. The emperor and royal princes and nobles had separate bazaars close to their tents.[11] These royal movements were widely reported by European travellers. The wide-scale movements of Mughal and other emperors and notables became a theme of visual representation with some early European residents and artists. Gentil's Collection (mostly furnished by Indian artists) had paintings of a visit made by the 'zenana of Muhammad Shah' in which the ladies were shown indulging in various forms of recreation, and also of an entourage of Mughal Emperor Shah Alam II with his sons, who were on a visit to Shuja al-Daula, ruler of Oudh.[12] The plate below, sketched by Zoffany, shows the march of Haider Beg, minister of Asaf al-Daula, nawab of Oudh (1785–90), passing through Patna on his way to meet Governor General Cornwallis. Such entourages usually consisted of a motley collection of animals (such as elephants and horses), foot soldiers with their wives and attendants, a *nautch* group, fakirs, bearers, vegetable sellers and even missionaries and doctors. An Englishman who accompanied Asaf al-Daula for four months between October 1793 and January 1794 on a hunting expedition says that the whole party 'consisted of about 40,000 men, and 20,000 beasts; composed of 10,000 soldiers, 1,000 cavalry, and near 150 pieces of cannon; 1,500 elephants, 3,000 carts or hackeries, and an innumerable train of camels, horses, and bullocks'.[13]

The show of extravagance so categorically emphasized by Lord Valentia was best reflected in the convoys of governor generals. Similar to Mughal practices, the colonial 'royal' entourage consisted of thousands of people and a motley of objects. As *mansabdars* and other officers of the empire accompanied the emperor or princes previously, now governor generals were followed by a retinue of staff, both civil and military (and also chaplains and doctors). The size of the fleet used to be equally impressive. William Hodges described Warren Hastings' upland tour undertaken in 1781 as 'comprising a very large fleet, consisting of every variety of the boats of the country but one'.[14] Lord Hastings' upcountry tour in 1814–15, again on the River Ganga, was a matter of visual display with a large flotilla of boats.[15] The river fleet of Lord Amherst's tour in 1827–28 consisted of a number of officers, a regiment of infantry and a group of bodyguards,

---

10 Views of Lord Valentia, as expressed at the inaugural ceremony of Government House in 1803. Quoted in Jagmohan Mahajan, *The Raj Landscape: British Views of Indian Cities* (New Delhi, 1988), 45.
11 Abul Khair M. Farooque, *Roads and Communications in Mughal India* (Delhi, 1977), 88–92.
12 Archer, *Company Paintings*, 119–20. Another set showing the procession of Shah Alam II from Lucknow to Delhi on page 124.
13 'An Account of a Hunting Party', *AJ* 1 (1816): 539.
14 Hodges, *Travels*, 38.
15 See for instance a watercolour drawing of the procession by the Patna artist Sita Ram. Add. Or. 4711, *P&D*.

Plate 8. Haider Beg, with the Company's Lucknow resident and Zoffany on a march

© British Library Board, Wilmot Corfield, *Calcutta Faces and Places in Pre-Camera Days* (Calcutta, 1910), shelfmark: W 4399, page 28.

comprising 600 horses. Altogether, the fleet consisted of twenty pinnaces and about 700 other boats of various descriptions.[16] Later, Lord Auckland's upcountry trip in 1837 was, as one reviewer put it, 'a major operation involving carriages, boats, palanquins, riding horses, some 850 camels and 140 elephants'.[17] Emily Eden, describing her outings in the Upper Provinces, wrote of, 'nine Europeans of steady age and respectable habits, going galloping every morning at sunrise over a sandy plain, followed by quantities of black horsemen and then by ten miles of beasts of burden carrying things'.[18] Even non-viceregal processions, like those of the Daniells in which there were only fifteen Europeans, comprised some 3,000 attendants and camp followers.[19]

---

16 Raleigh, '*The Log of a Griffin*', 2. Raleigh accompanied in the capacity of doctor. He arrived in Calcutta on 7 July 1826, was appointed surgeon to Lord Amherst in 1828 and remained in the Bengal Medical Service for fourteen years. He died on 22 January 1865. The typescript transcript of his diary is kept together with the handwritten one. I am following the pagination given on the top right-hand side of the typescript. The typescript is full of errors and hence it is advisable to check it against the handwritten manuscript.
17 Dorothy Middleton, 'Review', *The Geographical Journal* 150, no. 1 (1984): 105. [Henceforth *GJ*.]
18 Mahajan, *The Grand Indian Tour*, 111.
19 Evan Cotton, 'The Daniells in India', *BPP* 37, no. 3, pt 1 (1929): 2.

By the closing decades of the eighteenth century such tours had become a regular and standardized administrative ritual that involved meeting native chiefs and princes en route. The ritual started with a salute of guns for the travelling officer.[20] The fleets were further honoured with gun salutes from troops lined up on the riverbanks. The native rulers often came down a few stations from their seats of authority to receive the governor generals. The dignitaries were received with pomp: the nawab vizier of Oudh announced the arrival of Lord Valentia by posting a messenger on the road, announcing: 'Lord Saheb ka bhanja, Company ka nawasa teshrif laia.'[21] When the tour came to a halt, camps were thrown up in the most splendid way, in a display of grandeur, and *durbars* (royal ceremonial space displaying ruler's authority) were held where gifts and visits were exchanged.[22] While a good number of studies exist on durbar practices and the rituals of authority that were followed (and invented) during colonial times, very few have focused on the 'rituals of travelling' that rehearsed many of the similar practices and notions of hierarchy and authority. The undeniable purpose was to uphold British paramountcy vis-à-vis the natives; the gesture of nawabs and *rajas* (native rulers and princes) travelling from their seats of power to receive the head of the colonial government was symbolic of their subordinate position, which the European well understood. When the raja of Hurdwar came down to receive the party of A. Deane, one of his servants presented gold *mohurs* (coins) on a napkin that Deane and his colleagues touched with the tips of three fingers. The mohurs then were taken away, on which Deane remarked: 'It is merely a form in the person offering, to denote that he [the raja] acknowledges himself an inferior.'[23]

Time and again it was claimed that it was necessary to follow 'the etiquette of [the] oriental visit', which indeed was done; but I argue that these rituals of travelling meant

---

20 In 1801, Marques Wellesley was given a salute of nineteen guns from the ramparts of Fort William on his departure to the Upper Provinces. 'Journal of the Route of the Marquis Wellesley to the Upper Provinces', *The Asiatic Annual Register* 4 (1802). [Henceforth *AAR*.] The tour started on 15 August 1801. The same number of guns were fired in salute for Lord Moira when he returned to Calcutta from his upcountry tour. See *AJ* 2 (1816): 205.

21 'Lord [Wellesley] sister's son, and the grandson of Mrs Company has arrived.' The Hindi version does not indicate the gender of the Company. The natives often personified the Company as 'company bahadur', which in my view indicates its masculine gender. This excerpt provided in the *AAR* 9 (for the year 1809) (1811): 484.

22 Interestingly, the objects of communication had also become the items of gift, and this was not of colonial origin. Wellesley had gifted two large state tents, ornamented with embossed cloth of British manufacture to the *wazir* of Oudh. 'Journal of the Route of the Marquis Wellesley', 69. In pre-colonial times the means of communication were seen as 'sites' and 'things' that delineated political boundaries, rights and privileges. Around 1670, Aurungzeb prohibited the European-style use of ribbon and frills in boats and palkis. Again, in 1693–94, when he sent a glazed palki to Prince Azam Shah, it was ordered that 'excepting those who had been granted palkis by him, none of the Princes, Shahzadas and amirs should come in a palki within the gulalbar'. Later, orders were issued at the imperial court and in provinces disallowing the Hindus except the Rajputs to 'bear arms, or ride elephants, palkis, or Arab and Iraqi horses'. How efficiently these rules were implemented is another issue, but the orders convey the imperial intention to maintain specific hierarchies in which the modes and means of travelling also played a role. References are from *Maasir-i- Alamgiri*, 66, 214, 224.

23 Deane, *A Tour*, 188.

more than just impressing the native mind. The natives, as Raleigh informs us, watched with curiosity the large fleet from the banks but such rituals also rehearsed and reinscribed the notion of rank, hierarchy and power within the colonial bureaucracy. The first component of such 'rituals of travelling' was the strict organized movement under the supervision of the quartermaster general (QMG).[24] Every morning the boats left at a stipulated time after the firing of the guns. Times for breakfast and dinner were fixed. The large mess pinnace *Elvira* was the gathering place for the governor general, ladies and the household staff. A large white flag was hoisted to indicate the mealtimes. There was a separate state band boat named the *Bon Vivant* which travelled alongside the *Elvira* while the band played during dinner time. Not everyone was allowed to dine aboard the *Elvira*, thus maintaining bureaucratic divisions within the 'sahibs'. On the approach of the fleet the senior officials of the place, similar to native chiefs, went to receive the governor general, as the judge of Patna did by going down four coss. A strict order of progression of boats was observed; once Raleigh and his friends' boats came in advance of the *Soona Mouchee* (Sona Mukhi, Golden Face), Amherst's pinnace, upon which an order was issued that 'for the future all boats were to keep in the rear of the Governor General's pinnace'. After Allahabad, when the travel progressed by road, the QMG made an arrangement similar to that of the mir manzil of Mughal times in getting the tents pitched well in advance followed by strict rituals, such as a military call in the morning followed by gunfire to indicate the start of the march, and an evening gunshot at eight to signal the prohibition against any person entering the camp. The protocols of invitation were crucial not only between Europeans and natives[25] but also amongst Europeans, as is evident from the fact that the general of the Bareilley district was not able to dine at Hawkins' house (Hawkins was a senior civil servant at Bareilley) where the governor general was staying. The reason was that the military was not invited for the dinner.

Soon after Amherst's period of office, when Bentinck became governor general, the rituals of travelling, as part of broader transformations in colonial policy, underwent a 'Spartan' change.[26] Oriental etiquette and pompous displays were becoming more sober, partly as a result of new ideological moorings and partly as a result of financial stringency, about which the Court of Directors never forgot to remind the Indian government. In the seat of British paramountcy (Calcutta) Bentinck astounded his colleagues by freely riding about in an ordinary coat with no escort, or 'on occasion even setting off from Government House for a walk with an umbrella under his arm'.[27] He adopted the same attitude while on tour. Without any parade or show, he was frequently seen walking in or near the camp unattended. The new mantra of power and authority was to do away with 'tinsel and trappings of useless pageantry', which, not surprisingly, attracted the

---

24 Some of the details presented here are from Raleigh, *'The Log of a Griffin'*, 2–3, 15, 20–22, 24.
25 For instance, if a native prince asked the governor general for a visit, the latter was not allowed to 'stir from his tent' even if he starved sitting there 'till an "istackball" or embassy came to fetch him'. It was the regime of protocols that prevented Auckland from going to see the Delhi Palace. Mahajan, *The Grand Indian Tour*, 39–40, 66, 95.
26 'The Governor General', *AJ* 5 (1831): 126. This phrase was used by the journal editors, of which they were supportive.
27 Philips, 'Introduction', *BC*, I, xiv.

notice of both natives and Europeans. One important aspect of the travelling ritual, which he abolished, was the practice of *nazar* or gift exchange. Gifts were still exchanged but, under the new system, individuals were not allowed to keep them; the gifts became the property of the Company-state, later to be auctioned, with the proceeds going to the Company treasury. In fact Bentinck had to form a committee while on tour to investigate the disputes that arose over the division of 'spoils'.[28] Eden's account does not give the impression that in his tour Auckland followed the Spartan shift, but deviations from the fixed itinerary — something which was not observable before — did happen, although they brought with them serious remonstrations. When Auckland and his sisters decided to join a large congregation of people onshore, the senior officers panicked and protested 'that they could be murdered amongst other things'. They argued that there was no protocol for governor generals to either appear without a regiment or to visit this mela, to which Eden replied that 'they had created a precedent'.[29] By this time, the early nineteenth-century romance with opulence was rapidly fading away; Eden found this opulence and grandeur indubitably irritating and desired to return to 'our dear little villa at Kensington Gore'.[30] Moreover, many of the cadets who felt encouraged to join the EIC because of its reputation as a medium to get rich quickly, a view that circulated widely in England, were disillusioned on their arrival in India.[31]

Not surprisingly, these changes were not well received by local officials. Nor did practices change overnight. Reportedly, the collector of Ragunathpur marched with 'an elephant, eight cars, two cabriolets, a particular car for his child, two palanquins, six saddle and carriage horses, sixty or eighty porters to carry him, independent of at least sixty household servants' with 'glasses and glittering plates packed and unpacked from morning till night and clean linen changed four times a day'.[32] Strings of 'reforms of retrenchment' (which affected pecuniary provisions, for example, the abolition of nazar and the cutting of the *batta* system by half) made Bentinck so unpopular that Hawkins felt happy to learn that he was leaving. And if we rely on his account, Hawkins represented a view held by a considerable section of the officers, both in the army and in the military: Bentinck might have proved a good servant to his masters in Leadenhall Street, commented Hawkins, but he was 'by no means a favorite Master to us in India'.[33]

In spite of this criticism, which was directed towards one person, in general these tours helped not only to fulfil the function of display of authority but also to cement a sense of bond and solidarity among resident Europeans, who otherwise led a relatively

---

28 Mutual suspicion was rife. Lady Amherst had held a durbar to receive the ladies of the chiefs of Sindh in which no male members were allowed. Raleigh commented that as Mr Stirling (who was part of the tour and might be the person in charge of the nazar) 'was not admitted and could consequently not see whether the Ladies made any presents, it is to be hoped that Lady and Miss Amherst this time took all the advantage of their dignified position'. Raleigh, '*The Log of a Griffin*', 43.
29 Eden, *Up the Country*, 26.
30 Mahajan, *The Grand Indian Tour*, 19–20.
31 Anon., 'A Cadet's Debut in Calcutta', *AJ* 10 (1833).
32 Jacquemont, *Letters from India*, 154–5.
33 Hawkins, *Diaries and Letters*, B 365/5, 13. So great was the angst that on the difference of opinion pertaining to his statue epigram, a letter was sent to the editor of the *Englishman*, in

isolated life, being posted in some distant stations. This was done by meeting them, whenever the governor general's convoy halted, and by organizing dinners and balls. These provided resident Europeans with a cheerful occasion during which they could see a European face and to hear a word in their own language, which sometimes they had missed for months. The lonely lives led in far-flung districts often created feelings of horror, dread and a deep pessimism of dying without any European at hand.[34] Hawkins himself wrote extensively on his solitary life in Rungpoor, which he made bearable by indulging in sport (hog hunting being the favourite of many of the Europeans at this time) and reading. His duties as district magistrate were so excessive that it was only on Sundays that he was able to drop his official character and indulge in some recreation.[35] From the late eighteenth century some such isolated members of the colonial machinery – who became the 'old hands' of India in later memories – had become nodal points in generating, amassing and categorizing the 'information bytes' of colonial rule, and also in furthering the paternalist figure of the Raj.

Going into the Interiors

Francis Buchanan had already made a name for himself with his survey in South India in 1800 after the defeat of Tipu Sultan and thus was rightfully asked to survey the regions of eastern India in the early decades of the nineteenth century (1807–14).[36] A botanist by profession, Buchanan nonetheless was asked to submit an exhaustive description of each of the districts of Bengal, comprising its history, society, religion, land, agriculture,

---

which the following epigram was proposed:

Oh Rogers, dear Rogers, pray lend us a hand,
Of the surplus you'll perhaps get a slice;
A Statue they want of the *Nob* of the land,
So for God's sake let's have it of *Ice*.

The context of using ice arose because one Mr Rogers, an American, had come to Calcutta with two ships of ice which, although giving delight and enjoyment to some of the inhabitants of the city fell short of meeting the demands of the Calcutta folk. Ibid., 13–14.

34 Eden, *Up the Country*, 110–11. Seeing this, Eden wrote to her sister 'Never send a son to India! My dear M [Mary], this is the moral.' Henry Cotton, who joined the Civil Services in 1867, reminisced about his days in charge of a subdivision where, because he did all ordinary office work in Bengali, he did not 'for weeks and months together spoke [any] other language'. Henry J. S. Cotton, *Indian and Home Memories* (London, 1911), 71.

35 Hawkins, *Diaries and Letters*, B 365/5, 2–7. The response of the author of the following piece was similar; he started studying and sketching to keep up with the ennui and solitude in stations where he did not see a 'white face' for more than two years. Anon., 'The Collector', *AJ* 5 (1831): 274. In the second part of this article, published in the next volume, the author made similar complaints of living 'amidst the usual groupe of black faces in the seclusion'. See 36.

36 However, to begin with, he was also one of the isolated Company servants. His first posting in the Bengal medical establishment was at Luckipore 'one of the most isolated posts in the company's eastern jurisdiction'. Marika Vicziany, 'Imperialism, Botany and Statistics in Early Nineteenth-Century India: The Surveys of Francis Buchanan (1762–1829)', *MAS* 20, no. 4 (1986): 631.

Plate 9. A touring official

© British Library Board, D'Oyly, *Behar Amateur Lithographic Scrap Book*, add shelfmark, plate 13.

Plate 10. Heber's journey

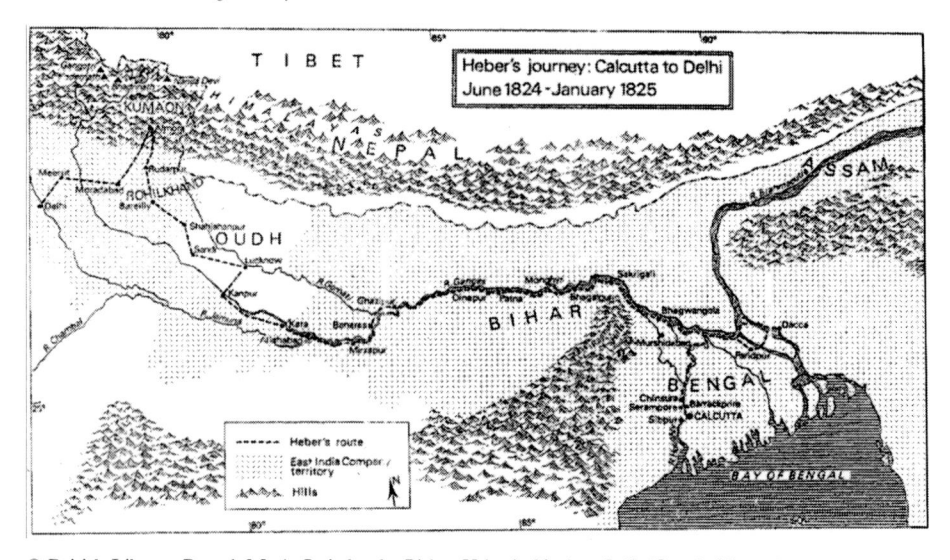

© British Library Board, M. A. Laird, ed., *Bishop Heber in Northern India* (Cambridge, 1971), map 1.

GOING INTO THE INTERIORS 67

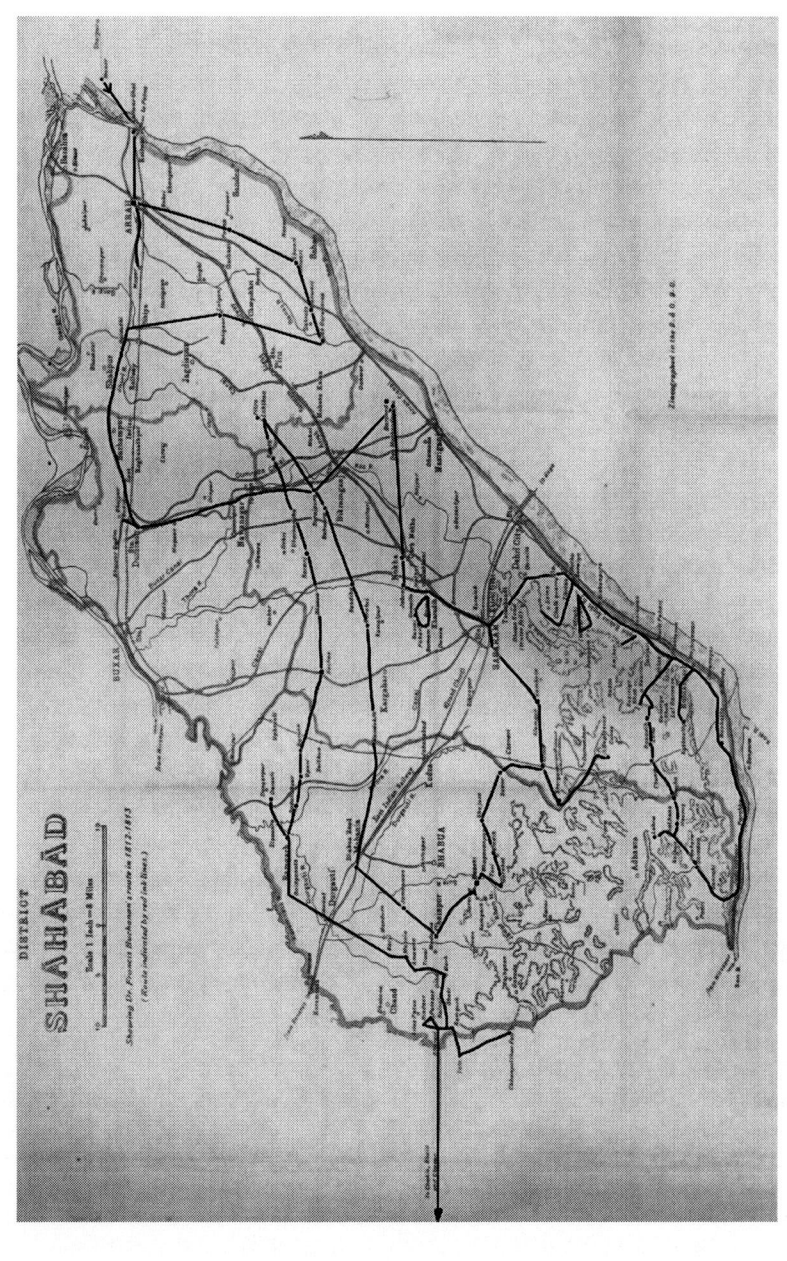

Plate 11. Buchanan's visit in Shahabad

© British Library Board, C. E. A. W. Oldham, ed., with notes, *Journal of Francis Buchanan kept during the Survey of District of Shahabad in 1812–1813* (Patna, 1926), map opp. page 1.

topography, industry, trade and communication. Unlike picturesque or vice-regal tours, those undertaken either by persons like Buchanan under specific instructions or by different lower-level officials as part of their administrative duty were characteristically of a different nature. These were 'statistical touring', with the following features. First, they were shorn of regal paraphernalia; they were relatively isolated and individualized acts of inspection and reporting. Second, because of this, rather than imposing authority and command, they represented a contested zone of authority, flow of information and colonial control. They were symptomatic of an empire that was restless. Third, the information based on such tours had wider economic and political implications than that which was given in accounts of 'picturesque' or vice-regal tours. And fourth, they charted unknown territories; they were not conducted only along main routes. Plates 9, 10 and 11 below, but especially the last two, give an idea of the nature of travelling in terms of routes traversed. While Heber's itinerary represents the route that was fairly often taken by most of the higher administrative officials, Buchanan's zigzagged route marked by a black line gives an idea of interior tours.

While accumulating a diverse range of knowledge, Buchanan, as Vicziany has argued, filled what had earlier been blank spaces 'with the names of towns, major villages and hills'.[37] This knowledge, however, did not come easily, which is perhaps the reason some scholars have questioned the credibility of his statistical information,[38] which was often impressionistic – he collated information on the basis of his 'belief' and 'understanding'. For instance, regarding the mica quarried in the hilly areas near Rajauli in Gaya, he said, 'I *understand* that one of them [workers] takes the mine for a certain sum annually... The amount taken *must* be pretty considerable.'[39] His account in the case of the indigo factories in the Shahabad district was similar: 'I have failed in procuring any particular statements from the owners of the factories, but, so far as I can learn, the speculation, for some years at least, has not been advantageous.'[40] Thus the reliability of his information can be called into question. Against this view, Vicziany's own explanation is that 'Buchanan was too much the European; there were things which he simply didn't want to know about, whilst much of what he saw he wanted to transform into English or Scottish.'[41] Another implication of this debate that goes beyond the above two contentions is to raise the issues of the limitations faced by these travelling members of the colonial bureaucracy. Not infrequently, knowledge was concealed from them.[42] It was not just that Buchanan or other members of the

---

37 Ibid., 648.
38 Vicziany takes up the criticism made by Amiya Bagchi.
39 *Journal of Francis Buchanan Kept During the Survey of the Districts of Patna and Gaya in 1811–12*, ed., with notes and intro., V. H. Jackson (Patna, 1925), 68 (emphasis added).
40 Francis Buchanan, *An Account of the District of Shahabad in 1812–13* (Patna, 1934), 315.
41 Vicziany, 'Imperialism, Botany and Statistics', 654. Notwithstanding, Buchanan occasionally surprises his readers by showing his sensitivity towards indigenous topographical categories. While for many, and for him too, the country in general appeared 'flat', he was, however, aware that the term *Des* (the low country as used to distinguish from *Pahar*, the mountains and hills) implied supposedly an excellence over the hills. *Account of the District of Shahabad*, 8.
42 He referred to the indifference of natives in telling him the exact nature and quantity of produce of the land. Ibid., 14, 315.

English officialdom intentionally refused to see things but that natives still commanded the flow of knowledge when these sojourners were met in the interiors. They had to depend on such information as was given: writing about the air and the weather of the Shahabad district, Buchanan said, 'Here, as in Behar, on this subject I must rely on the reports of the natives.'[43] On another occasion he admitted that the geography of the regions of south Shahabad was 'still imperfect'.[44] This limitation questions the assumed controlling position of a white man either while traversing or living in a region in relative isolation.[45] This type of touring therefore brings out a slightly different facet of colonial administrative mechanism wherein the flow of knowledge, the degree of control and the freedom to be completely self-reliant were not easily attained.

Precisely because of the implications of this limitation, the importance of district officers' interior tours was time and again emphasized, right from the beginning of colonial rule.[46] No less significant was the objective of striking a personal chord with the native population, which again was thought to be best achieved through tours and seeing things 'first hand'. It is true that the 'paternalist school' of the bureaucracy, as it flourished in the North-Western Provinces (NWP) and in the Punjab, did not develop well in Bengal, but the importance of the circulation of administrative personnel was recognized and pushed through. Jacques Pouchepadass tells us that '[t]he practice of camping developed after the Company had decided in 1771 to do away with Clive's system of "dual government" in Bengal'. Further, in 1783, the new Committee of Revenue (later renamed the Board of Revenue) 'finally issued orders to all Collectors to tour their districts so as to gain a practical knowledge of local revenue usage, which varied from pargana to pargana, and to form a personal estimate of the state of the crops and of their likely produce for the current year'.[47] However, even before this formalization, especially in seemingly 'trouble-hit' areas, collectors were doing the rounds of their districts. Augustus Cleveland, whom Hodges had accompanied, went on a tour of the Jungle Terry areas of the Bhagalpur district in February 1782.[48] Before him, James Browne had toured the southern division of the Jungle Terry with a battalion and 'in person examined into the past and present state of everything respecting the

---

43 Ibid., 34.
44 Ibid., 9.
45 As late as in 1852, an attempt made by an Englishman to obtain the lease of copper mines in the Singhbhum region proved abortive. Haughton himself had tried to convince the zamindars of the advantages of 'employing European skill and capital', but was rebuked on the plea that 'the 'Sahib Logue [officials] once admitted, soon become masters of their estates.' Haughton, 'Memorandum on the Geological Structure', 114. Earlier, Duncan also had faced similar problems from the local zamindars, who bribed and decoyed his workmen into destroying his operations and building. In Duncan's own words, his experiments were 'effectually interrupted'. Bcl, F/4/489 11862.
46 Jacques Pouchepadass' brilliant essay covers many facets of the touring activities of colonial district officials. 'Itinerant Kings and Touring Officials: Circulation as a Modality of Power in India, 1700–1947', in Markovits et al., *Society and Circulation*.
47 Ibid., 261–2.
48 Hodges, *Travels*, 87.

Mountaineers'. Such 'personal enquiries' helped him furnish the future plan of action that eventually received government's approval.[49] Still earlier, a European appointed in 1770 to superintend the collection of revenues had set out on a 'personal visit' in 1772–73 to induce the defiant chieftain Juggernath Deo to pay off his balance.[50] In colonial discourse, acts of touring, especially in regions like the Jungle Terry, assumed a greater significance; they not only had administrative utility but were seen as 'bringing civilization' into an otherwise barbaric space.[51]

The following decades saw increasing importance attached to tours. Although socio-religious and cultural observations were part of the knowledge assemblage, it was trade, commerce, agriculture, revenue, local markets and *gunges* (market), price fluctuations, commodity production and communication that became the main subjects of reporting.[52] The monopolistic nature of trade and the willingness on the part of the EIC to diversify its business put demands on officers to tour their districts and report on conditions of production and trade.[53] And for all this a want of 'good local knowledge of the District' was always stressed.[54] To further strengthen the power of the collector, the office of Dewani was abolished under Regulation XV of 1813. The reason given was 'to annihilate the influence which the designation of Head Native Officer and the nature of the situation in many instances, enabled the Dewans to exert with most pernicious effects'.[55] Simultaneously, it required collectors to directly oversee matters of revenue

---

49 J. Browne, *A Description of the Jungle Terry Districts: Their Revenues, Trade and Government with a Plan for the Improvement of Them* (London, 1788), 3. I am citing from a typescript transcript prepared by Prof. K. K. Datta and deposited in the Library of the Bihar State Archives (BSA).
50 Ibid., 55.
51 See 'Appendix E. Extract from Mr. Sutherland's Report to the Secretary to Government, Judicial Department, Fort William, on the Hill People', in James Long, *Unpublished Records of the Government*, ed. M. P. Saha (Calcutta, 1973), 746. First edn 1869. [Henceforth *URG*.] Warren Hastings had applauded the 'settlement' of the Jungle Terry in the following words: 'By the battalion employed in the Jungleterry, a tract of country which was considered as inaccessible and unknown and only served as a receptacle to robbers, has been reduced to government, the inhabitants civilized, and not only the reduction of the revenues, which was occasioned by their ravages, prevented, but some revenue yielded from this country itself, which a prosecution of the same measure will improve.' 'At the Council', Fort William, 3 December 1774, in G. W. Forrest, ed. *Selections from the Letters, Despatches, and Other State Papers preserved in the Foreign Department of the Government of India, 1772–1785* (Calcutta, 1890), vol. 1, 138–9.
52 See, for instance, K. K. Datta, *A Handbook of Bhagalpur District Revenue Records, 1774–1855* (Patna, 1975).
53 J. Fombelle, the judge-magistrate of Bhagalpur, noticed the 'illicit' cultivation of opium 'in the several remote parts of the country' during his tour. 'Letter form Fombelle to George Tucker, Secretary to the Government in Revenue and Judicial Department', 7 October 1800, in K. K. Datta, ed., *Selections from the Judicial Records of the Bhagalpur District Office (1792–1805)* (Patna, 1968), 294. [Henceforth Datta, ed., *BR*.] In the late 1780s, the Court of Directors had directed the commercial resident to obtain precise information on cotton and tobacco production in the country. Such information relied on reports of collectors and magistrates. 'Extract of a Letter from the Governor General in Council', 20 March 1789, in P. C. Roy Chaudhury, *Muzaffarpur Old Records* (Patna, 1959), 91. [Henceforth *MOR*.]
54 'Letter from Revenue Board to H. Parry, Collector of Tirhoot', 30 March 1813, *MOR*, 270.
55 *MOR*, 284–5.

collection. The move towards making local officers the 'embodiment of the state' was further emphasized by making it mandatory for deputy collectors to 'be able to read and speak the vernacular language of the Districts to which they may be appointed'.[56]

This mounting emphasis manifested itself in recognizing the utility and the existing limitation in acts of touring and knowledge gathering. In 1815, the magistrate of Saran acknowledged that the 'interior of this District which is very extensive...has never to the best of my knowledge [been] visited...by an European officer of the government'.[57] It also helped in locating loose links in the administrative machinery; in 1839, the touring commissioner of Patna noted that the officially defined links between district magistrates and *daroghas* (sub-inspectors or constables, usually native) existed only on 'paper'.[58] As a result, by the 1850s collectors were repeatedly reprehended for neglecting their duty. This neglect arose in part because of a cut in the travel allowances of officers who received less then Rs. 23,000 per annum.[59] Furthermore, from 1859 onwards, in the aftermath of the 1857 'Mutiny', arguing that tours were growing into a strictly codified administrative routine, Pouchepadass suggests a political reason, connected with the mutiny, behind it.[60] Notwithstanding, my understanding is that the constant reminders, which are discernible from the early 1850s, were because of the issues we have discussed so far, namely, the spatial politics relating to the demarcation of zones of knowability and unknowability, the resolution on the part of the Company-state to minimize its dependence on 'natives' (whether this happened or not is a different issue), and not least, to streamline the administrative structures of knowledge acquisition. The formalization of both, the act of touring and the format of reporting, is evident in a series of letters and correspondences between commissioner and collectors in which the former asked the latter to submit in advance details of the works undertaken during their winter tours.[61] The collectors were directed to submit a brief plan of their conduct before leaving on tour.[62] The renewed emphasis also brought up the issue of the careful preservation of records; it was stressed that 'half of the benefit of these results is lost' due to the lack of keeping the records properly. A standard format of reporting emerged whereby officers

---

56 Under Regulation IX of 1833. *Circular Orders of the Sudder Board of Revenue at the Presidency of Fort William...from September 1837 to the end of 1850* (Calcutta, 1851), 17; Pouchepadass, 'Itinerant Kings', 257. During his times, Bentinck had expressed resentment against the 'patronage system' through which civil service cadets were appointed; his argument was that the system failed to promote acquiring 'knowledge of the relevant Indian languages and laws'. Philips, ed., 'Introduction', *BC*, I, xxiii.
57 Anand Yang, *The Limited Raj: Agrarian Relations in Colonial India, Saran District 1793–1920* (Berkeley, LA, and London, 1989), 94.
58 Ibid., 94.
59 The cut in allowances was introduced in 1840. A Circular Order of 17 October 1851 brought up this point. The Order also made it obligatory on them to 'traverse at least one third of the district during each cold season'. 'Extract from a Despatch from the Hon'ble Court of Directors to the Government of India in the Revenue Department', 17 September 1856, *Patna Commissioner Record Series*, vol. 238, 1855, BSA. [Henceforth *PCRS*.]
60 Pouchepadass, 'Itinerant Kings', 268.
61 *PCRS*, vol. 590, 1853–54.
62 'Letter to the Collectors of the Division of Patna', 29 November 1856, ibid.

were asked to arrange their tour reports under the following seven categories: 'Crime & Criminals', 'Roads and Communications', 'Ferries', 'Planters, Zamindars', 'State of the Country – Cultivation, Crops etc.', 'Education' and 'Miscellaneous Remarks'.[63] The importance of communication and trade is not only obvious in the choice of categories but also in the fact that officers were required to mark their routes on the skeleton map of the district, with the dates of their visits (very similar to what Buchanan had done earlier). One copy of the report was to go to the senior officer; another was meant for deputy officers in the respective districts. Commissioners, in turn, were required to proceed on 'inspection tour' and submit their reports.[64]

Of course, it would be erroneous to circumscribe the ramifications of these tours to commerce, trade and communication alone; but what is interesting for our analysis here is that local-level touring provided a vital link between 'knowledge' and 'action'. Increased mobility brought the centres of commerce under observation. Although spaces such as *chauks* (intersection of four streets, usually becoming a vibrant market place), bazaars, haats and gunges were seen as sites of 'numerous annoyances'[65] (and paradoxically also of much gossip and rumour, which made the colonial bureaucracy paranoid), since they were also important nodes of marketing, officers were routinely asked to monitor them closely. The collector of Saran, for instance, was asked to maintain a general register of commercial transactions and to insist on individuals possessing bazaars or haats to deliver to him their full accounts.[66] Such commercial feedback helped the Company to take measures to improve or introduce the cultivation and production of different commodities which they considered remunerative.[67] This concern was pushing the Company-state to also improve the means of communication, to which we turn now, and which, as argued above, is usually erased in the accounts of the early days of Company administration.[68]

The following section, which adopts a region-specific approach has two purposes. First, it lays down the details of the networks of roads and other forms of communication that existed in Bihar on the eve of the colonial rule and their fate through the course of next fifty to sixty years. To understand the nature of the changes that social groups underwent (Chapter 5) or the mercantile networks encountered (Chapter 6) it is important

---

63 See 'Letter from the Commissioner of Circuit for the Division of Patna to the Magistrates of the Division', 3 September 1856, *PCRS*, vol. 473, 1856; 'Letter from the Officiating Secretary to the Board of Revenue, Lower Provinces to the Commissioner of Revenue, Patna Division', 23 December 1856, *PCRS*, vol. 238, 1855.
64 Order was passed in 1853. *PCRS*, vol. 238, 1855.
65 Anon., 'The Collector', *AJ* 6 (1831): 33.
66 'Letter to the collector of Saran', 26 April 1790, *MOR*, 36.
67 In 1790, at the instigation of the Board of Trade, the governor general in council proposed to improve the quality of cotton produced in Tirhut by importing the Dacca seeds. *MOR*, 96. In 1792, one John Patterson, described as 'well conversant with the culture and management of sugar production in West Indies' was engaged for twelve years by the EIC to expand the production of sugar in Bihar and Bengal. Ibid., 112.
68 'Nothing was done by the East India Company during the early period of its rule, to improve upon the shattered condition of the communications.' *History of Road Development in India*, compiled and published by Central Road Research Institute (New Delhi, 1963), 31.

to have a basic 'background layout' of the communication web of this region. The second reason is an apparent critique of the first one but is rather closer to the nature of the methodology this book aspires to suggest, which is, to not just take communication as a background framework to fill in the analytical hues related to trade, market, social differentiation and so on but to interject it at different levels of analysis of which it forms an integral part of the interlinked stories of colonial rule. The appropriate place for this discussion could arguably have remained the beginning of a chapter on something like 'regime of communication and circulation in Bihar' but it has been intentionally presented here to argue that communication was an important medium and aspect of colonial governance in the ways in which the early colonial state mobilized its bureaucracy to collect knowledge. It was integral to the knowledge related to trade and commerce, together with political concerns on strengthening the empire. In the latter aspect, communication became an important site of control and negotiation. Construction of roads was one aspect of developing communication; maintaining and repairing them was another. Probably, in the South Asian climate, the latter was more crucial. Once again, the tussle over power and authority over issues related to construction and repair illuminates the social history of how colonial rule was consolidated. Rather than serving the conventional function of providing background details, the following section places communication at the intersecting cusp of very many histories – knowledge production, trading and taxation policies, social and economic authority, and, not least, ecological setting – within a region that historically came to constitute its patterns of circulation of people and commodities. It is important to remember that networks of communication are not pre-given structures of transport and mobility.

Company Rule, Communication, Bihar

Keeping ecological and topographical factors in mind, we can see Bihar as divided into three zones. One, the area of wet, riparian north Bihar, comprising the districts of Saran, Champaran, Tirhut, Purnea and others; two, Gangetic Bihar including the districts of Bhagalpur, Monghyr, Patna and Shahabad; and three, the hilly areas of Rajmahal and further down towards the area of Chota Nagpur.

Rennell's *Description* gives an idea of the existing networks of communication inherited by the Company-state.[69] There were three main routes that connected Calcutta and Benares. The first ran along the southern bank of the Ganga via Murshidabad, Rajmahal, Bhagalpur, Monghyr, Patna, Arrah, Buxar and Ghazipur. This was the old Mughal road (also called the Gangetic route), which was the one taken by most of the travellers discussed above.[70] When Shershah acceded to power he made a diversion to this road to accommodate his hometown, Sasseram. From the old Mughal road, a route branched off from Patna, followed the eastern bank of the River Soane for the most part,

---

69 James Rennell, *A Description of the Roads in Bengal and Bahar* (London, 1778).
70 See also W. Oldham, 'Routes: Old and New, from Lower Bengal up the Country', *BPP* 28, nos. 55–6 (July–December 1924): pt 1, 26. This road was also shown in Van den Broucke's map drawn around the year 1660. Jean Deloche, *Transport and Communications in India Prior to Steam Locomotion*, 2 vols, trans. James Walker (Delhi, 1993). Above reference is from vol. 1, 37–8.

passed through Arwal, Samsernagar, Daudnagar, crossed the Soane below Daudnagar, and went up to Benares via Sasseram. This road was 565 miles in length.[71] The third passed through Burdwan, Serampore, Curukdea, Gaya, Tekari, Daudnagar and finally Benares.[72] There were two more routes to Patna other than the Mughal road. One went through Burdwan, Nagore, Sarhaut, Deoghar, Chacki and Behar; the second, via Burdwan, Serampore, Curukdea, Nawada and Behar.[73] From this road from Deoghar, one branch went straight to Monghyr. This route, William Oldham says, was followed by Hindu pilgrims.[74] Though the exact route is not clear, in 1821 the raja of Tanjore used one of these routes on a pilgrimage from Calcutta to Gaya, Benares and Allahabad, going to Deoghar and Patna as well.[75] Thus, it is evident that these were the routes that not only existed but were also frequently used. Rennell also traced a trunk line passing through the southern parts of Bihar, from Midnapur, Hazaribagh, Singhbhoom, Palamow and then one branch going to Sherghatty and another to Daudnagar. Oldham describes this as one of the highroads of the Muslim times across the Chota Nagpur (see Plate 12).[76]

The area of north Bihar also had important major roads. One, like the Mughal road, ran parallel to the northern bank of the Ganga.[77] Another ran from Hajipur, opposite Patna on the Ganga, to Bettiah, passing through Muzaffarpur. Darbhanga was well connected with three places on the Ganga: Hajipur, Mowah and Monghyr. Similarly, Purneah was connected with Monghyr and Cargola on the Ganga. They also were connected themselves by a road leading to Malda and then further to Dhaka on the eastern side and to Jaunpur on the west.[78] Saran was connected through land routes with the province of Oudh. Ellis, the Patna factory agent who in 1763 attempted to besiege the city in anticipation of Mir Qasim's attack, used the land route to find shelter in the territory of the nawab of Oudh.[79] The area of north Bihar was also well connected with Nepal. A Select Committee proceeding of 1767 referred to a 'New Route to Nipal', that started from Hajipur and passed through Darbhanga, Bawah, Sidley and Danpebah. The Company and the raja both looked at the supply of water and other provisions at different stations. The road was described as 'very good'.[80] In addition to these roads, rivers such as the Gogra, the Gandak and the Kosi, all discharging into the Ganga and navigable throughout the year, were important mediums of communication for north

---

71 Rennell, *Description*, 9.
72 Ibid., 9–10.
73 Ibid., 56–8.
74 Oldham, 'Routes: Old and New', pt 1, 26.
75 'Enclosed in a Letter from G. Swinton, Secretary to the Government to Mr. Sutton, Surgeon to the Raja of Tanjore', 7 March 1821, in K. K. Datta, ed., *Selections from Unpublished Correspondence of the Judge-Magistrate and the Judge of Patna, 1790–1857* (Patna, 1954), 131. [Henceforth Datta, ed., *Selections*.]
76 Oldham, 'Routes: Old and New', pt 1, 26.
77 Anil Kumar, *Trade in Early Medieval Eastern Bihar, c. A.D. 600–A.D.1200* (Patna and New Delhi, 2001), 90.
78 Chatterjee, *Merchants, Politics and Society*, 15.
79 P. C. Roy Chaudhury, *Sarkar Saran, Based on Old Correspondence Regarding Saran District in Bihar from 1785 to 1866* (Patna, 1956), 2.
80 *URG*, record no. 975, 21 July 1767, 698–9.

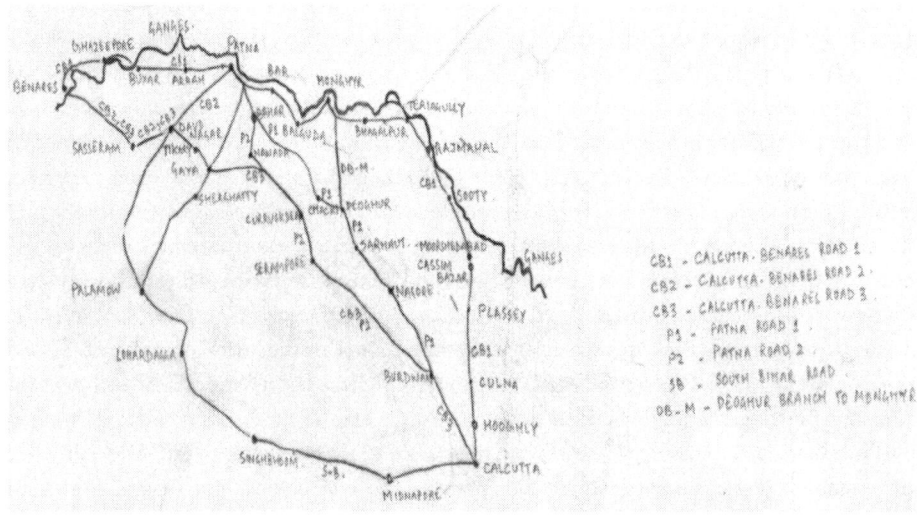

Plate 12. Major highways in Bihar, south of the Ganga

© British Library Board, sketched from James Rennell, 'A General Map of the Roads of Bengal, 1778', in Rennell, *Description*, shelfmark: T35013.

Bihar. In fact, as we will see later in this chapter and further in Chapter 6, ferries were more important than land transportation in this wet, riparian part of Bihar.

The Company inherited these structures of communication, which over a period of time underwent certain changes. The reasons for such changes were diverse: the selective interest which the Company took in their upkeep, the institutional limitation of relying on zamindars and other local notables, the hierarchic nature of the 'colonial management' rigged with internal contradictions, and a relatively well-defined trade and commercial priorities were a few of them.

There is very little information on the modalities of communication management from the period before the Company rule. From B. K. Sarkar's and other accounts it appears that both native rulers and zamindars shared this responsibility, although the latter were responsible for maintaining, and not constructing, roads. This comes out from the discussion that took place over *kabooleats* (deeds) in the early colonial period. For instance, the collector of the Bhagalpur district blamed the zamindars for not maintaining the roads in spite of being bound by the kabooleats.[81] In return, zamindars collected taxes on

---

81 Bejoy Kumar Sarkar, *Inland Transport and Communication in Medieval India* (Calcutta, 1925). See 'Letter from G. Dickinson, Collector of Bhaghalpur to Fombelle, Judge-Magistrate of Bhagalpur', 16 June 1800, in Datta, ed., *BR*, 285. The words of the kabooleat as entered into by the zamindars of the Rangpur district in 1786–87 were: 'I will take care in the repairs and protection of the highways within my boundaries that Travellers and the people employed in cultivation may pass with ease and safety…will not collect any revenue from the Ryots on account of Syarchilarita (a custom on grain & c. carried overland) Guliahmangun (a custom on boats)'. W. Firminger, ed., *Bengal District Records: Rangpur, vol. 6, 1786–87 (Letters Issued)* (Calcutta, 1928), nos. 103–4, page 107.

roads and rivers. They also maintained registers of boats and manjhees (head boatmen) in their respective districts, which apparently helped them track down cases of robbery.[82] Subsequently, when the EIC attained sovereign power in Bengal and Bihar, it forced the zamindars to repair the roads, arguing that such a role was established by the original rule of the country. But this was also a period of clash of interests between the Company and the zamindars, in particular over the proliferation of the *choukies* (check points) in collecting these taxes. Earlier, Aurungzeb had abolished many duties, such as *rahdari* (road tax) and *sayers* (a set of other taxes, see below). One of the reasons was that under the pretence of searches the excise officers 'used to practise astonishing outrages on the modesty of women'.[83] It is not known when these taxes resurfaced (or even if they ever disappeared in spite of Aurungzeb's directive) but by the time the Company took over the administrative reins, they were almost ubiquitous. As a result, the Company abolished the rahdari in 1773. The reason, however, apparently was not as 'moralistic' as it was for Aurungzeb. Before 1772, when the Company gave up the dual governance, its traders and suppliers had to undergo 'exorbitant exactions' at different choukies.[84] Yet even after the abolition the custom persisted; Mr Brooke, the collector of customs at Patna, in 1785 reported that zamindars did not desist from levying and collecting rahdari duties. To stop this, the government ordered the collector not only 'to oblige the immediate offender to refund the money so exacted, but to inflict corporal punishment upon him on the spot'. The order further stated that 'the zamindar, choudhury, talukdar, and other proprietors of the pargana, or portion of land, where the offence was committed, shall be punishable by a confiscation of the whole or part of his land by the Governor-General and Council'.[85] A merchant who made a complaint in this regard said that in bringing grain and seed to Patna, he had to pay rahdari dues at Sasseram, Daudnagar, Arwal, Bekram and Duriarpur. Similar complaints were also made by other merchants.[86] Surprisingly, and quite paradoxically, before it had abolished the rahdari, in 1766, the Company also had made it clear to the zamindars 'not to grant lands for roads, tanks, & c, & c, without leave from the President and Council'.[87] On the one hand the traditional role of zamindars in maintaining roads was consistently invoked by the colonial rulers;

---

82 Sarkar, *Inland Transport*, 3–11. On collection of transit duties by zamindars in the Mughal period, see M. N. Gupta, *Analytical Survey of Bengal Regulations and Acts of Parliament Relating to India, up to 1833* (Calcutta, 1943), 305.
83 *Maasir-i-Alamgiri*, 316. Reportedly, the loss of revenue to the Mughal treasury arising from the abolition of rahdari amounted to Rs. 25 *lakhs* per annum, 16.
84 See *URG*, record nos. 111 (February 1753), 695 (12 February 1763), 53, 460 respectively.
85 J. Reginald Hand, *Early English Administration of Bihar, 1781–1785* (Calcutta, 1894), 50. The merchants of Darbhanga complained about Raja Madho Singh, who used to charge Rs. 10 for each boat and 2 *annas* for bullocks. 'Copy of Petition from Merchants of Darbhanga to Revenue Board', 5 October 1789, in *MOR*, 95. See also 'No. 154: Extract of the Commissioners' Plan for the Management of the Customs', which mentioned that 'notwithstanding the repeated orders of the government there are still some zamindars who "extort money from the merchants"'. Walter K. Firminger, ed., *Bengal District Records: Rangpur, vol. 2: 1779–1782 (Letters Received)* (Calcutta, 1920), 125.
86 Hand, *Early English Administration*, 50.
87 *URG*, record no. 863, 3 September 1766, 590–91.

on the other the financial strings that supported those actions were redefined. At times, zamindars did relent under force, as in 1770–71 when the zamindars of Shahabad district agreed to voluntarily pay a small sum towards the upkeep of roads but excused themselves from providing any personal supervision of the work. Instead, this work was done by the nearest *tehsildar* (a native revenue and judicial official). Such arrangements produced confusion and laxity, so that the collector noted that accounts were kept neither of the sum collected nor of receipts of roads that had been maintained.[88]

Why did the Company abolish the rahdari? Why did it prohibit zamindars from making grants for public works? One reason, as pointed out above, was that Company agents were forced to pay excessive dues to the zamindars; but this was not the only reason. From the late 1760s the Company was also concerned with the declining trade of Bengal and the abusive powers of its own officers and *gomasthas* (agents). Recurrent appeals were made from Henry Vansittart, Clive and Hastings – governors of Bengal – to check the misuse of *dastaks* (passes allowing free trade) as well as the power of the gomsathas, who 'being under no control of their masters...set themselves up for Judges and Magistrates, hear disputes between the inhabitants and extort fines, force the merchants to buy their goods at more than market-price, and to sell what they require as much below it'.[89] As a result, the Company tried to make 'inland trade' completely free.[90] It is not a coincidence that Hastings, on his tour up the Ganga, noticed this misuse: 'almost on every trading boat and storehouse flew the English flag without warrant'.[91] In 1773, Hastings came up with a proposal with two main points: first, to abolish the choukies; and second, to abolish the distinction of dastaks.[92] These were the essential steps towards what Hastings described as 'free trade', which only meant 'opening up the inland trade' for the native merchants, a cause which had earlier led Siraj al-Daula and Mir Qasim, the nawabs of Bengal, to resist the Company's growing trade and abuse. As a result, in the 1773 Regulation all the choukies were abolished and only five customhouses were retained at Calcutta, Hooghly, Murshidabad, Dhaka and Patna, the places notably situated on the River Ganga.

These two decades, the 1760s and 1770s, had thus two main features. First was the curtailment of the power of zamindars to collect dues and taxes on the country's trading routes. This also deprived them of the extra collection that they usually invested in public works. Very broadly, two types of taxes were collected by zamindars. One was the rahdari tax that we have noted above, and second was the group of duties commonly called sayers. The nature of this collective duty ranged from charges on pastures and fruit trees to tolls

---

88 'Letter from the Collector of Shahabad to H. Wood, Acting Accountant to the Board of Revenue', 31 January 1813, *PCRS*, vol. 126, 1812.
89 'Governor Vansittart on Europeans Trading', *URG*, record no. 630, 1 February 1763, 404–5.
90 'Clive's Minute on the Salt Trade', *URG*, 3 September 1766, 591–4. Three commodities that they wanted to make 'free' for native merchants were salt, betel nut and tobacco. *URG*, record no. 978, August 1767, 701.
91 A. Mervyn Davies, *Life and Times of Warren Hastings*, reprint (Delhi, 1988), 45. First published 1935.
92 'Letter from Hastings to Josias Dupre', 9 March 1773, in G. R. Gleig, *Memoirs of the Life of the Right Honourable Warren Hastings* (London, 1841), vol. 1, 304.

on shops, charges on imports and exports, weight of merchandise and transport by land or ferries. Sayers were abolished in 1790.[93] H. T. Colebrooke criticized this move because he firmly believed that this collective tax, at least partially, helped in maintaining rural markets, gunges and roads.[94] The second feature of these two decades was the evolution of 'free' and 'regulated' trade. The Company tried to 'free' inland trade from the increasing monopoly of the European collectors and Indian gomasthas but at the same time secured a monopoly over the export trade in salt and opium. The Company's prioritization of long-distance, high-value export commodities had an effect on the structure of communication networks. The Company's preoccupation, on the one hand, with export commodities and its dependence on one channel of communication, the Ganga, and, on the other hand, curtailing the zamindars' extra monetary benefits (part of which trickled down into maintaining roads and ferries), reoriented the existing communication network. The fact that the Company set up all the five choukies along the places situated on the Ganga testifies to this fact. They were established to check the validity of the *rowannahs* (documents under which goods passed). Kumkum Chatterjee affirms that 'Patna's long-distance trade (the export of saltpeter, opium and cotton piece-goods to Calcutta for shipment overseas) was completely dependent on the Ganges'.[95] To better understand this let us look at the shipment volumes of saltpetre in one season in 1781–82. In September 1781, 40,000 *maunds* of saltpetre were dispatched for Calcutta from the Patna factory. The following month, 50,000 maunds were dispatched. In November of the same year 20,000 maunds (in 10,000 bags) were dispatched. From the invoice for October we learn that the whole consignment was escorted by one *havildar* (native constable) and six *sepoys*. The cost of escort and contracting boats for the month of November was the high sum of Rs. 10,999-5-9. Many other commodities were sent down the river to Calcutta. For instance, in June 1781, 200 bales of cloth, which included the famous amberties of Patna, were dispatched on eight boats. This was followed by fifty bales on 3 September 1781 and ninety bales of cloth and 300 maunds of turmeric (on five boats) on 19 October.[96] One should also recall the transport of opium from Ghazipore and Patna factories that went along the river. The 'Opium Fleet' as it was called, consisted of boats 'preceded by small canoes, the crews of which sound[ed] the depth of water, warn[ed] all boats out of the channel by beat of drum, and proclaim[ed] that the Opium of the "Companee Bahadoor" claims a passage down the river'. This scene and account sketched by Sherwill further informs us about the timber rafts floated down from the Nepal forests that were used for making packing cases for the opium.[97]

---

93 Gupta, *Analytical Survey*, 310.
94 H. T. Colebrooke, *Remarks on the Present State of the Husbandry and Commerce of Bengal* (Calcutta, 1795), 45–8.
95 Chatterjee, *Merchants, Politics and Society*, 51.
96 India Office Records (IOR) G/28/17, AAC, British Library. A. Deane impressionistically remarked on passing more than 200 merchant vessels, laden with grain, in just one day. *A Tour*, 230. Earlier in her account she mentioned counting 'sixty sail of vessels laden with merchandize' from a place just down from Bhagalpur town. She said, 'the traffic on it [the Ganga] is scarcely credible to those who have not witnessed it'. See page 58. Another traveller also noted many heavy vessels downstream on the Ganga filled with bales of cotton. Anon., *Journal*, 85–6.
97 *Illustrations of the Mode of Preparing the Indian Opium Intended for the Chinese Market, from Drawings by Captain Walter S. Sherwill* (London, 1851), text facing 'The Opium Fleet'.

Plate 13. The opium fleet on the Ganga

THE OPIUM FLEET,
DESCENDING THE GANGES EN ROUTE TO CALCUTTA.

© British Library Board, Sherwill, *Illustrations of the Mode of Preparing the Indian Opium*, shelfmark: X 850.

One of the fallouts of this export trade for the province of Bihar was its reorientation towards Calcutta; consequently, it became part of the imperial trade network, mostly as a supplier of high-priced commodities that were globally exchanged. Patna was losing its trading linkages with places to the west.[98] Colebrooke was once again perceptive of this change: 'It must however be not concealed,' he said, 'that by the effect of the monopoly, Bahar has lost the market of the western countries, which formerly were supplied from thence, but now furnish some opium to the British provinces.'[99] In the seventeenth century, Patna not only had trading links with regions to the north, such as Nepal, Bhutan, Sikkim and Tibet (not to mention Bengal and Orissa to the east), but had regular commercial contacts with Agra, Lahore, Surat, Masulipatnam, Balasore, Tipperah, Benares and Janupur to the west.[100] The shift in the region's ties was not causally linked to communication; however, communication channels and their nature

---

98 Patna was well connected to Agra, Allahabad and Benares, both by river and land routes, the latter going as far as to central Asia and west Asia. See, J. N. Sarkar, 'Economic Life in Bihar, 1526–1757', in Syed Hasan Askari and Qeyamuddin Ahmad, eds, *Comprehensive History of Bihar*, pt 2 (Patna, 1987).
99 Colebrooke, *Remarks on the Present State of the Husbandry*, 79.
100 Ahmad Raza Khan, 'A Brief Survey of Trade and Commerce in Bihar during the Seventeenth Century', *Indian History Congress Proceedings* (1978), 473–80.

(i.e. the practicability of the Ganga as the main trade route in this region), along with a set of policies on trading regulations was crucial in redefining the circuits of exchange.

Apart from the conflict between the Company-state and zamindars and prioritization of specific trade commodities, another source of confusion was the internal fissures in the structures of colonial authority. This was best manifest in Hastings' attempt to construct the NMR. The search for a better direct line from Calcutta to the River Karmanasha started in 1763.[101] The reasons apparently were two: first, to check the Maratha raids, which generally followed the southern Bihar routes; and, second, to improve the conveyance of dak that hitherto followed the circuitous Shershah's road. Lieutenant Nicholl was deputed to survey the region, but he died before finishing his work. So, in November 1766, one Captain Douglass was deputed to examine the passes through the hills of south Bihar. The repeated Maratha incursions required the Company to maintain a battalion at Ramgarh, which was situated on the southernmost trunk line traced by Rennell. It was against the backdrop of this contest that Hastings asked Captain Crawford to enquire into the possibility of a high road, a direct line from Calcutta to Chunargarh. Crawford submitted his report in 1781, which was then forwarded by Hastings to the Court of Directors, which rejected the plan. Hastings, however, defiantly proceeded to execute his ideas by entrusting Captain Rankin with the construction work. The Court of Directors remained 'astonished at this measure' but also conceded by directing the Calcutta government not to exceed Rs. 16,000 per annum for maintaining the road.[102] (See Plate 14 for the alignment of the NMR together with the GTR.)

The first major colonial investment in communication came about in total defiance of the higher authorities.[103] The NMR proved to be a successful venture, although some travellers raised doubts about the ingenuity of the course selected. A. Deane cast her suspicion in the following words:

...Government is making a new military road up the country another way... but can Government induce the natives to form villages on it, so great a distance from their sacred and favourite river? And if not, how are travellers, particularly natives, to procure supplies? They answer, The distance will be so much lessened. But who, in undertaking

---

101 The following account is based on Oldham unless otherwise mentioned. Oldham, 'Routes: Old and New'.
102 Much more astonishing for the Court of Directors was the Calcutta Government House whose construction had started in 1798 but which they knew nothing about until the plan and elevations were transmitted to them in a letter from the governor general in council dated 27 February 1804. The building cost £167,359, which came as a shock to the directors. Mildred Archer, *British Drawings*, 38–9. So shocking was the 'scandal' that soon it became a topic of poetical interest: 'At that vast palace cumbersome and grand, Which rising owned a Wellesley's plastic hand, (Loud moaned the Court o'ver vast expense incurred, "And spare, oh! spare our purses", was the word!).' 'Life in India', 483.
103 Irrespective of what Lord Valentia had to say the Court of Directors were clear in not following the 'pomp, magnificence and ostentation of the Native Governments'. Sore about the issue of the Government House it directed the Indian establishment that 'in future, no *new* and *expensive* buildings should be commenced, without their previous consent'. Archer, *British Drawings*, 40.

a journey of nearly a thousand miles, would not be glad to go a few miles more, in order to pass a pleasant day in some friendly habitation?[104]

Deane was partly right, and, of course, partly wrong. Military movement did soon commence; after only three years we hear of troops marching on this road at fourteen miles per day. Bazaars also sprang up on certain sections of the road. It seems that the construction was followed by a great progress of cultivation and an increase of habitants on the high-road side. Reportedly, the jungle was cleared, and *cutchery* (courts) and bungalows were erected.[105] But it took a while for other kinds of travelling to switch to this road. When on 21 February 1803 Valentia started his upcountry visit, he took to the old route because the NMR still did not have dak bungalows at regular intervals; the whole stretch provided only three stops.[106] Forrest also, who started his upcountry visit on 2 December 1807, took to the old route running along the Ganga. One of the reasons was that the supplies were more abundant on this line than on the new one.[107] However, gradually the NMR became the Company's dak-line. G. C. Mundy, travelling with others, took this road in 1827. It seems that by this time, the road was increasingly used by the British. Mundy referred to 'a family travelling southwards with all their household equipages, who treated these with rather more than plentiful and luxurious meal than our palankeen stores have afforded them'.[108] Thomas Williamson praised this route and its upkeep – grass and jungle free – which made the journey of 400 miles from Calcutta to Chunar comfortably possible in five days.[109] A. Deane herself noted Mecca pilgrims on this road.[110]

A distinct pattern therefore emerged in this period, which should, however, be treated as a model of explanation rather than reflecting absolute historical truth. For colonial needs of trade in imperial commodities, the Ganga became the main route; for facilitating military marches through a shorter route, the NMR was built, which slowly gained popularity not only for military marches but also with general travellers; and third, the old Gangetic route running along the Ganga retained its position as a chief pathway in this region. The reason, as already hinted by Deane, was that this old route had secured establishments for accommodation and supplies. From the point of view of the state, therefore, the priorities or the necessities to heavily invest in the upkeep of different types of local and lateral networks were limited; movement of goods and troops along a few select major routes (the Ganga and the NMR) fulfilled its basic needs. Further, even when the Company wished to develop or upkeep the local networks, it felt constrained by

---

104 Deane, *A Tour*, 36.
105 Oldham, 'Routes: Old and New'.
106 'Accepted Travellers', 285–6.
107 Forrest, *A Picturesque Tour*, 125.
108 Mundy, *Pen and Pencil Sketches, Being the Journal of a Tour in India*, vol. 1 (London, 1832), 4–5.
109 Thomas Williamson, *The East India Vade-Mecum*, 2 vols (London, 1810). Above reference is from vol. 1, 321.
110 '…who appeared lying flat on their faces, with scarcely any clothing on them, [with] the bones almost staring through the skin'. She does not say if this was because of lack of supplies on the road or otherwise. Deane, *A Tour*, 191.

Plate 14. NMR and GTR

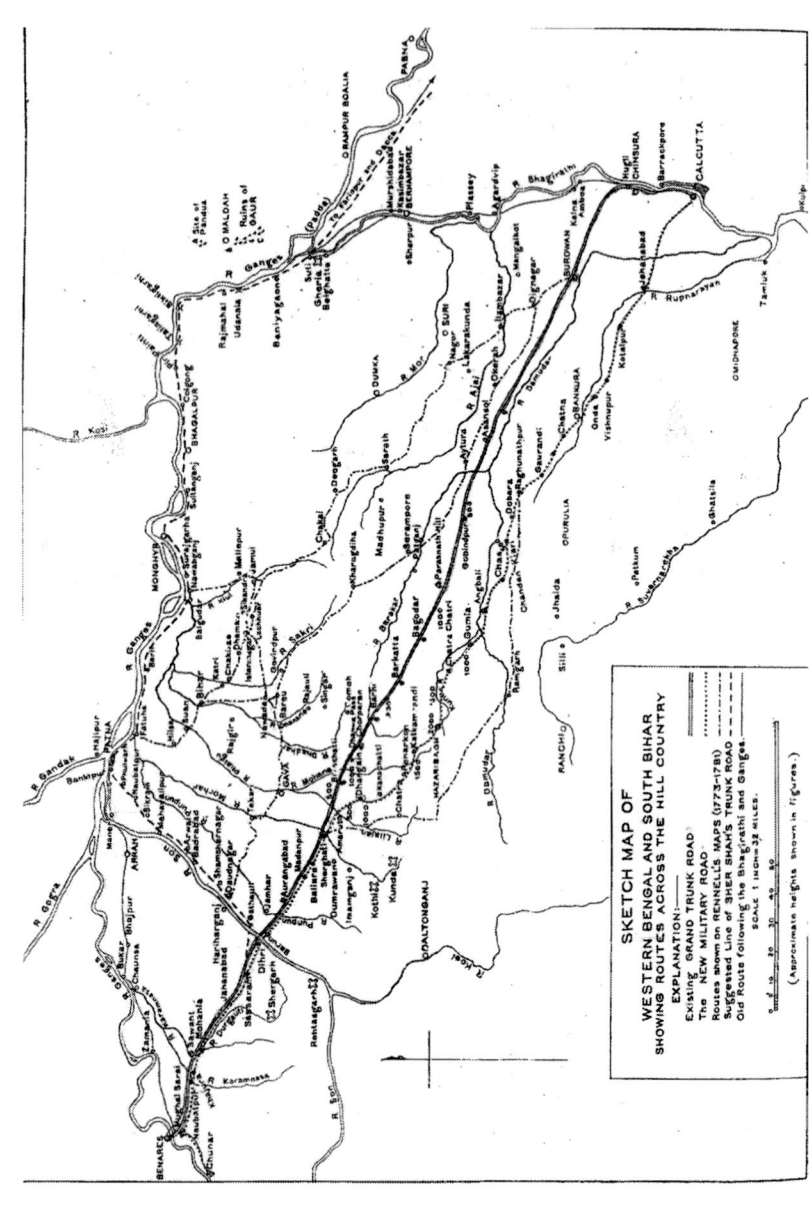

incessant reminders from the directors to maintain 'economic vigilance'. The maximum the Company was allowed to spend on all such heads, that is, roads and buildings (both civil and judicial) and fortifications, was not more than Rs. 100,000 annually.[111] The directors suggested raising money for building and repairing roads through community taxation, an idea that was contested by the Bengal authorities. The latter declared this as 'inexpedient and premature'.[112] By the 1820s, disagreement between the two bodies had turned bitter. A series of indictments and clarifications followed. On being specifically asked by the Court of Directors not to invest surplus revenue on public works, the Bengal government cast 'doubts' about some of the principles of British rule hitherto followed, underscoring the immense benefit that works such as roads and canals would bring to the trade, population and wealth of India. On this, the directors reminded the Bengal government not to forget where the final authority lay.[113]

This dispute forced the lower-level touring officials to explore alternative ways of raising funds. John Fombelle, judge-magistrate of Bhagalpur, apologetically made an appeal to use the 'dewany and foujdary fines', making clear that his intention was 'not to subject government to any expense on this account'.[114] To further save expenses, the practice began of employing convicts on the roads.[115] Although the authorities (in London) opposed any considerable investment in road building, local officials in the colonial Raj, who were convinced of the necessity of good roads, kept pressing the Indian government, which was reflected in a representation made by the Court of Circuit in 1796. Following this, the governor general in council directed Fombelle to 'pay particular attention to the preservation of the roads and prohibit the zemindars and other landholders from ploughing them up, or making any encroachments on them'.[116] In 1790–91, a Road Fund was formed in the Shahabad district. The collectors were asked to report on the conditions of existing roads, which made their winter tours very important. The Shahabad collector, A. Mclland, drew up one such report in 1794.[117] He listed six principal roads in his district, those being: first, the section of the NMR crossing through Shahabad; second, between Buxar and Culwar (Koelwar) ghat; third, the thoroughfare from Patna to Dinapore (present-day Danapur) to stations leading up to Ghazipore (present-day Ghazipur) and Benares; fourth, from Arrah to Sasseram; fifth, from Sasseram to Nasrigunj; and the sixth from Babhua in Chainpur to Mohannea. Leaving two of them aside (the NMR and the Patna–Danapur–Benares road), the

---

111 In contrast, investment on military purposes was allowed up to Rs. 4,00,000. 'Extract Military Letter to Bengal', 26 August 1801, Bcl, vol. 1115, 1829–30 F/4/1115 29886.
112 'Extract Judicial Letter from Bengal', 30 January 1813, Bcl, vol. 407, 1813–14, F/4/407 10147.
113 Bcl, vol. 962, 1827–28, F/4/962 27348.
114 'Letter from Fombelle to Barlow', 14 January 1796, Datta, ed., *BR*, 168.
115 More on this in Chapter 7.
116 'Circular from Henry St. George Tucker, Sub-Secretary to Government in the Judicial Department to Fombelle', 8 April 1796, Datta, ed., *BR*, 180.
117 'Letter from A. Mclland, Collector Shahabad to John Rawlins, Secretary to the Board of Revenue', 3 October 1794, in *Letters sent from Shahabad Collector, 1794–95*, vol. 22, BSA. I am thankful to Peter Gottschalk for bringing this letter to my notice.

rest were local, intra-district roads. Brooke, the previous collector of Shahabad, had finished work on some of these in the year 1793. He exhorted the necessity of good roads and devised a way to raise funds by asking zamindars to voluntarily contribute 1 per cent of their revenue. The zamindars reportedly 'voluntarily entered into an Akrarnamma' (agreement) and subscribed to the fund from which Mclland did some repair works.[118] By 1813 a separate Road Committee had come into existence. This lower-level initiative nevertheless lacked the government's sanction. Nor was it taken up by any other district, at least until 1813. The annual receipt of the fund was meagre, generally amounting to Rs. 9,000–10,000 annually.[119] However, a circular of 1800 in the name of the governor general purported to extend the agriculture and commerce of the country by facilitating communication between principal cities and towns. The three main instructions given to magistrates to report upon are quoted below verbatim:

> To give an account of the roads, how and in what manner they were repaired, what roads were particularly necessary and how they could best be made, whether by convicts or otherwise, what regulation was necessary to avoid encroachment and keep them in repair, whether zamindars could do it without taking it to be a hardship, whether the construction of any bridge was necessary and at what expense.
> To report on the conditions of ferries, who maintained the boats, how the expenses were being met, what arrangements were necessary for the future regulation of ferries.
> If water communication could be improved by cleaning or deepening the river beds and could it be executed by convicts and at what expense.[120]

This 'good intention' was often accompanied by unwillingness to increase the expenditure. As a result, to raise money, taxes were levied on boats. Under Regulation VII of 1801, a duty was imposed of one anna per ton on country vessels, called *dhonies*, carrying goods in the River Hooghly. In 1806 (under Regulation XVIII) a toll was levied on all boats passing through the Eastern Canal (Tolly's Nullah), and certain other *khals* (ponds, tanks) near Calcutta. In 1813 (under Regulation IV), tolls were imposed on boats plying their trade on the rivers Ichamati, Mathabhagna and Churni; the stated object was to defray expenses incurred on improvements to the rivers.[121] A few years later, under Regulation XIX of 1816, the

---

118 Some of the zamindars did not want to contribute; one such was Ramkissen Lal. 'Letter from Shahabad Collector to A. Seton, President and Member of the Board of Revenue', 24 April 1813, *PCRS*, vol. 125, 1806–13. There were two other local roads, one, a ten-mile stretch from Brookgunge on the Ganga to Arrah; and the second, an eight-mile stretch from the Koelwar ghat on the River Soane to Arrah. Both of them were passable in almost all the seasons and were kept up by voluntary contributions. 'Letter from D. Burges, Shahabad Collector to General Garslin, President and Member of the Road Committee', 13 June 1813, *PCRS*, vol. 126, 1812.
119 'Letter from D. Burgees to R. Rocke, Acting President and Member of the Board of Revenue', 27 August 1813, ibid.
120 'Order of the GG in Council contained in the Letter from Revenue and Judicial Department to W. Cowper, President and Member, Board of Revenue', 1 May 1800, Roy Chaudhury, ed., *MOR*, 184–5.
121 Gupta, *Analytical Survey*, 316.

government committed itself to providing better and safer travelling facilities. It first tried to directly manage the ferries through collectors, but it seems that the excessive duties with which the collectors were already burdened led to a revision of the regulation; ferries were now farmed to the highest bidders, who were mostly zamindars.[122] This brought financial profits, which signifies that the capacity of the notable natives to minutely monitor and regulate the means of communication other than the thoroughfares was greater than that of the 'white sahibs'. From 12 April to the end of November 1817, when the ferries were under Company management in the Saran district, the total collection was Rs. 4,897, increasing to Rs. 13,000 when the farming system was adopted.[123] Paradoxically, in the colonialist understanding, this might be one of the reasons why the zamindars remained the favourite scapegoat when it came to attributing blame for poor communication. This was precisely the content of the replies submitted by the collectors in response to the 1800 Circular. For instance, the collector of Tirhut accused the zamindars of 'not discharging their obligation to repair roads'. The reply of the collector of Saran was similar; he lamented the bad condition of the roads yet pinned his hope on zamindars 'who have been and still are bound by their engagements to repair and maintain the roads in their respective zamindaries'.[124] Most of these letters were apologetically written; improvements were necessary but it was considered better if they could be carried out 'without our honourable masters being put to the expense of one single rupee for this important advantage to the state and to the community at large'.[125] An earlier proposal to invest 1 per cent of the revenue – Rs. 800,000 annually according to an estimate of the combined revenue of Bihar, Bengal and Orissa at four *crores* – on roads and bridges never materialized.[126]

Two broader conclusions can be drawn from the above analysis: one, apart from the growing realization that a good communication network was important for the growth of trade, the colonial bureaucracy struggled to raise sufficient funds for it; two, and a related reason for this failure, was the divided nature of the bureaucracy itself.[127] The nexus of both these factors, however, paradoxically altered the situation that had developed just three decades previously.[128] The inland duty, abolished by Hastings to promote trade, was re-established in 1801 and gradually extended to all important

---

122 See 'Letters from R. Chamberlain, Secretary to the Commissioner's Office, Behar and Benares to W. Laing, Collector, Shahabad', 2 September 1817, 10 September 1817, 18 September 1816, *PCRS*, vol. 19, 1812–17; 'Letters from Chamberlain to W. Money, collector of Behar', 11 February 1817, 13 December 1817, *PCRS*, vol. 415, 1817.
123 'List of Ferries established in the district of Sarun', *PCRS*, 1818, vol. no. not given.
124 'Letter from I. R. Elphinstone, Collector of Sarun to the Secretary to the Government', ibid. This letter from 1801 is kept in the 1818 bundle.
125 Ibid.
126 'Letter from D. Burges, Shahabad Collector to General Garslin, President and Member of the Road Committee', 13 June 1813, *PCRS*, vol. 126, 1812. A definite miscalculation is at hand here: either the investible amount would be four lakhs or the total revenue eight crores.
127 As late as the 1820s, when Elphinstone (in the Bombay presidency) had proposed to make roads, a member of his own council wrote back to the Court of Directors, saying, 'the silly young nobleman actually talks of making roads!' Tremenheere, *On Public Works*, 49.
128 The following account is based on Gupta, *Analytical Survey*, 312–47, and Charles Trevelyan, *A Report upon the Inland Customs and Town-Duties of the Bengal Presidency* (Calcutta, 1834).

towns in the Bengal presidency. All articles liable to the duty had first to be brought to the official *godown* (warehouse), and paid for, after which a rowannah was secured. This was the procedure both for imports and exports within/from a town. So in place of five customhouses, under Regulation X of 1810 toll centres were now established in many other towns, such as Monghyr, Patna, Purneah, Bhagalpur, Muzaffarpur, Chapra, Arrah and Gaya. In Patna alone, not less than sixteen choukies existed, all attached to the Patna customhouse.[129] These must have generated some funds but certainly one of the motives behind this shift was neither 'philanthropic' nor 'welfarian'. According to Regulation XI of 1801, the foreign goods that came to Calcutta passed duty free into the 'interiors' if such goods were 'articles of British growth, produce or manufacture', whereas country goods 'exported' from Calcutta to the 'interiors' were charged. In other words, one of the reasons for the proliferation of choukies was to bar or to make it difficult for the home-produced goods to find their way into the different nodes of market (and thus to make it easier for imported goods).

It seems that, after 1800, communication and taxation worked hand in hand to expand the reach of British products. If we compare this drive with the thrust of the promotional literature of the 1830s to 1840s to open the country to British goods, then we can also argue that the effort to 'open up the interior' started much earlier. In this drive, structures of taxation and networks of communication became two important tools. And if we accept this proposition, then we would also have to acknowledge that the resuscitation of the interior as a closed zone and its opening up were simultaneous processes of colonial spatial discourse, in which the factors of economy, mobility, trade, aesthetics and communication all played an equally important role. There are, however, two points of difference in this comparison. In the earlier phase, even when communication was high on the agenda of 'improvement' and was looked upon as an important factor in increasing the commerce and cultivation of the country, little could actually be done because of the limited sphere of the state's activity. However vigorously it tried to improve the roads and to 'fix' the zamindars' responsibilities, it in fact achieved little. It also failed to convince the London authorities of the utility of improved communication. The Company therefore could not bring in the changes it desired. But within this limited space, it introduced a series of new regulations that brought in some shifts; the most notable amongst these was the reorientation of the trading links of Patna in particular and Bihar in general. The second point of distinction is the instability and loss of understanding on the part of the Company-state in the earlier phase in dealing with the whole issue of communication, trade, commerce, revenue and 'opening up'. Its vacillating nature becomes evident when, again by the 1830s, it started reconsidering doing away with the proliferation of choukies. By the 1830s, the idea of free trade had come full circle. On being asked about the practicability of dispensing with choukies, the Saran collector replied:

> My full conviction of the benefits which commence and general improvement [that] must experience [follow] if they [chokies] are dispensed with…the searches impede the

---

129 'Letter from Collector, Government Customs to R. M. Tilghman, Secretary to the Board of Revenue, Patna', 15 June 1824, *PCRS*, vol. 176, 1820. Most of these choukies were established along the Ganga and the Dewah (present-day Gogra) to prevent the illicit trade in salt.

inland river trade...it [sic, searches] is too often feared as a cloak for oppression and extortion, without by any means benefitting the public revenue in the proportion in which it harasses the merchants who are subjected to it.[130]

Conclusions

In this chapter 'interior' has been approached in a specific way. It has been shown, first, how personnel of the raj moved in the interiors to gather knowledge; second, how the policies, mainly related to taxation and communication, helped the products to circulate in or reach the interiors. Since in this 'opening up' drive, the initiatives of the local-level officers remained crucial and much of what they prescribed was generated through their acts of touring, we conclude this chapter by reflecting on the changing nature and meanings of the tour itself, the point with which we began this chapter. Changes in the technology of mobility were thought to enhance control at the local level. The growth in bureaucracy was also at this time making touring a prominent activity.[131] But, paradoxically, as Pouchepadass has rightly argued, over the course of the nineteenth century, while improvement in communication might have led to an increased mobility at the local level, it nevertheless led to an erosion of the personal touch which the 'old hands' of British administration had somehow managed to establish. He argues that 'touring tended to become a series of rushes out and back to headquarters, instead of more leisurely marches from one village to another'.[132]

Such a change came more gradually than it at first sight appears. The magistrates were still going into the interiors, inspecting police thannas, taking stock of agricultural conditions and public health, reviewing the work of dispensaries, and making recommendations on 'new roads' to connect the district well.[133] The element of personal touch through physical presence had also not completely ceased.[134] Writing in 1870

---

130 'Letter from Collector of Saran to W. Ewer, Commissioner of Revenue, Saran Division', 5 June 1832, *PCRS*, vol. 94, 1832.
131 The following account gives an idea of the enhanced circulation of personnel. In one winter season in the Gaya district there were four officers who were on tour. The magistrate of Gaya was out between 1 November 1870 and 28 February 1871; Mr Newbery, officiating first-class magistrate in charge of the Sherghatty subdivision between 7 November 1870 and 19 February 1871; a Bengali deputy magistrate of Nawada, Baboo Bimal Charan Bhattacharya, between 21 November 1870 and 24 March 1871 (the magistrate had also gone to the Nawada subdivision), and another native deputy magistrate, Moulvi Delwar Hossen Ahmed, in charge of the Aurungabad subdivision, was on tour for about six weeks. 'Letter from A. V. Palmer, Magistrate, Gaya to Commissioner of Patna', 21 April 1871, P. C. Roy Chaudhury, *Gaya Old Records* (Patna, 1958), 307–10. [Henceforth *GOR*.]
132 Pouchepadass, 'Itinerant Kings', 270. A range of new techniques of communication was responsible for that. If the telegraph diminished the acquaintance of officers with their districts, the advent of cars and telephones made the collector increasingly remote from his environment. Ibid., 270.
133 *GOR*, 284–5.
134 In 1871, on a visit by the assistant collector of Bhudruck (in Orissa), the *ryots* (peasants) complained to him about the illegal exactions made by the zamindars. Subsequently, a petition was forwarded to John Beams, the collector of Balasore, who directed his subordinate to 'make strict inquiry into the truth'. *SOR*, 224. Also see 'Tour Diary of W. C. Costley,

Chesney regarded the 'isolated community' – collector-magistrate and his two assistants with the district judge – as embodying 'all the functions of government with which the people of each district have any practical experience'.[135] Henry Cotton reminisced how as a subdivisional officer in the Nuddea district of Bengal from 1869 into the 1870s he acquired from camp life local knowledge, which he utilized in the assessment of income tax, which was then a new imposition. And this was done in circumstances when 'we had no assistants, no old registers and nothing to guide us in making a first assessment'.[136] These local nuggets of information were crucial for Hunters' multivolume *Statistical Account of Bengal*, published in the 1870s.

This personal touch was, however, often mixed with a 'perpetual fear of things done behind the back'.[137] 'Native conspiracy' was always suspected but, interestingly, 'speed' was something which was criticized, quite akin to the woes expressed on the loss of the picturesque. The difference was that this set of ruminations dealt with 'administrative' and not 'aesthetic' characteristics. Beams criticized Richard Temple for mishandling the 1866 famine crisis because Temple: '[I]n his usual theatrical way rode at the rate of fifty or sixty miles a day through the districts, forming as he said, an opinion on the condition of the people and the state of crops.' He further continued: 'What kind of opinion or what kind of observation could be formed by riding at a gallop along a road, no one could make out.'[138] Contrast it with the case existing a few decades earlier, when the government had made it clear that officers travelling during their public duty need not 'prolong their march beyond the rate of 15 miles in each day'.[139] The coming of the railways seemingly affected the vice-regal tours more than the 'statistical touring'.[140] The governor generals and viceroys now preferred not to tour by road, a probability that Emily Eden had foreseen: 'Now that India has fallen under the curse of railroads, the splendour of a governor general's progress is at end.'[141] Though private discomfort was compensated by first-class carriages providing the best possible facilities, public grandeur, which created a spectacle-on-the-march that constituted and represented authority, was

---

Deputy Magistrate of Sherghatty for the Cold Weather of 1866', 17 March 1866, *GOR*, 288–9. Costley took a large number of *fouzdary* and *abkari* cases during his tour. When John Beams retired from Champaran, apparently the ryots did not trust any other magistrate, but insisted on the authorities sending back the 'Chasmawala' (man with specs). *Memoirs of a Bengal Civilian by John Beams*, new edn (Delhi, 1984), 184. During one of his tours in the 1870s, Edward Lockwood, magistrate of Monghyr, 'got an invitation from the Manjhi or chief Santhal (Manjhis were the village headmen) to have a day's jungle-fowl shooting under his guidance in the hills'. Lockwood, *Natural History, Sport and Travel* (London, 1878), 81.

135 George Chesney, *Indian Polity: A View of the System of Administration in India*, 2nd edn (London, 1870), 209–10.
136 Cotton, *Indian and Home Memories*, 95.
137 *Memoirs of a Bengal Civilian*, 212.
138 Ibid., 232.
139 'Bengal Occurrences for July 1805', *AAR* 8 (for the year 1806): pt 1, 20.
140 For that part of the Prince of Wales' visit made by railways in India, it was said, 'days and nights in the atmosphere of gilded and golden saloons, surrounded by every luxury that the imagination could desire'. *Five Months with the Prince*, 68.
141 Eden, *Up the Country*, v–vi.

now greatly diminished.[142] And with this there came, at least for many civilians who lived to see the changes from the early to the late nineteenth century, the loss of personal touch. 'The good old times' for Cotton had become a bygone era, where after the camp he would have sat with the 'grey bearded householders of the village, garrulous old men gossiping of everything – the quarrels with their landlord, the dacoity in the neighbouring dwelling, the rice crop gathered in the garner...the pestilence in April...the rates of rent and labour...the rise of river'. He sadly concluded about the latter days: there was 'no one word of information, no look of sympathy, no expression of confidence and no friendly voice'.[143] This anxiety was best expressed in W. Oldham's lines: 'And now the shrein [sic] of the motor horn is heard all along the great road [the GTR] in place of the pious, thankful call of "Ram! Ram!" Can we wonder why the officers of olden days knew the country more intimately than their modern successors?'[144]

Of the variety of initiatives, ranging from picturesque voyages to geological surveys and from vice-regal trips to winter tours, that were made in the attempt to get to know the country, we have observed that there was no single way of representing space. Even within the romantic journeys driven by the dominant mode of the contemporary aesthetic values we saw that the gaze was not altogether flattening. However, what we now proceed towards speaks strongly of the objectifying impulses of colonial rule. One could treat this as yet another instance of the immanent contradictions of colonialism, but this will be only a partial explanation if one does not explain the reasons for this contradiction. The contradictions we are talking about are related to the processes of knowledge formation of routes and roads and their representation on maps. As noted earlier, even in the world of localized circuits of administrative mobility, routes and roads were a prime object that not only formed part of the textual corpus of the colonial knowledge-pool but were also significantly represented in the visual mediums (maps). In the next chapter we look at the modalities in which a more specific genre of topographical knowledge evolved and how that knowledge was represented in the visual mediums.

---

142 'Public grandeur and private discomfort' is Eden's expression. She named her tent the 'Misery Hall' and Auckland named his the 'Foully Palace'. Ibid., vi, 53 respectively. Many other accounts give an idea of 'public discomfort'. For instance see, Deane, *A Tour*, 10, 218; Raleigh, *'The Log of a Griffin'*, 37. But for some, such marches, especially the tent life, was fairly comfortable with commodious tents supplied with every available necessity in a liberal quantity, with two or three servants waiting on an officer's arrival to shave and dress him, and finally with the provisions to serve an excellent breakfast. Captain John Luard, *A Series of Views in India; Comprising Sketches of Scenery, Antiquities and Native Character, Drawn from Nature and on Stone* (London, 1833), 1095.
143 Cotton, *Indian and Home Memories*, 96.
144 Oldham, 'Routes: Old and New', 31.

Chapter 4

KNOWING THE WAYS

Neither the accumulation of route knowledge nor the compilation of such was 'colonial' in origin. Imperial marches and journeys under Mughal rule often employed a class of people who measured the roads. Further, such calculations were followed by building coss minarets at regular intervals. This practice was followed not only when monarchs and kings travelled at a leisurely pace but also, as is evident from the hasty march of Shah Azam, in times of speedy journeys over a wide geographical distance. The prince, who took nineteen days travelling from Patna to Delhi, was constantly accompanied by twelve troopers, four footmen, one *chobdar* (mace carrier), one *jarib-kash* (road measurer) and two *ghariwalas* (time keepers).[1] A famous text of the Mughal period is *The Chahar Gulshan*, written in 1759–60 by Rai Chaturman Saksena. It was a route table, together with, as Irfan Habib has suggested, 'cartographic' elements.[2] Similarly, a map showing the northwest frontier regions together with Kashmir and the north of India, which, R. H. Phillimore suggests, dates between 1650 and 1730, 'records the stages and distances between these towns [shown on the map], the crossings of the great rivers and the main passes through the border hills'.[3] Registers of marches depicting actual measured distances (of course often without inflections and latitude) were kept, which James Rennell generously admitted as being superior to the vague report or judgement.[4] Certain safarnamas (travel accounts) also gave information on routes and stages,[5] and diaries gave information on itineraries. Yusuf Ali Khan, who wrote the *Tarikh-i Bangala-i Mahabat Jangi*, also wrote *Majmu'a-i Yusufi*, two sections of which contain a diary of the itinerary that 'relate to the events connected with Yusuf Ali's journey from Murshidabad to Patna in the company of Mir Qasim'.[6] Early colonial administrators and surveyors, in particular, made frequent use of a range of 'native' sources to supplement their own works, which evidently proves that

---

1 *Maasir-i-Alamgiri*, 113. On the practices of road measurement and building coss minarets, see Farooque, *Roads and Communications*, 28–31. Also, Jadunath Sarkar, *The India of Aurangzib (Topography, Statistics and Roads) Compared with the India of Akbar* (Calcutta, 1901).
2 Irfan Habib, 'Cartography in Mughal India', *The Indian Archives* 28 (January–December, 1979): 95.
3 R. H. Phillimore, 'Three Indian Maps', *Imago Mundi* 9 (1952): 111.
4 R. H. Phillimore, *Historical Records of the Survey of India*, 5 vols (Dehra Sun, 1945–68), vol. 1, 10. (Henceforth *HR*. Further references are to vol. 1 unless otherwise mentioned.)
5 Latif's safarnama, the title of which reads 'Sair-ul-Manazil Wal-Bilad Wal Amsar' also denoted that it was an account of the various stages, cities and areas visited by him. N. D. Ahuja, 'Abd-al-Latif Al 'Abbasi and his Account of Punjab', *Islamic Culture* 41 no. 2 (1967): 97.
6 Abdus Subhan, 'Tarikh-i Bangala-i Mahabat Jangi of Yusuf Ali Khan', *Islamic Culture* 40, no. 4, pt 2 (1966): 188.

the culture of making maps, maintaining route diaries, fort plans, and what Susan Gole has called 'picture narratives' was fairly well established in pre-colonial polities, especially among the Marathas and the Mughals.[7] Sometimes independent travellers also marked their routes on these picture narratives, which were used as *paubhas* (wall hangings). One such example is a paubha made by one Shri Chikidhi in 1802, which showed him, his wife and their son on a journey through various stages to Kathmandu, suggesting that marking routes and making space intelligible was not strictly restricted to political usages alone.[8] The Company-state's willingness to acquire all sorts of knowledge, as reflected in Hastings' statement, is no more surprising: 'Every accumulation of knowledge,' he said, 'and especially such as is obtained by social communication with people over whom we exercise a dominion founded on the right of conquest is useful to the state.'[9] Territorial acquisition and the gradual bureaucratization of colonial rule after 1757 made the knowledge of routes necessary. The fluid political condition of the late eighteenth century required the Company-state to possess knowledge about various passes, routes and ghats (mountain passes) in order to augment its military efficacy. As a result, the phase of route surveys started just after the 1757 Battle of Plassey.

This process was almost simultaneously accompanied by the publication of such marches and journeys, individually as articles in contemporary journals or as compilations. Further, this textual compilation was often accompanied by the visual display of routes on maps, which had their own politics of representation. Yet these route books were clearly not the sole provider of information on roads and rivers; such information was scattered in almost all the types of sources we have discussed so far. But here we have a corpus of printed materials that specifically provided information only on the existing communication network. I contend that this aspect distinguishes them from other sources, though not in the sense that the information presented was either radically *different* from or *new* in relation to other sources, such as the travelogues or the district revenue surveys, but different and new in terms of the emergence of the new genre of 'road books', which in many ways anticipated the mid-nineteenth-century travel guides and travel books. And so it is with maps. The maps that we discuss here primarily (indeed only) aim to show networks of roads. True, such networks were shown on other types of maps as well, for example in geological, revenue and trigonometrical maps, but their function, however overlapping, was not self-professedly to point out the roads on the maps in the same manner as did the 'communication maps'.[10] Apart from the information on routes collected through district-level tours, a route survey

---

7 Susan Gole, *Indian Maps and Plans: From Earliest Times to the Advent of European Surveys* (New Delhi, 1989); Prasad P. Gogate and B. Arunachalam, 'Area Maps in Maratha Cartography: A Study in Native Maps of Western India', *Imago Mundi* 50 (1998).

8 Gole, *Indian Maps*, 68.

9 Kapil Raj, 'Colonial Encounters and the Forging of New Knowledge and National Identities: Great Britain and India, 1760–1850', *Osiris*, 2nd series, 15 (2000): 122.

10 The purpose of this clarification is to explain that the arguments in this chapter are not, as could mistakenly be alleged, based on comparing the incomparable, which is, picking up the examples from different genres of texts and maps. In other words, the analysis presented here builds upon a similar type of texts, what has been defined as 'route and road books' and of maps, defined as 'communication maps'.

was an important and in fact more specific way of gathering information. The following section does not provide a descriptive account of such surveys, since this has already been done by Matthew Edney in his seminal work;[11] it rather concentrates on raising some issues regarding their mechanisms and implications. By the former, I mean specifically to revisit the often-discussed and perhaps 'tiresome' debate on the role of natives in the formation of colonial knowledge. The need to revisit this issue stems from the recent approach that uses the concept of 'circulation' in understanding the nature and processes of knowledge formation in the colonial set-up. But later and by implication I want to address some of the issues related to the historiographical contention about mapping and space, a point which we explore in the third section of this chapter, where we engage with maps.

Route Surveys: Mechanisms and Implications

One of the motives behind surveys was to 'ensure the safety and regularity of communications'.[12] Of course, in doing so the larger aim was to improve the understanding about the topography and geography of India. The immediate colonial implications of such surveys were based on military necessity; the territorial acquisition in Bengal and subsequent wars with Mysore in the south prompted the Company-state to have surveys made of these regions.[13] Henry Vansittart, the then governor of Bengal, wanted the acquired territories to be carefully surveyed and so made contact with Rennell who when at Madras was slowly making his name in the field of surveying.[14] Later, Clive continued to give Rennell support and encouragement.

The 'Maratha incursions' into Bengal had made it necessary for the Company-state to safeguard the frontiers of its newly acquired territory. The aim was to know the hill passes both along the Balasore (Orissa) region and southwest Bihar, which were the usual entry zones for Marathas into Bengal. In 1760, in the wake of the Maratha incursion into the region of Burdwan and Balasore, one Captain White was asked to keep a journal of his marches and to employ, if possible, an officer 'who understands enough of drawing to describe the roads' and 'the situation of every large village or other remarkable object'.[15] In 1766 Colonel Richard Smith was posted at Sasseram in Bihar 'to observe and report on the movements of the Marathas and to keep watch over the roads and passes in Bihar'.[16] In the same year, de Gloss, who earlier had made surveys of parts of Burdwan and Midnapur in Bengal, was recalled and sent to Smith to undertake a survey of the Bihar roads and hill passes along the River Soane.[17] Another motivation was linked to

---

11 Edney, *Mapping an Empire*.
12 Raj, 'Circulation and the Emergence of Modern Mapping: Great Britain and Early Colonial India, 1764–1820', in Markovits, et al., *Society and Circulation*, 30; G. F. Heaney, 'Rennell and the Surveyors of India', *GJ* 134, no. 3 (September 1968): 318.
13 *HR*, 2, 4.
14 Rennell Rodd, 'Major James Rennell. Born 3 December 1742. Died 20 March 1830', *GJ* 75, no. 4 (April 1930): 292.
15 *URG*, record nos. 534, 491 and 509, pages 334–5, 313, 321 respectively.
16 R. R. Diwakar, ed., *Bihar Through the Ages* (Bombay, 1959), 587.
17 See *HR*, 22–5 for other initiatives taken during this time.

Bengal's internal political set-up; when Mir Qasim had fled to Oudh, the British did not pursue him because they did not know the routes. As a result, James Nicholl, whom we encountered above in the discussion about the construction of the NMR, was sent to survey the roads between the River Karmanasha and Calcutta.[18] If one aspect of these surveys was to know the colony better, the other, clearly related, was to safeguard it from other European powers. Surveying thus was also a part of inter-European conflicts and power struggles played out in the field of knowledge acquisition in South Asia. For instance, Nicholl went to Balasore with a detachment of sepoys to prevent French ships that were then in the Bay of Bengal from getting supplies and provisions (wood, water, etc.) from the nearby villages; on this same trip he was asked by his superior, Major R. Knox, to survey the mouth of the River Pipli.[19] In 1766, the Company asked the Court of Directors to employ a surveyor of roads.[20] By 1767 Rennell was appointed surveyor general. The Company, accepting the need for accurate surveys, both for military operations and 'in coming at a true knowledge of the value of possessions' exuded great enthusiasm by 'employing everybody on this service who could be spared and were capable of it [survey]'.[21] Not restricted to Rennell alone, the most celebrated surveyor, 'the era of route surveys continued till the end of the eighteenth century'.[22]

It is well known that in these survey operations the European understanding of Indian topography was not devoid of 'native' input. But the use of native maps, texts and skills did not detract from the conviction that 'Indians did not like surveys'. Upon the refusal of the nawab of Carnatic in the 1770s to allow the British to carry a general survey of his area, Robert Kelly of the Madras Infantry remarked in 1782: 'The Natives of India never think of surveying large territories or of settling their boundaries in anything like straight lines.'[23] Such claims, rather than depicting the truth, hide a complex network of exchange and recognition, ignorance and accusation that were all part of the native–European knowledge circulation regimes. In recent years, the concept of 'circulation' or 'co-constitution' has been adopted for understanding this exchange process.[24] No one

---

18 S. C. Hill, 'Major Randfarlie Knox, Dilawar Jang Bahadur: A Memoir', *JBORS* 3, pt 1 (1917): 152.
19 Ibid., 132.
20 *URG*, record no. 858, 588.
21 Ibid., record no. 929, 639.
22 Heaney, 'Rennell and the Surveyors of India', 319. These could be seen as part of an emerging genre, which Matthew Edney calls 'geographical narratives'. Such surveys became the rage among all sorts of colonial officials, civil and military, who contributed their accounts as 'Journal of a March' or 'Journal of the Route' to the leading journal – *The Asiatic Society of Bengal* – of the period. Edney, *Mapping an Empire*, 64–78.
23 Gole, *Indian Maps and Plans*, 36. And yet how little Kelly's own work – 'an excellent atlas of South India' – was appreciated is proved by the fact that the EIC declined to publish it. Ibid., 36, fn. 29.
24 The idea of 'contact zone' is from Pratt, *The Imperial Eyes*; the historiography of 'collaboration' goes back at least to the 1960s, starting with studies on nationalism and coming down to the information-gathering system under colonialism in India. For co-constitution and circulation of knowledge in the case of South Asia, see Markovits et al., *Society and Circulation* and Raj, *Relocating Modern Science*.

would deny (and as it has been convincingly shown in some of these studies) that natives did contribute in various ways to the formation of knowledge during colonial times. Similarly, it is now fairly well established that texts, maps and other artefacts of knowledge circulated across time and space. What remains nevertheless important is to tease out the nature of that circulation, both in terms of power relations between natives and Europeans on the one hand, and in terms of the usages of texts and maps on the other. One strand adopted for analysing this co-constitution is to place 'colonial knowledge' under the larger rubric of universalism that marked the period. Continuing in the same paragraph (part of which is quoted above), Hastings noted it:

> ...is useful to the state: it is the gain of humanity: ...it attracts and conciliates distant affections; it lessens the weight of the chain by which the natives are held in subjection... Every instance which brings their real character home to observation will impress us with a more generous sense of feeling for their natural rights, and teach us to estimate them by the measure of our own.[25]

A second strand, which comes out clearly in Raj's work, is not only to look at the native input (which indeed is one of the strongest points in Bayly's *Empire and Information*) but also to thematize such contributions under the 'trust' and 'civility' that existed between collaborators of all colours. He rightfully asks us to identify and enquire into 'the nature of the vectors of knowledge transmission'.[26] There is certainly no dispute that circulation itself is the locus for both the formation and dislocation of knowledge. However, the analysis should go beyond identifying circulation as a site in itself into interrogating the 'politics' that make and remake that site continuously, the processes which it not only affects but also gets affected by. Thus Raj's approach seemingly addresses one part of the story, the other part requires us to ask: what was the nature of the axes along which the vectors of knowledge transmission moved and rotated? Raj acknowledges the presence of asymmetries of power,[27] but nowhere in his work are the implications of such asymmetries explored; the implications which will require, conceptually and theoretically, asymmetries to be treated as part of the same body of circulation that constituted knowledge. Few of his own examples can in fact be read otherwise. For instance, Raj shows how crucial it was for Jardin and probably for all other Europeans to make friends with local organized knowledge communities (as Jardin did with fakirs) in order to get to know Hindustan. The obverse side of this logic would mean that those who failed to do so became victims of marginalized reach or of 'segmented circulation'. In fact, the fate of Jardin's monumental work shows precisely how the text failed to

---

25 Quoted in Michael J. Franklin, 'General Introduction and [meta]historical Background [re] presenting "The palanquins of state; or, broken leaves in a Mughal garden"', in Franklin, ed., *Romantic Representations of British India* (Oxford, 2006), 13. For a useful discussion on the role and functions of surveys cutting across the needs and limits of foreign rule, see Peter Robb, 'Completing "Our Stock of Geography" or an Object "Still More Sublime": Colin Mackenzie's Survey of Mysore 1799–1810', *Journal of the Royal Asiatic Society* 8, no. 2 (1998): 184–5.
26 Raj, *Relocating*, 10.
27 Ibid., 13, 90–92.

enter into the circuits of knowledge transmission. The second example can be extracted from what Raj succinctly describes as 'flight of maps', which were conspicuous in the late eighteenth century. These maps, which were privately owned or used for decorating the walls of the living rooms of leading officials, again point towards the limitation of circulation. We will come to our first concern (the nature of asymmetrical exchange between natives and Europeans) shortly, but to end this present discussion, one could look at an example to see that the circulation of texts and maps were considerably segmented in our period. Jean Baptiste Joseph Gentil, who had spent twenty-five years in India from 1752 to 1777, ten of which as the official French agent at the Court of Oudh, personally presented his manuscripts with twenty-one maps to the king of France with these words: 'Today, when your glorious reign has given to the name of France the greatest renown in all parts of the globe, this is the time to make use of your victory to enlarge the commerce of the nation. This volume can help fulfil this design.'[28] Yet his texts and maps were hardly used by someone like Rennell. According to Gole, Gentil's atlas failed to produce any influence on the European cartography of India. Rennell was certainly aware of Gentil's work; he had used Gentil once, quoting a longitude reading of Pondicherry.[29] Traditional Anglo–French rivalry (and guarding maps and charts from 'foreign' nations) could be one of the explanations, but there are examples when the boundaries were breached. Rennell himself was using Jean d'Anville's work (who was commissioned by the French East India Company to produce a map of India); he in turn had relied considerably on Jesuit missionaries' travelogues and maps.[30] Robert Orme, an EIC officer, was in contact with another Frenchman, Anquetil Duperron, who had published his *Description geographique et historique de l'Inde* in 1787. The failure of Gentil's work to enter into the circulatory ambit could also be because of the change in political conditions in France, yet this again does not explain why his memoir, published by his son in 1822, remained 'almost unknown'. Such proofs of lack of circulation also existed closer to home, in the colonial context; for instance, Rennell did not acknowledge the works of Nicholl and Knox. The reasons will probably never be known; they may stem from his intentional choice not to use their surveys, or from the unavailability of the reports. What it does leave us with is the fact that we must recognize the limits of circulation and integrate this factor into our discussion on any aspect of knowledge production. We will return to this point.

To return to our earlier question of native input, we will start with Rennell, whose career, as argued by Andrew Cook, can be seen in two phases. First came the years he spent in India. This phase was directed towards making surveys, editing and compiling different route journals kept by army personnel, and bringing them together in maps.

---

28 Gole, *Maps of Mughal India: drawn by Colonel Jean-Baptiste-Joseph Gentil, agent for the French Government to the Court of Shuja-ud-daula at Faizabad, in 1777* (London, 1988), 4.
29 Ibid., 3.
30 Prominent among them were Father Monserrate (1536–1600), Joseph Tieffenthaler (1710–85), Father Bouchet (who made a map of south India in 1719), and the Jesuit Boudier (who provided the exact positions of Delhi, Agra and Madras). Gole, *Early Maps*, 37; Barrow, *Making History*, 90–91. Also, Jean d'Anville, *A Geographical Illustration of the Map of India*, trans. William Herbert (London, 1759), 22.

Two publications belonged to this phase.[31] In fact, during his stay in India itself, after 1770, Rennell was occupied less with surveys and more with map compilation.[32] The second phase, marked by the publication of his *Memoir*, was driven towards the larger pursuit of laying the foundations for the cartographic knowledge of the geography of India. In his published works, both in the *Description* and in the *Memoir*, he refused to give the natives any role in the collection of information. For instance, in his 'Preface' to the first edition of the *Memoir*, he remarked, 'it ought rather to surprise us that so much geographical matter should be collected during so short a period; especially where so little has been contributed towards it by the natives themselves, as in the present case'.[33] Similarly, in his 'Preface' to *Description*, he said 'no information whatever can be derived from them [native guides], and as for the peasantry, or ryots, they cannot be supposed to know the roads beyond the circle of markets which they frequent'.[34] But in his travel diary, which was published much later, he unequivocally accepted meeting a boatman during his river survey 'who seemed to be an intelligent Fellow', and one from whom he received information about creeks and the weight of boats that could pass through them.[35] Thus, in a journal that was kept on a daily basis, he accepted meeting an intelligent native, whereas in the *Memoir*, which showcased his lifelong enterprising engagement in a colony to a wider European audience, he was unwilling to allow the natives any contributory role. Yet in the same *Memoir* he gave further information on the native contribution, this time in terms of texts, not personnel. He acquired the knowledge of the Punjab region from a Persian map, which was a 'valuable acquisition' conveying 'a distinct idea of the courses and names of the five rivers, which we never had before'.[36] Similarly, it was details from the itinerary of Ghulam Muhammed, a sepoy officer under Captain Camac, which were used for learning about the routes between Bengal and Deccan. For finding out about the area of Bundelkhand, Rennell used what he called a 'Hindoo map of that country'. The picture of both borrowing and repudiation that emerges from this account is thus contradictory. Part of it can be explained, as has been done above, by closely looking at the nature and readership of the text, which might have framed the contours of the narratives not only for him but also for many other officials in allowing (or not allowing) them to openly accommodate and accept the native contribution. Most of the time, as Edney has argued, they did not.[37] Beyond that, what also appears true

---

31 James Rennell, *Description* and *A Bengal Atlas*. The latter was published first in 1780, was then lost and subsequently republished in 1781. See Andrew S. Cook for an exhaustive account of the different publications and their contents. Cook, *Major James Rennell and A Bengal Atlas (1780 and 1781)* (India Office Library and Records Report, 1976). Both these publications came out after he had returned to England in 1777, but according to Phillimore he produced numerous manuscripts and maps when he was in India. Ibid., 10–11.
32 Cook, *Major James Rennell*, 9.
33 Rennell, *Memoir of a Map of Hindoostan; or the Mogul's Empire* (London, 1785), iv. The first edition came out in 1783, the preface of which is reproduced in the second edition. In subsequent citations I will not point out the editions unless necessary for making a point of shift. The page numbers cited are from the second edition.
34 Rennell, *Description*.
35 La Touche, ed., *The Journal of Major James Rennell*, 21.
36 Rennell, *Memoir*, vi–vii, 57.
37 Edney, *Mapping an Empire*, 81–2.

is that this contradictoriness, which was also typical of Hodges' account, was one of the chief characteristics of early colonial rule in India.

To present another example of this contradictory character, which now relates to the implication part of the survey text as outlined above, let us go back to Rennell again. In writing the *Memoir* his aim was, in his own words, to examine 'some positions in the former system of Indian Geography; and some illustrations of the present one'.[38] So for bringing the ancient and the modern together, he was not only using the recent survey reports but also engaging with ancient texts on geography and topography, ranging from Ptolemy to Abul Fazl. Of peculiar interest here is his take on Abul Fazl's *Ain-i Akbari*. To him the *Ain-i Akbari* constituted the 'register of highest authority' and Akbar a monarch of great interest and wisdom, who regulated the empire and conducted enquiries to ascertain revenue, population, produce, religion, arts and commerce of each individual district.[39] A quotation from the *Ain-i Akbari* on the title page of the *Memoir* is worth noting: 'These objects cannot be attained solely by means of the wealth of individuals; they require also the patronage and encouragement of Monarchs.' Rennell was seemingly invoking the authority of the *Ain-i Akbari* to elicit the support of the Court of Directors for field surveys in India – support that was so clearly unforthcoming.[40] Yet of the same text in the same edition, he said: 'From such kind of materials [*Ain-i Akbari*], nothing very accurate can be expected, and therefore I have never had recourse to them but in a very few cases, where every other species of information has failed.'[41] In spite of this bias, what is noticeably significant is that, like Gentil before him, Rennell had drafted his 'new' cartographic space on the older politico-spatial divisions of India as detailed in the *Ain-i Akbari*, which is a classic example of layered spatial configuration in the early colonial period. The demarcation of territorial space, for instance in terms of subahs and sarkars, followed Mughal praxis. The reasons to do so, in Rennell's own words, were:

> In the division of HINDOOSTAN into soubahs &c., I have followed the mode adopted by the emperor ACBAR, as it appears to me to be the most permanent one: for the ideas of the boundaries are not only impressed on the minds of the natives by tradition, but are also ascertained in the AYIN ACBAREE; a register of the highest authority.[42]

The textual authority of the *Ain-i Akbari* was thus not the only reason; in the spatial representation and arrangement of the 'new' territories to the wider British readership (which indeed was the objective of Rennell's *Memoir*) it was necessary to follow what

---

38 These words appeared in the title of the second edition of the *Memoir*.
39 Rennell, *Memoir*, iii, 2.
40 On his return to England the Court of Directors reduced Rennell's pension, granted by Warren Hastings, from £600 to £400. This, however, was restored in 1781 because the 'Court was thoroughly ashamed of their conduct'. Also, the court did not publish the *Bengal Atlas* at its own expense. Rather 'they allowed it to be brought out by a subscription of the Company's servants in India. Though Rennell was advanced a small sum of £150 for engraving the maps, he had to give the Court a bond to repay them in eighteen months.' C. R. Markham, *Major James Rennell and the Rise of Modern English Geography* (London, Paris and Melbourne, 1895), 61.
41 Quoted in Gole, *Map of Mughal India*, 7.
42 Rennell, *Memoir*, iii.

'traditional' political divisions in the Mughal Empire remained. And this was not a one-off instance; an essay describing the manners of the inhabitants of India saw India through the politico-spatial framework of the Mughal Empire. The territory of India, described as 'within the Ganges', included the whole subcontinent, but separate territorial units such as Bengal and Deccan, the author argued, were usually outside the control of the political machinery of the Mughals.[43] The late eighteenth-century European understanding of territory and its control was coloured by what had existed earlier, and was also reflected in the distinction that was maintained between Hindustan and Bengal in many of the travel writings of the period, a point noted in Chapters 1 and 2.

This does not mean that through this continuum the objective of upholding British victory and conquest or superiority was diluted either in the territorial or topographical representation through maps or in picturesque versions of landscape depictions. Nor did it mean that the emerging spatiality of territory (in the political sense), which was largely driven by British wars and acquisitions, kept the space static or essentially hinged to earlier Mughal praxis. For instance, Rennell himself subsequently pointed out that since the Mughal Empire had now been dismembered:

> ...a new division of its province has also taken place, by which means some soubahs now form a part of the dominions of three or more princes and very few are preserved entire. These modern divisions are not only distinguished in the map by the names of the present possessors, but the colouring also is entirely employed in facilitating the distinctions between them. So that the modern divisions appear, as it were, in the fore ground and the ancient ones in the back ground, one illustrating and explaining the other.[44]

But what emerges from a close perusal of the processes through which this objective (of British rule and superiority) was attained points towards protracted, negotiated and often contradictory ways. Even if read literally, the 'modern' was mapped *on to* and not *over* the 'ancient'; each explained the other, thus highlighting a processual continuum rather than a sharp break. In one of his recent articles, Matthew Edney has argued that the processes of mapping and the act of viewing and reading maps amount to a denial of space. The former includes the imposition of an idealized optic of geographical and cartographic practices that found local/indigenous practices 'incorrect', and the latter, in his own words, mean: 'In bringing a distant place to hand, the map reader ignores the realities of geographical space.'[45] This denial of space is seen as denial of history. The imposition of categories (to understand space), vision and the techniques of 'western scientific approach' of mapping over existing native practices is too obvious to deny;

---

43 'Account of the Manners of the INHABITANTS of India within the Ganges', *Weekly Miscellany; or Instructive Entertainer* 2, no. 38 (June 1774): 281.
44 Rennell, *Memoir*, iii–iv.
45 Edney, 'Bringing India to Hand', in Felicity A. Nussbaum, ed., *The Global Eighteenth Century* (Baltimore, 2003), 65. Further, it is also argued that gridding leads to the transformation of places into spaces. John Rennie Short, *Making Space: Revisioning the World, 1475–1600* (Syracuse, 2004), 3, 9, 10.

however, it is necessary to acknowledge two things. First, as seen above, the early colonial initiatives did not discard the pre-existing spatial practices and divisions, particularly those related to the notions of territorial administration. This meant that the history which this set of representation was 'creating' was also aware of the preceding historical set-up and of the changes that were gradually taking place. Second, by looking at the textual corpus of the processes of mapping, that is, the survey reports or the winter tour reports, it is hard to discern the denial of 'realities of geographical space' (the epistemological claims to understand those realities could differ).[46] Connected to this is also an idea, as some recent scholarship, especially anthropological, has brought to our attention, that the realities of 'spaces' and 'places' could mean two different things:[47] history, manners, customs, trade, agriculture, revenue, kinship, patterns of mobility, vegetation and so on, which seemingly constitute the 'reality of space' for Edney, could also be the lived experiences of a place, which keep reconstituting themselves and that particular locality.[48] And the textual corpus of mapping provided copious information on such subjects, definitely guided by its own objectives, but nonetheless without making space appear blank. Edney's reference in this discussion might appear to some as unjustified because he is not talking about textual mediums. His concern is with the visual products, the maps. However, as we have argued before, in this phase of colonial rule the diverse impulses of knowledge acquisition cut across a rigid division of mediums. So a travelogue carrying a descriptive account also had picturesque sketches and a cartographic piece showing the routes. For example, Deane's account carried a guidebook for river travel together with a map. Also, very possibly the author, either him/herself or through commissioning a set of native artists, prepared a set of albums showing a variety of themes. When dealing with the nature of 'colonial state–space' and to make sense of it through practices of mapping that included surveys which in turn included both textual and visual forms of knowledge production, it is necessary to consider sources in their totality (and also of course in their fragmented attributes wherever they appear so) before making any generalization about the nature of that space. Since the practice of route surveys was in many ways intricately related to the production of communication maps, an enquiry into our theoretical understanding (which, in this case is the idea of denial of space) acquires significance. This qualification

---

46 Regarding the imposition of the Western scientific approach as argued by Edney, see also the critique offered by Raj, *Relocating*. However, Raj fails to acknowledge Edney's discussion, which figures in the second half of his (Edney's) book and that shows how the rhetoric of 'scientificity' was marred by the structural limitations of colonial rule and therefore had to undergo severe compromises. Even by this qualification Edney nonetheless can be seen as suggesting that colonial situations 'contaminated' an otherwise 'scientific' enterprise. Edney, *Mapping an Empire*.
47 Erich Hirsch has developed the understanding of place as 'foreground actuality', which means the concrete actuality of everyday social life ('the way we now are') and space as 'background potentiality', which means 'the way we might be' referring to the 'context and form of experience beyond the everyday'. See Hirsch, 'Introduction', in Hirsch and Michael O' Hanlon, eds, *The Anthropology of Landscape: Perspectives on Place and Space* (Oxford, 1995), 1–30.
48 I am here using the concept of Locality as developed by Arjun Appadurai in *Modernity at Large: Cultural Dimensions of Globalization* (Minneapolis, 1996), ch. 9.

in no way diminishes the significant contribution from the field of cartographic studies in helping us understand the nature of space. Arguably, mapping is a practice that by bringing land arranged in a gridded space into hand or within sight, 'fixes' the places on the space and also in time. The coordinates of grid – latitude and longitude – become, in some way, the identity of the place.[49] In this regard maps present a 'new space of visibility'.[50] While sharing many of the premises of this approach, which in a way are part of the processes of objectification that we outlined at the beginning of this book, I do want to emphasize that such spaces of visibility had different indexes of formation in different overlapping mediums. What appears as new spaces of visibility on maps (visual medium) in this particular case did not reflect in the textual corpus (route surveys and tour reports). And, with greater accumulation of knowledge about routes, the visual and the textual diversified according to the purposes and readerships, thus presumably giving rise to varying notions of spaces within colonialism.

Route surveys lacked the technical precision to 'correctly' map the region, and therefore by the turn of the eighteenth century there was a growing discontent with this practice. Their importance, however, lay in the fact that they were the only secure medium of accumulating knowledge about roads and routes in the 'interiors'. It is also equally true that '[b]oth the route survey and the resultant map [were] linear in nature: both reveal[ed] a regular unfolding of a narrow band of landscape',[51] but again, such tours and surveys were also part of 'knowing the interiors', which the early colonial state deemed so necessary. Rennell's *Description* was an example of this growing necessity. By the turn of the century, such publications became conspicuously visible, if not popular.

Road Books

It is difficult to ascertain why road books and books of routes and stages came increasingly to be published, but travelling patterns in the early colonial state and the state's policies on communication and the organization of route surveys may offer us some clues. First, the move towards compiling the knowledge of routes, both existing and new ones, corresponded with the growth of territorial boundaries and the expansion of the British Empire. Troop movements required information about provisions available on routes, which some of these books furnished. Second, the stability of the empire was accompanied by increased mobility, or, as Rennell had put it, 'people employed by government [were] more sojourners'.[52] In our analysis of administrative mobility in the previous chapter

---

49 On this see Peter Robb, 'Completing "Our Stock of Geography"', especially section v. This fixation if looked upon as a process is also borne out by many other practices than just the imposition of geometric lines and grid. Most important amongst them was the dialogue with ancient texts, the best example of which in this period was the overdrawn discussion on the 'exact site' of Palibothra/Pataliputra/Patna. See William Francklin, *Inquiry Concerning the Site of Ancient Palibothra, conjectured to lie within the limits of the modern district of Bhaugulpoor, according to researches made on the spot in 1811 and 1812* (London 1815).
50 I borrow this phrase from Christian Jacob, *The Sovereign Map: Theoretical Approaches in Cartography throughout History*, trans. Tom Conley and ed. Edward H. Dahl (Chicago and London, 2006), 2.
51 Edney, *Mapping an Empire*, 94.
52 Rennell, 'Preface', *Description*.

we noticed that tours of higher officials were often planned excursions leading to acts such as the hurried transformation of roads or the clearing of jungles around residential areas.[53] The fixed itinerary and prior planning required precise knowledge about routes. Third, by the early decades of the nineteenth century, the native and private dak system was giving way to the colonial dak system, which required more detailed information about routes and roads.[54] Fourth, routes and knowledge of them apparently were also a site of contestation between state and 'natives', particularly in areas where the reach of the colonial state was limited. Surveyors' accusations of being misled can be read as an intentional act of unwillingness on the part of natives to divulge too much information. As we have seen, mistrust and collaborative dependence, the features of early colonialism, were two sides of the same coin.[55] Fifth, there was growing distrust of native route guides. An early nineteenth-century correspondence of St Fort George gives us some idea of how the corps system of route guides was organized and how it was changed and why.[56] It was a three-tier organization comprising native informants working under the command of the QMG. At the lowest level were the privates, above them the second guides, and at the top, the first guides. The existing system had three heads or first guides, five second guides and fifty privates. The three head guides were employed in the QMG office, their services being confined to translating and assisting the QMG in arranging reports of routes from the divisions.[57] The remaining two, the second guides and the privates, surveyed the roads and passes specified by the QMG. There was growing dissatisfaction among military officers with this set-up; the commander-in-chief reported: 'It was hopeless to attempt to form a body of guides who can afford that precision of information requisite for the secured movement of troops which entirely results from a daily and the most recent intercourse and is scarcely ever to be admitted in a satisfactory reliance except from a Resident in that Quarter.'[58] This reliance on the resident was accompanied with the charges that the privates' knowledge was based on recollection and memory and perishes

---

53 To 'get rid of nuisances' on the eve of the visit of the lieutenant governor of Bengal to Bhagalpur in 1854 the local magistrate ordered the clearing of the jungles. See Datta, *A Handbook*, 44.
54 In some pockets the zamindari dak prevailed as late as the 1850s. *GOR*, 142. As per Regulation XV of 1817, the official reports were not to be conveyed through zamindari dak but through the collector. But in 1855 the collector of Shahabad noted that the conveyance through zamindari dak 'has become the custom and the sudden prohibition would entail much inconvenience to the government and the public'. 'Letters from/to Shahabad Collector for the month of August 1855', *PCRS*, vol. 590, 1853–54.
55 Interestingly, this was also a feature of the pre-colonial states. For instance, Marathas used the 'Modi' as a secret script to annotate their maps so that the Mughals could not decipher them. Gole, *Indian Maps*, 34.
56 The following account is based on 'Regulations for the corps of guides regarding route surveys', Bcl, F/4/201 4547, vol. 201, 1807–08. A Madras soldier, John Pringle, had set up a military corps of guides earlier. It was probably the same institution which one Captain Blacker wanted to change. See *HR*, 4.
57 It appears from the account that these were Brahmins by caste, because while discussing the mode of punishment it was expressed that flogging would hurt their caste sentiments.
58 'Commander-in-Chief to the Quarter Master', 3 May 1805, ibid. The frustration of English officers owing to the alleged dereliction on the part of harkaras (messengers) is mentioned also by Bayly, *Empire and Information*, 68.

with their deaths. As a result, the new system proposed to have three first guides, twelve second guides and only thirty-six privates. Seven second guides with twenty-one privates were to accompany different army battalions; the rest were under the direct supervision of the QMG. The reduction of the number of privates, it was suggested, was to be compensated by the maintenance of written records.

The above case does not signify a complete decline in the practice of hiring natives for survey works. On the contrary, natives were used throughout the nineteenth century. What did shift was the spatial theatre of their activities: for the lesser known areas, or in T. G. Montgomerie's words, for 'countries which are not yet accessible to Europeans', where it was still hazardous for the white sahibs to travel, natives were sent to gather topographical reports. This fact also shows that while the credibility of route surveys might have declined in the heart of British possessions, it was still the only secure means of finding out about unknown or frontier regions. The trained native surveyors, commonly known as Pundits, arguably became 'instruments' of mapping. These frontier regions were Tibet, Central Asia and Eastern Turkistan.[59]

The close association of the QMG office with the army establishment makes it clear that a set of road books were specifically meant to provide information for troops on the march. One such publication appeared in 1814, produced by QMG Colonel John Paton.[60] Meant for assisting the movement of troops, this book was widely used within the EIC military establishment: within seven years it ran into its third edition. Revisions were undertaken, at the behest of the government of India, to show recent political changes and the extent of the territory added. Two hundred and fifty copies of the third edition were authorized to be published, out of which 179 were said to be 'necessary for immediate issue'. Six of those were to be sent to members of the Board of Commissioners for India affairs, the remaining to be kept in the depot of the QMG's office.[61] This clearly shows that the readership of this book was very limited and was restricted to official circles. The third edition was updated; a 'supplement' was added, giving information about 200 new routes. It also gave information on the stages and availability of bazaars, either at those stages or at nearby villages where supplies could be procured. Most of the 'new' routes, or more precisely the routes about which knowledge had been newly acquired, were in the region of Central India, showing the current political expansion that the Company had made. Some of the routes connected with places such as Hazaribagh, Palamow and Chitra in south Bihar. However, there was no map in the book.

In 1838 *Revised Tables of Routes and Stages* was published. Compiled from documents in the QMG's office and other details procured from local authorities, this book appears to be a revision of the above work. Again, the kind of the information given suggests that it was a guidebook for troops and had a limited official readership, primarily military. It gave details on camping grounds, water supply, the availability of boats or ferries at *nullahs* (streams) for 'crossing a regiment' and so on. Besides a map, this volume had a

---

59 See Raj, *Relocating*, ch. 6. The above quote is from T. G. Montgomerie, 'On the Geographical Position of Yarkund, and Some Other Places in Central Asia', *JRGS* 36 (1866): 166.
60 John Paton, *Tables of Routes and Stages Through the Several Districts, Under the Presidency of Fort William*, 1st edn (1814). I have consulted the third edition (Calcutta, 1821).
61 'A Revised Edition of John Paton's Routes', Bcl, F/4/710 19375, vol. 710, 1823–24.

'Polymetrical Table showing the number of stages between the military stations through out the Presidency of Fort William and the Governorship of the NWP', compiled by Major William Garden, the army's deputy QMG.

Rennell's *Description*, which was published before the above two works, was, however, of a slightly different nature. Although based on extensive survey reports, he still preferred to call it 'a complete travelling guide'. The book was not produced through any military establishment initiative and thus had no reason to be used only within the limited military circle. By calling it a general travelling guide, Rennell most plausibly meant not only to address the book to the civilians and military men living in India but to attract the readership from his home country, at least from amongst those who had India-centric interests or were planning and willing to make a career in India. It definitely, therefore, had a wider readership than the first two books mentioned above. The information given in *Description* also is not military specific; for instance, we do not find information (as in the two above) on things like encampment grounds or the provision of supplies for marching troops and so on. On the face of it, the book appears to be the first of its kind in providing information on different routes for European travellers, which of course consisted of new cadets arriving to join the service in India.

To this later trend of the travelling guide belongs another book, published in 1828.[62] This was undoubtedly meant for general travellers. The book was purposely designed in a 'convenient size', which travellers could carry easily and the plates were coloured to assist them in readily recognizing the routes. In the 1828 version (it seems to be a re-edited version; the exact date of the first edition is not known) the size of the maps and the book were cut down. Information about dak stages, travelling rates, the distances between major cities and the length of journeys were given. Another edition of this book came out in the 1830s (again, the exact year is not known), but it was not a revised edition; the number of plates (112) and the rates of travelling remained the same. Apart from the plates showing the routes mentioned in the text, the volume carried a general skeleton map showing the 'principal' roads (see Plate 17). Even the 1838 *Revised Tables of Routes and Stages*, though giving textual information about many routes (thus fulfilling its military purposes) showed only 'principal' routes on the map. Similar travelling guides were also published for river routes. One such was the *Illustrations of the Rivers Hooghly and Ganges*.[63] This gave information about the routes and distances from Calcutta to Kanpur, the details of intermediate stations together with the cities, towns and villages situated on the either side of the Ganga. Another such guide was prepared by A. Deane for the River Ganga, which was appended in her travelogue.

Three years before, in 1825, John B. Seely had published *The Road Book of India*, or what he called the 'East Indian Traveller's Guide'.[64] It was not a government publication. Seely was employed in the Bombay army and later became military secretary. But he had carried out all surveying work on his own since 1809 and had always 'the desire of compiling a map of India'. Seely's work is of interest for more than one reason. First, because of his claim that 'nothing of this kind [a road book] had ever before been attempted'.[65] He thus

---

62 *Illustrations of the Roads Throughout Bengal Including those to Madras and Bombay* (Calcutta, 1828).
63 I have not been able to locate this book. The reference to this work is available in the list of 'Oriental Literatures' published from the Asiatic Lithographic Press, Calcutta, contained in the *Illustrations*.
64 J. B. Seely, *The Road Book of India Or East Indian Traveller's Guide* (London, 1825).
65 Ibid., x.

overlooked the work of Rennell and Paton. (We can assume here that however limited the readership of Paton's work had remained, Seely, on account of being a military officer, must have known about such a publication.) Second, his work shows how the period in general was marked by a culture of exploration, surveys, map making and publishing road books, which did not necessarily draw upon the government's initiative. Third, the book resembled the modern-day travelling guide, as it not only described routes but gave a synoptic overview of historical and statistical information together with the idea of informally prescribing the things to see. The history reconstructed in Seely's notes legitimized British conquest. For instance, while describing Monghyr, he said: '[i]t became the headquarters of that *perfidious tyrant* Cossim Ali Khan [Mir Qasim]; but the straight forward *integrity of the British, aided by the justice and firmness* of their councils, soon reduced his power'.[66] But such legitimating endeavours came with cautions. For Patna he remarked:

> Here the infamous German adventurer, Summers (Sumroo) massacred in cold blood 203 persons belonging to the British factory, – a dreadful instance of Europeans being allowed to settle in the interior and a cautionary example to the advocates for colonization in India.[67]

Some of the publications about roads and routes were neither travelling guides nor aids for army movements but departmental records, brought together and published for future reference. One such was the *Statement*, published in 1854.[68] Of all the books surveyed here, this was the only one that gave information on the construction years of different roads, expenses incurred and trade carried. Information about authority and the supervising institutions was also given.

Another trend in this period was the publication of handbooks for travellers, most of whom were Company servants.[69] Such books not only gave route information but also a general sketch of important towns, detailing the availability of general amenities such as hotels and shooting options to amuse travellers; the location of post offices; the 'adroitly [sic] of Indian thieves'; the 'bad effects of alcohol and women in [the] India[n] climate'; and so on. The genre was not new, as we know that Thomas Williamson's *East India Vade-Mecum* provided a similar account in a much more detailed way, ranging from Indian customs to the Indian climate.[70] The newness nevertheless was in its conciseness,

---

66 Ibid., 25–6 (emphasis added).
67 Ibid., 16.
68 *Statement Showing the Roads in the Province of Bengal under the Department of Public Works* (Calcutta, 1854).
69 Vires Acquirit Eundo, *A Handbook of Useful Information for Officers and soldiers of the British and Hon. East India Company service in India, and for travellers proceeding through Bengal and the Punjaub* (London, 1853).
70 Thomas Williamson, *The East India Vade-Mecum*, 2 vols (London, 1810). The necessity or usability of such vade mecums is attested by the publication of J. B. Gilchrist's *Guide*, which admittedly was a 'digest of the work of Williamson'. The book claimed to present an improved knowledge with new additions. In fact, some of the sections, like the 'appendix' and a chapter on steam navigation were new but generally the improvements or additions were rare. J. B. Gilchrist, *The General East India Guide and Vade Mecum; for the Public Functionary, government officer, private agent, trader or foreign sojourner, in British India, and the adjacent parts of Asia immediately connected with the Honourable East India Company, Being a Digest of the work of the late Capt. Williamson, with many Improvements and Additions* (London, 1825).

in filtering out a large volume of knowledge into a pocket-size book. Road books thus gradually gave way to more general handbooks or guidebooks. Murray's handbook went a step further by providing not only the aforesaid information but by adding a thirty-five-page dialogue, consisting of translations of simple sentences into five different languages of India.[71] A traveller new to a place would have found such route books very helpful. With increasing suspicion of 'Blacky [who] strives to possess himself of every thing in the shapes of knives, blankets, woollen clothing, boots etc they [the new arrivals] may be possessed of, in exchange for cheerots, or about one-fourth of their value in money',[72] such publications had become an essential requisite of travel.

In these publications (travellers' guides and handbooks), if the object of knowledge was 'India', the target readership were Europeans, specifically travellers unfamiliar with India's history, antiquity and social customs. Such handbooks offered prescriptive advice as to what to see. By doing this, they also produced an India of their own interests, an India of 'every imaginable variety of scenery', of 'rich historical associations', of 'rich produce', of 'a land of ruined cities'.[73] However, two aspects should be acknowledged here. First, this was as much an attempt to essentialize India as it was in finding in it the remains of Europe's own past. Thus, it was said that in one of the ruined cities of India 'the antiquities of a whole European province might be collected'.[74] Second, such publications were part of the larger trend of publishing travel guides, route books and handbooks on different countries, including Britain. Even in Europe, as Murray says, 'the small remains of some ruined cloister, of the mouldering walls of a solitary castle, [were] sought out with eager interest'.[75]

What do route books signify in terms of knowledge about communication and its dissemination? Evidently, the knowledge base of the colonial state had expanded broadly between the 1770s and 1830s. Paton's work and the 1838 *Revised Tables of Routes and Stages* prove this. While the various editions of these two books signify that the military needs of the colonial state were met (needs which had become compelling because of territorial expansion from the late eighteenth century), general travelling guides signified the emergence of a relatively diverse readership. While the first gave dense information on various routes, the second discussed 'principal' roads. Two reasons can be proposed for this, the most obvious being that the latter were meant for popular usage so there was no need for these publications to show a dense communication network. The second formulation, however, goes deeper than this practical reasoning and reflects a set of factors related to the policies of the colonial state, general travelling patterns as they

---

71 John Murray, *A Handbook for India* (London, 1859). Separate volumes were intended for the three presidencies of Calcutta, Bombay and Madras. The two volumes on Bombay and Madras were published in 1859. The dialogues have been presented in Telgu, Tamil, Marathi, Gujrati and Kanarese. See pt 2, 540–75.
72 Eundo, *A Handbook of Useful Information*, 17.
73 Phrases taken from Murray, *A Handbook for India*, pt 1, i–ii.
74 Ibid., ii.
75 Ibid. For the prescriptive quality of these travel guides in Europe, see Rudy Koshar, '"What Ought to be Seen": Tourists' Guidebooks and National Identities in Modern Germany and Europe', *Journal of Contemporary History* 33, no. 3 (1998).

emerged amongst Europeans from the late eighteenth century, the limitations of finance and investment, and so on. We will now analyse these aspects in conjunction with some reflections on 'communication maps'.

Drawing Routes on Maps

Historians of cartography have argued for the centrality of maps and map making in imperial projects of conquest. R. Craib's useful review of the major works done on cartography says, 'geography and cartography were implicated in conquest and colonisation'.[76] The transformation of land into territory and the identification of space by marking places on the map are a few of the ideas given to us by such studies. This was as true for establishing colonial control (and imperialist projects) as for the government of early modern Europe, which 'increasingly relied on cartography as a means for territorial expansion, facilitation of rule and administrative control'.[77]

Pippa Biltcliffe, however, cautions us against over-reading imperialist currents in maps. By examining the life of the map engraver Walter Crane, she comes to the conclusion that the Imperial Federation Map of 1886 engraved by him was not simply a 'text' of imperial power (as argued by Brian Harley) but 'depicted a complex matrix of imperialism, a complex interplay between imperialism and aspiration for general reform'.[78] Along similar lines is the argument of Michael Biggs, who acknowledges the 'confluence of interests in accumulating knowledge [by cartographers] and aggrandizing power [of the state]' but refuses to see cartography 'merely a means to the end of state building' or as a tool representing power.[79] Unlike Ian Browne, who establishes a monocausal relationship between cartography and power in which the former is a tool of the latter (for representation), Biggs' contention that cartography itself helped to shape power is more convincing.[80] But, undeniably in the colonial

---

76 Raymond B. Craib, 'Cartography and Power in the Conquest and Creation of New Spain', *Latin American Research Review* 35, no. 1 (2000): 13.
77 Ibid., 14.
78 Pippa Biltcliffe, 'Walter Crane and the Imperial Federation Map Showing the Extent of the British Empire (1886)', *Imago Mundi* 57, no. 1 (2005): 67. For Harley's position in general see his, 'Maps, Knowledge, and Power', in Denis Cosgrove and Stephen Daniels, eds, *The Iconography of Landscape: Essays on the Symbolic Representation, Design and Use of Past Environments* (Cambridge, 1988).
79 Michael Biggs, 'Putting the State on the Map: Cartography, Territory and European State Formation', *CSSH* 41, no. 2 (1999): 380–85.
80 An interesting anecdote that brings out the interplay between map and power is that Hastings, while passing through Bihar during his downstream journey from Benares to Calcutta in 1781, took out a map of Bihar to assess the dimensions of the provinces of Tirhut and Hajipur. The immediate necessity of such an assessment arose because of the 'symptoms of zamindars' revolt at these places'. Seeing an early necessity of European superintendence he then made G. F. Grand the collector of Tirhut. This incident shows how maps were used to 'assess' the power (or lack of it). See Grand, *The Narrative of the Life of a Gentleman Long Resident in India* (1814), repr. with intro. by Walter Firminger (Calcutta, 1911), 113. Maps otherwise were also part of the visual representations of scenes of treaty formalization. In one of the sketches of the Gentil's Collection, a British man is shown holding out a map during the treaty made between the nawab and the British in 1765, an occasion on which Gentil was also present. Archer, *Company Paintings*, painting no. 20.

context, cartography more often than not linked issues of civilization (development), commerce and colonialism.[81]

These studies have nevertheless largely remained content with arguing for the crucial role maps played in transforming/representing land into territory, and understanding space through marking a series of places and towns. It can be argued that simply showing places did not make the space intelligible; a grid of communication connecting those places was equally necessary, if not more so. A unified representation of territory was required to show how places connected to each other. Territory needed routes to keep it intact. In order to control those places the state required mobility, which could be furnished by maps *with communications*. In his recent study, Chad Haines has drawn attention to some of these issues. He argues that, 'colonial mapping of a frontier and its binding into a territory was landscaped along the routes constructed, controlled and traversed into and out of frontier'.[82] Such a concern was not only prevalent for frontier regions but also for the empire in general, even in its mainland. That it was crucial to show links between places on the map becomes evident from Rennell's 'Table of Distances' added to his second edition of the *Memoir* (see Plate 15). And this map in his *Memoir* was surely not meant for restricted circulation (unlike some of the road books that were issued for military purposes). In the first edition of the *Memoir* itself, he clearly stated that the subsequent widening field (territorial and military) of British dominions in India through 'wars, alliances and negotiations' necessitated 'a map of Hindoostan explaining the local circumstances of political connections'. Such explanations, further, were meant to strike the imagination of the home audience 'with the splendour of victories in that quarter of the globe'.[83] He selected 168 cities on the basis of their current and future political significance. Further, he selected twelve cities that he considered of the greatest political consequence (British presidencies and the courts of native princes), forming for each of them a separate table in which distances between them were shown.[84] On this table a grid of roads showing the 'respective positions of all the places' was formed.[85] The roads shown on the map were without windings and inflections; they were mere lines joining places together. But they were important because they made visible the connections between places and made distances intelligible.

Taking Rennell's other map, which was published in *Description*, we notice a rather wide and dense representation of network of routes (Plates 15 and 16). It is possible that Rennell's own role as surveyor encouraged him to meticulously trace and draw every possible route on the map. If we recall our discussion from the previous chapter, we would see that at least four major routes, in addition to some cross-routes, were shown on his map. In contrast to this, the 1828 *Illustration*, which like Rennell's was a guidebook for general travelling, listed only two roads from Calcutta to the NWP that passed through Bihar, one the NMR and the other the old Gangetic route (Plate 17).

---

81 See for instance, Thomas J. Bassett, 'Cartography and Empire Building in Nineteenth-Century West Africa', *Geographical Review* 84, no. 3 (July 1994).
82 Chad Haines, 'Colonial Routes: Reorienting the Northern Frontier of British India', *Ethnohistory* 51, no. 3 (2004): 536.
83 See 'Preface' of the first edition of the *Memoir*.
84 Rennell, *Memoir*, 117–19.
85 Ibid, xi.

Plate 15. Principal roads and divisions of Hindustan by James Rennell

© British Library Board, Rennell, *The Memoir*, 117; also as Maps C.26.e.4.

Is Rennell's idiosyncratic penchant the only factor that explains this shift or did something else change between the 1770s and 1820s? As outlined in Chapter 3, in spite of its concern to improve local roads, the early colonial state did not meet much success in this endeavour. But thanks to early route surveys of people such as Nicholl and others, it did manage to build a thoroughfare, the NMR, which soon became the main artery of military movement. Until the 1810s general travellers kept to the old Gangetic route. By general travellers we mean Europeans, particularly the resident British who travelled up and down the country, or those who had recently come as cadets to join the Company service. Thus, most of these 'travellers' took to either of these two routes, which then became the 'principal' routes. As a consequence, the travelling pattern of Europeans was a factor behind some routes becoming principal. I say 'some routes' to pinpoint the processes of exclusion of other routes as depicted by Rennell. It could be argued

Plate 16. Roads of Bengal presidency

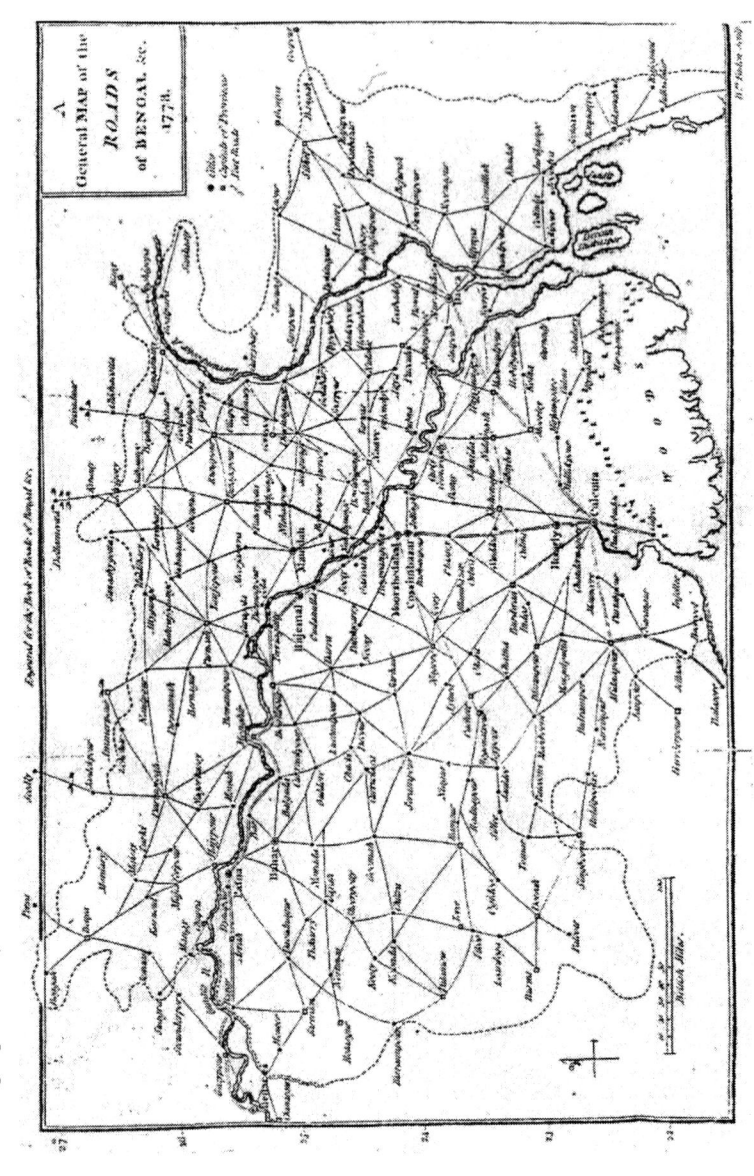

© British Library Board, Rennell, *Description*, shelfmark: T35013.

Plate 17. Principal roads

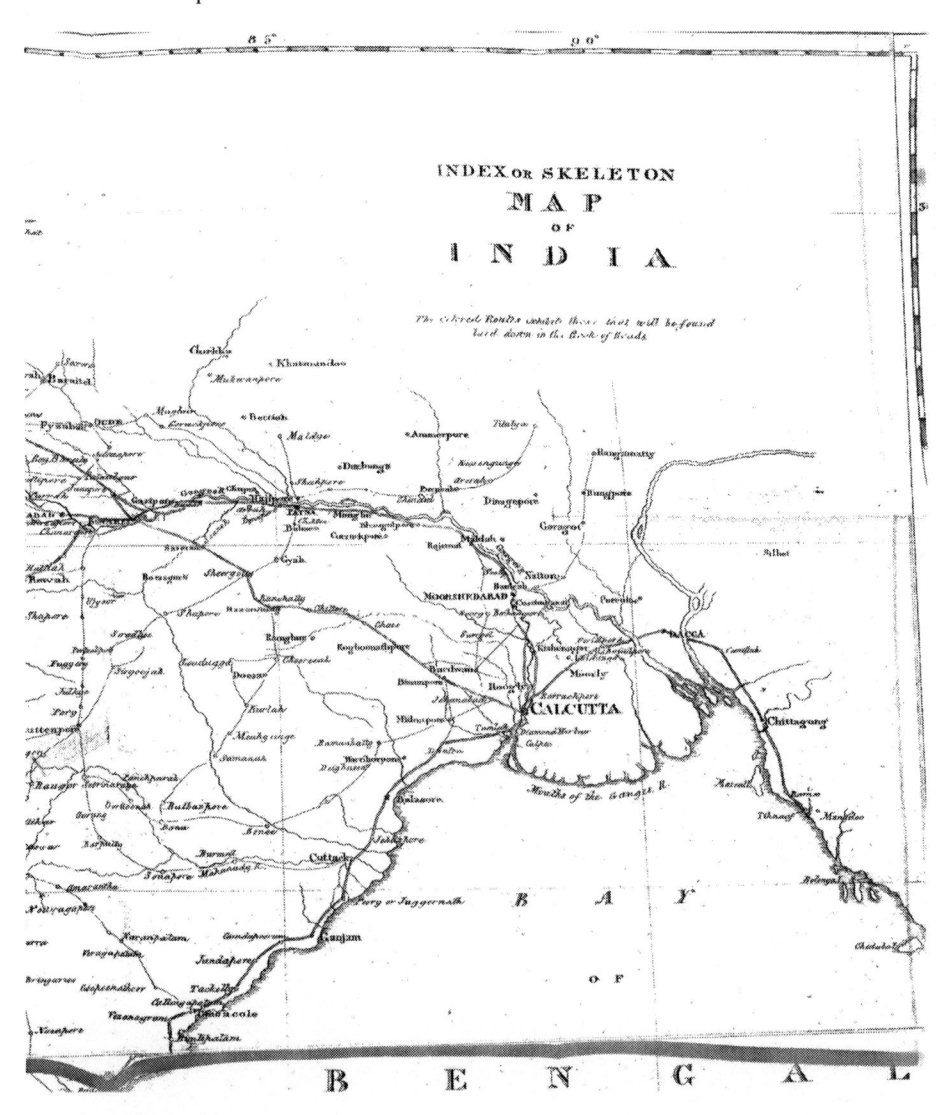

© British Library Board, *Illustration*, shelfmark: V 9498.

at this stage that these routes decayed over time and thus did not qualify to be listed as 'principals'. There is some truth in this proposition, but it should be qualified. Although references to people travelling on these other highways is not as forthcoming as for the other two routes, that is, the NMR and the old Gangetic route, we do have the example of the raja of Tanjore travelling with his party in the early 1820s to the pilgrimage sites of Gaya, Benares and Allahabad. Instead of travelling by the two principal routes he took one of the other routes that connected Burdwan with Patna, going through Serampore, Curukdea, Nawada and Behar. The reason for the paucity of such references may well lie in the nature of the sources rather than with actual travelling practices. Since most of the

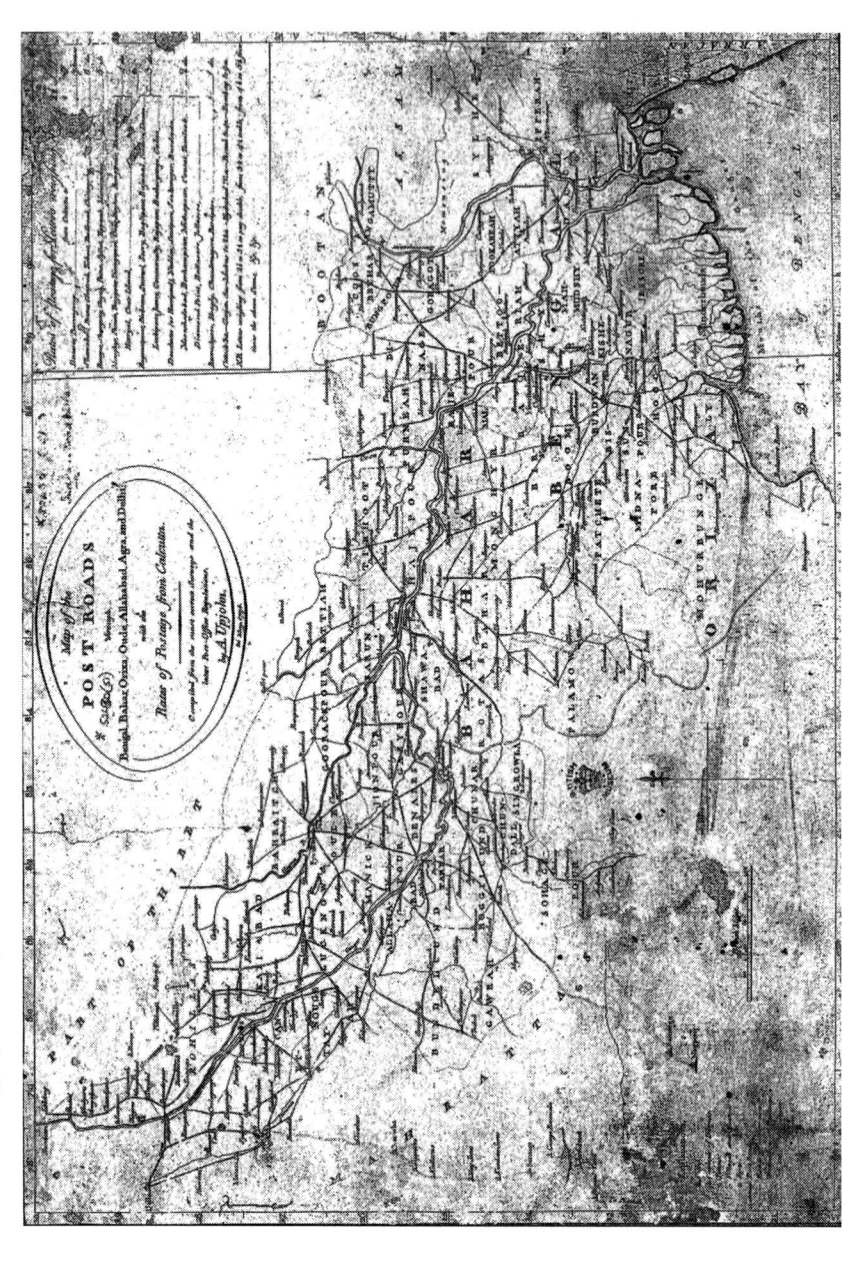

Plate 18. Post roads in Bengal presidency

sources relating to travelling practices and the routes taken are European in origin, we know little about the conditions of other routes. Yet it is possible to form a fairly decent opinion if we look at the network of dak services at the turn of the eighteenth century, which is best given in a map made by A. Upjohn (Plate 18). This map shows the post roads that interestingly cover all the highways traced by Rennell. We have a reason to believe that these routes were regularly used for this service because Upjohn also gives us the rates of postage.[86] Nevertheless, these routes declined over time because of the EIC's financial limitation and its concentration only on the NMR. The books and maps with 'principal' routes on them therefore did not *create* their (roads') principal positions. They rather reflect the interlinked histories of travelling, Company policies and the politics of investment. But this way of inscripting maps with only principal routes did create a hierarchy of routes, which was perpetuated in a series of successive maps, thus pushing other routes into oblivion.

These successive maps represent a further widened readership. By the beginning of the nineteenth century, large family publishing firms in London were doing brisk business in map production. They published maps of all the known places of the world, catering to the ever-growing demand of map readers and collectors. Travellers' companions, itinerary books, atlases, maps of post roads and post offices, and globes were some of the forms in which knowledge about the 'old and new' world was circulated.[87] The market was ripe for the 'newly opened' areas, and imperial connections kept up a special interest in India. Here again we speak only of the genre of 'communication maps' and include only those maps that deliberately showed India's communication networks. In particular we examine the maps issued by one family firm, that of Wyld, which had not only become a household name amongst the map-using public but had also become 'the haunt of the rich, the powerful, and the famous'.[88]

James Wyld, who had many credits to his name, established the firm. In 1812 he was supposedly the first to introduce lithography into map printing. One of the founding members of the Royal Geographical Society, he was also geographer to George IV, William IV and the Duke of York. After his death in 1836, his son, also named James, took charge of the firm. In 1840, James published a map of India in which the route network shown was remarkably dense.[89] However, this detailed description of roads was subsequently given up, and like the maps in general travelling guides, his maps also concentrated on principal roads. In 1848, he published a map, showing post roads and dak stations, which was very similar to the work discussed above (1828 *Illustrations*).[90] The 1850 edition of this

---

86 A. Upjohn, *Map of the Post Roads through Bengal, Bahar, Orixxa, Oude, Allahabad, Agra and Delhi* (Calcutta, 1795).
87 A very interesting example of this readership is Francis Hawkins' choice of materials while onboard to India. He first finished reading 'Clarks Travels' and then picked up 'Robertson's America'. While on the journey he had become an avid map reader; he traced down all the villages and cities mentioned by Clark on a map. Mss Eur. B365/2 ff. 1–24, vol. 2, 36.
88 David Smyth, 'The Wyld Family Firm', *The Map Collector* 55 (1991): 38. The following account is based on this unless otherwise mentioned.
89 James Wyld, *Map of India* (London, 1840).
90 James Wyld, *India Shewing the Post Roads and Dawk Stations* (London, 1848).

map showed no change. Under the same title, one more map was published in 1860.[91] In all these maps, for the region we are concerned with, there are three 'Post and Bangy and Military Roads': one, the GTR; two, a section of the old Gangetic route; and, three, a road from Patna to Sherghatty via Gaya. For the area of north Bihar, a road from Patna to Muzaffarpur also came into this category. Among the 'Post Roads and Routes', apart from a few roads in north Bihar, a section of the GTR between Burdwan and Hazaribagh, and from there to Burhee on the GTR was shown, as Upjohn showed more than half a century earlier. Sometimes the NMR was shown under 'Post Roads and Routes'. By way of a very broad comparison with the Upjohn's map, two things are clear. First, the earlier post roads had deteriorated and hence were no longer represented. For instance, Upjohn had showed a post road from Burdwan via Nagore, Sarhaut, Deoghur, Ghidoore and Bahar. In Wyld's map of 1848 places such as Ghiddore, Sarhaut, Bahar and Curukdea were all free standing. Second, with the construction of the GTR (which had started in the early nineteenth century and was completed in the 1830s; see Chapter 6), the NMR was becoming less important. It had ceased to be a military road and had become, as some of the maps showed, just a post road.

An interesting point in all these Wyld maps was the route of the railway line. In the earlier maps, true to the debates of the period, the proposed railway route shown was the direct line from Calcutta to the NWP with a branch line to Rajmahal (1848 and 1850 maps). However, even in the 1860 map, when the circuitous route along the Ganga had not only been developed but trains had started running along it, the same alignment was shown. This shows how easily unrevised maps were published. Contrast it with Collins' map of 1858 or with Cruchley's map of 1857,[92] which showed the Gangetic railway route as the proposed line. Most surprising is the fact that Wyld's previous map of 1857 had shown the correct railway lines.[93] Another instance of such 'acts of omissions' comes from the Cruchley map wherein the GTR is not shown at all. Are these just 'omissions' or do they say something about the nature of knowledge production and representation?

Conclusions

On the basis of these 'communication maps' it is difficult to make any generalization about the representation of space. Different types of maps for different types of readerships presented spaces in different ways. While road books produced for military movements together with Rennell's communication map, which was not limited to military usage, showed dense networks of communication, general travelling books with maps concentrating on principal roads showed relatively more blank spaces. This was by and large also the representational schema of maps produced in the metropolis (London) of the empire. We have already explained some of the reasons why and how some routes became principal. One of the natural offshoots of this nature of representation was to

---

91 James Wyld, *India Shewing the Post Roads and Dawk Stations* (London, 1860). See also H. G. Collins, *Enlarged War Map of India Shewing the Civil and Military Stations, Post and Bangy Roads, Railways, Routes & C.* (London, 1858).
92 C. F. Cruchley, *New Map of India with the Roads, Railways and Military Stations* (London, 1857).
93 Wyld, *Map of India: India Shewing the Post Roads and Dawk Stations* (London, 1857).

inscribe a fixed hierarchy of roads in which importance was given to those constructed under the colonial rule (the NMR and later the GTR). The obverse side of such representation was the gradual omission of routes existing from an earlier period, both in reality as well as in representation. This trend, which is clearly observable from the 1820s onwards, curiously sits very comfortably with the strong emerging discourse, as seen in Chapter 2, of a 'roadless India' around the same time.

What this chapter has tried to do is to bring together two aspects of colonial knowledge formation: the knowledge acquired and the knowledge represented. The knowledge acquired had a defined administrative agenda and requirement that was reflected in the Company-state's initiative to gather information about different routes; it also catered to purposes that went beyond rigid administrative utility. One was to meet the general travelling needs of Europeans in India. Another was not strictly limited to travellers but extended to a burgeoning European, especially British, readership. In our discussion of the nature of knowledge production we stressed the limits of circulation, of which I argue 'acts of omissions' were a part. One of the questions we posed was when and how did objects, people, skills, texts, maps and ideas enter into the 'circulatory' ambit. Another question relates to the nature of the reproduction of texts and maps and their role in knowledge production. We observed above that sometimes the texts were not revised. The same was true of maps. Not every map showed the results of newly discovered knowledge. This stands in contrast to the Latourian notion of the cycle of accumulation of which the argument is that 'at each translation of traces onto a new one something is *gained*'.[94] Our contention is that atrophication of knowledge was also a part of this translation or reproduction. The production of maps was not only a function of knowledge production alone; it had its own logic of circulation, which was governed by the volume of demand, accessibility to print technologies, and, not least, the profit that could be earned in the map bazaar. Until the turn of the eighteenth century, maps of the Indian subcontinent were privately owned and were used to adorn the walls of the Company's offices. Much to the dislike of the Court of Directors, which strenuously kept reminding its officials to deposit such maps in its collection, Vansittart and Clive each took home the maps prepared by Rennell as their private property. Through Vansittart, Rennell's maps came into Robert Orme's possession, and Orme used them to annotate his copy of Rennell's journal; but only a small part of Orme's collection reached the EIC in 1801. We have some stray references about the court acquiring maps from private collections, but their present whereabouts are neither known nor have transactions yet been verified.[95] Gradually, the Court of Directors tightened the 'flight of maps' and ensured that all maps were deposited in its own collection.

---

94 Bruno Latour, *Science in Action: How to Follow Scientists and Engineers through Society* (Cambridge MA, 1987), 236.
95 See Raj, 'Circulation and the Emergence', 46–50, and Cook, *Major James Rennell*, 11. Raj's uncritical acceptance that on an accidental discovery of the maps possessed by a lady of rank, the Court of Directors purchased them for £100 (48), is doubtful in the light of Cook's reservation that 'the claim has not been verified yet'. The maps in contention were the Rennell 'Original Surveys of the Lower Provinces of Bengal and Bahar'. See Cook, *Major James Rennell*, 11, fn. 39.

The technique of lithography helped to reproduce 'impressively accurate maps'. Raj argues that '[l]arge-scale reproductive techniques, like lithography, rendered maps much plainer, shearing them of their classical aesthetic appeal and thus of the demands of the market for art'.[96] However, while arguing this, he overlooks the simultaneous process of the reproduction of old plates. Reproduction of knowledge ensured circulation but it did not mean revision. The recycling of knowledge was part of the circulation of knowledge. For instance, Laurie and Whittle's publication 'A New Map of Hindoostan from the Latest Authorities' in 1794, which claimed to exhibit all the military roads and passes, did not show the NMR, which was built thirteen years before this map was published (Cruchley's example, given above, shows the same feature). The reason was that this map used old plates from Rennell.[97] Such unrevised publications continued. On the dissolution of Faden's firm, the Wyld family firm acquired all Faden's maps and reissued Rennell's map in 1824.[98] The implication of this recycling process that forms part of knowledge circulation emphasizes the non-linear relationship between knowledge produced and knowledge gained, that is, successive texts and maps did not secure or mean successive additions to the existing knowledge pool.

The approach adopted in this chapter has been to unpack the category of circulation on the one hand and to look at the contradictions involved in the act of knowledge formation on the other. One theme that has emerged from this analysis, especially in the field of native input, was Europe's increasing suspicion of the native contribution. Apart from their own sojourns in the interior and their reliance on native guides, of whom they were suspicious, the British officials also added to their knowledge of routes from a variety of mobile groups. One such group was fakirs and sanyasis who, with their extensive trading linkages, served to furnish not only route but also trade information to early colonial officials. The roads and routes for which information was considered so vital by the colonial administration were not only material artefacts but also the pathways of networks of mobility. The early Company-state not only aspired to know the directions of these routes but also to control the diverse patterns of mobility that thrived along them. In the following chapter we look at the attitude of the colonial administration towards some of these mobile groups.

---

96 Raj, 'Circulation and the Emergence', 51.
97 *A New Map of Hindoostan* (London, 1794).
98 Smyth, 'The Wyld Family Firm'. Wyld generally used to revise the editions but many times he published old maps without revisions. For example, Faden's 1786 'Map of the Country Around London' was published in 1824 without changes. See Smyth, 33–4.

Chapter 5

CONTROLLING THE ROUTES

While the image of the indolent native who could be induced to move only by necessity thrived as typical throughout the early phase of colonial rule,[1] in fact there existed a diverse range of mobile people and groups of which the Company-state was well aware. Men-on-the-road were a source of information for diverse areas of knowledge that many Company officials made use of, but such people's very mobility also made the Company-state anxious. They signified a 'decentred core' of power that, because of their travelling propensity, appeared threatening to the Company-state, both in regard to its exercise of authority and its control of revenue. As in other fields, this anxiety led the EIC to come up with a set of regulations to check and contain this diverse pattern of circulation. One natural outcome of this growing urge to regulate mobility was the formulation of stricter notions of crime and criminality. Peripatetic groups such as the banjaras, sanyasis and fakirs were, by the end of the first half of the nineteenth century, cast in the mould of criminal groups. This recasting, however, was not, as many current historiographical conventions would explain, an artefact of a paranoid colonial mindset, but was linked to the histories of mobility and disruption of prevailing patterns of trade and transport, and the livelihoods supported by them, consequent to colonial settlement and, in this region (eastern India), also to some extraneous factors such as the rise of the Gurkha kingdom in Nepal. By looking into this history, this chapter also addresses one more facet of the debate in the colonial 'change or/and continuity' paradigm by both rescuing from and indicting early colonial rule for the things it did. The arguments made in favour of a significant 'break' as symbolized by the coming of colonial rule, which apparently led to the eruption of or rise in crime, are found inadequate to explain the fluid political conditions that developed from the mid-eighteenth century. Hence, the 'changes' of the late eighteenth century need to be situated in, if not unqualifiedly linked to, the earlier period. But it cannot be denied that the following decades did witness a change. This was at the level of new priorities and new policies devised and implemented by a state that was colonial in nature.[2] The effects of these policies, which created a regime of regulation, proved detrimental in the long run for some mobile communities.

---

1 Deane, *A Tour*, 37. See also Chapter 2.
2 I am aware of the preponderance of what William Pinch has called the inclinations of postmodernist and postcolonial scholarship (and, if I may add, the standard nationalist underpinnings) towards perceiving 'only discontinuities' and precisely in response to that I argue for situating the late eighteenth-century developments in the century's earlier decades. See Pinch, *Warrior Ascetics and Indian Empires, 1500–2000* (Cambridge, 2006), 17. However, I would also like to stick to the use of the word 'colonial', which he has intentionally avoided (in his own words). It is so because the changes that accompanied the beginning of a new state (with all its limitations) were nonetheless colonial in their implications.

Most studies on crime done in the context of South Asian colonialism have focused on the mid- or late nineteenth century. They have either explained crime through the functioning of an authoritative utilitarian notion of paramountcy[3] or through the emergence of a dominant colonial discourse on criminality that had both the elements of 'the exigencies of colonial transformation and the prevalent European ideas'.[4] Legal intervention, in particular the Criminal Tribes Act (CTA) of 1871, has remained an important entry point in understanding colonial ideas about criminality. However, an overreliance on this framework has led to the argument that 'crime in India was not seen as a result of irreversible heredity or genes, but arising from social causes'. Further, arguably, this search for 'social scientific causes' linked crime, as one author argues, 'to the introduction of railways, the new forest policy, repeated famines and so on'.[5] The problem with this framework arises at two levels: first, even in the early colonial period crime was seen in its immediate social historical context (and therefore I argue that we should look at this period more closely); and, second, the late nineteenth-century search for 'scientific' reasons drew heavily upon the idea of 'race', which indeed traced the criminal propensities to genes.[6] Thus, amidst reforms of 'criminal tribes', we find voices in the late nineteenth century arguing, 'All Bowries have been from ages past and are still by profession *inveterate* and *irreclaimable* robbers.'[7] In this chapter, I suggest we look at the 'pre-history' of mobility to better understand the colonial productions of native criminality. Beyond dispute is the fact that notions of power and authority, on the one hand, and the 'villainized' representations of communities on the other were the factors involved. I do not intend to suggest that scholars have not taken into account the factor of mobility. Nigam has argued: 'The experience in Punjab and the North Western Provinces suggested that if the predatory tribes were to be controlled, their mobility would have to be restricted.'[8] The argument presented in this chapter is, however, different from this. Here, I argue that the check on the mobility of peripatetic groups was not only an after-effect (or factor) of establishing control but was a cause in shaping notions of criminality.

This approach also distances us from theories that reproduce the centrality of dominant 'colonial categorizations' in the making of criminality around certain groups. For instance, in the case study of Maghiya Doms, Anand Yang has shown how, by the 1860s and 1870s their 'criminality' had been 'discovered'.[9]

---

3 Radhika Singha, 'Providential Circumstances: The Thugee Campaign of the 1830s and Legal Innovation', *MAS* 27, no. 1 (1993). One could also turn to Sandria Freitag's argument of exclusive notion of authority as devised by the British in India. Freitag, 'Collective Crime and Authority in North India', in Anand Yang, ed., *Crime and Criminality in British India* (Arizona, 1985).
4 Sanjay Nigam, 'Disciplining and Policing the "Criminals by Birth"', pts 1 and 2, *IESHR* 27, nos. 2–3 (1990). Quotation is from pt 1, 131.
5 Meena Radhakrishna, *Dishonoured by History: 'Criminal Tribes' and British Colonial Policy* (Delhi, 2001), 6–8.
6 See Nigam, 'Disciplining and Policing', and Yang, 'Introduction', in Yang, ed., *Crime and Criminality*.
7 Major E. J. Gunthorpe, *Notes on Criminal Tribes residing in or frequenting the Bombay Presidency, Berar, and the Central Province* (Bombay, 1882), 2 (emphasis added).
8 Nigam, 'Disciplining and Policing', pt 1, 138.
9 Yang, 'Dangerous Castes and Tribes: The Criminal Tribes Act and the Maghiya Doms of Northeast India', in Yang, ed., *Crime and Criminality*.

In the 1810s, when Buchanan was writing, this group was not described as a 'tribe with criminal propensities'. Yang quotes Sherring, who was writing in the 1840s, to further prove his point of 'discovery' as Sherring 'does not...hint of any traits which could add up to a picture of a "criminal tribe"'. However, by 1871 this caste was declared 'criminal'. Thus both in Yang's account and through him in colonial accounts, we get an impression of a linear flow (in time) of colonial knowledge about caste on the one hand and crime on the other. This association of course was central to the development of colonial understanding in this period, but a problem arises when the colonial authorities are, in our historiographical accounts, pushed to 'discover' a 'criminal caste'. Colonial discourse on criminality was certainly based on castes, but the selection of tribes and castes which were labelled as 'criminals' had also to do with the history of how crime was perceived in preceding decades. It is therefore prudent to look into the socioeconomic and political fabric of the late decades of the eighteenth century in order to understand notions of authority and power and shifting representations as engendered by the colonial state that came to stabilize by the second and third decades of the nineteenth century. Unfortunately, Yang does not elucidate the history of Maghiya Doms in this sense.

One thing is certain: crime on the major routes and highways did not start with the coming of Company rule. Even before the Company had taken over the revenue and judicial charges, there were repeated calls for 'safe passage'. The oft-repeated anxiety about safe passage in the late eighteenth century begs us to ask whether the roads and major routes were unsafe in the preceding period. The general consensus will be 'yes'. Both Jean de Thevenot and G. F. G. Careri, who visited India in the late seventeenth century, complained about the difficult travelling conditions because of highway robberies.[10] Francisco Pelsaert also mentioned the presence of rebellious chiefs, thieves and robbers 'who did not hesitate to pillage up to the very gate of Ahmedabad, Burhanpur, Agra, Delhi and Lahore'.[11] A *firman* (order) issued by the Mughal ruler Jahangir confirmed the presence of the practice of road robbery:

> In as much as thieves and robbers carry off people's goods in isolated places, it is ordered that new qasbas should be populated and the Jaghirdars are directed, wherever they find considerable areas of waste and uninhabited land, to arrange to provide masjids, dharamsalas, and water-tanks so as to populate these areas.[12]

---

10 Surendra Nath Sen, *Indian Travels of Thevenot and Careri* (New Delhi, 1949), 94, 216. Before them, Peter Mundy described the country between Agra and Ahmedabad as 'Thevish'. Ibid., lx. C. A. Bayly has also noted: 'Roads had always been dangerous around Delhi and Agra even at the height of the Mughal empire.' Bayly, *Rulers, Townsmen and Bazaars: North Indian Society in the Age of British Expansion 1770–1870* (Cambridge, 1983), 91.

11 Quoted in K. N. Chaudhuri, 'Some Reflections on the Town and Country in Mughal India', *MAS* 12, no. 1 (1978): 86.

12 Ibid., 86. In fact, death was the punishment prescribed for highway robberies in Mughal times. Kartik Kalyan Raman, 'Utilitarianism and the Criminal Law in Colonial India: A Study of the Practical Limits of Utilitarian Jurisprudence', *MAS* 28, no. 4 (1994): 745.

We also have some evidence from the earlier period of refractory zamindars keeping a 'band of robbers' with whom they infested roads and plundered boats on the rivers.[13] Jahangir's directive is interesting in one more sense. He was suggesting a link between such crimes and 'unregulated' and uninhabited spaces, not typically in terms of the people residing in those places being plunderers and looters by default (which was also a prevalent belief at this time) but in ways in which such places provided safe hideouts. Besides safeguarding the routes,[14] the measures taken by the native rulers during the pre-colonial times included regulating the 'recalcitrant spaces', chiefly jungles. The clearance of jungles had not only a military purpose (to facilitate the movement of armies),[15] but was also associated with the idea of inhabiting such places to minimize the risk of plunder and robbery. Such places, as that in the vicinity of Palamow in south Bihar, had also become infamous for general travelling, which is evident from a folk saying, as recorded in the *Tarikh-i Daudia*: 'Ancha langhe aur Bhadoi tab jino ghar ae batohi' (Only after passing Ancha and Bhadoi, the traveller can be sure of arriving home safely).[16] Jungles as a refuge for robbers and as a space of lawlessness was not a colonial stereotype; Bhimsen when returning from Ramgir, lost his way in the thick jungle, and on falling upon a *darwesh* (mendicant), thought he belonged 'to the class of robbers'.[17]

Highway robbery and looting, both in medieval times in places like Gujrat, Central India and in north India in late pre-colonial times (to be precise, in the first half of the eighteenth century) remained enmeshed in the political struggle between rival powers.[18] Norbert Peabody has argued that banditry, looting and thievery were manifestations of internal political disorders between raja and chieftains and between chieftains and chieftains.[19] C. A. Bayly has provided a fruitful analysis by suggesting a relationship

---

13 Charles Stewart, *The History of Bengal* (London, 1813), 382. This trend of keeping *lathials* (lierally, men with stick; henchmen) could more fruitfully be seen as part of village militias and the widespread presence of militant ruralized north Indian peasantry, which was a crucial aspect of the region's polity and economy. This militarization in fact increased, as Richards has pointed out, from the mid-seventeenth to mid-eighteenth century. John. F. Richards, 'Warriors and the State in Early Modern India', *JESHO* 47, no. 3 (2004), 397.

14 Murshid Quli Khan had erected guard houses at Katwah and Moorshidgunge for the protection of travellers. Stewart mentioned that 'During Murshid Quly Khan's government, travellers were protected on the roads.' Stewart, *The History*, 405.

15 In the Daud Khan's expedition to Palamow in Bihar a number of woodcutters were part of the army; they cleared the jungles to prevent the enemy from setting an ambush. Khan Bahadur Saiyid Zamiruddin Ahmad, 'Daud Khan Quraishi, Governor of Bihar and Founder of the Town of Daudnagar', *JBORS* 4, no. 3 (1918): 288–9. The Mughals had an established institution of 'Dakhili troops', a part of which, according to the *Ain-i Akbari*, was handed over to the mansabdars but were paid directly by the state. The troops consisted of matchlock bearers, carpenters, iron workers, bhistees (water carriers) and so on. Farooque, *Roads and Communications*, 23, fn. 9. See 22–3 on the role of woodcutters.

16 Ibid. 292. I have slightly altered the translation, which in the original is: 'only after he had passed Ancha and Bhadoi, you can be certain of the wayfarer reaching home'.

17 *Tarikh-i-Dilkasha*, 91–2.

18 See Nandini Sinha Kapur, 'The Bhils in the Historic Setting of Western India', in Rudolf C. Heredia and Shereen F. Ratnagar, eds, *Mobile and Marginalized Peoples: Perspectives from the Past* (New Delhi, 2003), 160.

19 Peabody, 'Cents, Sense and Census: Human Inventories in Late Pre-colonial and Early Colonial India', *CSSH* 43, no. 4 (2001): 840.

between the local decline in agricultural production (occasionally exacerbated by famines) and 'banditry'. He says: 'Mercenaries and tribal people such as Bhattis, Mewatis and the corporations of mercenary adventurers known as Pindaris had to turn to outside looting and plunder when rent extracted from their home territories was no longer sufficient to maintain their style of life.'[20] The fluid political condition and the emergence of successor states, as they are called now, intensified such incidences. This was a period of, to borrow Pinch's phrase, 'military entrepreneurship', which saw groups of militant warriors, such as gosains, becoming crucial in pre-colonial state formation. The colonial state inherited and encountered rather than constructed this set of 'armed mobility'. In fact, in the early days, the state found it hard to come to any understanding of the 'vast multitudes' of Asiatic armies and how frequently they moved around in groups. Colonial officers were both baffled and impressed by this form of mobility, as one of them explained: 'the whole country is put in motion, and the strictest orders are given for all provisions to be brought into the camp'.[21]

However, with the advent of colonialism, between the 1760s and 1850s, a few of the notions related to 'native' mobility were recast. First, towards the end of this time spectrum, crime had increasingly come to be seen as an inherent part of the native character or Indian civilization. Indian/native criminality was not only traced back to ancient times, it was also said to be hereditary and professional. Singha has shown that there was a definite drive by the mid-nineteenth century to constitute criminality in communitarian terms.[22] Seemingly, such generalizations and stereotypes were accentuated more in response to *thuggee*, which was seen as a pan-Indian affair and which in turn required measures at an all-India level. Thuggee provided a powerful optic for classifying criminality: on the one hand the late eighteenth-century gosains, banjaras, *multanis*, and many others were objectified as the larger brotherhood of thugs,[23] on the other, the late nineteenth- and early twentieth-century 'robbers' and 'criminal tribes and castes' became 'second-generation' thugs. Writing in 1924, Edwardes said: 'In some cases,

---

20 Bayly, *Rulers, Townsmen and Bazaars*, 91. However, this functional relationship between 'decline' and 'crime' does not explain the condition of the late eighteenth-century Benares, which in the words of Ali Ibrahim Khan, the city administrator, was a period of peace and security. Yet, highway robberies in and around the city were frequent. When Khan was requested by one Sayyid Ali Akbar Khan of Lucknow to send him clothes worth Rs. 2,000 from Benares, he was informed by the *Daroga-e-Dak* (inspector of post) of Benares that roads were unsafe for the despatch of goods. Later, instead of sending all the *thaans* (rolls of cloth) together, it was decided to send them one at a time. Shayesta Khan, ed. and trans., *The Holy City of Benares as Administered by a Muslim Noble: Social, Religious, Cultural and Political Conditions, 1781–1793. (Translation of letters of Ali Ibrahim Khan written to the Maratha chiefs, the trustees of Mandirs & others.)* (Patna, 1993), 12–13.
21 'Account of the Manners of the INHABITANTS', 281. For similar expressions of surprise and baffle for south India, see the translations of German missionaries' observations in Ravi Ahuja, 'Labour Unsettled: Mobility and Protest in the Madras Region, 1750–1800', *IESHR* 35, no. 4 (1998): 387.
22 Singha, 'Providential Circumstances', 84–5.
23 A very interesting observation is the handwritten interpolation on the title page of *Narrative of Ajeet Singh, a Noted Dacoit in the North Western Provinces of India* (Agra, 1843), in which, after the word 'Dacoit', was added the word 'Thag', followed by a definition of the latter.

recorded in the later years of the last century, the criminals were proved to have belonged to families of Thag stranglers.'[24] The second important element was the association of crime with wandering people. Wandering mendicants and mobile vagrant groups were most liable to be classed as criminals. William Sleeman remarked that 'bands of thieves in the disguise of Gosains and Byragies are to be found in all parts of India; and these men often commit murder... Other bands wander about as Banjaras, Khunjurs, Nats, &c. &c. &c.'[25] More than forty years before, banjaras, who had helped the Company with their efficient lines of supply in winning the war of Seringapatam, were now classed as a 'criminal' group that indulged in looting and murdering travellers.[26]

What this meant was that armed mobility and conflicts that were part of the state formation and political struggles were now detached from their context. Ajeet Singh, a noted *dacoit* of the NWP in the early nineteenth century, complained that unlike his forefathers who committed robbery 'honourably', the new political conditions of the last twenty years had turned him and others like him into 'night robberers'. Clearly, the emphasis was on the loss of political imperatives that made raiding, looting and plundering an integral systemic adjunct of eighteenth-century politics.[27] The shift can also be discerned in the ways that the same terms, albeit with different meanings, were used. If, for Thevenot, who was travelling in the seventeenth century, there were some fakirs who were 'rogues and wretches' whose whole business was to molest travellers, for Tulsidas in the same century, the gosains were masters of deceit, 'scheming and guileful,' and 'hypocritical'.[28] Very interesting is the account given by Kim Wagner in which he quotes a poem by Surdas (1478–1583) which evidently shows that the notion of 'thag' as a group category who 'lure[s] a pilgrim with laddus...[and] takes his money and his life' had existed long before.[29] It is crucial here, without denying the existence of such terms, to account for the shifts in meanings that happened during the colonial times. The recasting of mobility as an important feature of criminality and then through that, not only branding a few communities as criminals but ahistoricizing their practices was a new development. It was akin to what Ajay Skaria has argued about the notion of jungli: in the pre-colonial times, *'jangli* was not about some chronologically prior state of nature, some prediscursive base which civilization transcended and overcame; wildness had no relation to time or evolution, nor even was it the Other of civilization'.[30] All these features became prominent in colonial ways of explanation.

---

24 S. M. Edwardes, *Crime in India* (London, 1924), 39.
25 Sleeman, *Thugs and Phansigars of India* (Philadelphia, 1839), 46, fn.
26 In 1819, Captain Briggs had said: 'the first time, however...they were employed...which I recollect, by the British government, was in the first war with Tippoo in the years 1791–92... It was to the timely supply of provisions brought by the Banjaras...that the safety of the British army may be ascribed.' Captain Briggs, 'Account of the Origin, History, and Manners of the Race of Men called Bunjaras', *Transactions of the Literary Society of Bombay* 1 (1819): 183.
27 *Narrative of Ajeet Singh*, 4.
28 For Thevenot see Sen, *Indian Travels*, 94; for Tulsidas, see Pinch, 'Gosain Tawaif: Slave, Sex, and Ascetics in Rasdhan, ca. 1800–1857', *MAS* 38, no. 3 (2004): 594.
29 Wagner, *Thuggee: Banditry and the British in Early Nineteenth-Century India* (Hampshire and New York, 2007), 27.
30 Skaria, 'Being Jangli: The Politics of Wildness', *SIH* 14, no. 2 (1998): 196.

This account of a shift in perspective must be followed by a caveat. How far these stereotypes were 'colonial' is unclear for two reasons: first, even in seventeenth-century England vagrancy was seen as a crime. In fact, lodging or harbouring vagrants or pedlars also constituted a crime.[31] Metropolitan ideology therefore had a part to play in the colonial officers' understanding of eighteenth-century South Asian mobility. However, it does appear that in the South Asian context it was not their marginal position in society that led to wandering groups being cast as criminals (i.e. the case of social banditry) but their circulatory nature that brought them within the ambit of criminality. Precisely because of this subcontinental mobility, as Pinch has argued, these groups had become 'attractive agents for people of means to project force, inflict punishment, carry valuables, or transmit valuable information'.[32] Second, we do not know much about 'perceptions' of non-colonial imperial powers such as the Mughals or other pre-colonial states towards mobile groups and their practices. This is a theme that needs further exploration. However, speaking both from the viewpoint of groups and spaces, there was a strong impulse (and one can trace this as far back as Maurayan times) to regard or equate certain spaces – border and frontier areas – and certain groups such as the Atavikas with barbarism and savagery on the one hand and robbers and thieves on the other.[33] And, closer to the late medieval period, there are references to Brahmins despising the Bhils or Kolis as a 'predatory tribe'. In addition, the strategy of disguise, which the Europeans themselves were using to travel in far-flung regions, also had a strong presence in the South Asian context, the most celebrated example going as far back as the epic age of Ramayana when the learned demon-god Ravana tricked Sita to cross over the *Lakshman rekha* by disguising himself as a *sadhu* (sanyasi/fakir). To further complicate the issue, it has been rightly asserted – again in the case of Bhils – that they 'were not just represented and categorized as wild within colonial discourse, they saw themselves as such even in pre-colonial times'.[34]

Mobile Trading Groups and Regimes of Regulation

Transformations in the representation of certain groups such as the banjaras and gosains by the 1820s and 1830s are beyond dispute. Similarly, the fact that the notion of communitarian and not individual responsibility of crime was solidifying in this period is too evident to deny. To cite one example, the case of multanis fits in well here:

> Multanis of Central India were described by Malcolm in 1823 as carrier traders in cattle who also engaged in some cultivation, and placed among the 'civil classes' of Muslims even though they were armed. Sleeman described them in 1836 as a class of 'ancient thugs', said to call themselves Naiks, and to travel and trade as Brinjaras, and Ramsay in 1850 termed them 'a tribe of Dacoits'.[35]

---

31 J. A. Sharpe, *Crime in Early Modern England, 1550–1750*, 1984, 8th impression (London, 1996), 84.
32 Pinch, *Warrior Ascetics*, 67.
33 Aloka Parasher-Sen, 'Of Tribes, Hunters and Barbarians: Forest Dwellers in the Mauryan Period', *SIH* 14, no. 2 (1998): 177–9.
34 Neeladri Bhattacharya, 'Introduction', *SIH* 14, no. 2 (1998) (special issue on 'Forests, Fields and Pastures'): 167.
35 Singha, 'Providential Circumstances', 91, fn. 35.

Malcolm's description of thugs was also similar. He said they were 'disguised as religious mendicants, as tradesmen, or as soldiers looking for service' who had 'horses, camels, and tents, and are equipped like merchants; some dressed like soldiers others as beggars, byragees, or holy mendicants'.[36] But, as Singha has pointed out, this trend of communitarian identification and responsibility did not emerge suddenly in the 1830s. Long before then Hastings had introduced a special provision that extended the punishment for dacoity from an individual offender to his family and his village.[37] The word 'disguise' used both by Sleeman and Malcolm hides more than they tell us about the anxieties and propensities of colonial rulers to identify groups committing the crime. Gosains, sanyasis, fakirs, banjaras and other mobile groups, who were largely peripatetic traders and merchants, then became easy targets to be described as 'plunderers and raiders'.[38] It seemed a simple conclusion for the authorities: people on the road must have committed the crime on the road. Nor were zamindars beyond suspicion, not for having committed crimes themselves but for being co-sharers of exploits and protecting people involved in such acts. The disbanded lathials of these zamindars were also engaged in such crimes. The issue here is not to establish the veracity of whether sanyasis, fakirs or gosains committed crimes of plunder – they certainly did.[39] More important here is to pinpoint the fact that because of their wandering nature, they were easily identified and classified as criminals. The term 'disguise' also suggests a reversal of identity. Thus, for some colonial officials people from these groups (or the whole of the group) were primarily thugs who carried on their trade of plunder and murder disguised as mendicants, merchants and traders. This change in perception was accompanied by a change in the occupational profile of these communities. Loss of occupation in some circumstances, severe dislocations caused by natural factors such as famine and droughts in others, and, not least, the control of circulatory patterns by the colonial state made the situation worse for certain groups and classes who then turned to robbery and other crimes.

By the 1830s and 1840s, banjaras were increasingly seen as a criminal group. In the late eighteenth century, by contrast, they were described as a people of 'useful class' without whom the army was 'helpless'.[40] So helpful did they prove to be that the Company thought of encouraging them to permanently reside in a territory. The officials knew about the wandering nature of this group but this did not pose a problem in conceptualizing a permanent residency for them. So, it was argued: 'Altho' they lead a wandering life and carry in general most of their families with them, they always have a home and live under a particular government of whom they consider themselves, from having a certain Establishment the subjects, and in whose service they are always ready

---

36 Quoted in D. H. A. Kolff, 'Sanyasi Trader–Soldiers', *IESHR* 8, no. 2 (1971): 218.

37 Singha, 'Providential Circumstances', 85.

38 Official letters of this period are full of expressions such as 'ravagers', 'pernicious tribes' and 'vagabond plunderers', particularly for sanyasis and fakirs. See Jamini Mohan Ghosh, *Sannyasi and Fakir Raiders in Bengal* (Calcutta, 1930), 39.

39 In many of the expeditions in the 1810s and 1820s, Ajeet Singh approved of disguise as a banjara or mendicant. *Narrative of Ajeet Singh*, 8, 13, 14, 15, 18, 25, 27, 29, 31–4.

40 'Extract of Military Letter from Fort St. George', 2 January 1799, Bcl, vol. 59, 1799–1800, F/4/59, 1913.

to engage.'[41] Nearly two decades later, the usefulness of this class was in doubt. Stewart, writing in 1813, praised Ali Vardy Khan for attacking and routing 'a band of robbers, called Bunjareh' when he arrived at Patna as the governor of Bihar in 1729–30. Stewart added, 'under the pretence of purchasing grain and other commodities, (Bunjareh) laid the country through which they passed under heavy contribution, and plundered the collectors of revenue'.[42] Whether Ali Vardy Khan saw banjaras simply as plunderers and looters is difficult to ascertain, but they appeared so in the eyes of Stewart.[43] Writing in the same period, Briggs said that the banjaras were a class of people who had for a long time been in the occupation of transporting merchandise of all kinds.[44] But they had picked up certain 'predatory habits', which was not in this period seen as a part of their character but something explained through historical conjecture. He noted: 'The grant that they pretend to have received from Aurungzeb…has furnished them with pretexts for their general predatory habits. Wherever they go in times of peace they are most cruel robbers on the highways, for they seldom spare the life if any resistance is made.'[45] They were also said to be 'devotedly fond' of *bhang*,[46] a commodity that Sleeman later identified with highway robbers.

However, the discursive context in which crime and mobility was seen in the earlier decades was different from how identities solidified in later years. Very interesting is the inherent tension exhibited in Edward Balfour's account of migratory tribes. Writing about the 'Binjarries' he acknowledged that changing politico-economic aspects (such as the cessation of wars which were 'periods of activity among them'), 'have done much to make the Binjarries poor'.[47] But he quickly added:

> They were at all times considered a bold and formidable race, and when traversing the country with herds of bullocks transporting grain and salt, they frequently perpetrated robberies in gangs, and they are not over-scrupulous in committing murder on these occasions, if they meet with opposition, or deem it necessary for their security. With the approaches of poverty, too, vice has grown apace; many are convicted of stealing cattle and children, and Thugs have also been detected among them.[48]

---

41 'Extract of General Harris' Minute', 30 October 1798, ibid.
42 Stewart, *The History of Bengal*, 421.
43 Singha's account supports Ali Vardi's punitive raid on the banjaras, but it appears from her account that groups such as banjaras were chastised when 'they made expeditions on their own account, or if they supported some recalcitrant chief'. In other words, raids were part of the larger political conflict rather than as correctives to narrowly defined criminality. Singha, *A Despotism of Law: Crime and Justice in Early Colonial India* (New Delhi, 1988), 25.
44 Briggs, 'Account of the Origin', 172.
45 Ibid., 190–91. Possibly there was an element of truth in this remark. A Mughal commander had once said to the banjara leaders: 'I do not mind if you burn my crops and poison my wells, so long as you feed my armies.' Bayly, *Rulers, Townsmen and Bazaars*, 29.
46 Briggs, 'Account of the Origin', 181.
47 Edward Balfour, 'On the Migratory Tribes of Natives in Central India', *JASB* 13, pt 1 (1844): 2–3.
48 Ibid., 3.

Evidently, although Balfour was willing to attribute the vices of murder and dacoity to the factor of poverty, the latter was only a contributory element. More important were racial (and physical) traits together with age-old habits. The reversal of identity became complete when Cumberlege applied the logic of 'second generation' thugs to them.[49]

Also of note are omissions of immediate historical explanations in the latter day texts, such as that of Cumberlege in the late nineteenth century, which encouraged certain groups to become 'petty thieves'. In contrast, the earlier texts, the early nineteenth-century ones, could be used for understanding the changing historical conditions that affected these groups. For instance, Sherwood, who, while regarding thuggee as a practice of 'ancient origin', still provided a clue as to its more immediate historical explanation. He raised three important points. First was the change in political masters. The destabilization caused by this change made the atmosphere conducive for the thugs to operate. Second was the immediate withdrawal of subsistence resources (caused by the political change), which pushed some people to take up criminal activities. And third was improved communications, which helped such activities to spread.[50]

On being arrested the thugs themselves attested to the colonial view that thuggee was their professional ancestral activity. But it would not be difficult to ascertain that their identity was an acquired one.[51] In his confession, one Sahib Khan, a thug from north India who had been practising thuggee for twenty years, informed: 'once we drove bullocks and were itinerant tradesmen, and consequently of lower cast'. On being asked if he thought there was any truth in his assertion that his ancestors drove bullocks, he replied, 'I think there is. We have some usages and traditions that seem to imply that our ancestors kept bullocks, and traded, but how I know not.'[52] A more detailed conversation quoted below brings out two points clearly. First, the identity and practice of thug and thuggee was an acquired one and there was a close connection between them and their wandering/itinerant/trading nature. Second, and quite paradoxically, the thugs themselves used the logic of 'disguise', thus legitimizing their

---

49 N. R. Cumberlege, *Some Account of the Bunjarah Class* (Bombay, 1882), 32. He was the district superintendent of police in Berar. He tried to imitate Sleeman in many ways. He gave descriptions of the ritual practices of banjaras, the deities they worshipped, and tried to suggest a connection between them and their occupation of robbery. According to him, as other criminal tribes worshipped Mahakali, banjaras also visited a Kali temple at a place called Pohara. Another deity worshipped was Mitthoo Bhukia. This deity was believed to have lived in the Central Provinces and was 'worshipped only by the dacoit now, as the most clever, never detected dacoit handed down by their ancestors'. On the employment of measuring technique and postulation of hierarchies (in terms of caste, class, clan and tribe) among the banjara class carried by British authorities, see R. G. Varady, 'North India Banjaras: Their Evolution as Transporters', *South Asia* 2, nos. 1–2 (1979).
50 Sleeman, *Thugs and Phansigars*, 38.
51 Singha, in her 'reading' of confessions also suggests that 'though the approvers talk of antiquity of their acts, their accounts of actual attacks do not go further back than the early nineteenth century'. 'Providential Circumstances, 100.
52 Sleeman, *Thugs and Phansigars*, 122–3.

own perception and that of the colonial understanding of being hereditarily involved in thuggee.

> Question by Sleeman: Have you Hindoostan men any funeral ceremonies by which your origin can be learnt?
>
> Inaent (a Hindoostan Thug): No funeral ceremonies; but at marriages an old matron will sometimes repeat, as she throws down the *toolsee* (leaves regarded auspicious in ritual-religious ceremonies), 'here's to the spirits of those who once led bears, and monkeys; to those who drove bullocks, and marked with the *godnee*, and those who made baskets for the head'.
>
> Q: And does not this indicate that your ancestors were Khunjurs, itinerant tradesmen, wandering with their herds and families about the country?
>
> Sahib khan: By no means. It only indicates that our ancestors after their captivity at Delhi were obliged to adopt those disguises to effect their escape. Some pretended to have dancing bears and monkeys, some to have herds of cattle, and to be wandering khunjurs, but they were not really so, they were high cast Musulmans.
>
> On this Feringeea, a Telingana thug, said, 'you may hear and say what you please, but your funeral and marriage ceremonies indicate that your ancestors were nothing more than khunjurs and vagrants about the great city'.
>
> Inaent: It is impossible to say whether they were really what is described in these ceremonies, or pretended to be so, that they performed these offices for a time is questionable, but I think they must have been assumed as disguises.
>
> Feringeea: But those who emigrated direct from Delhi into remote parts of India, and did not rest at Agra, retain those professions up to the present day, as the Mooltanies.
>
> Sahib khan: True, but it is still as disguise to conceal their real profession of Thuggee.
>
> Feringeea: True, and under the same guise they practiced their trade of Thuggee round Delhi before the captivity, and could never have had any other.
>
> Sahib Khan: I pretend not to know when they put on the disguise, but I am sure it was a disguise, and that they were never really leaders of bears and monkeys.[53]

It is clear from this that what Feringeea was saying had an element of truth. The then 'hereditary thugs' might have been itinerant tradesman, who on loss of their occupation took to roadside robbery. Interestingly, it was also thought that the wealth of such itinerant groups as banjaras and multanis was amassed through thuggee.[54] Also, there were always fresh recruits in the group. Sahib Khan and Nasir remembered meeting their old acquaintance Mudee Khan, who had migrated to Deccan and had formed a new group, which comprised of 'weavers, braziers, bracelet-makers, and all kinds of ragamuffins, whom he had scraped together about his new abode on the banks of the Herun and Nurbudda rivers, in the districts of Jebulpore and Nursingpore'.[55]

Seen in this context we can say that the histories of trade and trading communities on the one hand and the histories of identities on the other were reshuffled in a period of over

---

53 Sleeman, *Thugs and Phansigars*, 142–3.
54 Ibid., 223.
55 Ibid., 132.

fifty years. In all this, the regulation of communication played an important role. Securing a safe passage, about which early Company rule was so concerned, also indicated an attempt to regulate certain patterns of circulation. The Company was willing to promote only those forms of mobility that did not clash with its agenda of rule and revenue collection; others, which did not fall into its scheme, were dubbed as 'illegal' and hence criminal. In Chapter 3 we saw how a new monopolistic nature of trade emerged, which reflected the creation of a new power hierarchy. (This monopoly later became an object of criticism and was withdrawn from all but three commodities: salt, saltpetre and opium.) This restrictive monopoly extended both to production and distribution. The authorities described any infringement of the monopoly as amounting to 'illegal production' and 'smuggling'. One such instance was the 'smuggling' of 'Maratha salt' into Bengal from Nagpore (Nagpur).[56] The districts most 'affected' were Midnapur, Beerbhoom, Burdwan, Ramghur and Behar. The logic was simple. It was smuggling because the salt imported into the Company's territory of Bengal was eating up the revenue that the Company derived from the sale of its monopoly salt.[57] Cunningham, the superintendent of the Western Salt Choukies, estimated that 'many years ago forty or fifty thousand bullocks were employed in the trade'. According to him, in those days the annual importation of the Maratha salt probably exceeded 200,000 maunds. He claimed that the quantity imported in recent years had declined to 100,000 maunds but this was the amount smuggled through one of the choukies at Bulrampore situated in Nagpore. Though expressing his inability to calculate the exact quantity, Cunningham loosely put the amount at 600,000 maunds annually for the whole province, which was considerable by any standards. The reach of the 'smuggled' salt was widespread. In places like Raghunathpur, Peethorea, Choreah and Lohardagga in south Bihar no Rowannah salt (Company salt) was brought in. Through these places Maratha salt was conveyed from Nagpur to Chatra, an important trading place on the NMR. In the districts of Palamow and Ramghur, both Rowannah (imported from Patna and Chatra) and Maratha salt were consumed. The quantity traded and the number of bullocks employed proves that this trade was very significant before the Company declared a monopoly on salt. Apart from 'zamindars and more respected ryots [who] were proprietors of bullocks', the reference to the high number of bullocks used in this trade suggests the involvement of groups such as banjaras. It is well known that these banjaras who moved in *tandas* owned thousands of bullocks. Cumberlege mentioned that the banjaras earlier had a monopoly over the transport of salt in Berar, the Central Provinces and the Deccan.[58] It is beyond dispute that after coming so close to the Central Provinces, these men, with the support of wealthy zamindars, would not have carried the salt further into the western and southern districts of Bengal and Bihar.

---

56 The following account is based on 'Arrangements for the Prevention of an Illicit Trade in Salt in the districts under the Superintendent of the Western Chokies', Bcl, vol. 133, 1802–03, F/4/133, 2412.

57 The superintendent said that in 1800–1801, smuggled salt sold at as little as Rs. 1–13 maund of 62 *sicca* weight to the seer in Midnapur and Burdwan. He did not give the price of Company salt but said that 'this among other circumstances may have influenced the price of salt at the Company's sales', ibid.

58 Cumberlege, *Some Account*, 32.

Since this trade had now become illegal it needed to be checked. Cunningham suggested a series of measures for this. These included setting up choukies all along the road and major ghats through which the salt passed. The NMR became the dividing line. From the western extremity of the Bishenpore parganna (in Burdwan) to Hazaribagh in the Ramghur district, the NMR was to be considered as the northern boundary of the Western Salt Choukies. Accordingly, 'all salt transported or sold to the north of this Road, was to be free from search or molestation but all salt transported or sold either upon the said Road or to the south of it [were] required to be accompanied with Rowannahs or chars'.[59] From Hazaribagh to Kenda, situated at 3–4 coss to the northeast of Chatra, the same road was declared the boundary of the salt districts under the same rules. The role of manning the channels of communication was intertwined with the purpose of controlling crime, as it was claimed that no other line was as well set up as the NMR to prevent infiltration. This was because all the Rowannah salt brought to Chatra was transported on this road. It was therefore also thought expedient to establish a choukie at Chatra to distinguish between the Rowannah and the illicit salt. Salt choukies were established in various districts. Later, Regulation X of 1819 empowered the magistrates to seize illegal salt.[60] One Mr Palauden was deputed as a special officer to check the illicit transportation of salt from Benares into Bihar. All other magistrates of places like Saran, Shahabad, Patna, Tirhut and Ramghur were directed to afford assistance to Mr Palauden. During his survey, Buchanan approved of the means taken to stop the 'contraband' trade in salt, 'a good deal of [which] was imported from the west of India'.[61]

There were three official reasons given for smuggling. First was the inefficiency of the salt daroghas and their involvement in this trade. Second, a reason that explained the first, the daroghas were found inefficient because of their low salaries. Therefore, allegedly they did not pay sufficient attention to checking this 'smuggling'. Third, it was argued that Company salt was imported in inadequate amounts, which forced the people to buy smuggled salt. But one of the prime reasons, which the Company failed to register, was that it had interfered in an area of trade long established in the country.

Amongst notable contributions in this scholarly debate on crime, Singha has explained the construction of criminality in colonial times through the exigencies of authoritarian reform, which she argues started from the time of Bentinck.[62] Nigam has emphasized colonial dominance and classification. For the early colonial period, with which this chapter is concerned, Stewart Gordon's emphasis on 'structure and process of state formation' is more useful. He rightly concludes that, for understanding the nature of crime, 'a theory that is the product of a study of eighteenth-century Indian institutions and social and political conditions, rather than Victorian morality, is called for'.[63] However, Gordon's suggestion that activities of 'thugs' or marauding groups 'depended on the weakness of the authority of any

---

59 'Arrangements for the Prevention of an Illicit Trade in Salt in the districts under the Superintendent of the Western Chokies', Bcl, vol. 133, 1802–03, F/4/133, 2412.
60 Chaudhury, *Sarkar Saran*, 7.
61 Buchanan, *An Account of the Districts of Behar and Patna*, vol. 1, 283.
62 Singha, 'Providential Circumstances', 88–9.
63 Stewart Gordon, 'Scarf and Sword: Thugs, Marauders, and State-Formation in Eighteenth Century Malwa', *IESHR* 6, no. 4 (1969): 413.

government above the local level' needs some qualification.[64] It was not always the weakness of the supra-local authorities that helped such activities thrive; the changes brought about by these authorities also created conditions for criminality. Our discussion makes it clear that mobility and its different functional forms were important factors behind the early colonial need to check the incidences of crime and to define that crime. Existing forms of mobility were important factors in marking and ascribing certain groups with criminal attributes. Since these groups were not only mobile but were also a potential threat to the state's revenue base, it was predictable that they would be closely watched by the colonial state. Conceptualizing crime across India from the 1820s onwards was thus heavily influenced by ideas of mobility. The idea of regulation and mobility went deep down at the very local levels of transactions; the trade of *feriwalahs* (peddlers) dealing in brass and bell-metal vessels in the Shahabad district was under scrutiny. As this trade was thought 'liable to abuse by facilitating the disposal of stolen goods' it was prohibited in several districts.[65] Not only that, 'any person of the profession like, banker, *shroffs*, gold and silversmiths, and brazier, purchased any of the articles like jewels, ornaments of silver, gold or brass, or utensils of copper or brass, which may be proved to have been stolen, or from a person of bad character knowing him to be so shall be sentenced by the magistrate to six months imprisonment and hard labour on the public roads'.[66] We argue that established networks of trade and mobility in which groups such as feriwalahs and banjaras operated helped the colonial state visualize crime such as thuggee at the pan-India level, which of course then was meant to dissolve the local specificities. In other words, mobility not only came under surveillance when crime was 'detected' or 'proved'; it was rather an integral part of the discourse through which the colonial state understood criminality in India. We now turn to some other peripatetic groups and their fate.

Gosains, Sanyasis and Fakirs

Leaving aside some early 'revolts, uprisings and rebellions' in late eighteenth-century Bengal,[67] from 1772–73 a series of anxious reporting began on dacoities in the Rangpur district. In March 1773, the Rangpur assistant collector reported 'ravages [committed] by the decoits' in the district.[68] Two months later, in May, the collector of the same place reported 'a despatch of treasure been stopped by dacoits numbering two hundred and fifty, who have surrounded, destroyed, and cut off two villages'.[69] In June, we hear again 'that a sirdar with a body of decoits were establishing a Haut in the Barbund District, and committing outrages in that neighbourhood'.[70] Although these letters referred to

---

64 Ibid., 415.
65 Buchanan, *An Account of the District of Shahabad*, 435.
66 Datta, ed., *BR*, 336–7.
67 We are referring to the Chuar rebellion and the peasant insurrection in Rangpur. See Chattopadhyay, *Crime and Control*, 14–15.
68 'Letter no. 208, from Peter Speke, Rungpore Assistant Collector to Hastings', 14 March 1773, *Bengal Revenue Council Consultations*, P/49/39. [Henceforth *BRCC*.]
69 'Letter no. 438, from C. Purling, Collector, Rungpore to Hastings', 10 May 1773, *BRCC*, P/49/39.
70 'Letter from Herbert Harris, Collector, Rungpore to Hastings', 23 June 1773, *BRCC*, P/49/40.

the arrest en masse of *sardars* and dacoits, they did not say much about them. The 1774 minute of George Vansittart, however, did hint at occupational dissonances that were swelling up the ranks of these dacoits.[71] The resumption of the *Chaukeraun zameen*, or lands allotted to the *thannadars* and *pykes* for their services in guarding the villages and districts against robbers, had deprived them of their livelihood and had forced them to become dacoits.

The period also witnessed 'incursions' of sanyasis and fakirs. They were making extortions at different gunges and in villages.[72] But in this period they were not communally seen as robbers and plunderers. The state pledged to support the sanyasis in their trade, in taking up agriculture or in any 'other useful employments'. But for that it was necessary for them to '*fix* their habitations in the province'.[73] The government recognized the variety and utility of travel these fakirs and sanyasis undertook. An interesting account of one of these sanyasis/fakirs, named Praun Poory, has been given to us by Jonathan Duncan who recorded the sanyasi's account in May 1792 through a servant's intercession.[74] Duncan described Poory as a 'very intelligent man and a great traveller'. As recalled by the sanyasi himself, Praun Poory was a native of Kanauj who left his father's place at the age of nine and became a fakir under one Munsur Ali Khan. The time period of his travels, based on his anecdotes, probably started a little before the 1750s, lasting possibly until the 1770s. His travels can be classified into four phases, each covering 'new' places. The first phase of the journey was southwards to Rameshwaram, travelling through Kalpi, Ujjain, Burhanpur, Aurungabad, Elora, Poona, Seringapatnam, Malabar and Cochin. After reaching Rameshwaram he went via the Coromandal coast to Jaggarnath Puri in Orissa. He returned to Rameshwaram again, this time to proceed to Ceylon where he spent some time before returning to Cochin. He gave descriptions of routes and towns and the merchants residing in different cities. His second phase can be discerned in his itinerary starting from Bombay (which he reached from Cochin), which finally took him to Moscow, but in a zigzag fashion. He went to Multan first and

---

71 'Minute and Plan of the President, George Vansittart, for the establishment of Phouzdars for detecting Decoits', *BRCC*, P/49/45.
72 Reportedly about Rs. 3,000 was extorted by these sanyasis at Govindgunge. 'Letter no. 199 from Speke to Hastings', 23 February 1773, *BRCC*, 1773, P/49/38. Numerous instances of such 'plundering acts' are referred to in Firminger's edited series of Bengal district records. The Calcutta Council noted in 1773: 'A set of lawless banditti known under the name of Sanyasis or Fakirs have long infested these countries and under the pretence of religious pilgrimage have been accustomed to traverse the chief past of Bengal, begging, stealing and plundering wherever they go and as it best suits their convenience to practice.' Ghosh, *Sannyasi and Fakir*, 9, fn. 1.
73 'Letter from the Chief and Council at Patna to Hastings', 24 May 1773, *BRCC*, P/49/40.
74 Jonathan Duncan, 'An Account of Two Fakirs, with their Portraits', *AR*, 5, 1799. A few others described him as 'celebrated Pran Puri', whom they suspected, the Greeks would have regarded as a gymnosophist (a naked philosopher). 'Review of the *Sketches of India*', 600. There seems to be some confusion on the exact year of publication of vol. 5. In my article 'Mobility, Control and Criminality in Early Colonial India, 1760s–1850s', *IESHR* 45, no. 1 (2008), I gave the date 1802. William Pinch in his *Peasants and Monks in British India* (Berkeley, Los Angeles, and London, 1996), 221 has given the date of 1808. One probable reason for this discrepancy is that the *Asiatic Researches* were published both from Calcutta and London. The year 1799 is the date of the London publication, which I am using here.

Plate 19. Praun Poory

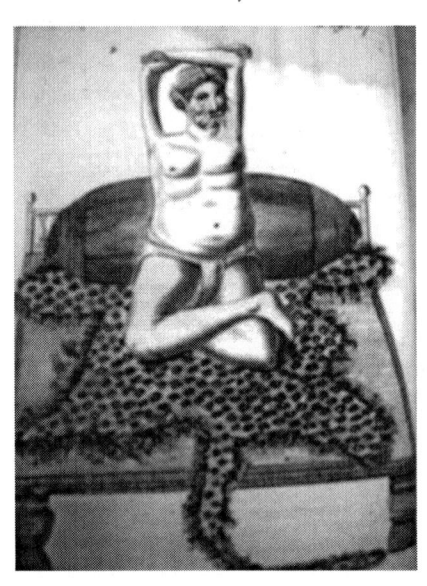

Plate 20. Perkasanand

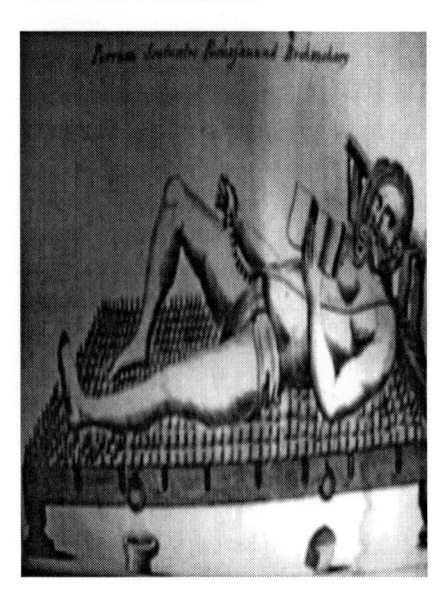

© British Library Board, Duncan, 'An Account'.

© British Library Board, Duncan, 'An Account'.

then turned eastwards to Hurdwar, proceeded to Kabul and reached the borders of the Caspian Sea through Bamian, Khorasan and Herat. There, he said he met Ahmad Shah Abdali, who allegedly consulted him for treating his ulcer on the nose. Praun Poory was aware of the fact that from Moscow one could reach Petersburg in one month, and from there one could proceed towards Great Britain. However, he decided to return, though not along the same route; he chose to go back through Persia along the coast (which makes it obvious that he made a sea journey as well) to Surat. From Surat he reportedly again went to Makha (Mecca?) and came back. The third leg of his journey was in the northwest direction towards Balkh, Bokhara, Samarqand, Badkashan, Kashmir, Gangotri and Jamunotri. He vividly described the source of these two rivers (the Ganga and the Jamuna). The final phase of his journey was now northwards towards Nepal and Tibet and then to Lake Mansarovar (which Moorcroft and Hearsey tried to reach a few years later). It was from this phase that he carried some despatches for Warren Hastings that secured him a rent-free *jaghir* (land) in Benares. Duncan reported that although he was now 'settled' in Benares he still 'makes short excursions into different parts of India, and occasionally as far as Nepal'.[75]

Another sanyasi, Perkasanand Brahmachari, who related his account to Duncan in August 1792, was not as highly regarded by Duncan as Praun Poory but he too had allegedly travelled far and wide. In his first phase he went to Nepal and Tibet and then to Lake Mansarovar, from where he proceeded to Kashmir. He stayed in Kashmir for some time for devotional purposes and also to undertake his studies. Unlike Praun Poory,

---

75 Duncan, *An Account*, 45. The sketches were made by Duncan himself, which are reproduced from his article.

Perkasanand was inclined towards self-penance, which is reflected (see Plate 20) in his wilful act of sleeping on a bed of iron-spikes, a practice he had followed for more than thirty-five years. From Kashmir he travelled to Tibet, Sindh, Allahabad and Benares. In his next phase he went to Puri and then to Rameshwaram; from there he went to Surat and boarded a ship to go to Muscat. He came back to Surat and stayed there for two years before finally deciding to settle in Benares. Like Praun Poory, he also received a provision from the government to reside in Benares. The theme of 'settlement' and the undertaking of 'religious' duties, which Perkasanand argued was one of the reasons he had come to settle in Benares, were not the only factors behind British curiosity and attraction to these figures. The fact that the sanyasis and fakirs were widely travelled and were able to furnish details of regions that were not under direct British control was no less important. People of this group were used for military intelligence purposes.[76] The overlapping itineraries of both these persons, at least for Nepal and Tibet, must have had to do with the extensive trade linkages the sanyasis had with those regions. George Bogle, who undertook a mission to Tibet in 1774, described gosains as the 'trading pilgrims of India' whose 'humble deportment and holy character heightened by the merit of distant pilgrimages and their knowledge of remote regions brought them great favours'.[77] Another sanyasi figure, perhaps the most celebrated in administrative circles, was Puran Gir. He accompanied Bogle both on this mission and on his second one in 1779. Again, in 1783, he accompanied Turner on the mission to Tibet. In 1785, he was sent independently to Tibet as a representative of the Company. On all these occasions, he was not only instrumental as a guide and an interpreter for these English missions but also in securing the goodwill of the lama for opening the dialogue between Tibet and the EIC.[78] Interestingly, because of the widespread travel in which gosains, sanyasis and fakirs participated, they became figures of legitimacy for many early European travellers. In their visits to Tibet, Moorcroft and Hearsey had disguised themselves as gosains. When returning, when they resumed their European dress, they were arrested by Gurkha soldiers. On being asked about the reason for putting on a disguise, the travellers replied: 'it was the custom for travellers to disguise themselves, and that by no other means could they have entered Tibet'.[79] For his help, Puran Gir was rewarded with a grant of land, rent free, in Hooghly, to build a temple with a garden.[80]

---

76 Bayly, *Empire and Information*, 69, 106.
77 'Memorandum by Mr. Bogle on the trade of Thibet', in G. W. Forrest, ed. *Selections*, vol. 1, 252. Bogle reportedly had said that 'in his journey to Tibet he had to rely mainly on the informations supplied by the Sannyasis about the roads, the climate and the people'. S. C. Sarkar, 'A Note on Puran Gir Gosain', *BPP* 43, nos. 85–6 (1932): 84. For a lucid treatment of Bogle's journey, see Kate Teltscher, *The High Road to China: George Bogle, the Panchen Lama and the British Expedition to Tibet* (London, 2006).
78 Sarkar, 'A Note on Puran Gir', 83–6.
79 Hugh Pearse, 'Moorcroft and Hearsey's Visit to Lake Mansarowar in 1812', *GJ* 26, no. 2 (1905): 182–6. However, for entering into Tibet even Puran Gir had to acquire a passport from the Tibetan authority, which allowed and pledged to take care of his necessities during the journey. See Gaur Das Bysack, 'Notes on a Buddhist Monastery', *JASB* 59, no. 1 (1890).
80 First *sanad* (deed) dated 12 June 1778. Bysack, 'Notes', 98.

Wearing disguise was equally true for intelligence missions on which natives were employed. A comprehensive report on Nepal, ranging from military establishments and the strength of the army to trade and towns, was furnished by 'a very intelligent man who was [in] every way qualified to act in the capacity of a spy'. Not surprisingly, this man, who spent more than three months in finding the details needed by the Company-state, was 'disguised' as a fakir.[81] The inimical relationship between the Company and Nepal was one important reason behind such disguises. On earlier missions to Tibet we do not hear of Bogle or Turner disguising themselves as gosains. The reason could be because they did not enter Tibet from Nepal but from Bhutan. But to go without a disguise could also have been made possible by the presence of Puran Gir. For, when Bogle was held up in Bhutan by messages from the Tashi lama asking him to go back, it was Puran Gir who went forward to Tibet, persuading the lama to allow Bogle and Hamilton to enter also.[82] But the presence of an Englishman became a matter of concern for the lama; he said to Bogle: 'I wish the Governor will not at present send an Englishman. You know what difficulties I had about your coming into the country and how I had to struggle with the jealousy of the Regent and the people of Lhasa. I would wish that the Governor would rather send a Hindu.'[83]

Similar to the multiplicity of the peripatetic behaviour of sanyasis and fakirs, the practice of dacoity and the identity of a dacoit was also diffused and ambiguous in this period. Officially, *decoit sardar* and *gang* were terms commonly used for referring to the people involved in robbery, but Hastings asked for a prudent application of such terms. He said, 'if a careful distinction be not made, the Reiott [ryot] who impelled by strong necessity in a single instance invades the property of his neighbour, will with his family fall a sacrifice to this Law, and be blended in one common fate with the professed Dacoit'.[84] Even in the Rangpur case noted above, the collector made a difference between sanyasis and dacoits. He confessed that the withdrawal of the sepoys on account of driving out the sanyasis was one major cause for the boldness of dacoits.

But for all this, prudence in colonial understanding was tempered with ideas of unregulated mobility and crime practised by wandering sanyasis and fakirs. This was partly because when robberies did occur, the districts of Rangpur and Purneah also suffered sanyasi 'uprisings'. Basudeb Chattopadhyay has tried explaining the causes of this 'uprising' by highlighting the *break* which Company rule brought with it. This break was both at the level of agriculture and trade. So, he explains, on the one hand the

---

81 See 'No. 91 Letter from D. H. McDowell, Collector, Rangpur to John McPherson', 23 July 1786, Firminger, ed., *Bengal District Records: Rangpur*, vol. 6, 92–7.
82 Sarkar, 'A Note on Puran Gir Gosain', 84.
83 As quoted in D. B. Dislaskar, 'Bogle's Embassy to Tibet', *The Indian Historical Quarterly* 9 (1933): 422.
84 Chattopadhyay, *Crime and Control*, 21. In the light of this remark, Ranjan Chakrabarti's assertion that 'the British administrators however, attributed the unprecedented rise in the number of crimes in early colonial Bengal to the character of the Indians' needs qualification. Chakrabarti himself has quoted Colebroke, the judge of the Murshidabad Court of Circuit, saying in 1801: 'it was not disposition to idleness or an aversion from labour which made dacoits. All Persons convicted of this crime, except a few instances, are found in the class of peasants.' Ranjan Chakrabarti, *Authority and Violence in Colonial Bengal, 1800–1860* (Calcutta, 1997). Quotations are from 187–8 and 186 respectively.

rent-free lands given to the sanyasis (by the Bengal nawabs before the Company administration) were resumed and on the other the Company's monopoly affected their trade.[85] However, if we follow the chronology carefully, we need to look at some alternative reasons other than the two mentioned above. Chattopadhyay says, 'the partial resumption, envisaged by Cornwallis in the *baze zamin* Regulation of 1788 aroused resentment among the rent-free-tenure-holding Sanyasis'.[86] We are then led to ask, if the Regulation was passed in 1788 why were the sanyasis 'infesting' and 'making incursions' into Rangpur and other neighbouring districts in 1773? Erosion of trading profits appears more relevant, but the Company was not always an instigator of such disruptions. The rise of the Gurkha kingdom in Nepal in the early 1770s disrupted the trade of gosains. Bogle informs us that these gosains, having extensive establishments in Nepal, were then driven out of the kingdom, 'many of them the wealthy inhabitants being stripped of their possessions and forced to flee'.[87] Even the terms used were 'incursion' and 'infestation', signifying that they came from outside. In all likelihood, these sanyasis who suffered at the hands of the Gurkhas were plundering the villages of the neighbouring districts, leading to a serious revenue deficiency in the colonial state.

The activities of sanyasis and fakirs during this period also need to be situated in their context of early and mid-eighteenth-century politics. Gosains, sanyasis and fakirs had by this time developed into a military and mercenary group. In the early eighteenth century they had fought battles against rulers and princes and had emerged victorious.[88] Their success with arms probably encouraged rulers of distant areas – from western India to Bengal – to recruit them as mercenaries. They had their own spy system. These mobile itinerant groups thus amalgamated the professions of trade, money lending, military adventure and pilgrimage.[89] The Company-state recognized this complex nature of circulation when it came to using them for amassing knowledge, but armed mobility was something it could not permit. It had first-hand experience at the decisive Battle of Buxar in 1764, in which sanyasis were also part of the forces fighting against it.[90] Possession of arms was a matter of grave concern for the state. In 1773 Hastings therefore instructed collectors to regard all persons travelling with arms through the country as enemies of the government. This was later modified and applied only to sanyasis and fakirs, since merchants and other travellers also carried arms with them.[91]

Let us once again juxtapose colonial and pre-colonial approaches to underline the colonial changes: in the reign of Aurangzeb, local landlords and military officials were

---

85 Chattopadhyay, *Crime and Control*, 10–13.
86 Ibid., 11.
87 Forrest, ed., *Selections*, vol. 1, 253.
88 Jadunath Sarkar, *History of Dasnami Naga Sanyasis* (Allahabad, n.d, probably 1950s), 87.
89 Bernard Cohn, 'The Role of Gosains in the Economy of Eighteenth and Nineteenth Century Upper India', *IESHR* 1, no. 4 (1963–64): 175–82; Pinch, *Warrior Ascetics*, 59–103.
90 Sarkar, *Dasnami Naga*, 164–6. In fact, according to an Italian traveller Marco della Tomba who was writing in 1773, sanyasis presented the strongest opposition 'the English ever had'. Pinch, *Warrior Ascetics*, 76.
91 Ghosh, *Sannyasi and Fakir*, 64–5.

warned 'that no obstacle or hindrance be put in their [sanyasis] ways, so that they may travel without molestation from one province to another'.[92] Elsewhere Pinch is more inclined (and not mistakenly) to associate British perception and regulation of ascetic groups to a post-Enlightenment definition of religion, which equated asceticism with monasticism, which meant a quiet, celibate and sedentary life. Thus, according to Pinch, the British modes of regulating sanyasis were based on what they thought them to be – ascetics who *should* be nearer to the pursuit of religion than political power.[93] In the setting up of this regulating regime, this chapter argues that the factor of armed mobility was also equally, if not more, important from the viewpoint of the Company-state.

A series of such regulations should be seen as a part of the contestation for power and authority. The colonial state wished to retain and impose an exclusive sense of authority that clashed with that entertained by groups such as sanyasis and fakirs. Sanyasis referred to a sanad granted to them by the Prince Shah Shuja in 1659. This document provided and legitimized the customary authority that sanyasis entertained. Some of the clauses of the sanad are quoted verbatim here:

> Clause 1. Wherever you wish to go out for the guidance of the people or for travel into the cities, countries, divisions, and all sorts of places where you may like to go according to your free will and inclination you may take all the articles of the *Julus*, e.g. Banners, standard, flags, poles, staffs, mahi and muratil etc.
>
> Clause 4. You will be entitled within the countries of Bengal, Bihar and Orissa to confiscate as you like properties to which there is no heir or pirpal or rent-free tenures.
>
> Clause 5. When you pass through any tract of the country, the landlords and tenants will supply you with provisions.
>
> Clause 7. No cess or contribution of any kind will be levied.[94]

The sanad, which was granted to one Sultan Hasan Muria Burhana in 1659, appears to be a historically valid document. Burhana was a powerful Madari fakir living in the area of Dinajpur in Bengal.[95] A very similar sanad was referred to by banjaras, allegedly granted to them by 'Asip Khan, the Wuzeer of Shahjahan' (Asaf Jahan, the prime minister of Mughal emperor Shahjahan), which said:

Runjan ka pani, chuppur ka ghans,
din ko teen khoon muaf,

---

92 Pinch, *Warrior Ascetics*, 72.
93 Pinch, 'Gosain Tawaif', 594.
94 Ghosh, *Sannyasi and Fakir*, 22.
95 The full text of the sanad appeared in the *JASB* 72, no. 3 (1903), the abstract of which appeared recently in Atis Dasgupta, 'The Mughal Grant of a *Sanad* to Madari Fakirs: Historical Significance', *Journal of the Asiatic Society* 49, no. 2 (2007): 100.

aur jahan Asiph Jan ke ghore,
wahan bhungi-jungi ke bael.[96]

[Access to water from the royal sources and straw for shelter; excused from two to three murders a day; the bullocks of banjaras stand where the royal horses of Asaf Jahan do.]

Farooque further informs us that Bhangi and Jungi were two *nayaks* (leaders) who supplied Asaf Jahan's army in his Deccan campaigns in 1630. This epithet inscribed on a copper plate and engraved in gold letters reportedly still exists in Hyderabad.[97]

Thus, travelling with arms, confiscating properties and asking for contributions were the ideas that the wandering groups took as their natural rights. For the Company it was the violation of law and a challenge to its authority. As a result, an attempt was made to check their mobility. In 1775, the sanyasis were stopped from entering into Bihar from the western side (the NWP). The Company was also wary of the movement of fakirs in this part of the country. In a letter written to Rani Bhowani, zamindar of Natore in 1772, Majnu Shah, the leader of the fakirs, deplored that the English had obstructed them in visiting shrines and other places. The English feared that such places were used for organizational meetings and the distribution of arms.[98] Further, many of the rich sanyasis had given loans to zamindars. The failure to repay the loans made zamindars the target of sanyasis' and fakirs' depredations and plunder, but Company officials generally sided with the zamindars, making the sanyasis appear villains.[99]

One crucial distinction between the colonial and pre-colonial nature of statecraft was that, in the latter, wandering armed groups were not disqualified from enjoying a share in the wealth of the countryside, whereas in colonial times the state theoretically maintained and institutionally tried to implement exclusive control of the revenue. As a result, these groups were slowly drawn into the ambit of colonial surveillance. Of course, disproval of sanyasis and gosains was also a feature of pre-colonial times; a poem ascribed to Kabir (the great poet of fifteenth- and sixteenth-century north India) chastised them for being gunners, making wars and becoming millionaires.[100] We also have earlier noted Surdas' view on thag. Such accusations and characterizations in the tone of this poem, and also from what Pinch has suggested, were a reflection of their false claims to religiosity, their practising false *siddhas* (ways) and being lovers of *maya* (illusion). Although colonial authors also questioned their asceticism, what apparently became a crucial threat was their widespread armed mobility. After all, Hastings made concessions

---

96 Cumberlege, *Some Account*, 14; Farooque, *Roads and Communications*, 68. Translation mine.
97 Farooque, *Roads and Communications*, 67–8. Such sanads and claims remind of Wagner's take on the constitution of colonial knowledge on thuggee in which the approvers themselves had a crucial role in shaping the British opinion. Wagner, 'The Deconstructed Stranglers: A Reassessment of Thuggee', *MAS* 38, no. 4 (2004): 950.
98 Chattopadhyay, *Crime and Control*, 14.
99 'Letter from Colebrooke to Major Lewis Smith, Commanding 5th Battalion Native Infantry, Tajpore', *Bengal Criminal and Judicial Consultations*, P/128/1. [Henceforth *BCJC*.] Also, Chattopadhyay, *Crime and Control*, 13.
100 Wagner, *Thuggee*, 27.

on the prohibition of movement only to those ascetics who were '*fixed* inhabitants' and practised their religion quietly.[101] Pinch, however, is unwilling to regard the British as 'primary authors of cultural and religious change in modern India' but he does accept that they were 'clearly instrumental in the decline of the gosain power in Rasdhan'.[102] Another study on gosains has argued that by the 1830s they were reduced to mere political pensioners.[103] Similarly, fakirs were also becoming 'great thieves'; Fanny Parks described the figure of fakir as: '[e]xternally he is a saint, but internally a devil'.[104] But as noted above, since a distinction was made between sanyasis' depredations and other sorts of robberies, we now examine who these later individuals were and how they were being described and controlled.

Mobile Sardars

If, on the one hand, already existing groups were cast as criminals, then, on the other, there were also cases of non-itinerant, non-trading groups involved in travelling highway crime. The official reports were often silent on the actual identity of these persons. Most probably, the state did not have the necessary tools to acquire knowledge about them and hence ended up calling them sardars and gangmen. It appears that the term sardar essentially referred to a headman of the group found involved in crimes such as robbery or looting. But, being the head of the collective, and also because of the limited reach of the colonial state, these sardars or other members of the group were regarded by colonial officials as providers of crucial information. George Vansittart expressed the lack of information in explicit terms: 'To me it has only come through the channels of private information, as I do not recollect to have heard the slightest intimation of them from the zamindars, farmers or other officers of the Revenue, which may appear extraordinary.'[105] Another factor that prevented the state from acquiring knowledge was the groups' rapid mobility; the Rangpur collector expressed his limitation by acknowledging that sardars never stayed long enough in any one place for the authorities to get to know them.[106] The forests and 'impenetrable jungles' became a shelter for the robbers.[107] The passes on the main highways like the NMR were said to be 'infested by robbers who travelled in parties of twenty or thirty', thus signifying a lack of control.[108]

---

101 Pinch, *Warrior Ascetics*, 196.
102 Pinch, 'Gosain Tawaif', 595.
103 Jaya Chowdhury, 'The Gosains and the Company, 1780–1830' (unpublished MPhil dissertation, Centre for Historical Studies, Jawaharlal Nehru University, 1997).
104 Fanny Parks as quoted in Joachim K. Bautze, ed., *Interactions of Culture: Indian and Western Painting 1780–1910, The Ehrenfeld Collection* (Alexandria: Arts Service International, 1998), 52.
105 'Minute and Plan of the President, George Vansittart', *BRCC*, P/49/45.
106 'Letter no. 208, from Peter Speke, Rungpore Assistant Collector to Hastings', 14 March 1773, *BRCC*, P/49/39.
107 'Letter no. 23, From Magistrate of Ramghur to Cornwallis', 12 September 1793, *BCJC*, P/128/6.
108 'Letter no. 24, Translation of an Arzee from Jugmohun Banerjee', 3 September 1793, *BCJC*, P/128/6.

The increasing incidence of crime affected the trading communities; in 1785 a petition was submitted by the merchants of Bihar criticizing the government for its recent decision to reduce the force, which left them in a 'defenceless state, in consequence of which many robberies have been committed'.[109] Chattopadhyay attributes the 'sudden outbursts of violence' to the decline in zamindari and *fouzdari* establishments. The waning fouzdari power of zamindars was taken note of by the governor general in council.[110] The council accepted that the utmost confusion prevailing in the country was due to the abolition of the local jurisdictions exercised by the zamindars in their respective zamindaries.

Over the past two decades or so, scholars have tried to explain the increase in crime in this period as the result of institutional changes. John McLane considers the Permanent Settlement Act of 1793 as a significant event responsible for the rise in banditry.[111] Without denying these explanations, one also needs to take into account a more realistic picture of early colonial rule, which was plagued with severe limitations. Vansittart deplored that he could not recollect an instance when guilt was proved by evidence at a court trial rather than by a sardar's own confession, which he accepted was often obtained by improper means.[112] Due to the lack of information, zamindars were often held accountable. In 1809 it was proposed: 'the proprietor of the estate should be called upon to apprehend and deliver them [persons concerned in the robbery] up within a specific time or at the expiration of that period report fully the measures he had adopted on the occasion and the causes of the failure or omission'.[113] It was further proposed that zamindars 'should also be required to take from the Mandal, or principal persons of the village, a moochulka, engaging to apprehend and deliver up *all persons of bad or suspicious character*'.[114] These registers were then to be deposited in the magistrate's office. The state adopted a two-pronged strategy: first it was proposed to arrest the sardars, or, in the words of the Beerbhoom magistrate, to 'apprehend a few villains';[115] and, second, as this was not always an easy task, since the 'inhabitants dreaded fear to give any information', the state embarked upon a policy of keeping details about 'bad and suspicious persons'. No wonder many innocent men were frequently punished on the mere basis of suspicion.[116]

The later colonial stereotypes thus emerged partly from a lack of intelligence and partly from a compulsion to simplify categories in order to impose control and authority.

---

109 Hand, *Early English Administration*, 77–8.
110 'Minute from General Clavering, Colonel Monson, and Mr. Francis, Proceedings of the Secret Select Committee', 18 October 1775, Forrest, ed., *Selections*, vol. 2, 432–3.
111 McLane, 'Bengali Bandits, Police, and Landlords after the Permanent Settlement', in Yang, ed., *Crime and Criminality*.
112 BRCC, P/49/45.
113 'Extract of a Letter from the Senior Judge of the Calcutta Court of Circuit to the Magistrate of Zillah Jessore, 9th March, 1809', Datta, ed., *Selections*, 297–8.
114 Ibid. (emphasis added).
115 'Letter no. 9 from C. Keating, Magistrate, Beerbhum to Fort William', 22 April 1793, *BCJC*, P/128/1.
116 The magistrate of Midnapur brought this to the notice of the administration. Chakrabarti, *Authority and Violence*, 72.

One category frequently invoked was caste, and a way of reaching an understanding was 'testimony'. The following testimony taken by the magistrate of Agra in 1809 from a sister of one Tara, a member of the Buddhak caste, makes the point clear:[117]

> Q: What is your name?
> A: Gungeea.
> Q: Are you of the Budhick cast?
> A: I am.
> Q: What relation are you to Tara Budhick, who was confined in the jail at this station?
> A: I am his sister.
> Q: What mode of life did Tara pursue?
> A: He was a professed robber.
> Q: How do you know?
> A: The whole of the cast of Budhicks are robbers.[118]

This testimony, which is similar to that relating to thuggee presented above, complicates the issue of the production of colonial knowledge. However, a number of sources and incidents suggest that dacoity and the identity of dacoits were much diffused in this period. In 1793, the magistrate of Shahabad reported 'numerous gangs of dekoits infesting [the] river [the Ganga] between Buxar and Chuprah [Chapra]'.[119] Although he talked about 'gangs', soon he reported an incident in which a group of Bengali pilgrims returning from Brindaban were attacked, leaving two of them dead; this was said to be the work of ryots living near the Ganga.[120] The high prices that then prevailed in many districts where crime was reported was an important reason behind the 1793–94 dacoities.[121] A few years later, in 1802, the judge-magistrate of Midnapur made similar connections between crime and agricultural prices: 'The crimes have not increased still more, is owing to the providential occurrence of number of years of plenty. In any calamity of season, I have no doubt crimes would increase to a most alarming degree.'[122]

---

117 'Extract of the Evidence of Gungeea, submitted by the Magistrate of Agrah on 29th May 1809', Walter Firminger, *The Fifth Report from the Select Committee of the House of Commons on the Affairs of the East India Company*, vol. 2 (Calcutta, 1917), 718.

118 Surprisingly, the magistrate of Etawah (not far from Agra) on 17 May 1810 had said: 'while the "class of Badhaks are in most instances robbers it does not follow that every man who has the misfortune to be born a Badhak should be by nature a Dacoit"'. Quoted in Wagner, *Thuggee*, 52. In the next thirty years, although a settlement colony was planned for them in the Terai region, official views had hardened. The Buddhaks themselves allegedly reported: 'Once a Budhuk, always a Budhuk, and all Budhuks are always dacoits.' *The Annals of Indian Administration* 6 (1862): 283. [Henceforth *AIA*.]

119 'Letter no. 4 from Magistrate of Shahabad to Cornwallis', 19 April 1793, *BCJC*, P/128/1, 51–3.

120 'Letter no. 5 from Henry Revel to T. Brooke', 15 April 1793, *BCJC*, P/128/1, 53–6.

121 'Introduction', Datta, ed., *BR*, ix. This is plausible because in 1793 such cases of robberies on the Ganga were also reported from the Bhagalpur district.

122 Quoted in Chakrabarti, *Authority and Violence*, 66.

Robberies persisted throughout the period but, again, during 1820–21 they increased.[123] In one of the cases, in February 1820, a boat laden with mercantile treasure was looted between Patna and Monghyr.[124] In another, in 1819, a gang of almost 200 people under one Mihirban was said to have travelled from Oudh to Calcutta. He was arrested together with 165 of his men and later sentenced to death.[125] Three reasons were given for the increase in highway robbery. First was the want of English supervisors and the changes occasioned by the temporary absence of magistrates. Second was the release of a considerable number of 'prisoners of suspicious character' under Regulation VIII of 1818. And, third, was the high price of grain in 1819–20.[126] The number of robberies had also increased in the districts of Nuddea, Rangpur, Rajshaye and Midnapur in Bengal, and Ramghur and Behar in Bihar.[127] Both Shakespear, the acting superintendent of police in the Lower Provinces, and Mr Macnab, an officer on a special duty to inquire into causes of the increased robberies in Ramghur, asserted that this increase was because of the high prices of grain. The findings of Mr Macnab read:

> Mr. Macnab didn't ascribe the rise to any deterioration in the general efficiency of the police, or to the *organization of any regular bands of robbers*, or to other causes of permanent character, on the contrary the facts stated by him confirm that the robberies in question, as well as others which occurred at the same period of time in the neighbouring districts of Behar and Patna, generally originated in the high price of grain, and in the distress to which the lower orders of the people were in consequence reduced.[128]

High prices prevailed not only in Bengal and Bihar but also in Benares and other districts of the region.[129] However, going against the findings of the deputed officer, the Court of Directors remarked: 'If *plundering tribes* are thus harboured in the neighbouring territory, it must be extremely difficult for our government to guard against incursions like those of Mihirban.'[130] The court thus stuck to its opinion that these robberies were the handiwork of organized plundering tribes.

---

123 'Letter from J. B. Elliot, Officiating Judge, Patna Court of Circuit, to Tippet, Magistrate of Patna', 7 August 1822, Datta, ed., *Selections*, 211. In 1821, there were twelve highway robberies in the Saran district that reduced to three in 1822. Chaudhury, *Sarkar Saran*, 20. McLane's observation that 'by 1815, dacoity in most Bengal districts had declined to a small fraction' needs qualification. McLane, 'Bengali Bandits', 44.
124 'Extract Judicial from the Court of Directors to the Bengal Government', 11 April 1826, *Selections of Papers from the Records at the East India House, Relating to the Revenue, Police, and Civil and Criminal Justice under the Company's Governments in India* (London, 1826), vol. 4, 15.
125 Ibid., 15–16.
126 Ibid., 8.
127 'In Midnapore, Nuddea, Ramghur, Behar, Dinagepur, Rungpore and Rajshaye, seventy-six dacoities were reportedly committed in 1818, and two hundred and forty-five in 1819. Total number of "heinous crimes" in those districts was reported to be five hundred and sixty-five in 1818, and seven hundred and ninety one in 1819.' Ibid., 11.
128 Ibid., 7 (emphasis added).
129 'Letter from W. B. Bayly, Acting Chief Secretary to the Government of Bengal to the Magistrate in the Division of Benares and Bariely', 27 January 1818, Datta, ed., *Selections*, 193.
130 'Extract Judicial from the Court of Directors to the Bengal Government', *Selections of Papers*, 15–16.

By the late years of the eighteenth century many depredations reported in Bihar were said to be the work of Oudh gangs. The Bhagalpur magistrate noted one such case in 1799 in which twenty-five persons from Futtyghur travelled down the river to Murshidabad. A few of them and their boats were seized in Monghyr.[131] Charles Boddam, magistrate of Saran, gave information about different gangs active in the province. One was headed by a person named Behary Rawut who operated in the region of Gaya and Daudnagar (mid-south Bihar) before killing a darogha at Siwan in north Bihar. In one case he killed two Brahmins in the Bhagalpur district and stole their diamonds. We are fortunate at least to have the names of his accomplices: Manik Ray, Gumbeera Ray and Munsa Ray, who also were said to have 'long infested the Behar province'.[132] Inquiries pointed the finger at networks of gangs; supposedly Behary Rawut and his gang had received intelligence on the intended route of the Brahmins from some of their associates at Benares. Many travellers also reported on the high incidence of crime in the Upper Provinces; Deane categorically stated that the Oudh region has many thieves who murder as well plunder.[133] Raleigh made a similar observation: for Meerut, he said that travelling without escorts was unsafe because frequent robberies accompanied with murder were committed. Although in the 'thuggee' case the Europeans boasted that they were never attacked, in the case of theft they openly admitted being targeted, so much so that even the tent of Governor General Lord Amherst was not spared.[134] It would, therefore, be too far-fetched to believe that the cases of robberies were 'colonial constructions'. There were many *arzees* (petitions) submitted by the natives who were robbed. One such was by Munshi Muhammed Taha who was robbed near Rajmahal in 1792.[135] These examples can be multiplied. Yet what remains in doubt is the representation of strong camaraderie and gang brotherhood that emerges from the colonial sources. In this regard, we are unfortunate in having little information on who these people were, and how and why they took to robbery. The social history of crime in these cases is thus based on one side of the story, that is, on colonial impressions. Yet, by sifting through them closely we can observe that the identities of dacoits, as would be expected, remained ambivalent. None of these travellers who were writing at the apogee of thuggee conceptualization used the word 'thug' for these thieves. The Shahabad magistrate complained of ryots coming down from Gorakhpur who perpetrated robberies along the bank of the Ganga.[136] In the same year (1793), the house of a shroff in Chapra was looted, supposedly by 'a party of twenty or twenty five men armed with tulwars, spears, and bows and arrows'. The acting magistrate of Saran 'imagined' that they had come from Gorakhpur, as some hatchets to

---

131 'Letter from J. Fombelle, to H. Doughlas, Magistrate of Patna', 12 September 1799, Datta, ed., *Selections*, 295.
132 'Enclosure no. 2, letter dated Chupra 1 May 1795, from Charles Boddam, Magistrate of Saran, to John Fombelle', Datta, ed., *BR*, 120–22.
133 Deane, *A Tour*, 84.
134 Raleigh, *'The Log of a Griffin'*, 46. There were other instances of officials' tents being cut and boxes taken away in spite of guards placed around. See page 28.
135 Datta, ed., *BR*, 8.
136 'Letter no. 6, from T. Brooke, Magistrate, Shahabad, To Henry Revel, Collector of Government Custom', 19 April 1793, *BCJC*, P/128/1, 57–8.

open the chests that were discovered on the spot were the manufactures of Gorakhpur.[137] The *ghautwal* (derived from *ghautwallies*, meaning small zamindaries in which the area was divided) sardars of Jungle Terry district were also suspected for committing murder and robbery in this region. However, James Browne, the collector of the Jungle Terry districts, had a different impression; he claimed that for most of the robberies the hill people had to bear the blame even when they were not involved. This, as he explained, was because of the famine of 1770 when many people from the lowlands fled to the hills, where hardy grains were still plentiful. They lived in the hills until the famine was over, but on their return were not accepted by their fellow caste-men. Being defiled in the company of hill men they turned to robbery.[138] Thus, although robberies were conducted by the people from the lowlands, because of the 'savage' image of the hill people, it was the latter who were often labelled as robbers.

For this period we can identify the names of some sardars, which gives some clues as to their caste and occupational status. There were seventy-seven sardars in the list we are referring to, and 2,365 accomplices. Of these seventy-seven, eleven were from Baugdis (Bagdi), Doom (Dom) and Haurey (Hari) castes and eight from Bowrey caste.[139] McLane says that these castes were among the lowest classes. For instance, Bagdis were labourers, fishermen, cultivators, palanquin bearers and sweepers; Haris (Haureys) were swine keepers and sweepers.[140] Chakrabarti says that village *chaukidars* were recruited from these castes. The abolition of the traditional village chaukidari system did not accompany the abolition of the fouzdari rights of zamindars.[141] It is no surprise, then, that colonial officers were suspicious about the involvement of chaukidars in such crimes.[142] What is remarkable is that, as early as the late eighteenth century, caste had become an index for understanding criminality. Such equations strengthened over the next few decades and matured by the mid- and late nineteenth century. By the 1840s these castes had become 'hereditary dacoits', as Dampier, the superintendent of police mentioned in his report, prepared in 1843.[143]

---

137 'Letter no. 3, from I. Lumsden, Acting Magistrate, Saran to G. H. Barlow, Register to the Nizamat Adawlat, Fort William', 14 June 1793, *BCJC*, P/128/3, 413–16. Okeden was of the view that at Ghazipur the natives were the 'greatest thieves of any parts of the district'. Okeden, *Diary*, 19.
138 J. Browne, *Description of the Jungle Terry Districts*, 86. The above is an interesting account of the mix of economic hardships and cultural regulations.
139 'Letter no. 9 from C. Keating, Magistrate, Beerbhoom to Fort William', 22 April 1793, *BCJC*, P/128/1.
140 Henry Waterfield, writing in 1871, informed that Bagdees were chiefly employed as fishermen and labourers; Harees was a 'scavenger' caste; and Baurees were employed in the Lower Bengal as palkee bearers. *Memorandum on the census of British India, 1871–72* (London, 1871), 23.
141 Chakrabarti, *Authority and Violence*, 172–3.
142 According to Abbas Sarwani, author of the *Tarikh-i Sher Shahi*, Sher Shah was also convinced that theft and highway robbery were committed either at the instance of village headmen or with their knowledge. Raziuddin Aquil, 'Salvaging a Fractured Past: Reflections on Norms of Governance and Afghan-Rajput Relations in North India in the Late Fifteenth and Early Sixteenth Centuries', *SIH* 20, no. 1 (2004): 12.
143 Chakrabarti, *Authority and Violence*, 156.

Guarding the Routes

Control of routes went alongside the process of identifying and controlling crime. Cases of disputes and harassment while travelling also occurred before Company rule. Frequent complaints were made by Company traders against cases of boat seizures and other trading difficulties. The annual Maratha raids were a constant source of 'plunder and depredations' of Company boats.[144] There were also other factors peculiar to Bengal, which the Company inherited. Mughal firmans did not guarantee the Company complete freedom and safe trading in Bengal. Local rulers always disrupted the trade and asked for a *peshkash* (gift or tribute). The Patna factors always had to give presents to the nawabs to prevent the saltpetre boats from being seized. The Company became reconciled to this state of affairs, accepting that 'the best way to avoid the difficulty was not to procure an imperial order which could take more than a year to negotiate but to make presents to the officials concerned'.[145] Things did not improve for the Company even in the early eighteenth century. There were cases of English merchants forbidden to purchase saltpetre and who, on defiance, were imprisoned.[146] As a result, the Company used guards as escorts in the trade of saltpetre from Patna to Calcutta. In September 1713, one Mr Benson was shot dead and a soldier wounded when 13,000 maunds of saltpetre was coming down the Hugli River to Calcutta. The Patna factory was closed in 1715, and the reasons given were the vexations and extractions of the nawabs. The fluid political condition forced the Company to enter into fresh negotiations and pay bribes each time.[147] Furthermore, the change in political regimes and actors, together with constant war, led the disbanded soldiers 'to pillage the country and exercise violence even in the middle of its capital'.[148]

Faced with these circumstances, whenever possible the Company challenged the authority of Bengal nawabs by blocking the Ganga and bringing the government over to its own terms.[149] The native merchants supplying the Company complained about their own rulers who detained goods and charged exorbitant fees at various choukies.[150] A 1763 letter noted a seizure of bullocks laden with Company saltpetre near Saran. Those coming from Ghazipur were seized by the nawab's amils.[151] These are not isolated cases. The point here is that trading disruptions existed long before the Company took over the charge of the revenue and administration of the territory. The fluid political scene

---

144 *URG*, 'Consultations', April 25 1748, record no. 13, 8–9.
145 N. N. Raye, *The Annals of the English Settlement in Bihar* (Calcutta, 1927), 38–50; *The Conduct of the East India Company with respect to their Wars & c.* (London, 1767), 10.
146 A. F. M. Abdul Ali, 'Patna – Her Relations with the John Company Bahadur', *BPP* 41, nos. 81–2 (1931): 38.
147 Raye, *Annals*, 131–3.
148 Ibid., 136.
149 *The Conduct*, 12–13.
150 *URG*, 'Consultations', February 1753, record nos. 14, 111, 146, at pages 9, 53 and 68 respectively.
151 *URG*, record no. 695, 12 February 1763, 460. This letter also noted the seizure of boat by a darogha and fleeing of all *assamies* (merchant-brokers) who were given money by the Company to supply saltpetre.

that the Company inherited was no less important a factor in the growth of highway crime than the regulative measures taken by the Company in the following decades. The zamindars defied authority whenever they could, thus making the situation worse for the Company. For instance, in 1765, the Company served a notice on the zamindar of Bettiah, asking him to pay his revenue dues.[152] A close look at the settlement of the Jungle Terry district illustrates this point.[153]

The lack of political settlement and centralized authority had already made the hill chiefs of this area 'rebellious', and they made repeated 'depredations' during the early 1770s. The ghautwals were formerly subject to several rajas, to whose territories their ghautwallies belonged. They paid a little tribute as a mark of feudal obedience and were bound to oppose all invasions; to attend to their rajas with all their followers in arms when summoned; and to check violence and irregularity committed within their boundaries. One of their primary duties was to keep the ghats safe. With the decline of the rajas, these ghautwals became independent and 'went to war among themselves on family quarrels and all those who had greatest force plundered their neighbours'. They also plundered the people of neighbouring lowlands and travellers on the road. The neighbouring districts of Rajmahal and Bhagalpur were the worst affected, as one Mr Harwood asked for an additional force to protect those districts 'from the depredations of the banditti who inhabit the neighbouring mountains'.[154] The travellers and boats could not pass with safety between Bhagalpur and Farruckabad without the danger of being plundered.[155] Cultivation had also decreased and the amount of revenue declined.

Following this, in 1773, Captain Brooke initiated a military operation against these ghautwals and brought them under control. The measures he introduced included disarming the 'feudal soldiery' and seizing the jaghirs of the zamindars. A few years later, Browne, who became the collector of this district, also 'assembled all the zamindars and made a settlement with them to release the ryots from a load of imposition, and induced them to undertake the cultivation of a great quantity of land which had fallen waste for a number of years'. However, the military operation went in tandem with an overt conciliatory approach. Although these hill men were described as 'savage', they were often given presents, gifts, turbans and khillats as marks of incorporation into the British system of governance. Hastings applauded the success of the Company administration on various levels. He referred to 'civilization', to opening up the inaccessible area and bringing it under control, and to the setting up of a mechanism for regular revenue extraction and ending depredations and robberies.[156]

---

152 The letter noted that during the time of Mir Qasim, the Bettiah zamindar used to pay their revenue regularly at around Rs. 6–7 lakhs; now, allegedly, they paid 'nothing but a few timbres'. The zamindar was warned to pay off his balances or face the English army. *URG*, record no. 808, 1765, 544.
153 The following account is based on Browne, *Description of the Jungle Terry Districts*, unless otherwise mentioned.
154 'Extract of the Proceedings of the Council of Revenue', 8 December 1772, Forrest, ed., *Selections*, vol. 1, 25.
155 Thomas Shaw, 'On the Inhabitants of the Hills Near Rajamahall', 102.
156 'At the council', Fort William, 3 December 1774, Forrest, ed., *Selections*, vol. 1, 138–9.

The jungles and the hilly areas were recalcitrant spaces not only because their inhabitants committed robberies but also because they provided a shelter for robbers. The association of the forest with lawlessness and of its inhabitants with an 'indolent race' was not of colonial origin; this idea was in wide circulation in late eighteenth-century England and also in India.[157] A settled agricultural pursuit was always promoted as the Other of vagrant, wild activities. The wild nature of the landscape remained a dominant trope in explaining the inability of colonial rule in pursuing dacoits and checking highway robberies. Most conspicuously, it figured in discussions on thuggee. Javed Majeed has argued that many passages describing the landscapes in Meadows Taylor's *Confessions of a Thug* evoke intractable jungles and wilds, which were difficult to traverse. Majeed is inclined to read in such representations an attempt to show 'the density of Indian society with all its complexities'.[158] Alternatively, the representation of untamed landscapes could simply be interpreted as spaces showing the limitation of colonial control and simultaneously as areas they eagerly wanted to control. This was the reason why Sleeman regarded unsafe roads and the total disappearance of serais during the early years of Company rule as one of the factors that made the 'practice of Thugee so practicable'.[159]

The Company, following on from its experiences of trading disruptions and also in order to curb the mobility of both individuals and a few circulatory groups, started taking measures to safeguard routes. In the 1790s, the cases of robberies in Raghunathpur had led to an increase in the number of *burkandazes* (police escorts) from ten to twenty in each of the police jurisdictions at Raghunathpur and Chass on the NMR. In the same period, the Shahabad collector also proposed establishing guard boats to patrol the Ganga between Buxar and Chapra. Monitoring individuals' movements was also on the agenda. Regulation III of 1821:

> ...empowered the magistrates and the subordinate police authorities to compel all persons who may be inhabitants of the remote district of the British provinces, or a subject of a foreign state, and may be found travelling within their respective jurisdictions without any reasonable object, to return such persons under a suitable guard, from station to station, to the district or territory from which they may appear to have advanced.[160]

---

157 Stephen Daniels, 'The Political Iconography of Woodland in Later Georgian England', in Denis Cosgrove and Stephen Daniels, eds, *The Iconography of Landscape: Essays on the Symbolic Representation, Design and Use of Past Environments* (Cambridge, 1988), 44.
158 Majeed, 'Meadows Taylor's Confessions of a Thug: The Anglo-Indian Novel as a Genre in the Making', in Bart Moore-Gilbert, ed., *Writing India, 1757–1990: The Literature of British India* (Manchester, 1996), 91.
159 Sleeman, *Thugs and Phansigars*, 52.
160 'Extract Judicial from the Court of Directors to the Bengal Government', 11 April 1826, *Selection of Papers*, vol. 4, 16. It is not a matter of coincidence or conjecture that soon we find the prevalence of chaukidars in the visual material, especially by those who were posted in this area. In an album of 121 lithographic sketches made primarily by Alexander Francis Lind (and others, particularly by his wife) while posted in Gaya in 1824–25, two of them (pages 14 and 18) showed 'Chokeedar or Watchman'. On page 14, the chaukidar is shown standing in front of a hut, watching the road with a background of dense foliage. On page 18, he is armed with a sword and shield, attentively watching a man passing by. P 2984, *P&D*.

In 1827, the magistrate of Saran was asked to submit a report on the construction of outposts on the Saran–Ghazipur road, which was 'notorious' for robberies. The *dafadars* were required to submit a monthly statement of all passers-by to the thannadars, who in turn had to submit the report to the superintendent of police, Lower Provinces.[161] Considering the importance of ferries in the districts of north Bihar, each ghat had a police officer to check the incidences of crime there.[162]

Initially, the measures taken did not prove sufficient. Officials from time to time complained about the inadequacy of the police establishment, especially in the districts adjoining the Ganga. In a letter to the chief secretary in the judicial department dated 15 August 1803, Wintle, the Bhagalpur magistrate, described the police establishment as 'insufficient'.[163] The alacrity of the gangs denied the police any chance to catch them. Before Wintle's time, in 1796 Fombelle had on enquiry found that the police guard boats were 'very ill calculated to cope with or pursue boats of the force and description of those generally used by dacoits'.[164] He was also told by the darogha of Monghyr about the inability to control 'the money thefts daily committed' because of the easy affordability the Ganga provided for escape, particularly in the rainy season.[165] Wintle reiterated the necessity of better guard boats by summing up that the gangs 'are presently out of the reach of the police officers'. He proposed to station four guard boats each at Rajmahal, Pointee, Bhagalpur and Monghyr. In addition, he also suggested establishing a small police chouki at Suffiabad because this was apparently the place where travellers generally stopped to rest and were then robbed. The additional thannah at Sicri Gully established in 1802 was also said to be 'inadequate to protect so great an extent of high road as from Telliagurhi to the Ghogah, more than half of which passes through a jungly country almost entirely uninhabited, and where chowkeedars are of course necessary to protect travellers merchants'.[166] The four river choukies were established by Cleveland (probably in the 1770s). However, seemingly these measures did not improve the situation; the want of good guard boats was repeatedly expressed in this period.[167] On Wintle's recommendation, in 1795 a fifth chouki was added at Gangapersaud.[168]

The expanding mobility of dacoits (for example the Oudh connections) on the one hand and changing colonial perceptions from the 1820s and 1830s in terms of seeing this crime as an integrated all-India practice on the other, forced the state to take further policing measures. The concern to provide a safe travelling environment with patrolling and guarding was confounded by the fact that these gangs disappeared into the jungles that surrounded the roads whenever they were chased. In particular, the Sicri Gully and Telia Gully passes were beset with thick jungles that apparently provided safe hideouts to those who committed robbery. As a result, the colonial state held firmly to its belief that any measures implemented to stop

---

161 Chaudhury, *Sarkar Saran*, 19.
162 Ibid., 48.
163 Datta, ed., *BR*, 335–6.
164 Datta, ed., *BR*, 181.
165 Ibid., 292.
166 Ibid., 353.
167 Ibid., 399.
168 Ibid., 158–62.

Plate 21. An armed watchman

© British Library Board, Archer, *British Drawings*, vol. 2, plate 69.[169]

crime had to be accompanied by the clearance of jungles, at least at some distance on both the sides of the road.[170] In time, it was also realized that the regular police force was inadequate in controlling crime. As a result, a new force, called the road police, was established. A new set of rules for the control, management and conduct of the road police on the GTR was circulated in 1853.[171] Magistrates were held responsible for the supervision and control of the road police in their respective jurisdictions through which the GTR passed.[172] The rules further required a *jamadar* to frequently visit the different posts in his charge. On the occurrence of any crime on the road the magistrate was expected to enter upon the case directly so that the parties suffer no unnecessary detentions. The focus on the GTR was for at least two reasons. First, post-1830s, it had become the main line of communication on which troops and

---

169 Sketched by George Chinnery in 1810. The piece does not mention the name of the road, but it is highly likely that the sketch depicted the growing patrolling exercises either on the NMR or on the old Mughal Gangetic road.
170 Ibid., 332–3.
171 *GOR*, 56.
172 The jurisdiction was divided as follows. From Sulkeea to Hurripaul was under the charge of the magistrate of the suburbs of Calcutta. From Gyretty to the junction of the road at Hurripaul and thence to Jehanabad was under the magistrate of Hooghly. From Jehanabad to Gorye Nullah was under the magistrate of Jungle Mehals, and from the Gorye Nullah near Chass to the bank of the River Soane was under the magistrate of Ramghur. From the River Soane to the River Karmanasha the road was under the jurisdiction of the magistrate of Shahabad. 'Judicial Department Resolution', 8 May 1828, in Datta, ed., *Selections*, 319.

travellers progressed; second, the government bullock trains and mail-cart trains that began to run on this road in the 1840s had also been subject to looting. In 1855 it was reported that 'road robberies in the bullock carts and bullock cart trains were common'.[173] How far these measures improved conditions remains doubtful. When Mr Davies, who was inquiring into the reasons for the rise in road robberies, paid a surprise visit up the road to Baroon, he found a good portion of the road police establishment neglectful of their duties and often asleep in the different station houses – for which he imposed a severe fine. At Aurungabad he found the jamadar and his entire establishment asleep at 3 o'clock in the morning.[174] By 1855–56 robberies had increased on the GTR.[175] Two years previously views were different. The Sherghatty magistrate had remarked that 'the result of establishing the Road Police as regards the safety of life and property has been highly satisfactory'.[176] The commissioner of revenue, Patna, forwarded the views of one Mr Seton who claimed that 'he did not think that he ever in Europe travelled along a road where the sense of personal safety and immunity from violence was more generally felt by travellers of all descriptions'.[177] It is surprising to see that the favourable response of the earlier years changed completely between 1853 and 1855. It is possible that the earlier statements stemmed from the excitement and buoyancy generated by this new establishment. Alternatively, the Kol and Santhal rebellion of 1855–56 led to the increase in 'crime', leading to a change in perception. This new experiment of having road police, however, soon hit controversy. The regular local police and the new road police were at loggerheads. With the establishment of the latter, the former were denied the easy gains they had been making from cart and hackery men. 'Consequently,' Davies stated, 'almost every report that the road police made and which the local police were required to investigate, were wilfully falsified [by the latter].'[178] As a result, in 1856 these two forces were amalgamated. But even this measure failed to produce the desired results, so that the old system was reverted to in 1860.[179] But now European constables were to replace Indian *sowars* (police mounted on horses) throughout Raniganj in Bengal to the River Karmanasha at the border of Bihar and UP.[180]

Conclusions

A complex set of commercial, military and political imperatives created a nexus between mobility and crime. Although the early state was dependent on inherited structures

---

173 *GOR*, 140. The government bullock train was first started in 1845 between Benares, Delhi, Meerut, Agra and other places. Later it was extended towards Calcutta. In the same period the mail carts began to operate. See W. H. Carrey, *The Good Old Days of the Honourable John Company 1600–1858* (Calcutta, 1964), 282.
174 *GOR*, 57–8.
175 See 'Letter from the Commissioner of Circuit for the Division of Patna to the Magistrate of Behar', 29 May 1856, *PCRS*, vol. 473.
176 *GOR*, 58.
177 'From the Commissioner of Revenue, Patna to the Secretary to the Government of Bengal', n.d, *PCRS*, vol. 455, 1854.
178 *GOR*, 58.
179 Ibid., 63.
180 Ibid., 64.

and experienced limited control, in the long run it brought about crucial changes, especially for mobile communities. Moreover, in the overall pattern, the changes it ushered in curtailing the fouzdari powers of the zamindars was reflected in the growing incidence of crime. The state was willing to allow only those patterns of exchanges that did not affect its revenue or which did not clash with its notion of authority. By the 1820s and 1830s, the belief in thuggee as a widespread crime across India that worked through extended criminal networks was forcing officials to see in it other incidences of crime. Like the mirror image of gypsies in Europe at the beginning of the nineteenth century, groups such as *bazeegurs*, nuts, gosains and banjaras gradually crystallized into becoming hereditary thugs,[181] which then became the referent for numerous dacoits and sardars. The practice of thuggee described by Sleeman was used for identifying road dacoits. Officials were now instructed to look out for distinct external markers to identify criminals. If earlier they recognized sanyasis by their 'matchlocks and tulwars',[182] according to the new rules the road-police force had now to look for all upcountry men (people from the NWP) without much luggage or with only a *lota* (a vessel) and clothes.[183]

Although the peripatetic activities of groups such as banjaras, gosains and sanyasis were severely diminished by the 1830s and 1840s, 'gang robbery' by 'professional groups' continued throughout the nineteenth century. Caste became the main marker in identifying such groups. The primacy given to caste was partly a result of colonial simplification (which in turn stemmed from the limitation of rule) and partly a result of information derived from 'approvers' through testimony. One of the serious outcomes of the centrality of a caste-based analysis of crime was the marginalization of voices that privileged local causes. From time to time such voices were heard, for instance that of Mr Davies in the 1850s, who concluded his inquiry by saying that frequent highway robberies were 'caused by persons of the immediate neighbourhood'.[184] This view disproves the other dominant view of 'mobile sardars' working through strong and extensive gang-based networks. Another voice was that of the magistrate of Champaran in Bihar, who reasoned that the increase in crime in 1868 was due to high prices.[185] In spite of this, the view remained firmly entrenched that 'once a dacoit is always a dacoit! [and] that he will never settle down to ordinary pursuits for his livelihood!'[186]

---

181 David Richardson, 'An Account of the Bazeegurs, a sect commonly denominated Nuts', *AR*, 7, 1803.
182 This was one of the measures that Lieut. Col. Muir adopted in 1775 to keep a check on the movement of sanyasis. Ghosh, *Sannyasi and Fakir*, 69.
183 *GOR*, 56. Lota or *kamandal* was a very common object which supposedly many of the travellers carried. Deane observed that while travelling 'each man fastens his *lota* round his waist'. *A Tour*, 241. In the visual repertoire the association of gosain and sanyasi with this object comes out very strongly. See, for instance, the frontispiece illustration of a Panduram and a Yogey in the first volume of the book written by someone who had never been to India. Thomas Pennant, *The View of Hindoostan*, 2 vols (London, 1798).
184 *GOR*, 57.
185 *Annual Report on the Police of the Patna Division: Champaran District* (Calcutta, 1867–68), 2.
186 'View of Mr Cockrell, Magistrate of Tirhut', ibid., 90.

Postscript

The story of crime and criminality can easily be continued into the twentieth century with some fascinating shifts that, again, came with changes in the means of communication. A new category – railway thugs – evolved during this period. Faster means of communication made it harder to nab the 'criminals'. The rationale behind this postscript is to briefly outline some of these shifts, one of which is related to the banjara community and another to the practice of travel and thuggee. With the rise of anthropological pursuits in the late nineteenth century, culminating in various compilations of 'tribes and castes', banjaras, from being a peripatetic class, metamorphosed into a lost picturesque group. In the words of William Crooke, writing in 1918: 'With the almost complete disappearance of the Banjara tanda or caravan from the roads of Northern India and the Deccan, the traveller misses one of the most picturesque types of Indian life.'[187] It is interesting to see how, with the marginalization of the group of which earlier the focus was on the males of the community – on their sturdiness, boldness and habitual drunkenness – came a shift in the subject of interest. Now women and in particular their dress and ornaments became the main subject of interest.[188] Before Crooke, this change is manifested in a sketch of four banjara women in which the object most highlighted is their 'picturesque' attire and ornaments.[189] Crooke also had used a European lady to exposit the picturesque beauty of banjara women's dress and other accessories.

In 1884 a drama in Hindi, written in four parts, was published in Benares.[190] Only the last two parts relate directly to our discussion here, but to summarize the background, the story is about a travelling company of one Bharos Das and his mother with two attendants (Khawasin and Ghaasi) who travel to Benares from Allahabad by train. Bharos Das left his mother with the two attendants at the house of one Ramdutt Pandit and proceeded to meet his superior. On their stay in Benares, Ghaasi went to a nearby pool or lake to fill his pitcher. Here he was approached by a Durjan thug, who through Ghaasi's dialect (he was humming a song) recognized him to be a *pardesi* (outsider). Durjan invited Ghaasi for a *chillam* (joint) and tried to befriend him. Soon they were joined by Banke, a friend of Durjan. After squeezing out the necessary information, Durjan and Banke together with two other friends, Jaalim and Dandi, hatched a plan to sell a *kangwariya* (some sort of utensil or

---

187 William Crooke, 'The Head-dress of Banjara Women', *JBORS* 4, no. 3 (1918): 247.
188 Instances like this provide ground for argument, which is appropriate here, that the 'picturesque' as an aesthetic category did not decline between, say, the late eighteenth and the late nineteenth centuries; it rather kept reinventing itself on different terrains, in landscape, community, groups, and not least, history.
189 It was done by John Griffiths (1837–1914). He first studied at the National Art Training School and later at the Royal College of Art. He worked on the decorations for the South Kensington Museum. In 1865, he was appointed to the Sir Jamsetji Jijabhai School of Art, Bombay, where he became the principal in 1875. The banjara painting was made in 1879. Kattenhorn, *British Drawings*, 150.
190 Harischandra Kulshreshtha, *Thugee ki chapet bagee ki rapet, (prahasan), chaar ankon mein* (Benares, 1884).

152   COMMUNICATION AND COLONIALISM IN EASTERN INDIA

Plate 22. Banjara women

BANJARA DRESS.
[The lady wearing it is a European.]

BANJARA DRESS AND "HORN."

BANJARA CLOTHING AND HEAD-DRESS.
[The lady wearing the dress is a European.]

© British Library Board, Crooke, 'The Head-dress of Banjara Women'.

women's ornament) to the mother of Bharos Das. The next day, Durjan and Jaalim, disguised as merchants, arrived at the house and managed to broker a deal for Rs. 150. As soon as they took the money, Banke and Dandi, disguised as policemen, appeared on the scene and arrested the two. Khawasin asked for the money, at which Banke shut her up and commanded that if her claim was right, she should collect the money from the police station the next day. All four then left the house. Ramdutt on his arrival came to know the reason for the commotion: अरे राम अरे राम, हेय ईश्वर बड़ा अनर्थ ये ना सौदागर है ना सिपाही है, ये ठग है जो सदैव दीन अविग्यों को यो ही सताया करते है। (Hey Lord! This is a big misery. These are neither merchants nor policemen. They are thugs who always inflict suffering on weak and ignorant (people) in this way).

On being asked by the mother to report the matter to the police, Ramdutt replied, पुलिस इत्यादि इस का कोई कुछ नही कर सकता। अब सन्तोष रखना चाहिए। (The police etc. cannot do anything about this. One should now reconcile yourself to the loss). The drama ends on this line of Ramdutt: अब धैर्य धरो, भावी प्रबल होता है। (Have endurance, fate is invincible).

This drama not only affirms that the act and perception of thuggee persisted but also tells us something significant about colonial claims and paradoxes. First and foremost, the story signified the failure of the state. The colonial state long ago congratulated itself for having abolished thuggee (of course with the contradiction that many still harboured the view 'once a robber always a robber'), yet in the general perception thuggee not only kept happening to the 'weak and the ignorant' but the police in particular or the state in general could not do much about it. In fact, as this story shows, the police provided a good disguise. This erosion of authority is evident also at the beginning of the drama. When Bharos Das alighted from the train he had to bribe the policemen twice: first, to request one of the policemen to drop his mother safely at the Pundit's house; and, second, to get a ticket from the crowded ticket counter. One could not miss the similarity in excitement on seeing an opportunity: when Durjan heard Ghaasi singing, he said to himself ई का हो भाई! कोई परदेसी जान परत बा!!! (What an opportunity brother! He seems to be an outsider). On listening to Bharos Das saying that he would continue his journey, the policeman said to himself, आज तो खुदा चाहे तो गेहरे हाथ मारेंगे अच्छा सिकार है। (God willing, today I can do a good deal, (he) seems to be a good prey). The only operative difference was that the policeman, because of his authority (coming from his uniform and a stick in his hand), could directly ask Bharos Das to 'grease his palms' whereas Durjan and his friends needed to wear a disguise in order to deceive. But overall, the state with its police institution suffered from the lack of legitimacy in containing the practice of thuggee, which Ramdutt Pandit has summed up well: to reconcile yourself to it, as destiny is invincible.

This story also 'regains' thuggee from its colonialist understanding of 'systemic' crime – a few people of one group identifying a traveller on the highway, then accompanying and befriending him (rarely her), strangling him and finally robbing him of his possessions. The thuggee represented in this drama is simply an act of cheating and deceiving, akin to the pre-colonial understanding of it. Here there is no highway and no strangulation. There is, of course, mobility and also an element of strangeness (newcomers identified through their zubaan), which emboldened Durjan and his friends to deceive. There is also befriending. But primarily it was a deceitful act which, interpreted from a colonial perspective, might appear to be a case of professional hereditary gang robbery and/or thuggee, which in turn might have led to the perception that this could be identified by easy markers of categorization such as caste.

Chapter 6

CHANGING REGIME OF COMMUNICATION, 1820s–60s

Broadly summarizing, so far we have covered the 'history of communication' from three perspectives: one, the nature and policies of the early colonial state towards communication between the 1760s and 1820s; two, the formation of a knowledge pool about roads and routes; and, three, the regulative measures adopted towards certain mobile groups. In evaluating the policies adopted towards communication we looked closely at the nature of trade, which influenced if not completely determined the course of action. We noticed the formation of one trunk line, the NMR, and also a growing interest in improving district-level communication networks. We argued (see Chapter 2) that a growing conviction in the idea of 'roadless India' became strong from the 1820s. This chapter carries the story forward into the next four decades until the railways come into the picture. An ardent belief in lack/absence/inadequacy of communication and the need for improvements propelled the colonial state to invest in public works during the period under review. This was the time when the GTRs were made and ferry communication was improved. Unfortunately, the colonial emphasis on railway building from the 1840s has also affected the historiography of transport in India. This is arguably because of the litany of discourse that divided Indian history into pre-steam and post-steam; needless to say, the latter represented recent 'modern' technology, promising a change in society and economy. In accounts following such divisions, the binary of old and new is reiterated. In other words, the new – represented by railways and steamships – overshadow parallel developments in the older technologies of transport, that is, roads and ferries.[1] This chapter is devoted to looking more closely at the 'older' means of transport and the transformation they underwent in response to colonial needs. The nature of 'needs' in this period is similar to that observed in Chapters 2–4, that is, trade and military requirements. A new language of ideological legitimation was crystallizing during this period, in which public works were attaining new meanings. The increased investment was part of and accompanied this ideological dressing.

Ideas of Public Work

The growing difference of opinion between the metropolitan authority and its Indian representatives, in which the latter cast doubt on the 'principles' of rule as advocated by

---

1 See Arnold for questioning this binary, *Science, Technology and Medicine*, 105–7. Tirthankar Roy has rightly remarked, 'A systematic history of roads and road transport in India remains to be written.' Roy, *The Economic History of India, 1857–1947* (Delhi, 2000), 265.

the former, signalled a change in the policy towards communication.[2] Increasingly, the justification for the colonial rule and its authority came to rest upon two ideas: first, the moral and material advancement of the colony; and, second, public works. The two were, of course, closely related.[3] Ahuja has identified three important features of the phrase 'public works': one, they conceal the 'contradictory social interests involved in the production of built environments for purposes of transport by asserting their "naturalness", general utility and contribution to an assumed "common good"'; second, they became the source for providing basic political legitimacy for the colonial rule; and third, while excluding the native population from the forces whose opinion had to be considered, 'it left considerable leeway for the interpretation of the actual composition of the "public"'.[4] Further, amongst the modifications that arose out of the colonial nature of political economy in which 'public works' emerged in India, Ahuja singles out two most important points: one, the 'built lines of communication did not have to "pay for themselves" in the same way as in Britain' (of course alluding to the guarantee system under which the railways were introduced in India); and two, they signified a much more active and coercive policy pursued by the state.[5] None of these observations made by Ahuja is disputable. However, a deviance from his understanding in actually locating the temporal divide that saw the most revolutionary changes in India's communication infrastructure around and after the 'Mutiny' of 1857 – a chronological understanding not very distinct from that of Goswami – is possible. Ahuja concedes that the aggressive strategic orientations of 'public works' started in the early 1850s, and that the 1857 event reinforced rather than created the needs of communication transformation;[6] in my understanding, as described in Chapter 2 and also below, an important change was taking place from the 1820s. One of the ingredients of this change was a growing emphasis on the non-military character of 'public works', to distinguish them from more overtly pronounced 'military works'. The military considerations did not disappear, as was evident in the debates around the introduction of railways in India, but it did reflect a growing uneasiness of particularly India-based colonial bureaucrats, for whom the lack of good communication was a scandal on the face of the British Empire. Consequently, what followed was not only a few cosmetic changes such as the introduction of a few steamboats on the Ganga, but also a much refined mechanism of 'local communications' was on the rise. The 1857 event did sharpen the acute lack but the mix of ideological trajectories of the preceding period – utilitarianism – and the concurrent paradoxical conservatism in the aftermath of 1857 was ever present. Therefore, when it is proposed in this work that the period from the 1820s onwards witnessed a

---

2 'Extract Territorial Finance Letter from Bengal', 19 October 1826, Bcl, vol. 962, 1827–28, F/4/962, 27348. This sentiment was vociferously expressed by Arthur Cotton who was extremely critical of the Court of Directors' approach adopted so far in the matter of public works. See Arthur Cotton, *Public Works in India, Their Importance; with Suggestions for their Extension and Improvement* (London, 1854), 5–23.

3 There were many advocates of this view, for instance, see Anon., 'Our Future', *CR* 30 (1858): 450–52.

4 Ahuja, *Pathways of Empire*, 82–5.

5 Ibid., 91.

6 Ibid., 92–3.

growing definitional (influenced by ideological change) dissociation between the military and the public works, I do not suggest that military 'needs' or military 'justifications' of good communication disappeared or even became marginal; they continued throughout the period, but these needs and justifications did not limit the meaning of the term in this period. The utilitarian values and the ideology of 'improvement' generated criticisms that tried to free 'public work' in its *nature* and *characterization* (and not necessarily needs and justifications) from its overt military meaning.

In the late eighteenth century, although public works remained a widely used descriptive category, in fact it consisted largely of military works. The building of barracks was one such instance.[7] Another important field of activity of such public works was the management of provisioning supplies to the marching armies. The army officers in charge of transport, often to the displeasure of the civil authorities, coerced neighbouring villagers into providing not only provisions but also free labour. And this was justified under the term 'public service'.[8] The Company was aware of and tried to stop abusive practices of forced free labour and seizure of provisions, but the focus was on amending the practice rather than challenging the idea of the military implications of public works. In 1782 a Minute was passed to stop this 'pernicious practice of seizing and pressing the inhabitants to serve as coolies or otherwise'. It also enjoined collectors to apprehend the offenders, both native and European officials, and to send them for trial to the nearest military station.[9] Again, in 1806, according to Regulation XI, the commanding officer of a corps requiring supplies was directed to forward an indent to the collector, requesting provisions in advance. The absence of any streamlined system of supply has been explained in terms of, first, the financial limitations of the Company and, second, the lack of demand for such.[10] This explanation, however, is only partially true. Financial limitations and the limitation of authority in procuring supplies did exist and were reflected in the adoption of the contract system but the need to have a regular supply system was in fact acutely felt, which is obvious from a string of proposed reforms. As a further redressal measure, the Commissariat Department was set up in 1809, but recurrent complaints about harassment of ryots did not cease. The forcible unpaid requisition of supplies by troops on the march was noticed by Bentinck during his upcountry tour in 1829, following which he then formed a committee to stop this practice.[11] In 1833 again, an order was passed that the articles of supply should be provided by contract; but very few contractors came forward and hence the order allowed the storage and sale of the articles by government officers.[12]

---

7 For instance, a cavalry cantonment to be made in Ghazipur in the first decade of the nineteenth century was described as 'public work'. 'Extracts from the Indian Correspondence during the last 30 years relative to disbursements upon public works', Bcl, vol. 1115, 1829–30, F/4/1115, 29886.
8 'Rules and regulations for the transport of troops and stores by boat to the army stations', Bcl, vol. 191, 1806–07, F/4/191, 4260.
9 See 'No. 351 Minute of Council', 11 July 1782, Firminger, ed., *Bengal District Records: Rangpur, vol. 2: 1779–1782*, 250.
10 Major Madan Paul Singh, *Indian Army under the East India Company* (New Delhi, 1976), 124.
11 'The Governor General', 126–7.
12 See 'Appendix A: Extract of a Letter from Major J. Steel, Superintendent of Cantonment Police, NWP to the Secretary to Government, NWP', *Circular Orders of the Sudder Board of Revenue*, 473.

Even when a blurred distinction was maintained between investment in buildings of a judicial and civil nature (which included roads) and military installations, in terms of priority the latter took the larger financial share.[13] The upper limit of investment for military buildings and works was Rs. 4 lakhs, while for civil and judicial buildings it was 1 lakh. Some of the share of military funds must have found its way into road building because of the close entwinement of communication and military needs. In fact, as has been noted in Chapter 4, the need to collect, preserve and publish information on routes also had a strong connection with the movement of troops. It is no surprise that the first thoroughfare built by the Company-state was called the *New Military Road*. The administrative organization of works such as road building also points towards a close nexus. True, initiatives to repair roads in the districts came largely from local officials, but at the higher level two departments were closely linked with road construction and management, the Military Board and the QMG office. The opinion of the Military Board was supreme in the selection of routes.[14] In 1829, a subordinate branch of the Department of Public Works was set up under the Military Board.[15] This was the practice even in Bentinck's time, from whence we can trace the crystallization of the idea of 'public good' and 'public works'. Gradually, however, over the next two decades the Military Board ceased to be the caretaker of public works. The criticisms that emerged in this period – that Company officers neglected road building – sought to accentuate the case of 'internal improvements' of the country, which included better road communication in particular and greater emphasis on public works in general. The military imperatives and control of military personnel came under criticism. The chief engineer of Bengal categorically stated that the reason behind the lack of good roads was that the expenditure hitherto remained confined to 'military works', especially the provision of 'accommodation for troops'.[16]

This growing dissociation between military and public led to certain changes. First, in some aspects of troop movement, we see a further drive towards regularization. Existing rules required the Company to pay for the provisions of all sorts of articles, but more often than not articles like fuel, straw and cooking pots were not paid for. In such cases, zamindars were the immediate suppliers, with the burden eventually falling on the ryots. Intermediate officers such as thannadars and *chaudharies* (and other subordinate officials of the revenue and police departments) coerced suppliers into providing 'triple the number required'. This, on the one hand, led to the 'oppression of the people' and, on the other, 'to the loss of Government who were eventually supplied with the very worst carriage'.[17] As a result, especially in the NWP, *burdasht khanas* were set up along the roads

---

13 'Military Letter to Bengal', 26 August 1801, Bcl, vol. 1115, 1829–30, F/4/1115, 29886.
14 'The Bengal Military Board to R. M. Stephenson', 17 September 1844, *SD*, 74.
15 'General Orders by the Right Honourable The Governor General in Council', 10 July 1829, Das Gupta, ed., *The Days of John Company*, 351.
16 *Report by the Chief Engineer, Bengal on the Progress of Public Works, for the Year 1858–59* (Calcutta, 1859). [Henceforth, *RCE*.] For example, in 1859, the expenditure on new military works was about Rs. 2,760,000 whereas on civil works it was only Rs. 510,000. Ibid., 1. This trend changed; in 1861 the investment in new military works was Rs. 850,000 whereas in civil work it was Rs. 2,080,000. *RCE*, 1860–61, 1.
17 'Extract from a Report from the Officiating Magistrate of Zillah Cawnpore', in *Circular Orders of the Sudder Board of Revenue*, 169.

in 1847–48. These were supply houses run by contractors who sold commodities 'at the rates of the day'. These contractors were given sanad directly by the collector and hence were less inclined to submit to the demands of native officials. Such an arrangement reportedly eased the burden on the zamindars and the ryots.[18]

A second emerging change in the idea of public works, which was put forth as a hallmark of superior Western civilization, was the growing belief in the superiority of the English as supervisors of such works. The persistent and probably inconsequential reminders to zamindars to fulfil their 'customary' duties were giving way to the idea of pursuing public works under European overseers:

> [That] the work cannot be entrusted to the zameendars or to the village prodhans or to the salaried jemadar appointed by the assistant commissioner... any such arrangements would aid only in embarrassment and disappointment; the road will be badly made by forced or ill paid labour and the money allowed for this purpose would be misappropriated.[19]

The collector of Rangpur in 1830 emphasized the need of collectors' and magistrates' 'superintendence in person' of such works.[20] Similar views were expressed back in 1813: 'an intelligent and active' European superintendent was needed to amend the problems of management of road making at the lower level. A Mr Luthbridge was suggested to replace Peerchand Roy, who, according to the Shahabad collector, had 'satisfactorily' conducted the work of construction and supervision of a bridge at Brookgunge in the same district. However, since his satisfactory conduct did not mean he kept the job, we must assume that Peerchand Roy was less 'active and intelligent' than Mr Luthbridge![21]

However, how far this rule was uniformly practised remains unclear. The commissioner of Chota Nagpur claimed that: 'All the new roads lately constructed in this part under Order No. 29 dated 6th January 1851 and No. 374 dated 15th February 1851 of government have been made under an European overseer who has some experience in road making', but the senior assistant commissioner of Singhbhum (which formed part of the Chota Nagpur area) wrote to the commissioner on 3 January 1856 that 'he has secured the services of an effective "native" overseer and is commencing to build the road to Chota Nagpur which lies within his division'.[22] The shortage of European personnel

---

18 Reportedly, in the district of Furrackabad, this system gave 'great relief to the zamindars and villagers'. See 'Appendix A: Extract of a Letter from Major J. Steel, Superintendent of Cantonment Police, NWP to the Secretary to Government, NWP', *Circular Orders of the Sudder Board of Revenue*, 474.
19 'Extract from a Letter from the Commissioner of Chota Nagpur to the Secretary to the Government of Bengal', 19 March 1855, *SOR*, 79–80.
20 'R. Nisbet to Captain Benson', 31 January 1829, *BC*, I, 148–50.
21 'Letter From D. Burges, Collector, Shahabad to R. Rocke, Acting President and Member of the Board of Revenue', 27 August 1813; 'Letter from Robertson to D. Burges', (date illegible), *PCRS*, vol. 126, 1812.
22 *SOR*, 79–80, 280–81.

and the allegedly overburdened administrative routine of magistrates and collectors made it difficult for them to supervise road construction, which then would have led to a compromise in the belief in the inherent superiority of the English. Although Nisbet, the Rangpur collector, exhorted his fellow men to personally supervise the works, he himself devised a shared hierarchy of supervision. On being asked by Bentinck about the method of making and repairing roads and bridges, Nisbet replied that the roads within five or six miles of the station (Rangpur) were made and kept in repair exclusively by convicts (most probably under direct magisterial supervision). But more distant roads were first made by the convicts and then 'placed under the superintendence of different zamindars through whose estates it passed and they in turn vested the management in their village officers (gomasthas and patwaris) who caused the different ryots in each village to keep in repair as much of the road as run along the fields'.[23] To secure the goodwill of natives, Nisbet advised the magistrates to be polite towards zamindars through 'little management' and 'frequent personal communication'. Another notable change, suitably for justifying the state's claims to 'public works', was on its way: through committees and its personnel the state *built* the roads and then tried convincing native landholders or even merchants in some cases[24] to keep them in good repair, whereas earlier, the collectors carried on the work of repair and construction while the funds came from the landholders[25] (or at least this was attempted and sometimes met with some success as was the case of the Shahabad Road Fund). Now, in addition to European supervisors (who were mainly to supervise construction), zamindars were increasingly asked to repair the works. The limitation of the colonial state forced it to change its tone too; if earlier the zamindars were reproached for not observing their customary duty of road making, now they were approached in a conciliatory manner to maintain roads by 'securing the good wishes and cooperation of landed proprietors through little management', as the Rangpur collector put it.

But for all this, the rhetorical idealism of the state — either at the level of posturing itself as the sole or dominant institution providing public works and public good or at the associated level of being civilizationally and scientifically composed of an advanced community (of white Europeans) to supervise such works — suffered at the hands of financial limitations. As a result, the state always looked for and welcomed outside monetary help, especially from natives. Public work did provide a new kind of legitimacy to the state but it did not entirely remain the preserve of the state. In general, the native community was criticized for its lack of interest in taking up the cause of public works,[26] but it was also encouraged to do so under the name of 'charity'. The idea of community taxation was already ruled out by the Bengal government. In such a situation, any contribution was more than welcome. Raja Sukhmoy's contribution of Rs. 150,000 is a case in point. The raja had proposed building a road from Calcutta to Jaggarnath Puri,

---

23 *BC*, I, 148.
24 In 1815, the collector of Saran reported of only one bridge being worthy of notice in the whole district, which was maintained by a native trader. 'Letter from Collector, Sarun', (date illegible), *PCRS*, vol. 76, 1817.
25 See 'Letter from D. Burges, Collector, Shahabad to Major General Garslin, President and the Member of the Road Committee', 13 June 1813, *PCRS*, vol. 126, 1812.
26 Das Gupta, *The Days of John Company*, 295.

the revered site of pilgrimage in Orissa. The government happily allowed the raja to do so, for it was argued that 'so large a donation will not be obtained from the Hindoos generally by small subscriptions, and as the work appears to be one of vast utility, your lordship in council will probably be disposed to acquiesce in the raja's wish of being the sole contributor, besides government'.[27] But the raja made certain demands before going ahead with the investment. First, no native beside himself, he insisted, should be allowed to have any concern with the expense, and his name, along with that of the government, should be the only ones to appear as contributors of the construction of the road. Second, the raja, his family and his followers should be exempted from paying the pilgrimage tax while going to the Jaggarnath temple. His gomasthas and people carrying *bhoges* (offerings) should also be exempted from the same. Third, the raja's name should be inscribed in Sanskrit, Persian and Bengali on each of the bridges erected.[28] All these demands were termed 'reasonable' by Buller, who categorically stated: 'Work is of such utility that anything of the kind which would contribute to the rajah's gratification should be allowed.'[29] The raja's sons, Raja Shib Chunder Rai and Raja Narsinh Chunder Rai, also made a donation of Rs. 1,04,000 for 'charitable' works, a part of which was used for constructing staging bungalows and public serais on the road between Benares and Kanpur. Such donations put the natives on 'the fairest path to distinction'.[30]

Public works had become a source of gratification for native elites and the colonial state willingly allowed, in fact, encouraged this to happen. Not surprisingly, public works also became the site of contestation not only between the native elites and colonial state but also amongst the former. On the sidelines of the Santhal uprising of 1853–55, the 'principal inhabitants' of the province of Bihar from zillah Azimabad submitted a petition to the government giving three reasons for the prevailing sense of resentment in the whole of the 'Hindoostan', out of which one was 'the destruction of Musjeeds and the Temples of the Hindoos for formation of road'.[31] While this explains the native sentiments, of course in a very conjectural way, towards some of the measures of public works, Raja Sukhmoy's categorical demand that the raja of Khurda ought 'not to be allowed to interfere or have any power with respect to the above [road]' and hence his name alone should appear on the inscriptions, shows that public works had become a site of rivalry amongst the natives. The social posturing behind philanthropic works was important. Inscribed stone tablets served as memorabilia of philanthropy for posterity. Bayly has argued that even amidst the dominating force of gradgrinding British empiricism, vernacular tracts and texts had a space for Indian reconstructions of their own world.[32] One such reconstruction, he argues, was a disposition towards pious public works; especially so far as recasting women's Dharmic (loosely translated into religious) duties was concerned.[33] W. Bingham,

---

27 'To Minto, Governor General in council', 11 December 1810, letter signed C. Buller (translator of raja's letter and a member of the Board of Revenue), Bcl, vol. 367, 1813–14, F/4/367, 9206.
28 'Letter by Sukhmoy', 9 December 1810, translated by Buller, ibid.
29 'To Minto, Governor General in Council', 11 December 1810, ibid.
30 Das Gupta, *The Days of John Company*, 140.
31 'Appendix B' in K. K. Datta, *Anti-British Plots and Movements Before 1857* (Meerut, 1970), 120.
32 Bayly, *Empire and Information*, 235.
33 Ibid., 237.

an Anglo-Indian official of the Shahabad district, also attested to the religious connotations of public works: 'even now, to build a temple or a mosque, plant a grove, erect a serai, dig a tank, or construct a well, are the most common ways in which the Hindoo or Moslem of northern India shows his gratitude for favors received from his Maker, or if childless, tries to perpetuate his name'.[34] 'Reconstruction' of notions of public charity might be true for native social elites in this period, but such notions had existed earlier so far as native rulers were concerned. For them, such works (public works, such as building roads and serais) not only fulfilled the feelings of piety and charity but also, understandably, were crucial in showcasing 'imperial aspiration and representation'.[35] Public works of a charitable nature had always carried a religious connotation. For instance, consider the following inscription at the Great Kuttra at Dacca:

> Sultan Shah Suja was employed in the performance of charitable acts. Therefore Abdool Kasim Tubba Hasseinee Ulsumaree, *in hopes of the mercy of God*, erected this building of auspicious structure, together with twenty-two dookans, or shops, adjoining, to the end that the profits arising from them to be solely appropriated by the agents and overseers to their repairs, and the necessities of the indigent, who on their arrival are to accommodated with lodgings free of expense. And this condition is not to be violated, *lest on the day of retribution the violator be punished.*[36]

The period under review shows similar features. One Banwari Lal of Chapra made an extensive gift to the government of lands and buildings for serais. In return, he was given the title of shah. The collector of Saran was asked to hold a durbar and confer a sanad on Banwari Lal.[37] A native of Poona built a bridge across the River Karmanasha, which had long formed a natural boundary between the Bengal presidency and the NWP. As the river was situated across the GTR, it had to be crossed in order to get to Benares (from the east) or to Gaya (from the west). The river being considered impure (the literal meaning of the river's name being one which pollutes fate or religious deeds), it therefore required a bridge.[38] Religious sentiments were well expressed in the stone tablet, explaining that the bridge was made 'to prevent the feet of pious pilgrims from touching its polluted waters'.[39]

It would be a mistake to see the secular connotation of 'public works' as opposed to the religious flair of 'charity'. Throughout the nineteenth century both streams acted in tandem rather than in dissociation. From the viewpoint of pilgrimage, it has been argued that 'increased religiosity' (with the betterment of communication) showed that the 'pursuit

---

34 W. R. Bingham, *Canals for Irrigation and Navigation in India, particularly for Behar & C* (Calcutta, 1860), 14.
35 Wayne E. Begley, 'Four Mughal Caravanserais Built during the Reigns of Jahangir and Shah Jahan', *Muqarnas* 1 (1983): 170.
36 The building was made in 1644–45 ad. Translation reproduced from Joachim K. Bautze, ed., *Interactions of Culture*, 228 (emphasis added).
37 Roy Chaudhuri, *Sarkar Saran*, 46.
38 Williamson, *The East India Vade-Mecum*, 253–4.
39 Bingham, *Canals for Irrigation*, 64, fn.

of civilizing mission [through communications, which Rudyard Kipling thought would stop donations to Brahmins] created...results very different from the intentions of the colonial rulers'.[40] If the issue of religiosity is approached from the viewpoint of public works and charity this claim needs to be qualified. The 'secular' pursuit of the civilizing mission was already aware of, and in fact more than not complied with, 'philanthropic-religious' gestures; in other words, it would be fallacious to assume that the 'intentions' of the colonial rulers were only 'secular' in promoting public works. The *parwana* (deed or title) granted to Raja Sukhmoy congratulated him for 'showing attachment to the British government' and helping 'promote and protect the happiness and welfare of its [British] Hindoo subjects in the exercise of their religious faith and worship'.[41] Financial needs mitigated not only the claim to scientific and moral superiority of the Europeans in supervising works but also the secularizing imperatives of the civilizing mission. And the state did earn the wrath of missionaries for doing this. James Peggs, a missionary at Cuttack, charged British rule with promoting idolatry through pilgrimage.[42] However, a shift in the nature of works that constituted 'public' did take place, although it was very subtle and protracted. From building tombs, gateways, tanks, serais and wells, the objects of public good in the second part of the nineteenth century broadly constituted hospitals, dispensaries, roads, schools and public clocks. Still, it was not the historical truth that natives did not put money to public utilities that many of the colonial officials believed in, but the secularizing idioms of public works of later years that explains the surprise of Colonel Sykes, who, writing in 1867, commented that now natives contributed to 'public utilities of European origin', such as charitable hospitals, clocks, water supply, roads and even a church.[43]

In general, public work was also fast becoming an index of good administration, which is another instance of how it was gradually transcending its narrow military character. Good roads in the district came to symbolize the image of an efficient magistrate. However, as in present-day India where visits of ministers or higher officials are preceded by hurried overnight facelifts of roads and public buildings (and most amusingly by painting roadside trees), colonial times were no different. Before the inspection tour of the lieutenant governor of Bengal in the cold season of 1852–53, the officials of the various districts in Bihar, such as Behar, Patna and Saran, were directed to improve the condition of the roads. The commissioner of revenue provided the details of the itinerary and asked the magistrates 'to put roads in some order'.[44] If good roads symbolized efficiency then obviously the bad ones became a site for criticism of the administration. The most important group, leading the accusations, was of the indigo planters in north Bihar.

---

40 Ahuja, 'The Bridge-Builders', 111.
41 'Parwannah granted to Sukhmoy Roy', 30 December 1810, Bcl, vol. 367, 1813–14, F/4/367, 9206.
42 James Peggs, *Ghaut Murders in India* (London, 1828), 3–4.
43 W. H. Sykes, 'Statistics of Sums Given by Native Gentry in India for Charitable and Educational Institutions and for Works of Public Utility', *Journal of the Statistical Society of London*, 30, 4, December 1867. [Henceforth *JSSL*.]
44 'Letter from Commissioner of Revenue to Collector and Magistrate of Patna'; 'Letter from Commissioner of Revenue to Collector and Magistrate of Behar', both dated 1 November 1854, *PCRS*, vol. 455, 1854.

John Freeman, an indigo planter who had lived in Bihar and Bengal for more than twenty-five years, charged the Company with neglecting the development of roads: 'with the exception of a celebrated strategical one, and a few others of an ornamental character, there are no roads throughout the entire of Bengal'.[45] The 'strategical' one alluded to was the GTR. To safeguard their trading interests the planters had invested in road making. A. Wyatt's account attests to 'several roads kept in repair by the indigo planters intersecting the pergannah and leading to different factories' in the district of Tirhut.[46] As road building was not undertaken with any sort of formal understanding (as with zamindars), the sphere of management seemed to be divided. The principal roads and thoroughfares were managed by the Ferry Fund Committee (FFC) while the 'several smaller roads were kept up in excellent repair by the planters'. These were either the crossroads connecting the factories or the approach roads from factory to ferry ghats. The involvement of private interests once again points to the fact that although the state drew its legitimacy from 'public works' it also simultaneously encouraged non-state actors to participate in the act of 'public good'.

Roads and Ferries

In the Bengal presidency alone, Rs. 4,933,082, at the annual average rate of Rs. 548,120, was invested in public works between 1837–38 and 1845–46. These figures did not include expenditure on military works. In the NWP, the investment was around Rs. 6,460,556, at the annual average rate of Rs. 717,839 in nine years.[47] In Bengal, the larger share was devoted to roads, bridges and embankments; in the NWP, roads and canals were significant. The following table shows the investment made in the Bengal presidency.[48] It would be next to impossible to work out the Bihar share from the accumulated Bengal figures.

The emphasis in this period was on thoroughfares. The construction of three main grand trunk lines was undertaken in these two decades. First, was the GTR (the Calcutta–Delhi–Lahore–Peshawar road); second was the Bombay–Agra road; and,

---

45 Freeman, *British India*, 15. Before Freeman, H. T. Colebrooke, representing the interests of private planters, had criticized the Company rule. Colebrooke, *Remarks on the Present State of the Husbandry*.
46 A. Wyatt, *Geographical and Statistical Report of the District of Tirhoot* (Calcutta, 1854), 9.
47 Probably, this was the reason why NWP officials took pride in their initiatives to improve communication in the province. Henry Elliot, who later became the foreign secretary to the government of India, wrote in 1848: 'I speak only with reference to my own presidency – NWP. Bengal is said to be a quarter of a century behind it in every symptom of improvement, except mere English education. To the NWP at least cannot be applied the taunt, that we have done nothing compared with the Mohammedan emperors. With respect to roads, bridges, and canals even here in the very seat of supremacy, we have hundreds of good district roads where one never existed before; besides the 400 miles of Grand Trunk Road, which is better than any mail road of similar extent in Europe, and to which the emperors never had anything, in the remotest degree to be compared. In canals we have been fifty times more effective.' Bingham, *Canals for Irrigation*, 11.
48 W. H. Sykes, 'Expenditure in India on Public Works from 1837–38 to 1845–46', *JSSL* 14, no. 1 (March 1851). Table compiled from this article. The figures for 1846–47 to 1849–50 have been taken from Edward Thornton, *Statistical Papers Relating to India* (London, 1853), 88.

Table 1. Public works expenditure in Bengal between 1837 and 1850

Year	Roads and bridges	Embankments	Canals	Total
1837–38	149,274 (50.63%)	115,812 (39.28%)	29,733 (10.08%)	294,820
1838–39	139,232 (41.05%)	129,759 (38.26%)	70,119 (20.67%)	339,111
1839–40	196,732 (53.53%)	140,915 (38.35%)	29,705 (9.64%)	367,354
1840–41	256,096 (58.58%)	145,626 (33.31%)	35,449 (8.10%)	437,172
1841–42	816,162 (78.79%)	190,589 (18.39%)	29,108 (2.81%)	10,35,860
1842–43	339,400 (56.57%)	224,506 (37.42%)	36,020 (6.00%)	599,926
1843–44	302,674 (55.22%)	192,326 (35.08%)	53,105 (9.68%)	548,106
1844–45	445,894 (67.57%)	171,987 (26.06%)	41,490 (6.28%)	659,872
1845–46	446,984 (68.62%)	135,859 (20.85%)	68,513 (10.51%)	651,358
1846–47	465,274	–	–	–
1847–48	523,923	–	–	–
1848–49	525,970	–	–	–
1849–50	465,250	–	–	–

third, the Calcutta–Bombay mail road. Work on the first road was completed by the late 1830s, while that on the remaining two started in 1840.[49] Providing connectivity over vast geographical regions was prioritized. In 1830, with a view to connecting the two important towns of Bengal and Bihar, that is, Burdwan and Patna, a proposal was made to make a direct thoroughfare road. It was to be eighty miles shorter than the existing route to Patna via Hazaribagh and Sherghatty. The government accepted the political and commercial advantages of such a direct route, as the line passed through the rich areas of rice cultivation, but Bentinck declined to sanction the construction. Instead, he requested that the existing route between the two towns be improved.[50] Another important trunk route constructed in this period, which passed through the northern districts of Bihar, was the Darjeeling cart road. The following table shows the relative importance of highways vis-à-vis other public works for the year 1854–55.[51]

---

49 Thornton, *Statistical Paper*, 81–2.
50 'Bentinck Minute on Road Improvement', 21 August 1830, *BC*, I, 498–9.
51 Table compiled from 'Table II', in Colonel Sykes, 'Notes on Public Works in India', *JSSL* 21, no. 2 (June 1858). All figures in pound sterling.

Table 2. Public works expenditure in different presidencies, 1854–55

	Trunk lines	Secondary roads	Ferries and bridges	Dak bunglows	Navigable canals and rivers	Repair	Total
GOI	7,970	–	–	–	–	–	7,970
Bengal	59,473	3,019	3,959	493	2,001	26,964	95,912
NWP	3,702	164	–	352	–	7,885	12,105
Punjab	272,583	51,577	9,282	98	–	633	334,175

The astounding difference between Bengal and NWP on the one hand and the Punjab on the other is striking and a theme that needs further investigation, but so far as the Bengal presidency, especially the regions south of the Ganga in Bihar, was concerned, the GTR became the main military and commercial line. It followed the existing NMR with certain diversions, but the construction of this road led to the abandonment of the NMR 'for ever'.[52] This was, however, a slow process. The NMR continued to be used even after the GTR was made. The practice that emerged was of travelling along the new alignment of the GTR as far as Burdwan and then striking west across to Bankura, joining the NMR and following that onwards to Sherghatty and Benares. This was the route taken by Victor Jacquemont in 1828–29.[53] In the 1838 *Revised Tables of Routes and Stages*, all the stages on the NMR are said to have had bazaars of different sizes, whereas none was mentioned for the GTR. Other details, such as the availability of water and encamping ground for troops were not given either for the GTR.[54]

The condition of the NMR had nonetheless begun to deteriorate. Oldham says that by 1837, of fifty-eight bridges in the Hooghly district only thirty-two were standing. The dak bungalows were in a bad state of repair. The furniture was decaying and being stolen. The *Revised Tables of Routes and Stages* also referred to broken bridges and annual flooding of the road.[55] Travellers' accounts of this period attest to the declining condition of the NMR. Fanny Parks, who travelled along this road in 1826, mentioned the decaying condition of Dhangain, a place on the NMR:

> Dhungye! Dhungye! With hills so high,
> A sorry place art thou;
> Thou boasts not e'en a blade of grass,
> Enough to feed an hungry ass,
> Or e'en a half-starved cow.[56]

---

52 Oldham, 'Routes: Old and New', pt 1, 35.
53 Jacquemont, *Letters from India*, 128.
54 *Revised Tables of Routes and Stages*.
55 Ibid., 164.
56 Oldham, 'Routes: Old and New', pt 2, 25. Mundy also gave similar accounts of desolated appearance. Mundy, *Pen and Pencil Sketches*, vol. 1, 5–8. During his geological survey near the Dhunghye pass, Sherwill mentioned that the region was covered with thick forests, 'which destroyed some men' of his establishment. Sherwill, 'Note on the Geological Features of Zillah Behar', *JASB* 15, no. 169 (1856): 56.

The realignment of the GTR, which resulted in the desolation of the NMR, was under way from as early as 1804. The impulse came from finding a route that would pass through Barrackpur, Chinsura, Hooghly and Burdwan. In 1805, the new road was opened between Calcutta and Barrackpur. The construction was further extended and in the 1820s troops were marching along it. By 1836, it was metalled beyond Burdwan. By 1838, the section passing through the Hazaribagh district was made but not metalled; and all the larger bridges across streams and rivers remained to be built.

The construction of the GTR led to a shift in colonial policy. The GTR gained primacy amongst existing routes but, also, new routes were now made to provide connections with the GTR. In 1854, the Shahabad FFC proposed to erect thirty-five stone and masonry bridges on the road between Tiloothoo and Sasseram. The idea was to 'bring the produce of that part of the country at all seasons to the GTR'.[57] The sources showing increased economic activities along this road are nonetheless impressionistic. For example, in 1853, the magistrate of Behar was asked to issue instructions to the deputy magistrate and the police to prevent obstructions on the road, particularly at the *chutties* (halting places) where carts frequently drew up in a manner that impeded the passage of the road. The police were asked to stop the carts and carriages left standing on the road and thus prevent traffic obstruction.[58] In another example, J. Steel, superintendent of police and supplies on the GTR, remarked in 1850: 'on the whole of the Grand Trunk Road...there is such a great and increasing traffic'.[59] The change in route thus had the potential of affecting the local economy by realigning trade networks. The sources, to repeat, are too meagre to construct a detailed picture. The GTR had also become the main dak line. Bullock train services had started. This created a prospect of enhanced economic investment; one Tunti Mal formed an Inland Transit Company and started the horse dak service between Calcutta and Kanpur in April 1850. By the mid-1840s the mail-cart service was also established along the entire length of the road.[60] F. W. Simms, who came to assess the practicability of railways in India, referred to the recent improvements in the areas continuous to the GTR, which before the road, were 'abandoned to the beasts of forest'.[61] Another traveller in 1845 described the GTR as one 'which may compete with the best in Europe'.[62]

---

57 'From the Commissioner of Revenue, Patna to the Secretary to the Government of Bengal', 1 June 1854, *PCRS*, vol. 455, 1854.
58 *GOR*, 140. At these chuttees, *puraos* (shelter for hackery) were also built. The first of its kind was built in Govindpur in 1855. The successful experiment ('they were used to such an extent that they are not half large enough for the number of Hackeries seeking shelter in them') encouraged the building of five more puraos in the Govindpur subdivision alone (in the current district of Dhanbad in Bihar) on the GTR. Government of Bengal (GOB), Public Works Department (PWD), General Branch (GB), prodgs 37–8, June 1859, Record Room of the Water Resource Department (*RRWRD*), Patna.
59 See 'Appendix A: Extract of a Letter from Major J. Steel, Superintendent of Cantonment Police, NWP to the Secretary to Government, NWP', *Circular Orders of the Sudder Board of Revenue*, 472.
60 Carrey, *The Good Old Days*, 282–4. The cruelty against horses by these companies was also reported in 1854. 'Letter from the Commissioner of Revenue to the Government of Bengal', 5 December 1854, *PCRS*, vol. 455, 1854.
61 'Report on the Practicability of Introducing Railways in India', *SD*, doc. no. 55, 149.
62 Leopold Von Orlich, *Travels in India Including Sinde and the Punjab*, trans. H. Evans Lloyd, 2 vols (London, 1845; repr. Lahore, 1976). The above reference is from repr., vol. 1, 38.

The emphasis on building major thoroughfares did not totally eclipse the importance of local roads in this period. We have earlier noted the establishment of a Road Fund in Shahabad in the late eighteenth century. Though based on voluntary subscriptions by the zamindars, the collector approved of its utility and urged for similar institutions in other districts. He noted, 'It is not yet too late to establish in every Zillah in our possession a similar cess to the one that has so long been established in this Zillah.'[63] The amount generally generated through this fund was about Rs. 9,000–10,000 per year. In 1816, an Act was passed for levying toll on the passage of persons and property over rivers and lakes: 'The Act laid down that after meeting the charges of the ferries the surplus receipts should be applied for the maintenance of an efficient Police, the safety and convenience of travellers, the facility of commercial intercourse, the expeditious transport of troops, the repair and construction of roads, bridges and drains, the erection of serais and other works of a like nature.'[64] Further, under Regulation VII of 1822 and IX of 1833, a cess of 1 per cent on all temporarily settled estates was levied, in order to form a 'Road Fund'.[65] Mr Stockwell, the postmaster general, had prepared a report on the roads to Benares for Bentinck. Stressing the commercial significance of roads, he lamented that 'too little regard has been paid to the improvement of roads in the interior'. He emphasized the need for free and easy access to and from principal marts. For that he proposed to ask the executive officers in their circle to send in the reports on the conditions of roads.[66] Bentinck suggested the formation of a board of 'able and scientific individuals'. He also ordered the preparation of a skeleton map tracing all the different roads of Bengal, both earthed and metalled.[67]

Another institution to look after the local networks of communication that grew up roughly in the same time period was the FFC. The actual date of its formation is not known, but it was some time around the late 1810s, when the Regulation of 1819 was enforced directing collectors to provide free and safe communication. Here again, although the state took upon itself the charge of 'providing safe communications' and therefore appropriating the revenue generated from them, the collectors were advised to 'employ the agency of the established ghaut manjees in all practicable cases'. Emphasis was put on adhering to customary practices such as allowing free passages to persons not having the means to pay the tolls.[68] For districts south of the Ganga, for instance in Gaya, where several rivers were used for navigation by local people, the need to provide safe boats was stressed. It was said candidly in 1856 that 'any loss that is suffered and any life that is sacrificed for want of good and safer boats is, I think, discredit to govt and however important roads and bridges may be life and property are still more so'.[69] A few years

---

63 'From D. Burges, Shahabad Collector to Major General Garslin, President and Member of the Road Committee', 13 June 1813, *PCRS*, vol. 126, 1812.
64 'Roads in Bengal 1860–61', *The Annals of Indian Administration* 5 (1861): 439. [Henceforth *AIA*.]
65 *The Imperial Gazetteer of India: The Indian Empire (Economy)*, new edn (Oxford, 1907), vol. 3, 404.
66 'Bentinck's Minute on Roads', 27 July 1829, *BC*, I, 261–2.
67 See 'Bentinck's Additional Minute on Roads', ibid.
68 'From Commissioner's Office, Behar and Benares to W. Money', 11 February 1817, *PCRS*, vol. 415, 1817.
69 *GOR*, 140–41.

later the commissioner of Patna went so far as to suggest that the provision of good boats would be preferable even if it brought a reduction in profits from the ferries.[70]

Local roads were crucial in bringing products to the thoroughfares. The concept of feeder lines came with the development of the railways, but the want of good district roads was freely expressed during this period, resulting in the construction of at least a few. The forty-six-mile long Bellia road, leading from Monghyr to Tirhut, was commenced in 1843–44. The annual estimated traffic on this road was about 700 carriages, and 1,160 horses.[71] But for most of the roads of north Bihar, we do not know the actual date of construction. In all probability, these lines had existed from before the Company rule but were raised and in some cases widened by the FFCs. Also, these were, at best, *kutcha* (unmetalled) roads.[72]

A uniform pattern of width was followed depending upon the importance of the places that the roads connected. The width varied from twenty-four, twenty and fifteen feet. Most of the roads leading from Muzaffarpur to places such as Motihari, Dulsing Serai, Mullye and Hajipur were twenty-four feet wide. The roads that were more locally important were fifteen feet wide.[73] The repair or construction was done in gradual stages depending upon the availability of funds and other resources. For instance, a road in the Singhbhum district in the 1850s was first made a 'good fair-weather road' and was to be upgraded into an all-weather road only if funds were allotted.[74] In general, these roads were not metalled. Thus, there were only three metalled roads in Bihar during our period of study. First was the second division of the GTR from eastern Barakar to the River Karmanasha. This was thirty feet in breadth, fifteen feet *pucca* (metalled) in centre and 7.5 feet kutcha on two sides. Second was the Patna branch road, seventy-eight miles in length, which connected Patna with Dhobi (a place on the GTR). It was thirty feet wide with sixteen feet pucca in the centre.[75] And third was the Soree–Bhagalpur road, the southern section of which was fifty-four miles in length, thirty-two being already metalled by 1859–60. This work was abandoned, however, since with the coming of the railways in the late 1850s, the northern section, from Bowsee to Bhagalpur, was completed first.[76]

In north Bihar, ferries were important because many of the rivers were navigable for most of the year. Regulation XIX of 1816 enjoined the government to provide better travelling facilities, including the safety of the ferries. Three years later, section VII of Regulation VI of 1819 reiterated the government's responsibility for providing safe and commodious means of transit. Partly under such policy guidance and partly because of

---

70 Ibid., 143.
71 *Statement Showing the Roads in the Province of Bengal*, 28–9.
72 We do have this kind of information for some other roads also. A road from Burhee to Hazaribagh, 22 miles in length, connecting Hazaribagh to the GTR, was a kutcha road. Similarly, the Surwah road from Gaya to Kooslah (on the GTR), 18 miles in length, was a kutcha road. Ibid. 52–3.
73 See ibid., 30–43.
74 *SOR*, 280.
75 *Statement Showing the Roads in the Province of Bengal*, 64–5.
76 *RCE*, 1859–60, 17. This was a part of the Burdwan–Soree road. This was not entirely newly built. A road from Nagore (close to Soory) to Bhagalpur had existed, which A. Upjohn in his map had described as of 'inferior note'. The lower section of this road, that is, the Burdwan–Soree section, is shown as a 'post road', meaning, that it was of better quality than the other.

the navigability of the rivers for the bulk of the year, the ferries did much better in north Bihar. The districts of riparian north Bihar surpassed other districts in terms of revenue collection. Nearly twenty rivers and lakes intersected Tirhut. The collector reported in 1817 that in the eighteen thannahs of Tirhut there were about 500 ghats.[77] The Company was primarily interested in establishing ferries on thoroughfares[78] but the region as a whole profited from such establishments. Revenues from the ferries were invested in building and repairing roads. By the 1850s there were numerous instances of collectors reporting on 'good roads' in the districts of Saran and Tirhut.[79] Much correspondence refers to investments on both the local roads and the thoroughfares connecting different districts. For instance, the Champaran FFC requested permission to invest Rs. 10,910 to reconstruct and erect new bridges on the road from Seegawli to Ruxaul. This was to facilitate trade with Nepal as the Nepalese government had constructed a 'good road' from the foot of the hills through the Terrai to join the proposed road at Ruxaul.[80] The following table shows the collection (in rupees) of ferry charges in different districts of Bihar.[81]

The collections of north Bihar districts such as Saran (which also included Champaran in this period) and Tirhut were much greater than the districts lying along the Ganga.[82] It was because of these large collections and subsequent investment that magistrates, collectors and revenue surveyors described the roads of north Bihar as either 'good' or 'excellent'. Compare for instance what the Saran collector and the joint magistrate had to say in 1801 and 1859 respectively:

> The roads in this district, except those in the vicinity of Chapra which are annually repaired by the magistrate are in a very bad state being scarcely anything more than paths leading from one village to another.[83]
>
> Sarun is almost an island. So numerous are the ferries that people are already taxed actually beyond the requirement of the district. With 880 miles of road in good order throughout the year our ferry collections are in excess of our expenditure.[84]

---

77 H. R. Ghosal, 'Tirhut at the End of the Eighteenth and the Beginning of the Nineteenth Century (1790–1820)', *Journal of the Bihar Research Society* 39, no. 4 (1953): 368.
78 'Letter from I. Wemyss, Saran Collector to Rocke and Haring, Members of the Board of Commissioners in Behar and Benares', 12 September 1818, *PCRS*, vol. no. not given.
79 For instance, see 'Letter from the Commissioner of Revenue, Patna to the Secretary to the Government of Bengal', 14 June 1854, *PCRS*, vol. 455, 1854.
80 'Letter from the Commissioner of Revenue to the Secretary to the Government of Bengal', 17 April 1854, *PCRS*, vol. 455, 1854.
81 Table compiled from *Correspondence Related to the Ferry Funds in the Lower Provinces* (Calcutta, 1857), 3.
82 We have figures for two districts, Patna and Saran, for the years 1852 and 1853. The Saran collection was Rs. 20,503 and 21,300 respectively, while that of Patna Rs. 16,305 and 17,112 for the same period. 'Letter from the Commissioner of Revenue to Secretary to the Government of Bengal', 15 May 1854, *PCRS*, vol. 455, 1854.
83 'Letter from I. R. Elphinstone, Collector Sarun, to the Secretary to Government', 29 December 1801, *PCRS*, vol. no. not given, 1818.
84 'Letter from Joint Magistrate, Chupra to the Commissioner of Patna', 22 December 1859, *PCRS*, vol. 18, 1859.

Table 3. Ferry collections in districts of Bihar, 1855–56 to 1858

District	1855–56	1858
Tirhut	46,120	47,824
Monghyr	8,861	9,058
Bhagalpur	9,084	18,856
Purneah	4,067	5,511
Saran	23,972	24,557
Champaran	10,131	10,909
Patna	15,779	16,783
Shahabad	9,536	5,726
Behar	2,647	2,053

In contrast, the roads of Patna in the later phase (1850s) were said to be in a 'disgraceful state'.[85] The commissioner observed in 1856:

> The means of inter-communication appears to have been entirely neglected in this district [Patna] for many years… it would be a most important benefit to the country if they could now be extended.[86]

The Mughal Gangetic route between Patna and Bhagalpur passing through Monghyr reportedly remained inundated during the rains and impassable for a *buggy*. It had allegedly not been repaired for a long period.[87] This seems probable, because Deane complained about the bad condition of the through road around Patna.[88] The roads were so bad that the collector of Patna had to apply to the commissioner-general of Dinapore for elephants in order to remit treasure to the collector of Behar.[89]

One of the reasons for the uneven state of the roads between north Bihar and, say, the Patna district was the positive contribution of local institutions such as the FFCs in north Bihar; they managed almost all the roads of north Bihar.[90] It is necessary here to take into account the ecological factor that made this possible. The fact that many of the rivers and streams were navigable for a great part of the year in north Bihar was an important factor. This meant that ferry collections in north Bihar provided enough funds to maintain the roads. Such huge collections, as the above table shows, were not

---

85 'Letter from the Commissioner of Circuit for the Division of Patna to the Secretary, Ferry Fund Committee, Magistrate', 21 January 1857, *PCRS*, vol. 473, 1856.
86 'Letter from the Commissioner of Circuit for the Division of Patna to the Magistrate of Patna', 21 April 1856, ibid.
87 *Statement Showing the Roads in the Province of Bengal*, 28–9. The annual traffic on this road was about 1,000 carriages and 1,700 horses.
88 Deane, *A Tour*, 60.
89 The roads did not even allow the use of carts. 'Letter from the Collector of Behar', no. 645, 22 October 1856, *PCRS*, vol. 590, 1853–54.
90 *Statement Showing the Roads in the Province of Bengal*, 28–43.

made in districts such as Monghyr, Bhagalpur, Shahabad and Behar. Since there were no tolls on the Ganga (duties were levied on goods but the income was not invested in communication management) the collections in the adjoining districts were low. The numerous hill rivers in district like Shahabad were not taxed. The water was appropriated by rich landowners for irrigation purposes, not for navigation.[91] Older institutions like the 'Road Fund' in the same district depended on voluntary subscriptions. The role of planters and zamindars also made a difference. Zamindars, as seen above, were denied the income from customary collections (rahdari and sayers), which prevented them from maintaining local roads. Planters, on the other hand, although highly critical of the Company, were active in maintaining roads that benefitted them in north Bihar. On top of this, the period under review did not see any change in the approach of the higher authorities based in London. The struggle between the colonial authorities located in India and those in England continued, which constrained any significant investment in public works. The Court of Directors despatch of 18 June 1852 illuminates this point:

> We have not overlooked the compensating circumstances, that within the period under review, considerable outlays have been made in the prosecution of Public Works, such as must eventually contribute largely to the improvement of Her Majesty's Indian territories. But as the larger portion of the cost of these Public Works is applicable to such as are in progress only, and which will call for similar outlays in future years, we cannot but regard with much anxiety the existing deficiency; and we feel the importance of impressing in the strongest manner upon your consideration, the necessity of using your most strenuous endeavours to effect by every practicable economy and retrenchment consistent with the due administration of the public service, *such reductions of charge and debt* as may conduce to the restoration of a favourable balance between the receipts and expenditure of the Indian finances.[92]

Steamships

Amidst these measures taken to improve the 'older' means of communication, the new technology of steamships was also making its way. One of the first proposals to introduce steamships on the Ganga came from an American, Robert Fulton, in 1812. Fulton, who had tried his 'unique combination of machinery and arrangement on the Seine' in 1802, through an emissary in 1812, approached a banker friend of Earl of Moira, the newly appointed governor general of the EIC, with the idea of establishing steamboats for passengers and merchandise from Calcutta to Patna. Very striking is the language of the 'opening', as was later to be seen in the case of railways; in the letter, Fulton said: 'The facility which they [steamboats] would give to the transportation of troops, the merchandise and produce of the country, is not now to be calculated'. He added that profits would be enormous.[93] This plan, however, did not materialize. Steamships, as we recall from our previous discussion, started plying the Ganga in the 1820s. The first experimental voyage

---

91 Bingham, *Canals for Irrigation*, 40–46.
92 Cotton, *Public Works*, 22–3.
93 Henry T. Bernstein, *Steamboats on the Ganges: An Exploration in the History of India's Modernization through Science and Technology* (Calcutta, 1960), 26–7, direct quote from page 27.

of the *Hooghly* took place in 1828. The investment in trunk lines and successful functioning of local institutions like the FFCs went hand in hand with a more ambitious project of running steamships. One of the first steamboats made in India was for the nawab of Oudh, and was designed to travel at the speed of seven or eight miles per hour. However, it soon fell into ruin.[94] Later, the two trial runs of the *Hooghly* convinced the authorities to introduce the tug system. The nature of Indian rivers, in our case the Ganga, made this change imperative. Steamers in India were basically steam-tugs, which drew *accommodation boats* or *flats*. The former were vessels that carried passengers, spice, light packages and parcels; the latter were for freight. Only one of these two was able to be tugged at a time by the steamer, meaning that the freight and the passengers were never conveyed together by the same steamer.[95] G. A. Prinsep had predicted the following advantages of employing steamers for river navigation: first, their role in carrying treasure (government revenue from different districts to Calcutta) safely, which would save considerable amounts of money on boat hire and escorts; second, steamers would lessen the chances of river robbery; and, third, they would help save money on account of boat allowances and batta given to officers, mainly to the junior ranks, for joining their stations.[96]

The metanarratives of modernity that influence our historical enquiry usually lead us to assume that wide-reaching changes were brought about by the introduction of steamships. On the larger imperial canvas of trading links and empire building, some of the changes do indeed seem to be radical; but in the more localized set-up of the Gangetic river system a more cautious approach is appropriate. Morris D. Morris has given the following reasons for the 'casual and insignificant feature' of the introduction of new technology 'on a still almost entirely traditional economic landscape': first, the scale of markets was far too limited (and also markets were not well integrated); and, second, it was advantageous to use labour rather than productive labour-saving technology.[97] Other reasons included the lack of adequate technical skill and the special difficulties in adapting to local conditions. The introduction of the tug system illustrates the last point. In the same volume, a rather sketchy treatment of the north Indian transport system nevertheless says that space on steamships was quite expensive, thus restricting their use to special goods and European travellers.[98] David Arnold has also pointed out

---

[94] Prinsep, *An Account*, 3. Bernstein nonetheless informs us that the steamboat remained in use even 'several years later'. Bernstein, *Steamboats*, 1. For a systematic and chronological account of development of steamships, see Bernstein, *Steamboats*, ch. 2.

[95] Albert Robinson, *Account of some Recent Improvements in the System of Navigating the Ganges by Iron Steam Vessels* (London, 1848), 23–4; Prinsep, *An Account*, 65–6. For details of experimental voyages and discussions on making technology adaptable to suit the Ganga, see Bernstein, *Steamboats*, ch. 3, and especially on the tug system, 70–79.

[96] Prinsep, *An Account*, 44–5; Bernstein, *Steamboats on the Ganges*, 47–9. On the last head (on boat allowances) in 1823–24, the government spent Rs. 52,000 for king's officers, and Rs. 106,768 for Company's; in 1826–27, the expense had gone up to Rs. 74,044 and Rs. 310,260 respectively. Bernstein, *Steamboats*, 48.

[97] Morris, 'The Growth of Large-Scale Industry to 1947', in Dharma Kumar, ed. (with editorial assistance of Meghnad Desai), *The Cambridge Economic History of India*, vol. 2 (Cambridge, 1983), 564. [Henceforth *CEHI*.]

[98] Tom G. Kessinger, 'Regional Economy: North India', ibid., 258.

the limitations of this new technology. For instance, he argues that '[t]he Ganges was not navigable by steam above Allahabad and barely beyond Mirzapur',[99] which proves to be true if we look at a journal kept during the experimental voyage of the *Megna* with the flat *Soorma* in tow.[100] The steamer's experimental itinerary was from Allahabad to Kanpur, from Kanpur to Gurmukteshwar Ghaut and then back to Allahabad via Kanpur. The average speed on the first leg of the journey was seventeen miles a day and for the second leg, seven miles a day. In the downward journey the first leg (from Gurmukteshwar to Kanpur) was covered at the speed of eleven miles a day and the second at twenty-five miles a day. In the downward journey the *Megna* covered the greater part of the journey without her flat, because while towing it the *Megna* often grounded ashore or on sand beds. The speed of the vessel does not seem to be astonishing (one should bear in mind the government instruction of 1805 that officials were *not required* to prolong their march beyond the rate of fifteen miles a day, which means that if desirable it was capable of being done). Second, the *Megna* kept drifting when anchored at night by almost a mile. Third, the pilots for the most part of the journey were clueless about the right channel to follow: 'it is impossible for any eye, European or Native, with the strong glare of the water and under the rays of burning sun, to detect the course of the channel'.[101]

The above experience was, however, carried out on the river section above Allahabad. On the Calcutta to Benares or Mirzapur section initial success was mixed. The *Comet*, the steamer in the fleet of Governor General Amherst, launched in February 1826 on the River Hooghly, had to be sent back to Calcutta because it was unable to overcome the river currents.[102] In other cases, steamers had some success in carrying the treasury or in helping officials on their inspection tours.[103] The limitedness of the role also comes through the fact that the capacity for passenger accommodation was limited, owing to the large amount of space deemed necessary for a cabin passenger in India – the average being cabins for sixteen passengers, with their servants.[104] The overall picture, considering the economy of working up the new technology, was unfavourable. Captain Johnston, who came to London as Bentinck's representative to make a case for steam navigation on the Ganga in front of the Court of Directors, admitted that 'goods would travel by steamer at rates 60% or 70% higher than on country boats [though at three and four times the speed]'.[105]

Some engineers, such as Albert Robinson, had spent some time in the United States and wanted to bring their experience to India. In 1844, Robinson came to India and conducted a survey of the river from Allahabad downwards, and with his friends formed a company, the Ganges Steam Navigation Company (GSNC). The most important change this Company achieved was to do away with the double vessel system, which government steamers and steamers of another rival company, the General Inland Steam Navigation

---

99 Arnold, *Science, Technology and Medicine*, 104.
100 J. Digney, *Journal of an Experimental Voyage up the Ganges, on board the Honorable Company's Steamer "Megna"* (Calcutta, 1846).
101 Ibid., 24.
102 Raleigh, '*The Log of a Griffin*', 10, Prinsep, *An Account*, 18.
103 Prinsep, *An Account*, 23.
104 Robinson, *Account*, 25.
105 Bernstein, *Steamboats*, 72.

CHANGING REGIME OF COMMUNICATION, 1820s–60s   175

Plate 23. Government steam tug with accommodation flat

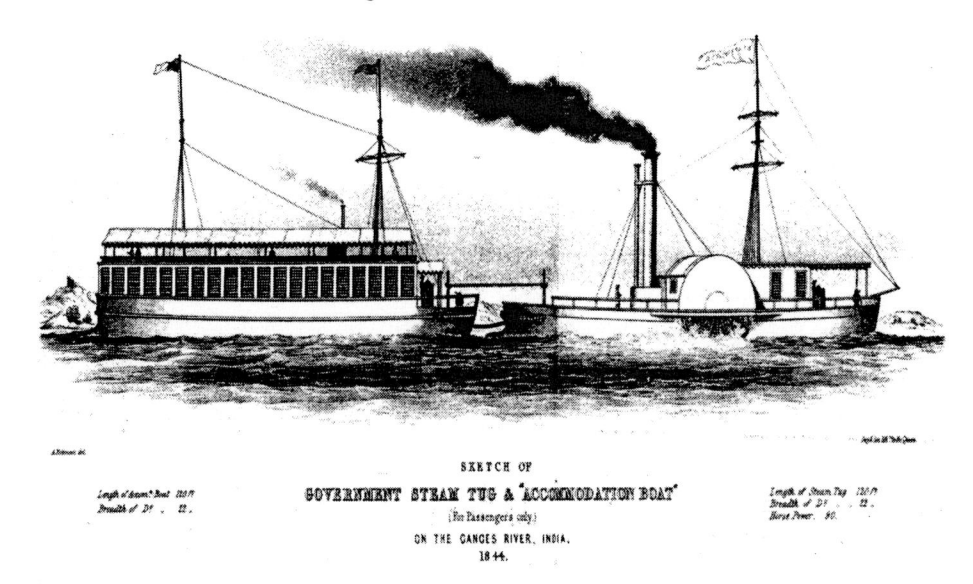

© British Library Board, Robinson, *Account*.

Plate 24. GSNC's the *Patna*

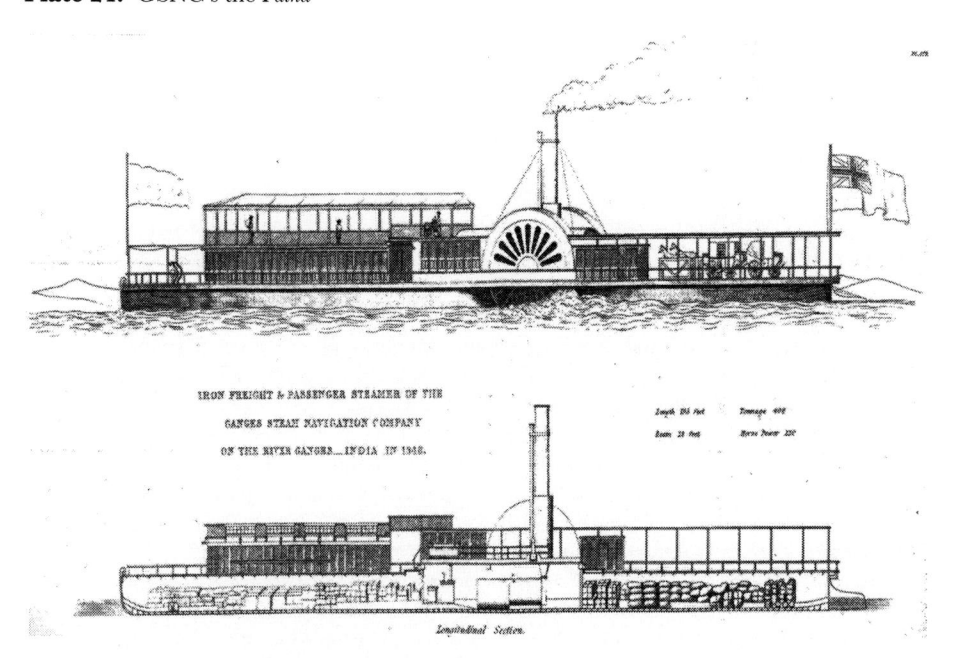

© British Library Board, Robinson, *Account*.

Company (GISNC), were still following. The steamers of the latter, however, were more powerful than those of the government and were able to tow two small cargo vessels at once, the passenger cabins being on board the steamer.[106] The GSNC had a fleet of five steamers; the first two steamers were named the *Patna* and the *Benares*. The passenger capacity did not vary much; in the *Patna* there were only twelve passenger cabins. In her first voyage there were thirty-five passengers. In the second, there was said to be more but the exact figure is not known. Steamer fares were high, thus defeating one of the Prinsep's ideas to save the cost on the batta granted to the junior officers. The latter still found it economical to travel by budgerow or by dak.[107] Soon, three more steamers, the *Chunar*, the *Mirzapore* and the *Ghazeepore*, were introduced by the GSNC. According to Robinson, who wrote his account in 1848, these three were designed for cargo only. Our anonymous traveller, whose account we discussed in Chapter 2, travelled down from Benares to Calcutta on the *Mirzapore* in August 1853.[108] He was appreciative of the private competition, which according to him led to some improvement in steamboat travelling – the boats were cleaner, roomier and swifter, and cabins neatly carved and venetianed. It is puzzling to understand how, if the *Mirzapore* was a cargo steamboat, there were passengers. A few conjectural explanations can be offered. First, it might be the case that the steamer was designed as a cargo ship (in terms of carrying relatively larger quantities of freight than the first two steamers) but might have been provided with some cabins as well. The second, which seems more plausible, is that within five years (Robinson was writing in 1848 and the anonymous traveller in 1853) the GSNC had lost two of its steamers, so to cover the losses and to meet passenger demand (which seemingly was only European) it is possible that some cabins were added later on.

The loss of the steamers or tug boats was the second difficulty that all the parties – government and private companies – faced. Until the 1840s (and here both Robinson and

106 Robinson, *Account*, 31.
107 Joachim Hayward Stocqueler, *India: History, Climate, Productions; with a full account of the Origin, Progress and Development of the Bengal Mutiny, and Suggestions as to the Future Government of India* (London, 1857), 88. There remains, however, a contradiction. Robinson says that on government steamers the charge was fixed at £30 for a cabin passenger for the whole distance (supposedly from Calcutta to Mirzapur), which did not include provisions; the passengers arranged their own bedstead and bedding. A. Deane in her tour guide for the River Ganga says that a budgerow of sixteen oars (the price varied according to the number of oars, ranging from Rs. 97 to Rs. 176), could be hired at Rs. 157 a month. The cost of hiring a cook boat and a luggage boat would respectively be Rs. 22 and Rs. 35 a month. Taking two months as an average for computing the cost of the travel between Calcutta and Benares, the total amount would be Rs. 428 (obviously excluding the provisions). The contemporary conversion rate, which in the early nineteenth century was about £1 = Rs. 10, would suggest that boat travelling was not cheaper than travelling by steamship. See Robinson, *Account*, 26–7 and Deane, 'A Guide up the River Ganges', appended in *A Tour*, 269. This guide was much later republished in the *BPP* 31, nos. 61–2 (January–June 1926) (author unknown). The cheapness of steam vessels is also attested by another estimate: for a journey between Calcutta and Allahabad of 800 miles, taking on average two and a half months, the rates for hiring Dacca pinnace were from Rs. 1400 to Rs. 1200, of a lesser class from Rs. 1,000 to Rs. 900. The best type of budgerow was available for Rs. 650, and a smaller one for Rs. 450. These sums included the wages of boatmen but hire for a cooking or luggage boat, which was essential, cost another Rs. 150. Bernstein, *Steamboats*, 16.
108 Anon., Mss Eur. B 242.

Bernstein are incorrect in saying that there was no private competition before 1844;[109] the Calcutta Steam Tug Association was formed in 1836) the Indian rivers presented a set of difficulties that constantly led to loss of steamers and subsequent capital loss.[110] As mentioned above, the GSNC had already lost its two steamers; the GISNC also had lost its one steamer, the *Sir Herbert Maddock* in the Hooghly. The shares of the GINSC had fallen to one-fourth of their cost. Subsequently, it bought over the *Assam*, which was earlier meant to strengthen the labour flow into Assam tea plantations but had failed to prove profitable. Although the tug system had been adopted to meet the local specificities of the Indian rivers – the system which was also subsequently improved by doing away with the two-vessel system – it was soon realized that the imported experience of engineers like Robinson had limitations. His knowledge of American rivers had resulted in building large and long steamers; for instance the *Mirzapore* and the *Ghazeepore* were each 250 feet in length. As a result, they drew too much water to be profitably employed during the dry season. The *Patna* and the *Benares* were each 190 feet in length. The total cost of these four vessels was £41,371 with a high cost of per ton carrying capacity. The largeness also resulted in further loss; a 250-foot-long tow boat of the GSNC was lost in the Sunderbans. The reconsideration in the 1850s of many of these fallouts had made one thing clear: what was needed for Indian rivers was light drafts and not speed. Also, it was accepted that the new technology was not going to displace existing means; instead, their complementarity was stressed: 'For many years to come the native boats must be the means of conveying the great bulk of Indian produce either to the termini of the railways, or to those stations on the main channels of the great rivers which can be reached by the large steamers employed.'[111] The writer of these words, Andrew Henderson, who had long been involved with the subject of navigation in the Bengal rivers, suggested a plan for making four small tow vessels of relatively smaller length (100 feet) at the relatively meagre cost of £7,000. The design of these vessels was based on the models of native boats, the *Katoora*, the *Dacca Pulwar* and the *Tumlook*. What evidently emerges from this discussion is that from the 1830s to the 1850s, the new steam technology had failed to convincingly adapt itself to local conditions.

I have not come across any source or writing, including the most comprehensive one by Bernstein,[112] that gives a clear idea of the share and contribution of steamships in the constitution of Gangetic trade in this period, which had expanded considerably over the last hundred years.[113]

---

109 Bernstein, *Steamboats*, 112.
110 Andrew Henderson, 'On River Steamers, their Form, Construction, and Fittings, with reference to the necessity for improving the present means of Shallow Water Navigation on the Rivers of British India', *Report of the Twenty-Eighth Meeting of the British Association for the Advancement of Science* (London, 1859), esp. 274–6. Long before, in June 1832, while transferring treasure from Benares to Calcutta, the government had lost the *Berhampooter*. Bernstein, *Steamboats*, 80.
111 Henderson, 'On River Steamers', 271. A 'Carrying Company of Dehlie' providing carts drawn by two camels was proposed to bring packages from Allahabad (beyond which steamers practically did not go) to Delhi up the GTR. Bernstein, *Steamboats*, 115.
112 In his own words, it is not possible to determine the economic consequences of steamships on the Ganga. Bernstein, *Steamboats*, 113–14. This tellingly reflects upon the state of research in this field, as Bernstein's book, published more than five decades ago, still remains the sole scholarly account of steamships on the Ganga.
113 Kessinger, 'Regional Economy: North India', 252–7.

The impetus to build large cargo steamships does point towards this increase but how far they were successful in capturing the trade in bulk commodities that were often transported by boats is difficult to determine. Certainly the capacity of these ships was greater; the freight capacity of the flat was between sixty and one hundred tons of dead weight, varying with the season or depth of the river. In comparison, that of the native boats was five to sixty tons.[114] There is, however, a set of data that gives some idea of the share of steamships in the trade for the year 1844, though this relates to only government steamers, as the two main private companies had not yet come into operation. At the Jungypur toll on the River Bhagirathi, the only point other than Calcutta where returns were registered, 50,320 boats were recorded, the tonnage of which was 796,213. This excluded boats carrying troops, stores, ammunition and opium. The boats that arrived at Calcutta through Sunderbans, which were taxed at the Tolly's Nullah, in the same year numbered 125,000, the total tonnage of which was 1,316,970. Added together, the total tonnage was 2,113,183. Boats under twenty-eight maunds were excluded from this calculation, which would considerably increase the total share of boats in the trade. The seven steamers that altogether made upwards of thirty-nine trips in the same year carried 2,027 tons of cargo. In their downward journey they carried 675 tons. They carried 2,500 passengers. The government steamers at this point concentrated on meeting military necessities, which partly explains this very low figure of tonnage. With the introduction of more steamers under private enterprise the share must have gone up, but it still seems that native boats transported the bulk of the traffic.[115]

The benefit in military movements through steamers is certainly recognizable. In 1825, the employment of the *Enterprise* in the Burmese War saved the government some six lakhs of rupees, which otherwise would have gone on securing boat contracts. The cost of boat hire paid for the conveyance of troops in 1825–26 amounted to Rs. 572,422. In the following year it amounted to Rs. 456,922. Captain Johnston estimated that in 1827 more than 28,000 tons of boats had been employed for the conveyance of troops and stores by the government, principally on the Ganga. The cost involved in sending one European regiment by boat to Kanpur was little less than Rs. 50,000.[116] Apart from the transport of troops and storage, and also leaving aside the upcountry tours and travels that usually employed a great number of boats for a longer period of time, there were some other permanent costs involved with boat hire. For instance, four large covered boats were kept in constant employment for the conveyance of stamps to the different district stations at a charge of Rs. 118 per month. Together they amounted to Rs. 16,000 annually. This cost was also predicted to be saved once steamers had started running, but we do not know if this happened.[117]

The time taken was also greatly reduced: on average, a native boat took one and a half to two months to reach Benares, while steamers took three weeks. The downward journey on boats was quicker in the wet season; a distance of 800 miles from Allahabad to Calcutta

---

114 Bernstein, *Steamboats*, 14.
115 Figures taken from Robinson, *Account*, 18–19 and 'Appendix C', 76. The profits made by the steamers should not be taken as an index of their 'successful' displacement of boat traffic. The booking space for freight was usually auctioned. In 1844, the minimum rate for measurement goods was £6 per ton of forty cubic feet; the rate after auction sometimes went as high as £20 per ton measurement. Robinson, *Account*, 26.
116 Prinsep, *An Account*, 46–7.
117 Ibid., 47.

was covered in about twenty days.[118] The time reduction, given that other factors remained constant, would theoretically mean better market integration and less price fluctuation, but again, the exact influence of steamships on the working of the economy remains only a guesstimate. In the area of governance, it definitely led to a speedier conveyance of mail;[119] it also afforded better convenience and security in sending treasury to Calcutta, so much so that gradually, as Bernstein states, 'Indian merchants were entrusting their commercial remittances to the Steam Department.'[120] Yet steam technology neither worked in nor led to a kind of market perfection where its effects were categorically visible. Steam still was greatly affected by the nature of harvest, wind, monsoon and, not least, the river itself. Leaving treasury out, which also had a seasonal pattern to its remittance depending on the revenue collection and harvest, the downstream journeys of steamships were almost empty. Amongst upstream loads, medical and military stores, and items of 'luxury and necessity' for European communities living in the 'interiors' of the country were the important parts of the cargo. Of commodities shipped to Calcutta, Bernstein lists opium, indigo and lac but he does not provide any regular set of statistics that can help us ascertain the role of steamships. Additionally, if we rely on Sherwill's account, then we will be led to believe that opium was still transported by boats. The reason was plain economic – the boat charges were still much cheaper, which is evident from the comparative cost figure provided by a civil engineer in 1849. The cost of carrying goods down the river in country boats was 1.15 pence per ton per mile; carrying goods up the river in the same was 1.59 pence per ton per mile; and cost by steamer was 2.05 (taking into account the fluctuating nature due to the auction of space). The overland mode was the most expensive: 3.05 pence per ton per mile.[121]

Piloting steamers in the Ganga was still far from perfected; the diversity of the nature of this river never ceased to present difficulties. The manifold channels and sunken materials such as trees, boats and even a temple at Mirzapur, very often obstructed steamers' progress.[122] By the late 1840s, when railway projects had secured governmental approval, steamships were sidelined in the debate over the opening up of the interiors. The constant obstructions and delays and instances of steamers going aground that filled the newspapers of the period rendered their value 'very uncertain'.[123]

---

118 Ibid., 21.
119 Still, the services of boats were regarded as necessary even in the districts that were situated on the thoroughfares. For the Gaya district, which had the benefit of the GTR passing close by, it was reported that during the rainy season great difficulty was experienced in the conveyance of mail. The deputy magistrate of Sherghatty therefore recommended the employment of boat and rafts with boatmen or mullah (mallah) at the following streams – Buttanch, Poonpoon, Ramrekha, Kurrubar, Barbee, Doomree, Kookoohee and Iurhee. *GOR*, 141.
120 Bernstein, *Steamboats*, 92.
121 Ibid., 97–9; rates from 100.
122 *Operations for the Improvement of the Navigation of the Ganges from Revelgunge to Allahabad, during the seasons 1852–53, and part of 1853–54* (Roorkee, 1855).
123 'Notes and Suggestions on Indian Affairs', *The Dublin University Magazine*, November 1849, 610. On smaller stretches, as for crossing the river, steam-propelled ferryboats were tried.

Conclusions

In this chapter we discussed the subject of means and modes of communication through the ideas of new and old forms and mediums of transport and technology, and the changes, realignments and limitations they underwent. The period from the 1820s to the 1850s saw the crystallization of the idea of public works, which in turn led to an enhanced governmental concern and investment towards improving the existing means of communication, that is, roads and ferries, but also to introducing and experimenting with newer means, chiefly steamships. The prime concern in this period remained on thoroughfares; the overland connections worked through relaying or constructing grand trunk routes whereas the Ganga retained its place of importance as an imperial highway connecting Calcutta, the seat of governance, with the expanding territorial boundaries of the EIC in northern India. Steam's role in providing that connectivity was almost unanimously accepted by the decision makers of the time. The manifold histories of steamships in this period – economic, cultural and scientific – is still a subject that awaits in-depth research; in the section presented above the aim was to contextualize its working within the factors it encountered – the existing flotilla of native boats designed for specific purposes of carrying passengers and goods; the rain and the wind; and the nature of the river.

The above account nevertheless also provides a window to take into account the professional groups who ran this transport infrastructure. The little details regarding the boat traffic, for instance, suggests the presence of a large community of boatmen in the late eighteenth and early nineteenth centuries; Rennell had estimated that there were 30,000 boatmen in Bengal. The coexistence of boats and steamers was a feature of this period but it is important to ask if the introduction and expansion of steamer services, at least to some degree, meant the displacement of this huge community of boatmen. Did steamships make some of these people redundant? The existing literature on boatmen or *mallahs* is too scanty to offer any definite answers; in addition, the kind of sources used in this book also offer very little information on boatmen or dandies – as they were called by Europeans – to form a holistic picture of their adaptation to and displacement from the new steam technology. The picture becomes a bit clearer towards the end of the nineteenth century when railways began to displace the older means of communication. But to move on with our present discussion, we will very briefly and broadly present a sketch on the 'labour pool' of this transport infrastructure that included roads and rivers, with the idea that analysis of forms of spatial constructs of and along the lines of infrastructures must recognize the intense labour and labouring practices that made them possible in the first instance.

For instance, the Patna–Hajipur route was selected for an experimental line for steam ferryboats but later the idea was dropped because of the uncertainty of profit. Instead, paddle ferryboats were suggested. See 'Letter from the Commissioner of Circuit, Patna to the Magistrate of Patna, Saran and Shahabad', 7 January 1855, *PCRS*, vol. 455, 1854; 'Letter from Russell to the Commissioner of Circuit', 7 April 1855, *PCRS*, vol. 632, 1855. But steamer ferryboats were definitely plying in the 1870s as travellers crossed the Ganga at Patna by steamer before continuing their journey to Darjeeling. Viscount Hinchingbrook, *Diary in Ceylon and India, 1878–79* (London, 1879).

Chapter 7

OF MEN AND COMMODITIES

This chapter looks at two issues: one, the groups and people that made and managed the transport infrastructure; two, the commodities that travelled along these lines. While the first set of concerns tells us how roads were made and how the river transport infrastructure operated, the focus on the second informs us how these roads and rivers were used. Obviously, there were diverse usages of these communication lines, some of which we have seen earlier in relation to peripatetic trading groups; the thrust of the argument in this chapter is to look at the nature of networks – commodity spread, mercantile ties, sites of exchange such as melas and so on – to understand the relationship between means of communication and patterns of exchange. By doing so, this chapter aims to stimulate thinking about emerging spatial configurations, especially along trade networks, in terms of a more diverse and vibrant field of activity of which colonial necessities, which for a want of a better descriptive term can be called the 'macro-networks' of communication, were a part. This vivid field of activity has been characterized here as 'nested networks'. The nexus of capital investment, prioritization of certain routes (as seen in Chapter 4) and interest in long-distance imperial commodities' trade obviously highlighted the primacy of macro-networks but they were both adapting to and changing the existing nature of trading networks.

Men at Work

The history of road builders is still a fairly new field of research in South Asian history writing.[1] The main characteristic of road-building projects, according to Chitra Joshi, was the use of convict labour and 'an increasing consolidation of military jurisdiction over the questions of control and management of [convict] labour'.[2] This was largely true, as she has shown, for the first half of the nineteenth century. Further on, this form of labour had certain specific elements to it: first, it invited an elaborate system of surveillance and control from the state; second, its paradoxical nature: the workforce needed to be fixed and immobile while at the same time – because of being employed on roads – flexible and mobile; third, the absence of women and children on the worksite left gendered imprints on the culture of the work; fourth, increased mortality due to overwork; and, fifth, the use of escape as

---

[1] One of the leading historians of labour, Chitra Joshi, is currently working on this theme; the preliminary findings were recently published as 'Fettered Bodies: Labouring on Public Works in Nineteenth-Century India', in Marcel van der Linden and Prabhu P. Mohapatra, eds, *Labour Matters: Towards Global Histories, Studies in Honour of Sabyasachi Bhattacharya* (New Delhi, 2009).

[2] Ibid., 4.

a mode to break away from both conviction and hard labour.[3] The earliest references to the employment of convicts for construction and repair works are from the 1790s;[4] the complete absence of any scholarly work on the pre-colonial situation makes it difficult to juxtapose the change, if any, that was taking place in the field of labour mobilization during the early colonial rule. In other words, we do not know if imprisoned labour was used before the colonial rule for such practices, or, if so, what the ideological premises of it were. But with some clarity, we can definitely answer a more fundamental question, which is, why the colonial state was using convict labour for public works. Amongst other factors that have also been discussed by Joshi, and which prominently figured in the debates amongst colonial officials, two were most important: the cost-effectiveness of employing convict labour, and the connection between the idea of punishment and physical labour. The argument made by one set of colonial officials that it was cheaper to employ convicts than hire labour, as argued by Joshi and also explained below, is, however, difficult to sustain.[5] The judicial and legal framework in which the ideology behind the use of convict labour was framed was more important than the economic justification.[6] The purpose behind employing convicts was to give them 'some punishment adequate to their crime'.[7] Hence they were employed on public works (the construction of buildings, for instance), public military roads, clearing river beds and so on. Magistrates were to employ convicts '*on all occasions* upon the public roads or other public works under sufficient guard'.[8] Working along these guidelines, Wintle used convicts for repairing the 'High Road' passing through his district (Bhagalpur) and also for clearing the nearby jungles.[9]

Throughout the first half of the nineteenth century, military and the judicial views differed on the subject: the former fiercely supported the idea of employing convicts on public works and the latter urged for reforming and even abandoning this practice.[10] Nonetheless,

---

3 Ibid., 4–7.
4 Many letters refer to the employment of prisoners for making roads. See 'Letter from Mr. Henry Lodge, Magistrate, Bhagalpur to Mr. G. H. Barlow, Registrar to the Nizamat Adalat', 29 June 1793; 'Letter from Mr. John Fombelle, Judge Magistrate of Bhagalpur to Sir John Shore, Governor General in Council', 11 January 1794; 'Letter from Fombelle to William Douglas, Judge of Moorshedabad Court of Circuit', 15 January 1795; 'Letter from Fombelle to Barlow', 26 February 1795, Datta, ed., *BR*, 21, 50, 77 and 101 respectively.
5 Joshi, 'Fettered Bodies', 7–10.
6 This line of argument is therefore not very different from Joshi's, who suggests that 'Labour strategies in public works in nineteenth-century India thus bring out the connected histories of labour, crime and punishment.' Under the utilitarian impulse of legal reform, this connection definitely became more pronounced and contested during the period of the 1830s (as Joshi shows) but this was not the period of genesis of this debate. The practice of employing convicts and the differences within colonial officialdom surfaced long before the growth and popularity of utilitarian ideals. Joshi, 'Fettered Bodies', direct quote from page 13, see also 10–12.
7 'Letter from R. Graham, Acting Collector of Tirhoot to Charles Buller, Sub-Secretary to the Board of Revenue', 30 May 1800, *MOR*, 176.
8 'Letter from Registrar to the Moorshedabad Court of Circuit to James Wintle, Magistrate, Bhagalpur', 29 June 1803, Datta, ed., *BR*, 323 (emphasis added).
9 'Letter from J. Wintle, Magistrate, Bhagalpur to G. Dowdeswell, Secretary to Government in the Judicial Department', 2 August 1803, ibid., 333.
10 See Joshi, 'Fettered Bodies'.

within the corpus of legal–judicial views a distinction was made between the nature of crime and the required punishment.[11] For 'limited imprisonment' (following relatively non-serious crimes), the utility of 'hard labour' was appreciated. It was seen as a process of habituating convicts to the ethos of work and industry, which would help them when released. As a form of punishment, 'hard labour' was the logic behind working absconding dandies on public roads for three months.[12] But for more serious crimes pertaining to 'horrid cruelty and murder', which invited 'perpetual imprisonment', the notion of 'hard labour' was questioned. It was argued that, when working in open makeshift jails, convicts would find recreation in passing through bazaars and gossiping with the shopkeepers. Working in the open also provided them with an opportunity for escape. For these reasons, in cases of serious punishment close confinement was advocated. Both these punitive forms nonetheless aimed at disciplining convicts. If working them on the sites of public utilities was thought to instil the habit of 'work and industry', keeping the convicts within closed walls was intended to force them to be introspective. Additionally, close confinement was also thought to be a suitable lesson for fellow prisoners. The Nizamat Court, however, dismissed these suggestions.[13] First, it said that unlike Europe, the climatic conditions of India did not allow prisoners to be kept in closed cells; second, the court argued that labour on public roads with the servility attached to it would be a more fitting conduct than would be found within closed walls. Doubts were also raised that public works would come to a stop because regular releases from the jails exceeded the number of convictions.[14]

A debate then ensued about the employment of convicts on public works. It is difficult to ascertain whether the debate was sparked off because of the necessity of penal and juridical reforms or because of the financial cost involved in employing convicts. Nonetheless, the two were interlinked. Working the convicts on the road required mobile jails. The Dinajpur magistrate reported that one jail cost around Rs. 800.[15] This was the primary cost. For constructing a road from Dinajpur to the Ganga, which was one hundred miles long, two jails were to be subsequently constructed eight miles apart. Further, to cover the whole distance the jails needed to be moved five times each. The expense of each removal was calculated at 20 per cent of the primary cost, thus amounting to Rs. 1,600 for ten removals. Spending Rs. 2,400 on convicts alone for building the road was perhaps too much for the Company to sanction. Added to this was the cost of burkandazes required for watching the prisoners at work. The governor general in council found it 'very expensive'. Consequently, the council forbade the employment of convicts at any considerable distance from the place of their confinement. It did, however, allow them to be employed within the local jurisdiction of the magistrate. But while passing this judgement the council made it clear that the degree of punishment should not be lessened.

---

11 'Extract of Report of the Third Judge of the Court of Circuit for the Division of Dacca', 10 October 1797, Bcl, vol. 39, 1798–99, F/4/39, letter nos. 965–75.
12 'Rules and Regulations for the Transport of Troops', Bcl, vol. 191, 1806–07, F/4/191, 4260.
13 Bcl, vol. 39, 1798–99, F/4/39, letter nos. 965–75.
14 Datta, ed., *BR*, 333.
15 Bcl, vol. 39, 1798–99, F/4/39, letter nos. 965–75.

Apart from cost, the other serious issue involved was the attempt by the prisoners to escape from work.[16] By the turn of the eighteenth century, the council had already started exploring alternative avenues for employing convicts.[17] Mines appeared as a useful site where convicts could be guarded relatively easily. The coal and iron mines in the district of Beerbhoom, and tin and copper mines in Ramghur, were discussed as probable options. Other areas and enterprises considered were stone quarries at Chunar and repairing the embankments.[18] But for a few local magistrates, like that of Bhagalpur, roads were still the first priority.[19]

Gradually in this period we start hearing about coolies (in the sense of 'hired/free labour') working on the road. For two roads surveyed in the 1790s in the Hooghly district, the magistrate argued that the cost of employing coolies would be less than the total expense of guarding the prisoners. Consequently, he was allowed to withdraw the prisoners and get the work done by hiring coolies. The word 'coolie' during this period was used in different ways. Coolies were said to come from a race or tribe in western India, called Koli. But they were also thought to be kinsfolk of Kols, a tribe in the Chota Nagpur area.[20] The military department made frequent requests for the provision of coolies to carry baggage and other military equipments. It is in this sense that Deane's travelling party hired twenty coolies, who were 'people from the bazaar, at so much per diem, to carry furniture for the tents'.[21] Even dandies were mentioned as coolies. Similarly, the palanquin bearers were also referred to as coolies. It seems that in this early phase the word did not signify any fixed occupation, but it did denote a form of hard labour based on a cash-wage relationship. They were *hired* and were paid for, for whatever work they were employed to do.

By the 1810s and 1820s, we repeatedly hear about Dhangers, who were hired, for instance, on repair works in the Shahabad district in the year 1812.[22] We further hear about them in 1819, employed in the same district for making roads.[23] Not much is known about the work organization of this particular group (whether they moved in groups or individually, whether

---

16 The magistrate of Hooghly typically remarked: 'Were they [convicts] employed near Hooghly, I could not be uneasy in this head, but three hundred and fifty felons, stationed near jungles from 15 to 30 coss distance from Hooghly under a guard of only eighty burkandazes, on a duty which will take them nearly two seasons leaves them opportunities to escape which they could not avail themselves of any where else.' 'Extract Bengal Judicial Consultations, from C. A. Bruce, Magistrate, Zillah Hooghly to Henry George Tucker, Sub-Secretary, Fort William', 5 January 1798, ibid.
17 Datta, ed., *BR*, 268.
18 'Resolution of the Governor-General in Council', Bcl, vol. 39, 1798–99, F/4/39, letter nos. 965–75.
19 'Letter from Fombelle to Thomas Pattle, Richard Rocke, and Edward Colebrooke, Judges of Murshidabad Court of Circuit', 8 April 1800, Datta, ed. *BR*, 271.
20 Henry Yule and A. C. Burnell, *Hobson-Jobson: The Anglo-Indian Dictionary* (London, 1886). The quotation is from the Wordsworth edition (Hertfordshire, 1996), 249–50.
21 Deane, *A Tour*, 240.
22 'Letter from D. Burges, Collector, Shahabad to R. Rocke, Member of the Board of Revenue', 22 December 1812, *PCRS*, vol. 126, 1812.
23 'Estimate of the expense which may probably be incurred by the Road Fund for July', *PCRS*, vol. no not given, 1819. The employment of 240 Dhangers on various roads cost Rs. 600.

they were recruited by sardars or directly through local officials and so on). As with coolies, Dhanger appears to be a generic term: 'the name by which members of various tribes of Chutia (Chota) Nagpur, but especially of the Oraons are generally known when they go out to distant provinces to seek employment as labourers ("coolies")'.[24] By 1871, they were described as an 'industrious light-hearted race chiefly found in Lohardagga'.[25]

But convicts continued to be employed. In the Saran district, Roy Chaudhury says: 'all the important bridges and roads between 1820 and 1830 were made by convicts'.[26] But for a road of prime importance like the NMR, the Military Board was doubtful of the efficiency of convicts in repairing the roads.[27] The board was also apprehensive about magistrates' supervision: 'the Board cannot recommend that the charge of this important line of road should be committed to the magistrates and the repairs executed by convicts'.[28] Alternatively, native agents were employed on a monthly salary of Rs. 20–25 to superintend the repair works in the divisions entrusted to them. But the Board's proposal was later modified. The agents were retained but the judicial department made it clear that '[t]he road will be superintended by magistrates in their respective divisions with the assistance of the native sircars or agents adverted to by the Military Board'.[29] The resolution also allowed magistrates 'to depute parties of convicts for the repairs of the road in their respective districts, or to employ hired labourers when a sufficient body of convicts cannot be spared'.[30] The GTR in the 1830s was also built with the help of convicts under the command of Captain George Thomson.[31] Between 1833 and 1838, about 13,000 convicts were employed on a continuous basis on the great trunk and other roads.[32] Again, in 1843 the employment of convicts on public works was described as legitimate.[33]

Two changes were evident by the 1820s. Coolies were increasingly chosen over convicts, although the latter were still employed. The reasons are obscure. Perhaps the free labour market had not fully developed to get all the work done by the hired coolies, for, as late as the 1860s and 1870s engineers were complaining about the difficulty of procuring labour for repair works on roads like the GTR and the Patna branch road.[34] The problem of

---

24 Yule and Burnell, *Hobson-Jobson*, 296.
25 Waterfield, *Memorandum on the Census*, 25.
26 Roy Chaudhury, *Sarkar Saran*, 40.
27 'Extract from a Letter from the Secretary to the Military Board', 11 December 1827, Datta, ed., *Selections*, 316–17.
28 Ibid., 317.
29 'Judicial Department Resolution', 8 May 1828, ibid., 318.
30 Ibid., 319.
31 'Letter from Thomason to Lee Warner', 17 September 1833, *PCRS*, vol. no not given, 1833. Using convicts was much cheaper than hiring coolies for this road. This surprisingly stands in contrast to what the officials were advocating in the late eighteenth and early nineteenth centuries. See George Thomson, *Sketch of two Lines of Road between Burdwan and Benares* (Calcutta, 1836).
32 Thornton, *Statistical Papers*, 88.
33 'Letter from J. Hawkins, to A. Smelt, Sessions Judge of Patna', 17 March 1843, Datta, ed., *Selections*, 323.
34 'Behar Circle, Annual Progress Report', Gaya, 13 May 1862 in *Report Showing the Progress made during the year 1861–62 in Public Works under the Bengal Government* (Calcutta, 1862), 37–8. Also, *Progress Report of the Public Works Department*, Bengal, (Buildings and Roads Branch) for 1871–72, 21. [Henceforth *PRPWD*.]

labour shortage was acutely felt on another important route, the Ganges–Darjeeling road. The seasonal cycle of work that corresponded with the harvest season was an important factor for labour shortage. The engineer complained that in contrast to the cold season the number of workmen fell in the season of Holi (a festival corresponding with the season of harvest).[35] The second reason for keeping to the practice of employing convicts may have been purely economical, although in the above cases it is clear that the expenses involved in working convicts was greater than employing 'free labour'.

The second change discernible in this period was the declining role of magistrates in public works. The resolution referred to above restored their supervisory powers but their importance was slowly declining in the wake of engineers taking over the role of supervision. In the case of the GTR, when a separate superintendent was placed, the council argued:

> ...this arrangement will give more useful results than that of continuing local improvements under the magistrate who never can have time to direct the labour of the prisoners advantageously and they must be generally deficient in knowledge of the proper principles on which all roads and improvements of that kind should be made...[36]

Both these points hint towards the increasing formalization and institutionalization of public works. In 1856, the commissioner reported: 'The outdoor labour of the convicts has been entirely discontinued.'[37] Prison labour was now increasingly employed on works such as making baskets and ropes. The proceeds from the sales, however, went into clearing and repairing the roads. By this time, the management of roads had passed from the magistrates' hands to those of executive engineers. The Public Works Department (PWD), set up in 1853, created its own divisions and circles and entrusted work to its engineers. The role of magistrates did not dwindle away completely but it definitely shrank. Their role became confined to serving as secretaries to different local bodies such as the FFC.

In the visual ethnographic archive of this period the figure of the boatman/dandie/coolie, as variously they were called, is conspicuous, suggesting their important role in the transport infrastructure of the time and the region. Rennell had, in 1780, estimated that about 30,000 boatmen were involved in the task of inland navigation in Bengal.[38] Subsequently, a text of 1836 gave the figure of 350,000 for the whole of the Ganga.[39] Even if these figures seem inflated, the fact that boatmen remained an important group of transport workers is beyond dispute. Though many travelogues give stray references to these boatmen they are not sufficient to reconstruct a complete picture of their work

---

35 'Extract from a Letter no. 3, from T. Login, Executive Engineer, Ganges and Darjeeling Road, to Major Maxwell Superintending Engineer (SE) 2nd Circle', *RCE*, 1859, 8–69.
36 'Letter from C. Macsiween to Lee Warner', 6 April 1833, *PCRS*, vol. no not given, 1833.
37 'Letter from the Commissioner of Circuit for the Division of Patna to the Magistrate of Patna', 9 April 1856, *PCRS*, vol. 473, 1856.
38 S. Bhattacharya, 'Eastern India I', in *CEHI*, 271.
39 *Memoir on the Agricultural and Commercial Capabilities of Bengal in Observations with reference to the establishment of the East India Sugar and Agricultural Company, Extracted from various sources, with original calculations, and remarks* (London, 1836), 5.

Plate 25. A dandy

a Dandy of the River Ganges or Exquisite of the fresh Water

© British Library Board, Hawkins, *Diaries and Letters*, Mss Eur. B 365/4 ff.1–28.

organization, methods of employment and forms of resistance. They do, however, provide a glimpse into the world of these mobile workers. These boatmen were not boat owners; they most probably worked on the contract system. The boats belonged to wealthy and landed zamindars, merchants or well-to-do boatmen. On a typical upcountry trip with a budgerow, a luggage boat, a cook boat and also often a separate boat carrying horses, the crew consisted of six to twelve men called dandies, along with a headman called a manjhee. The frequent and widespread practice of river travel must have offered lucrative business opportunities, which is evident by the fact that in the early nineteenth century one Messrs. Barber & Co. at the Old Fort Ghaut in Calcutta hired boats with boatmen to transport the newly arrived Company employees. An agency such as this was paid in advance and the dandies also received half of their payment in advance. To travel through the auspices of an agency was in fact recommended; it supposedly provided security against dandies' desertion, 'a circumstance by no means unusual on this voyage'.[40] However, paradoxically, this advance payment was also regarded as a reason for frequent desertion.[41]

---

40 Deane, *A Tour*, 269.
41 Ibid., 270; Reginald Heber, *Narrative of a Journey through the Upper Provinces of India from Calcutta to Bombay, 1824–25* (London, 1828; repr. New Delhi, 1993), vol. 1, 210.

Even to the European eyes the work done by these dandies involved immense physical labour. For the whole journey, which normally took one to three months, these dandies, owing to the unfavourable stream currents, had often to track the boats with long ropes from the shore. Bishop Heber spared a few words on their physical appearance:

> Our own men, though all in the prime of youth, well fed, and with figures such as statuary might delight to model after, themselves show too many symptoms of the ill-effects occasioned by their constant vicissitudes of water, sun, and toil. The backs and skin of many of them were scaly, as if with leprosy, and they spoke of this complaint as a frequent consequence of their way of life...[42]

The nature of the work involved a great risk of loss of life, which is evident through an interesting fact that 'Calcutta's river insurance companied were accustomed to charge the same three and a half percent premium on merchandise bound eight hundred miles up to Allahabad as upon a ten thousand mile sea-voyage to England.'[43]

A long period of travelling in a new country made Europeans dependent on these dandies for getting to know places and gathering general information about the country. Many travellers carried guidebooks and other 'scientific equipment' such as telescopes, but informal conversational exchange was a regular feature. On many accounts Heber was informed on a variety of matter by his boatmen.[44] It was owing to this nature of dependence and exchange that Deane warned her readers: 'It is always desirable to keep his [manjhee] in good humour, by attending a little to his advice, as on his depends in a great measure both your expedition and comfort on the voyage.'[45] Usually officers who had been living in India for some time also carried their servants with them. In that case the head servant worked as the intermediary between the manjhee and the travelling officer/s. Stawasy Khan was the head servant on the boat of Hawkins and his friend. The form of dependence is evident in Hawkins' amusing account of his head servant's act of approaching these officers, for instance, to convey the manjhee's view on mooring the boat for the night halt if he (the manjhee) had found a good place: 'The truth I suspect is that master Stawasy is getting very hungry and is anxious to get on shore to dress his dinner.'[46]

Perhaps the dandies were aware of this dependence, which they utilized in their favour by pressing their demands about advance payment. Okeden mentioned the 'boatmen mutiny' when his dandies refused to take him further without an advance payment. He was eventually forced to comply with their wish.[47] This was not an isolated case; other travellers also mentioned the mutinous moments that sometimes were avoided by accepting their wishes and sometimes by the use of force and threat. When the dandies of the anonymous traveller threatened to desert, the burkandazes were called in to arrest

---

42 Heber, *Narrative*, 120; Bernstein, *Steamboats*, 16–17.
43 Bernstein, *Steamboats*, 20.
44 Heber, *Narrative*, 105, 107.
45 Deane, *A Tour*, 273.
46 Hawkins, Mss Eur. B 365/4 ff. 1–28, 4.
47 Okeden, *Diary*, 16.

the 'mutineers' in case they persisted with their threat.[48] Amidst informal exchange between the travelling Europeans and the rowing dandies a zone of mutual suspicion existed. Hawkins' suspicion of Stawasy Khan's own interest (driven by hunger) to moor the boat was not of an alarming nature, but often the officers suspected dandies for intentionally delaying the journey.[49] This suspicion arose because of the fact that dandies and manjhees somehow were indispensable to the officers who were on the river for two to three months. No wonder that in his *Vade-Mecum*, Williamson included dandies amongst groups such as *dubhashis*, merchants and shroffs and characterized them as 'cunning and profit mongers who at the first instance would not leave any opportunity of making even smallest advantage from these fresh youths'.[50] The prevalence of bad weather added to the bargaining power of the manjhees in deciding the course of travel. For the same anonymous traveller it was because of inclement weather that a council of manjhees was called near Rajmahal. Much to the dismay of the officers, the majority of them decided not to proceed, a decision that had to be reluctantly accepted by the officers.[51] Any generalization based on the above account would be untenable, but it does seem that such suspicion and dependence, together with a consensual belief that advance payment led to frequent desertions, created a tension-ridden situation between dandies and their European masters. Sometimes this tension manifested itself in the violent postures adopted by European officials; in a fit of anger the friend of Hawkins broke all the cooking pots of the dandies. It is thus no surprise to see Heber commenting that 'one fertile reason of boatmen's desertion was the ill conduct of Europeans, who often stimulated them [dandies] to do things which, in their weak and clumsy boats, were really dangerous, and against all law or right, beat them when they refused or hesitated'.[52]

Any avid reader of the late eighteenth- and early nineteenth-century travelogues will be aware of the typical characterization of dandies' 'cooking practices', which I will pass over here to focus on a more important aspect of their regularization, which appeared to happen because of their propensity to desert and the dependence-driven anxiety felt by travelling officers. There was one more reason: the concern with providing safe travelling conditions was making manjhees accountable for their behaviour. Under Regulation XIX of 1816, officials were not only required to report on the number of ferries and tolls levied but also to provide the number and size of boats maintained at various ghats.[53] Under the same regulation collectors were further directed to fix the wages of the boatmen.[54] The collectors in turn asked important individuals in their districts, such as the indigo planters, to submit statements giving the number and size of boats employed at their factories with the names of the manjhees.[55] The Company's own necessity in transporting 'imperial commodities' such as saltpetre and opium required a

---

48 Anon., *Journal of a Voyage*, 38.
49 Major James Bayley, Mss Eur. D 970, 5.
50 Williamson, *The East India Vade-Mecum*, 151.
51 Anon., *Journal of a Voyage*, 37.
52 Heber, *Narrative*, 211.
53 *MOR*, 304.
54 Ibid., 306.
55 Ibid., 309.

fairly regularized and accountable system of boat hiring, for we do have certain evidence that the Company entered into contracts with manjhees directly.[56] Sometimes disputes amongst manjhees led to the detainment of boats that carried military supplies, thus exposing the early Company-state to the risks involved in overly depending on boatmen.[57] At the same time there is also evidence of complaints made by native merchants against manjhees, the former accusing the latter of taking their full advance and still refusing to convey the goods. It was also suspected that manjhees connived in letting a few of the dandies escape, thus making it more difficult for merchants to get their goods transported. Whatever the reason, it appears that recurrent desertion had taken place on an alarming scale, which led to proposals investing European custom officials with greater power to deal with complaints.[58] As a result, not only were manjhees made accountable for their own behaviour, but they were also held responsible for dandies' behaviour and conduct. '[They] were required to deliver a list of name and places of their dandies, and sign the agreement.' Detailed information about dandies' residences including their villages, parganas and districts were to be submitted. The agreement read:

> I will not permit or induce any of the dandies of my boat to abscond during the voyage under the penalty of forfeiting the sum of…payable to me at (the destination), and that in the event of the Hon'ble Company being put to any expense for the hire of dandies in consequence of any of my people absconding my boats shall be liable to confiscation.[59]

The second reason for the shift towards regularization was the factor of 'mobility', an issue which we dealt in Chapter 5. Similar to other peripatetic groups, boatmen also came under colonial suspicion and scrutiny, at least for being collaborators if not direct perpetrators in many of the river dacoities. By 1872 the Mallah caste was added to the list of the 'Criminal Tribes'.[60] There is often an inclination among scholars to regard 1857 as a break point after which, arguably, the British discourse of criminality came into prominence; but I will argue, along the line of arguments presented in the previous chapter, that the British way of understanding criminality as entwined with mobility developed much earlier, in fact as early as British rule began to establish itself in the late eighteenth century. This time line difference is necessary to bear in mind because it helps to pinpoint shifts in colonial discourse. For instance, the accounts of William

---

56 Datta, ed., *Selections*, 168.
57 Ibid., 192.
58 Montgomery Martin, *The History, Antiquities, Topography and Statistics of Eastern India*, 3 vols (London, 1838), vol. 2, 578. My reading of the paragraph written originally by Buchanan and produced by Martin substantially differs from Assa Doron's. The quote which he produced in full refers to merchants' problems and the issue of the desertion of dandies allegedly facilitated by manjhees. I do not see any hint of the boatmen's 'moral degradation' in this paragraph, which Doron suggests. Assa Doron, *Caste, Occupation and Politics on the Ganges: Passages of Resistance* (Surrey, 2008), 35.
59 'Rules and Regulations for the Transport of Troops', Bcl, vol. 191, 1806–07, F/4/191, 4260.
60 Doron, *Caste, Occupation and Politics*, 30.

Crooke associate mallahs with a ritually inferior position in the caste hierarchy by giving details of their 'polluting' dietary habits. Apart from fish and meat, the mallahs allegedly also ate rats, tortoises, crocodiles and practised excessive alcohol consumption.[61] This is the prevalent view in the late nineteenth and early twentieth centuries. If we look at descriptions of cooking practices as reported by several travellers of an earlier period, we do not find any trace of the dandies' 'derogatory' and 'polluting' practices. The boatmen reportedly did not cook their food on board; they ate only some parched rice while onboard and prepared their dinner ashore in the evening after mooring their boats. This practice was so strictly observed that at times, when rain did not permit them to prepare their dinner, they did not eat at all. This was true for the 'Hindu' members of the crew; the Muslims reportedly ate onboard.[62] This was also a common theme in pictorial representations of this group: in one of the Eastern India-style watercolours dated 1785–90 a dandy is shown preparing his dinner on the banks of the river. The person is preparing the food in an earthen vessel. He wears only a *dhoti* with his hair tied at the top of the head (the image suggests he is a Hindu).[63] In another sketch referred to above (Add.Or.2672), the members of the crew are shown in two different dress styles: one group is in long *kurta* and *khalta paijama* with a *topi* or a headwear; another just in dhoti. The group of dandies comprised of both Muslims and Hindus, a fact that was not lost on the early travellers, but in the ethnographic and enumerative descriptions of the period when Crooke was writing, the 'religious' composition (I am not intending here to suggest religious *segregation*, the emphasis is on religious *composition*) of the crew had given way to caste descriptions. This observation does not intend to suggest a linear shift from 'community and religion' to 'caste and tribe' but only intends to highlight the changing context of colonial knowledge practices; the former set of texts and images emerged from the travelling practices (at least in the case of dandies) and the latter from a growing anthropological pursuit to understand 'things Indian'.

In the lack of any substantive study, the occupational displacement that came into play with the development of steam power is yet to be established. Based on the fieldwork that is contextualized in the historical sources of the late nineteenth and early twentieth centuries (mainly the census reports), Smita Tewari Jassal's article on mallahs offers an interesting insight. Mallahs were classified in Class B of the Criminal Tribes Act (CTA), meaning that although they were 'criminals' they had recently settled down to agriculture, in contrast to tribes classified under Class C that required resettlement and transportation.[64] The upshot of this argument, which Jassal has mentioned at the beginning of her article, is that a lot of occupational diversification, including settlement to agriculture, had already taken place before the 1871 census and the passing of the CTA. According to her, one of the prime reasons, which she just lists (and does not explore), was the construction of the GTR (leading to the decline in river traffic) and the subsequent advent of the

---

61 Ibid., 32–3.
62 Brainerd, *Historic Incidents*, 39; Forrest, *A Picturesque Tour*, 124; Deane, *A Tour*, 11. Williamson talks about the unhygienic way in which dandies prepared their curry, 151–3.
63 Add. Or. 2732, *P&D*.
64 Smita Tewari Jassal, 'Caste and the Colonial State: Mallahs in the Census', *Contributions to Indian Sociology* 35, no. 3 (2001): 340–42.

railways.[65] The ways in which this occupational diversification – from being transport workers to agricultural labourers – took place is still a matter of general speculation. It does not appear that the competition from road and railway networks was strong enough, at least in the period of the 1860s and 1870s, to have led to any massive or substantial sectorial shift. Some of the experienced boatmen did find their way into becoming part of the steamship establishment; their experience made them worthy of being employed as pilots.[66] In the 1830s, around 500 people were employed in the steam department. The difficulties involved in running steamships led owners/managers to seek the help of 'native pilots'. People such as Robinson, who compared navigation on the Ganga with that on the Mississippi, where a regular pilot establishment existed, disregarded the utility of 'local knowledge'; yet it seems that native pilots remained indispensable until the late 1860s. Stationed along the river, they provided useful knowledge about hidden shoals.[67] But as Bernstein concludes, the unavailability of sources renders it extremely difficult to chart the actual historical change in the status and occupation of boatmen.[68] Nonetheless, the factor of regularization of boatmen was something conspicuous in this period: a set of rules for river navigation passed in 1867 required each boatman to 'provide details, such as caste, patrilineal descent, place of residence and the "length of the river under his pilotage"'.[69] At best we can assume that some of these boatmen were co-opted into the new steam service, while some lost their jobs on account of growing regularization (and displacement) and others still continued in their role as mobile transport workers. The phase of decline in the river transport (due to the railways) is a feature of a much later period. Therefore, if we accept Jassal's argument that the occupational diversification of mallahs into the agricultural sector happened before the 1870s, the reasons are then not primarily in the change of circulatory regimes taking place with the coming of the railway – as its effects, vis-à-vis the river transport, start becoming sharper only by the turn of the century. This understanding of the shifts and patterns of circulation that thrived in this region is based on the idea of 'nested' networks, to which we turn now.

Nested networks

With mounting emphasis on connecting 'interiors' with thoroughfares, we need to ask if trading patterns and linkages also changed with the new configurations in the transport structure. One way to approach this issue is through the nature of commodities. The history of communication in this period – not only communication infrastructure but also the social dynamics of trade connections – was intricately related to the nature of commodities. Commodities such as salt and saltpetre, which the colonial state was directly interested in, forced the state to control existing trade networks and to regulate the means of communication. The fate of banjaras and the patrolling of the NMR is a

---

65 Ibid., 321.
66 Bernstein says that the 'collectors and magistrates of riverside districts were responsible for recruiting river pilots from among local boatmen and fisherfolk'. Bernstein, *Steamboats*, 84.
67 Doron, *Caste, Occupation and Politics*, 39.
68 Bernstein, *Steamboats*, 113–14.
69 Doron, *Caste, Occupation and Politics*, 39.

case in point. The state was not helplessly 'limited' in its scope. It was, however, limited or unconcerned (not in terms of knowledge but in terms of 'controlling' them) when it came to commodities that circulated in nested networks. These commodities did not elicit any direct concern from the state. It is difficult to ascertain the degree of benefit these networks derived from recent changes made in the field of communication. Most probably they benefitted, in particular, from the good state of the roads maintained by the FFCs in north Bihar and from the metalled thoroughfares such as the GTR. For instance, after two ferry roads were raised and bridged in the 1850s in the Champaran district of north Bihar, a significant increase in traffic was reported.[70] In order to study this world of nested networks we will chiefly rely on revenue and statistical surveys of the districts of Bihar published in the 1840s and 1850s, supplemented by other sources.[71]

A road running in a south–north direction, that is, from Gaya to Patna, crossed the district of Behar.[72] For most of the southern parganas of this district, this was the crossing road. The villages of these parganas sent grain towards the Ganga from this road. The road, however, was in such poor condition that only pack bullocks and not wheeled carriages could travel along it. Another road ran southwest to northeast, leading from Hazaribagh and Ramghur and crossing through the pargana Puchrookhee. One southern pargana, Jurrah, was rich in talc, which was quarried and exported to the Patna market. Daudnagar, situated on the right bank of the River Soane, was an important trade centre. Paper, carpets and *suttranjies* (a type of woven carpet) were important manufactures exported to Patna, Danapur, Ghazipur, Benares and other cities.[73] The Shershah's trunk road, also called the Benares trunk road, which ran along the Ganga to Danapur from where it passed along the banks of the Soane, connected Daudnagar with the cities mentioned above. The region also traded locally and with more distant places in resinous products. Lac, *dhoona* (formed from the extracted piece of the sal tree) and *kuth* (obtained by boiling the bark of the khaibur tree) were three important products that were brought from Immamgunge in the Sherghatty subdivision and Rajauli in the

---

70 'From the Commissioner of Revenue to the Secretary to the Government of Bengal', 22 March 1854, *PCRS*, vol. 455, 1854.
71 There might have existed, as Bayly has argued, a wide gap in the expansion of revenue information between the NWP and Bengal, the latter providing a 'striking contrast of sluggishness'. For him, this was due to the domination of large zamindars in the countryside and the absence of paternalist officialdom as promoted by Thomason in the NWP. But for our purposes of knowing the local routes and local trade networks, the revenue and statistical reports are not inadequate. Bayly, *Empire and Information*, 221.
72 W. S. Sherwill, *Statistics of the District of Behar* (Calcutta, 1845). The following account is based on this source unless otherwise mentioned.
73 Suttranjies and Daudnagar carpets, among other manufactures, found a place in the Memorandum prepared by the Gaya collector, giving the list of the *bona fide* works of arts and industry of the district to be sent to the Paris Exhibition of 1867. *GOR*, 6–7. However, by the late 1870s this industry had declined. The commerce of Gaya with other districts was said to be 'rare'. W. W. Hunter, *A Statistical Account of Bengal: Districts of Gaya and Shahabad*, vol. 12 (London, 1877), 41. [Henceforth Hunter, *AGS*.] Paper is also mentioned as a trading commodity in Mughal times. Irfan Habib, *An Atlas of the Mughal Empire: Political and Economic Maps with detailed Notes, Bibliography and Index* (Delhi, 1982), sheet 10B.

Nawadah subdivision. They were obtained from forests in neighbouring areas and were also supplied from Hazaribagh, Chatra, Palamow and Palkot.[74] A large trade in lac and dhoona was carried on with Calcutta, Patna, Arrah, Mirzapur, Chapra and Muzaffarpur. Considerable trade in kuth existed with Mirzapur. The annual supply in maunds from Immamgunge and Rajauli in these products was:[75]

Table 4. Trade in resinous products in Bihar

Places	Lac	Dhoona	Kuth
Immamgunge	7,000	5,000	4,000
Rajauli	5,000	4,000	–

Chatra was the principal mart in the Hazaribagh district. Even when the roads did not allow carts to travel along them, the annual trade of Hazaribagh district was about Rs. 55 lakhs.[76] The importance of this thriving trade encouraged local authorities to connect up with adjoining places. Proposals were made to make three roads, one from Aurungabad to Daudnagar, another from Gaya to Rajauli, and a third from Arwal to Jehanabad.[77] In the southernmost part of this region, the Chota Nagpur area, Chaibassa was an emerging important trade centre. For the import of salt into Chota Nagpur region, which mainly came from Orissa, it was proposed that two roads be improved, one from Chaibassa to Chota Nagpur and another from Chaibassa to Keiparrah (a place in the central Cuttack). The proposal came after the huge increase in the traffic of salt was noted in the early 1850s.[78] Two more roads were proposed to connect Chaibassa with Midnapur and Bankura. The latter was said to be of 'much importance to the trading community', since by this road almost the whole of the raw silk trade was conveyed on country carts to Raghunathpur, Sona Mookhee and Rajgunge, the last two situated in the Bankura district.[79] Already by the 1850s, in the region of the *Damin-i Koh* (formed in 1832–33, the territorial boundary of *Damin-i Koh* spanned across the districts of Bhagalpur, Murshidabad and Beerbhoom), Bengali merchants, together with merchants from places such as Shahabad, Chapra, Bettiah and Arrah were settled and carrying on a brisk trade in commodities including rice, mustard, oilseed, salt, tobacco and cloth.[80] So far as south Bihar is concerned, the picture that emerges from the above description is of vibrant trade

---

74 Even in the Mughal period these forests had served as rich source of gumlac. Shireen Moosvi, 'Man and Nature in Mughal Era', *Indian History Congress Symposia Paper 5* (Delhi, 1993), 11.
75 'Letter from J. S. Drummond, Officiating Collector, Gaya to the Commissioner of Revenue for the division of Patna', 12 December 1866, *GOR*, 28–9.
76 G. Hunter Thompson, 'Report on the District of Hazareebaugh, surveyed during seasons 1858–59 to 1862–63', *AIA* 8 (1864): 333–4.
77 'Letter no. 446, from Drummond to the Commissioner, Patna division', 25 July 1866, *GOR*, 12.
78 'Extract from a Letter from the Commissioner of Chota Nagpur to the Secretary to the Government of Bengal', 19 March 1855, *SOR*, 79–81.
79 Ibid.
80 Datta, *Anti-British Plots*, 44–6.

linkages between different nodes of 'interiors' and between them and the big cities that were situated on the principal lines of communication. These trading nodes and marts were connected with places in Bengal and Orissa on the one hand and with UP on the other. From the point of view of spatial dynamism, far from being a *tabula rasa* these spaces were not only inhabited but also widely traversed by merchant communities. Further, 'colonial intervention' in terms of improved communication leading to the forging of a new 'colonial state–space' was not meant to 'clean up' but to strengthen those ties.

The Ganga remained the main axis of trade for the districts adjoining it. Among the products from the eleven parganas of Monghyr lying north of the river, tobacco was a major commodity, the soil of these parganas being particularly favourable for its growth.[81] Trade in tobacco was carried out with Benares, Kanpur, Patna and Ghazipur. The *mahajans* (traders, moneylenders) from these regions made advance payments to the cultivators, who upon reaping their crop in March and after deducting the amount of advance, sold their produce to the mahajans. Many thousands of maunds of tobacco were conveyed by boat to the NWP every year. Imports into these parganas were principally of wheat, pulses of different kinds and saltpetre, all coming from the west (NWP), and salt from the east (Calcutta). The southern parganas produced grain – chiefly rice and wheat – for export. Mahua petals obtained from the adjoining forest areas (Chukye pargana) were also exported. 'Considerable traffic' in dried Mahua fruit had prompted Mr Birch, the magistrate of Monghyr, to keep the road in repair. However, no amount was sanctioned for this.[82] The twelve parganas lying south of the Ganga were rich opium-producing areas; the total number of *beegahs* (unit of land measurement) under poppy cultivation was 20,315, producing 4,040 maunds of opium.[83]

From the seven river ghats of Patna, considerable trade was carried on in cloth, grain, sugar and rice.[84] The region of Shahabad provided lime, which amounted 'to many thousands of tons annually', which were then sent by boat down the River Soane to all the principal towns and cities on the Ganga. The lithographic stones used in the office of the surveyor general of India travelled in this way.[85] The deep valleys of the south of the Shahabad district, which

---

81 W. S. Sherwill, *General Remarks on the District of Monghyr* (Calcutta, 1848), 2. Account based on this source unless otherwise mentioned. Tobacco was also exported in large quantities from one of the southern parganas called Ooturkund.
82 GOB, PWD, GB, proceedings 91–2, June 1859, *RRWRD*.
83 In the early nineteenth century, Monghyr's trading importance had attracted attention: Sita Ram, the painter who accompanied Lord Hastings in his upcountry tour, drew nine out of twenty-three sketches on Mongyhr in the first volume of the Hastings collections (which is missing). Out of those nine, three showed the houses of native merchants, one a bazaar of Monghyr (confectioners and flower sellers) and another a vegetable and grain market. The importance of Monghyr as a river station is attested to by many travellers. Within ten minutes of being on the banks, reported a traveller, the 'swarms of traders in these articles [guns, furniture and other hand wares] flocked to the boats'. Anon., *Journey*, 69.
84 H. L. Thuillier, *Statistics of the District of Patna* (Calcutta, 1847), 1–2.
85 Sandstones from the Shahabad region were used for flooring the Asiatic Society's Museum in Calcutta. Bingham, *Canals for Irrigation*, 54–6. These were also tried as lithographic stones, but were considered too siliceous and thin. Sherwill, 'Geological Notes on Zillah Shahabad, or Arrah', *JASB* 16, no. 1 (January–June 1847): 282.

were described as 'almost impenetrable to man' afforded 'excellent shade and pasture to large herds of buffaloes', which had a significant role in the production of the *ghee* (clarified butter) in this region that was supplied to markets in Benares and Mirzapur.[86] 'Indurated Reddle' or Geru, as it was called in the native language, which was used for the purposes of dyeing or as a pigment, was carried in great quantities on bullocks to Benares, Patna and other cities.[87] Fine veins of mica were worked in the district of Behar and the produce was exported to Patna.[88] From the Kharakpur Hills, lying south of Monghyr, quartz rock was quarried for millstones and sent to Monghyr, from where it was 'exported in great quantities to Bengal and other parts of India'.[89] In the early nineteenth century, Bhagalpur was famous as a big mart of 'yellowish-white cloth pieces', which were in vogue amongst the Turks of Basra and Baghdad.[90] Dakatiyas, a group of people in the Shahabad district, specialized in the trade of holy water from the Ganga, which was brought in from Allahabad and sold on the way to Baidyanath (Deoghar) at Rs. 8 a load.[91]

Chapra and Revelgunge were two important towns in the Saran district.[92] Apart from the production and trade in indigo, opium and saltpetre, there were other minor trade networks. Revelgunge, situated at the confluence of the Ganga and the Dewah (Gogra), was an important mart where saltpetre and other commodities such as grain were collected before being despatched to Patna in the east and Benares, Ghazipur and Mirzapur in the northwest. Chapra was also well connected with towns such as Hajipur, Muzaffarpur and Ghazipur in the north and northwest of the Ganga, and with Arrah, Patna and Danapur on the Ganga. One village of Doomaeegarh in the pargana Manghee (Manjhi) was a famous wood mart where timber was collected in large quantities from Gorakhpur. It was also famous for boat making, the range varying from one to 2,500 maunds in tonnage.

Chapra, situated on the banks of the Ganga, remained an important entrepôt town for commodities from both sides of the river. Large quantities of cotton, Kashmiri shawls and Benares brocades were imported from the northwest for shipment to Calcutta, while English goods, such as woollens, cottons and chintzes arrived at Chapra from Calcutta to be distributed into the 'interiors'. There were several native agency houses, the principal ones engaged in this trade being those of Banwari Lal, Bhgawan Dass and Ujodea Persaud (Ayodhya Prasad). As we will see in the next chapter, even with the coming of the railways, this river trade and the prime position that towns such as Patna and Chapra commanded by virtue of being situated on the river — and thus acting as entrepôts — continued to be vital.

---

86 Ibid., 280.
87 Ibid., 283.
88 Sherwill, 'Note on the Geological Features of Zillah Behar', 55.
89 Sherwill, 'The Kurruckpoor Hills', *JASB* 31, no. 3 (1852): 197.
90 Behbahani, *Mir'at Ul-Ahwal-i Jahan Numa*, 128.
91 Francis Buchanan, *An Account of the District of Shahabad*, 185. Before Buchanan, Hodges too, when in Deoghar, had commented about 'a considerable trade in holy water', the price of which varied 'in proportion to the distance of the place where it is sold from the river'. Hodges, *Travels*, 94.
92 A. Wyatt, *Statistics of the District of Sarun consisting of Sircars Sarun and Champarun* (Calcutta, 1847?). The account is based on this source unless otherwise mentioned.

There were many important local bazaars situated in the 'interiors' of north Bihar carrying on a brisk trade with neighbouring regions. Important among them were Allygunge, Meergunge and Maharajgunge, which were not only connected to places on the Ganga but with towns further north such as Motihari and Bettiah. This zone of trade networks often appeared to be situated in 'interiors' (from the Calcutta- or the Ganga-oriented perspective) but, if seen on its own, presents a picture of a well-knit trading complex, the extent of which went as far north as Nepal. Allygunje was noted for its manufacture of bell-metal vessels and chintzes. A much-frequented good cart road passed through Allygunje via Meergunge, Burragaon and Buthooa to Gorakhpur. Meergunge was an entrepôt for grain from the north and northwest, which was then exported to Patna and elsewhere. Yang mentions that there were several Patna merchants who had agents in Meergunge for linseed, cotton and *gur* (jaggery).[93] Good roads connected all the important towns such as Ghazipur, Gorakhpur, Seegawli, Bettiah, Mullye, Muzaffarpur, Chapra and Patna.

Further north in the Champaran district were five principal roads. The first ran from Chapra, Muzaffarpur and Patna to Motihari, Seegawli and Bettiah; the second connected Gorakhpur with Bettiah; a third ran from Bettiah via Ramnagar to Tribeni and Nepal; a fourth from Motihari to Mullye and then to Nepal; and a fifth, the high road, from Seegawli to Kathmandu. Thus all the important towns in north Bihar were on the one side well connected with the frontier regions and the kingdom of Nepal, and on the other with places such as Patna and Chapra on the Ganga. Besides, there were numerous cart roads and bullock tracks, which intersected the Champaran division. The principal river, the Gandak, which skirted this subdivision to the south and southwest, was navigable throughout the year for boats of 1,000 to 1,500 maunds tonnage (37 to 55 metric tons). The chief commodities passing through the river, such as rice, oilseed, opium and indigo were mainly meant for export. The principal imports were salt and cotton from Calcutta.

Tirhut had some 'excellent roads' throughout the district during this period.[94] Coarse rice from Dacca, Calcutta salt and NWP cotton were the chief imports. The principal exports were indigo, sugar, wheat, barley, oats, fine rice, oilseeds, hides and horns to Calcutta and neighbouring places. Tirhut also sent tobacco to Patna and other places. Tobacco from Sureysa pargana was famous for its pungency and strength. The Gandak was the principal river of transport. Besides, secondary rivers such as the Bya, the Boor Gandak and the Bagmati were navigable for about six months of the year for smaller boats of 500 and 600 maunds tonnage (18 to 22 metric tons). In many of the parganas, these rivers were navigable throughout the year for much larger tonnage. Muzaffarpur was the most well-connected town in this district. Roads linked it not only with towns situated on the Ganga, such as Patna, Chapra and Monghyr, but also with Kathmandu, Darbhanga and Purneah. 'Several excellent roads leading to qasbah towns, and indigo factories' existed in the district.

---

93 Yang, *The Limited Raj*, 122.
94 Wyatt, *Geographical and Statistical Report*. The account is based on this source unless otherwise mentioned.

The annual or biannual fairs at many of these local bazaars and gunges were times of increased trading interactions. At many places in north Bihar — as at Myhsee, Mullye, Halo-Koaree, Shewhur, Ramnagar, Buguhua, Gobindgunj, Kisureea and Tribeni — biannual fairs were held during the months of *Fagun* and *Chaitra* (corresponding to the harvest seasons of February and March).[95] People from different places including Nepal, Gorakhpur, Azimgarh and Saran amassed and traded in cloths, vessels, iron ores, iron vessels, manufactured iron goods (such as knives) and drugs. Shilajit ('native sulphate of Alumina from the Aluminous rocks') was the most important article among these medicinal drugs.[96] Found throughout the lower, central and upper hills of Nepal in considerable quantities, shilajit was brought by the Bhooteas, the Murmis and other hill people of Kathmandu, to be exchanged with the merchants of that city for money or other articles. From there, Newar merchants and other *beoparis* (merchants) brought it down to the Gangetic plain.[97] The expanse of shilajit trade was extensive and also overlapped with the pilgrimage circuit; we are told that apart from the merchants of Bihar it was also carried by the 'horse merchants of the Punjab' and fakirs who distributed it to every pilgrim centre from Jaggarnath to Mansarowar and from Rameshwar to Dwarika.[98]

The annual fair held in the village of Sitamarhi in the pargana Muhila of the Tirhut district was famous for its large collection of bullocks. Traders from adjoining villages and from Nepal flocked to buy, sell and barter goods.[99] Mullye on the Nepalese frontier became an important emporium of trade with Nepal. Grain, cotton and clothes were imported from Nepal. In return, the Nepalese traded for cotton and clothes. The British troops at Mullye provided safety to the native merchants and dealers. The village of Choohurree, situated about three miles north of Bettiah, excelled in the manufacture of straw and bamboo mats, baskets and large and small bamboo ribbed *chattahs* (umbrellas) covered with coloured wax cloth, which met with ready purchasers at Bettiah, Muzaffarpur, Chapra and Patna, for both private use as well as for export to Bengal and the NWP.[100] There were several minor native agency houses in Bettiah dealing in grain, sugar, cloths and other commodities. Though Europeans were mainly involved in indigo production, some of them were also resident dealers in grain, seeds, horns and hides.

Conclusions

Different types of market connections and exchange networks had existed, which the Company-state was coming to know. These included the trading connections between

---

95 Wyatt, *Statistics of the District of Sarun*, 3.
96 J. Stevenson, 'Notice of a Native Sulphate of Alumina from the Aluminous Rocks of Nipal', *JASB* 2 (1833): 321.
97 A. Campbell, 'On the Native Alum or Salajit or Nepal', *JASB* 2 (1833): 482.
98 Ibid., 484.
99 Wyatt, *Geographical and Statistical*, 20.
100 In previous centuries, bamboos from the forest of Rohtas and Patna were of durable quality, and were also used for palanquin poles. The availability of bamboo sustained many professional castes in UP and Bihar, who were engaged in making fans, baskets and boxes. Moosvi, 'Man and Nature in Mughal Era',16–18. See also Habib, *An Atlas*, sheet 8B.

north Bihar and Nepal,[101] between local markets and the gunges of north Bihar and places such as Ghazipur and Gorakhpur in the NWP, and between Chota Nagpur and Jungle Terry areas on the one hand and Orissa and Bengal on the other. It is quite evident from the account presented above that the commodities that were traded were both items of 'local' nature – (locally produced and consumed) but traded over a wide geographical area such as lac and dhoona – and items of an 'imperial' nature such as indigo, opium and English clothes. Both these forms of commodity traversed the same pathways and most probably were also handled by the same set of merchants. These merchants were both natives and Europeans. This picture of 'high' and 'popular' commodities, of Europeans and native merchants, created a network of circulation in which the colonial state was not absent. Agency houses and traders had to accommodate themselves within a larger pattern of trade dictated by imperial imperatives. The penetration of English manufactured clothes in these gunges and markets compelled them to do so. But there were many other commodities such as tobacco, kuth, vessels, ropes and baskets and so on, whose trade, and quite an extensive one, existed simultaneously with those of 'high' commodities. Such coexistences were not without contestations.

To stretch this point a little further, trading relations between Bihar, Nepal and Tibet present an interesting case of contested authority. As noted above, the gosains controlled the larger portion of trade with Nepal and other Terai regions in the eighteenth century. Bogle reasoned that gosains' knowledge of remote and unknown regions, together with their appearance as holy pilgrims, made them the most acceptable group for this trade.[102] Another community that controlled the trade between Bengal and Tibet was the Booteas. The common route for this trade was through Cooch Behar. Another route through which the trade with Nepal and Tibet was carried out was through Mirzapur and Benares.[103] Right from the beginning, the Company was interested in accumulating knowledge about and profiting from this trade. Bogle's successive missions were part of this agenda; he was sent on a second trip 'to endeavour to establish free and lasting trade relations with the kingdom of Tibet and other states to the north of the company's possessions'.[104]

In 1791, before William Kirkpatrick mounted his fact-finding mission in 1793,[105] the Company had tried to conclude a commercial treaty with Nepal via Jonathan Duncan, the Benares resident. The collectors of Saran and Champaran were asked to supply information about trading commodities. The circulation of Nepalese pice amounting to Rs. 25,000–30,000 in the district of Muzaffarpur alone proves the flourishing trading ties.[106]

---

101 Apart from the connections detailed above, in the late eighteenth century, the Patna Sicca rupee was the most common coin in Nepal. See 'No. 91 Letter from D. H. McDowell, Collector, Rangpur to John McPherson', 23 July 1786, Firminger, ed., *Bengal District Records: Rangpur, vol. 6, 1786–87 (Letters Issued)*, 92–7.
102 'Memorandum by Mr. Bogle on the Trade of Thibet', 252–4.
103 Ibid., 353–4. See also 'Letter from Hastings to John MacPherson', 21 October 1784, Forrest, ed., *Selections*, vol. 3, 1117.
104 Schuyler Cammann, 'The Panchen Lama's Visit to China in 1780: An Episode in Anglo-Tibetan Relations', *The Far Eastern Quarterly* 9, no. 1 (1949): 4.
105 Bayly, *Empire and Information*, 100.
106 *MOR*, 30.

Keen on tapping into these profits, the Company removed the customhouse choukie situated at Seegawli on the way to Nepal. However, the Company was not successful; repeated allegations of lack of protection and the levying of 'arbitrary and exorbitant duties' were made against the Nepalese government.[107] Political animosity further hindered the official commercial ties between the Company-state and the Nepalese government. From 1787 to 1815 the Gurkhas made 'frequent in-roads' into 'British territories'; in 1813, for instance, they came down to Muzaffarpur, seizing almost 200 villages.[108] As a result, on 22 July 1815, a Circular was passed informing the Saran magistrate to restrain all commercial intercourse with Nepal, especially in war-like stores. Throughout the mid-nineteenth century, presents and delegations were exchanged but the relationship between the Company-state and the Nepalese authorities did not improve. In 1854, the Nepalese government assembled troops on the Bihar border to 'obtain reparations' from the officers at Tirhut for some injuries done to the subjects of Nepal.[109] By the 1820s–1830s, gosains had virtually lost their control of this trade; the Company, however, did not take over. Giving details of the Nepalese trade in 1831, resident B. H. Hodgson dismissed the idea of an extension of trade through arms or diplomacy.[110] Hodgson reported that general Europeans not attached to the Residency were not allowed to attend the Nepalese festival of Pasupati Kshetra at Kathmandu, which nonetheless was attended by 'lakhs of people from plains' (of Bihar). The indigo planters of north Bihar did try to gain a foothold in local trade but the articles they traded in were different from those exchanged with Nepal. The chief articles exported to Nepal were European broadcloths (crimson, green, orange, liver and brown coloured), cutlery, pearls, coral, diamonds, emeralds, indigo and opium,[111] while the planters traded mainly in sugar, indigo, saltpetre, hides and horns, grain and oilseed.[112] The large assembly of traders and merchants at different fairs and the presence of native agency houses suggest that the trade with Nepal was largely in the hands of native merchants. Also the sustained political uneasiness between the Company-state and the Gurkha rulers did not put an end to the networks of trade in which merchants from north Bihar and Nepal participated.

As pointed out earlier, these networks and their merchants probably benefitted from the improvements in the communication network, especially in north Bihar. But communication facilitated trade if transit duties were low. In the late eighteenth century, according to Trevelyan, tariffs on goods were paid as trade progressed.[113] In other words, tariffs were charged in each pargana as the goods entered into them, the sum being small. Local trade therefore had to pay lower tariffs than long-distance trade. The 1808 Commission on Tariffs changed this system. The commissioners took for their standard the aggregate of all the instalments, which were levied on goods proceeding to the greatest distance, and applied it on the whole internal trade of the country. In other words, local

---

107 Ibid., 114–17.
108 Roy Choudhury, *Sarkar Saran*, 16.
109 Datta, ed., *Selections*, 23.
110 *AIA* 6 (1858): 90–93.
111 Ibid., 93.
112 Wyatt, *Geographical and Statistical*, 11.
113 C. E. Trevelyan, *A Report upon the Inland Customs and Town-Duties of the Bengal Presidency* (Calcutta, 1834), 2–3.

trade was made as much dutiable as long-distance trade. This system hurt local business, as Trevelyan notes:

> ...the intercourse between adjoining districts in the interior is positively burdened with heavier duties than the trade between England and India. English metals and woollens are admitted free, and nearly all other articles at 2½ percent, and on the export side, indigo, cotton and tobacco are free, while other articles are charged 2½ percent; but in the trade carried on between the most contiguous places in the interior, metals are charged ten percent, and other articles from five to ten percent.[114]

This system further required merchants to secure the rowannahs from the customhouses, but the choukies retained the right to check the specifications of the commodities entered into the rowannah. As a result, even if a customhouse was located 100 miles away and a choukie a mile off, the merchandise had to be taken to the customhouse before passing through the choukie.[115] In Bengal and Bihar, this scheme proved effective for the British, as the Ganga was the main trading line, compared to the NWP where the trader had a choice of routes.[116] This structure of taxation was instrumental in bringing in a change in the social composition of merchants in Bihar and Bengal. Trevelyan reports that in these provinces inland trade was concentrated in the hands of a few rich merchants at the cost of petty traders. This explains the emergence of native agency houses in places such as Chapra and Tirhut, which dealt extensively in the long-distance import-export business. With the abolition of choukies in the 1830s (under the pretext of making inland trade free) this picture changed. With fewer regulations and increasing investment in communication, a favourable atmosphere emerged for these networks. Soon, however, the existing circulatory regime witnessed the entrance of a new technology, that of railways. We now move towards the last chapter, where we examine the nature of the trends outlined in this chapter in relation to the introduction of railways.

---

114 Ibid., 4–5.
115 Ibid., 12–13.
116 Ibid., 28–9.

Chapter 8

THE WHEELS OF CHANGE

In our final chapter we set out to examine the role of railways in the larger matrix of communication policy and the effects they cast, in particular, on trading and commercial patterns. Clearly, the unity of empire and the steady flow of external trade were twin functions closely associated with the railways. Not surprisingly then, some scholars have therefore described the Indian railways as a crucial project of colonial rule.[1] Politically, the Punjab wars in the 1840s reinforced the need for speedy means of communication. Simultaneously, the needs of industrializing Britain were pressing hard to 'open up the interiors', both for the supply of raw materials from the colony and for the sale of British-manufactured finished goods.[2] For these reasons, the railways became the site of a fierce contestation between groups of different ideological pursuits. For a majority of colonial officers and policymakers the railways remained a tool of development,[3] but for many others, especially Indian nationalist critics, they symbolized an instrument of economic exploitation and the draining of wealth.[4] This divide resonates in several works on the economic history of nineteenth-century India.[5]

The core of this chapter aims at addressing a few of the issues outlined above. It is difficult to discard our common-sense understanding that railways as the 'wheels of change' formed an inseparable part of the colonial project of rule, but any discussion of the relationship between railways and late nineteenth-century India within the framework of communication and circulation does need to address certain basic issues. In studying such a relationship there has been a strong tendency to look at railways alone at the cost of neglecting the part played by other means of communication. Such lopsidedness arises partly from the fact that our understanding of communication, society and the economy is still very much trapped in colonial justificatory discourses. But nor does the nationalist critique help in appreciating the contextualized effects of this new technology.

---

1 Ian Kerr, 'Introduction', in Kerr, ed., *Railways in Modern India*.
2 Though dated, two articles are seminal in their treatment of the reasons behind introducing the railways in India: W. J. Macpherson, 'Investment in Indian Railways, 1845–1875', *Economic History Review* 8, 2nd series (1958); Daniel Thorner, 'Capital Movement and Transportation: Great Britain and the Development of India's Railways', *Journal of Economic History* 11, no. 4 (1951).
3 By the late decades of the nineteenth century it had become proverbial that 'railways make trade'. G. Balachandran, 'Introduction', in Balachandran, ed., *India and the World Economy 1850–1950* (New Delhi, 2003), 11 and 36, fn. 25.
4 The writings of Dadabhai Naoroji and R. C. Dutt still enjoy the canonical position. Naoroji, *Poverty and Un-British Rule in India* (London, 1901); Dutt, *The Economic History of India*, 2 vols (London, 1903).
5 For example Michelle Burge McAlpin, *Subject to Famine: Food Crises and Economic Change in Western India, 1860–1920* (Princeton, 1983).

Hence, our first aim is to situate railways within the larger pattern of the development of the communication grid.

It is perhaps this fascination with the railways alone that explains why most questions in the field of transport history in India have so far been framed in terms of 'competition' between the railways and other means of communication. Tirthankar Roy says, 'It is not surprising that the railways destroyed them [older systems of transport] without much resistance.'[6] Mukul Mukherjee has come to the conclusion that in Bengal the railways, by gradually superseding existing means of communication (carts and boats), affected both regional price differentials and annual price fluctuations.[7] Such conclusions have become consensual. Ian Derbyshire in his study of the UP has also arrived at two similar conclusions: first, that railways, by scoring an edge over other available forms of communication, namely roads and rivers, opened up a number of new marketing possibilities that brought down the spatial differences in regional prices; second, they created an upward movement in price levels.[8] However, Derbyshire goes further in his investigation by not only looking at the changes in the volume of trade, but also at the spatial shifts in the patterns of production. Thus he argues that there was a shift in cash-crop production from the former productive region of the eastern UP to the high-yield areas of the Doab. Market extension is another theme often studied under the umbrella of the effects of railway development. Both at the national and regional level, like the UP noted above, expansion in terms of increased acreage under cultivation, together with regional specialization and the commercialization of agriculture, are described as important effects of the development of the railways.[9]

This chapter sets out to qualify our understanding, which is largely framed in terms of 'competition and contestation', by proposing to assess railway-induced changes from the perspective of 'alignments' and 'realignments'. Ellen Gumperz's study on Bombay has shown how the multiple functions of a city or a region changed once better means of transport were introduced. One of the effects was the decline in the economic importance of the Dharwar region but its simultaneous rise in political importance.[10] Derbyshire's thesis on regional configuration also leads us towards substituting 'reconfiguration' for absolute decline or gain. Regional specificities are often sacrificed to sweeping generalizations, which are made in respect both of routes and networks of merchants

---

6 Roy, *The Economic History of India*, 263. Roy qualifies this by adding that destruction was at the level of long distance; short-distance routes changed very little, as they attracted very little government investment. Ibid., 263.
7 Mukul Mukherjee, 'Railway and their Impact on Bengal's Economy, 1870–1920', *IESHR* 17, no. 2 (1981).
8 Ian Derbyshire, 'Economic Change and the Railways in North India, 1860–1914', *MAS* 21, no. 3 (1987). A previous study on the same region suggested a directly proportionate relationship between increase in trade and commerce on the one hand and growth in transportation on the other. Dharma Bhanu, 'Economic Condition of the People in the North-Western Provinces, 1830–1860', *Indian History Congress Proceedings*, 19th session, 1956.
9 See John Hurd, 'Railways' in *CEHI*; Roy, *The Economic History of India*, 264–5.
10 Ellen McDonald Gumperz, 'City-Hinterland Relations and the Development of a Regional Elite in Nineteenth Century Bombay' in Kerr, ed., *Railways in Modern India*, 113.

and traders. In his review of works on the nineteenth-century economy, G. Balachandran has warned us: 'While the nineteenth-century integration of regional economies into a putative world economy weakened or displaced some agents, such as most famously the bankers to the East India Company in Bengal, smaller agents from less exposed centres were less adversely affected.'[11]

The framework of realignment also helps us gain a better understanding of the nature of the market integration of varied commodities. In the case of the textile industry, as Tirthankar Roy has elsewhere argued, the growth in transportation opened up hitherto inaccessible markets to imported clothes (which is one nationalist critique of the railways destroying traditional industry) but better connectivity also gradually integrated markets for handloom clothes thereby stimulating their internal trade.[12] Similar is the contention of Konard Specker in his study of Madras handlooms in the nineteenth century. He argues: 'Finally, the same railroads which hastened the penetration of imported textiles into Indian market assured these Kornadu products a market in the whole of south India from Madras to Cape Comorin.'[13] In the case of local manufactures, Roy has also shown that by the late nineteenth and early twentieth centuries, the railways allowed brass, for example, to enter into a market that 'had probably grown since the advent of railways'. Among other factors, he says, by providing cheaper transportation the railways created greater demand by integrating the markets for brass products.[14] But in other regions, the effects of the railways were adverse. Sumit Guha, in his study of the Central Provinces' textile industry, points out that the availability of British imported textiles in Nagpur city increased with the advent of the railways. As a result, 'Nagpur weavers lost the partial protection afforded by the high cost of inland transport.'[15] Therefore, this chapter does not suggest that the railways did not affect the nature of existing industries but it does aim to understand this shift as a web of complex adaptations that followed such encounters and contestations. In evaluating the effects of transport, one needs to be commodity- and region-specific.

The case of contestation was not only restricted to older commodity production centres and the people involved with them, and to the easy and fast transportation of goods by the new instrument of steam technology. This contestation extended to competing means of communication themselves. This chapter does not intend to underplay the fact that the

---

11 Balachandran, 'Introduction' in Balachandran, ed., *India and the World Economy*, 28.
12 Tirthankar Roy, 'Introduction', in Roy, ed., *Cloth and Commerce: Textiles in Colonial India* (New Delhi, Thousand Oaks and London, 1996), 22.
13 Specker, 'Madras Handlooms in the Nineteenth Century', in Roy, ed., *Cloth and Commerce*, 194.
14 Such benefits of the railways were often accompanied by spatial relocations. For regional shifts in brass manufacturing centres in Bombay see Roy, 'Home Markets and Artisans in Colonial India: A Study of Brass-Ware', *MAS* 30, no. 2 (1996): esp. 366, 362–3, 368.
15 Sumit Guha, 'The Handloom Industry of Central India: 1825–1950', in Roy, ed., *Cloth and Commerce*, 222. However, as Guha has pointed out, railways alone did not worsen the conditions of Nagpur weavers. Their dependence on handspun yarn and the competition they faced from the Indian mill-machine yarn was also responsible. Otherwise, he says, in the weaving sector, there was expansion during the 1870s and 1880s. See 226–9.

railways became the central organizing feature of the communication grid that led to the decline in the importance of some of the existing means of communication. For instance, in spite of the fact that the GTR was the 'saviour-line' during the 1857 events that helped the colonial state regain its losses, the state's communication policy shifted in favour of the railways.[16] The first roads to be constructed were those that connected with the railways. The 1879 Inspection Report of the Hazaribagh division of the GTR said: 'The work done on the GTR is disgraceful, wasteful, and useless.'[17] This decline was well attested to by local officials who complained about the loss of the GTR's 'military grandeur'. A. V. Palmer, the magistrate of Gaya, deplored the poor condition of the GTR, saying that, 'The railway may be more speedy but it must not be forgotten that the railway is liable to be torn up and rendered useless in a day, that the Grand Trunk Road must always remain the most important chain of communication between the metropolis and the NWP.'[18] However, the story of relative decline in importance of any particular road was not restricted to the railways alone; the gradual decline of the NMR once the GTR had become the main line of communication is a case in point. In other words, the displacement of one line of communication is not necessarily a function of a 'better' technology of the other, but part of broader political choices, economic investments and cultural practices.

The view of contestation apparently borrows from an even larger debate on the nature of the world economy in the nineteenth century. The conventional understanding is of the contestation of the 'dual economy': foreign capital and institutions posited against 'native'/Indian institutions in which the latter finally yields to the former.[19] This approach, however, has been challenged from different viewpoints and from different positions. First, it has been shown that eighteenth-century India was 'highly mobile and by no means tied to its village communities from time out of mind'.[20] Therefore, native capital, enterprise and the expanse of circulation was extremely vibrant before the establishment of colonial rule. Although Morris D. Morris's theses that colonial rule in nineteenth-century India was not

---

16 I have dealt with the issue of 'communication' and the 1857 'Mutiny' in greater detail in Nitin Sinha, 'Forged Linkages and the "Spectre" of 1857: A Few Instances from Bihar', in Sharmistha Gooptu and Boria Majumdar, eds, *Revisiting 1857: History, Myth, Memory* (New Delhi, 2007).

17 GOB, PWD, GB (Communications), B Proceedings, file no. 14 of February 1879, *RRWRD*.

18 *MOR*, 168.

19 Again in the case of communication one can see these views reflected in the writing of Henry Dodwell. For him, the railways invaded the village community. It brought Indian villagers 'into contact with things that they would naturally never have heard of'. In the Indian context, this invasion was sudden and abrupt because 'the English country-folks only approached the railway by the easy stages of the wagon and the mail coach but in India it descended without nearly so much preparation'. Thus, a clear binary of self-sustained village economy on the one hand and railways (as an invasive force) on the other was set up. Henry Dodwell, 'Economic Transition in India', *The Economic Journal* 20, no. 80 (1910): 614–18. The quotation is from page 618.

20 Some of the works that comprehensively summarize the debate and give a convincing critique of the 'dual economy' are Rajat Kanta Ray, 'Asian Capital in the Age of European Domination: The Rise of Bazaar', *MAS*, 29, 3, 1995; David Washbrook, 'Progress and Problems: South Asian Economic and Social History', *MAS*, 22, 1, 1988; M. D. Morris, 'Towards a Reinterpretation of Nineteenth-Century Indian Economic History', *Journal of Economic History* 23, no. 4 (1963).

necessarily exploitative and destructive still holds true for some scholars, the basis of his argument has been considerably revised. For him, eighteenth-century India represented an era of 'political instability' with 'insignificant commerce'.[21] Historiographically, this view is no longer valid.[22] Second, most scholars have accepted that by the mid-nineteenth century the colonial regime was more effectively transforming Indian economy than hitherto. Yet it did not completely 'destroy' 'native' capital or, as Rajat Kanta Ray has shown, the money and financial markets and institutions. Third, in his estimate of the mutual struggle for control and survival between the world system of international trade and the world of rural localized trade, Neeladri Bhattacharya has concluded that the former could not have incorporated the latter just by eliminating it.[23]

My arguments take clues from these studies and their conclusions to suggest that the nature of interaction between the 'new communication networks' (that is, railways) and existing ones should be assessed by going beyond the framework of competition. Of course, adaptation came with resistance, but an overemphasis on the railways has prevented us from looking at the role of other networks, which not only existed but also contributed to the growth of commodity circulation. After all, and even at the risk of an overstatement, Morris's argument that the 'railways tapped only restricted portions of the country, and their impact on the economy was limited by the unwillingness to develop feeder lines' cannot be dismissed altogether.[24]

Politics of Funds, Alignments and Priorities

In 1858–59, of the total expenditure made under the heading 'New Works', Rs. 2,760,000 was invested on military works and Rs. 510,000 on works of a civil nature. Much of this was expended on providing better halting grounds on the GTR (especially on the second division of the road that passed through Bihar), on improving barrack amenities, on making bungalows for officers in charge of supplies at halting stations and, not least, on making a commissariat station.[25] A few years earlier, too, the condition of the camping grounds was a subject of concern among officials.[26] Following this, sheds were erected at halting stations in 1859.[27] In the following year three toll houses at Nooneah, Muggrah and Burhee were completed on the GTR, and two more were under construction at Doorgowtee (Durgawati) and Baroon.[28] A sudden but short-lived rise in the investment

---

21 Morris, 'Towards a Reinterpretation', 610. Low agricultural productivity and insignificant commerce in the eighteenth century are the building blocks on which Morris suggests that the nineteenth-century India under the colonial regime was not necessarily exploitative, as there was improvement in both the sectors.
22 See Washbrook, 'Progress and Problems'.
23 Neeladri Bhattacharya, 'Predicaments of Mobility: Peddlers and Itinerants in Nineteenth-Century Northwestern India', in Markovits et al., *Society and Circulation*, 164–5.
24 Morris, 'Towards a Reinterpretation', 616.
25 *RCE*, 1858–59, see 1–13.
26 'From the Commissioner of Revenue to the Secretary, Government of Bengal', 25 August 1854, *PCRS*, vol. 455, 1854.
27 *GOR*, 142.
28 *RCE*, 1859–60, 18.

made on the GTR was the result of the experience of the 1857 event. Gradually the share of investment started declining. The GTR remained a prime line but only for places such as Lohardagga, Hazaribagh and so on, situated in south Bihar. The mid-Bihar region, for instance places around the River Soane, was now linked with the railways through direct feeder lines. This was a change in policy from that followed in the early 1850s, where roads were planned to connect places such as Tiloothoo, situated on the banks of the Soane, of the same region (mid-Bihar), with the GTR.[29] But even amidst this shift regional variations persisted.

The following details would make the pattern evident. Surveys continued to be conducted to connect places in south Bihar with the GTR. One proposed line ran from Ranchi to Govindpur, on the GTR; a second from Hazaribagh to Bagodar, again on the GTR.[30] Until now improvement of GTR-centric connectivity was also deemed important to improve trade. For instance, it was proposed that the existing track between Chatra and Chauparan (on the GTR) should be converted 'into a good road for the wheeled traffic as it was a 'very important line of traffic'.[31] But the condition of the road remained deplorable. Works on bridges and causeways, for example, only progressed with much delay. In 1861, the PWD of the Bengal government was asked to amend existing defects on the road. The areas of major concern were the bad state of the road, the condition of the ferries on the unbridged rivers, and the difficulty in securing coolie labour attached to the ferries.[32] The inspecting officer remarked that he saw 'no obvious progress since 1854' when he last passed along the road. Partly this was explained by the suspension of works between 1856 and 1859 due to the 1857 'Mutiny' and uprisings in south Bihar and partly because of the heavy floods of 1861. Reportedly, almost 5,000 people were stranded for three days on the road in the month of October when nearly all the rivers of the region were flowing high.[33]

In 1861 the postmaster of Benares, Mr Dillon, also made a survey of the mail traffic between Raneegunge and Benares and voiced strong resentment about the ferry system provided on the rivers intersecting the GTR. He reported that there was just 'one old rickety country boat' to be shared on three rivers. Travellers sat on the coach boxes of their carriages, which were driven by coolies. Mr Dillon quipped: 'Fancy ladies have to resort to such measures on the principal road of India.'[34] Good strong flat-bottomed boats were substituted for bad native boats, but in general the condition of the road remained bad.[35] In the Ramghur division the repairs were so badly executed that the executive engineer conceded that 'the portion of road in this division is at present in a

---

29 'From the Commissioner of Revenue, Patna to the Secretary to the Government of Bengal', 1 June 1854, *PCRS*, vol. 455, 1854.
30 *RCE*, 1860–61, 17–18.
31 GOB, PWD, GB, proceedings 140–42, January 1862, *RRWRD*.
32 GOB, PWD, GB, proceedings 71–3, January 1862, *RRWRD*.
33 'Report from Captain J. Mead, Executive Engineer 2nd Division GTR to SE, Behar Circle, Lower Provinces', 26 October 1861, ibid.
34 'Extract from the Report from Mr Dillon', 9 December 1861, GOB, PWD, GB, proceedings 110–11, January 1862.
35 *RCE*, 1862–63, 39.

worse state than I have ever known of it'. He accepted that it would take more than one year to repair the neglect of the previous season.[36]

The gap between intended improvement and practical ineffectiveness is self-evident. Officers found it easy to blame the bad condition of the road either on disruptions caused by natural disasters such as floods or by unstable political conditions. Nevertheless, there were serious structural and institutional factors involved too. Not only was the GTR said to be in a bad state of repair but similar complaints about other roads of imperial status were also made. One of the main excuses cited for not getting works finished on time was the shortage of labour and lack of funds. Thus, reportedly, the progress on the Hazaribagh–Burhee road was not satisfactory because of a labour shortage.[37] The opening of another road, the Ganges–Darjeeling road on 1 July 1861, was delayed because of a shortage of skilled labour.[38] The labour problem was often accompanied by difficulty in procuring materials such as bricks. Even in a place nearer to Calcutta, great difficulty was experienced in finding brick makers in sufficient numbers.[39] Absenteeism during religious festivals and agricultural cycles was considered the prime reason behind the labour shortage. The coolies on the Ganges–Darjeeling road worked in the cold weather when agricultural activities were minimal and avoided returning to work in the hot season, which corresponded with increased agricultural activity.[40] The Patna branch road also suffered from a lack of labour and carriages, both of which reportedly were 'exceedingly scarce in the district'. Every attempt to meet the demand was met only with partial success.[41]

However, only a few officials were able to identify the effect of railway construction work in creating a shortage of labour for working on roads. For instance, the simultaneous construction of the Bowsee–Bhagalpur road and the Bhagalpur railway line and station made it difficult to keep masons working on the road because they found it more lucrative to work on the railways (at Rs. 25–30 per cubic feet) than to finish the road masonry at a lesser rate.[42] The shortage in supervisory hands was another contributory factor. In 1879, in the Bhagalpur district, only Rs. 5,195 was spent out of Rs. 40,254 earmarked for road construction and repair. The reason for the funds lying unutilized was the inability of the superintending engineer to get through all the projects. Later, an additional person was appointed.[43] Under-utilization of funds was a feature of other districts as well. In the season 1878–79, Chota Nagpur division was allotted Rs. 107,376 but the amount utilized was the meagre sum of Rs. 31,225. The ratio of amount expended on 'original works' compared with sums invested on 'repair works' was lesser, signifying that out of the expended sum the under-utilization of funds applied relatively more to road building than to repairing.[44] Sometimes, the

---

36 *RCE*, 1861–62, 37.
37 *RCE*, 1860–61, 14; *RCE*, 1859–60, 80.
38 *RCE*, 1860–61, 68–9.
39 Ibid., 15.
40 *RCE*, 1858–59, 68–9.
41 *RCE*, 1861–62, 38.
42 GOB, PWD, GB, proceedings 168–70, January 1862, *RRWRD*.
43 GOB, PWD, GB, (Local Commns), part vii of file no. 14 of June 1879, *RRWRD*.
44 GOB, PWD, GB (Local Communications), part v of file no. 14 of June 1879, *RRWRD*.

local committees' power was restricted; this was the reason cited by the Lohardagga officer behind his district's Road Cess Committee's ability to bring in 'alterations [only] in a petty way, year by year'.[45] But this was largely true for a 'poor region', as the commissioner of Chota Nagpur had described the area; for, in districts such as Purneah, Bhagalpur and Monghyr, works progressed satisfactorily and reportedly 'the cess-payers appreciate[d] that they are gaining real, useful and practical advantage from what they pay'.[46]

Internal differences regarding matters of engineering and the organization of work was another reason that hampered work. Frequent complaints about 'unscientific alignments', 'blunders of amateur engineering' and 'unnecessary expenditure' were made. The management was lax, as was evident from a letter written by the superintending engineer who complained that no work specifications were given to subordinates or to contractors.[47]

To overcome the problem of labour shortage the contract system was started. In the initial years this method was found to be useful and was appreciated. It was said: 'the class of men, whom it is most desirable to encourage as contractors, are beginning to awaken to a conviction of its advantages and profits'.[48] However, soon the system presented its own set of problems, the most disturbing of which was the supply of inferior quality materials. As noted by G. Campbell, lieutenant governor of Bengal:

> By far the most frequent and flagrant of public works failures seem to be due to bad lime; it is in this respect that almost all our works seem to be so immeasurably inferior to those of our native predecessors. Most of the failures are probably due to fraud on the part of contractors, & c. but still the failure of our lime is so general and contrasts in so marked a way with the excellent lime used for old native works, that it seems to me that we either do not or cannot make good lime or cannot afford it, and the subject requires the most anxious consideration.[49]

Supply of bad-quality stones was also mentioned. The problem seemed so menacing that the superintending engineer in fact proposed to punish or dismiss the erring overseers and subordinates.[50] However, the contract system continued, as is evident from the sources of the period of the late 1870s;[51] also from the growing economic prosperity of certain castes such as Noniyas, who earlier were involved in the saltpetre trade, but

---

45 'Letter from Lieut. W. Samuells, Deputy Commissioner, Lohardagga to Commissioner, Chota Nagpur', 14 May 1885, GOB, PWD, GB (Communications), file no. 6 of March 1885, *RRWRD*.
46 GOB, PWD, Road Cess (Accounts), file no. 27 of February 1885, *RRWRD*.
47 'Letter from SE to Commissioner, Chota Nagpur', 6 March 1885, GOB, PWD, GB (Communications), file no. 6 of March 1885, *RRWRD*. He was referring to certain deviations made on the Ranchi–Daltongunj road, which cost Rs. 5,000 but was later abandoned.
48 *RCE*, 1862–63, 32.
49 'Minute by the Hon'ble Lt Governor of Bengal, G. Campbell', 16 August 1872, *PRPWD*, 1871–72.
50 GOB, PWD, GB (Communications), file no. 6 of March 1885, *RRWRD*.
51 GOB, PWD, GB (Local Communications), part v of file no. 14 of June 1879, *RRWRD*.

in the late nineteenth century had 'acquired considerable wealth through contracting with the British government for earthworks, brick-making and other "traditional" tasks associated with their caste'.[52] There seems to be some modification attempted in this field: in the Chota Nagpur division, zamindars were engaged for supplying materials but this too proved a 'failure'. The contractors had their own set of complaints; they charged the overseers for not paying their dues and arrears.[53] Overall, the state officials failed to perfect the system of contractorship and devise a working relationship between labourer, contractor and overseer.

The next important factor behind 'bad roads' of this period was lack of funds. On the amount allocated for road works, the 1866–67 *Annual Report of the Bengal Presidency* reported: 'Large as these sums are they go but a small way towards keeping pace with the development of the country, and they barely meet the most urgent wants of the provinces under the Bengal government.'[54] In the following year, the need of greater funds for local roads was also raised.[55] The magistrate of Gaya candidly accepted this fact and the impending result:

> The allotment is so small and there are so many roads which are little better than tracts that the only result of distributing money over the roads would be simply to fritter it away without producing any material benefit and under these circumstances it is much better among the expenditure as to provide for its application where it is most needed and to ensure at least one road and that the most important in the district being made really passable for traffic.[56]

To overcome this problem, local merchants were often encouraged to contribute funds for making roads. For instance, when the railways came to Patna, the need of a good road from the railway station to the main market area of the city (chauk) was felt. The government insisted on having it built by the railway company, but the latter refused. At this, an attempt was made to convince local merchants to contribute to the funds; this was equally unsuccessful. As a result the plan was shelved.[57] In general, although the earlier investment trend had reversed, that is, more was now expended on civil than on military works, the coming of the railways at virtually the same time as funding needs for road construction increased, influenced the way these funds were distributed. In some of the districts of Bihar, particularly those situated on the banks of the Ganga, the condition of the roads was already reportedly bad in the 1840s–50s, implying that the politics of funding as it emerged due to the coming of the railways was not an originary

---

52 Catherine Servan-Schreiber, 'Tellers of Tales, Sellers of Tales: Bhojpuri Peddlers in Northern India', in Markovits et al., *Society and Circulation*, 280.
53 GOB, PWD, GB (Communications), file no. 6 of March 1885, *RRWRD*.
54 *Annual Report on the Administration of the Bengal Presidency* (Calcutta, 1866–67), 82. [Henceforth *AARB*.]
55 *AARB*, 1868–69, 312.
56 *GOR*, 156.
57 Railway Bengal Proceedings (RBP), proceedings 34–42, September 1863, P/163/31, AAC, British Library, London.

but a contributory factor. This, however, does not overrule the fact that broadly the development of roadways now depended on how far they functioned as routes connecting with the railways. The need to promote India's external export trade, and the deep interest of British capitalists in railway investment in India, was too powerful to allow road construction to have an independent space in policymaking. At best, roads were seen as subservient to the railways. However, I wish to emphasize the difference between roads assuming a *subservient* position in the colonial policy and the role they still played (in spite of the existence of railways) in commercial exchanges, a point which is often ignored in standard historiography. It is precisely at this point of divergence – between stated and intended policy on the one hand and the actual historical use of the roads – that the description of 'nested' networks given in the previous chapter fits in well.

As shown in Chapter 2, the railways promised to open up the interiors. Thus stated the opening line of R. M. Stephenson's Report prepared in 1844: 'The development of the resources of British India had engaged my attention for a period considerably antecedent to my visiting that country [India].'[58] Further, he noted:

> The extent to which *in the several districts* in which we look forward to see this means of conveyance generally introduced, the *cultivation* of indigo-opium, sugar, rice and grain, are cultivated, and *whence* saltpetre, shell, lac, drugs, minerals, and spices are brought, and for which the return at present received in salt, and European goods are so considerable, will be fully entered upon in the consideration of each particular line…[59]

Bearing in mind the italicized words, we can safely assume that Stephenson wanted the railways to go into the production areas 'where indigo-opium and sugar are cultivated' or from 'where saltpetre is brought'. The economic geography of Bihar, as discussed in previous chapters, leaves no doubt that north Bihar was the leading production zone of indigo, opium and saltpetre, the three main export commodities of the colonial economy. By 1810 there were twenty-five indigo factories in Tirhut and no less than 10,000 maunds were sent to Calcutta annually.[60] Purneah was also a leading producer of indigo. Almost seventy-five factories existed there at the time of Buchanan's survey.[61] Saltpetre was another important product of the Tirhut region. Of three main factories, two, Singhea and Mow, were in Tirhut; the third, Chapra, was in the Saran district. The principal trade centres of the Tirhut district were Lalganj, Hajipur, Muzaffarpur, Darbhanga, Dalsingserai, Beguserai, Rosera and Teghra.[62] Saran was the leading producer of saltpetre. The usual mode of communication was the Gangetic route. Goods were first sent down to Patna from any of the three rivers, the Gandak, the Dewah (Gogra) and the Buri Gandak, and were then sent down to Calcutta.

---

58 'Letter from R. M. Stephenson along with his Report on the Practicability and Advantages of Railways in British India to Wilberforce Bird', 26 November 1844, *SD*, doc. no. 41, 83.
59 Ibid, 86–7 (emphasis added).
60 Ghosal, 'Tirhut at the End of', 373–4.
61 Shyam Behari Singh, 'Economic Conditions (1757–1858)', in K. K. Datta, with Jatashankar Jha, ed., *Comprehensive History of Bihar*, vol. 3, pt 1 (Patna, 1976), 461.
62 Ibid., 375.

Complete unanimity had existed among the early promoters that the railway should connect Calcutta with the NWP. However, differences persisted over the actual course of the route. Stephenson had suggested six routes but soon the discussion centred around two only. One was the 'direct route' from Calcutta to Mirzapur passing alongside the GTR, the other was the circuitous route running along the Ganga. Of the 2,75,000 tons of merchandise of sugar, cotton and salt transported between Calcutta and the NWP, only about 20,000 tons were carried by land; the rest was sent by boats on the River Ganga.[63] However, Mr Simms, who was sent to India in 1846 by the Court of Directors to ascertain the most practical route, suggested the direct line. This line was to run parallel to the GTR, but, to make it more effective, he suggested making four branch lines; the first, from a point near Burdwan to Rajmahal; the second, from five miles eastward of Sherghatty passing northward through Gaya, Patna and Dinapore; the third, from the valley of the Soane to the coalfields westward of Rohtasgarh; and the fourth, from nine miles east of Chunar to Rajghat opposite Benares. The last one, he thought, was not immediately necessary.[64]

Knowing that the Gangetic line had been suggested earlier, Simms argued that his proposed direct line would have a more 'ultimate favourable result' by not only capturing the Gangetic trade through branch lines but also by 'bringing forward a country now much neglected and which contains mineral wealth and possesses great capabilities'.[65] Although no direct line was suggested for the region of north Bihar, he assumed that the branch lines to Patna and Rajmahal would accommodate and attract the trade of regions such as Purneah, Malda, Rangpur, Dinajpur and Tirhut. Of course, the least he suggested for this region was to construct terminal stations opposite Patna and Rajmahal on the northern banks of the Ganga.[66] Simms's proposed line was opposed on the basis that it did not pass through a single town of importance or emporium of trade. The debate over the exact line to be followed continued over the next few years. J. Bourne, an engineer in the East Indian Railway Company (EIRC) favoured the direct line.[67] Another view was held by W. P. Andrew who supported the idea of connecting Calcutta with Rajmahal by rail and then utilizing the services of an 'improved class of steam vessels' from Rajmahal to Mirzapur on the Ganga, which 'would be free of physical impediments of weighty character'.[68] The idea was to supersede the difficulties of navigation in the lower part of Bengal where 'the Ganges split up in different channels and streams' making goods transit extremely hazardous.

---

63 Bourne, *Railways in India*, 49–50. The figure of land share in trade as given by one Macintyre and Company was also between 10,000 and 22,000 tons. See 'Reply from G. Ashburner', in *SD*, doc. no. 25, 49.
64 F. W. Simms, 'Report on the Practicability of Introducing Railways in India', in *SD*, doc. no. 55, 147–9.
65 Ibid., 149.
66 Ibid., 144–7.
67 Bourne, *Railways in India*.
68 W. P. Andrew, *Railway in Bengal (Being the Substance of a Report addressed to the Chairman of the East India Company in 1849)* (London, 1853).

Andrew's proposal to utilize two different modes of transport needs further elaboration. Mr D. W. Leod, chairman of the Great Western Bengal Railway Company (GWBRC), of which Mr Andrew was a member, was also the chairman of the GISNC.[69] It was this association that led Andrew to advocate only a partial construction of railways, complemented by the use of steamers. The proponents of the direct line rejected this idea on the grounds that 'if the railway is to have the impediment of an intermediate land carriage, and an intermediate transhipment – as any severed piece of the line must have – it is impossible that a competition with the river can be maintained with success, and without the river traffic the line must be a failure'.[70] Andrew, on the other hand, forcefully resisted this idea by referring to 'insurmountable physical obstacles' that the direct line would encounter. The 'pestilential jungle-covered hills', he argued, were not the only impediments; the line would allegedly suffer from a 'want of population in 250 miles of the regions to be traversed'.[71] Bourne and Andrew represented the views of two competing companies, the EIRC and the GWBRC. The latter, formed in mid-1845, was the biggest rival of the EIRC. GWBRC's proposal to build a railway line from Calcutta to Rajmahal was based on a proposal from the 1830s to dig a canal from Calcutta 'to tap indigo and sugar production of Rajmahal'.[72] None of these plans eventually succeeded. The direct line was given up in favour of the Gangetic circuitous route, based on the conclusion that the railways could only capture the river trade if they ran alongside the river. Thus the potential commercial benefits of steam technology were dependent on its proximity to the old medium of communication. The following map shows the proposed lines; the thick line on the right side represents the GWBRC's proposal, the thin lines the proposal made by Simms. Plate 27 shows the actual lines; the line on the extreme right shows the 'loop line' – originally this was the direct line completed in 1862 but it became the 'loop line' after the construction of the 'main line' in 1871 (shown by the middle line on the map). The dotted line on the extreme left shows the 'grand chord line' built in 1906. The dark black line shows the Ganga.

---

69 'Letter from D. W. Leod, Chairman of the Great Western of Bengal Railway Company to the Court of Directors of the EIC', 9 February 1847, *SD*, doc. no. 71, 210–11.
70 Bourne, *Railways in India*, 13.
71 Andrew, *Railway in Bengal*, 11–12.
72 See 'Note of Letter from the Great Western Bengal Railway Company to the Court of Directors', 21 June 1845, *SD*, doc. no. 50, 128. Even after their amalgamation in 1847(?), differences continued between the two companies. Contemporary magazines such as the *Railway Chronicle* or the *Morning Chronicle* reported stories of mutual accusations. After the slump of the late 1840s in the London capital market, the differences became bitter. Andrew raised the question of the financial insolvency of the EIRC, to which many shareholders responded by asking the EIRC to make the financial details of the Company public. Because of the ongoing slump, the government by October 1847 reduced the amount of deposit to £100,000. The continuing slump forced it to further reduce the amount to £60,000, which the EIRC managed to pay in November 1848. See W. P. Andrew, *A letter to the Chairman of the Honourable East India Company, with Extracts from the public papers and Remarks* (London, 1848). See Thorner, *Investment in Empire*, for a lucid treatment on these negotiations.

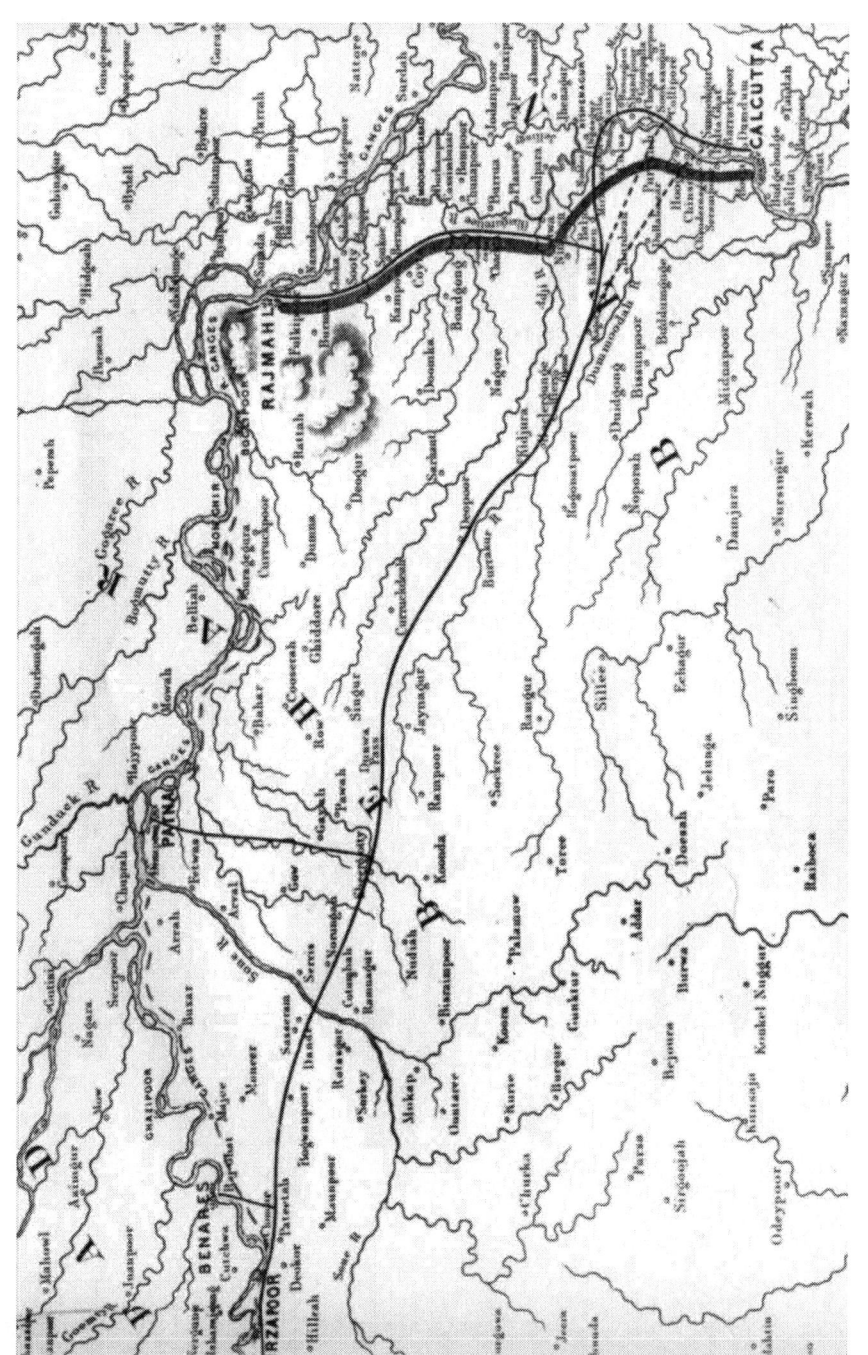

Plate 26. Map showing the proposed railway lines in Bengal presidency

© British Library Board, Bourne, *Indian Railways*.

Plate 27. First railway lines in Bengal presidency

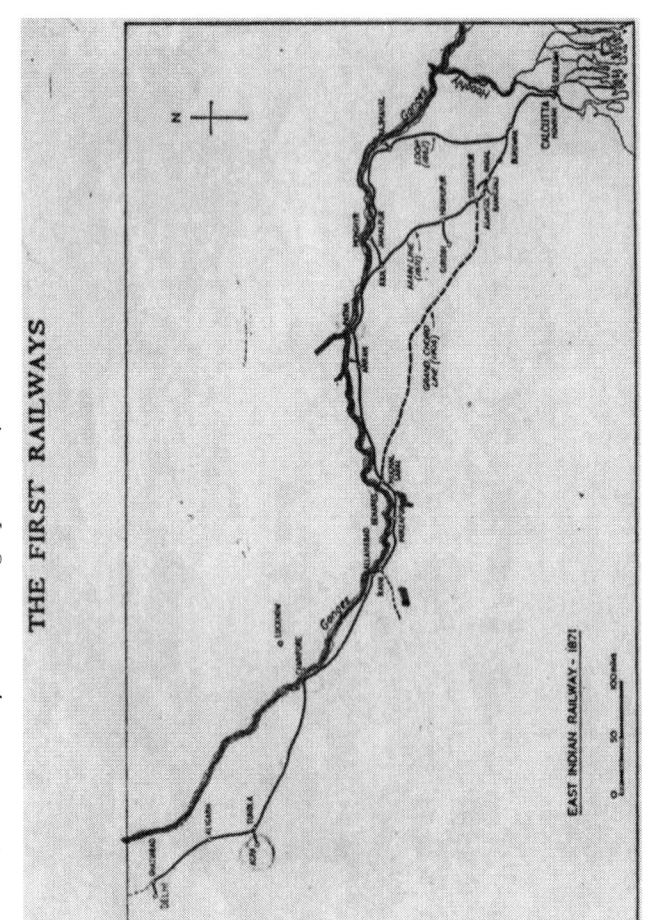

© British Library Board, J. N. Westwood, *Railways of India*, page 19.

'Lateral Communication' and Trade

The following table shows the opening of the EIR with dates.

Table 5. Opening of the EIR

From	To	When opened	No. of miles
Howrah	Hooghly	15 August 1854	23
Hooghly	Pundooah	1 September 1854	14
Pundooah	Raneegunge	3 February 1855	83
Burdwan junction	River Adjai	3 October 1858	20
River Adjai	Synthia	3 September 1859	25
Synthia	Rajmahal	15 October 1860	82
Undal	Baboosole	1 May 1861	3
Teenpahar junction	Bhaugulpoor	1 November 1861	69
Bhaugulpoor	Jumalpoor	10 February 1862	33
Jumalpoor	Monghyr	10 April 1862	5
Jumalpoor	Dinapoor road	17 November 1862	113
Dinapore road	End of Bengal div.	22 December 1862	74
		Total	544

Source: 'From G. Turnbull, Chief Engineer, to the Agent, EIRC', 19 December 1862, RBP, prodg 44, January 1863, P/163/30.

With railways came the policy of road classification into imperial or local. The idea was to 'build roads in a direction which will enable them to feed rather than to compete with the newer means of communication'.[73] The leading feature of the imperial road system was 'to provide one main line of road, at least in each district, which shall pass through the principal town or station and be continuous, that is in connection with the main line of the next district'.[74] To start with, trunk roads and their branches formed part of the projected system. However, imperial branch roads not only provided road-to-road connection but also road-to-railway linkages. On the other hand, railway feeders were defined as 'system of local roads, as feeders which shall place all the most important towns and marts of the districts in communication with railways'.[75] The funds for imperial roads came from the central government; the funds for local roads and feeders initially came from ferry fund collections, road tolls and other local funds. It was, nevertheless, soon realized that local funds were not adequate. Therefore, it was decided to divert some of the imperial funds to construct railway feeders. The reason given was that, without these 'lateral communications', railways would not be able to take advantage of the rich tracts of the country.[76] Gradually, local funds were confined almost entirely to maintaining and

---

73 *Imperial Gazetteer*, 406.
74 *AARB*, 1860–61, 58.
75 Ibid., 60.
76 GOB, PWD, GB, proceedings 20–26, January 1862, *RRWRD*.

improving ordinary district station roads (connecting with the railways) and other works of a local nature.[77]

In Bihar, the main imperial road was the GTR. Next in importance were the imperial branch roads. Among them, one was from Burhee on the GTR to Hazaribagh; the second, from Dhobee on the GTR via Gaya, Patna and Hajipur to Muzaffarpur; the third, from Baroon on the GTR to Bihta (a railway station on the EIR); the fourth from Dehri (on the GTR) to Arrah (on the EIR); and the fifth from Bhagalpur (on the EIR) to Soree. Thus we can clearly see that most of the imperial branch roads were designed to connect places on the GTR with the EIR. The purpose was to attract the trade of the GTR to the railways. In north Bihar there were two imperial branch roads. One was the Darjeeling trunk road (from Cargola via Purneah to Darjeeling); and the second, the Tirhut trunk road (starting from opposite the Monghyr railway station to Batsura via Muzaffarpur, Motihari and Bettiah).[78] In addition to these, there were six railway feeders under construction.[79]

As pointed out earlier, finishing work on those roads that connected to the railways got priority. One such case was with the Bhagalpur–Soree imperial line. The fifty-four-mile long southern section of this road was metalled for thirty-two miles and sanction received and materials collected to start work on making the wooden bridges. Soon the work was stopped as it was decided to complete the northern section first, from Bowsee to Bhagalpur, because this section connected with the railways.[80] The hierarchy of roads also meant hierarchized management. The imperial roads were supervised directly by the PWD. For instance, the Muzaffarpur–Hajipur road, which was thirty-four miles in length, was transferred from the supervision of local officers to the PWD 'with a view to its being kept up as an Imperial road and railway feeder, connecting Patna with the fertile districts north of the Ganges'.[81] Similarly, a road from the GTR through Behar to a railway station in the Patna district was transferred to the PWD for the purposes of making it an imperial line of communication.[82] The policy of communication had moved a long way from the 1820s–30s. If we recall Nisbet's words, we should realize that as late as the 1830s colonial officials were pinning their hopes on zamindars to play a significant role in road management. In the three decades that followed, it became clear to the government that it had itself to devise a well-defined structure of communication management. The picture which then emerged was that of shared responsibility in which imperial roads were maintained by the PWD and the local ones mainly by the FFCs.

At this time, several other roads were surveyed with a view to connecting places to the EIR. A preliminary comparative survey was made on two roads, one from Baroon, on the right bank of the Soane, to the EIR at Bihta, and a second from Dehree, on the left bank of the Soane, to Arrah.[83] The idea was to connect the towns situated on the Soane with the EIR. The former was approved as an imperial road, thus requiring further surveys and estimates. A survey and estimate was also under preparation for a road from Burhait, in the

---

77 *AARB*, 1863–64, 67.
78 *AARB*, 1860–61. Information taken from the map annexed in the report and account, 58–9.
79 Ibid., 60, 78.
80 *RCE*, 1859–60, 17.
81 *RCE*, 1860–61, 17.
82 *RCE*, 1861–62, 174.
83 Ibid., 17.

Santhal hills, to Bahawah station on the EIR. A preliminary survey and report was made on the road from Monghyr to Muzaffarpur, and for a line of road from Barh on the EIR, northward towards Darbhanga.[84] Construction was started on the Giridih road to connect the Giridih EIR station to Doomree on the GTR. The Hazaribagh–Bagodar road, being the continuation of the Giridih road, further helped connecting Hazaribagh to the EIR.[85]

A few of the roads listed above were constructed to connect regions of south Bihar with the railways that ran alongside the Ganga. For regions nearer to the river and the railway line, for instance, at Shahabad, a scheme of the 'Ganges Fair-Weather Railway Feeders' was adopted. According to this scheme, 'the old tracks from the Ganges that had fallen into disuse from time beyond record were to be opened and connected with the railway stations by modifying them and changing their directions here and there'.[86] It is important to recall here that most of the roads, which these reports claimed to have *constructed*, had existed earlier. The change, of course, was in the technology and conditions of road building. For instance, the Hazaribagh–Bagodar road had existed as a fair-weather road but it was now to be upgraded as a first-class line or an imperial branch road, meaning that it was to be metalled.[87] The Soree–Bhagalpur road had also existed but it was improved as a metalled road. Two roads, one from Baroon to Bihta and another from Dehree to Arrah were also old tracks, but by the 1860s were in a 'dilapidated condition' with a few masonry drains and no bridges.[88] The best example of neglect comes from the southwest region of the Gaya district. This region earlier had a flourishing trade not only in cotton manufactures but also in commodities such as grain, ghee and silk with places such as Palamow, Sirgoojah and Mirzapore (in the Nagpur district). As noted earlier, Daudnagar on the River Soane was an important centre of this trade. It was, however, asserted that:

> These roads have been allowed to fade away off of the earth nothing have [sic] been done to keep up. Nothing was ever done to a place what had been allowed to die out. In the beginning of 1866 there were actually no roads in the Arungabad subdivision save only the GTR. In 1866 a road was marked out (but not made), by a ditch one foot wide and deep. Excepting this, I can hear of no expenditure whatever at any time for any roads in the S. W. of the district till 1868.[89]

We will take up the case of the GTR to see some of the effects of the realignment that happened because of the railways. Although from time to time money was spent on its upkeep,[90] overall investment was inadequate. The toll rates were apparently too high to

---

84 Ibid., 18.
85 *PRPWD*, 1871–72, 21.
86 *RCE*, 1861–62, 177.
87 *PRPWD*, 1871–72, 21.
88 *GOR*, 144.
89 Letter dated 15 June 1869. The author is not known but most probably it was written by the magistrate of Gaya. *GOR*, 303–5. Quote from page 305.
90 In the early 1860s, extensive repair works were undertaken 'owing to the heavily laden cotton carts that had cut the road'. The proceeds from tolls went into improving the road. *AARB*, 1863–64, 63.

be of any use. Given the ruined condition of one of the bridges, the Lilajun bridge, the magistrate doubted whether the rates of four annas per cart and three pice per person should be continued.[91] In the Gaya district, the GTR ran for about sixty-six miles from Baroon to the west to a little beyond Bullooa Chuttee to the east. Since the opening of the EIR, the amount of traffic on this stretch of the road considerably declined. In 1871, the daily average of through traffic did not exceed twenty bullock carts per day in dry weather and one-third of that during the rainy season.[92] If we consider dry and rainy periods of six months each, then the total figure of bullock carts passing through would be around 4,800. We can compare this with the figures available for 1862–63, when altogether (including two-, three- and four-bullock driven carts) 7,089 carts had passed through the road.[93] These figures, however, are too fragmentary to suggest any general picture. For instance, in the period between July 1870 and July 1871, 7,483 bullocks, 6,359 carts, 93,222 men and 3,000 tattoos had crossed the Soane ferry on the GTR.[94] This, then, does not suggest a drastic fall in the traffic. What does appear to have been the case is that the traffic fluctuated according to seasonal patterns and that certain sections of the road experienced a decline in the traffic, depending on the way other networks developed. The traffic recorded at Sasseram for the section of the road between Sherghatty and the River Karmanasha was also 'certainly very light for so great a road'.[95] On yet another section, between Barkata and the River Karmanasha, the traffic was described as 'now so insignificant' as to entertain any idea of establishing toll bars. It was said that such toll bars would 'injure the local trade without in anyway adding to the railway traffic'.[96] On the Hazaribagh section too, the 'through traffic' was 'so small that it may be put down as nil': 'such a thing as an upcountry cart being seen on the GTR is now quite unknown'.[97] Similarly, the Hazaribagh–Burhee road, which had started as an imperial line in the 1860s, carried 'very little traffic' by the 1880s, which led the government to maintain this line just as a 'gravelled' and not a metalled road.[98]

Because of declining traffic, officials were uncertain about continuing investment in the GTR. The case of the bridge over the Lilajun River serves as a good example: built in 1852–53 it was destroyed in the 1855 flood. In 1862, a proposal was made to restore it. The government approved of the project but the superintending engineer (SE) cast doubt on two grounds: first, on the premise of securing suitable foundation for the bridge; and, second, in consequence of the diminishing traffic on the GTR. The project nevertheless was pushed through but the work was not started until 1867–68.[99] The declining traffic

---

91 *GOR*, 167.
92 Ibid.
93 The figures were recorded at the Sherghatty toll gate. *AARB*, 1863–64, 63.
94 GOB, PWD, Communications, proceedings 35–8, January 1873, *RRWRD*.
95 'Letter from R. P. Jenkins, Commissioner of Patna to Secretary, Government of Bengal', 22 August 1871, GOB, PWD, Communications, proceedings 35–8, January 1873, *RRWRD*.
96 GOB, PWD, Communications, proceedings 29–32, January 1873, *RRWRD*.
97 'Letter from H. M. Boddam, Deputy Commissioner, Hazaribagh to E. Dalton, Commissioner, Chota Nagpur', 22 February 1872, ibid.
98 GOB, PWD, GB (Communications), file no. 13 of January 1885, *RRWRD*.
99 *AARB*, 1867–68, 135–6.

and uncertain conditions also led to the decline in the former importance of certain places on the GTR. The magistrate of Gaya requested to transfer the subdivisional office from Sherghatty (situated on the GTR) to Jehanabad because of the decline in use of the GTR. The Patna branch road (from Patna to Gaya) was becoming more important and hence the subdivisional establishment was now 'urgently required' at Jehanabad (situated on this road).[100] This was also one of the important pilgrim routes. In a single day almost 6,000 people were counted on this road. By 1875, this route was described as one of the 'most crowded thoroughfares in the province'.[101] The receipts from pilgrims arriving at Bankipur railway station (Patna) to continue their onward journey to Gaya by this road amounted to Rs. 5,000–7,000 per week in the pilgrim season. Later, a part of this road, from Patna to Jehanabad, was taken over by the railways and for the rest of the route a new embankment was thrown up, which crossed the length of the road four to five times.[102] But this happened only after much deliberation on the role of the railways in enhancing the district's export trade. It was always feared that the railways might not be profitable because Gaya did not export much oilseed.[103]

However, this story of decline had another side. The 'nested' network continued to thrive on the zigzagged communication web. The GTR still maintained its importance in the regional circuit of south Bihar. With the coming of the railways, its utility was reconfigured. It served more for regional than for through traffic. In the 1880s, according to the road traffic registered at Sherghatty alone, the amount of shell lac imported into Gaya was 3,044 maunds for the first two quarters of 1887. The railways transported 1,379 maunds of lac for one quarter of the year. Road transport was still preferred for bulkier commodities such as rice; the amount transported was 2,377 maunds for two quarters in comparison with

---

100 *GOR*, 194. By the mid-1880s, Jehanabad was considered as the 'best paying good station on the Gaya line'. GOB, PWD, GB (Communications), file no. 3 of October 1885, *RRWRD*.
101 GOB, PWD, Local Communications, proceedings 6–27, November 1875, *RRWRD*. In the early 1870s, traffic registration on this road began. For four months, between September and December 1875, traffic from Patna to Gaya under Class I (goods of utmost priority such as the English piece goods, seeds, grains, salt, opium, lac, ghee and so on) amounted to 2,712 tons and the export from Gaya to Patna amounted to 2,384 tons. Although these figures were only for four months, they comprised the busiest season of the year because of coinciding with the pilgrim season. No wonder that almost all the English piece goods from Patna were consigned in September, as in that month pilgrims from all over India gathered at Gaya. Hunter, *AGS*, 118.
102 GOB, PWD, General (Communications), B proceedings 12, March 1879, *RRWRD*. With the coming of the railways, in the early 1880s, it was believed that pilgrimage to Gaya more than doubled. Ahuja, 'The Bridge-Builders', 110. Of course, the pilgrim mobility diversified and increased with the coming of the railways, but this was not always the case. An interesting account was reported by the collector of Monghyr in 1873, when he was camped at a place called Goraghat: 'I counted in one line ninety bullock carts, each containing five or six women or children, returning from a pilgrimage to Parasnath in Hazaribagh. The pilgrims told me they came from the country about Agra, and that by the time they got home six months would have been spent in the pilgrimage. They appear to have some hidden dislike to the railway; but they said they did not use it in consequence of the trains not suiting as regards time.' W.W. Hunter, *A Statistical Account of Bengal: Monghyr and Purniah* (London, 1877), vol. 15, 54–5. [Henceforth *AMP.*]
103 'Minute by Richard Temple', 14 November 1874, GOB, PWD, Local Communications, proceedings 6–27, November 1875, *RRWRD*.

710 maunds imported into Gaya by the railways for one quarter of 1887.[104] Places such as Sasseram on the GTR were still important entrepôts.[105] Piece goods, grain of all kinds, sugar, betel, forest products and melted butter entered Shahabad on pack bullocks along this road and were distributed at important marts like Nasriganj.[106] Two important marts in south Bihar, Chatra and Hazaribagh, did their trade through the GTR. Commodities such as wine, piece goods and salt averaging 2,500 maunds per month were imported into Hazaribagh from the east while the district exported oilseed, hides and ghee amounting roughly to 2,000 maunds per month. Imports into Chatra were greater than this: salt and piece goods coming from Burdwan amounted to 8,000 maunds per month.[107]

The nature of trade in the town of Behar presents some interesting features in this period. The town was neither situated on any railway line nor on the banks of any river. But, since 'all the traffic between Patna, Gaya, Hazaribagh and Monghyr passed through Behar... the travelling traders offered their goods for sale here, as they passed through the town'.[108] Of the 8,346 houses in the town of Behar, almost one-quarter were owned by cloth and grain merchants and, amongst the former, twenty-eight families were recognized to have considerable trade in imported European cloth as well as in country goods procured from Benares, Dacca and Murshidabad.[109] The patterns of circulation were far from railway-centric in this period. Talc or mica was brought from Hazaribagh to Rajauli, a town in the Gaya district, which was well connected with Behar and Nawada by a metalled road. Almost 178 tons worth £2,500 was sent to Calcutta annually. Ghee was also made and sent in skin bags to Calcutta.[110] About one-quarter of the rice produced and one-half of the wheat produced in the Gaya district were exported to other districts.[111] In imperial products such as imported piece goods, the railways took the lead over existing means; it was stated that 'neither steamers nor country-boats get any of the piece-goods traffic between Calcutta and the Upper Provinces'.[112]

The most compelling importance of roads and rivers was discernible in north Bihar, at least until the 1880s. Apart from a small line built by the Tirhut estate in 1874 (a famine-relief line) the whole region continued to trade through roads and ferries as before. The nature of the circulation of goods in this period was also similar to

---

104 GOB, PWD, file W 25 and W 25 KW of January 1886, *RRWRD*.
105 In 1872–73, the imports into Sasseram amounted to 95,698 maunds (3571.85 metric tons), valued at Rs. 1,98,553, and exports to 35,253 maunds (1315.79 metric tons) at the value of Rs. 66,603. Local gunges such as Nasrigunj and Harihargunj were also important trading centres, the former for bamboos and woods and later for paper manufacturing, which was, however, declining. Hunter, *AGS*, 205–6.
106 Hunter, *AGS*, 264.
107 GOB, PWD, Communications, proceedings 29–32, January 1873, *RRWRD*. Hazaribagh also had a regimental bazaar which required a regular supply of provisions. GOB, PWD, GB, proceedings 69–70, January 1862, *RRWRD*.
108 W. W. Hunter, *A Statistical Account of Bengal: Districts of Patna and Saran* (London, 1877), vol. 11, 35. [Henceforth *APS*.]
109 Ibid., 75.
110 Hunter, *AGS*, 61.
111 Hunter, *AGS*, 82–4.
112 *AARB*, 1872–73, 238–9.

that existing earlier. Trade in goods such as cotton, mustard oil and rice from Patna; perfumes from Ghazipur; tobacco from Gorakhpur and Tirhut; knives and basketwork from Muzaffarpur and so on, were carried by two types of merchants. One were the established baniyas and telis, mainly grain traders and oil traders, 'who quite ran two shops, one in Bihar and one in Nepal or Bengal, and could afford caravans to carry their goods', and the other were the small peddlers (*paikars*) 'who walked along the roads with goods in their *jholi* (bags), and often traded in small objects such as mirrors, combs, needles, handkerchiefs, fancy jewels, ribbons and candles'.[113] The world of peddlers, whose itineraries extended from the Punjab to Bengal and to Nepal Terai thrived mainly on road networks.[114] Ferries remained important, connecting different gunges and facilitating the movement of goods inward and outward. In the parts of the Bhagalpur district that was north of the Ganga, there was a large bazaar at Murliganj, where the Marwari merchants had established branches with their headquarters in the Shahabad district. Commodities such as salt, sugar, paddy, oilseed, spices and so on were carried through numerous ghats.[115] In north Monghyr, that is, in the parganas lying north of the Ganga, the little Gundak was the 'most important trade route'. This was navigable throughout the year for boats of four tons, and in the rainy season for boats of up to seventy tons.[116]

If for certain commodities the railways and roads complemented each other by dividing their spheres of operation, for others they both failed to bring about the desired change. The cotton trade from Bihar and Bengal was one such case. At the level of policymaking, communication and export trade were seen as inseparable. From the 1830s, the cotton trade and better roads (and later railways) became part of the same explanatory discourse. It was argued that the long duration of travel on bullock carts damaged the cotton badly before it reached the port of either Bombay or Calcutta.[117] The Cotton Associations of Liverpool, Manchester and Glasgow made similar complaints. Mr Bell, a statistical reporter reviewing the conditions of inland communication in Bengal, accepted the

---

113 Schreiber, 'Tellers of Tale, Sellers of Tales', 286–7. For distant trade in 'local' products, see also Biharilal 'Fitrat', *Aina-i-Tirhut*, edited by Hetukar Jha in *Mithila in the Nineteenth Century* (Darbhanga, 2001), 113–17. This volume also contains a helpful account by Surendra Gopal, 'The Importance of Aina-i-Tirhut in Urdu Historiography'. Hindi translation in the text is by Ijharul Imam. *Aina-i-Tirhut* was originally written in the 1880s. Contracts for public works, money lending and trade were three important ways of making money in this particular district. Many Khatris (Agarwals) who had migrated from the area of Azamgarh, NWP, were settled in this district. One, for instance, was Ayodhya Prasad, who also had written *Riaz-i-Tirhut*. He worked on the Darbhanga estate before starting his own business in English imported goods. His brother, Mahadel Lal, was also an owner of a shop of English goods and a print house. 'Mahajani karobai' (the occupation of money lending) was the most important occupation among the members of the Sahu caste. For instance, one Manohar Lal Sahu, allegedly made only Rs. 40,000 from his zamindari but more than 10 lakhs rupees from Mahajani. See 'Fitrat', *Aina-i-Tirhut*, pt 3, 177–89.
114 Bhattacharya, 'Predicaments of Mobility', 194.
115 W. W. Hunter, *A Statistical Account of Bengal: Bhagalpur and Santal Parganas* (London, 1877), vol. 14, 93. [Henceforth *ABSP*.]
116 Hunter, *AMP*, 21.
117 *The Cotton Trade of India: Can India Supply England with Cotton* (London, 1839).

positive utility of numerous navigable streams but deplored the state of the roads.[118] During these years, the government accepted the promotion of cotton cultivation as a 'national object' but expressed their limitation in constructing and maintaining metalled roads. Auckland, governor general of India, conceded that 'the expense of forming and keeping up metalled roads throughout our territories must be so enormous, and can so little be relieved by any possibility of repayment, as to be apparently beyond the limits of all prudent outlay on the part of the state'.[119]

Better transport facilities were not only considered necessary to enhance the quality of cotton exported but also to open up new areas of production. Besides transport, technology was also crucial. The government had decided to depute three American cultivators and four machine workmen to the Bengal presidency to develop better-quality cotton. New varieties of cotton were introduced; for instance, an Egyptian variety was tried in Sasseram.[120] Regions in western and central India were more important for cotton production but Bihar's role was not inconsequential in the previous decades. In 1789, through the circuitous route of Flanders and Denmark, 2,000,000 lbs of raw cotton reached the English market from India for the first time. In 1790, a report on the culture and manufacture of cotton wool, raw silk and tobacco in India, suggested that 1,328,000 lbs of cotton were grown in Shahabad. Patna and Tirhut grew 320,000 lbs and 216,000 lbs respectively.[121]

The cotton shipment from Bengal declined between the 1830s and 1850s but it was thought that the railways, along with better roads, could reverse this process.[122] Further, the American crisis of the 1860s rekindled the hope of the authorities in India.

To augment the supply of cotton, the government came up with a cotton road scheme. It passed a resolution on 28 February 1862 ensuring the provision of a special grant for improving routes between cotton-producing districts and shipment ports. Another Home Department Circulation mentioned: 'Government will gladly aid every well considered plan for improving any roads that are likely to be of use in extending the cultivation of, or trade, in cotton.'[123] The region of south Bihar, specifically Palamow and Toori, received special attention. Altogether they exported about 2,000 to 3,000 maunds of cotton but good roads were thought to further boost the production and supply. Regions such as Shahabad and Patna, which in the late eighteenth century had provided a considerable amount of cotton, had already registered a shift in the crop production. From the early

---

118 *The Cotton Trade of India: Its Future Prospects* (London, 1840?), pt 2, 81. The pagination follows from the first part, which unfortunately remains unlocated.
119 G. H. Huttmann, *Official Papers Connected with the Improved Cultivation of Cotton* (Calcutta, 1839), 24.
120 *Report of the Cotton Committee of the Agricultural and Horticultural Society of India* (London, 1840), 68–9.
121 Major General Briggs, *The Cotton Trade of India: Its Past and Present Condition, Read Before the Royal Asiatic Society, 16 November 1839* (London, 1839), 4–6.
122 See 'Letter and Memorandum from the Chamber of Commerce and Manufactures of Manchester to the Court of Directors', 17 June 1847, and 'Memorandum on Indian Railways from Major J. P. Kennedy to the Court of Directors', 14 September 1852, SD, doc. nos. 79 and 161, pages 290–92, 507 respectively.
123 GOB, PWD, GB, proceedings B, 251–3 and K. W., January 1862, *RRWRD*.

Table 6. Supply of cotton from Bengal between 1834–35 and 1849–50

Year	From Bengal to England	From Bengal to countries other than England
1834–35	3,051,190 lbs	25,858,616 lbs
1835–36	11,681,706 lbs	45,997,884 lbs
1838–39	2,100,346 lbs	17,464,702 lbs
1845–46	12,154 lbs	7,691,580 lbs
1849–50	27,306 lbs	1,817,971 lbs

Source: Thornton, *Statistical Papers*, 68.

decades of the nineteenth century these regions were primarily known for their opium cultivation. To return to the cotton story, produce from the eastern part of the Palamow district went to Chatra and that grown westward was taken to Sherghatty. Merchants who paid advances to the Khywars and Cherows tribes, engaged in cotton production, built *golahs* (storehouses) in the central positions in this district. A comprehensive road scheme was suggested to link important market towns where cotton was collected.[124] The road connecting Chatra to Chauparan, a place on the GTR, which was the first portion of the road connecting Palamow to the GTR, was undertaken. The track already existed but had recently been reclassified as an imperial line; Rs. 47,387 were estimated for its improvement.[125] Chota Nagpur was allotted Rs. 24,000 for improving the road from Lohardagga to the new imperial road at Chatra. This road arguably was to 'open out a sealed country where cotton is grown'.[126] Other 'cotton producing tracts' such as Kundah in Hazaribagh were to be connected to Chatra.[127] Plans were also proposed to connect the GTR with the places in the Central Provinces on the one hand and with the Soane valley on the other. This opening up, arguably, was to give the Soane valley the same status as the Mississippi as a cotton-producing country.[128]

Much of this, however, proved, to be wishful thinking. By 1865, it was realized that the 'cultivation of cotton in Bengal, *as a rule* was insignificant and unimportant'.[129] The soil in eastern India was not conducive to cotton cultivation in general and thus the project of 'cotton roads' failed to achieve the desired results.

---

124 Account based on 'Letter from Commissioner of Chota Nagpur to Secretary to the Government of Bengal', 12 July 1861, GOB, PWD, GB, proceedings 143–6, January 1862, *RRWRD*.
125 Imperial lines were those that were completely bridged and metalled. Out of Rs. 47,387 only Rs. 12,380 was provisioned in the budget. The estimate for metalling the road was Rs. 17,583 but the budget approved of only Rs. 10,357. GOB, PWD, GB, progds. 140–42, January 1862, *RRWRD*. Also, 'No. 194, Bengal Budget Orders, 1864–65', RBP, April 1864, P/163/32.
126 Government of India (GOI), PWD, GB, proceedings 7–8, March 1862, 117–22, National Archives of India. [Henceforth NAI.]
127 GOB, PWD, GB, proceedings 143–6, January 1862, *RRWRD*.
128 GOB, PWD, GB, proceedings B, 251–3 and K. W., January 1862, *RRWRD*.
129 *AARB*, 1864–65, 142 (emphasis added).

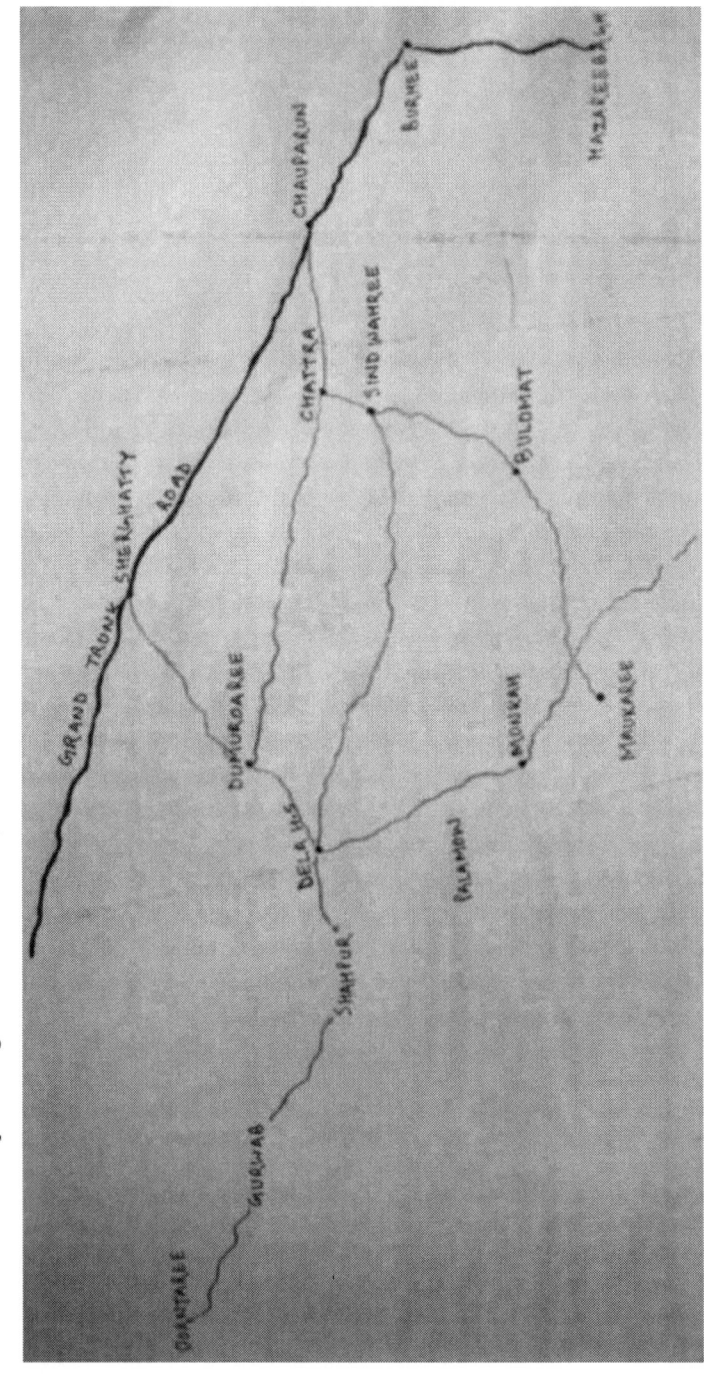

Plate 28. Sketch map showing cotton road scheme, 1860s

Source: GOB, PWD, GB, proceedings 143–6, January 1862, *RRIWRD*.

The railways did, however, capture the cotton trade between NWP and Bengal. The receipt of goods sent from the NWP in the second half of 1862 increased by 63.7 per cent in comparison with the corresponding half of the previous year. The increase, the traffic manager claimed, was mainly derived from the conveyance of the staple produce of the country. Amongst those, cotton was central. The receipts from cotton showed an increase of Rs. 63,502 over the corresponding period of the previous year.[130] The cotton transported was of unscrewed quality, or packed in what was called 'country bales', which not only took more wagon space but also needed covered wagons. The difference in terms of occupied space was huge: about 3 lbs of country-bale cotton could be packed per cubic foot while 25 lbs of the screwed variety could be packed as sea freight and 18 lbs by the railway conveyance.[131] In a full capacity covered wagon, which was of 148 maunds, unscrewed cotton could make only 35.5 maunds. By comparison, the screwed variety could make 86 maunds.[132] It was therefore unprofitable for the railway company to carry unscrewed cotton. Because of this, despite being a free export commodity (that is, non-dutiable), cotton was initially placed in the second category of the railway freight system, which meant that the charges were half a pie per mile. Later, it was shifted to the fourth class, in which one pie per mile was charged. In other words, transport costs increased.

On one level, this shift represented the feeble negotiating power of the colonial state vis-à-vis the EIRC, which was a private company, because in spite of the state's objective to furnish England with Indian cotton, the private company prioritized its own principle of profit maximization. However, on the other hand, this shift showed how subtle the effects of communication were on commodity production. It is true that cotton production in Bengal did not increase substantially, but the railway tariffs led to the establishment of cotton presses for screwing, which was described as 'being freely used'.[133] Altogether, so far as the eastern part of India is concerned, this particular commodity did not respond well to the availability of the better means of transport. T. Login, the executive engineer of the 7th division, GTR, stated: 'Cotton from Saharanpur, Jugadree, Kurnaul, Panipat, and even Delhi are *now* carted to Ferozepore to be boated down the Indus, rather than sending it by rail to Calcutta, it is self evident that in spite of the moderate charges on the EIR, a still lower rate is necessary to secure the cotton trade.'[134] Cotton is one example taken here to illustrate the connected history of commodity, production, transport and communication. Any account of impact of communication thus has to be specific in terms of commodity production and distribution. Other commodities possibly would have reacted to the changes in transport in different ways. Immediately after the introduction of the railways, twenty-five chests of manufactured opium were experimentally sent to Calcutta from Rajmahal. The contents were not completely damaged but 'the upper

---

130 'From B. Smyth, Traffic Manager, to Deputy Agent, EIR, NWP', 14 October 1863, GOI, PWD, Railway Proceedings A, proceedings 42–4, January 1864, NAI.
131 Ibid.
132 Ibid. and 'Note by Captain Taylor on the Subject of a Proposal to Increase the Tariff-Rate for Unscrewed Cotton, 20th March 1863', RBP, proceedings 10 and 12–15, December 1863, P/163/31.
133 RBP, prodg. 15, December 1863, P/163/31.
134 T. Login, *Traffic on Roads, Railways and Canals in India* (Roorkee, 1867), 15 (emphasis original).

layer of cakes in the chests [were] more or less exposed to view owing to the "trash" with which cakes had been covered'.[135] It was, however, not only the matter of packaging but also of economy. Sending opium from Patna to Calcutta by the river cost Rs. 1-13 per chest as opposed to Rs. 7-8-3 by rail. Still, the government continued with its policy of transporting opium by the railways; the secretary of state approved this measure: 'Though water transit of opium is cheaper than railway, greater risk in water transit justifies increased cost of railway.'[136]

Apart from the favoured treatment that the railways began to receive, another problem that persisted with river navigation was the shift in the course of the rivers themselves together with the hazards created due to silting. In Chapter 6 we noted some of the difficulties faced by steamers. These problems continued throughout the period. For instance, officials of the Gulzarbagh godown at Patna often complained that 'scarcely a day passes without some vessel running aground in the neighbourhood of the landing stages'.[137] The constant change in the river course forced the merchants to shift their bases: many traders, especially Bengalis, left Colong in 1875 when the Ganga, which earlier had flown just under the town, entirely receded and left a 'broad bank of loose sand' in its place.[138] The same was true for other rivers; the most fertile parts of the sub-Tarai rice tract in the Bhagalpur district, which had a great grain mart at Nathpur, were 'completely devastated by the changes in the course of the Kusi river'.[139] This trade, however, was relocated to Murligunj and Kishengunj, the former making use of the numerous ghats on the changed course of the River Kosi. The shift in the stream was followed by spatial changes. At Balua, which formerly was an inland market, trade increased because it was brought within two miles from the Kosi, but at Birpur on the Nepal frontier, what had formerly been a brisk trade declined because merchants feared further encroachment from the river.[140]

Gradually, railways began to take over through trade. The rise in the merchandise carried by rail was considerable and kept increasing throughout the period.[141] In particular, the trade in English cotton goods started choking the line in the early 1860s; merchants complained of their goods being stranded at different stations for more than two months.[142] As a result, not only were the number of lines doubled but a more direct

---

135 *AARB*, 1863–64, 38.
136 'Letter from Secretary of State to Governor-General in Council', 31 December 1878, GOB, PWD, GB (Communications), file no. illegible, 1879, *RRWRD*. There was some merit in this view. In 1862, the sub-deputy opium agent of Chapra had despatched two boats containing 213 jars, besides two pots of opium. The storm, however, wrecked the boats, and though 205 jars were recovered only 27 of them (that is, 27 maunds) were 'found in a good condition'. GOB, Revenue Department, Miscellaneous Branch A, proceedings 18–38, July 1862.
137 GOB, PWD, GB (Communications), file no. illegible, 1879, *RRWRD*.
138 Hunter, *ABSP*, 85.
139 Ibid., 23. See also Christopher V. Hill, *River of Sorrow: Environment and Social Control in Riparian North Bihar, 1770–1994* (Ann Arbor, MI, 1997).
140 Hunter, *ABSP*, 94.
141 There were occasional periods of slump owing to famines and floods, such as the one in 1866–67 and again in 1870. G. Huddleston, *History of the East Indian Railway* (Calcutta, 1906), 57, 64.
142 GOI, PWD, Railway A, proceedings 6–11, April 1865, NAI.

route, the Chord line, was opened in 1871. This line ran through the districts of Bankura, Purulia, Santhal Pargana, Bhagalpur and Monghyr. The stations were selected without any data of traffic recorded for them.[143]

Railways were also becoming popular among local merchants for despatching their goods to port towns. For instance, the merchants of Surjgarh, situated at the junction of the rivers Ganga and Keul in the Monghyr district, petitioned the EIRC to make a road from there to Kujrah, a station on the EIR. The merchants expressed their desire to send their goods, which amounted to 10,000 maunds per day, directly to Howrah, as they experienced inconvenience in sending the goods first to Monghyr and then by boat and steamer to Calcutta. The proposal was finally accepted and the project, described as a 'local railway feeder', was given a grant of Rs. 30,700.[144]

However, even amidst the growing role of the railway in trade, a complementary pattern in the circulation of goods was discernible. We can only construct an impressionistic picture, for, as late as the 1870s, the data on different channels of communication was inadequate.[145] To fill this gap, arrangements were made in 1873 to register trade on the Ganga past Sahibgunge, a place in Bihar situated on the river.[146] That year, about 43,000 boats passed through Sahibgunge. In the first half of the year upstream traffic was extensive, whereas in the second half downstream traffic was extensive. Rice and oilseed were two articles that together made up for more than half of the entire Gangetic traffic. Rice was brought up from Calcutta for consumption in Bihar and Benares in the first half of the year, whereas oilseed was sent down to Calcutta in the second half of the year for export. The second half of the year was unproductive for the railway, as the swollen rivers afforded cheap transport for bulk commodities. The products despatched in 1872 from the EIR from the Bhagalpur district illustrates this point. For the first six months of the year the total amount of grain sent that included edibles and pulses was 287,614 maunds whereas the amount sent in the second half of the year was 136,735 maunds. The amount of seeds varied from 152,546 maunds to 25,596 maunds in the same period. This was the amount carried by the railways. Exclusive of this, the river carried 315,675 maunds of oilseed in the whole year. Almost all the wheat exported from this district was 'carried in equal proportion by rail and boat'.[147]

Some of the figures for mail transport across India are interesting, a sector with which the political utility of the railways (and also steamships) was closely associated since the first discussions on introducing railways to India. In the fiscal year 1860–61, mail travelled over 43,570 miles, of which 36,784 were done by boats and runners, 5,740 by cart and on horseback and only 1,046 by the railways. For the fiscal year ending 31 March 1874,

---

143 GOI, PWD, Railway A, proceedings 113–19, May 1866, NAI.
144 RBP, proceedings 67–70, December 1863, P/163/31.
145 *AARB*, 1871–72, 131.
146 *AARB*, 1872–73, 238. The importance of Sahibgunge had actually increased in the 1860s owing to the railways. It had become a changing station for travellers coming from Calcutta and continuing their journey to Darjeeling. RBP, proceedings 11–13, 16, January 1863, P/163/30.
147 Hunter, *ABSP*, 183–7.

mail travelled over 54,000 miles, of which 44, 857 were done by boats and runners, 4,003 by cart and on horseback and 5,739 by railway. In using these figures one should bear in mind that there were many parts of India that still did not have any railways. Data exclusively related to the Bengal presidency would have given a clearer picture, but still the importance of the older means and ways of conveyance is proven beyond doubt.[148]

At least in the first twenty years of their operations, railways had synchronized their role with other modes of communication, mainly the rivers. In spite of being connected with the railways, Patna remained 'the largest river-mart in Bengal', facilitating the exchange, distribution and circulation of goods that came from Calcutta by rail. The cost of transport and the nature of commodities worked together as factors in delineating the complementary nature of the modes of communication. The Patna trade demonstrated this feature: the city received salt mostly by the railways. Hides, which were spoiled due to the exposure to humid conditions of water transport, were also shifting to the railways. But for commodities such as rice, which came from northern and eastern Bengal, or oilseeds, which went downstream from Patna, the Ganga remained the main means of transport.[149] Agricultural produce such as indigo, opium, oilseed and grain were collected at Patna and then despatched to Calcutta. Revelgunge, an important town in the 'nested' network, continued to be a major river mart, by performing the same function of collection and despatch of goods for not only the districts in Bihar but also for the NWP and Oudh.[150] Other towns in the Patna district that were supported in great measure by river traffic were Danapur, Fatwa and Barh. The gunges on the riverside, especially at Patna, such as Marufgunj, Khwajah Kalanghat, Rikabgunj and Gulzarbagh, were emporiums for grain and other commodities.[151] The latter also had an opium godown, where all the poppy grown in the province of Bihar was manufactured. For the regions of central-west Bihar the Soane continued to be an important medium. Nasrigunj, situated close to this river in the Shahabad district, owed its commercial prosperity to the trade in timber, bamboos and rope fibre. In 1872–73, 3,900,000 bamboos, worth £3,900, were floated on rafts down the Soane to Patna.[152]

Conclusions

This chapter questioned the 'railway-centric' approach from three perspectives. First, it argued that in spite of the fact that railways had become the dominant centralizing feature of post–mid-nineteenth-century communication policy, official wisdom in developing complementary modes, that is, roads as 'feeder lines' for railways, was not altogether missing. Railways went through a gestation period of at least twenty-five to thirty years before realizing the radical effects ascribed to them. From the very early years of the introduction of railways, it was clear that they alone would not 'open up' the country.

---

148 *Five Months in India*, 79.
149 Hunter, *APS*, 26–7.
150 Hunter, 'Preface', *APS*.
151 Ibid., 20.
152 Hunter, *AGS*, 264.

How far and how much the other means of communication attracted investment is, however, a different story. Second, the chapter assessed the role of communication, and here the argument was not restricted to the railways alone, but linked to the shifting histories of different commodities. Commodity production and distribution was not dependent on the means of communication alone. Alternately, better means of communication did not necessarily ensure a rise in commodity production and its circulation, as is proved in the case of cotton. Lastly, the chapter suggested a sensitive approach towards identifying regional diversity. The GTR's importance in thoroughfare trade gradually declined but it remained important for the regions of south Bihar in providing connections with important trading centres in Bengal and Orissa. North Bihar, the heart of the production zone for many imperial commodities, did not see any regular railway connection until the 1880s, the time when the Bengal and North-Western Railway began to develop their lines. For other commodities such as rice and oilseed – the two leading export commodities with extensive through traffic – river transport remained important. Yet for many other commodities, ranging from baskets to perfume, talc and tobacco, roads and ferries were often the ways that integrated them into wider trading circuits.

The more obvious changes associated with the railways started becoming conspicuous from the 1880s; the density of the lines and the connectivity of the places then expanded and diversified. The railways also became instrumental in the growth of urban clusters; towns such as Jamalpur, Mokama and Khagaul in Bihar developed because of the railways.[153] Some of these grew into changing stations, followed by bazaar establishments; others such as Jamalpur came into existence as industrial workshop towns that attracted labour from neighbouring villages.

But until the 1880s, so far as trade was concerned, a general complementariness existed between different means of communication. Colonial officers were aware of the limitation of the new technology; John Strachey, a late nineteenth-century official, commented: 'It is difficult for railways to contend with the cheap water-carriage; they do not diminish the usefulness of the rivers or materially lessen the traffic which they carry.'[154] However, railways opened up many new possibilities, all of which are extremely interesting for the social history of the late nineteenth century. We will conclude by very briefly pointing at some of them. As mentioned in Chapter 5, the 'crime scene' had already started changing with the coming of the railways. One of the first cases of robbery committed on the railways was on 9 September 1863, when a man got into the covered wagon of a goods train and threw off two boxes before jumping off when the train started moving. As seen by the *chaprasie* (peon), he had nine other accomplices waiting on the ground. The train was standing at the Gooskarah station in Raneegunge in Burdwan district; the boxes contained linseed. A person named Goribullah Sheikh was convicted and sentenced to six months' imprisonment. The other eight were acquitted because of lack of evidence, and one person absconded.[155] From the viewpoint of the colonial state, the new technology questioned the efficacy of the 'regime of regulations' imposed

---

153 Hunter, *APS*, 86–90.
154 Strachey, *India: Its Administration and Progress*, 406.
155 RBP, proceedings 41–8, November 1863, P/163/31.

on 'illegal' trade. A case in point relates to opium dealers and how they used railways for their benefit. The vendors at Hooghly had shops in districts such as Bhagalpur and Monghyr. The people at these shops purchased opium directly from the cultivators and sent it in parcels by rail, which 'violated' the state monopoly. In order to check this, an Opium Smuggling Preventive Establishment was formed. It employed six detectives who were given free railway tickets to travel in order to investigate violation of the state's monopoly.[156]

Another important facet of railway development was an increase in cases of bribery. In 1865 it was said that the practice of bribery had existed for the last two years, and that it had now become a 'gigantic system'.[157] Station masters were the usual suspects. However, traders eager to despatch their goods were also blamed for paying extra money to secure wagon space. Officers posted in various districts and in railway establishments were directed by the government to conduct enquiries. Interestingly, by the following year, what had been a very clear acceptance of the prevalence of bribery had turned into 'widespread rumour'. One after another, the consulting and deputy consulting engineers of Bengal refuted the prevalence of bribery; they said that although it was commonly spoken of there was no evidence for it.[158] The colonial state might have had vested interests in downplaying the existence of bribery but if we recall the story of thuggee from Chapter 5, in which policemen asked for bribes to help Bharos Das get his railway ticket, it would leave little doubt that in the interlinked histories of trade, travel, commodity and transport many new practices emerged and many existing ones, like the 'illegality' of trade, were set in a new context.

---

156 GOB, Finance Department, Opium A, proceedings 9–10, July 1869, BSA.
157 GOI, PWD, Railway A, proceedings 122–5, February 1866, NAI.
158 GOI, PWD, Railway A, proceedings 31–6, March 1866, NAI.

CONCLUSION

This book in no way claims to represent the 'right' way of writing the history of communication. There could, and possibly do, exist many other ways in which this theme can be approached. I will use this conclusion to broadly reflect on the general outcome of this research but also on the possibilities of further 'opening up' the theme of communication in diverse directions.

One of the possible ways in which this account could be rewritten is by enlarging the field and scope of enquiry by including post and telegraph, which was introduced in roughly the same period as more focused debates on good roads, and later the railways, began to emerge, that is, in the 1830s.[1] Roads, railways, and post and telegraph constituted the triumvirate of the new technological basis of 'communication' in colonial India. That the dak system had existed long before is undisputable, but the technological spread of services of postal and telegraphic communication that catered to a wider social base constitutes a fascinating area of research. In what ways this new technology fostered new types of mobilities and sociabilities by enabling migrant workers to remit money back home is one example in which the social and economic impulses of the nineteenth century can be understood through the intervention of technology. More conventionally, the role of the dissemination of telegraphic command in the consolidation of colonial rule would prove useful in understanding the techniques of governmentality that the colonial state promoted from the mid-nineteenth century. This might provide a refreshing change from the current dominant approach, which tries to understand issues of governmentality only by analysing the discursive regime of colonial rule.

The history of technology is part of the history of communication, particularly if the latter is more conventionally understood in terms of means of transport. In this regard, this book, while addressing the diversity of the themes connected with the issue of communication, has focused on one of the technologies of its time, that is, steam. The role of steam both in inscribing the marker of the civilizational gap between the metropolis and the colony, as well as its practical limitation and importance in the overall communication network, has been presented here in depth. However, any new technological intervention works within its historical, political, economic and, not least, ecological set-up. Steam-driven ships encountered a river of a dramatically different nature; they, together with railways, further encountered a set of highly developed systems of boats manufactured according to varied functions. Also, in order to earn profits, they had to tap into the structures of mercantile networks and commodity circulation. All these

---

1 This book has used Deep Kanta Lahiri Choudhury's unpublished MPhil thesis. For a greater exposition of his ideas see his recent book.

factors working together create a picture of complementariness existing amongst diverse means of communication. The history of communication presented in this work is not based on the fulcrum of 'transition' and 'subsequent replacement', that is, one technology, one mode dominating and replacing the other.

The diversity this book deals with exists not only at the level of multiple modes of communication but in the very set of historical processes these modes interacted with. We are referring to the way communication has been presented here as an integral part of many other concerns of the colonial state: forms of travelling, regulation, knowledge gathering, capital investment and, not least, trading activities. This has been done with an eye to contributing to the hitherto neglected or scarcely researched fields, of which three themes are the most important: colonial policy on road development, Bihar's history of communication network and trading patterns, and sojourning lives of local-level officials of colonial bureaucracy. However, the main concern behind writing this book was not to look out for thematic newness. For even if some of the themes such as travel, mapping and crime, for instance, have been the focus of research, few approaches have placed them into dialogue with each other. In this regard, communication appears not only as a descriptive category but also as an analytic category to interlink the diverse yet connected histories of trade, travel, transport and social space. The initial research questions that eventually took concrete shape were simple: if travel constituted one of the important ways of 'writing cultures', then did the ways of travelling affect (or not) such accounts? Did ways of seeing have any relation to ways of travelling? If travel was an important medium of colonial knowledge production, then what forms of travel existed and how different were they from each other? If there existed a growing concern for safeguarding routes, then how did the colonial state perceive existing forms of mobility: what was the nature of the relationship between different mediums of communication and how did they interact? And so on. In trying to answer each of these sets of questions, the interconnectedness between the themes became clear.

This interconnectedness is between communication and aspects of governance. Here we have described how communication was integrated into the contexts of travelogues, official tours, cartography, 'men-on-the-road', public works and trade. The book is not arranged chronologically in a conventional sense, but a historical and chronological development of the colonial ideas and practices about and related to communication does come through. The book starts with the late eighteenth-century accounts of travel and trade, of tours and surveys, followed in the middle sections by accounts of the changing technology of metalled roads and steamships together with changing ideological pursuits, and ends by looking at the nature of the overall communication grid including railways, as it existed in the late nineteenth century.

The effort to bring cultural practices such as travel and forms of representation together with economic descriptions on trade and trading networks had a definite agenda, which to put it simply, is the outcome of dissatisfaction with the current wave of history writing in South Asia which treats them far too strictly and separately than required.[2] The necessity of marrying 'culture' or 'cultural' with 'economy' is therefore partly in

---

2 This point has been discussed in the Introduction.

response to this approach but also partly explicable by the nature of interconnectedness outlined above. While 'reading *with* the grains' of colonial accounts, it became apparent that the 'opening up of the interiors' had to remain the entry point when writing this book. Rather than being a 'flash in the pan', the discourse of 'opening up' pervaded colonial policies in significant ways. Whether the regions were opened up or not is a different question, but the fact that changes in communication policies, as they started appearing from the 1820s, were significantly driven by a conviction in this discourse is undeniable. That this 'opening up' was further intricately related to discussions on imperial trade, commodity production, better linkages between the regions and so on, made it clear that 'economy' was centre stage in this discussion. Therefore, the economic aspects have remained a constant field of enquiry in this book, even when the discussion has seemingly followed cultural lines. For instance, Chapter 3, while dealing with forms of administrative travel, also deals explicitly with the nature of trade and taxation. Collecting information on trading circuits was one of the tasks of district-level officials during their winter tours. Attempts like the formation of the Road Fund, the Circular towards improving the means of communication at the district level, and formation of the Ferry Fund Committee were linked with questions of transit duties, inland trade, and free and unfree trade. However, I also believe that economic accounts *without* their discursive and cultural justifications, contestations and ambivalences would not have fully served the purposes of this study. The cultural logic/representations/justifications of economic and technological changes were part of the processes and contexts in which those changes were seen and implemented. Thus, any discussion, on economic effects of steamships and railways for example, should take into account the ways in which they simultaneously constituted and contributed to the discourse of imperialism, colonialism and civilizational progress. This has fundamentally remained the reason why the policies and their effects as described in this book, have been studied wherever possible in association with their ideological contexts. This commitment and understanding explains Chapter 2's lengthy treatment of forms of travelling and the nature of gaze; the reason behind this again lies in the reckoning that 'interior' has to be 'unpacked'. In this case, too, the enquiry began by asking simple, if fundamental, questions: was interior a pre-given category? Was it fixed or flexible? What were the genealogies of this category before their regular appearance in discussions on sources related to making roads and railways (and improving trade and governance)? Did it surface in other genres of literature, and if yes how? Did communication have any role in defining/shaping/promoting this spatial category? And so on.

One of the ways in which I traced the meaning of the term 'interior', by following its imprint in the sources used here, was by looking at the forms of spatial descriptions as they emerged from the late eighteenth century. What became evident was that travel, ways of travelling, visual representations, the powerful influence of the picturesque ideology that shaped the contemporary 'gaze' on the nature of landforms, and the administrative impulse to control newly acquired territory, all played a crucial role in the languages of legitimation of colonial rule, in which interior emerged as one of the powerful categories. Being flexible, because there was no 'fixed' zone which was defined as 'interior', there was also a definite urge to objectify the spaces. The issue of objectification in colonial times has been dealt with in the Introduction and Chapter 1 and need not be repeated here, but it must be reiterated that, in current historiographical practice, particularly that dealing with colonial times and focusing more on 'ruptures' than on continuities, the need to contextualize the processes of this objectification – spatial or social – is barely achieved. This work nevertheless shares the limitations offered by its own critique – that is, of starting the story of colonialism from the time when colonialism itself started – and has tried to, however briefly, explore the pre-colonial practices and trace the early colonial developments, either in terms of breaks or continuities in that trajectory of historical progression. As argued here, the affective nature of space in pre-colonial times gradually started changing under the aegis of 'processes of objectification' during colonial times. Acts such as travel and mapping, for instance, played an important role in those processes. In all these, as Chapter 2 shows, means of communication, either by river or roads, remained crucial in (un)enabling and stabilizing the gaze. However, looking solely at travelogues together with visual productions to understand the nature of the space might lead to the generalization that the colonial gaze was all too powerful in creating a category *just for the sake of legitimation*. The practice of 'going into the interiors' served a timely reminder that the interior was as much a category resurrected from *without* as it was a space seen from *within*. The trope of the 'unknowability of interior' was simultaneously made contradictory by the attempts to know as much as was possible about it. This approach not only justified bringing cultural forms of representation together with the economic issues related with communication, but opened up the question of colonial knowledge production and the nature of early colonial rule.

If asked to draw one conclusion about the nature of early colonial rule in India, that is, approximately between the 1760s and 1820s, I would point to its contradictory character. This in no way dismisses the 'coloniality' of colonial rule or presents an apologia that colonial rule in this period was inherently (and innocently) handicapped by its limitations. What it does mean in the simplest terms is that colonial rule could not bring about all the changes it wished to, yet nevertheless did bring about considerable change. While the zamindars could never be either forced or convinced to substantially contribute to the making and repairing of roads, the mobile communities that threatened the financial and administrative powers of the colonial state were by and large 'tamed'. In any assessment of the nature of early colonial rule, the opposing weights of 'institutions' and 'revenue' need to be taken into account. Institutional continuity with its ethos of responsibility dating from pre-colonial times more often than not did not sit comfortably with the revenue-accumulation aspirations of the colonial state. Thus, although zamindars were incessantly reminded of their 'traditional' duties of road building/repairing, their options to generate revenue through sayers and rahdari were cut. I used these examples, and the point of the opposing pull between institutional continuity and revenue accumulation, merely to illustrate one form of 'contradictoriness'. Others, as they existed and have been shown in this book, related to different nodes of power hierarchy within the colonial state's structure. That between the Indian and London authorities was the most obvious, at least when it came to issues of developing communication.

The nature of this contradictoriness took on a different character when it was positioned vis-à-vis the natives. Contradictions sometimes became accusations, for instance the natives were accused of keeping roads in a bad state of repair. This example of accusation is pertinent here for two reasons: one, the dominant belief in this view somehow, although unsuccessfully, tried to mitigate the role of the early colonial state, which was as much responsible for the decay and neglect of roads, perhaps more, as were the native chiefs and landlords. The second reason is that such labellings create a necessity for not limiting our historical analysis to either justifying or dismissing such claims; they ask us to go further into identifying the locations of such accusations in conflicting and competing ideologies. The accusation behind a 'roadless India' needs elaboration in this direction. In the late eighteenth-century political set-up, roads served different purposes for different groups. In late eighteenth-century Bihar, various landed notables competed for power. Mir Qasim was able to subdue certain zamindars, such as Bishen Singh of Siris and Kutumb (Bhojpur area) or the raja of Bettiah in 1762, but such measures had only a temporary effect. Mir Qasim's defeat at the hands of the British in 1764 again gave the zamindars a chance to revive their authority, fortifying themselves, usually by making mud forts and digging moats around them. The roads and passages to such forts were deliberately cut off and access was made difficult. During Buchanan's survey of the districts of Bihar, he mentioned such forts, many of which were in ruins. For instance, there were eighty-six mud forts in just one division (Hilsa) of the Gaya district.[3] Keeping roads in a poor state of repair was thus part of the political power game amongst zamindars, and between them and the state power represented first by the Bengal nawabs and then the EIC. However, when the EIC gained absolute power it needed to know about those roads and routes. As shown in Chapter 4, the era of route surveys signalled this necessity. The change in the political set-up shaped the role of communication. Early colonial rule needed good and open roads for easy and rapid troop movement. They also needed to know and control the roads precisely because of the zamindars' rebellious tendencies. Their experience with zamindars, particularly with those in the hilly and jungle areas, reinforced this need.[4] This was the reason why 'keeping the roads open' was one of the clauses in almost every settlement made with 'refractory' zamindars. For instance, in a settlement with the Hos of the Singhbhum district in 1827, the latter agreed to 'keep the roads throughout the country open and safe for travellers'.[5] How far these goals were realized is again a different matter. We have seen that almost until the 1850s the state was dependent on zamindars for supplying provisions for troops on the march. The vulnerability became obvious in times of crises, for instance, during the Chait Singh's revolt in 1781 when the state found it difficult to move its equipment via boats. Even after more than seven decades, such problems, to a large extent, remained. In the 1857 'Mutiny', the state faced a difficult time in curtailing the 'hidden mobility' of 'rebels' and also in maintaining a hassle-free chain of supply between Bengal and the NWP. One reason behind this limited control was the colonial state's interest in only imperial commodities that in turn attracted its attention to only a few select thoroughfares (including the Ganga). This was reflected in the measures

---

3 Buchanan, *An Account of the Districts of Behar and Patna*, 233.
4 Hand, *Early English Administration of Bihar*, 13.
5 Diwakar, ed., *Bihar Through the Ages*, 604.

taken to guard routes; the police patrol system was first developed on the Ganga in the late eighteenth and early nineteenth centuries and later was adopted for the GTR.

Just as the meaning of roads has to be contextualized, so too does that of technology. In colonial eyes, the macadamized roads of Europe must have made the Indian kutcha roads appear to be non-roads, or 'roadless'. However, if we go back to some seventeenth-century European representations of Indian roads, the issue would require a reassessment. Thomas Roe, who came to India in the early seventeenth century, had to say the following about a segment of the Badshahi road (Shershah's GTR from Sonargaon in Bengal to Rohtas in the Punjab): 'it is all a plain and the highway planted on both sides with trees like a delicate walk, it is one of the great works and wonders of the world'.[6] Travernier, travelling in India in the same century, regarded travel conditions in India as 'not less convenient than…that one may be carried in comfort either in France or Italy'.[7] Laying the blame on the natives for the alleged roadless state of India was the dominant representation, but as seen in Chapter 2, this discourse was internally fractured. It is best represented in the candid admittance of one Mr Sibley, who had served in the Bengal presidency: 'In the district I was most familiar, the roads were actually in a worse condition than during the period of the native rule, and relatively, comparing roads in Bengal with roads in England a hundred years ago and now, they were then much superior.'[8] Thus part of the blame lies in the functioning of British rule in these hundred years, which is precisely the time period of this book. India's peculiarly long rainy seasons damaged kutcha roads, which required regular repair works. The shortage of funds and the politics of realignment led to neglect on the part of the colonial state. Existing roads began to decay, and the state found it difficult to invest even Rs. 6,000–8,000, the amount needed to repair the old routes of Hajipur–Muzaffarpur, Muzaffarpur–Singhea and Muzaffarpur–Darbhanga.[9] The use of metal technology was restricted to trunk lines. This is the reason why, as late as 1898–99, out of the 2,440 miles of roads in the district of Saran and Champaran, only 109 miles were metalled and the remaining 2,331 unmetalled.[10] In the Patna division, by the end of 1883–84, out of the 8,098 miles of roads under the charge of several districts and branch committees, only 917 miles were metalled. Some 3,334 miles were in the second-class category (i.e. roads partially bridged but not metalled), 1,124 were third class (neither bridged nor metalled) and 2,722 were village roads.[11]

Limitations in the application of technology, however, do not suggest immobility, as was often argued by colonialists. This book deconstructs colonial ideas of a 'static' Indian society. A high degree of internal movement of people and goods was in evidence. Some

---

6 Sarkar, *Inland Transport*, 33. A study on the transport system of eighteenth-century Bengal also suggests that Bengal nawabs contributed towards making roads. Tilottama Mukherjee, 'Of Roads and Rivers: Aspects of Travel and Transport in 18th century Bengal' (unpublished MPhil dissertation, Centre for Historical Studies, Jawaharlal Nehru University, 1997).

7 Sarkar, *Inland Transport*, 58.

8 Tremenheere, *On Public Works*, 46. The view of another person, named Mr Greaves, was similar. Ibid., 43–4.

9 *MOR*, 133.

10 *Report on Public Works: Roads and Buildings, Bengal Presidency*, 1889–90, V/24/3336, British Library.

11 GOB, PWD, Road Cess Accounts Branch, file no. 8 of March 1885, *RRWRD*.

forms of mobility declined, as was the case with mobile communities. This also meant that the laying down of new 'fixed' routes by the colonial state – via roads (primarily the metalled trunk lines) and railways – did not simply open up new communications, but simultaneously either closed down or re-routed others. As Chapter 8 has shown, the building of railways led to the decline in the importance and maintenance of some roads. However, the picture is more nested than this. For instance, the railways did both: they undercut the previous transport routes and also stimulated the formation of new ones. The effects did not flow in one direction with the new technology 'displacing' earlier ones. On the contrary, not only did new technology have its own limitations of implementation, as was noted in the case of steamships on the Ganga, it also revitalized old ones to create complementary relationships.

Towards the end of this conclusion, let us now turn to new leads in the field of communication history. I am aware that this book has not comprehensively covered 'native responses' to the changing web of communication. It engages only with those groups that featured in the arena of colonial policies on communication. Zamindars, contractors, merchants, social elites, coolies, dandies, guides and mobile communities are groups scattered throughout the book. Part of the reason for this apparent omission lies in the fact that distinct changes in the patterns of mobility, as induced by the railways, started developing clearly after the 1870s–80s, the period where this work ends. A more profound reason is that the aim of the book has been to understand the colonial exigencies behind the development of communication, its rhetoric and policy, its interests and investments. However, the field of native travelling experience is interesting and vast, and has been gradually attaining scholarly attention. The groups that can be looked at from this viewpoint and the themes that can be addressed are myriad. Women, labour, artisans, peasants and pilgrims are the most obvious ones. The richness of the sources available for such a study is overwhelming. To illustrate this point further: the issue of either legitimacy and/or resistance to the new technology remain usually confined to 'high' debates on economic fallouts. However, the popular recollection of this technological device, railway, (often known as *dhuwangaadi* in the Bhojpuri belt of Bihar and UP, *dhuwan* meaning smoke and *gaadi* a car or a wagon) can potentially open up the field beyond the paradigms of economic drain and exploitation. Consider, for instance, the following lines by Ambikadutt Vyas (b. 1915 according to the Vikram Samvat, which would roughly correspond to 1857–58), who was the head pundit in the government zillah schools at different places such as Bhagalpur and Chapra:

रानी बिक्टोरिया के राज बड़ा भारी रामा ।
फईल गईले सब सन्सरवा रे हरी ॥
जहाँ देखो तहाँ चले धुआँकस रामा ।
चारो ओर लागल बाटे तरवा रे हरी ॥

[The rule of the queen Victoria is full of wonders,
It has extended all around the world,
Wherever you look the railways are running
Everywhere are spread the telegraph wires.]

The expression of one Kavi Tanki (poet Tanki) of the Gaya district was similar. Writing in the nineteenth century, he not only praised the construction of railways and bridges that gave employment to thousands, but also exclaimed that this 'wonder' is liked by all:

चलल रेलगाड़ी रँगरेज तेजधारी,
बोझाए खूब भारी हहाकार कईले जात बा ।
वईसे सब सूबा जहाँ बात हो अजूबा,
रँगरेज मनसूबा सब लोग के सुहात बा ।

[Off goes the train, with fierceness and rush,
Mighty it looks, creates thunderous sound on its way.
Reaches all the corners (subahs), where it is marvelled as a wonder,
This piece of work is admired by all.]

In yet another folksong written by Saheb Das of the Shahabad district, we find a positive acceptance of the new technology in its role played in helping people reach wherever they wished to go:

कहे कवि 'साहेब दास' अजब चाल रेल के,
जे जहाँ चाहे ताके तहाँ पहुँचवले बा ।

[So says the poet 'Saheb Das': wondrous is the railways' nature,
It brings people wherever they wish to go.]

In another set of folksongs of which the central subject is women, the engagement with this new technology does not revolve around the issue of acceptance and wonder but highlights technology's role in causing separation. Bhojpuri women, whose husbands went to 'Purab' (basically Calcutta) as either seasonal migrant workers or on a relatively permanent basis, suffered pangs of separation. These womenfolk dreaded the new technology not only because of the separation that it caused but also because of the possibility that their men would bring a *sawatiya* (second wife) from Bengal (Calcutta). However, this possibility of travel also opened up a world of desires; the women expected their men to bring 'new commodities' (mainly saris and ornaments) when returning home. How far these voices reflected the desires of women or the fear (and desires) of migrant men is a tricky question. Most of the folksongs were 'authored' by men and hence are liable to be read in reverse.[12] Whatever the case may be, such popular representations have the potential of addressing the key social issues of late nineteenth-century India in ways that have not been widely adopted so far. This book has tried to suggest that the history of communication would (and should) not only be the history of transport infrastructure, but forms a part of the history of technology, circulation, mobility, travel, commodities, and, not least, potentially also of gender.

---

12 Durgashanker Prasad Singh, *Bhojpuri ke Kavi aur Kavya*, ed. Vishwanath Prasad, 1st edn, (Patna, 1957), 2nd edn (Patna, 2001). I am collectively giving the page references for all the songs: Ambikadutt Vyas (186); Kavi Tanki (149); Saheb Das (149–50).

BIBLIOGRAPHY

I. Primary Sources

A. Unpublished government records

Asia and Africa Collections, British Library, London
Bengal Criminal and Judicial Consultations, 1793–95.
Bengal Railway Proceedings, 1863–75.
Bengal Revenue Council Consultations, 1773–75.
Board's Collections, 1796–1858.

National Archives of India, New Delhi
Government of India, Home Department, Public Works, 1850–54.
Government of India, Public Works Department, Proceeding Volumes, 1860–62.
Government of India, Public Works Department, Railway Proceedings, 1863–79.
Government of India, Public Works Department, (General, Communication, Traffic, Establishment, Accounts, Miscellaneous), 1863–79.

Bihar State Archives, Patna
Government of Bengal, Revenue Department (Agriculture and Miscellaneous) Proceedings, 1859–1901.
Government of Bengal, Finance Department, 1869.
Letters sent from Shahabad Collector, 1794–95.
Patna Commissioner Record Series, 1806–60.

Record Room of the Water Resource Department, Old Secretariat, Patna
Government of Bengal, Public Works Department, General Branch, 1859–62.
Government of Bengal, Public Works Department, General Branch – Communications, 1872–1904.
Government of Bengal, Public Works Department, General Branch – Local Communications, 1879–85.
Government of Bengal, Railway Department, Railway Branch, 1898.
Government of Bengal, Road Cess, Accounts Branch, 1885.
Government of Bengal, Roads and Building Department, Communications Branch, 1892–95.

B. Maps

Maps, British Library, London
Collins, H. G. *Enlarged War Map of India Shewing the Civil and Military Stations, Post and Bangy Roads, Railways, Routes &c. with a Table of Distances* (London, 1858).
Cruchley, C. F. *New Map of India with the Roads, Railways and Military Stations* (London, 1857).
Joseph, Charles. *A New and Improved Map of the First Portion of the Grand Trunk Road from Calcutta and Benares* (Calcutta, 1855).
A New Map of Hindoostan (London, 1794).
School Room Map of Hindoostan by the Scottish School Book Association (London, 1852?).

Sketch Map Shewing the Principal Roads through the Presidency of Bengal and the Lieutenant Governorship of the Western Provinces (1850).

Upjohn, A. *Map of Post Roads through Bengal, Bahar, Orixxa, Oude, Allahabad, Agra and Delhi* (Calcutta, 1795).

Wyld, James. *Map of India* (London, 1840).

_____. *India Shewing the Post Roads and Dawk Stations* (London, 1848).

_____. *India Shewing the Post Roads and Dawk Stations* (London, 1850?).

_____. *Map of India: India Shewing the Post Roads and Dawk Stations* (London, 1857).

_____. *India Shewing the Post Roads and Dawk Stations* (London, 1860).

C. Private papers

MSS Eur, British Library, London

Anon. (1821). Mss Eur. E 271.

_____. (1853–54). Mss Eur. B 242.

Bayley, James. (1808–14). Mss Eur. D 970.

Hawkins, Francis James. (1806–1860). Mss Eur. B 365.

Okeden, William Parry. (1821–41). Mss Eur. A 210.

Raleigh, Edward Ward Walter. (1827–28). Mss Eur. D 786.

D. Published government reports and documents

The Annals of Indian Administration. Years consulted 1856–74.

Annual Administration Reports for Roads and Buildings and Railways, Government of Bengal, Public Works Department. Years consulted, 1894–1900.

Annual Progress Report of the Works under the Chief Engineer of Bengal for the year 1874–75.

Annual Report on the Administration of the Bengal Presidency. Years consulted 1860–73.

Annual Report on the Police of the Patna Division: Champaran District, for the year 1867–68.

Buchanan, Francis. *An Account of the District of Purnea, 1809–10* (Patna, 1928).

_____. *An Account of the Districts of Behar and Patna in 1811–12*, 2 vols (Patna, 1934).

_____. *An Account of the District of Shahabad, 1812–13* (Patna, 1934).

_____. *An Account of the District of Bhagalpur, 1810–11* (Patna, 1939).

Correspondence Related to the Ferry Funds in the Lower Provinces (Calcutta, 1857).

Datta, K. K., ed. *Selections from Unpublished Correspondence of the Judge-Magistrate and the Judge of Patna, 1790–1857* (Patna, 1954).

_____, ed. *Selections from the Judicial Records of the Bhagalpur District Office (1792–1805)* (Patna, 1968).

_____. *A Handbook of Bhagalpur District Revenue Records, 1774–1855* (Patna, 1975).

Firminger, Walter, ed. *Bengal District Records: Rangpur, vol. 1: 1770–79* (Calcutta, 1914).

_____. *The Fifth Report from the Select Committee of the House of Commons on the Affairs of the East India Company*, vol. 2 (Calcutta, 1917).

_____, ed. *Bengal District Records: Rangpur, vol. 2: 1779–1782 (Letters Received)* (Calcutta, 1920).

_____, ed. *Bengal District Records: Rangpur, vol. 6: 1786–87 (Letters Issued)* (Calcutta, 1928).

Forrest, G. W., ed. *Selections from the Letters, Despatches, and Other State Papers Preserved in the Foreign Department of the Government of India, 1772–1785*, 3 vols (Calcutta, 1890).

Gupta, Anil Chandra Das, ed. and comp. *The Days of John Company: Selections from Calcutta Gazette, 1824–1832* (Calcutta, 1959).

Gupta, Hiralal, ed. *Fort William-Delhi House Correspondence, 1777–81*, vol. 8 (Delhi, 1981).

Hunter, W. W. *A Statistical Account of Bengal: Bhagalpur and Santal Parganas*, vol. 14 (London, 1877).

_____. *A Statistical Account of Bengal: Districts of Gaya and Shahabad*, vol. 12 (London, 1877).

_____. *A Statistical Account of Bengal: Districts of Patna and Saran*, vol. 11 (London, 1877).

_____. *A Statistical Account of Bengal: Monghyr and Purniah*, vol. 15 (London, 1877).
Huttmann, G. H. *Official Papers Connected with the Improved Cultivation of Cotton* (Calcutta, 1839).
The Imperial Gazetteer of India: The Indian Empire (Economy), vol. 3, new edn (Oxford, 1907).
James, J. F. W. *Final Report on the Survey and Settlement Operations in the District of Patna (1907–11)* (Patna, 1914).
Jones, W. H. *Circular Orders of the Sudder Board of Revenue at the Presidency of Fort William…from September 1837 to the end of 1850* (Calcutta, 1851).
Journal of Francis Buchanan Kept During the Survey of the Districts of Patna and Gaya in 1811–12, ed. with Notes and introduction by V. H. Jackson (Patna, 1925).
Journal of Francis Buchanan Kept During the Survey of the District of Bhagalpur in 1810–11, ed. with notes and introduction by C. E. A. W. Oldham (Patna, 1930).
Login, T. *Traffic on Roads, Railways and Canals in India* (Roorkee, 1867).
Long, James. *Unpublished Records of the Government*, ed. M. P. Saha (1869; repr. Calcutta, 1973).
McClelland, J. M. *Report of a Committee for Investigating the Coal and Mineral Resources of India* (Calcutta, 1838).
Memoir on the Agricultural and Commercial Capabilities of Bengal in Observations with Reference to the Establishment of the East India Sugar and Agricultural Company, Extracted from Various Sources, with Original Calculations, and Remarks (London, 1836).
Operations for the Improvement of the Navigation of the Ganges from Revelgunge to Allahabad, during the Seasons 1852–53, and part of 1853–54 (Roorkee, 1855).
Paton, John. *Tables of Routes and Stages Through the Several Districts, under the Presidency of Fort William* (1814; repr. Calcutta, 1821).
Phillips, C. H., ed. *The Correspondence of Lord W. C. Bentinck, Governor General of India, 1828–35*, 2 vols (Oxford, 1977).
Phillips, C. H. and B. B. Misra, eds. *Fort William-India House Correspondence: Foreign and Secret, 1782–86*, vol. 15 (Delhi, 1963).
Progress Report of the Public Works Department, Bengal (Buildings and Roads Branch). Years consulted 1871–74.
Report by the Chief Engineer, Bengal on the Progress of Public Works. Years consulted 1858–62.
Report of Proceedings in the Public Works Department. Years consulted 1860–65.
Report of the Cotton Committee of the Agricultural and Horticultural Society of India (London, 1840).
Report of the Progress made during the Year 1862–63 in Imperial Public Works under the Bengal Government (Calcutta, 1863).
Report on Public Works: Roads and Buildings. Bengal presidency. Years consulted 1888–92.
Report Showing the Progress made during the Year 1861–62 in Public Works under the Bengal Government (Calcutta, 1862).
Revised Tables of Routes and Stages through the Territories under the Presidency of Bengal and the Lieutenant Governorship of Agra (Calcutta, 1838).
Roy Chaudhury, P. C. *Sarkar Saran, based on Old Correspondence Regarding Saran District in Bihar from 1785 to 1866* (Patna, 1956).
_____. *Gaya Old Records* (Patna, 1958).
_____. *Singhbhum Old Records* (Patna, 1958).
_____. *Muzaffarpur Old Records* (Patna, 1959).
Selections of Papers from the Records at the East India House, Relating to the Revenue, Police, and Civil and Criminal Justice under the Company's Governments in India (London, 1826).
Settar, S., ed. *Railway Construction in India: Select Documents*, 3 vols (New Delhi, 1999).
Sherwill, W. S. *Statistics of the District of Behar* (Calcutta, 1845).
_____. *General Remarks on the District of Monghyr* (Calcutta, 1848).
Statement Showing the Roads in the Province of Bengal under the Department of Public Works (Calcutta, 1854).
Statistical Atlas of India, 2nd edn (Calcutta, 1895).
Thomson, George. *Sketch of Two Lines of Road between Burdwan and Benares* (Calcutta, 1836).

Thornton, Edward. *Statistical Papers Relating to India* (London, 1853).
_____. *A Gazetteer of the Territories under the Government of the Viceroy of India*, rev. and ed. Roper Lethbridge (London, 1886).
Thuillier, H. L. *Statistics of the District of Patna* (Calcutta, 1847).
Touche, T. H. D. La, ed. *The Journals of Major James Rennell* (Calcutta, 1910).
Trevelyan, Charles E. *A Report upon the Inland Customs and Town-Duties of the Bengal Presidency* (Calcutta, 1834).
Tripathi, Amales, ed. *India Record Series, Fort William-India House Correspondence and Other Contemporary Papers Relating thereto (Public Series), 1793–95*, vol. 12 (Delhi, 1978).
A View of the Present State and Future Prospects of the Free Trade and Colonisation of India (London, 1828).
Waterfield, Henry. *Memorandum on the Census of British India of 1871–72* (London, 1875).
Wyatt, A. *Statistics of the District of Sarun consisting of Sircar Sarun and Champarun* (Calcutta, 1847?).
_____. *Geographical and Statistical Report of the District of Tirhoot* (Calcutta, 1854).

E. Contemporary works, pre-1900

'Accepted Travellers', *Calcutta Review* 24 (December 1856).
'An Account of a Hunting Party', *Asiatic Journal* 1 (1816).
'Account of the Manners of the INHABITANTS of India within the Ganges', *Weekly Miscellany; or Instructive Entertainer* 2, no. 38 (June 1774).
'Account of the Peninsula of the INDIES within the Ganges: Being that Part of Asia where the chief European Settlements are situated, and the Seat of the War in India', *Royal Magazine*, August 1761.
Address of Mr. Holt S. Hallett upon New Markets and extension of Railways in India and Burmah, delivered before the Ipswich Chamber of Commerce, on the 25th January 1887 (London, 1887).
Andrew, W. P. *A Letter to the Chairman of the Honourable East India Company, with Extracts from the Public Papers and Remarks* (London, 1848).
_____. *Railway in Bengal (Being the Substance of a Report addressed to the Chairman of the East India Company in 1849)* (London, 1853).
Anon. 'India: Its Products and Improvement', *Calcutta Review* 30 (January–June 1858).
Arnold, Edwin. *India Revisited* (London, 1886).
Ayrton, Fredrick. *Some Considerations on the means of Introducing Railways into India, in connection with the Incidental Principles of Legislation, as applied in the Proposed Bill for the Establishment of the Great Indian Peninsula Railway Company* (London, 1847).
'Autobiography of Sheikh Mohammed Ali Hazir (1692–1779)', *Asiatic Journal* (new series) 4 (1831).
Balfour, Edward. 'On the Migratory Tribes of Natives in Central India', *Journal of the Asiatic Society of Bengal* 13, no. 1 (1844).
Behbahani, Ahmad. *Mir'at Ul-Ahwal-i Jahan Numa* [trans. A. F. Haider, *India in the Early Nineteenth Century: An Iranian Travel Account* (Patna, 1996)].
Bell, Horace. *Railway Policy in India with a Historical Sketch* (London, 1894).
Bingham, W. R. *Canals for Irrigation and Navigation in India, particularly for Behar & C* (Calcutta, 1860).
Boulnois, C. 'East India Railway', *Calcutta Review* 31 (July–December 1858).
Bourne, John, *Railways in India*, 2nd edn (London, 1848).
Brainerd, J. A. and Wright, Caleb. *Historic Incidents and Life in India* (Chicago, 1867).
Briggs, Captain. 'Account of the Origin, History, and Manners of the Race of Men called Bunjaras', *Transactions of the Literary Society of Bombay* 1 (1819).
Briggs, Major General. *The Cotton Trade of India: Its Past and Present Condition, read before the Royal Asiatic Society, 16th November 1839* (London, 1839).
Browne, J. *A Description of the Jungle Terry Districts: Their Revenues, Trade, and Government with a Plan for the Improvement of Them* (London, 1788).

Bysack, Gaur Das. 'Notes on a Buddhist Monastery', *Journal of the Asiatic Society of Bengal* 59, no. 1 (1890).
'A Cadet's Debut in Calcutta', *Asiatic Journal* 10 (1833).
Campbell, A. 'On the Native Alum or Salajit or Nepal', *Journal of the Asiatic Society of Bengal* 2 (1833).
Chesney, George. *Indian Polity: A View of the System of Administration in India*, 2nd edn (London, 1870).
Clarke, Hyde. *Colonization, Defence, and Railways in Our Indian Empire* (London, 1857).
Colebrooke, H. T. *Remarks on the Present State of the Husbandry and Commerce of Bengal* (Calcutta, 1795).
Colebrooke, R. H. 'On the Course of the Ganges through Bengal', *Asiatic Researches* 7 (1803).
'The Collector', *Asiatic Journal* 5 (1831).
Collins, I. G. *An Essay in favour of the Colonization of the North and North-West Provinces of India with regard to the question of Increased Cotton Supply and its bearing on the Slave Trade* (London, n.d., c. 1859–60).
The Conduct of the East India Company, with Respect to Their Wars & C. (London, 1767).
Cotton, Arthur. *Public Works in India, Their Importance; with Suggestions for their Extension and Improvement* (London, 1854).
The Cotton Trade of India: Can India Supply England with Cotton (London, 1839).
The Cotton Trade of India: Its future Prospects, pt 2 (London, 1840).
Cumberlege, N. R. *Some Account of the Bunjarah Class* (Bombay, 1882).
d'Anville, Jean. *A Geographical Illustration of the Map of India*, trans. from French by William Herbert (London, 1759).
D'Oyly, Charles. *Amateur Repository of Indian Sketches, Part I* (Calcutta, 1828).
———. *Behar Amateur Lithographic Scrap Book* (1828).
———. *Selection from the Early Experiments of the Bahar Amateur Lithographic Press* (1828).
———. *Sketches of the New Road in a Journey from Calcutta to Gyah* (Calcutta, 1830).
Daniell, Thomas and William Daniell. *A Picturesque Voyage to India; by the way of China* (London, 1810).
Danvers, Juland. *Indian Railways: Their Past History, Present Condition and Future Prospects* (London, 1877).
Davidson, Edward. *The Railways of India with an Account of their Rise, Progress and Construction* (London, 1868).
Davies, A. Mervyn. *Life and Times of Warren Hastings* (repr. Delhi, 1988).
Deane, A. *A Tour through the Upper Provinces of Hindostan; Comprising a Period between the Years 1804 and 1814: with Remarks and Authentic Anecdotes to which is Annexed, a Guide up the River Ganges with a Map from the Source to the Mouth* (London, 1823).
Digney, J. *Journal of an Experimental Voyage up the Ganges, on board the Honorable Company's Steamer 'Megna'* (Calcutta, 1846).
Duncan, Jonathan. 'An Account of Two Fakirs, with their Portraits', *Asiatic Researches* 5 (1799).
Eden, Emily. *Up the Country: Letters written to her Sister from the Upper Provinces of India*, 2 vols (London, 1866).
Eundo, Vires Acquirit. *A Handbook of useful Information for Officers and Soldiers of the British and Hon. East India Company Service in India, and for Travellers Proceeding through Bengal and the Punjab* (London, 1853).
'A Fair on the Ganges', *All the Year Round* 5, no. 122 (August 1861).
Firminger, Walter K., ed. *The Diaries of Three Surgeons of Patna (1763)* (Calcutta, 1909).
'Fitrat', Biharilal. *Aina-i-Tirhut*, ed. Hetukar Jha in *Mithila in the Nineteenth Century* (Darbhanga, 2001).
Five Months with the Prince in India Containing a Glance at the Inner Life of the Inhabitants, and Narrating the Chief Romantic and Picturesque Incidents in Connection with the Visit of the Prince of Wales (London, 1876).

Forrest, Charles Ramus. *A Picturesque Tour along the River Ganges and Jumna in India, Consisting of Twenty-Four highly finished and Coloured Views, a Map, and Vignettes, from Original drawing made on the Spot: with Illustrations, Historical and Descriptive* (London, 1824).

Francklin, William. *Inquiry Concerning the Site of Ancient Palibothra, Conjectured to Lie within the Limits of the Modern District of Bhaugulpoor, according to Researches made on the Spot in 1811 and 1812* (London, 1815).

Frazer, R. W. *British India* (London, 1896).

Freeman, John. *British India or A Reply to the Memorandum of the East India Company: Or An Insight into British India* (London, 1858).

Gilchrist, J. B. *The General East India Guide and Vade Mecum; for the Public Functionary, Government Officer, Private Agent, Trader or Foreign Sojourner, in British India, and the Adjacent Parts of Asia immediately Connected with the Honourable East India Company, Being a Digest of the Work of the Late Capt. Williamson, with many Improvements and Additions* (London, 1825).

Gleig, G. R. *Memoirs of the Life of the Right Honourable Warren Hastings* (London, 1841).

'The Governor General', *Asiatic Journal* 5 (1831).

Grand, George. F. *The Narrative of the Life of a Gentleman Long Resident in India*, with an introduction by Walter Firminger (1814; repr. Calcutta, 1911).

Gunthorpe, Major E. J. *Notes on Criminal Tribes Residing in or Frequenting the Bombay Presidency, Berar, and the Central Provinces* (Bombay, 1882).

Halliday, Fred Jas. *Letters Indicating Practical Means for the Extensive Development of Cheap Railways in India* (Calcutta, 1849).

Halls, John James. *Two Months in Arrah in 1857* (London, 1860).

Hand, J. Reginald. *Early English Administration of Bihar, 1781–1785* (Calcutta, 1894).

Hathron, Captain J. G. *A Handbook of Darjeeling* (Calcutta, 1863).

Haughton, J. C. 'Memorandum on the Geological Structure and Mineral Resources of the Singhbhoom Division', *Journal of the Asiatic Society of Bengal* 23, nos. 1–7 (1854).

Heber, Reginald. *Narrative of a Journey through the Upper Provinces of India from Calcutta to Bombay, 1824–25* (1827; repr. New Delhi, 1993).

Henderson, Andrew. 'On River Steamers, their Form, Construction, and Fittings, with Reference to the Necessity for Improving the Present Means of Shallow Water Navigation on the Rivers of British India', *Report of the Twenty-Eighth Meeting of the British Association for the Advancement of Science* (London, 1859).

Hinchingbrook, Viscount. *Diary in Ceylon and India, 1878–79* (London, 1879).

Hodges, William. *Travels in India during the Years 1780, 1781, 1782, and 1783*, 2nd edn (London, 1794; repr. Delhi, 1999).

Illustrations of the Mode of Preparing the Indian Opium Intended for the Chinese Market, from drawings by Captain Walter S. Sherwill (London, 1851).

Illustrations of the Roads throughout Bengal Including those to Madras and Bombay (Calcutta, 1828).

Jackson, Welby. 'Memorandum on the Iron Works of Beerbhoom', *Journal of the Asiatic Society of Bengal* 14, pt 2, no. 166 (December 1845).

Jacquemont, Victor. *Letters from India Describing a Journey in the British Dominions of India* (London, 1834; repr. Delhi, 1993).

Jervis, Thos. Best. 'Memoir on the Origin, Progress, and Present State of the Surveys in India', *Journal of the Royal Geographical Society of London* 7 (1837).

Johnston, J. H. 'Communication between the Ganges and Hoogly, & C.', *Journal of the Royal Geographical Society of London* 2 (1832).

Jordan, F. J. *Postal Guide Containing the Chief Public Regulations of the Post Office, Telegraph and Railway*, 3rd edn, rev. and enlarged (Calcutta, 1864).

'Journal of the Route of the Marquis Wellesley to the Upper Provinces', *Asiatic Annual Register* 4 (1802).

Khan, Abu Taleb. *The Travels of Mirza Abu Taleb Khan in Asia, Africa and Europe during the Years 1799, 1800, 1801, 1802, and 1803*, English trans. Charles Stewart (London, 1810).

Kulshreshtha, Harishchandra. *Thugee ki Chapet Bagee ki Rapet, (Prahasan), Chaar Ankon Mein* (Benares, 1884).
'Life in India', *Asiatic Journal* 2 (1816).
Lockwood, Edward Dowdeswell. *Natural History, Sport and Travel* (London, 1878).
Luard, Captain John. *A Series of Views in India; Comprising Sketches of Scenery, Antiquities and Native Character, drawn from Nature and on Stone* (London, 1833).
Macgeorge, G.W. *Ways and Works in India* (Westminster, 1894).
Mann, James A. *The Cotton Trade of India* (London, 1860).
Markham, C. R. *Major James Rennell and the Rise of Modern English Geography* (London, Paris and Melbourne, 1895).
Martin, Montgomery. *The History, Antiquities, Topography and Statistics of Eastern India*, 3 vols (London, 1838).
Maxwell. 'Colonization in India', *Calcutta Review* 31 (1858).
Memoirs of a Bengal Civilian by John Beams (London, 1961; new edn Delhi, 1984).
Monier-Williams, Monier. *Modern India and the Indians: Being a Series of Impressions, Notes and Essays*, 2nd edn (London, 1878).
Montgomerie, T. G. 'On the Geographical Position of Yarkund, and Some Other Places in Central Asia', *Journal of the Royal Geographical Society of London* 36 (1866).
Mundy, G. C. *Pen and Pencil Sketches, being the Journal of A Tour in India* (London, 1832).
Murray, John. *A Handbook for India* (London, 1859).
Narrative of Ajeet Singh, a Noted Dacoit in the North Western Provinces of India (Agra, 1843).
'Notes and Suggestions on Indian Affairs', *The Dublin University Magazine*, November 1849.
Oldham, Thomas. 'Notes upon the Geology of the Rajmahal Hills: Being the Result of Examinations Made During the Cold Season of 1852–53', *Journal of the Asiatic Society of Bengal* 23, no. 3 (1854).
Orlich, Leopold von. *Travels in India Including Sinde and the Punjab*, English trans. H. Evans Lloyd, 2 vols (London, 1845; repr. Lahore, 1976).
'Our Future', *Calcutta Review* 30 (1858).
Peggs, James. *Ghaut Murders in India* (London, 1828).
Pennant, Thomas. *The View of Hindoostan*, 2 vols (London, 1798).
Piddington, Henry. *A Memoir on the Proposed Improvements in Indian Cotton addressed to the Right Honourable Lord Auckland* (Calcutta, 1840).
Prinsep, G. A. *Remarks on the External Commerce and Exchanges of Bengal, with Appendix of Accounts and Estimates* (London, 1823).
_____. *An Account of Steam Vessels and of Connected Proceedings with Steam Navigation in British India* (Calcutta, 1830).
'Queries Respecting the Human Race', *Journal of the Asiatic Society of Bengal* 13, no. 2 (1844).
Reasons for Railways in Madras and Bombay and against the Exclusive Favour of Government to those in Bengal and Agra, 2nd edn (London, 1847).
Rennell, James. *A Description of the Roads in Bengal and Bahar* (London, 1778).
_____. *Memoir of a Map of Hindoostan; or the Mogul's Empire*, 2nd edn (London, 1785).
'Report of a Route-Survey made by Pundit, from Nepal to Lhasa, and thence Through Its Upper Valley of the Brahmaputra to Its Source', *Journal of the Royal Geographical Society of London* 38 (1868).
'Review of Journal of a Voyage in 1811 and 1812 to Madras and China', *Asiatic Journal* 2 (1816).
'Review of Sketches of India; Or Observations Descriptive of the Scenery, & C. of Bengal. written in India, in the Years 1811, 12, 13, 14; together with Notes on the Cape of Good Hope and St. Helena, written at those Places in February, March and April, 1815', *Asiatic Journal* 2 (1816).
'Review of Tracts, Historical and Statistical, on India by Benjamin Heynes', *Asiatic Journal* 2 (1816).
Richardson, David. 'An Account of the Bazeegurs, a Sect commonly Denominated Nuts', *Asiatic Researches* 7 (1803).

Robinson, Albert. *Account of Some Recent Improvements in the System of Navigating the Ganges by Iron Steam Vessels* (London, 1848).

Row, J. 'Geological Remarks during the March from Benares (Old Road) via Hazareebaugh, Bankoora and Burdwan to Barrackpoor', *Journal of the Asiatic Society of Bengal* 13, pt 2, no. 155 (1844).

Seely, J. B. *The Road Book of India Or East Indian Traveller's Guide* (London, 1825).

Shaw, Thomas. 'On the Inhabitants of the Hills near Rajamahall', *Asiatic Researches* 4 (1801).

Sherwill, W. S. 'Note upon a Curious Sandstone Formation at Sasseram, Zillah Shahabad', *Journal of the Asiatic Society of Bengal* 14, pt 2, no. 163 (1845).

———. 'Geological Notes on Zillah Shahabad, or Arrah', *Journal of the Asiatic Society of Bengal* 16, no. 1 (January–June 1847).

———. 'Notes upon a Tour through the Rajmahal Hills', *Journal of the Asiatic Society of Bengal* 20, no. 7 (1851).

———. 'A Short Notice of an Ancient Colossal figure carved in Granite on the Mandar Hill in the District of Bhagalpur', *Journal of the Asiatic Society of Bengal* 20, no. 3 (1851).

———. 'A Sketch of the Behar Mica Mines', *Journal of the Asiatic Society of Bengal* 20, no. 4 (1851).

———. 'The Kurruckpoor Hills', *Journal of the Asiatic Society of Bengal* 31, no. 3 (1852).

———. 'Note on the Geological Features of Zillah Behar', *Journal of the Asiatic Society of Bengal* 15, no. 169 (1856).

———. 'Notes upon Some Remarkable Waterspouts seen in Bengal between the Years 1852 and 1860', *Journal of the Asiatic Society of Bengal* 29, no. 4 (1860).

'Singular Customs at Arracan, in India beyond the Ganges', *La Belle Assemblee, or Bell's Court and Fashionable Magazine*, 1 August 1814.

Sketches of India; Or Observations Descriptive of the Scenery, & c. of Bengal. written in India, in the Years 1811, 12, 13, 14; together with Notes on the Cape of Good Hope and St. Helena, written at those Places in February, March, and April, 1815 (London, 1816).

Sleeman, William. *Thugs or Phansigars of India* (Philadelphia, 1839).

———. *Rambles and Recollections of an Indian Official* (Westminster, 1893); new edn ed. V. A. Smith, 2 vols (Delhi and Madras, 1995).

Solvyns, François Balthazar. *Les Hindoûs*, 4 vols (Paris, 1808–12).

Stephenson, John. *Treatise on the Manufacture of Saltpetre* (Calcutta, 1835).

Stephenson, R. M. *The Science of Railway Construction*, 4th edn rev. and augmented Edward Nugent (London, 1869).

Stevenson, J. 'Notice of a Native Sulphate of Alumina from the Aluminous Rocks of Nipal', *Journal of the Asiatic Society of Bengal* 2 (1833).

Stewart, Charles. *The History of Bengal* (London, 1813).

Stocqueler, Joachim Hayward. *India: History, Climate, Productions; with a Full Account of the Origin, Progress and Development of the Bengal Mutiny, and Suggestions as to the Future Government of India* (London, 1857).

Strachey, John. *India: Its Administration and Progress*, with a foreword by M. C. J. Kagzi (1888; repr. Delhi, 1997).

Sykes, W. H. 'Expenditure in India on Public Works from 1837–38 to 1845–46', *Journal of the Statistical Society of London* 14, no. 1 (March 1851).

———. 'Notes on Public Works in India', *Journal of the Statistical Society of London* 21, no. 2 (1858).

———. 'Statistics of Sums Given by Native Gentry in India for Charitable and Educational Institutions and for Works of Public Utility', *Journal of the Statistical Society of London* 30, no. 4 (1867).

Tanner. 'Native Coal', *Asiatic Journal* (new series) 5 (1831).

Tayler, William. *Brief Narrative of Events Connected with the Removal of W. Tayler from the Commissionership of Patna* (Calcutta, 1857).

Tremenheere, George Borlase. *On Public Works in the Bengal Presidency, with an Abstract of the Discussion upon the Paper*, ed. Charles Manby (London, 1858).

Valbezen, E. de. *The English and India: New Sketches* (2nd edn, Paris, 1875; repr. Delhi, 1986).

Vambery, M. *The Travels and Adventures of the Turkish Admiral Sidi Ali Reis in India, Afghanistan, Central Asia and Persia during the years 1553–1556* (London, 1899).
Wheeler, J. T. *A Short History of India and of the Frontier States of Afghanistan, Nipal and Burma* (London, 1894).
Williamson, Thomas. *The East India Vade-Mecum*, 2 vols (London, 1810).
Yule, Henry and A. C. Burnell, *Hobson-Jobson: The Anglo-Indian Dictionary* (1886; Herfordshire, 1996).

II. Secondary Sources

A. Published books and articles

Abdul Ali, A. F. M. 'Patna – Her Relations with the John Company Bahadur', *Bengal Past and Present* 41, nos. 81–2 (1931).
Ahmad, Khan Bahadur Saiyid Zamiruddin. 'Daud Khan Quraishi, Governor of Bihar and Founder of the Town of Daudnagar', *Journal of Bihar and Orissa Research Society* 4, no. 3 (1918).
Ahmed, Qeyamuddin. *Corpus of Arabic and Persian Inscriptions from Bihar (A.H. 640–1200)* (Patna, 1973).
Ahuja, N. D. 'Abd-al-Latif Al 'Abbasi and his Account of Punjab', *Islamic Culture* 41, no. 2 (1967).
Ahuja, Ravi. 'Labour Unsettled: Mobility and Protest in the Madras Region, 1750–1800', *Indian Economic and Social History Review* 35, no. 4 (1998).
———. '"The Bridge Builders": Some Notes on Railways, Pilgrimage and the British "Civilizing Mission" in Colonial India', in Harald Fischer-Tiné and Michael Mann, eds, *Colonialism as Civilizing Mission: Cultural Ideology in British India* (London, 2003).
———. '"Opening up the Country"? Patterns of Circulation and Politics of Communication in Early Colonial Orissa', *Studies in History* 20, no. 1 (2004).
———. *Pathways of Empire: Circulation, 'Public Works' and Social Space in Colonial Orissa, 1780–1914* (New Delhi, 2009).
Alam, Muzaffar. 'The Pursuit of Persian: Language Politics in Mughal India', *Modern Asian Studies* 32, no. 2 (1998).
———. *The Languages of Political Islam: India 1200–1800* (Chicago, 2004).
Alam, M. and S. Alavi. *A European Experience of the Mughal Orient: The I'jaz-I Arsalani (Persian Letters, 1773–1779) of Antoine-Louis Henri Polier*, paperback edn (New Delhi, 2007).
Alam, M. and S. Subrahmanyam. 'Discovering the Familiar: Notes on the Travel-Account of Anand Ram Mukhlis, 1745', *South Asia Research* 16, no. 2 (1996).
———. 'The Deccan Frontier and Mughal Expansion, ca. 1600: Contemporary Perspectives', *Journal of the Economic and Social History of the Orient* 47, no. 3 (2004).
Alam, M., F. N. Delvoye and M. Gaborieau, eds. *The Making of Indo-Persian Culture* (New Delhi, 2000).
Alavi, Seema. 'The Company Army and Rural Society: Invalid Thannah 1780–1830', *Modern Asian Studies* 27, no. 1 (1993).
Ali, M. Athar. 'The Evolution of the Perception of India: Akbar and Abu'l Fazl', *Social Scientist* 24 (1996).
Appadurai, Arjun. *Modernity at Large: Cultural Dimensions of Globalization* (Minneapolis, 1996).
Aquil, Raziuddin. 'Salvaging a Fractured Past: Reflections on Norms of Governance and Afghan-Rajput Relations in North India in the Late Fifteenth and Early Sixteenth Centuries', *Studies in History* 20, no. 1 (2004).
Archer, Mildred. *British Drawings in the India Office Library*, vol. 1 (London, 1969).
———. *Artist Adventurers in Eighteenth Century India; Thomas and William Daniell* (London, 1974).
Archer, Mildred and Ronald Lightbown, *India Observed: India as Viewed by British Artists, 1760–1860* (London, 1982).

———. *Company Paintings: Indian Paintings of the British Period* (London, 1992).
Arnold, David. *Science, Technology and Medicine in Colonial India* (Cambridge, 2000).
———. *The Tropics and the Traveling Gaze: India, Landscape and Science, 1800–1856* (New Delhi, 2005).
Asher, Catherine B. 'The Mausoleum of Sher Shah Suri', *Atribus Asiae* 39, nos. 3–4 (1977).
Asher, Catherine B. and Thomas R. Metcalfe, eds. *Perceptions of South Asia's Visual Past* (New Delhi, 1994).
Ashta, Mahesh Chandra. 'Passenger Fares on the Indian Railways, 1849–1869', *Indian Economic and Social History Review* 4, no. 1 (1967).
Askari, Syed Hasan and Qeyamuddin Ahmad, eds. *Comprehensive History of Bihar*, vol. 2, pt 2 (Patna, 1987).
Bagchi, Amiya Kumar et al. *Webs of History: Information, Communication and Technology from Early to Post-Colonial India* (New Delhi, 2005).
Balachandran, G., ed. *India and the World Economy 1850–1950* (New Delhi, 2003).
Ballantyne, Tony, ed. *Textures of the Sikh Past: New Historical Perspectives* (Oxford, 2007).
Ballantyne, Tony and Antoinette Burton. *Bodies in Contact: Rethinking Colonial Encounters in World History* (Durham NC, 2005).
Banerjee, Prathama. *Politics of Time: 'Primitives' and History-Writing in a Colonial Society* (New Delhi, 2006).
Barrow, Ian. *Making History Drawing Territory: British Mapping in India, c. 1765–1905* (Oxford and New Delhi, 2003).
Bassett, Thomas J. 'Cartography and Empire Building in Nineteenth-Century West Africa', *Geographical Review*, 84, 3, 1994.
Bautze, J. K., ed. *Interactions of Culture: Indian and Western Painting 1780–1910, The Ehrenfeld Collection* (Alexandria, 1998).
Bayly, C. A. 'Town Building in North India, 1790–1830', *Modern Asian Studies* 9, no. 4 (1975).
———. *Rulers, Townsmen and Bazaars: North Indian Society in the Age of British Expansion 1770–1870* (Cambridge, 1983).
———. 'Knowing the Country: Empire and Information in India', *Modern Asian Studies* 27, no. 1 (1993).
———. *Empire and Information: Information Gathering and Social Communication in India, 1780–1870* (Cambridge, 1996).
———. *Indian Society and the Making of the British Empire* (Cambridge, 1998).
Bearce, G. D. 'Lord William Bentinck: The Application of Liberalism to India', *Journal of Modern History* 28, no. 3 (1956).
———. *British Attitudes Towards India 1784–1858* (Oxford, 1961).
Begley, Wayne E. 'Four Mughal Caravanserais Built During the Reigns of Jahangir and Shah Jahan', *Muqarnas* 1 (1983).
Behal, Rana P. and Marcel van der Linden, eds. *International Review of Social History: Coolies, Capital and Colonisation: Studies in Indian Labour History*, suppl. 14 (2006).
Beinart, William. 'Men, Science, Travel, and Nature in the Eighteenth and Nineteenth Centuries Cape', *Journal of South African Studies* 24, no. 4 (1998).
Bernstein, Henry T. *Steamboats on the Ganges: An Exploration in the History of India's Modernization through Science and Technology* (Calcutta, 1960).
Bhanu, Dharma. 'Economic Condition of the People in the North-Western Provinces, 1830–1860', *Indian History Congress Proceedings*, 19th session, 1956.
———. 'Travel and Transport in the North-Western Provinces, 1830–1860', *Indian History Congress Proceedings*, 20th session, 1957.
Bhargava, Meena. 'Changing River Courses in North India: Calamities, Bounties, Strategies – Sixteenth to Early Nineteenth Centuries', *Medieval History Journal* 10, no. 183 (2007).
Bhattacharya, Neeladri. 'Introduction', *Studies in History* 14, no. 2 (1998).

_____. 'Predicaments of Mobility: Peddlers and Itinerants in Nineteenth-Century Northwestern India', in Markovits et al., *Society and Circulation: Mobile People and Itinerant cultures in South Asia* (New Delhi, 2003).

Bhattacharya, Sabyasachi. 'Cultural and Social Constraints on Technological Innovation and Economic Development: Some Case Studies', *Indian Economic and Social History Review* 3, no. 3 (1966).

_____. 'Eastern India I', in Dhrama Kumar with Meghnad Desai, eds, *The Cambridge Economic History of India*, vol. 2 (Cambridge, 1983).

_____. 'Introduction', in Rana P. Behal and Marcel van der Linden, eds, *International Review of Social History: Coolies, Capital and Colonisation: Studies in Indian Labour History*, suppl. 14, 2006.

Bhattasali, N. K. 'Bengal Chiefs' Struggle for Independence in the Reign of Akbar and Jahangir', *Bengal Past and Present* 35, pt 2, no. 70 (1928).

Biggs, Michael. 'Putting the State on the Map: Cartography, Territory, and European State Formation', *Comparative Studies in Society and History* 41, no. 2 (1999).

Biltcliffe, Pippa. 'Walter Crane and the *Imperial Federation Map Showing the Extent of the British Empire (1886)*', *Imago Mundi* 57, no. 1 (2005).

Brown, Katherine. 'Reading Indian Music: The Interpretation of Seventeenth-Century European Travel-Writing in the (Re)construction of Indian Music History', *British Journal of Ethnomusicology* 9, no. 2 (2000).

Bury, Harriet. 'Novel Spaces, Transitional Moments: Negotiating Text and Territory in Nineteenth-Century Hindi Travel Accounts', in Ian J. Kerr, ed., *27 Down: New Departures in Indian Railway Studies* (New Delhi, 2007).

Cammann, Schuyler. 'The Panchen Lama's Visit to China in 1780: An Episode in Anglo-Tibetan Relations', *Far Eastern Quarterly* 9, no. 1 (1949).

Carrey, W. H. *The Good Old Days of the Honourable John Company 1600–1858*, 2 vols (Calcutta, 1906–07; abridged edn, Calcutta, 1964).

Carter, Ian. *Railways and Culture in Britain: The Epitome of Modernity* (Manchester and New York, 2001).

Chakrabarti, Ranjan. *Authority and Violence in Colonial Bengal, 1800–1860* (Calcutta, 1997).

Chakrabarty, Dipesh. 'Foreword', *The Bernard Cohn Omnibus* (New Delhi, 2004).

Chandra, Bipan. 'Indian Nationalists and the Drain, 1880–1905', *Indian Economic and Social History Review* 2, no. 2 (1965).

_____. *The Rise and Growth of Economic Nationalism in India: Economic Policies of Indian Nationalism Leadership, 1880–1905* (New Delhi, 1966).

Chatterjee, Kumkum. 'History as Self-Representation: The Recasting of a Political Tradition in Late Eighteenth-Century Eastern India', *Modern Asian Studies* 32, no. 4 (1988).

_____. 'Trade and Darbar Politics in the Bengal Subah, 1773–1757', *Modern Asian Studies* 26, no. 2 (1992).

_____. *Merchants, Politics, and Society in Early Modern India, Bihar: 1733–1820* (Leiden, New York and Cologne, 1996).

Chattopadhyay, Basudeb. *Crime and Control in Early Colonial Bengal* (Calcutta, 2000).

Chaudhuri, K. N. 'Some Reflections on the Town and Country in Mughal India', *Modern Asian Studies* 12, no. 1 (1978).

Choudhury, Deep Kanta Lahiri. *Telegraphic Imperialism: Crisis and Panic in the Indian Empire, c. 1830* (Basingstoke, 2010).

Cohn, Bernard. 'From Indian Status to British Contract', *Journal of Economic History* 21, no. 4 (1961).

_____. 'The Role of Gosains in the Economy of Eighteenth and Nineteenth Century Upper India', *Indian Economic and Social History Review* 1, no. 4 (1963–64).

_____. *Colonialism and its Forms of Knowledge: The British in India* (Princeton, 1996), included in *The Bernard Cohn Omnibus* (New Delhi, 2004).

Colley, Linda. *Britons: Forging the Nation, 1707–1837* (Yale, 1992).

Collingham, E. M. *Imperial Bodies: The Physical Experience of the Raj* (Cambridge, 2001).

Conner, Patrick. *Twelve Oil Paintings by Thomas Daniell* (London, 1981).
_____. 'The Poet's Eye: The Intimate Landscape of George Chinnery', in Pauline Rohatgi and Pheroza Godrez, eds, *Under the Indian Sun: British Landscape Artists* (Bombay, 1995).
Cook, Andrew S. *Major James Rennell and A Bengal Atlas (1780 and 1781)*, India Office Library and Records Report, 1976.
Corfield, Wilmot. *Calcutta Faces and Places in Pre-Camera Days* (Calcutta, 1910).
Cosgrove, Denis and Stephen Daniels, eds. *The Iconography of Landscape: Essays on the Symbolic Representation, Design and Use of Past Environments* (Cambridge, 1988).
Cosson, A. de. 'The Early Days of the East Indian Railway', *Bengal Past and Present* 5, no. 11 (1910).
Cotton, Evan. 'The Daniells in India', *Bengal Past and Present* 37, pt 1, no. 3 (1929).
Cotton, Henry John Stedman. *Indian and Home Memories* (London, 1911).
Craib, Raymond B. 'Cartography and Power in the Conquest and Creation of New Spain', *Latin American Research Review* 35, no. 1 (2000).
Crooke, William. 'The Head-dress of Banjara Women', *Journal of Bihar and Orissa Research Society* 4, no. 3 (1918).
Dale, Stephen. 'The Poetry and Autobiography of the Babur-Nama', *Journal of Asian Studies* 55, no. 3 (1996).
Daniels, Stephen. 'The Political Iconography of Woodland in Later Georgian England', in Denis Cosgrove and Stephen Daniels, eds, *The Iconography of Landscape: Essays on the Symbolic Representation, Design and Use of Past Environments* (Cambridge, 1988).
Dasgupta, Atis. 'The Mughal Grant of a *Sanad* to Madari Fakirs: Historical Significance', *Journal of the Asiatic Society* 49, no. 2 (2007).
Datta, K. K. *Biography of Kunwar Singh and Amar Singh* (Patna, 1957).
_____. *The History of Freedom Movement in Bihar* (Patna, 1957).
_____, ed. *Selections from the Judicial Records of the Bhagalpur District Office (1792–1805)* (Patna, 1968).
_____. *Anti-British Plots and Movements Before 1857* (Meerut, 1970).
_____. *A Handbook of Bhagalpur District Revenue Records, 1774–1855* (Patna, 1975).
Datta, K. K. with Jatashankar Jha, eds. *Comprehensive History of Bihar*, vol. 3, pt 1 (Patna, 1976).
Datta, Rajat. *Society, Economy and the Market: Commercialization in Rural Bengal c. 1760–1800* (New Delhi, 2000).
Deloche, Jean. *Transport and Communications in India Prior to Steam Locomotion*, English trans. James Walker, 2 vols (Delhi, 1993).
Derbyshire, Ian. 'Economic Change and the Railways in North India, 1860–1914', *Modern Asian Studies* 21, no. 3 (1987).
_____. 'The Building of India's Railways: The Application of Western Technology in the Colonial Periphery 1850–1920', in Roy MacLeod and Deepak Kumar, eds, *Technology and the Raj: Western Technology and Technical Transfers to India 1700–1947* (New Delhi, Thousand Oaks and London, 1995).
_____. 'Private and State Enterprise: Financing and Managing the Railways of Colonial North India, 1859–1914', in Ian J. Kerr, ed., *27 Down: New Departures in Indian Railway Studies* (New Delhi, 2007).
Dewar, Douglas. *Bygone Days in India: With Eighteen Illustrations* (London, 1922).
Dewey, Clive. 'Images of the Village Community: A Study of Anglo-Indian Ideology', *Modern Asian Studies* 6, no. 3 (1972).
Digby, Simon. 'Iletmish or Iltutmish: A Reconsideration of the Name of the Delhi Sultan', *Iran* 8 (1970).
_____. 'The Sufi Shaykh and the Sultan: A Conflict to Claims of Authority in Medieval India', *Iran* 28 (1990).
_____. 'Some Asian Wanderers in Seventeenth Century India: An Examination of Sources in Persian', *Studies in History* 9, no. 2 (1993).
_____. 'Beyond the Ocean: Perceptions of Overseas in Indo-Persian Sources of the Mughal Period', *Studies in History* 15, no. 2 (1999).

_____. 'Before Timur Came: Provincialization of the Delhi Sultanate through the Fourteenth Century', *Journal of the Economic and Social History of the Orient* 47, no. 3 (2004).
_____. *Wonder-Tales of South Asia* (repr. New Delhi, 2006).
Dirks, Nicholas. 'Guiltless Spoliations: Picturesque Beauty, Colonial Knowledge, and Colin Mackenzie's Survey of India', in Catherine B. Asher and Thomas R. Metcalfe, eds, *Perceptions of South Asia's Visual Past* (New Delhi, 1994).
_____. 'Foreword', in *The Bernard Cohn Omnibus* (New Delhi, 2004).
'Discussion: Rennell and the Surveyors of India', *Geographical Journal* 134, no. 3 (1968).
Dislaskar, D. B. 'Bogle's Embassy to Tibet', *Indian Historical Quarterly* 9 (1933).
Diwakar, R. R., ed. *Bihar Through the Ages* (Bombay, 1959).
Dodwell, Henry. 'Economic Transition in India', *Economic Journal* 20, no. 80 (1910).
Doron, Assa. *Caste, Occupation and Politics on the Ganges: Passages of Resistance* (Surrey, 2008).
Dutt, R. C. *The Economic History of India*, 2 vols (London, 1903).
Dyson, Ketaki K. *A Various Universe: A Study of the Journals and Memoirs of British Men and Women in the Indian Subcontinent, 1765–1856* (Delhi, 1978).
Eaton, R. *The Rise of Islam and the Bengal Frontier, 1204–1760* (Berkeley and Los Angeles, 1993).
Edney, Matthew H. *Mapping an Empire: The Geographical Construction of British India, 1765–1843* (Chicago and London, 1997).
_____. 'Bringing India to Hand: Mapping an Empire, Denying Space', in Felicity Nussbaum, ed., *The Global Eighteenth Century* (Baltimore, 2003).
Edwardes, S. M. *Crime in India* (London, 1924).
Farooque, Abdul Khair Muhammad. *Roads and Communications in Mughal India* (Delhi, 1977).
Faruqui, Munis D. 'The Forgotten Prince: Mirza Hakim and the Formation of Mughal Empire in India', *Journal of the Economic and Social History of the Orient* 48, no. 4 (2005).
Finkelstein, David and Douglas M. Peers, eds. '"A Great System of Circulation": Introducing India into the Nineteenth-Century Media', in David Finkelstein and Douglas M. Peers, eds, *Negotiating India in the Nineteenth-Century Media* (London and New York, 2000).
Firminger, Walter K. 'Narrative of a Journey, etc. – I', *Bengal Past and Present* 13, nos. 25–6 (1916).
_____. 'Materials for a History of the Great Trunk Road – I', *Bengal Past and Present* 15, pt 1, no. 29 (1917).
Fischer-Tiné, Harald and Michael Mann, eds. *Colonialism as Civilizing Mission: Cultural Ideology in British India* (London, 2003).
Fisher, Michael H. 'The Office of Akhbar Nawis: The Transition from Mughal to British Forms', *Modern Asian Studies* 27, no. 1 (1993).
Flores, Jorge. 'Distant Wonders: The Strange and the Marvelous between Mughal India and Habsburg Iberia in the Early Seventeenth Century', *Comparative Studies in Society and History* 49, no. 3 (2007).
Forlong, J. G. R. 'The Life of Calcutta as a Seaport and the Mercantile Capital of Asia', *Geographical Journal* 16, no. 2 (1900).
Franklin, Michael J., ed. *Romantic Representations of British India* (London and New York, 2006).
Freitag, Sandria. 'Collective Crime and Authority in North India', in Anand Yang, ed., *Crime and Criminality in British India* (Arizona, 1985).
Gadgil, D. R. *The Industrial Evolution of India in Recent Times* (Calcutta, 1924).
Ghosal, H. R. 'Tirhut at the End of the Eighteenth and the Beginning of the Nineteenth Century (1790–1820)', *Journal of the Bihar Research Society* 39, no. 4 (1953).
Ghosh, Jamini Mohan. *Sannyasi and Fakir Raiders in Bengal* (Calcutta, 1930).
Gilbert, Helen and Anna Johnston, eds. *In Transit: Travel, Text, Empire* (New York, 2002).
Godrez, Pheroza. 'Nature's Tall Sentinels: Mountainscapes by British Artists in India', in Pauline Rohatgi and Pheroza Godrez, eds, *Under the Indian Sun: British Landscape Artists* (Bombay, 1995).
Gogate, Prasad P. and B. Arunachalam. 'Area Maps in Maratha Cartography: A Study in Native Maps of Western India', *Imago Mundi* 50 (1998).

Gole, Susan. *Early Maps of India* (New Delhi, 1976).
_____. *Indian within the Ganges* (New Delhi, 1983).
_____. *Maps of Mughal India: Drawn by Colonel Jean-Baptiste-Joseph Gentil, Agent for the French Government to the Court of Shuja-ud-Daula at Faizabad, in 1777* (London, 1988).
_____. *Indian Maps and Plans: From Earliest Times to the Advent of European Surveys* (New Delhi, 1989).
Gooptu Sharmistha and Boria Majumdar, eds. *Revisiting 1857: History, Myth, Memory* (New Delhi, 2007).
Gopal, Surendra. 'The Importance of Aina-i-Tirhut in Urdu Historiography', in Hetukar Jha, ed., *Mithila in the Nineteenth Century* (Darbhanga, 2001).
Gordon, Stewart. 'Scarf and Sword: Thugs, Marauders, and State-Formation in Eighteenth Century Malwa', *Indian Economic and Social History Review* 6, no. 4 (1969).
_____, ed. *Robes of Honour: Khil'at in Pre-Colonial and Colonial India* (Oxford and Delhi, 2003).
Goswami, Manu. *Producing India: From Colonial Economy to National Space* (Chicago and London, 2004).
Griffiths, Percival. *A History of the Joint Steamer Companies* (London, 1979).
Guest, Harriet. 'The Great Distinction: Figures of the Exotic in the Work of William Hodges', *Oxford Art Journal* 12, no. 2 (1989).
Guha, Sumit. 'The Handloom Industry of Central India: 1825–1950', in Tirthankar Roy, ed., *Cloth and Commerce: Textiles in Colonial India* (New Delhi, Thousand Oaks and London, 1996).
'A Guide up the River Ganges, from Calcutta to Cawnpore', *Bengal Past and Present* 31, nos. 61–2 (1926).
Gumperz, Ellen McDonald. 'City-Hinterland Relations and the Development of a Regional Elite in Nineteenth Century Bombay', in Ian J. Kerr, ed., *Railways in Modern India* (Delhi, 2001).
Gupta, M. N. *Analytical Survey of Bengal Regulations and Acts of Parliament Relating to India, up to 1833* (Calcutta, 1943).
Habib, Irfan. 'Cartography in Mughal India', *Indian Archives* 28 (1979).
_____. *An Atlas of the Mughal Empire: Political and Economic Maps with Detailed Notes, Bibliography and Index* (Delhi, 1982).
Haines, Chad. 'Colonial Routes: Reorienting the Northern Frontier of British India', *Ethnohistory* 51, no. 3 (2004).
Hall, Stuart, ed. *Representation: Cultural Representations and Signifying Practices* (London, Thousand Oaks and New Delhi, 1997).
Harley, J. B. 'Maps, Knowledge, and Power', in Denis Cosgrove and Stephen Daniels, eds, *The Iconography of Landscape: Essays on the Symbolic Representation, Design and Use of Past Environments* (Cambridge, 1988).
Harvey, David. 'Space as a Key Word', in Noel Castree and Derek Gregory, eds, *David Harvey: A Critical Reader* (Oxford, 2006).
Haynes, Douglas. 'Imperial Ritual in a Local Setting: The Ceremonial Order in Surat, 1890–1939', *Modern Asian Studies* 24, no. 3 (1990).
Heaney, G. F. 'Rennell and the Surveyors of India', *Geographical Journal* 134, no. 3 (1968).
Henningham, Stephen. 'Bureaucracy and Control in India's Great Landed Estates: The Raj Darbhanga of Bihar, 1879–1950', *Modern Asian Studies* 17, no. 1 (1983).
Hill, Christopher V. 'Philosophy and Reality in Riparian South Asia: British Famine Policy and Migration in Colonial North India', *Modern Asian Studies* 25, no. 2 (1991).
_____. *River of Sorrow: Environment and Social Control in Riparian North Bihar, 1770–1994* (Ann Arbor, MI, 1997).
Hill, S. C. 'Major Randfarlie Knox, Dilawar Jang Bahadur: A Memoir', *Journal of Bihar and Orissa Research Society* 3, no. 1 (1917).
Hirsch, Eric and Michael O'Hanlon, eds. *The Anthropology of Landscape: Perspectives on Place and Space* (Oxford, 1995).
History of Road Development in India, complied and published by Central Road Research Institute (New Delhi, 1963).

Hosain, Sheik Sajjad. *The Amir Hamza: An Oriental Novel*, pt 1 (Calcutta, 1892), republished as *An Oriental Novel Dastan-e Amir Hamza* (Patna, 1992).
Hosten, Rev. H. 'Relation of the Capuchin Missions in Egypt, Syria, Mesopotamia, Persia and East Indies (1644–47)', *Bengal Past and Present* 37, pt 2, no. 74 (1929).
Huddleston, G. *History of the East Indian Railway* (Calcutta, 1906).
Hurd, John. 'Railways', in Dharma Kumar with Meghnad Desai, eds, *The Cambridge Economic History of India*, vol. 2 (Cambridge, 1983).
Jacob, Christian. *The Sovereign Map: Theoretical Approaches in Cartography throughout History*, trans. Tom Conley and ed. Edward H. Dahl (Chicago and London, 2006).
Jafri, Sardar. 'Hafiz Shirazi (1312–1387–89)', *Social Scientist* 28 (2000).
Jassal, Smita Tewari. 'Caste and the Colonial State: Mallahs in the Census', *Contributions to Indian Sociology* 35, no. 3 (2001).
Jha, Jagdish Chandra. 'Early British Penetration into Chota Nagpur', *Journal of Bihar Research Society* 43, nos. 3 and 4 (1957).
Joshi, Chitra. 'Fettered Bodies: Labouring on Public Works in Nineteenth-Century India', in Marcel van der and P. Mohapatra, eds, *Labour Matters: Towards Global Histories, Studies in Honour of Sabyasachi Bhattacharya* (New Delhi, 2009).
Kapur, Nandini Sinha. 'The Bhils in the Historic Setting of Western India', in Rudolf C. Heredia and Shereen F. Ratnagar, eds, *Mobile and Marginalized Peoples: Perspectives from the Past* (New Delhi, 2003).
Kattenhorn, Patricia. *British Drawings in the India Office Library*, vol. 3 (London, 1994).
Kenny, Judith T. 'Climate, Race, and Imperial Authority: The Symbolic Landscape of the British Hill Station in India', *Annals of the Association of American Geographers* 85, no. 4 (1995).
Kerr, Ian J. 'Reworking a Popular Religious Practice: The Effects of Railways on Pilgrimage in 19th and 20th Century South Asia', in Ian J. Kerr, ed., *Railways in Modern India* (Delhi, 2001).
———, ed. *Railways in Modern India* (Delhi, 2001).
———. 'Representation and Representations of the Railways of Colonial and Post-Colonial South Asia', *Modern Asian Studies* 37, no. 2 (2003).
———. 'On the Move: Circulating Labor in Pre-Colonial, Colonial and Post-Colonial India', in Rana P. Behal and Marcel van der Linden, eds, *International Review of Social History: Coolies, Capital and Colonisation: Studies in Indian Labour History*, suppl. 14, 2006.
———. 'British Rule, Technological Change and the Revolution in Transportation and Communication: Punjab in the Later Nineteenth Century', in Tony Ballantyne, ed., *Textures of the Sikh Past: New Historical Perspectives* (Oxford, 2007).
———, ed. *27 Down: New Departures in Indian Railway Studies* (New Delhi, 2007).
Khan, Ahmad Raza. 'A Brief Survey of Trade and Commerce in Bihar during the Seventeenth Century', *Indian History Congress Proceedings* (1978).
Khan, Dargah Quli. *Muraqqa-e-Dehli*, English trans. Chander Shekhar and Shama Mitra Chenoy (Delhi, 1989).
Khan, Shayesta, ed. and trans. *The Holy City of Benares as Administered by a Muslim Noble: Social, Religious, Cultural and Political Conditions, 1781–1793, (Translation of Letters of Ali Ibrahim Khan written to the Maratha Chiefs, the Trustees of Mandirs & Others.)* (Patna, 1993).
Khobreakar, V. G., ed. *Tarikh-i-Dilkasha*, English trans. Jadunath Sarkar (Bombay, 1972).
Koch, Ebba. 'Dara-Shikoh Shooting Nilgais: Hunt and Landscape in Mughal Painting', *Freer Gallery of Art Occasional Papers*, vol. 1 (Arthur M. Sackler Gallery, Smithsonian Institute, Washington DC, 1998).
Kolff, D. H. A. 'Sanyasi Trader–Soldiers', *Indian Economic and Social History Review* 8, no. 2 (1971).
Kooiman, Dick. 'Meeting at the Threshold, at the Edge of the Carpet or Somewhere In Between? Questions of Ceremonial in Princely India', *Indian Economic and Social History Review* 40, no. 3 (2003).
Koshar, Rudy. '"What Ought to be Seen": Tourists' Guidebooks and National Identities in Modern Germany and Europe', *Journal of Contemporary History* 33, no. 3 (1998).

Kumar, Anil. *Trade in Early Medieval Eastern Bihar, c. A.D. 600–A.D. 1200* (Patna and New Delhi, 2001).

Kumar, Dharma, ed., with Meghnad Desai, *The Cambridge Economic History of India*, vol. 2 (Cambridge, 1983).

Kumar, Sunil. 'Assertions of Authority: A Study of the Discursive Statements of Two Sultans of Delhi', in M. Alam, F. N. Delvoye and M. Gaborieau, eds, *The Making of Indo-Persian Culture* (New Delhi, 2000).

———. 'The Ignored Elites: Turks, Mongols and a Persian Secretarial Class in the Early Delhi Sultanate', *Modern Asian Studies* 43, no. 1 (2008).

Laird, M. A., ed. *Bishop Heber in Northern India: Selections from Heber's Journal* (Cambridge, 1971).

Lal, Ruby. '"The 'Domestic World" of Peripatetic Kings: Babur and Humanyun, c. 1494–1556', *Medieval History Journal* 4, no. 1 (2001).

Latour, Bruno. *Science in Action: How to Follow Scientists and Engineers through Society* (Cambridge, MA, 1987).

Leask, Nigel. *Curiosities and the Aesthetics of Travel Writing, 1770–1840: 'From an Antique Land'* (Oxford, 2002).

———. *British Romantic Writers and the East: Anxieties of Empire* (Cambridge, 2002).

Lefebvre, Henry. *The Production of Space*, English trans. Donald Nicholsan-Smith (1974; repr. Oxford, 1991).

Lefevre, Corinne. 'Recovering the Missing Voice from Mughal India: The Imperial Discourse of Jahangir (r. 1605–1627) in his Memoirs', *Journal of the Economic and Social History of the Orient* 50, no. 4 (2007).

Linden, Marcel van der and P. Mohapatra, eds. *Labour Matters: Towards Global Histories, Studies in Honour of Sabyasachi Bhattacharya* (New Delhi, 2009).

Logan, Frenise A. 'Factors Influencing India's Ability to Maintain its Monopoly of the Cotton Export Trade after 1865', *Indian History Congress Proceedings* (23rd session, 1960).

Losty, J. P. 'A Career in Art: Sir Charles D'Oyly', in Pauline Rohatgi and Pheroza Godrez, eds, *Under the Indian Sun: British Landscape Artists* (Bombay, 1995).

———. 'The Place of Company Painting in Indian Art', in Joachim K. Bautze, ed., *Interactions of Culture: Indian and Western Painting 1780–1910, The Ehrenfeld Collection* (Alexandria, 1998).

Macpherson, W. J. 'Investment in Indian Railways, 1845–1875', *Economic History Review*, 2nd series, 8 (1958).

Mahajan, Jagmohan. *The Raj Landscape: British Views of Indian Cities* (New Delhi, 1988).

———. *The Grand Indian Tour: Travels and Sketches of Emily Eden* (New Delhi, 1996).

Majeed, Javed. 'James Mill's "The History of British India" and Utilitarianism as a Rhetoric of Reform', *Modern Asian Studies* 24, no. 2 (1990).

———. 'Meadows Taylor's Confessions of a Thug: The Anglo-Indian Novel as a Genre in the Making', in Bart Moore-Gilbert, ed., *Writing India, 1757–1990: The Literature of British India* (Manchester, 1996).

Mancke, Elizabeth. 'Early Modern Expansion and Politicization of Oceanic Space', *Geographical Review* 89, no. 2 (1999).

Mann, Michael. '"Torchbearers Upon the Path of Progress": Britain Ideology of a "Moral and Material Progress" in India', in Harald Fischer-Tiné and Michael Mann, eds, *Colonialism as Civilizing Mission: Cultural Ideology in British India* (London, 2003).

Markham, C. R. 'Review', *Geographical Journal* 38, no. 6 (1911).

Markovits, Claude, Sanjay Subrahmanyam and Jacques Pouchepadass, eds. *Society and Circulation: Mobile People and Itinerant cultures in South Asia* (New Delhi, 2003).

Marshall, P. J. 'Economic and Political Expansion: The Case of Oudh', *Modern Asian Studies* 9, no. 4 (1975).

———. 'Early British Imperialism in India', *Past and Present* 106 (1985).

———. 'British Society in India under the East India Company', *Modern Asian Studies* 31, no. 1 (1997).

———. 'The White Town of Calcutta under the Rule of the East India Company', *Modern Asian Studies* 34, no. 2 (2000).
———, ed. *The Eighteenth Century in Indian History: Evolution or Revolution?* (New Delhi, 2003).
———. 'British-Indian Connections c. 1780 to c. 1830: The Empire of the Officials', in Michael J. Franklin, ed., *Romantic Representations of British India* (London and New York, 2006).
McAlpin, Michelle Burge. 'Railroads, Prices and Peasant Rationality: India 1860–1900', *Journal of Economic History* 34, no. 3 (1974).
———. *Subject to Famine: Food Crises and Economic Change in Western India, 1860–1920* (Princeton, 1983).
McLane, John R. 'Bengali Bandits, Police, and Landlords After the Permanent Settlement', in Anand Yang, ed., *Crime and Criminality in British India* (Arizona, 1985).
Meston, Lord. 'Statistics in India', *Journal of the Royal Statistical Society* 96, no. 1 (1933).
Metcalf, Thomas R. *Ideologies of the Raj* (Cambridge, 1995).
Middleton, Dorothy. 'Review', *Geographical Journal* 150, no. 1 (1984).
Mohanty, Sachidananda, ed. *Travel Writing and the Empire* (Delhi, 2003).
Moon, Penderal. *Warren Hastings and British India* (London, 1947).
Moore-Gilbert, Bart, ed. *Writing India, 1757–1990: The Literature of British India* (Manchester, 1996).
Moosvi, Shireen. 'Man and Nature in Mughal Era', *Indian History Congress Symposia Paper 5* (Delhi, 1993).
Morris, Morris D. 'Towards a Reinterpretation of Nineteenth-Century Indian Economic History', *Journal of Economic History* 23, no. 4 (1963).
———. 'The Growth of Large-Scale Industry to 1947', in Dharma Kumar with Meghnad Desai, eds, *The Cambridge Economic History of India*, vol. 2 (Cambridge, 1983).
Mukherjee, Hena. *The Early History of the East Indian Railway 1845–1879* (Calcutta, 1994).
Mukherjee, Mukul. 'Railway and their Impact on Bengal's Economy, 1870–1920', *Indian Economic and Social History Review* 17, no. 2 (1981).
Mukherjee, Rudrangshu. '"Satan Let Loose upon Earth": The Kanpur Massacres in India in the Revolt of 1857', *Past and Present* 128 (1990).
Munshi, S. K. *Geography of Transportation in Eastern India Under the British Raj*, Centre for Studies of Social Sciences Monograph 1 (Calcutta, 1980).
Nair, Savithri Preetha. 'Science and the Politics of Colonial Collecting: The Case of Indian Meteorites, 1856–70', *British Journal for History of Science* 39, no. 1 (2006).
Naoroji, Dadabhai. *Poverty and Un-British Rule in India* (London, 1901).
Narain, V. A. 'Anglo-Nepalese Commercial Treaty of 1792', *Journal of Bihar Research Society*, 43, nos. 3 and 4 (1957).
Nayar, Pramod K. *English Writing and India, 1600–1920: Colonizing Aesthetics* (Oxford, 2008).
Nigam, Sanjay. 'Disciplining and Policing the "Criminals by Birth"', 2 pts, *Indian Economic and Social History Review* 27, nos. 2 and 3 (1990).
O'Hanlon, R. 'Manliness and Imperial Service in Mughal North India', *Journal of the Economic and Social History of the Orient* 42, no. 1 (1999).
Oldenburg, Veena T. *The Making of Colonial Lucknow, 1856–1877* (Princeton, 1984).
Oldham, W. 'Routes: Old and New, from Lower Bengal up the Country', 2 pts, *Bengal Past and Present* 28, nos. 55–6 (1924).
———. 'Review', *Geographical Journal* 71, no. 3 (1928).
Parasher-Sen, Aloka. 'Of Tribes, Hunters and Barbarians: Forest Dwellers in the Mauryan Period', *Studies in History* 14, no. 2 (1998).
Peabody, Norbert. 'Cents, Sense and Census: Human Inventories in Late Pre-Colonial and Early Colonial India', *Comparative Studies in Society and History* 43, no. 4 (2001).
Pearse, Hugh. 'Moorcroft and Hearsey's Visit to Lake Mansarowar in 1812', *Geographical Journal* 26, no. 2 (1905).
Pennell, T. L. *Things Seen: Northern India* (London, 1913).

Phillimore, R.H. *Historical Records of the Survey of India*, 5 vols (Dehra Sun: Survey of India, 1945–68).
———. 'Three Indian Maps', *Imago Mundi* 9 (1952).
Phukan, Shantanu. 'The Rustic Beloved: Ecology of Hindi in a Persianate World', *Annual of Urdu Studies* 15 (2000).
———. '"Through throats were many rivers meet": The Ecology of Hindi in the World of Persian', *Indian Economic and Social History Review* 38, no. 1 (2001).
Pinch, William. *Peasants and Monks in British India* (Berkeley, LA, and London, 1996).
———. 'Review: Same Difference in India and Europe', *History and Theory* 38, no. 3 (1999).
———. 'Gosain Tawaif: Slave, Sex, and Ascetics in Rasdhan, ca. 1800–1857', *Modern Asian Studies* 38, no. 3 (2004).
———. *Warrior Ascetics and Indian Empires, 1500–2000* (Cambridge, 2006).
Pouchepadass, Jacques. 'Itinerant Kings and Touring Officials: Circulation as a Modality of Power in India, 1700–1947, in Markovits et al., *Society and Circulation: Mobile People and Itinerant cultures in South Asia* (New Delhi, 2003).
Prasad, Leela. *Opposition to British Supremacy in Bihar – 1757–1803* (Patna and New Delhi, 1981).
Pratt, Mary Louise. *Imperial Eyes: Travel Writing and Transculturation* (London and New York, 1992).
Radhakrishna, Meena. 'The Criminal Tribes Act in the Madras Presidency: Implication for Itinerant Trading Communities', *Indian Economic and Social History Review* 26, no. 3 (1989).
———. *Dishonoured by History: 'Criminal Tribes' and British Colonial Policy* (Delhi, 2001).
Raj, Kapil. 'Colonial Encounters and the Forging of New Knowledge and National Identities: Great Britain and India, 1760–1850', *Osiris*, 2nd series, 15 (2000).
———. 'Circulation and the Emergence of Modern Mapping: Great Britain and Early Colonial India, 1764–1820', in Markovits et al., *Society and Circulation: Mobile People and Itinerant cultures in South Asia* (New Delhi, 2003).
———. *Relocating Modern Science: Circulation and the Construction of Knowledge in South Asia and Europe, 1650–1900* (Basingstoke, 2007).
Raman, Kartik Kalyan. 'Utilitarianism and the Criminal Law in Colonial India: A Study of the Practical Limits of Utilitarian Jurisprudence', *Modern Asian Studies* 28, no. 4 (1994).
Ramaswamy, Sumathi. 'Conceit of the Globe in Mughal Visual Practice', *Comparative Studies in Society and History* 49, no. 4 (2007).
Ray, Rajat Kanta, ed. *Entrepreneurship and Industry in India, 1800–1947* (Delhi, 1992).
———. 'Asian Capital in the Age of European Domination: The Rise of Bazaar', *Modern Asian Studies* 29, no. 3 (1995).
Raye, N. N. *The Annals of the English Settlement in Bihar* (Calcutta, 1927).
Reed, Robert R. 'The Colonial Genesis of Hill Stations: The Genting Exception', *Geographical Review* 69, no. 4 (1979).
Reeves, P. D., ed. *Sleeman in Oudh: An Abridgement of W. H. Sleeman's A Journey through the Kingdom of Oude in 1849–50* (Cambridge, 1971).
Richards, John. F. 'Warriors and the State in Early Modern India', *Journal of the Economic and Social History of the Orient* 47, no. 3 (2004).
Robb, Peter. 'Hierarchy and Resources: Peasant Stratification in Late Nineteenth Century Bihar', *Modern Asian Studies* 13, no. 1 (1979).
———. 'British Rule and Indian "Improvement"', *Economic History Review* 34, no. 4 (1981).
———. 'Law and Agrarian Society in India: The Case of Bihar and the Nineteenth Century Tenancy Debate', *Modern Asian Studies* 22, no. 2 (1988).
———. 'Peasants' Choices? Indian Agriculture and the Limits of Commercialization in Nineteenth-Century Bihar', *Economic History Review* 45, no. 1 (1992).
———, ed. *The Concept of Race in South Asia* (Delhi, 1995).
———. 'Completing "Our Stock of Geography" or an Object "Still More Sublime": Colin Mackenzie's Survey of Mysore 1799–1810', *Journal of the Royal Asiatic Society* 8, no. 2 (1998).

Rodd, Rennell. 'Major James Rennell. Born 3 December 1742. Died 20 March 1830', *Geographical Journal* 75, no. 4 (1930).

Rohatgi, Pauline. 'Preface to a Lost Collection: The Pioneering Art of Francis Swain Ward', in Pauline Rohatgi and Pheroza Godrez, eds, *Under the Indian Sun: British Landscape Artists* (Bombay, 1995).

Rohatgi, Pauline and Pheroza Godrez, eds. *Under the Indian Sun: British Landscape Artists* (Bombay, 1995).

Roy Chaudhury, P. C. 'Tirhoot during Early British Rule', *Journal of Bihar Research Society* 41, no. 4 (1955).

———. *Bihar in 1857* (Patna, 1957).

Roy MacLeod and Deepak Kumar, eds. *Technology and the Raj: Western Technology and Technical Transfers to India 1700–1947* (New Delhi, Thousand Oaks and London, 1995).

Roy, Tapti. 'Visions of the Rebels: A Study of 1857 in Bundelkhand', *Modern Asian Studies* 27, no. 1 (1993).

Roy, Tirthankar, ed. *Cloth and Commerce: Textiles in Colonial India* (New Delhi, Thousand Oaks and London, 1996).

———. 'Home Markets and Artisans in Colonial India: A Study of Brass-Ware', *Modern Asian Studies* 30, no. 2 (1996).

———. *Traditional Industry in the Economy of Colonial India* (Cambridge, 1999).

———. *The Economic History of India, 1857–1947* (Delhi, 2000).

Rudolf C. Heredia and Shereen F. Ratnagar, eds. *Mobile and Marginalized Peoples: Perspectives from the Past* (New Delhi, 2003).

Rycroft, Daniel J. *Representing Rebellion: Visual Aspects of Counter-Insurgency in Colonial India* (New Delhi, 2006).

Sandes, E. W. C. *The Military Engineer in India*, vol. 2 (Chatham, 1935).

Sarkar, Bejoy Kumar. *Inland Transport and Communication in Medieval India* (Calcutta, 1925).

Sarkar, Jadunath. *The India of Aurangzib (Topography, Statistics, and Roads) Compared with the India of Akbar* (Calcutta, 1901).

———. 'Travels in Bihar, 1608 A. D.', *Journal of Bihar and Orissa Research Society* 5 (1919).

———. 'A Description of North Bengal in 1609 A. D.', *Bengal Past and Present* 35 (1928).

———, ed. *Maasir-i-Alamgiri*, a work completed by Saqi Must'ad Khan in 1710 (Calcutta, 1947).

———. *A History of Dasnami Naga Sanyasis* (Allahabad, n.d, c. 1950s).

———, ed. William Irvine, *The Later Mughals*, 2 vols bound in one (New Delhi, 1971).

———, ed. *The History of Bengal*, vol. 2: *Muslim Period, 1200–1757*, 2nd impression (Dacca, 1972).

Sarkar, J. N. 'Patna and its Environs in the Seventeenth Century – A Study in Economic History', *Journal of Bihar Research Society* 34, nos. 1 and 2 (1948).

———. 'Restoration of Order in Manbhum after the Mutiny (1857–58)', *Journal of Bihar Research Society* 43, nos. 3 and 4 (1957).

———. 'Economic Life in Bihar, 1526–1757', in Syed Hasan Askari and Qeyamuddin Ahmad, eds, *Comprehensive History of Bihar*, vol. 2, pt 2 (Patna, 1987).

Sarkar, S. C., 'A Note on Puran Gir Gosain', *Bengal Past and Present* 43, nos. 85–6 (1932).

Schivelbusch, Wolfgang. *The Railway Journey: The Industrialisation of Time and Space in the Nineteenth Century* (Berkeley, 1986).

Sen, S. N. 'Steam Johnston', *Bengal Past and Present* 60, nos. 121–2 (1941).

Sen, Surendra Nath. *Indian Travels of Thevenot and Careri* (New Delhi, 1949).

Servan-Schreiber, Catherine. 'Tellers of Tales, Sellers of Tales: Bhojpuri Peddlers in Northern India', in Markovits et al., *Society and Circulation: Mobile People and Itinerant cultures in South Asia* (New Delhi, 2003).

Sharpe, J. A. *Crime in Early Modern England, 1550–1750* (1984; 8th impression, London, 1996).

Short, John Rennie. *Making Space: Revisioning the World, 1475–1600* (Syracuse, NY, 2004).

Singh, Durgashanker Prasad. *Bhojpuri ke Kavi aur Kavya*, ed. Vishwanath Prasad (1957; 2nd edn, Patna, 2001).
Singh, Jagdish. *Transport Geography of South Bihar* (Varanasi, 1964).
Singh, Major Madan Paul. *Indian Army under the East India Company* (New Delhi, 1976).
Singh, Nilu. *Social and Economic Development in Bihar, 1854–1885* (Patna, 2000).
Singh, Ram Briksh. *Transport Geography of Uttar Pradesh* (Varanasi, 1966).
Singh, Shyam Bihari. 'Saltpetre Industry of Zillah Tirhoot during the First Quarter of the Nineteenth Century', *Journal of Bihar Research Society* 37, nos. 3 and 4 (1951).
Singh, Shyam Narayan. *History of Tirhut: From the Earliest Times to the End of the Nineteenth Century*, with a foreword by Sir Haviland LeMesurier (Calcutta, 1922).
Singha, Radhika. *A Despotism of Law: Crime and Justice in Early Colonial India* (New Delhi, 1988).
_____. 'Providential Circumstances: The Thugee Campaign of the 1830s and Legal Innovation', *Modern Asian Studies* 27, no. 1 (1993).
Sinha, Nitin. 'Forged Linkages and the 'Spectre' of 1857: A Few Instances from Bihar', in Gooptu Sharmistha and Boria Majumdar, eds, *Revisiting 1857: History, Myth, Memory* (New Delhi, 2007).
_____. 'Contest and Communication: The Geography of Rebellion in Bihar', *Biblio: A Review of Books: A Special Issue on 1857* 12 (2007).
_____. 'Mobility, Control and Criminality in Early Colonial India, 1760s–1850s', *Indian Economic and Social History Review* 45, no. 1 (2008).
Skaria, Ajay. 'Being Jangli: The Politics of Wildness', *Studies in History* 14, no. 2 (1998).
Smyth, David. 'The Wyld Family Firm', *Map Collector* 55 (1991).
Soucek, Priscilla P. 'Persian Artists in Mughal India: Influences and Transformations', *Muqarnas* 4 (1987).
Specker, Konrad. 'Madras Handlooms in the Nineteenth Century', in Tirthankar Roy, ed., *Cloth and Commerce: Textiles in Colonial India* (New Delhi, Thousand Oaks and London, 1996).
Spencer, J. E. and W. L. Thomas. 'The Hill Stations and Summer Resorts of the Orient', *Geographical Review* 38, no. 4 (1948).
Spivak, Gayatri C. 'The Rani of Sirmur: An Essay in Reading the Archives', *History and Theory* 24, no. 3 (1985).
Stokes, Eric. 'The First Century of British Colonial Rule in India: Social Revolution or Social Stagnation', *Past and Present* 58 (1973).
Stuebe, Isabel. 'William Hodges and Warren Hastings: A Study in Eighteenth-Century Patronage', *The Burlington Magazine* 115, no. 847 (1973).
Subhan, Abdus. 'Tarikh-i Bangala-i Mahabat Jangi of Yusuf Ali Khan', pt 2, *Islamic Culture* 40, no. 4 (1966).
Subrahmanyam, Sanjay. 'Connected Histories: Notes Towards a Reconfiguration of Early Modern Eurasia', *Modern Asian Studies* 31, no. 3 (1997).
_____. *Penumbral Visions: Making Polities in Early Modern South India* (Ann Arbor, 2001).
Teltscher, Kate. *The High Road to China: George Bogle, the Panchen Lama and the British Expedition to Tibet* (London, 2006).
Thackston, W. M. *A Century of Princes, Sources of Timurid History and Art* (Cambridge, MA, 1989).
Thorner, Daniel. *Investment in Empire: British Railway and Steam Shipping Enterprise in India, 1825–1849* (Philadelphia, 1950).
_____. 'Capital Movement and Transportation: Great Britain and the Development of India's Railways', *Journal of Economic History* 11, no. 4 (1951).
Tillotson, G. H. R. 'A Fair Picture: Hodges and the Daniells at Rajmahal', in Pauline Rohatgi and Pheroza Godrez, eds, *Under the Indian Sun: British Landscape Artists* (Bombay, 1995).
_____. *The Artificial Empire: The Indian Landscapes of William Hodges* (Richmond, 2000).
Tiwari, R. D. *Railways in Modern India* (Bombay, 1941).
Varady, Robert, G. 'North India Banjaras: Their Evolution as Transporters', *South Asia* 2, nos. 1–2 (1979).

Vicziany, Marika. 'Imperialism, Botany and Statistics in Early Nineteenth-Century India: The Surveys of Francis Buchanan (1762–1829)', *Modern Asian Studies* 20, no. 4 (1986).
Wagner, Kim A. 'The Deconstructed Stranglers: A Reassessment of Thuggee', *Modern Asian Studies* 38, no. 4 (2004).
_____. *Thuggee: Banditry and the British in Early Nineteenth-Century India* (Hampshire and New York, 2007).
Wainwright, A. Martin. 'Representing the Technology of the Raj in Britain's Victorian Periodical Press', in David Finkelstein and Douglas M. Peers, eds, *Negotiating India in the Nineteenth-Century Media* (London and New York, 2000).
Washbrook, David. 'Progress and Problems: South Asian Economic and Social History', *Modern Asian Studies* 22, no. 1 (1988).
Westwood, J. N. *Railways of India* (Newton Abbot, 1974).
Yang, Anand. 'Dangerous Castes and Tribes: The Criminal Tribes Act and the Maghiya Doms of North-East India', in Anand Yang, ed., *Crime and Criminality in British India* (Arizona, 1985).
_____, ed. *Crime and Criminality in British India* (Arizona, 1985).
_____. *The Limited Raj: Agrarian Relations in Colonial India, Saran District 1793–1920* (Berkeley, LA, and London, 1989).
_____. *Bazaar India: Markets, Society, and the Colonial State in Gangetic Bihar* (Berkeley, LA, and London, 1998).

B. Unpublished dissertations

Appleby, L. L. 'Social Change and the Railways in North India, c. 1845–1914', unpublished PhD dissertation, University of Sydney, 1990.
Choudhuri, Deep Kanta Lahiri. 'Communication and Empire: The Telegraph in North India, c. 1830–1856', unpublished MPhil dissertation, Centre for Historical Studies, Jawaharlal Nehru University, New Delhi, 1997.
Chowdhury, Jaya. 'The Gosains and the Company, 1780–1830', unpublished MPhil dissertation, Centre for Historical Studies, Jawaharlal Nehru University, New Delhi, 1997.
Mukherjee, Tilottama. 'Of Roads and Rivers: Aspects of Travel and Transport in 18th Century Bengal', unpublished MPhil dissertation, Centre for Historical Studies, Jawaharlal Nehru University, New Delhi, 1997.
Varady, Robert Gabriel. 'Rail and Road Transport in Nineteenth Century Awadh: Competition in a North Indian Province', unpublished PhD dissertation, University of Arizona, 1981.

INDEX

Abdali, Ahmad Shah 132
Archer, Mildred 34n51, 35n51, 39n67, 45
Ahuja, Ravi xxiin18, xxvii–xxviii, xxxiii, xxxviii, 27n18, 156
Ain-i Akbari 98, 120n15; *see also* Fazl, Abul
Akbar (Acbar) 4, 11–12, 14n65, 20, 98
Akbarabad 11, 11n54; *see also* Rajmahal
al-Biruni 33: idea of Hindustan by 2n4; *Kitab-al-Hind* 2
al-Idrisi 33
Alam, Muzaffar xxvn23, 7, 14
Allahabad 28n23, 63, 74, 79n98, 111, 133, 151, 174, 176n107, 177n111, 178, 188, 196
Amherst, Lord 59–60, 61n16, 63, 142, 174
Andrew, W. P. 213–14
Anglo–Burmese War 28–9, 178
Appleby, L. L. xxiin17
Arnold, David xixn5, xxvn24, xxxvin44, 9n38, 18n78, 19n84, 26, 39, 57n3, 155n1, 173
Arrah 73, 83, 84n118, 86, 194, 196, 218, 219
Arwal 74, 76, 194
Auckland, Lord 50, 51n130, 61, 63n25, 64, 89n142, 224
Aurungzeb 2n2, 9, 41, 62n22, 76, 125

Bahar 46, 79, 114
Balasore 79, 87n134, 93–4
Balfour, Edward 125–6
Banerjee, Prathama xxi. xxin15
banjaras xxxvi, xxix, xxxii, 117, 121–2, 122n26, 123–5, 125n43, 125n45, 126n49, 127–8, 130, 136–7, 150–51, 152
Baroon 149, 207, 218–20
Barrackpur 39, 51–2, 167
Bayley, James 20n87, 38n65, 39, 47, 51
Bayly, C. A. xviii, 35, 57, 95, 119n10, 120, 121n20, 161, 193n71
bazaars 18, 48, 115, 183–4, 195n83, 231; in north Bihar, local 197–8, 223; during tours 60; founding of 15; in Hazaribagh,

military 222n107; on the NMR 81, 166; regulation of 72; on the roads 103
Behar 69, 128, 196; dacoity and robbery in 141–2; roads and ferries in 74, 111, 163, 167, 171–2, 218; trade of 193, 196, 222
Behbahani, Ahmed 16–17
Benares 129, 132–3, 141–2, 149n173, 151, 161–2, 208, 213; railways connecting 213; roads connecting 73–4, 79, 79n98, 83, 111, 166, 168, 193; road construction in 161–2; road safety in 121n20, 141–2; steamers connecting 174, 176, 176n107, 177n10, 178; trade of and with 193,195–6, 199, 222, 229; in travelogues 41, 47–8, 52
Bengal 15n67, 47n114, 65, 72n67, 79, 102n53, 143n140, 149, 198–9, 238n6; relationship with Bihar xxxvi–xxxviii, 45–6, 46n106; boatmen in 180, 186; boats of 42, 177; British views on condition of roads in 30–31, 158, 223, 238; cotton trade of 223–5, 227; districts, dacoity in 130–36; 140–41, 143n140; European travels to and from 35–8, 49–52; government towards steamships, early response of 29–30; early ironworks in 53; funds for roads in 83–6, 158, 160–62; colonial officials' isolation in 65n34, 65n35, 65n36, 88; Maratha salt into 128; difference between NWP and 69, 193n71; presidency, condition of and public expenditure on roads in 163–6, 208, 210–11, 237–8; railways in xxi, xxin15, 204–5, 214–17, 230–32, 240; rivers, navigation of 177, 213, 223, 228; in road construction, role of *zamindars* of 76–7; pre-colonial and colonial spatiality of 14–15; pre-colonial spatiality of 2–6; surveys and mapping in 93–4, 97, 168; colonial territoriality of 45–6, 46n106, 99; trade of and from 194–6, 198–9, 201,

223, 230–31; trade, politics and early colonial rule in 144, 237
Bentinck, Lord William 40, 58, 63, 129, 157–8; on 'patronage system' 71n56; on steam navigation and roads 28–30, 160, 165, 168, 174; change in travelling ritual by 63–4; unpopularity of 64
Bernstein, Henry T. 173n94, 177, 177n112, 179, 192, 192n66
Bettiah 74, 145, 145n152, 194, 197–8, 218, 237
Bhagalpur 29, 47, 54n146, 69, 70n53, 73, 75, 78n96, 83, 86, 102n53, 140n121, 142, 145, 147, 169, 169n76, 171–2, 182, 184, 194, 196, 209–10, 218–19, 223, 228–9, 232, 239
bhang 125
Bhimsen 2n2, 5, 13, 120
Bhooteas 198
Bihar xviii, xxxii, xxxvi, 37, 120, 125, 136–7, 167n58; cotton (piece-goods) in 70n53, 72n67,78, 78n96, 196–8, 213, 219, 223–6; late eighteenth-century communication network in 72–5; highway robberies and crime in 139–42, 149–50; Maratha raids in 80 railways in xxii, xxvi, xxxiv, 212–19, 223, 227–31, 239; regional historiography of xxxvii–viii; roads and ferries in xxiin18, xxxiv, 48n119, 72–5, 80–85, 103, 108, 114, 147, 161, 163–72, 193, 207–8, 211, 218–26, 231, 237; road repair in 75–7, 83–5, 168–72, 208–12; road and route surveys in 93–4, 107n80, 108, 208; topography and ecology of 45, 73; trade and trading ties of xxxiii, 79–80, 85–7, 128–9, 193–201, 212–13, 218–29; travelling picturesque representations of 46–7, 50, 120; *see also* Bengal
Bogle, George 133–5, 133n77, 199
bridges xvii, xxn8, 52, 85, 160–61, 160n24, 164–6, 164n47, 168, 170, 185, 218–20, 240; construction, native supervision of 84, 159; on the GTR 162, 167, 220; across the River Karmanasha, 162; across the River Lilajun on the GTR 208, 220; on the NMR 166–7; at Oodoonulla 40
British: conquest 15–16, 15n69, 20–21, 105, 107n80, 108; perception of ascetic groups 132–8; representation of power 59–65, 87, 99–100; science and enterprise 52–3, 94; topographical representation of 19n84, 33n45, 32–49, 99; trade, opening up of the interiors and 25–7, 27n19, 52–6, 85–7, 203–5, 212
Browne, James 69, 143, 145
Buchanan, Francis 47n114, 72, 119, 129, 190n58, 196n91, 212, 237: 'statistical touring' of 65–9; visit to Patna 16–17, 59; *see also* colonial knowledge
Burdwan xvii, 49, 52, 54–5, 74, 93, 111, 114, 128, 128n57, 129, 165–7, 169n76, 213, 217, 222, 231
Burhee 114, 169n72, 207, 209, 218, 220
Bury, Harriet xxi, xxin15
Buxar 47, 73, 83, 135, 140, 146

Calcutta xvii, xxxiii, 28n23, 34n51, 35, 40–41, 44, 46n106, 49–50, 52, 58–9, 61n16, 62n20, 63, 65n33, 77–79, 84, 86, 106n71, 107n80, 131n72, 131n74, 141, 144, 149n173, 177–80, 176n107, 177n110, 178–80, 187–8, 194–7, 209, 212, 222–3, 240; climatic discourse on 4, 15n67; as imperial centre 33, 33n45, 39, 80n102; railways to and from 114, 214, 227–9, 229n146, 230; roads to and from 73–4, 80–81, 94, 104, 108, 148n172, 160, 164–5, 167; steamships in/to/from 28–9, 172–6, 177n110, 213
Calcutta Steam Tug Association 177
Careri, G. F. G. 119
Cargola 74, 218
carts xxii, 31n37, 60, 149, 165, 167, 171n89, 177n111, 194, 197, 204, 219n90, 220, 221n102, 223, 229–30
Chahar Gulshan, The 91
Chaibassa 194
Champaran 73, 88n134, 150, 170–71; roads in 193, 197, 238; trade of 199
Chapra 86, 140, 142, 146, 162, 170, 194, 196–8, 201, 212, 228n136, 239
Chatra 128–9, 194, 208, 222, 225
Chatterjee, Kumkum xxxiiin38, 78
Chattopadhyay, Basudeb 134–5, 139
chaukidars 143, 146n160
Chinsura 41, 51–2, 167
Chota Nagpur 23, 24n4, 73–4, 159, 184–5, 194, 199, 209, 210–11, 225
choukies 76–8, 86, 86n129, 128–9, 144, 147, 200–201
Chunar 52, 80–81, 184, 213
circulation: knowledge production and xxv, xxvi, xxxi–xxiii, 73, 93–6, 115–16; of

INDEX 265

colonial maps xxviii, 92, 95–6, 104, 115–16; segmented nature of xxviii, 95–6; *see also* Latour, Bruno
Clarke, Hyde 27
Cleveland, Augustus 47, 55n154, 69, 147
Clive, Robert 69, 77, 93, 115
coal(fields) xvii, 26n16, 54–5, 54n146, 56n155, 184, 213
Cohn, Bernard 15
Collins, H. G. 114
colonial knowledge: Anglo–French rivalry 94, 96; caste and xxvii–iii, 119, 191; criminality and 119; natives' role in formation of xviii, xxx, 93–5, 137n97, 140; production of xxvi–xxviii, 18n78, 34, 39, 55, 115, 234; recycling of 116; of roads 101–7
colonial objectification 14–22; immanent contradictions in xxxv, 18, 21, 40, 89; spatial xxix–xxx, 1, 16, 22, 236
colonial picturesque gaze xxx, 18–22, 34, 35n51, 36n56, 40–2, 45–6, 49–56, 58–9, 68, 88–9, 99–100, 151, 151n188, 235; *see also* colonial knowledge; colonial state-space; colonial travel; Mackenzie, Colin
colonial state–space xxxv–xxxvi, xxxvin44, 100, 195; *see also* Goswami, Manu
colonial travel: accounts, colonial 17–21, xxxn31; British views on native 27, 30–32; disguise during 37–8, 123, 133–4;forms of xxx; notion of 'heathenscape' in 8–9; idea of interior and 1–2, xxix–xxx, 32–52; ideologies behind travel xxi–xxii, xxxi, xxxin34, 6, 9–11, 17, 55n152; means of communication and 34n46, xixn5, xix, xxiii–xxvi, xxxiv, 33, 40–41, 58, 172, 180, 202, 204–5, 217,231, 234–6; rituals of 10, 62–4; routinization of xxx, xxv, 17, 33, 58; *see also* Gangascape; roads, roadscape; tours
Commissariat Department 157
communication: and Bihar lateral growth of 217–30; approach towards history of xvi–xxv, xxiii, xxxiii–xxxiv, 155, 204–7, 233–4, 239–40; knowledge formation about means of 106–7; maps xxxi, 107–14; policy, colonial changes in xxxii–xxxiii; consolidation of rule and 57–8, 63–73, 87–9, 156–7, 178, 234; taxation and 85–7; *see also* crime; Grand Trunk Road (GTR); mobility; New Military Road (NMR); public works; railways;

roads, 'roadless India'; steam; steamships; steamship(s); travel
Cook, Andrew 96, 97n31, 115n95
coolies xvii, 157, 184–6, 185n31, 208–9, 239; *see also* roads, construction, colonial policy, investment, view and system of; dandy/dandies/boatmen
Colebrooke, H. T. 78–9
Cornwallis, Lord 60, 135
cotton: American crisis 224; associations in England 223; piece-goods, trade in 78; presses for screwing 227; road scheme 224–6; *see also* Bengal; Bihar
Court of Directors 24, 24n6, 29, 32, 63, 70n53, 80, 80nn102–3, 83, 85n127, 94, 98, 98n40, 115, 115n95, 141, 156n2, 172, 174, 213
crime: communication, mobility and xxiii, 117–19, 121–3, 125, 130, 134, 147, 149, 190; explanations for increase in 139–42, 150; colonial recasting of native 121–2, 124–5, 134, 153–4; in pre-colonial times 119–21, 135–8; in railways 153, 231; role of testimony 126–7, 140; *see also banjaras*; coolies; dandy/dandies/boatmen; *fakirs*; *gosains*; *mallahs*; *sanyasis*
Criminal Tribes Act (CTA) xxxii, 118, 191
Crooke, William 151–2, 191
Cruchley, C. F. 114, 116
Cumberlege, N. R. 126, 128

d'Anville Jean 96
D'Oyly, Charles 42–3, 48n122, 50, 55n152, 66
Dacca 72n67, 162, 176n107, 197, 222
dak: boats 178, 230; bungalow xxxi, 81, 166; roads (lines) 81, 113, 121n20, 164n47,166–7; services 80, 104, 113, 167, 176; system, colonial 102, 166–7, 233; travel by 40, 48; *zamindari* 102n54
Dalhousie, Lord 24
dacoits 89, 121n23, 122–4, 126, 126n49, 130–31, 134, 134n84, 140, 140n118, 141n123, 141n127, 142–3, 146–7, 150, 190
Danapur (Dinapore) 83, 171, 193, 196, 213, 217, 230
dandy/dandies/boatmen 20, 42, 42n93, 76, 176n107, 179n119, 180, 183–4, 186–92, 191n62, 192n66 239; bargaining power of 189; occupational dislocation of 191–2; regulation of 189–90, 192; ritual status of 190n58, 191; *see also mallahs*; *manjhees*

Daniell, Thomas and William Daniell 21, 33n45, 35, 35n52, 37, 37n61, 38, 47n114, 61; *see also* colonial knowledge; colonial picturesque gaze; colonial travel; interior/inland spatial category of
Danvers, Juland xx
Dar-al Aman 11
Dar-al Harb 8
Dar-al Islam 8
Darbhanga 74, 76n85, 197, 212, 219, 223n113, 238
Daudnagar 74, 76, 142, 193–4, 193n73, 219
Deane, A. 6–7, 21, 39, 41–2, 46–8, 62, 78n96, 80–81, 100, 104, 142, 150n183, 171, 176n107, 184, 188
Deccan (Dakkan) 1–3, 2n2, 2n4, 7, 9, 97, 99, 127–8, 137, 151
Delhi 1–2, 2n5, 6–7, 11, 13, 16, 20n87, 38, 39n67, 60n12, 63n25, 91, 96n30, 119, 127, 149n173, 164, 177n111, 199n10, 227
Derbyshire, Ian xxn8, xxiiin19, 204
Dhangain 166
Dhanger 184, 184n23; *see also* Bengal, early iron works; coolies
Dirks, Nicholas 18, 21, 35n51
Duperron, Anquetil 96
Duncan, Andrew 53, 53n144, 54

East India Vade-Mecum 105, 105n70
Eden, Emily 49, 51, 51n130, 61, 64, 65n34, 88, 89n142
Edney, Matthew 17, 19n84, 93, 94n22, 97, 99, 100, 100n46

Faden's firm 116, 116n98
fakirs xxix, 37, 41, 60, 95, 116–17, 122–4, 124n38, 130–38, 123, 131, 134, 136, 138, 198
Fazl, Abul 2n4, 4, 33, 98
feriwalahs xxvi, 130, 223
ferries xx, xxx, xxxii–xxxvi, xxxvii, 72, 75, 78, 84–5, 103, 147, 155, 164, 166, 168–71, 179–80n123, 180, 189, 193, 208, 217, 220, 222–3, 231, 235
Ferry Fund Committee (FFC) xxxiii, 164, 167–71, 173, 186, 193, 218, 235
Forrest, Charles Ramus 19, 21, 36n57, 44–5, 47, 50, 81
Forster, George 37
Fulton, Robert 172; *see also* steamships

Gangascape xxix, 29, 41, 44–9
'Ganges Fair-Weather Railway Feeders' 219
Ganges Steam Navigation Company 174–7
Gangetic route 58, 73, 81, 108–9, 111, 114, 171, 212
Gangetic trade 28, 177–8, 213–14, 229
Gaya 68, 74, 86, 87n131, 111, 114, 142, 146n160, 162, 168, 169n72, 179n119, 193–4, 193n73, 206, 211, 213, 218–22, 221n101–2, 237, 240
General Inland Steam Navigation Company (GISNC) 174, 176–7, 214
Gentil, Jean Baptiste Joseph 60, 96, 98, 107n80
ghats (riverbank): of Benares 47–8; in north Bihar, ferry 147, 164, 170, 223; of Patna 41, 43–4, 195, 230; on the River Kosi 228; sketches of 41, 44; on the River Soane (Koelwar) 83, 84n118
ghats/ghauts (mountain pass) 49, 92, 129, 145, 168
ghautwal 143, 145
Ghazipur 41, 46, 73, 83, 143n137, 144, 147, 157n7, 193, 195–7, 199, 223
Gir, Puran 133–4, 133n79
Giridih 219
Gole, Susan 92, 96, 102n55
Gorakhpur 142–3, 196–9, 223
Gordon, Stewart 129
gosains xxvi, xxix, 37, 121–4, 130, 133–8, 150, 150n183, 199–200
Goswami, Manu xxvii, xxxv–xxxvi, xxxvin44–5, 156
grain trade xxxvii, 75n81, 76, 78n96, 125, 193, 195–200, 212, 219, 221n101, 222–3, 228–30
Grand Trunk Road (GTR) 49, 89, 114, 148, 162, 164n47, 167, 169, 179n119, 193, 206, 208, 213, 219–20, 225, 227, 238; alignment of xxxiii–xxxiv, 80, 82, 167, 219 ; bad conditions of 179n119, 206, 208–9, 219; construction of xxxiii, 114–15, 164, 166–7, 185–6, 191; as imperial road in Bihar xxxvii, 114, 164, 169, 206, 218; regional importance of xxxiii, 114, 148, 167, 206, 208, 221–2, 231; renewed investment in 207–8; road police on 148–9; supply provisions on 166–7, 207; toll houses on 207; trade by 164, 167, 177n111, 193, 208, 213, 218–22, 225, 227, 231
Gully, Telia (Terria) 46, 147

INDEX

Gumperz, Ellen 204
Gurkha 38, 38n65, 200; kingdom in Nepal 117, 133, 135

haat 15, 72
Habib, Irfan 91
Hafiz 10, 10n47
Hajipur 74, 107n80, 169, 180n123, 196, 212, 218, 238
Harley, Brian 107
Hall, Stuart xxvi–xxvii
Hastings, Warren 70n51, 98n40, 107n80, 132, 138; abolition of *dastaks* and *choukies* by 77, 85; acquisition of knowledge 92, 95; measures taken to control crime 124, 134–5, 137, 145; NMR construction by 80; upland tour of 45, 60, 77
Hawkins, Francis James 37, 42n93, 63–5, 113n87, 187–9
Hazaribagh 74, 103, 114, 129, 165, 167, 169n72, 193–4, 206, 208–9, 218–20, 221n102, 222, 222n107, 225
Heber, Reginald 50, 66, 68, 188–9
Henderson, Andrew 177
highway/trunk roads 75, 75n81, 111, 113, 138, 165, 180, 193, 238; robbery on 119–20, 119n12, 121n20, 125, 138, 141, 141n123, 143n142, 145–6, 150, 153; *see also* Grand Trunk Road (GTR); New Military Road (NMR)
Hindustan (Hindostan) xxxviii, 2n2, 6, 95; in British travellers' understanding 3, 45–6, 99; in pre-colonial understanding 1–2, 2n2, 2n4, 6–7, 13, 22, 46n106; in Rennell's understanding 109
Hodges, William 18–20, 35–7, 35n52, 37n61, 40–41, 45–7, 47n114, 60, 69, 98, 196n91; *see also* colonial picturesque gaze; colonial travel; interior/inland spatial category of
Hodgson, B. H. 200
Howrah 217, 229
Humanyun 5

indigo xxvi, xxxiii, xxxvii, 59, 68, 163–4, 179, 189, 196–201, 212, 214, 230
inland trade 77–8, 201, 235
Inland Transit Company 167
interior/inland spatial category of xviii–xix, xxix–xxx, 22, 33, 46–7, 235–6; colonial knowledge of xxvi–xxviii, xxx, 52–8, 65–73, 87–9, 101, 116; communication and xxxiv, 23–32, 46–7, 49–52, 58–9,

83–7, 168, 179, 192, 203, 212; European community in 179; European travelling gaze and 33–49; opening up of xxiv–xxvi, xxxv, xxxvii, 23–32, 81–5, 179, 203, 235; trade within 192–8, 201

Jaggarnath 131, 198; road to 160–61
Jahan, Asaf 136–7
Jahangir 11n53, 119–20
Jacquemont, Victor 49, 166
Jassal, Smita Tewari 191
Jehanabad 148n172, 194, 221, 221n100
Johnston, James Henry 28; *see also* steamships
Joshi, Chitra 181–2, 181n1, 182n6
jungle: clearing of 15n67, 81, 102, 102n53, 102, 120n15, 148, 182; in picturesque representations 34, 42, 45–6, 49; as wild and impenetrable spaces xvii, xxvi, 17, 34, 42, 49, 56, 88n134, 120, 138, 146–8, 184n16
Jungle Terry: 47, tour of 69–70, settlement of 70n51, 145 role in highway robbery 143, 143n138
jungli 23, 122

Kathmandu: road to 92, 197–8; trade in 200
Kelly, Robert 94, 94n23
Kerr, Ian xxin12, xxxii–xxxiii
Khan, Abu Taleb 4, 6, 11n49, 46n109
Khan, Ali Vardy 125
Khan, Dargah Quli 1, 2, 6, 13, 16; *Muraqqa-e-Dehli* 1, 6, 13n61
khillat 10, 12, 14, 145
Khusraw, Amir 7, 10
Kishengunj 228
Knox, Major Randfarlie 94, 96

lathials 120n13, 124
Latour, Bruno xxxin34, 115; *see also* circulation
Laurie and Whittle 116
lithograph(y) 113, 116, 146n160
lithographic stone 195, 195n85
Lohardugga 128, 185, 208, 210, 225

Maasir-i-Alamgiri 3n11, 8
Mackenzie, Colin 19, 21; *see also* colonial knowledge; colonial picturesque gaze
Majeed, Javed 146
mallahs 179n119, 180, 190–92; *see also* dandy/dandies/boatmen; *manjhees*
manjhees 42n93, 76, 187–90, 190n58

maps 1–2, 14, 15n69, 17, 33, 45, 55, 66–7, 72, 73n70, 75, 89, 92n10, 96n30, 97n31, 98n40, 99–101, 102n55, 103–5, 107–16, 107n80, 115n95; in communication history, role of xxviii–xxxi; publication of xxix–xxxi, 97, 97n31, 108, 113–14, 116, 116n98, 168, 214–15, 218n78, 226, 234, 236; readership of xxxi, 104, 113–15, 113n87; showing roads on xxxi, 72, 92, 100, 104, 107–14, 168, 226; spatial objectification through 17, 33, 55, 89, 93, 99–101, 114, 236; *see also* Bengal, survey and mapping in; Mughal rule, mapping in; circulation, of colonial maps; communication, maps; Edney, Matthew; Rennell, James; roads, books

Maratha: maps 1, 92, 102n55; raids into Bengal 80, 93, 144; salt 128

McLane, John 139, 141n123, 143

merchants xxvi, 9, 25, 29, 131, 135, 187, 189, 239; in Bihar, Bengal UP, Nepal, network of 194–201, 204, 222–5, 228; complaints by 76, 76n85, 77, 87, 139, 144, 144n151, 147, 190, 190n58, 228; contribution to public works 160, 211; disappearance from Patna xxxiiin38; English 144, 199; Newar 198; use of steamships and railways by 179, 229; thugs disguised as 124, 153

Midnapur 74, 93, 128, 128n57, 139n116, 140–41, 194

Military Board 158, 185

military: xxxi, 10, 11n54, 21, 28, 42, 60, 63–4; marches on the NMR 81, 109; movement using steamers 178–9; operations in Jungle Terry 145; roads 114, 116, 166, 182, 206; roads, investment on 83, 83n111, 164, 207, 211; role in road surveys and public works 92–4, 102–8, 114, 120, 133–4, 155–8, 163, 181–2, 184, 190; *see also* Grand Trunk Road (GTR); New Military Road (NMR)

Mill, James xxxvi, 31, 31n35

Mirzapur 32, 174, 176n107, 179, 194, 196, 199, 213

mobility xviii, xxxiii, xxxvi–xxxvii, 86, 100, 149, 238, 240; colonial administrative 57–9, 87–9, 101, 108, 116; in crime, role of xxxiii, 117–19, 123, 125, 130, 138, 147, 153, 237; networks, colonial control over xxxii–xxxiii, 116–18, 123–30, 134–7, 144–9, 190; higher officials 59–65; lower-level officials 65–73; pre-colonial 10, 11n50, 26, 30, 119–23, 234; railway xxvi, xxxiv, 221n102, 239; types and networks of xxv–xxviii, 116, 234, 238–9

Monghyr 40–41, 52, 73–4, 86, 88n134, 105, 141–2, 147, 169, 171–2, 195–7, 195n83, 210, 217–19, 221n102, 222–3, 229, 232

Moorcroft and Hearsey 36, 38, 38n65, 132–3

Morris, Morris D. 173, 206–7, 207n21

moral and material xix, xxiv, xxxii, xxxiiin37, 23, 27, 56, 156

Mughal rule: comparison between British colonial and 14–17, 33, 46n106, 59–60, 63, 91, 98–9, 102n55, 144; crime under 119, 119n10, 119n12123, 125n45, 136; duties under 76n82–3; ideology of 11n53, 12–14; Iranians under 11, 11n49, 98; mapping in 1, 91–2; spatial perception under 3–10, 11n54, 12–14, 33, 98–9; tours under 60, 63; trade under 193n73, 194n74; troops 120n15; weakening of xxxiiin38

multanis 121, 123, 127

Mundy, G. C. 47n114, 81, 166n56

Murray's handbook 106

Murshidabad 41, 44, 46n109, 48n120, 73, 77, 91, 134n84, 142, 194, 222

Mutiny of 1857 31n38, 71, 156, 206n16, 208, 237

Muzaffarpur 74, 86, 114, 169, 194, 196–200, 212, 218–19, 223, 238

native(s): capital and merchants xxvi, 77, 77n90, 144, 160–63, 160n24, 190, 195–6, 198–201 206–7; criminality xvii, xxiii, xxxii, 1, 118, 121 (*see also* crime); guide xvii, 97, 116; maps, texts and personnel in colonial knowledge xviii, xxvi, xxviii, xxx–xxxi, 14, 19–20, 20n86, 68n42, 69, 71, 88, 91, 93–103, 116, 134; pilots 192; stereotypes about xx, xxiiin18, xxivn22, 6, 9, 21, 23, 26–7, 27n18, 30, 30n31, 31–2, 117, 123, 139, 143n137

nawabs 237, 238n6, xxiin18, 11n54, 39, 60, 62, 74, 77, 94, 107n80, 135, 144, 173

Nepal xxxiii, xxxvii–xxxviii, 1, 38n66, 74, 78, 79, 117, 132–5, 170, 197–200, 223, 228

'nested' networks xxvi, xxxiii, xxxiv, 181, 192, 212, 221, 230

INDEX 269

New Military Road (NMR) xxx–xxxi, xxxiii, xxxvii, 80, 108–9, 113–15, 128–9, 138, 146, 148n169, 155, 158, 166; construction of xxx, xxxviii, 80, 94, 116 decline of xxxiii,114–16, 166–7, 185, 193, 206; marches of army on 81, 109; travel by 48n119, 49, 49n123, 58, 81–3, 111
Nicholl, James 80, 94, 96, 109
Nigam, Sanjay 118, 129

oil traders 223
oilseed 194, 197, 200, 221–3, 229–31
Okeden, William Parry 39, 47, 143n137, 188
Oldham, W. 56, 67, 74, 80n101, 82, 89, 166
opium xxxvii, 70n53, 78, 128, 178, 195–200, 212, 221n101, 225, 230, 232; Smuggling Preventive Establishment 232; transport of xxxiii, 78–9, 179, 189, 227–8, 228n136
Orissa xxxviii, 79, 85, 87n134, 93, 131, 136, 161, 194–5, 199, 231
Orme, Robert 96, 115
Oudh (Awadh) xxiin17–18, 2, 39, 60, 62, 62n22, 74, 94, 96, 141–2, 147, 173, 230

Palamow 54, 74, 103, 120, 120n15, 128, 194, 219, 224–5
palanquins xvi, xxx, 38, 46, 59, 61, 64, 143, 184, 198n100
Patna xxxiiin38, 39, 41, 46n109, 48, 51, 59–60, 63, 71, 91, 101, 125, 141, 170n82, 172, 180n123: roads in 73–4, 83, 86, 111, 114, 149, 163, 165, 169, 171, 185, 193, 197, 209, 211, 213, 218, 221, 238; *ghats* of 43–4, 195; representation of 16–17, 105; style of painting 42n93, 48n122, 60n15; trade of xxxvii, 76–9, 86, 128–9, 144, 193–8, 199n101, 212–13, 222–4, 228, 230
Paton, Colonel John 103, 105–6
Peggs, James 163
Pelsaert, Francisco 119
Perkasnand 132–3
Persian 3, 3n11, 6, 7, 7n28, 11, 97, 132, 161
Phillimore, R. H. 91, 97n31
Pinch, William 117n2, 121, 123, 131n74, 136–8
Pouchepadass, Jacques 69, 69n46, 71, 87
Pratt, Louis Mary xxxn31, xxxi, 17–18, 18n78, 34, 94n24; *see also* colonial state–space

Praun Poory 131–3
pre-colonial: colonial and xxvii, xxix, xxxvi, 1, 5, 10, 14–16, 16n69, 22, 32, 57, 59–60, 122–3, 135, 137, 153, 182, 236; spatiality 1–14, 22, 92, 102n55 (*see also* Deccan (Dakkan)); Hindustan (*see* Hindustan (Hindostan); *Purab*; *wilayat*); mobility 26, 59–60, 121 (*see also* mobility, pre-colonial); times, means of communication in 62n22; times, regulation in 120; *see also* crime; Mughal rule
Prinsep, G. A. 28n23, 29, 51, 54, 173, 176
public works: xix, xxiv, xxvii, xxxv, 77, 234; idea of xxxii, 155–63, 180, 186; investment on xxxii, 83, 155, 160–65, 172, 210, 223n113; labour on 181–6; supervision of 186
Purab 6, 22, 46n106, 240
Purneah 74, 86, 134, 171, 197, 210, 212–13, 218

Qasim, Mir (Cossim Ali Khan) 74, 77, 91, 94, 105, 145n152, 237
quartermaster general 63, 102, 104, 158

rahdari 76, 76n83, 77, 172, 236
railway(s) xvii, xixn6, xxiin12, xxiin15, xxiin17–18, xxx, xxxv–xxxvi, 24–5n6, 30, 118, 153, 206n19, 229n146; building, colonial policy on 155–6; -centric approach, critique of xxiii–xxiv, xxxii, 203–7, 222, 230; complementary relationship between roads, rivers and xxiv, xxvi, xxxiv, 23, 32n40, 52, 169, 177, 180, 192, 196, 201, 203–8, 212, 214, 217–24, 229, 231–2, 234, 239; construction and labour 209; lines and projects, early 114, 167, 179, 213–17, 222; opening up the interior and 23–7, 32–3, 172, 207, 212; as symbol of civilization and progress xix, xx–xxii, 23–4, 53, 54n146, 235; travel xxi, 32, 51–2, 88, 88n140, 151, 221, 221n102, 239–40; thugs 151
Railway Company: East India 27n18; Great Western Bengal 214; North-Western 231
Raj, Kapil xxviiin29
Rajmahal 11, 11n54, 16, 35n52, 40–42, 46, 50–52, 55, 55n154, 56, 73, 114, 142, 145, 147, 189, 213–14, 217, 227
Raleigh, Edward Ward Walter 61n16, 63, 64n28, 142

Raghunathpur 128, 146, 194
Ramghur 128–9, 141, 141n127, 148n142, 184, 193, 208
Ranchi 208, 210n47
Rangpur 75n81, 130, 134–5, 138, 141, 159–60, 213
Regulation: of 1773 77; of 1788 135; of 1819 168
   III of 1821 146
   IV of 1813 84
   VI of 1819 169
   VII of 1801 84
   VII of 1822 168
   VIII of 1818 141
   IX of 1833 71n56
   X of 1810 86
   X of 1819 129
   XI of 1801 86
   XI of 1806 157
   XV of 1813 70
   XV of 1817 102n74
   XVIII of 1806 84
   XIX of 1816 84, 169, 189
Rennell, James: career in India and London 97; compilation of route knowledge by 93–4, 96–8, 101, 105; description of roads by 74, 80, 91, 108, 114; *Description of the Roads in Bengal and Bahar* 73, 101, 104; indigenous sources used by 97; maps drawn by 45, 75, 99, 108–10, 113–16; *Memoir of a Map of Hindoostan* 97–8, 108; survey of the Ganga by 44, 59, 180, 186; *see also* circulation, of colonial maps
resinous products 193–4
Revelgunge 196, 230
Revised Tables of Routes and Stages 103–4, 106, 166
rice 46, 89, 165, 191, 194–5, 197, 212, 221–3, 228–31
rivers xvii, xxiv–xxv, xxxv, xxxvii–xxxviii, 2, 3n9, 5, 5n18, 7n28, 9, 25, 28–9, 34, 40–51, 44n98, 44n100, 56, 58, 59n5, 60, 62, 73–4, 76–8, 79n98, 80, 84, 84n118, 87, 89, 91–4, 97, 100, 104, 120, 127, 132, 140, 142, 144, 147, 148n172, 149, 162, 166–74, 176n107, 177–9, 179n123, 180–82, 187–92, 192n66, 193, 195–7, 195n83, 196n91, 204, 208, 212–14, 217, 219–20, 222, 228–31, 233, 236; as cultural boundary 3, 3n9

river(s): the Bagmati 197; the Bhagirathi 178; the Buri Gandak 212; the Bya 197; the Canton 29; the Dewah (Gogra) 74, 86n129, 196, 212; the Gandak 44n100, 74, 197, 212; the Ganges 2–3n7, 16, 33–4, 40, 43–4, 46, 50, 56, 78, 99, 174, 186, 209, 213, 218–19; the Hugli 144; the Karmanasha 5n18, 80, 94, 148n172, 149, 162, 169, 220; the Kosi (Kusi) 3n9, 45n100, 74, 228; the Lilajun 220; the Pipli 94; the Soane 46, 73–4, 84n118, 93, 148n172, 193, 195, 208, 213, 218–20, 225, 230
roads:
   in Bihar, networks and importance of xxxvii, 23, 72–5, 83–4, 108, 115, 169–72, 192–8, 208, 218–30, 237
   books xxviii, xxx, 92, 92n10, 101, 103–6, 108, 114
   Cess Committee 210
   construction, colonial policy, investment, view and system of xix–xx, xxii, xxvi, xxx–xxxv, xxxvii, 26, 28, 30, 30n31, 31, 31n37, 53, 58, 73, 75, 77–8, 80, 83–6, 85n127, 155, 158–62, 164–72, 180, 186, 207–12, 236–8 (*see also* public works)
   convict labour on 83, 130, 181–6
   crime on (*see banjaras*; crime; fakirs; gosains)
   Fund xxx, xxxiii, xxxviii, 83, 160, 168, 172, 235
   guarding 129–30, 144–9
   as hallmark of civilization xviii, xxn9, xxv, 23–4
   making of principal 106–14
   military supply system on 157–9, 207
   police 148–50
   in pre-colonial times 14, 14n65, 75–8, 91, 119–20
   railways and xxi, xxii, xxiin18, xxxvi, 52, 88, 192, 204–9, 217–18, 223, 227, 229–30
   'roadless India' xxxi, xxiv, xxxi, 24, 27n18, 32, 115, 155, 237–8
   roadscape xxix, 47–9
   trade, opening and 25, 27, 53, 54n146, 83
   types of xxxiv, 26, 168–70, 217, 238
   ways of seeing and xxv, xxix, 34, 40, 42, 44, 46, 55n152, 133n77
road(s): Benares trunk 193; Bombay–Agra 164; Bowsee–Bhagalpur 209; Calcutta–Bombay mail 165; Darjeeling cart 165;

INDEX

Darjeeling trunk 218; Ganges–Darjeeling 186, 209; Hazaribagh–Burhee 209, 220; old Mughal (Gangetic route) xxxvii, 73–4, 148n169, 171; Muzaffarpur–Hajipur 218; Patna branch 169, 185, 209, 221; Patna–Gaya 221; Saran–Ghazipur 147; Shershah trunk 193; Soree–Bhagalpur 219; Tirhut trunk 218
Robinson, Albert 31n38, 174, 176, 176n107, 177, 192
Roe, Thomas 238
route: survey, journals kept during 96; *see also* roads, books; surveys
routinized gaze 35
routinized India 41
Roy, Tirthankar 155n1, 204–5, 204n6

safarnamas 5n18, 11n54, 90, 90n5
Sahibgunge 229, 229n146
salt: *choukies* 1289; contraband 129; EIC monopoly 78; Rowannah 128–9
saltpetre (saltpeter) xxxvii, 78, 128, 144, 144n151, 189, 192, 195–6, 200, 210, 212
sanyasis xxix, 116–17, 124, 124n38, 130–38, 150, 150n183; *see also fakirs*; *gosains*
Saran 71, 73–4, 85–6, 129, 141n123, 142, 160, 162, 200, 212; roads in 85, 147, 163, 170, 172n83, 185, 238; trade of 72, 144, 196, 198–9
Sasseram 47, 73–4, 76, 83, 93, 167, 220, 222, 222n105, 224
sayers 76–8, 172, 236
Seely, John B. 105; *The Road Book of India* 104
serais 146, 161–3, 168
Shah, Azam 9, 62n22, 91
Shahabad 67–8, 73, 77, 84, 102n5, 129–30, 140, 142, 146, 148n172, 159, 162, 171–2, 219, 230, 240; roads in 83, 160, 167–8, 184, 224; trade of 194–6, 195n85, 222–4
Shahabad Road Fund 160
Sherghatty 213, 220–21, 225
Shuja, Shah 136
Sicri Gully 40, 46, 147
shilajit trade 198
Simms, F. W. 167, 213
Singh, Ajeet 122, 124n39
Singha, Radhika 121, 124, 125n43, 126n51, 129
Singhbhum 23, 69n45, 159, 169, 237
Sleeman, William 122–5, 126n49, 127, 146, 150

Smith, Colonel Richard 93
Society and Circulation (Markovits et al.) xxv
Solvyns, François Balthazar 21, 37
statistical touring 68, 88; *see also* Buchanan, Francis; tours
Stephenson, R. M. 25, 25n6, 212–13
steam xixn7, 27, 54, 105n70, 173–5, 176n107, 179–80n123, 191–2, 213; civilizational discourse on xix–xx, 23, 31, 155, 233; navigation, Bentinck's minute 28–30, 30n29; technology of xx, xxii, xxiv, 27, 58, 177, 179–80, 205, 214, 233–4, 239
steamships xix, xixn7, xxiv, xxxiii, 23, 26n16, 29, 55, 156, 172–80, 229, 234, 235; boats and xxviii, xxx, 155, 180; cost of travelling by 32n40, 49–52, 173, 176n107; difficulty in piloting 192, 228; early colonial state's approach towards 28; Gangetic trade by 173, 177, 229, 233; military movement by; time taken by 51, 173; travel by 55; tug system of 173, 173n95, 177
steamship(s): the *Assam* 177; the *Benares* 176–7; the *Brahmaputra* 28; the *Chunar* 176; the *Comet* 174; the *Diana* 29; the *Enterprise* 29, 178; the *Ghazeepore* 176–7; the *Hooghly* 28–9, 51, 173; the *Megna* 174; the *Mirzapore* 52, 176–7; the *Patna* 175–7
Sukhmoy, Raja 160–61, 163
Surdas 122, 137
surveys: expansion in colonial knowledge through route xix, xxvii, xxx, xxxv, 93, 101, 103; geological 54, 89, 166n56; Maratha incursions and route 80, 93; route xxxv, xxxxviii, 1, 59n5, 92, 94, 100–101, 103, 109, 237; *see also* maps; Rennell, James
Sykes, W. H. 163

telegraph xxiv, 25, 27, 52, 87n132, 233, 239
Thevenot, Jean de 119, 122
thuggee 121, 126–7, 130, 137n97, 140, 142, 146, 150–54, 232
Tibet xxviii, 38n65, 79, 103, 132–4, 133n77, 133n79, 199
Tirhut 3n9, 72n67, 73, 85, 107n80, 129, 164, 170–71, 200–201; roads in 169–70, 197, 218, 222; trade of 197–8, 212–13, 223–24
tobacco 70n53, 77n90, 194–5, 195n81, 197, 199, 201, 223–4, 231

Thomson, George 185
tours: district level xxx, 92, 235; governor general xxx, 59, 88; purposes of collectors' 57, 59n5, 69, 71, 83; ritual of higher officials 62–4
Tumlook 177
Tremenheere, George B. 31, 31n35, 31n38, 58
Tulsidas 122

Upjohn, A. 112–14, 169n76

Valentia, Lord 15n67, 37n61, 59–60, 60n10, 62, 80n103, 81
Vansittart, George 131, 138
Vansittart, Henry 77, 93, 115
Varady, Robert Gabriel xxiin18, xxxvii
village community 26–7, 206

Wagner, Kim 122, 137n97
Wellesley, Marquis 62n20, 62n22
wheat 46, 195, 197, 222, 229

White, Captain 93
wilayat 3, 3n11, 9, 12, 22
Williamson, Thomas 81, 105, 105n70, 189, 191n62
Wyld family firm 113, 116

Yang, Anand xxiin16, 118–19, 197

zamindars 69n45, 72, 75, 84–5, 102n84, 107n80, 128, 137–8, 143, 145n152, 160, 187, 193n71, 211, 218, 237, 239; collection of *sayers* and *rahdari* by 76–7, 172 (*see also rahdari*; *sayers*); participation in crime 87n134, 120, 124; 'customary duty' of maintaining and repairing roads xxvi, xxx, 75–7, 75n81, 85–6, 164, 236; conflict between EIC and 76, 76n85, 80, 145, 150; declining *fouzdari* power of 139, 143; role in supplying provisions to marching troops 158–9; voluntary subscriptions by 80, 168